1987

DATABASE COMPUTERS
Principles, Architectures, and Techniques

DATABASE COMPUTERS
PRINCIPLES, ARCHITECTURES, AND TECHNIQUES

First Edition

Stanley Y. W. Su, Ph.D.

Professor and Director
Database Systems Research
and Development Center
Department of Computer and
Information Science and
Department of Electrical
Engineering
University of Florida

McGraw-Hill Book Company

New York St. Louis San Francisco Auckland Bogotá Caracas
Colorado Springs Hamburg Lisbon London Madrid Mexico
Milan Montreal New Delhi Oklahoma City Panama Paris
San Juan São Paulo Singapore Sydney Tokyo Toronto

To my parents
Sing Su and Shu-Hwei T. Su

My wife
Siew-Phek T. Su

And my sons
Li-Chiun and Li-Ming

This book was set in Times Roman by Publication Services.
The editor was David Shapiro;
the cover was designed by Scott Chelius;
the production supervisor was Denise L. Puryear.
Project supervision was done by Publication Services.
Arcata Graphics/Halliday was printer and binder.

DATABASE COMPUTERS
Principles, Architectures, and Techniques

1 2 3 4 5 6 7 8 9 0 HALHAL 8 9 3 2 1 0 9 8

ISBN 0-07-062295-7

Library of Congress Cataloging-in-Publication Data

Su, Stanley, Y. W.
  Database computers.

  (McGraw-Hill computer science series)
  Includes index.
  1. Electronic digital computers.   2. Data base
management.   I. Title.   II. Series.
QA76.5.S86   1988   005.74   87-32475
ISBN 0-07-062295-7

ABOUT THE AUTHOR

Stanley Y. W. Su received his M.S. and Ph.D. degrees in Computer Science from the University of
Wisconsin, Madison, in 1965 and 1968, respectively. He is a professor of Computer and Information
Sciences and of Electrical Engineering, and is the Director of the Database Systems Research and
Development Center, University of Florida.
    He was one of the founding members of the IEEE-CS's Technical Committee on Database
Engineering. He served as the Co-chairman of the Second Workshop on Computer Architecture
for Non-numeric Processing (1976), the Program Chairman and organizer of the Workshop on
Database Management in Taiwan (1977), the U.S. Conference Chairman of the Fifth International
Conference on Very Large Data Bases (1979), and the General Chairman of the ACM's SIGMOD
International Conference on Management of Data (1982). He is an editor of the IEEE's *Transactions
on Software Engineering*, the *International Journal on Computer Languages, Information Sciences:
An International Journal*, and an Area Editor for *Journal on Parallel and Distributed Computing*.

CONTENTS

PREFACE

In this information-oriented age, data has become one of the most important resources to both organizations and individuals. The availability, accuracy, timeliness, and completeness of data often determines the right or wrong decisions of organizations and individuals. The effective and efficient management of large quantities of data is a common problem found in most large business, scientific, engineering, and military applications. There is a growing demand for high-performance computers that are tailored for processing large databases efficiently. This demand arises due to the following two reasons: First, there is a constant effort toward building more powerful database management systems that can provide database users with better functionalities and ease of use through high-level data models and languages. However, the provision of better functionalities and ease of use by a database management system introduces considerable system complexity and processing overhead. Inefficiency and lack of functionality of the existing database management systems are commonly felt by the users of large database systems. Second, the conventional computers used for database management are not particularly suited for non-numeric processing since the primitive operations, i.e., machine instructions, of these computers are numeric in nature. Non-numeric operations required in database management are carried out by software. This causes operational inefficiency of the database management system and makes it difficult for the users to develop application programs and systems. There is a definite need for high-performance computers that can solve large database problems efficiently.

In recent years, the computer industry has made tremendous progress in processor, memory, and communication technologies. The result of this progress has been a rapid decrease in hardware cost to an extent that special-purpose as well as general-purpose computers structured specifically for processing database functions have become economically feasible. Hardware- and architecture-oriented solutions to database management problems have become viable and desirable alternatives to the traditional software means for solving database management problems. In the past two decades, there has been a considerable amount of research and development effort in the design and development of "database computers." Many systems have been proposed and some have been prototyped. A few commercial products have been in the market for a number of years. These research and commercial systems range from special-purpose processors for performing simple database operations to large multicomputer systems which support complex database management functions. There is growing interest and activity in research, development, production, and commercialization of high-performance computers whose hardware and architecture are tailored for database management functions.

The motivation for writing this book evolves mainly from the following: First, research and development on database computers has been rapidly progressing for the past two decades. There is much knowledge generated by many projects carried out in various countries. The principles, architectures, and techniques introduced by these projects have been reported separately in various technical reports, journals, conference proceedings, and manuals. Inconsistent and sometimes confusing notations and terminologies have been used by different authors of these technical papers. There is a need to assemble this knowledge in a single volume using consistent notations and terminologies and to make it available to computer scientists, engineers, and data processing professionals. Second, the field of database management has reached a stage of maturity. Many commercial database management systems for main frames, minicomputers, and microcomputers are available and regularly used by many large enterprises as well as small businesses. One limitation commonly felt by the users of these existing database management systems is that they are slow and lack functionalities. The use of high-performance database computers to support database management tasks is a natural solution. There is a need for all database and database systems designers, users, and managers to understand the present capabilities and limitations as well as the future potential of the new database computer technology. This book should meet this need. Third, courses in computer architectures and database management are widely taught in colleges and universities. The principles, architectures, and hardware/software techniques of database computers are the products of integrating these two matured fields of study. A course on database computers would be a natural extension of architecture and database management courses. It will demonstrate to students how the integration of hardware, architecture, and software techniques introduced in computer architecture and database management courses can produce high-performance computers for solving present and future database problems.

This book covers the principles, architectures, and hardware/software techniques used in five categories of database computers. The main features of this book are: (1) the problem-oriented classification of database computers based on different approaches for solving problems and eliminating the limitations found in conventional computers; (2) the use of consistent notations and terminologies to relate and present the architectures and techniques introduced in various database computers; (3) the presentation of architectures and hardware/software techniques using many examples and diagrams; (4) the integration and synthesis of the existing information on database computers, and (5) the analysis of algorithms for four representative database operations, which are executed in abstract models introduced for the different categories of database computers.

This book is designed for use as a general reference for computer users and data processing professionals or as a text or reference book for a course at the senior or graduate level. The material presented in this book can be used for a semester course or for two courses in the quarter system.

The nine chapters of this book are organized as follows: The first chapter defines the term "database computer," establishes the need and the motivations for research and development work in database computers, and provides a classification of these computers. Chapter 2 presents the basic concepts and functional requirements of databases and database management systems. Problems and techniques related to data modeling, data representations, query translation and modification, integrity and security control, concurrency control, and recovery are addressed. This chapter provides the background knowledge in database management to non-database readers and introduces the database examples used throughout this book. It also points out the complexity and causes of inefficiency found in the existing database management systems. Following these two introductory chapters, the principles, architectures, and hardware/software techniques of five categories of database computers are presented in the next six chapters. Chapter 3 describes three cellular-logic devices, CASSM, RAP, and RARES, and a magnetic bubble system designed at IBM's Yorktown Heights Research Center. Chapter 4 presents the concept and techniques of database filters using CAFS, SURE, and VERSO as examples. The filtering techniques used in DBC's mass memory and in DBM are also described. Chapter 5 covers associative memory systems and their application to database management. The key features of systems such as Logic Memory, ASP, STARAN, APCS, NON-VON, ASLM, and RELACS are presented. Chapters 6 and 7 are devoted to the category of computers called multiprocessor database computers. This category consists of two subcategories: systems with replication of functions and systems with distribution of functions, which are described in these two chapters respectively. Chapter 6 presents the main architectural features and techniques introduced by systems like MICRONET, EDC, MDBS, DBC/1012, GAMMA, REPT, HYPERTREE, NON-VON, CUBE-CONNECTED MULTICOMPUTER, DIRECT, GRACE, DBMAC, and SM3. Chapter 7 presents the main architectural features and techniques introduced in XDMS, IDM, IQC, iDBP, DBC, SABRE, RDBM, DELTA, DDM, CADAM, SYSTOLIC ARRAY, and VLSI TREE MACHINE. Chapter 8 presents text processors. First, the characteristics and general processing requirements in text processing are defined. Second, the basic structure of a text retrieval system is described. Text processing techniques such as full text scanning, inverted file and index processing, and superimposed coding are presented. Several term comparator designs and hardware systems for supporting these processing techniques are detailed. The general architecture of a few text processing systems such as EUREKA, GESCAN, and a list merging network are described. The final chapter, Chapter 9, summarizes the past accomplishments of this field of study, gives some factors that restrict the present growth of this field, and offers this author's view concerning the future prospect and possible research directions of database computers.

The author is grateful to a number of individuals for their encouragement and professional assistance. In particular, the author would like to thank Prof. C. V. Ramamoorthy, Prof. B. Berra, Prof. C. K. Baru, Dr. J. Banerjee, Prof. S. Ceri, Prof. Paul Fisher (Kansas State University), Prof. Lee Holloar (University of Utah), Eugene Lowenthal (Microelectronics and Computer Technology Corporation), and Prof. G. Wiederhold for their valuable comments and suggestions regarding the technical contents and organization of this book. Many students have helped in collecting reference materials and proofreading the manuscript and have offered suggestions for improving the clarity of presentation. In particular, the author would like to thank P. Hariharasubramanian, A. Azam, R. M. Yaseen, and C. Lee for their kind assistance. Sharon Grant, the author's long-time secretary, has been extremely helpful during the long writing and production process. Her clerical assistance is gratefully acknowledged. The author would also like to thank the editing and production staff of the McGraw-Hill Co. for their professional assistance in the production of this book. Finally, last but not the least, the author would like to thank his dear wife, Siew-Phek T. Su, for her encouragement, patience, and understanding during the preparation of this book. Without her support, the completion of this book would have been impossible.

Stanley Y. W. Su

CHAPTER
1

INTRODUCTION TO DATABASE COMPUTERS

The purpose of this chapter is (1) to provide a definition for "database computer," (2) to explain what motivates the research and development work on database computers, (3) to present a general model of a "conventional" computer system used for database management applications and point out the main limitations of such a system, (4) to describe the basic approaches taken by the existing database computers to either partially or fully solve some of these problems, and (5) to classify the existing database computers based on the approaches taken by them.

1.1 WHAT IS A DATABASE COMPUTER?

A *database computer* is a hardware, software, and firmware complex dedicated and tailored to perform some or all of the functions of the database management portion of a computing system. It can be a special-purpose functional processor used for performing specific database operations (e.g., the selection of a set of records from a given file satisfying some search conditions.) It can also be a single or multicomputer system dedicated to performing a variety of database functions such as query processing, data retrieval and updating, integrity and security control, and error recovery. A database computer can either be a stand-alone system or be a component of a larger system.

This definition is intended to include all configurations of hardware, firmware, and associated software, which are designed for the purpose of achieving efficient database management. We exclude the so-called distributed database management systems, which are built as a distinct layer of software with an interface to some existing homogeneous or heterogeneous data management utilities. In the computer science field, the term "database machines" is also frequently used

1

to refer to devices or systems designed specifically for database applications. In this book, the terms "database computer" and "database machine" will be used interchangeably.

1.2   WHY DATABASE COMPUTERS?

Research and development work on database computers has drawn great attention from both the academic community and computer industry in the past decade. Several commercial products such as CAFS, IDM 500, iDBP, and DBC/1012 have been introduced in the computer market in recent years and have been well received by computer users. A discussion of the three main reasons for the increase in research, development, and the subsequent commercialization of database computers follows.

1.2.1   The Need for Efficient and Effective Data Management

In a modern society, a large percentage of the work force is service oriented. Organizations as well as individuals need effective information systems to manage human services and to provide greater operational efficiency in the delivery of such services. Data has become one of the most important resources to both the organizations and the individuals since its availability, accuracy, timeliness, and completeness often determines whether the right or wrong decision is made.

The complexity of the problems we face today demands that data generated by the various disciplines of human endeavors be integrated and used as a whole to find appropriate solutions. This means that in most real situations large quantities of data need to be collected, stored, processed, and maintained in databases. Such large databases complicate the problems of data retrieval, updating, recovery, transaction management, and all other database management functions. Software solutions for these problems work reasonably well for small databases supporting many applications and for large databases supporting only a few applications. However, the labor-intensive cost, the time delays, and the reliability problems associated with software development and maintenance become prohibitive as large and highly shared databases emerge. Therefore, the search for hardware-oriented and architecture-oriented solutions to meet the need for efficiency is a viable alternative.

1.2.2   The Need for More Powerful Database Management Systems

In the database management area, there is constant effort toward creating more powerful database management systems (DBMS), that is, systems that provide better functionalities and ease of use through their support of high-level data models and languages. This drive is motivated by the need to improve user/programmer productivity and the desire to protect applications from changes in the hardware, software, and database structures of the systems. However, high-level data models and languages are supported by building layer upon layer of software that maps or translates the high-level data representations and commands into low-level storage representations and machine codes interpretable by the hardware. This mapping between levels is the main cause of inefficiency in database management systems running on existing computers. Typically, the wide gap that exists between the representations at the user level and the hardware level is bridged by software. Since one cannot require the user to communicate with the hardware in low-level data representations and commands, a reasonable solution to closing this gap is to build hardware that is capable of interpreting high-level data and commands.

Many database applications require real-time, multiuser access and manipulation of databases. The current rate of 10 to 100 requests per second handled by most of the existing database management systems is not adequate for future applications. The capacity to process 1,000 to 10,000 requests per second will be needed in the future. The existing single processors are too slow to meet this requirement.

1.2.3 The Advancement in Hardware Technologies and Price Reduction

In the past decade, the computer industry has made tremendous progress in processor, memory, and communication technologies. The result of this progress has been a rapid decrease in hardware cost to an extent that special-purpose machines and general-purpose computers that are dedicated to specialized functions have become not only economically feasible but also functionally desirable. We can expect the cost of memory, processors, terminals, and communication devices to continue to drop at a drastic rate. It is now the time to reevaluate the traditional role of hardware and software in solving database management problems.

1.3 THE CONVENTIONAL COMPUTER ARCHITECTURE AND LIMITATIONS

The architecture of a "conventional" computer (or the Von Neumann–type computer) is not particularly suitable for nonnumeric processing in general and database management in particular. There are a number of very serious limitations and bottlenecks in such an architecture. The simple model shown in Figure 1.1 will be used to discuss them.

In a conventional computer system, both programs and data are stored in a secondary storage device. They are moved to the main memory, via a controller, in order to execute the instructions of the programs using the data as the operands. The instructions are executed one at a time with frequent access to the secondary storage device to obtain new data and instructions. The general model of a conventional computer system shown in Figure 1.1 highlights the three areas with limitations (secondary storage, main memory, and processor) and the two potential bottlenecks (secondary storage to main memory and main memory to processor) that exist in such a system. These limitations are presented in left-to-right order (see Figure 1.1).

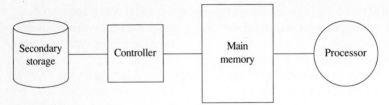

FIGURE 1.1
A general model of a conventional computer system.

1.3.1 Limitations of Conventional Secondary Storage Devices

Perhaps the most serious limitation of conventional secondary storage devices is their inability to process data locally. The read/write mechanisms of these devices are used only for data transmission and not for examining the contents of the stored data. A stored file needs to be transferred, via the storage device controller, to the main memory before the processor can examine its contents.

A second limitation of these devices is their speed. The speed of secondary storage devices is limited by the mechanical motion involved in the spinning of tapes or disks and the movement of disk arms, which take much more time than the switching of electronic devices. In addition, increasing the speed of mechanical devices is much more difficult than decreasing the switching time of electronic devices. Therefore, it is impossible for conventional storage devices such as tapes, disks, and drums to catch up with the speed improvement of the processor. In the conventional architecture, the speed of secondary storage will always be the determining factor in system performance.

The third limitation is that data transmission can only be done one physical block (i.e., a disk sector or a block of a magnetic tape) at a time through a single read/write head. Most of the existing storage devices do not have the parallel read capability. This limitation restricts data transfers and searches to serial processes.

The fourth limitation is that the data in secondary storage are stored and accessed by address rather than by content. These addresses are computed for each access, thereby adding an overhead time to the data access time. Data cannot be freely moved around inside the storage device in order to maximize the usage of the storage space without paying the high cost of keeping track of address changes. Only data contents, not addresses, are of interest to the database user. From the user's viewpoint, computation of these addresses is strictly an overhead expense.

1.3.2 I/O Bottleneck

Due to the limitations of the conventional secondary storage devices, data as well as programs need to be moved between the devices and the main memory at the speed of the storage devices. In database applications, large quantities of data are moved into the main memory for processing, and the computed results in the form of temporary files are moved out to the secondary storage. To "stage" the data and instructions in the main memory is very time-consuming. The I/O channel often becomes the bottleneck that degrades the performance of a DBMS.

1.3.3   The Limitations of the Main Memory

Database management systems generally support multiple users. Multiple application programs reside in the main memory at the same time. These programs together with the DBMS software occupy a large amount of main memory space. The programs operate on input data and generate output data that in turn occupy more main memory space. The space limitation of the main memory often forces input data to be brought in from the secondary storage in segments and output data to be written out periodically even if they are to be used again. Large programs are often divided into "segments" and/or "pages," which are moved in and out of the main memory by a time-sharing operating system. This is another main cause of system inefficiency.

Another limitation of main memory, as in the case of the secondary storage devices, is its lack of content addressing capability. Data stored in the main memory are retrieved by the processor via their addresses, without which they cannot be directly accessed. This limitation requires that either the system software or the application programs keep track of addresses and address changes through the use of pointers and/or complex data structures. Address computation and storage requirement for addresses are additional overhead time.

An additional limitation is that the main memory allows only a single processor to access its contents at a time. In a multiprocessor or a multicomputer system, it is often convenient to post messages and data in a memory that can be accessed simultaneously by more than one processor. The traditional memory with a single addressing mechanism does not allow this type of access.

1.3.4   Von Neumann Bottleneck

The architecture of the conventional computers has remained much the same as the one introduced by John von Neumann a generation ago. The control logic of a computer routes instructions and data from the main memory to a central processing unit (CPU) that executes the instructions, manipulates the data, and sends the results back to the memory. In this architecture, the movement of instructions and data between the main memory and the registers in the CPU is the limiting factor in determining the processing speed. A single instruction stream executed against a single data stream is simply too slow to process large databases. Some other architectural concepts need to be used in order to remove or relieve this bottleneck.

1.3.5   The Limitations of
Conventional Processors

Conventional Von Neumann–type processors were originally designed for numeric computations and, therefore, are unsuitable for database management applications that are inherently nonnumeric in nature. The instruction set of such processors contains primitive operations such as shift, add, subtract, multiply, and so forth. These are very low-level operations when compared to the operations typically required to process databases. In conventional systems, software is written to carry out the basic database operations (e.g., retrieve, update, sort, insert, delete, etc.) using the available low-level operations. Additional layers of software are built on top of these basic database operations to perform other DBMS functions. This fact explains the complexity of the existing DBMSs and the difficulty of developing application systems. If a processor can be built to perform the basic operations needed in database management, then much of the software can be eliminated and the system development and maintenance costs can be drastically reduced.

The sequential nature of a Von Neumann processor also limits performance. Most numeric as well as nonnumeric computational tasks can be divided into parallel subtasks. These subtasks can be executed concurrently in order to shorten the total time required for performing the tasks. Conventional processors cannot take advantage of such concurrency because of their one-instruction-at-a-time limitation.

1.4   DATABASE COMPUTER APPROACHES

The limitations and bottlenecks described previously have motivated many researchers to seek hardware and architecture solutions to database management problems. Many approaches have been proposed to remove or relieve these limitations and bottlenecks. In this section, the approaches taken are highlighted. The specific details will be discussed in subsequent chapters in which various database computers using these approaches or combinations of these approaches are described. These approaches are presented in the same order as the description of the limitations and bottlenecks in order to maintain a correspondence between the problems and their solutions.

1.4.1   Intelligent Secondary Storage Devices

One approach to eliminating the limitations of the conventional secondary storage devices for database applications is to build more intelligence into the secondary storage (i.e., to build more processing capabilities into the read/write mechanisms) so that data stored on the devices can be directly searched and manipulated. The idea is to make the devices intelligent enough so that they can select only the relevant data and transfer them to the main memory for further processing. This will reduce the staging problem discussed in Section 1.3.2.

There are several database computers that use this general approach. The so-called cellular-logic devices such as CASSM, RAP, and RARES seek to eliminate the limitations by using a processing element for each track of a rotating memory device such as a disk, a drum, a charge couple device (CCD), or a magnetic bubble memory. Figure 1.2 illustrates a general architectural model for

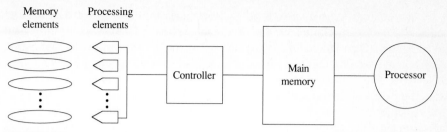

FIGURE 1.2
A general model of a system using an intelligent secondary storage device.

this approach. The intelligent secondary storage device contains an array of cells, each of which consists of a memory element and a processing element. In one revolution of the storage device, a simple search operation can be performed over the data contents of all the memory elements and thus over the data of the entire storage device. If the whole database is stored on a number of such storage devices, then the entire database can be searched in one revolution. More complex database operations can also be carried out by these devices, but they would involve more memory revolutions. Since the previously mentioned systems use a disk track as a memory element in their initial designs and use specially designed hardware logic as a processing element, they are often called logic-per-track systems. However, it should be noted that "cellular-logic" is a more general concept than "logic-per-track" since a memory element of a cellular-logic device can be something other than a disk track. It can be a shift register, a CCD memory, a magnetic bubble memory, or a memory element formed by multiple disk tracks.

The cellular-logic systems offer tremendous parallel processing capability since a small portion of a database, that is, a full track of data, can be processed by a dedicated processor. However, the cost of building such a device can be quite high. In order to reduce the number of such special purpose processors required for a large database, one can extend the memory element size. For instance, a single track can be extended to the entire surface of the disk. This would change the secondary storage device configuration from a fixed-head disk, with intelligence on each read/write head, to an intelligent moving-head disk on which the array of processing elements (the read/write heads) can be dynamically moved to a selected track. All the tracks under the processing elements form a cylinder, the contents of which can be processed in parallel. This is an alternative implementation of the general principle of intelligent secondary storage. An example of its use is in the mass memory design of The Ohio State University's database machine, DBC, which is an example of the so-called logic-per-head systems.

Another cellular-logic system using a modular, configurable, electronically timed magnetic bubble storage system has been studied at IBM's Yorktown Heights Laboratory. The system follows the general principle of cellular logic with the memory element in this case being a magnetic bubble chip with a modified major-minor loop organization. The processing capability is provided by some off-chip logic and "marker loops." Further details about this system will be discussed in Chapter 3.

The cellular-logic approach not only reduces the problem of data staging but also completely eliminates the overhead cost associated with locating data by addresses. Data stored in the memory element are systematically compared against some search conditions by the associated processing elements. Data can be searched and processed by specifying their contents rather than their addresses. Thus the overhead time of address mapping and maintenance is eliminated.

Chapter 3 will provide a more detailed explanation of this approach, including some implementation techniques of systems using this approach as well as its advantages and disadvantages. Chapter 3 will also introduce an abstract model for cellular-logic systems. The performance of several algorithms for four representative database operations in this model will be analyzed. Cost formulas for these algorithms will be derived.

1.4.2 Database Filters

The cellular-logic approach requires that a new storage device be built. This involves a considerable initial development cost and may result in a product that may not be compatible with existing storage devices. The database filtering approach aims at achieving the same filtering effect as the cellular-logic devices by using existing storage devices but with an intelligent controller. The controller is capable of searching and comparing all data read from secondary storage devices against some search conditions in order to determine the specific data that need to be forwarded to the host computer. A general architectural model of this approach is shown in Figure 1.3. In the figure, the database filter is shown to consist of two parts: (1) the hardware of a regular secondary storage controller and (2) special-purpose hardware for performing the data filtering tasks. In some proposed systems, these two parts are separated from each other and form two distinct processors.

The database filter operates in the following manner. Database commands are issued by the host computer (usually a general-purpose digital computer) to the filter, which reads a designated file from the secondary storage device. The records in the file are sequentially processed by one or more processing elements; and records, which satisfy some specified conditions, are selected and transferred to the host computer either for output or for further processing. Thus, unwanted data are filtered out by the database filter. Only the relevant data will constitute the traffic in the often-congested data channel between the secondary storage

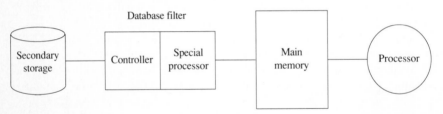

FIGURE 1.3
A general model of a system using a database filter.

and the main memory, thereby reducing the problem of channel congestion and eliminating the so-called I/O bottleneck.

The idea of database filtering is not limited to the selection of records. More complicated database operations can also be carried out by the filter. For example, the merging of two files or the selection of some specific data fields and values from each record of a file are reasonable operations for a filter.

Several database computers have been designed based on the concept of database filtering, and some incorporate the concept as a part of a more elaborate system. CAFS, VERSO, SURE, DBC, and DBM are some examples of such machines. In Chapter 4, the architectures and techniques used in these systems will be described. An abstract model for this category of database computers will also be introduced. Algorithms for four representative database operations will be analyzed, and cost formulas will be derived.

1.4.3 Associative Memory Systems for Database Management

One approach to remove some of the limitations of the traditional main memories described in Section 1.3.3 is to add intelligence to these memory elements so that the memory contents can be searched and retrieved in an efficient manner. Instead of having a central processor accessing each memory location sequentially in order to examine its contents (as in conventional computers), memories can be built with some logic associated with each memory word or bit so that the contents of the entire memory can be examined simultaneously. All memory words or bits that contain certain data can be marked for subsequent use. A general model of a computing system using an associative memory is shown in Figure 1.4.

The associative memories used in STARAN, NON-VON, and RELACS have these capabilities. They allow data to be retrieved by specifying their contents rather than their addresses. Such an addressing scheme is not only more akin to the way database users address their data, but it is also faster than address-based schemes since the overhead cost of address computations is completely eliminated.

The advantages of associative memories can be illustrated by an example. Suppose an instructor in a large class wants to find out the number of students who have not handed in their homework. One method is to ask each student, in turn, whether he or she has submitted the homework and to count the number of students

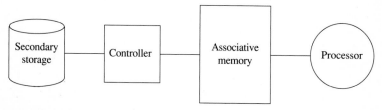

FIGURE 1.4
A general model of a system using an associative memory.

who answer no. A second method is to ask all those students who have not handed in their homework to raise their hands and to count the number of raised hands. The first method is similar to the way in which the conventional processors work, that is, sequentially. The second method resembles the approach used in associative memories. The teacher's question is similar to a search command broadcast to all memory locations (the students). The logic associated with each memory location (the intelligence of the students) is able to decide whether or not to flag the locations (to raise their hands). Counting the flags (the hands) would give the answer needed.

In Chapter 5, associative memory systems and several other systems will be described in greater detail. The applications of these memory systems in database management will be presented and illustrated, and their limitations will be discussed. Chapter 5 will also present an abstract model for associative memory systems. Based on this model, some algorithms for four representative database operations will be analyzed and cost formulas for these algorithms will be derived.

1.4.4   Multiprocessor Database Computers

The main cause of the Von Neumann bottleneck discussed in Section 1.3.4 is the sequential access of data words and instructions by the CPU from the main memory. One approach to remove or ease this bottleneck is to replicate the database management functions in a number of processors and to distribute data to these processors so that they can be processed by either the same or different functions in parallel. This basic approach taken by many multiprocessor and multicomputer systems will be referred to here as *multiprocessor systems with replication of functions*. Another approach is to distribute database management functions to a number of processors, each of which is tailored to perform one or a small number of functions efficiently. Data are distributed to these processors for processing. Thus, high computation efficiency can be achieved by functional specialization and parallel execution of these functions. Many existing database computers are designed based on this second approach. Such computers will be referred to here as *multiprocessor systems with distribution of functions*.

A general architectural model showing the relationship between main memories and processors appears in Figure 1.5. Different interconnection structures

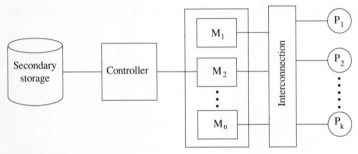

FIGURE 1.5
A general model for multiprocessor systems.

can be used to connect the memories and processors. A multiprocessor system allows a complex computational task to be divided into a number of subtasks that can be carried out by the processors concurrently with some intermittent synchronizations. Thus, the response time of the original task is reduced to the time needed for the largest subtask.

There are a number of database computers that employ the multiprocessor approach. Examples include MICRONET, DBC, DIRECT, REPT, HYPER-TREE, NON-VON, DBMAC, SABRE, RDBM, DBM, MDBS, SM3, GAM-MA, CUBE-CONNECTED MULTICOMPUTER, and several commercial products such as IDM, iDBP, and DBC/1012. The Japanese fifth-generation computer effort and other database machine projects have also resulted in a number of multiprocessor systems such as IQC, DELTA, GRACE, CADAM, and DDM. Chapters 6 and 7 describe these systems by dividing them into two categories: (1) systems with replication of functions and (2) systems with distribution of functions. The main architectural features and novel techniques used in these systems will be described, and their support of database operations will be explained and illustrated. Two abstract models will also be introduced for these two categories of systems. Analyses of some selected algorithms will be presented, and cost formulas for these algorithms will be derived.

1.4.5 Text Processors

The main limitation of conventional Von Neumann processors for database application, described in Section 1.3.5, is the mismatch between the computational capabilities of the processor and the processing requirements of an application. Text processing is a good example of such an application. The conventional processors do not provide direct support for text processing operations. They use complex software to perform these operations. An obvious solution is to build a processor that is tailored for text processing so as to close the gap between the application needs and processor capabilities. However, in building such a processor, it must be determined which capabilities and facilities will be used frequently and will prove cost effective. These will be built into the hardware. The others should be left for the software to handle. A processor designed for text processing, for example, should be able to process the common text processing operations efficiently (e.g., searching for a substring of characters).

In Chapter 8, text processing systems in which the central processors are specially designed for manipulating text will be examined. Text processing techniques including full text search, inverted file, indexing, hashing, and superimposed coding will be described.

1.5 CLASSIFICATION OF DATABASE COMPUTERS

There are many ways of classifying database computers. One method is based on the architecture classification proposed by Flynn [FLY72] in which all computer architectures fall into one of the following four categories:

1. Single instruction stream and single data stream (SISD)
2. Multiple instruction stream and single data stream (MISD)
3. Single instruction stream and multiple data stream (SIMD)
4. Multiple instruction stream and multiple data stream (MIMD)

This architectural classification will be used here to discuss the general architectural features of database computers. However, for the ease of grouping together those database computers that have similar design objectives, this text uses a problem-oriented and application-oriented classification scheme, which classifies database computers based on the various approaches taken for solving the problems described in Section 1.3. This enables the reader to relate the database computer solutions to the problems that they are meant to solve. The same principle is used to further divide a category into subcategories, each of which represents a different approach to solving some specific problem. Figure 1.6 shows a hierarchical classification of the database computers discussed in this book. Chapters 3 through 8 will present the basic principles, architectural features, and techniques of the database computers belonging to the five major categories shown in the figure. The fourth category, the multiprocessor database computers, is presented in Chapters 6 and 7, each of which describes a major subcategory.

It should be noted here that many database computers are designed to tackle a number of problems by using a combination of hardware techniques. These systems could have been classified in several different categories. However, in this text each of them is assigned to a single category based on the main architectural features and hardware techniques employed. Whenever appropriate, their secondary features and techniques will be mentioned in the presentations of other categories of machines.

1.6   SUMMARY

In this introductory chapter, the term database computer has been defined and the reasons why this subject has drawn substantial attention from both the academic community and computer industry have been explained. The limitations of the conventional computer systems that motivated the research and development work on database computers have also been described, and the approaches taken by the existing database computers in an attempt to either ease or eliminate the limitations and bottlenecks have been briefly outlined. As illustrated in Figure 1.7, the limitations of the conventional secondary storage devices can be eliminated to a certain extent by the use of intelligent secondary storage devices. The I/O bottleneck can be relieved either by reducing the amount of data to be moved through the I/O channel using the database filter concept or by moving data from the secondary storage to the main memory more efficiently using parallel input and output. The limitations of the conventional main memories can be removed by using more intelligent memory systems. The multiprocessor approach can be used

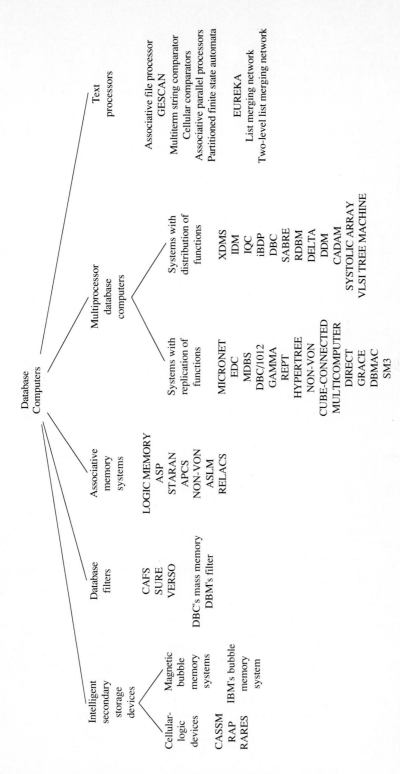

FIGURE 1.6
A hierarchical classification of database computers.

Database Computers

Intelligent secondary storage devices | Database filters | Associative memory systems | Multiprocessor database computers | Text processors

Cellular-logic devices
CASSM
RAP
RARES

Magnetic bubble memory systems

IBM's bubble memory system

Database filters
CAFS
SURE
VERSO
DBC's mass memory
DBM's filter

Associative memory systems
LOGIC MEMORY
ASP
STARAN
APCS
NON-VON
ASLM
RELACS

Systems with replication of functions
MICRONET
EDC
MDBS
DBC/1012
GAMMA
REPT
HYPERTREE
NON-VON
CUBE-CONNECTED
MULTICOMPUTER
DIRECT
GRACE
DBMAC
SM3

Systems with distribution of functions
XDMS
IDM
IQC
iBDP
DBC
SABRE
RDBM
DELTA
DDM
CADAM
SYSTOLIC ARRAY
VLSI TREE MACHINE

Text processors
Associative file processor
GESCAN
Multiterm string comparator
Cellular comparators
Associative parallel processors
Partitioned finite state automata
EUREKA
List merging network
Two-level list merging network

13

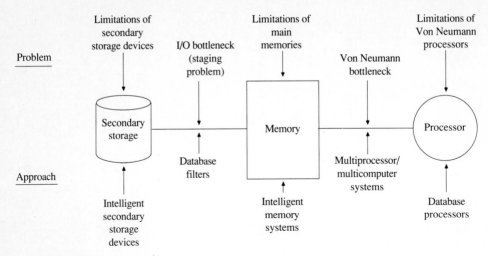

FIGURE 1.7
A summary of problems and database computer approaches.

to relieve the Von Neumann bottleneck, and new text processors hold promise to eliminate the limitations inherent in Von Neumann processors for text processing.

It should be stressed that several of the existing database computers use a combination of the basic approaches presented here. The architectures of these database computers can be considered to be combinations of subarchitectures that implement these basic approaches. The performance evaluation of database computer architectures can thus be carried out by using the performance parameters and cost formulas derived for the component subarchitectures.

1.7 BIBLIOGRAPHY

[BAN78] Banerjee, J., Hsiao, D. K., and Ng, F. K.: "Data Network—a Computer Network of General-purpose Front-end Computers and Special-purpose Back-end Database Machines." In A. Danthine (Ed.), *Proceedings of the International Symposium on Computer Network Protocols,* Liege, Belgium, 1978, pp. D6-1–D6-2.

[BAU76] Baum, R. I., and Hsiao, D. K.: "Database Computers—A Step Toward Data Utilities," *IEEE Transaction on Computers,* vol. C-25, no. 12, Dec. 1976, pp. 1254–1259.

[BER74] Berra, P. B.: "Some Problems in Associative Processor Applications to Database Management," *Proceedings of the 1974 AFIP National Computer Conference,* vol. 43, AFIP Press, Montvale, N.J., 1974, pp. 1–5.

[CHE78] Chen, T. C.: "Computer Technology and the Database User," *Proceedings of the Fourth International Conference on Very Large Data Bases,* Berlin, West Germany, Sept. 1978, pp. 72–86.

[COU72] Coulouris, C. F., Evans, J. M., and Mitchell, R. W.: "Towards Content Addressing in Data Bases," *Computer Journal,* vol. 15, no. 2, Feb. 1972, pp. 95–98.

[DEM85] Demurjian, S. A., and Hsiao, D. K.: "New Directions in Database-Systems Research and Development," *Proceedings of International Conference on New Directions in Computing,* IEEE Computer Society, Trondheim, Norway, Aug. 1985, pp. 188–197.

[FLY72] Flynn, M. J.: "Some Computer Organizations and Their Effectiveness," *IEEE Transaction on Computers,* vol. C-21, no. 9, Sept. 1972, pp. 948–960.

[HEA75] Heacox, M. C., Cosley, E. S., and Cohen, J. B.: "An Experiment in Dedicated Data Management," *Proceedings of the First Conference on Very Large Data Bases,* Framingham, Mass., 1975, pp. 511–513.

[HOL79] Hollaar, L. A.: "Text Retrieval Computers," *IEEE COMPUTER,* vol. 12, no. 3, 1979, pp. 40–52.

[HSI77] Hsiao, D. K., and Madnick, S. E.: "Database Machine Architecture in the Context of Information Technology Evaluation," *Proceedings of the Third International Conference on Very Large Data Bases,* Tokyo, Japan, 1977, pp. 63–84.

[HSI79] Hsaio, D. K.: "Guest Editor's Introduction: Data Base Machines are Coming, Data Base Machines are Coming!," *IEEE COMPUTER,* vol. 12, no. 3, 1979, pp. 7–10.

[HSI80] Hsiao, D. K.: "Database Computers," *Advances in Computers,* Academic Press, New York, vol. 19, June 1980, pp. 1–64.

[HSI83] Hsiao, D. K. (ed.): *Advanced Database Machine Architecture,* Prentice-Hall, Englewood Cliffs, N.J., 1983.

[HSI86] Hsiao, D. K.: "Super Database Computers: Hardware and Software Solutions for Efficient Processing of Very Large Databases," *Proceedings of the IFIP Congress '86.*

[HWA84] Hwang, K., and Briggs, F.A.: *Computer Architecture and Parallel Procesing,* McGraw-Hill, New York, 1984.

[LOW76] Lowenthal, E. I.: "The Backend (Data Base) Computer, Part I and II," Auerbach (Data Management) Series, Auerback Publishers, Princeton, N.J., 1976, 24-01-04 and 24-01-05.

[MAD75] Madnick, S. E.: "INFOPLEX—Hierarchical Decomposition of a Large Information Management System Using a Microprocessor Complex," *Proceedings of the 1975 National Computer Conference,* vol. 44, AFIP Press, Montvale, N.J., pp. 581–586.

[MAR76] Maryanski, F. J., Fisher, P. S., and Wallentine, V. E.: "Evaluation of Conversion to a Back-end Data Base Management System," *Proceedings of the Association for Computing Machinery,* pp. 293–297.

[OZK86] Ozkarahan, E.: *Database Machines and Database Management,* Prentice-Hall, Englewood Cliffs, N.J., 1986.

[SLO70] Slotnick, D. L.: "Logic per Track Devices." In J. Tou (Ed.), *Advances in Computers,* vol. 10, Academic Press, New York, 1970, pp. 291–296.

[SMI79] Smith, D. C. P., and Smith, J. M.: "Relational Data Base Machines," *IEEE COMPUTER,* vol. 12, no. 3, March 1979, pp. 18–38.

[SON81] Song, S. W.: "A Survey and Taxonomy of Database Machines," IEEE *Database Engineering,* vol. 4, no. 2, Dec. 1981, pp. 3–13.

[SU73] Su, S. Y. W., Copland, G. P., and Lipovski, G. J.: "Retrieval Operations and Data Representations in a Context-addressed Disc System," *Proceedings of ACM/SIGPLAN and SIGIR Interface Meeting,* Gaithersburg, Md., Nov. 1973, pp. 144–156.

[SU79] Su, S. Y. W.: "On Cellular Logic Devices: Concepts and Applications," *IEEE COMPUTER,* vol. 12, no. 3, March 1979, pp. 11–27.

[SU80] Su, S. Y. W., Chang, H., Copeland, G., Fisher, P., Lowenthal, E., and Schuster, S.: "Database Machines and Some Issues on DBMS Standards," *Proceedings of the 1980 National Computer Conference,* Los Angeles, Cal., AFIP Press, Montvale, N.J., 1980, pp. 191–208.

[YAU77] Yau, S. S., and Fung, H. S.: "Associative Processor Architecture—a Survey," *ACM's Computing Survey,* vol. 9, no. 1, pp. 3–28.

CHAPTER
2

DATABASE AND DATABASE MANAGEMENT SYSTEM ARCHITECTURE

Database computers are computer systems designed specifically for supporting database management functions. In order to understand and appreciate the purposes, the techniques, the strengths, and the weaknesses of existing and future database computers, it is important for the reader to be familiar with the characteristics, operations, and functions of databases and database management systems. The purpose of this chapter is: (1) to introduce the characteristics and applications of integrated databases and database management systems, (2) to define database contents and levels of data representation, (3) to categorize and describe the common database operations and their algorithms, (4) to present the general architecture of a DBMS, (5) to discuss and illustrate the main database management functions, and (6) to discuss the performance problems in database systems and stress the need and importance of managing data efficiently, which is one of the main objectives of database computers. This chapter also establishes the terminology and examples necessary for subsequent chapters.

This chapter is intended for those readers who are not familiar with the concepts and operations of databases and database management systems. Those who are familiar with them may choose to study only selected sections of this chapter. However, all readers should read Section 2.3 in detail since it introduces cost formulas for some primitive database operations. Many parameters and formulas used in this section are reused in the analyses of various categories of database computers to be presented in later chapters.

2.1 GENERAL CHARACTERISTICS AND APPLICATIONS OF DATABASES AND DATABASE MANAGEMENT SYSTEMS

Database management systems are typically used by an organization to efficiently and effectively process and retrieve data from an underlying database to support the operational and decision-making tasks of the organization. Therefore, it is important to put databases and DBMSs in the proper context of a generalized information system for supporting decision making. It is also important to examine their general characteristics and applications before taking a closer look at the structures and operations of databases in Sections 2.2 and 2.3 and the architecture and functions of a database management system in Sections 2.4 and 2.5.

2.1.1 Data Versus Information

Data are recorded representations of physical objects, abstract things, facts, events, or other observable entities that are useful for decision making. *Information* refers to those data that have been used by an individual or an organization to affect decision making. The advancement in data recording technologies in the past decades has made possible the permanent recording of voluminous data generated by all disciplines of human endeavors. The amount of data is growing at an unprecedented rate. We are faced with the serious problem of storing, maintaining, and managing these data and of making them useful for individuals and organizations in their decision-making process. Modern digital computers have been used as tools, in these respects, for establishing information systems for different applications.

A generalized model of an information system shown in Figure 2.1 was proposed by Yovits [YOV81] in which observable actions in an external environment are first recorded as data by an information acquisition and dissemination component. This component handles the tasks of acquisition, storage, and dissemination of data to a decision-making component. This component may represent a human decision maker, a committee, or an organization that receives the data, and it can either use the data for decision making or store the data in a memory for later use. The data used for decision making become information to the decision maker, who directs the course of action to be carried out by an execution component. The execution component is subject to the noise in the external environment so that the observable actions produced may not be the ones intended by the decision maker; thus, the system is nondeterministic. The observable actions produced can be transformed into data to be acquired again by the information acquisition and dissemination component. Information is measured by its interaction with the external environment since its interaction will result in some type of physical action that is measurable and observable. The physical action is a result of the decision-making process.

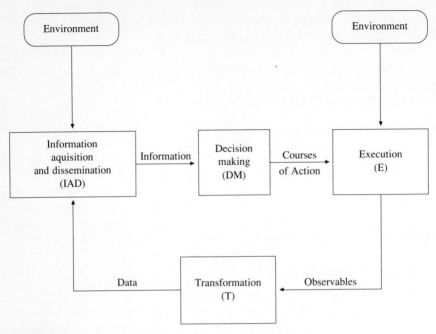

FIGURE 2.1
A generalized information system model. (Source: [YOV81], copyright ©1981, John Wiley and Sons, Inc., reprinted by permission of John Wiley and Sons, Inc.)

In the context of the information system model, a database management system is a computerized system that deals with the technological aspects of information acquisition and dissemination. Although the process of decision making, the execution of decisions, the effects of the external noises on execution, and the transformation of observable actions are not the functions of a DBMS, they are intimately related to it. Database management systems are not the only kind of systems that can be used to handle the acquisition and dissemination tasks of an information system. Others, such as the traditional file management systems, are also used often.

2.1.2   Database Management Systems Versus File Management Systems

Having put a database management system in the proper context of an information system and drawn the domain for it, this section will detail how the technical aspects of data acquisition and dissemination are handled in the conventional file management systems and how they are handled differently in DBMSs.

In the conventional file management system, data files are created and processed by programs written by the owners or users of the files. Files created by different users of an organization often contain redundant data. Also the

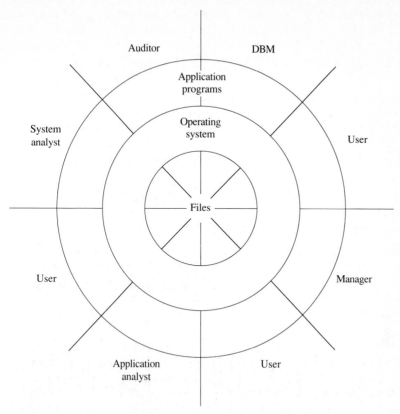

FIGURE 2.2
User-file interface in a traditional file system.

application programs often depend on the structural properties of the files, that is, the access path structures and the physical structures of the files are built into the program logic. Furthermore, the application programs interact directly with the operating system of a computer. Pictorially, the characteristics of a conventional file management system can be illustrated by Figure 2.2. The figure illustrates that each user uses a different set of programs to process different files through the software of an operating system.

There are a number of disadvantages associated with each of the characteristics of the conventional file management system. They can be summarized as follows:

1. Files are created and processed by special programs. It is not possible for a program to freely access arbitrary files in the system. In most real-world applications, it is often desirable and sometimes necessary for a user to freely access files across file boundaries. For example, before the manager of a company promotes an employee to a higher position, he or she may want to access several files pertaining to the employee. These files may include the

Employee Performance File for the employee's past and present performance, the Project File for the projects that he or she is currently involved in, the Medical File for health information, and so forth. Therefore, it is important that related files be easily accessible by an application program.

2. Files established by different branches of a large enterprise often contain a large amount of redundant data. Uncontrolled redundancy in files increases the cost of storage and complicates the problem of data updates and of keeping databases in a consistent state (i.e., without containing conflicting information).

3. Application programs are "dependent" upon the structures of the files they process, in the sense that these structures are built into the program logic. Any changes made in the file structure will entail changes to the application programs. Making changes to existing programs is extremely expensive and time-consuming.

4. Application programs interact directly with the operating system. No database management software other than the ones accessible through the operating system are available to the application programs. This means that the user or the programmer has to do much more, in terms of programming, in order to implement the data management functions.

In contrast to conventional file systems, a database management system allows data files to be integrated to avoid unnecessary redundancies. The users of a DBMS can access any file available in the system as long as the access does not violate security constraints. Multiple users can have access to the collection of files, with the possibility of each user or user group having a different "view" of the database. A view of a database may contain a subset of the set of integrated data files and/or files derivable from the set. It can also contain data items that are not in the original database but are derivable from the database. Furthermore, the application programs interact with the DBMS software, which provides various database management facilities to the programs. The accuracy, consistency, and security of a database are maintained by the DBMS rather than by the users' programs. Also, in a DBMS, changes made in the access strategy and in the physical organization of data do not require corresponding changes to be made in the application programs. This property is called *data independence* and is a very important concept of a DBMS. It will be discussed later in this chapter.

Based on this discussion, a database can be defined as a collection of integrated files containing data useful for decision making. A DBMS can be defined as a software package that provides all data management facilities for the creation, retrieval, manipulation, and maintenance of databases. Databases can be considered the center of a database system as illustrated in Figure 2.3. The user's application programs interact with a layer of DBMS software, which in turn uses the operating system software to create and manipulate the integrated files. Multiple users can have multiple views of a database and can have easy access to the integrated files subject to some integrity and security constraints.

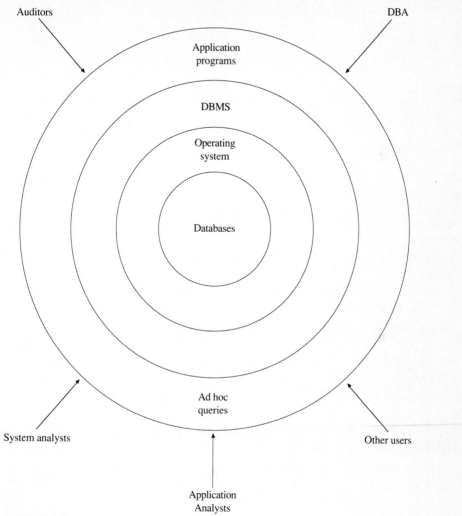

FIGURE 2.3
User-database in a DBMS.

The rigid partitioning of users, application programs, and files found in the conventional file systems as illustrated in Figure 2.2 does not exist in a DBMS.

2.1.3 Applications

Databases and database management technologies have very wide applications. Since, as was established in the preceding sections, databases and database management systems can serve as an important component of a general information system, all areas of human effort can use and benefit from these technologies. As illustrated in Figure 2.4, databases and a DBMS can be the basis of all application areas including CAD/CAM, information storage and retrieval, knowledge-

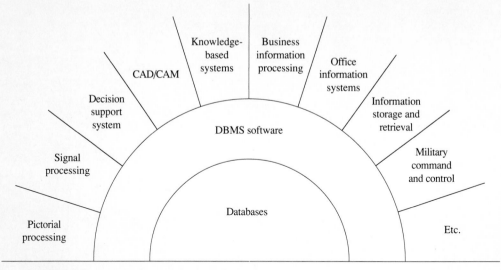

FIGURE 2.4
Databases and DBMS as the basis for other application areas.

based systems, decision support systems, business information processing, pictorial processing, signal processing, military command and control, and others. If the operations of databases and the functions of a DBMS can be made very efficient by using database machines, for example, it will be beneficial to all areas of computer applications.

2.2   DATABASE CONTENTS AND STRUCTURAL REPRESENTATIONS

In order to create, use, and maintain a database for the purpose of supporting the information and processing requirements of an organization, it is necessary to define or describe its information contents. The contents of a database can be described in terms of the structural properties, semantic constraints, and operations associated with the data objects to be stored in the database. The data objects that are described or defined are commonly called the *base data*. The description itself is commonly called the *metadata*, which is the data about the base data. In addition to these two types of data, a third type of data is generally added to the database to make the access to the other two types of data more convenient and efficient. This third type includes auxiliary data structures introduced in the implementation of a database (e.g., indexes, pointers, and linked lists). These three types of data make up the database as illustrated in Figure 2.5. The distinction between base data and metadata is not always clear since what may be defined as metadata by one user may be regarded as base data by another user. They can only be separated, somewhat subjectively, by the user or the database administrator (DBA) based on the nature of a specific application.

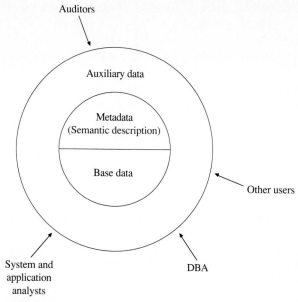

FIGURE 2.5
Three general types of data in a database.

The first two types of data are absolutely necessary for setting up a database, whereas the third type is not. It is this auxiliary data that many database machines attempt to reduce or eliminate since such data occupy additional storage space and complicate database updates. This will be discussed further in Section 2.2.4.

2.2.1   Semantic Description of a Database

In order to define or describe the semantic properties of a database, a proper tool is needed. Just as language is a tool for human beings to communicate ideas, a data model is a tool for defining or describing the contents of a database. A data model contains a set of constructs or mechanisms that can be used to define the meaningful relationships among data objects. For example, the popular relational model used in many existing DBMSs uses the relation as its main construct. The model introduced by the Conference on Data Systems Languages (CODASYL) Committee, called the CODASYL's network model [DBT71], is another data model that uses "record types," "sets," and "areas" as its basic constructs for defining a database. However, it is commonly recognized that the existing so-called data models are not "rich" enough in semantic constructs for a database designer or a database administrator to define the semantic contents of a database. For this reason, several models that are "rich" in semantic constructs have been introduced by researchers [CHE76, SMI77, HAM78, SU79, COD79, WIE79, HAM81, BRO81, SHI81, SU83, SU86, and HAL86] They are called *semantic models,* which are distinguished from the data models used in the existing DBMSs. These semantic models can be used as design tools for a database designer to define and describe a database. They can also be used as the underlying models for the implementation of DBMSs. In this section, the semantic association model (SAM∗) [SU83 and SU86] is used as a design tool to define an example database that will be used throughout this book to illustrate the design and operation of different database machines.

There are two main reasons for using SAM∗ for this purpose instead of using some other well-known models such as the aggregation and generalization model [SMI77], the entity-relationship model [CHE76], the functional model [SHI81], or the semantic database model [HAM81]. First, SAM∗ contains semantic constructs that capture most of the semantic properties recognized in these popular models. Second, the statistical aggregation operation to be described in Section 2.3.3 has been used as a benchmark operation for evaluating database computers. It is also used in this book for the analysis of abstract models for several categories of database machines. The distinction made in the field of statistics between *category attributes* and *summary attributes,* which is important in dealing with statistical aggregation operations, is not explicitly modeled by these popular models. SAM∗ uses *crossproduct* and *summarization* associations to mark the distinction.

In SAM∗, a database is defined by a network of *concept/object types,* each of which is defined in terms of other concept/object types. The grouping of concepts/objects for the purpose of defining another type is called an *association.* Based on the differences in the structural properties, semantic constraints, and operations associated with these concept/object types, the model distinguishes seven types of associations. These association types are the basic semantic constructs for modeling the complex structural and semantic relationships among the data objects of a database. Five association types are used in the following example.

Figure 2.6 is a graphic representation of a student database defined by a network of concept/object types, each of which is shown in the figure by a node. A node has a name and a label. The label is used to specify the association type by which the concept/object is defined. Each node or concept/object type has a set of occurrences associated with it. The set of occurrences forms a *domain.* The arcs leading out of a node represent the *attributes* of the concept/object type the node represents. The dashed arcs denote the key attributes or unique identifiers. A node pointed to by an arc is the domain from which the attribute draws its members. The label *M* stands for the *membership association* type in SAM∗, which defines a set of atomic concepts/objects. An *atomic concept/object* is a concept/object that cannot be broken down, and its meaning is assumed to be understood by the designer or user. It need not be defined in terms of other concepts/objects. For example, the *M* node named AGE defines a set of integer values. The meaning of age 25 need not be further defined. A membership constraint can be associated with an *M* node and used by a database designer to specify the legitimate values that form the set. For example, a university may restrict its enrollment only to students above a certain age.

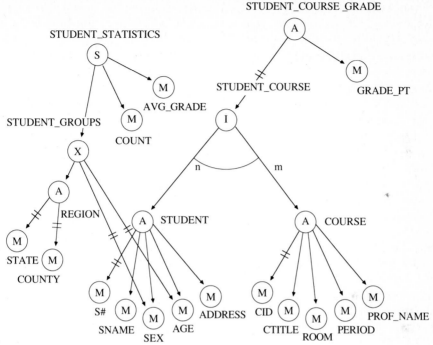

FIGURE 2.6
A conceptual design of a student database.

An *A* node in the network stands for an *aggregation association* type in SAM∗. Semantically, an aggregation association type defines a set of objects by their properties or characteristics. Structurally, it is a subset of the Cartesian product formed by its component sets. For example, the *A* node named STUDENT is defined by S#, SNAME, SEX, AGE, and ADDRESS, which are attributes of students. An occurrence of the *A* node (e.g., [16743, Joe Smith, Male, 24, '30 NE 10th St. Gainesville Florida 34102']), is a member of the Cartesian product formed by the sets named S#, SNAME, SEX, AGE, and ADDRESS. The word "aggregation," was first used in the model introduced by Smith and Smith [SMI77] and corresponds to the independent entity type of the entity-relationship model [CHE76].

An *I* node in Figure 2.6 stands for the *interaction association type* in SAM ∗. Semantically, it defines a set of facts that involve some action or interaction between two or more sets of objects. Structurally, it is again a subset of the Cartesian product formed by the component sets. For example, the *I* node named "STUDENT_COURSE" defines a set of facts stating which students take which courses. An occurrence of this node type is formed by an occurrence of STUDENT and an occurrence of COURSE. Since S# and CID can uniquely identify STUDENT and COURSE respectively, a pair of S# and CID (e.g., [23561,

C69]) can uniquely represent a STUDENT_COURSE occurrence. An occurrence of STUDENT_COURSE and an occurrence of GRADE in turn defines an occurrence of STUDENT_COURSE_GRADE.

Several semantic constraints are relevant to the interaction association type and can be defined by a database designer and used by a DBMS to enforce the integrity of a database. For example, students can be allowed to take many courses, and each course can be taken by many students. The so-called $n - m$ mapping constraint can be specified with the STUDENT_COURSE node as shown in the figure. Other mappings, $1 - 1$, $1 - n$, or $n - 1$, can also be used if, for some strange reason, a course can only be attended by one student $(1 - 1)$, a student can take many courses but a course can have only one student $(1 - n)$, or many students can be in a single course but a student cannot take more than one course $(n - 1)$.

Another semantic constraint associated with the interaction association type is called a *referential constraint* [DAT86]. It specifies that in order for an occurrence of that type to exist meaningfully in a database, the component values that form the occurrence must exist in the component types that define the *I* node. For example, if we record the fact that a student takes a certain course as an occurrence of STUDENT_COURSE, then that student must be an occurrence of STUDENT and that course must be an occurrence of COURSE. This type of constraint can be used by the DBMS to enforce the integrity of a database when it is first created or subsequently updated.

An X node in SAM∗ stands for a *cross product association type*. Semantically, it defines a number of categories of objects by taking all the possible combinations of the values of some attributes, called *category attributes* in the statistical data processing field. Structurally, it is a Cartesian product formed by its component sets. For example, the X node named "STUDENT_GROUPS" defines the categories of students by STATE, COUNTY, SEX, and AGE. An occurrence of an X node represents a category of objects rather than a single object. As a category, it is subject to statistical summarization that is modeled in SAM∗ by a separate association type called *summarization association*.

An S node, or summarization association, is defined by two subsets of concept/object types. One contains a single concept/object type that defines some categories of objects, and the other contains a set of concept/object types defining some statistical summary data of these categories. For example, the S node named "STUDENT_STATISTICS" records the counts and average grades of students categorized by STATE, COUNTY, SEX, and AGE. The S node and the data it represents can be subject to the statistical aggregation and disaggregation operations to be described in Section 2.3.3.

This semantic or conceptual description of the student database should exemplify the structural properties, constraints, and operations that can be used to characterize a database. Many other semantic properties recognized by SAM∗ and other semantic models are useful for an explicit and clear definition of the semantic contents of a database. A DBMS that is implemented based on a semantic model will provide a data definition facility for defining databases, a database manipulation facility to process the databases, and the necessary software to enforce the semantic constraints. Unfortunately, the existing DBMSs are implemented based on models that are at a relatively lower semantic level than the semantic models proposed by various researchers. As a result, many semantic properties cannot be expressed by the existing models and must be interpreted and distinguished by the application programs. This means that the individual application programs must bear the burden of bringing out the structural differences among the data objects, enforcing the integrity constraints, and ensuring that meaningful operations are performed on the data. Furthermore, since the underlying data model used by a DBMS is different from the semantic model used for database design, the result of a design (i.e., the semantic or conceptual description) must be transformed and stated in terms of the constructs of the data model used by a DBMS. In the next subsection, the relational model is used as the underlying data model to define some of the semantic properties discussed in this section.

2.2.2 Modeling a Database in a Database Management System

In a DBMS, a data definition language (DDL) is provided to the user for defining the semantics of a database. The nature and power of this language largely depends upon the underlying data model used by the DBMS. The set of language statements that defines a database is called a *schema.* Two types of schemata are of concern here: the conceptual schema and the external schema [ANS75]. The *conceptual schema* defines the database as seen by the database administrator. It represents the community users' collective view of the database, which is generally different from the individuals' views. An *external schema,* on the other hand, defines the database as seen by a particular user or a user group (i.e., an individual's view of the database). What a schema defines is a model of a database. The conceptual schema defines a conceptual model of the database, whereas each external schema defines an external model of the database.

Multiple external schemata can be defined for the community of users. These schemata not only define the database contents as seen by the different users, but also define the so-called mappings between the external schemata and the conceptual schema. The mappings are language statements specifying the way data defined by the external schemata can be derived from the data defined by the conceptual schema. The relationship between the above two types of schemata is illustrated in Figure 2.7.

2.2.2.1 CONCEPTUAL MODEL. The relational model introduced by Codd [COD70] will be used as the underlying data model of a DBMS to define the conceptual model of the student database given in the preceding section. The relational model was chosen over other popular models (e.g., the network and hierarchical models), because most existing database machines are designed to support the relational model. Figure 2.8 shows a conceptual schema of the stu-

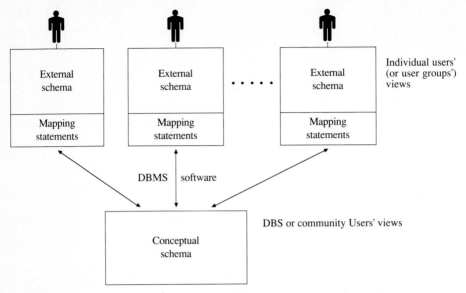

FIGURE 2.7
The relationship between the conceptual schema and the external schemata.

dent database. The DDL language used here is for illustration purposes. It does not correspond to any implemented language. The schema defines four relations, each of which contains a number of domains. A relation in the relational model can be formally defined as follows:

```
Domains
S#              INTEGER (5),
SNAME           CHAR (25),
SEX             CHAR (1) (M, F),
AGE             INTEGER (2) (16 ≤ X ≤ 70),
ADDRESS         CHAR (45),
CID             CHAR (7),
CTITLE          CHAR (20),
ROOM            CHAR (10),
PERIOD          INTEGER (1) (1 ≤ X ≤ 7),
PROF_NAME       CHAR (25),
STATE           CHAR (10),
COUNTY          CHAR (10),
COUNT           INTEGER (7),
AVG_GRADE       REAL(2.1) (0 < X ≤ 4),
GRADE_PT        REAL(2.1) (0 < X ≤ 4),
Relations
```

STUDENT (S#, SNAME, SEX, AGE, ADDRESS) KEY (S#),
COURSE (CID, CTITLE, ROOM, PERIOD, PROF_NAME) KEY (CID),
STUDENT_COURSE (S#, CID, GRADE_PT) KEY (S#, CID),
STUDENT_STATISTICS (STATE, COUNTY, SEX, AGE, COUNT, AVG_GRADE)
          KEY (STATE, COUNTY, SEX, AGE),

FIGURE 2.8
A conceptual schema of the STUDENT database.

Let D_1, D_2, ...D_N be sets, each of which contains a number of homogeneous data objects. A relation R is a set of ordered N-tuples $< d_1, d_2, ..., d_N >$, where $d_1 \epsilon D_1$, $d_2 \epsilon D_2$, ..., $d_N \epsilon D_N$. R is a subset of the Cartesian product denoted by $D_1 \times D_2 \times .... \times D_N$ where $D_1, D_2, ..., D_N$ are the domains of R and N is the degree of R.

In Figure 2.8, STUDENT, COURSE, STUDENT_COURSE, and STUDENT_STATISTICS are relations, and their domains are defined by specifying the characteristics of the data objects, which constitute the domains, together with their associated integrity constraints. A domain can be used in more than one relation in a database. It may have a slightly different meaning in each relation even though the same set of values are used to make up the relations. In this case, the domain is given different attribute names. For example, COURSE_NUMBER and PREREQUISITE_COURSE_NUMBER can be two attribute names given to the same domain CID and are used in different relations. However, in most cases, the attribute names are identical to the domain names, as is the case in the schema given in Figure 2.8. For the sake of accuracy in terminology, the names associated with the relations in a schema will be referred to here as the attribute names.

The schema in Figure 2.8 defines four relation types: STUDENT, COURSE, STUDENT_COURSE, and STUDENT_STATISTICS. The occurrences of the four relation types are loaded into the database when the database is created. Figure 2.9 shows some possible occurrences of these relation types in tabular form. An occurrence of a relation type is called a *tuple* in the relational model.

A relation in the relational model has the following properties:

1. Each tuple of a relation is unique. This property implies that the value or values of one or more attributes (a composite attribute) of a tuple can uniquely identify the tuple, that is, can distinguish the tuple from all the other tuples of the relation. More than one attribute or composite attributes may have the uniqueness property. They are called *candidate keys*. One of the candidate keys is declared as the *primary key* of the relation. For example, S# is the only candidate key and is declared as the primary key of the relation STUDENT in Figure 2.9 and can be used to uniquely identify each student. A *foreign key* is an attribute of a relation that is not a key to the relation but is a primary key of a related relation. For example, S# and CID in the relation STUDENT_COURSE of Figure 2.9 are foreign keys. They together form a primary key (a composite key) of the relation STUDENT_COURSE.

2. Each value in a tuple is an atomic element. This means that each value is a single element that cannot be broken down to smaller elements; it cannot itself be a relation.

3. The order of the tuples in a relation is insignificant. This means that changing the order of these tuples does not change the semantic contents of the relation. Thus, any order in which these tuples are processed will produce the same result. This property is used by some database machines (to be described later in the text) to place data in different memories and to process them independently, regardless of tuple ordering.

STUDENT

S#	SNAME	SEX	AGE	ADDRESS
14256	J.R. Jones	M	23	412 NW 5th St., Gainesville, FL. 32601
16242	J.C. Brown	F	21	1243 NE 10th Ave., Newberry, FL. 32401
17522	T.S. Larsen	M	26	1410 University Ave., Gainesville, FL. 32605
18600	H. Hsu	F	23	32 NW 11th Lane, Willston, FL. 34200
24010	S.H. Smith	F	24	4236 SW 13th Ave., Gainesville, FL. 32611

COURSE

CID	CTITLE	ROOM	PERIOD	PROF_NAME
CIS4121	Computer Organization	Larsen 210	2	T.B. Bronson
CIS6220	Compilers	Benton 211	4	S.B. Jensen
EE5417	Database Engineering	Weil 507	6	N.T. Yong
EE6967	Database Machines	Larsen 210	4	T.B. Bronson

FIGURE 2.9
Relations of the STUDENT database.

4. The order of the columns of a relation is insignificant as long as the relationship between the values and the attribute they are associated with is maintained. This property is also used by some database machines to process columns of data in an arbitrary order.

A relation in the relational model is a very simple and uniform structure for defining a database. However, some semantics of a database cannot be defined by relations, and others can only be implicitly defined. These semantic properties would have to be interpreted and handled by the users through their application programs. For example, the database defined by the schema in Figure 2.8 does not include all the semantic properties modeled by Figure 2.6 and discussed in Section 2.2.1. The relation STUDENT_STATISTICS models the X and S nodes of Figure 2.6. However, the semantic distinctions made between (1) category attributes (STATE, COUNTY, SEX, etc.) and summary attributes (COUNT and AVG_GRADE) and (2) STUDENT_GROUPS, which models groups of students, and STUDENT, which models individual students, are not made in STUDENT_STATISTICS of Figure 2.8. Also, the n-m mapping between STUDENT and COURSE in Figure 2.6 is not explicitly specified in the schema of Figure 2.8.

STUDENT_COURSE

S#	CID	GRADE_PT
16242	CIS4121	4.0
17522	EE5417	3.0
18600	EE5417	4.0
24010	EE6967	2.5
18600	CIS6220	3.0
14256	EE6967	4.0
17522	CIS4121	3.0
18600	CIS4121	3.0
14256	CIS6220	4.0

STUDENT_STATISTICS

STATE	COUNTY	SEX	AGE	COUNT	AVG_GRADE
Florida	Orange	M	22	1210	3.7
Florida	Orange	F	22	1219	3.0
Florida	Orange	M	23	1150	2.90
Florida	Orange	F	23	960	2.50
Florida	Alachua	M	22	2456	3.65
Florida	Alachua	F	22	2412	2.89
Florida	Alachua	M	23	2566	3.44
Florida	Alachua	F	23	1967	3.60
.	.	.	.	.	.
.	.	.	.	.	.
.	.	.	.	.	.

FIGURE 2.9
(continued)

2.2.2.2 EXTERNAL MODELS. The two examples in Figure 2.10 illustrate that multiple external schemata can be defined over a conceptual schema. Figure 2.10(*a*) defines a user's view of the database in which the course information is of no concern to the user. Only a selected number of attributes in the original STUDENT relation are of interest. Also, the user is only interested in the counts and average grades of student groups by sex and by age. Figure 2.10(*b*) defines another user's view in which the relation STUDENT contains some attributes from the original STUDENT, COURSE, and STUDENT_COURSE relations, and the counts and average grades of the student groups by state are of

Domains

S#	INTEGER (5),
SNAME	CHAR (25),
ADDRESS	CHAR (45),
CID	CHAR (7),
CTITLE	CHAR (20),
PROF_NAME	CHAR (25),
GRADE_PT	REAL (2.1) $(0 < X \le 4)$,
SEX	CHAR (1) (M, F),
AGE	INTEGER (2) $(18 \le X \le 45)$,
COUNT	INTEGER (7),
AVG_GRADE	REAL (2.1),

Relations

STUDENT (S#, SNAME, ADDRESS) KEY (S#),
COURSE_STUDENT (CID, S#, CTITLE, PROF_NAME, GRADE_PT) KEY (CID, S#),
STUDENT_GRADE_BY_SEX_AGE (SEX, AGE, COUNT, AVG_GRADE)
                   KEY (SEX, AGE),

Domains

S#	INTEGER (5),
SNAME	CHAR (25),
CID	CHAR (7),
CTITLE	CHAR (20),
GRADE_PT	REAL (2.1) $(0 < X \le 4)$,
STATE	CHAR (10),
COUNT	INTEGER (7),
AVG_GRADE	REAL (2.1) $(0 < X \le 4)$,

Relations

STUDENT (S#, CID, SNAME, CTITLE, GRADE_PT) KEY (S#, CID),
STUDENT_GRADE_BY_STATE (STATE, COUNT, AVG_GRADE) KEY (STATE),

FIGURE 2.10
(a) External schema 1 of the STUDENT database. (b) External schema 2 of the STUDENT database.

interest to the user. The external schemata contain some mapping statements that are usually defined using a data manipulation language (DML), another facility provided by a DBMS. These mapping statements allow the DBMS software to derive the relations of the external schemata from the relations of the conceptual schema or to translate a query issued by the user for processing against the external schemata to one that is suitable for processing against the conceptual schema.

The distinction made in a DBMS between the database defined by the external schemata and the one defined by the conceptual schema is necessary for two reasons: (1) to support multiple users' views of the database in which data are structured in accordance with the users' specifications and (2) to provide a means of data protection, since the DBMS will allow users to access only those data defined by their own views. However, it should be pointed out that the mapping or translation of queries and data between the external schemata and the conceptual schema is a very time-consuming process and is one of the main causes of inefficiency in existing DBMSs. The mapping process will be illustrated in Section 2.4.3, and the issue of inefficiency will be reexamined in Section 2.5.

2.2.2.3   INTERNAL MODEL. The structures of data seen by the end user and the database administrator, as represented by the external and conceptual schemata, can be quite different from the storage structure in which data are organized for efficient access purposes. In a DBMS, the storage structure of a database is defined by an *internal schema* in the ANSI SPARC terminology [ANS75]. Its relationship to the external and conceptual schemata is illustrated in Figure 2.11. The conceptual schema contains certain mapping statements to specify how the data defined in it correspond to the storage structures defined in the internal schema. The language used to define the storage structures of the database can be quite different from the DDL used for the external and conceptual schemata because of the differences in structures. Special storage structures are required to organize and store the data because it is very inefficient for conventional computers to directly process data using the structures defined in the conceptual schema. For example, the relation COURSE in Figure 2.9 contains a set of tuples. If it is implemented using the structure as defined, it will correspond to a sequential file of records. Retrieving all tuples of the relation that satisfy the conditions that PROF_NAME equals 'T. B. Bronson' or ROOM equals 'Benton 211,' amounts to sequentially processing each record of the entire file. This will be very time-consuming if the number of records is large.

To make the retrieval more efficient, a DBMS can use several data structures to implement the relation. A popular one is the index structure shown in Figure 2.12, which introduces two indices, one on PROF_NAME and the other on ROOM. The index file named "PROF_INDEX" contains a set of records, each of which stores a professor's name and a number of pointers to the records of the master file COURSE in which the professor's name can be found. The index file named "ROOM_INDEX" contains a set of records, each of which stores a

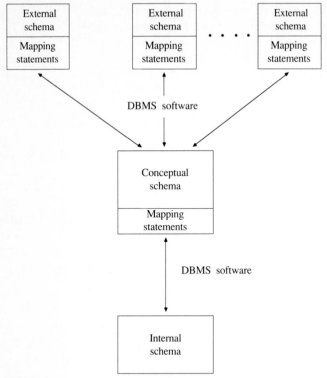

FIGURE 2.11
The relationships among external schemata, conceptual schema, and internal schema.

room number and a number of pointers to the records of COURSE in which the room number can be found. To respond to the retrieval request stated before, the DBMS software can search the PROF_INDEX for 'T. B. Bronson' and retrieve the associated pointers. It can then search the ROOM_INDEX for 'Benton 211' and retrieve another set of pointers. The set union of these two sets of pointers provides the locations where the COURSE records can be directly found and retrieved. Thus, the sequential access of the large COURSE file can be avoided.

While this indexing scheme offers a significant advantage in data retrieval, it also introduces an additional storage requirement for storing the index files. Furthermore, it makes database updates much more complicated since changes made on the values of PROF_NAME and ROOM in the COURSE file will require some corresponding updates in the index files if the database is to remain in a consistent state. The index files constitute the auxiliary data discussed in Section 2.2. They do not add any new information to the original COURSE file but are added to the database to achieve the needed efficiency in data retrieval.

The advantages of setting up the indices exist only if retrieval requests use the indexed fields in their search conditions. Otherwise, the master file COURSE still would have to be searched sequentially. For this reason, many physical

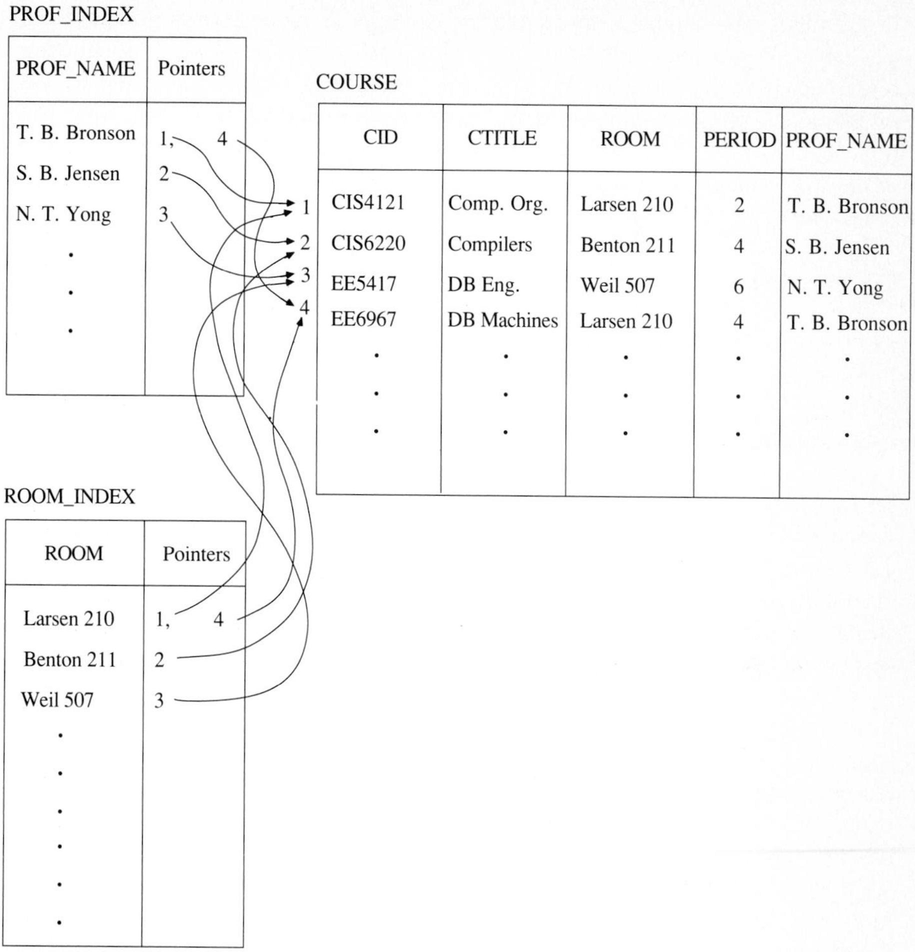

PROF_INDEX

PROF_NAME	Pointers
T. B. Bronson	1, 4
S. B. Jensen	2
N. T. Yong	3
.	
.	
.	

COURSE

	CID	CTITLE	ROOM	PERIOD	PROF_NAME
1	CIS4121	Comp. Org.	Larsen 210	2	T. B. Bronson
2	CIS6220	Compilers	Benton 211	4	S. B. Jensen
3	EE5417	DB Eng.	Weil 507	6	N. T. Yong
4	EE6967	DB Machines	Larsen 210	4	T. B. Bronson
	.	.	.	.	.
	.	.	.	.	.
	.	.	.	.	.

ROOM_INDEX

ROOM	Pointers
Larsen 210	1, 4
Benton 211	2
Weil 507	3
.	
.	
.	
.	
.	

FIGURE 2.12
An Indexed file.

implementations use a considerable number of these indices. If one is unable to predetermine which data fields will be used the most in search conditions, then indices may have to be introduced for all the fields of a file. This organization is called a *fully inverted file organization.* This structure, of course, uses even more storage space than a normal indexed file and makes database updates even more difficult. In general, all storage structures used in existing DBMSs for implementing a database defined by a conceptual schema support retrieval operations at the expense of storage requirements and ease of updates. Thus, the software overhead for processing and maintaining the auxiliary data cannot be overlooked.

It is somewhat misleading to call the structure shown in Figure 2.12 a storage structure since it does not represent the way in which data are physically organized in the main memory or in the secondary storage. A more accurate description, used in some database literature, is *access path structure,* since this structure represents how data can be accessed (i.e., the access path) without the details of the actual physical data organization. There are at least two other structural representations in most implementations of a data file: (1) the physical structure in the main memory, or the encoding structure, and (2) the physical structure in the secondary storage, or the access method structure.

The encoding structure. In order to process a file defined in the internal schema on a conventional computer system, it is necessary to read the records of the file from some secondary storage device to an I/O buffer in the main memory. Furthermore, the records must be moved from the I/O buffer to the data area of the application program that processes the file. The *encoding structure* is the data structure used to encode the records in the data area of a program. It deals with the way data are packed into machine words. This structure is dictated by the compiler and the hardware used. The compiler translates the program variables and their values into machine words, and the word width of the hardware determines the way data are packed in the machine words. As an example, the encoding structure of the COURSE file may resemble Figure 2.13. Here the string of characters 'CIS4121 COMPUTER ORGANIZATION...' is represented by placing two characters in each machine word. This structure represents another level of data mapping required in the existing implementation of a data file. The mapping in this case is handled by the compiler.

Access method structure. The data structure used to store a data file in the secondary storage can be quite different from that of the file defined in the internal schema. The structure is generally dictated by the characteristics of the secondary storage device (e.g., sequential access or random access). It determines how data in the file can be accessed from the secondary storage. In the conventional implementation, the access to a file in a secondary storage is handled by a piece of software in the operating system called an *access method routine,* which recognizes the device characteristics and the idiosyncracies of the particular structure used for the file. A file structure in a secondary storage is therefore called an *access method structure.*

There are a number of access method structures commonly used in the existing systems. They include the sequential access method (SAM), index sequential access method (ISAM), direct access method (DAM), overflow sequential access method (OSAM), and virtual sequential access method (VSAM). They are supported by the access method routines of the operating system. These routines in effect handle the data mapping between the encoding structures and the access method structures. They are used by the DBMS software to access and manipulate the files in a database. As shown previously in Figure 2.3, the DBMS accesses the database through the operating system.

As an example of access method structures, Figure 2.14 illustrates an ISAM structure of the COURSE file. In this structure, a file consists of three types of

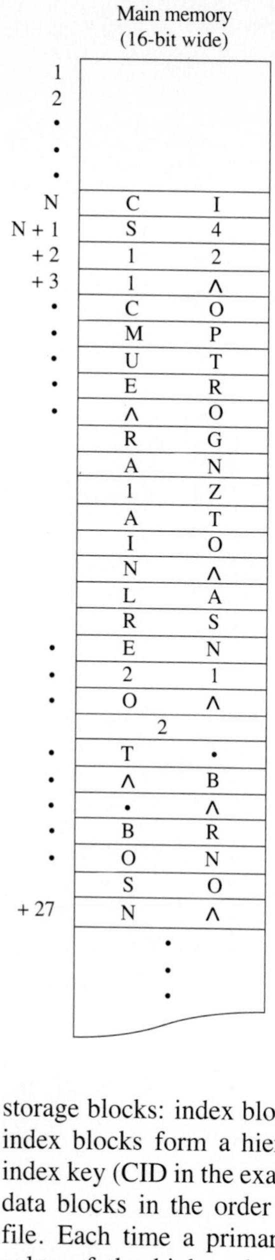

Main memory
(16-bit wide)

1		
2		
·		
·		
·		
N	C	I
N + 1	S	4
+ 2	1	2
+ 3	1	^
·	C	O
·	M	P
·	U	T
·	E	R
·	^	O
	R	G
	A	N
	1	Z
	A	T
	I	O
	N	^
	L	A
	R	S
·	E	N
·	2	1
·	O	^
	2	
·	T	·
·	^	B
·	·	^
·	B	R
·	O	N
	S	O
+ 27	N	^
	·	
	·	
	·	

FIGURE 2.13
A main memory layout.

storage blocks: index blocks, primary data blocks, and overflow data blocks. The index blocks form a hierarchical structure and contain the values of a selected index key (CID in the example). The COURSE records are loaded into the primary data blocks in the order of their key sequence during the initial loading of the file. Each time a primary data block is filled, an index entry representing the value of the highest key in that data block is established in an index block. When an index block is full, a new index block is used to store the indices, and a hierarchical structure of index blocks is established. Each parent node in the hierarchy contains the highest key values of the child nodes. The loading of the data records and the establishment of the index hierarchy from the leaf nodes to the root would continue until all data records have been loaded in sequential order.

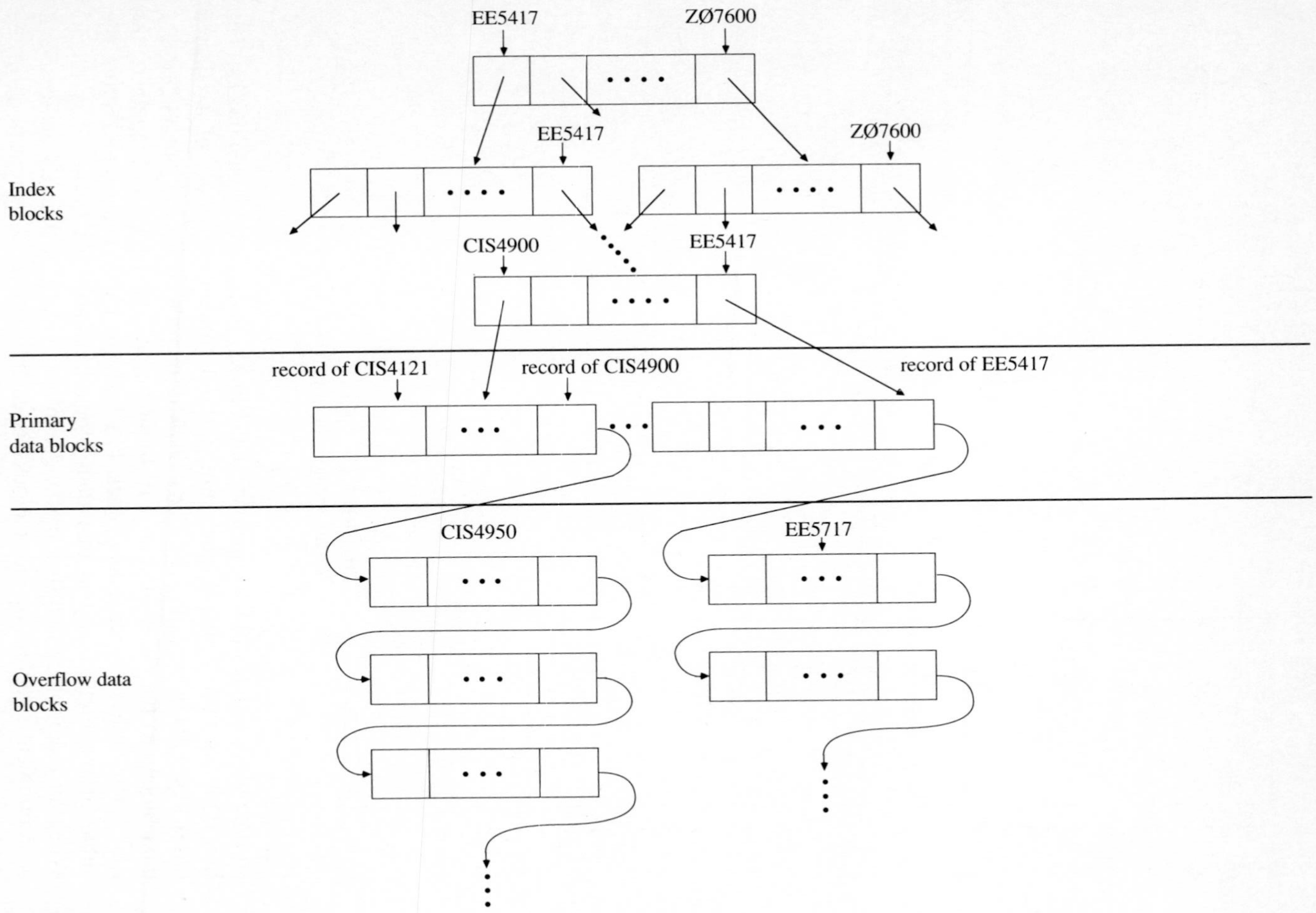

FIGURE 2.14
An index sequential access method (ISAM) file.

Index blocks

EE5417 ZØ7600 ZØ7600

EE5417 EE5417 CIS4900

record of CIS4121 record of CIS4900 record of EE5417

Primary data blocks

CIS4950 EE5717

Overflow data blocks

38

After the initial loading, the index hierarchy stays fixed. All subsequent insertions of new records will either go to the proper primary data blocks or to the overflow data blocks, depending on the key values of the inserted records. Overflow data blocks are used when there is no more space in a primary block. These blocks are chained to the corresponding primary data block. During the retrieval process, the index structure is used to reach a leaf node of the hierarchy containing the given key value. This leaf node contains an address pointer associated with the key value, which is used to access a primary data block. The primary data block and its associated overflow data blocks are then sequentially searched to retrieve the record.

*   *   *

To conclude this section on database contents and structural representations, it is important to remember that a database can be defined and stored in many different structures. These structures represent different levels of data representations for the same database. They are necessary for bridging the gap between the user's view of the database and what is actually stored in a computer. In a traditional implementation of a DBMS, the mappings between two adjacent levels are handled by the software of the DBMS, the compiler, or the operating system as illustrated in Figure 2.15. They are very time-consuming processes and represent a main cause of inefficiency in a conventional DBMS. Many database machines reduce the number of these levels by storing data in a structure very close to the user's view of the database and by processing the data using special-purpose hardware. Such machines will be described in more detail later in the text.

2.3 DATABASE OPERATIONS, ALGORITHMS, AND ANALYSES

Once a database has been designed and established by a DBMS, the user of the database can retrieve and manipulate the data in the database using a DML provided by the DBMS. The syntax and semantics of a DML are closely tied to the data model used to define the database. The language can be "high-level," in that the constructs of the language are very close to those needed in applications rather than those interpretable by the machine. It can be "non-procedural," in that the language requires the user to state only *what* operation he or she wants to perform rather than *how* this operation should be performed (i.e., access methods to be used, etc.). Some examples of high-level and nonprocedural languages are SQL [CHA74 and CHA76], QBE [ZLO75], and QUEL [HEL75, ALL76, and STO76]. There are also quite a few "low-level" and "procedural" DMLs such as the DML for the CODASYL's network model [ANS75], the DL/1 language of the IBM's IMS (a database management system based on a hierarchical model [MCG77 and KAP78]), and the algebraic language of the relational model [COD72a]. Regardless of their nature, all DMLs allow users to specify all the retrieval and

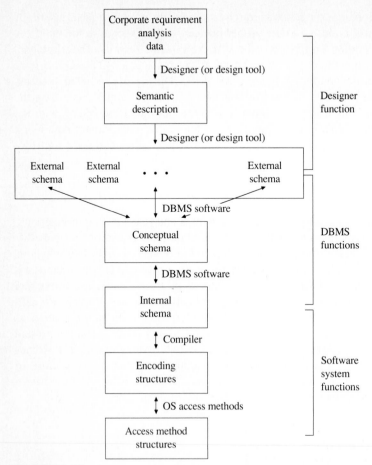

FIGURE 2.15
Levels of data representations of a database.

storage operations (e.g., insertion, deletion, and updating) that he or she might want to perform on the data objects defined in his or her external schema.

There are a number of primitive database operations that are necessary for retrieving and manipulating the data in a database. A high-level language statement can be translated into these primitives, which then carry out the intended operation. The following subsections classify these primitives into four categories and use the STUDENT database to illustrate the meaning of these operations. The categories are based on the amount of processing required by each of these operations. They are used in this book for the analysis of different categories of database machines. Since the relational model has been used to model the STUDENT database, the relational algebra [COD72a] will be used to describe these primitives. Similar database operations are commonly used to process databases defined by other data models.

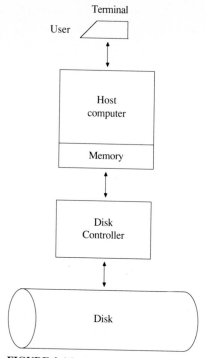

FIGURE 2.16
An abstract model of a conventional computer system.

The following subsections also provide the analyses of some popular algorithms for the representative operations in the previously mentioned categories. The analyses provided in this chapter will be done for the abstract model of a conventional computer system as shown in Figure 2.16. The model consists of a user terminal, a central processor with a main memory, a disk controller, and a disk. Similar analyses will be done in subsequent chapters based on the abstract models of various categories of database computers. The main purposes of these analyses are (1) to show how data and control information flow through the various hardware components of the the abstract models in order to show the architectural features of the systems represented by these models, (2) to identify the important parameters that can affect the performance of the different categories of database computers, (3) to show how algorithms, data distributions and placement on secondary storage devices, and architectural features are interrelated in determining the performance of a database computer, and (4) to provide readers some general guidelines on the analyses of algorithms and performance evaluations so that they can follow the techniques to conduct more detailed analysis and evaluation of systems using specific parameters and values that best represent their computing environment, database characteristics, and processing requirements.

This book makes no attempt to compare the performance of specific database computers for the following reasons. First, different computers have been designed for different purposes (e.g., to eliminate different bottlenecks of the conventional system). Second, they often use different hardware technologies in their design and implementation. The performance of one system will be drastically different if it adopts the technology used by another system. Third, the data organization, data distribution, and physical placement of data in secondary storage are often different. They have a great effect on the performance. Fourth, the algorithms used for performing primitive database operations are often different. Although, a considerable amount of analysis and evaluation papers on specific systems, and a few on the comparison of different systems, are available in the literature, the parameters and parameter values assigned to them are often different. Many different assumptions were made in these evaluations.

These and other differences among database computers make direct comparisons among them very difficult. The results of any direct comparison will not be very meaningful. In addition, the details about the architectures, algorithms, data organizations, processing techniques, technologies, and so forth of many existing database computers, which are needed for a thorough analysis and evaluation of database computers, are not available in the literature. It is not possible for us to fill in the missing information for the various systems.

For the purposes of analysis stated previously, this text will examine the performance of the abstract models introduced to represent different categories of computers instead of examining the performance of specific computers. Also, the analysis will be limited to data and control flows in these abstract models when algorithms for some representative database operations are executed. This limitation is chosen because transfer of data and control information such as commands, status, and synchronization messages are common to all architectures. The time components involved in these transfers can reflect the characteristics and limitations of these models.

2.3.1   Single-Pass Operations

This type of operation involves a single scan of the tuples of a relation, that is, each tuple is examined only once in the operation. The Select operation of relational algebra is a typical example of a single-pass operation. The following Select statement retrieves tuples, which satisfy the qualification conditions specified in parentheses, from the relation COURSE.

SELECT COURSE(PROF_NAME = T.B. BRONSON AND PERIOD = 2)

When this operation is performed on the relation COURSE shown in Figure 2.9, the first tuple with CID = CIS412 will be retrieved. The result of the Select is a relation shown in Figure 2.17 as BRONSON_COURSE.

The other single-pass operations frequently used in database applications are the so-called aggregation functions. They include taking the sum, count, average, maximum, and minimum of a set of attribute values. To compute these aggregation functions, it is necessary to access every tuple of a relation to extract

BRONSON_COURSE

CID	CTITLE	ROOM	PERIOD	PROF_NAME
CIS4121	Computer Organization	Larsen 210	2	T.B. BRONSON

FIGURE 2.17
The result of a SELECT operation.

the value of a specified attribute. However, a single pass through the tuples of the relation is sufficient to compute the function.

The abstract model of a conventional system will be used here to discuss the algorithm for the Select operation and its analysis. The algorithm for Select is very simple. Assuming that the relation is stored as a file in the secondary storage of a conventional system, logical pages of this file, which correspond to fixed-length, physical blocks of data, will be read one page at a time into the main memory and processed by the processor. Each tuple in a page will be examined to determine if it satisfies the search condition(s) specified by the Select command. Qualified tuples are then accumulated in an output buffer and transferred to the secondary storage when the buffer is filled. The result of Select is a relation L, which is stored on the secondary storage as a part of the database. It can be further processed by other operations or be transferred to the user.

This algorithm is not the most efficient one for the conventional system model. Usually, a DBMS will establish indices for some selected attributes of a relation, as has been discussed in Section 2.2.2.3. If a selection query makes reference to these selected attributes, the indices can be used to directly access a subset of tuples so that the entire relation does not have to be scanned. However, there is an overhead cost involved in setting up, accessing, and updating indices. Therefore, in the following analysis of the Select operation, the most straightforward algorithm will be used.

There are three major time components involved in this and all other algorithms to be described in this book. They are: (1) instruction flow time, denoted by $t[inst\_flow]$, (2) data processing time, denoted by $t[process]$, and (3) data collection time, denoted by $t[data\_collect]$. The key parameters used in the analyses of algorithms presented in this section are shown in Table 2.1.

An analysis of the Select operation for the conventional system model has been described by DeWitt [DEW81]. A selection query is received by the processor and is compiled into a set of instructions. Since the instructions are in the main memory ready for execution, the instruction flow time involves only the compilation time (some other database machine models may involve the transfer of the instructions to another processor or processors). Thus,

$$t[inst\_flow] = t[comp]$$

The time required to read a page of the relation R is given by

$$t[read\_page, R] = t[access] + t[I/O]$$

TABLE 2.1
Performance Parameters

Parameter	Definition
c_fac	Collision factor; a value greater than one to account for the extra processing needed due to collisions in hashing
jn_fac	Join selectivity factor; that is, the ratio of the number of tuples of L to the number of tuples of the crossproduct between R and S
L	Name of the resulting relation of an operation
m	Number of pages in relation R
q	Number of tracks in a disk cylinder
R	Name of a referenced relation
s	Number of pages in relation S
S	Name of the inner relation in a Join operation
sel_fac	Selectivity factor for the Selection operation; that is, the ratio of the number of selected tuples of a referenced relation to the number of tuples of that relation
t	Number of tuples per page of R or S
u	Total number of pages of L produced by joining relations R and S
w	Number of distinct categories of category attributes and values
x	Number of attributes involved in selection conditions
$t[access]$	Disk seek time plus latency
$t[comp]$	Compilation time for a simple query
$t[cpu]$	Time for comparing two values in registers or an arithmetic operation
$t[hash]$	Time for performing a hash function over an attribute value
$t[I/O]$	Track (page) read/write time
$t[lat]$	Disk latency time
$t[mov]$	Time for moving a tuple of R or S
$t[rev]$	Disk revolution time; also used as the time for reading or writing a page in the analysis
$t[s]$	Time to load a value from the memory to a register
$t[seek]$	Disk seek time
$t[tp\_out]$	Time for transferring a tuple to an output buffer associated with the user-interface device (e.g., a terminal)

where

$$t[access] = t[seek] + t[lat] \text{ and } t[I/O] = t[rev].$$

In the analyses given throughout this book, it is assumed that the pages of a relation are stored in consecutive disk tracks. The reading or writing of a relation will incur one $t[access]$ for the seek time and latency time involved in reading or writing the first page. The small amount of time for track-to-track or intercylinder head movement is ignored. This assumption means that the disk read/write heads are not moved away from the current position during the reading or writing of a relation due to other I/O operations in the system. In the case of an operation that involves the reading and writing of more than one relation, it is assumed that each relation is read from or written to a different disk unit; thus, there is no conflict in different I/O operations. It is assumed that there are q tracks in a cylinder of a disk and each track is the same size as a page. A cylinder-full of data is read and processed at a time. The time necessary to read an entire cylinder would be

$$t[read\_q\_pg, R] = q * t[I/O]$$

Here, the one $t[access]$ needed to position the read/write head at the beginning of the input operation has not been included. It will be added later in the final formula. The time required to process a tuple consists of two time components: (1) $t[s]$, for loading the value of an attribute specified in the selection command from the main memory to the processor's register and (2) $t[cpu]$, for performing the comparison operation. If there are x attributes specified in the selection command as the search conditions, the time necessary to process a tuple of R is

$$t[process\_tuple, R] = x * \{2 * t[s] + t[cpu]\}$$

where $x \geq 1$ and $2 * t[s]$ accounts for the time to load two values to be compared. During the processing of R tuples, if a tuple satisfies the selection condition(s), it is moved to an output buffer. If the selectivity factor is denoted by sel_fac, a real number whose value is between 0 and 1, then $q * t * sel\_fac$ tuples out of q pages would satisfy the search. These tuples need to be moved to the output buffer for transfer to the disk.

The time necessary to process q pages with t tuples each is then:

$$t[process\_q\_pg, R] = q * t * t[process\_tuple, R] + q * t * sel\_fac * t[mov]$$

Since the relation R has m pages and there are m/q loads of q pages of R to be processed, the time required to process the tuples of R is

$$(m/q) * t[process\_q\_pg, R]$$

As the tuples of R are being processed, the tuples that satisfied the selection conditions are moved to the output buffer. When the output buffer is full, the selected tuples in the buffer are written to the secondary storage. These tuples form the resulting relations L. The time required to write the relations L is

$$t[I/O, L] = \text{ceil}(m * \text{sel\_fac}) * t[I/O]$$

Here, ceil is the function that rounds a fraction number up to the next higher integer value, which is the number of pages of L that need to be written.

The total time required to process R would then be

$$t[\text{process}] = 2 * t[\text{access}] + (m/q) * \{t[\text{read\_}q\text{\_pg}, R]$$

$$+ t[\text{process\_}q\text{\_pg}, R]\} + t[I/O, L].$$

Here, $2 * t[\text{access}]$ accounts for the seek time and latency time involved in the reading of R and the writing of L.

The third main time component, $t[\text{collect}]$, also must be considered. Since, in general, the result of a selection operation is established in the database as a relation, qualified tuples of R have been written to the secondary storage. Since there are $\text{ceil}(m * \text{sel\_fac})$ output pages of the resulting relation L on the disk, it will take the following amount of time to read them back from the secondary storage.

$$t[\text{access}] + t[I/O, L]$$

The tuples in these pages need to be transferred to the user's terminal. There are $m * t * \text{sel\_fac}$ of tuples that need to be output. Therefore, the total data collection time would be

$$t[\text{data\_collect}] = t[\text{access}] + t[I/O, L] + m * t * \text{sel\_fac} * t[\text{tp\_out}]$$

Here, $t[\text{tp\_out}]$ is the time to output a tuple to the user at a terminal. Its value would depend on the device used for I/O and the method of data transfer (e.g., character, line, or block transfer). If a sophisticated terminal is used as the output device, then $t[\text{tp\_out}]$ will be the time for moving a tuple to an output buffer from which the terminal automatically extracts the buffer's contents. Assuming no overlap in the three main time components, the total execution time for this algorithm is

$$t[\text{select}] = t[\text{inst\_flow}] + t[\text{process}] + t[\text{data\_collect}]$$

In the case of an overlap between or among these time components or their subcomponents, the smaller time component(s) is ignored.

2.3.2   Multi-Pass Operations

Two operations are considered in this category: Projection and Join.

2.3.2.1   PROJECTION. One very common primitive operation in this category is the Project operation, which consists of two suboperations. The first suboperation is a single-scan operation that involves processing each tuple of a relation and selecting a subset of the attribute values. The result is a relation defined over the selected attributes or columns of the original relation. The second suboperation is a multipass operation that involves the elimination of duplicate tuples in the new relation obtained by the first suboperation. For example, examine the following Project operation performed on the COURSE relation of Figure 2.9.

PROJECT COURSE(ROOM,PROF_NAME)

This produces the relations shown in Figures 2.18(*a*) and 2.18(*b*), which are the results of the two suboperations.

The elimination of duplicates requires that each tuple of the relation, resulting from the first suboperation, be compared with all the other tuples in the relation in order to remove the duplicates. Since the two suboperations are quite different in terms of the amount of processing involved, many database machines treat the Project operation as two separate primitives, namely Projection and Duplicate_Elimination.

2.3.2.2 JOIN. The second common operation in this category is the Join operation, which involves two relations. It concatenates a tuple of one relation with the tuple of another relation if the value(s) of the specified attribute(s) in this pair of tuples satisfy some prespecified condition. The general format of this operation is as follows:

JOIN $R1$ **WITH** $R2$ **OVER** (A#B)

$R1$ and $R2$ are the names of the two relations, and A and B are attributes of $R1$ and $R2$, respectively. The # sign represents a comparison operator in the set $\{=, \neq, \geq, \leq, >, <\}$. For example, the following Join operation, performed on the relations COURSE and STUDENT_COURSE will produce the relation COURSE_TAKEN as shown in Figure 2.19.

JOIN COURSE **WITH** STUDENT_COURSE **OVER** (CID = CID)

This operation involves comparing each tuple of COURSE with every tuple in STUDENT_COURSE to determine if they can be concatenated to form a tuple of the resulting relation COURSE_TAKEN. If COURSE has n tuples and STUDENT_COURSE has m tuples, the number of comparisons involved would be $n * m$. The Join of two relations is performed very frequently in relational

COURSE

ROOM	PROF_NAME
Larsen 210	T.B. Bronson
Benton 211	S.B. Jensen
Weil 507	N.T. Yong
Larsen 210	T.B. Bronson

COURSE

ROOM	PROF_NAME
Larsen 210	T.B. Bronson
Benton 211	S.B. Jensen
Weil 507	N.T. Yong

FIGURE 2.18
(a) The result of projection. (b) The result of eliminating duplicates.

COURSE _TAKEN

CID	CTITLE	ROOM	PERIOD	PROF_NAME	S#	GRADE_PT
CIS4121	Computer Organization	Larsen 210	2	T.B. Bronson	16242	4.0
CIS4121	Computer Organization	Larsen 210	2	T.B. Bronson	17522	3.0
CIS4121	Computer Organization	Larsen 210	2	T.B. Bronson	18600	3.0
CIS6220	Compilers	Benton 211	4	S.B. Jensen	18600	3.0
CIS6220	Compilers	Benton 211	4	S.B. Jensen	14256	4.0
EE5417	Database Engineering	Weil 507	6	N.T. Yong	17522	3.0
EE5417	Database Engineering	Weil 507	6	N.T. Yong	18600	4.0
EE6967	Database Machines	Larsen 210	4	T.B. Bronson	24010	2.5
EE6967	Database Machines	Larsen 210	4	T.B. Bronson	14256	4.0

FIGURE 2.19
The result of a JOIN operation.

database systems (due to the "normalization" of relations [COD72b and DAT86]). This operation is very time-consuming, and its performance has thus been the focal point of many research efforts. Several join algorithms have been proposed and used in database machine studies. They are: (1) the nested-loop algorithm, (2) the sort-merge algorithm, and (3) the hashing algorithm.

The nested-loop algorithm. This is conceptually the simplest of the three. Two relations involved in a Join operation are called the outer relation R and the inner relation S, respectively. Each tuple of the outer relation is compared with all tuples of the inner relation over their join attribute(s). If the join condition is satisfied, a tuple of R is concatenated with a tuple of S to produce a tuple for the resulting relation L. The algorithm terminates after the last tuple of R has been processed against all tuples of S. In the actual implementation of the above algorithm, pages of tuples of both relations, instead of tuples of these two relations, are read from the secondary storage and processed in order to reduce the I/O time. A page corresponds to a physical block of data such as a disk track. Thus, the algorithm is sometimes called *nested-block–join*. In the nested-block–join, one page of R and q pages of S are read from the secondary storage. (Here, q is a system variable that may correspond to the number of tracks in a cylinder.)

The join attribute(s) of the R tuples are compared with that of every tuple in the q pages of S. Concatenations of tuples are formed in an output buffer if they satisfy the join condition. Whenever the output buffer is full, its contents are written to the secondary storage as the partial outcome of the resulting relation L.

After the first page of R has been joined with the q pages of S, another q pages of S are read and compared with the same page of R. This process continues until all the pages of S have been joined with the R page. At this time, the next page of R is read from the secondary storage, and the process of joining one page of R with all pages of S repeats. The algorithm terminates when the last page of R has been processed.

The sort-merge algorithm. In this algorithm, each of the two involved relations is retrieved from the secondary storage and its tuples are sorted over the join attribute(s) using one of many sorting algorithms. Upon the completion of the sorting operation, the two sorted streams of tuples are merged using one of many available merging algorithms. During the merge operation, if a tuple of R and a tuple of S satisfy the join condition, they are concatenated to form a tuple of the resulting relation L. The sorting and merging operations can be carried out by a single processor or a number of processors, depending on the system used. For sorting and merging algorithms, the reader is referred to Knuth [KNU75].

The hashing algorithm. Several hashing algorithms have been proposed in database machine literature [DEW85]. The most straightforward one will be described here, and others will be presented in subsequent chapters. In the simple algorithm, both relations are read from the secondary storage. The join attribute values of one relation are first hashed by a hash function h. The hashed values are used to address a hash table in which the attribute values are stored together with either the tuples or tuple identifications. The same hashing function is used for the join attribute values of the second relation. If an attribute value of the second relation is hashed to a non-empty entry of the hash table and one of the attribute values stored in that entry matches with the value, the join condition (assuming equality join) is satisfied. The corresponding tuples of these two relations are concatenated to form a tuple of the resulting relation, or a pair of tuple identifications are retrieved from the entry and are used to fetch the corresponding tuples. The process continues until all the tuples of the second relation have been processed. The accumulated tuples of the resulting relation are output to the secondary storage as the output buffer is filled.

A well-known problem associated with the hashing technique is the problem of collision, that is, different values are hashed to the same address. A variety of methods have been used to handle the collision problem.

The Join operation described here has been called "explicit join" in contrast to "implicit join," which involves an explicit join followed by a Project operation over the attributes of one of the relations. The main difference between these two types of joins is that the former requires a relation to be formed explicitly by concatenating attributes and values of both relations, whereas the latter can be done by marking those rows in the relation over which the projection is performed. Thus, the resulting relation is implicitly formed over the projected relation. The implicit join was used in several early database machines for traversal among relations (see Chapter 3). The implicit join is similar to what has been called "semi-join" in theoretical database literature.

Besides the Join operation, other frequently used operations in this category are the Union, Intersection, and Difference of two relations each having the same or comparable attributes. To find the union, intersection, or difference of two sets of tuples, the tuples of one must be compared with those of the other, thus involving a multipass scan of one of the relations. The Union operation in the relational algebra can be used for inserting one or more tuples into a relation, thus implementing one of the frequent storage operations, i.e., the Insertion operation. The Difference operation, on the other hand, can be used to delete tuples from a relation, thus implementing the Deletion operation.

The nested-loop–join algorithm and the sort-merge–join algorithm, which are considered suitable for use in a conventional system model, will be analyzed. These analyses resemble those presented by DeWitt [DEW81]. The Join operation is to be performed over relations R and S to produce a resulting relation L. R contains m pages and S contains s pages. A tuple of R is the same size as a tuple of S.

Nested-loop–join algorithm. The three main time components are t[inst_flow], t[process], and t[data_collect]. The instruction flow time, in the conventional system model, involves mainly the compilation time of the query. Thus,

$$t[\text{inst\_flow}] = t[\text{comp}]$$

The time necessary for joining the relations R and S consists of a number of subcomponents. The time required to read a page of relation R is

$$t[\text{read\_pg}, R] = t[\text{I/O}]$$

The time required to read q pages (one cylinder worth) of relation S into the primary memory is

$$t[\text{read\_}q\text{\_pg}, S] = q * t[\text{I/O}]$$

The comparison of join attribute values of the tuples in these q pages of S against the join attribute values of one page of R and the forming of the tuples of the resulting relation L will take the following time:

$$
\begin{aligned}
t[\text{jn\_Rpg\_Sq}] &= t * \{2 * t[\text{s}] + t[\text{cpu}]\} * q * t + \text{jn\_fac} * q * t * t * 2 * t[\text{mov}] \\
&= t * q * t * \{2 * t[\text{s}] + t[\text{cpu}] + \text{jn\_fac} * 2 * t[\text{mov}]\}
\end{aligned}
$$

where jn_fac is the selectivity factor of the Join operation. The time necessary to read the entire s pages of S relation and to join all their tuples with one page of R is

$$t[\text{jn\_pg}, R] = (s/q) * \{t[\text{read\_}q\text{\_pg}, S] + t[\text{jn\_Rpg\_Sq}]\}$$

The time for processing m pages of R, including the read time for the m pages, is

$$t[\text{process}, R] = m * \{t[\text{jn\_pg}, R] + t[\text{read\_pg}, R]\}$$

The number of pages of L produced by joining s pages of S with m pages of R is

$$u = \text{ceil}((\text{jn\_fac} * s * t * m * t)/(t/2))$$

Here, tuples of R and S are assumed to be the same size and the size of a tuple of L is twice as large as that of R and S. Thus, only $t/2$ tuples of L can fit into a page. The time required to write these u pages of L to the secondary storage is then

$$t[\text{I/O}, L] = u * t[\text{I/O}]$$

Thus, the processing time for joining R and S including the output time for L is

$$t[\text{process}] = (2 + m) * t[\text{access}] + m * t[\text{process}, R] + t[\text{I/O}, L]$$

Here, $(2 + m)*t[\text{access}]$ accounts for the seek and latency times involved in the reading of relation R, the reading of relation S(m times), and the writing of relation L.

The data collection time for this Join operation involves (1) the reading of u pages of L, which have already been written to the secondary storage, back to the main memory and (2) the transfer of their tuples to the user's terminal. The collection time required is

$$t[\text{data\_collect}] = t[\text{access}] + t[\text{I/O}, L] + m * t * s * t *\text{jn\_fac} * 2 * t[\text{tp\_out}]$$

where $2*t[\text{tp\_out}]$ is to account for the fact that a tuple of L is roughly twice the size of the tuple of R or S. The total execution time for this algorithm is

$$t[\text{Join\_nested\_loop}] = t[\text{inst\_flow}] + t[\text{process}] + t[\text{data\_collect}]$$

The Sort-merge–join algorithm. This algorithm is implemented in two phases. In the first phase, both R and S are sorted. In the second phase, the sorted relations are joined by merging the sorted tuples based on the join condition. As in the first algorithm,

$$t[\text{inst\_flow}] = t[\text{comp}]$$

The four-way external merge sort algorithm is used to sort R and S. This algorithm has been shown by Blasgen [BLA77] to be an efficient algorithm for a single-processor system. This sort algorithm requires $\log_4(m)$ subphases for processing R and $\log_4(s)$ subphases for processing S. In each subphase, all pages of R (or S) relation are read and written from/to the disk, and approximately $m/2$ (or $s/2$) two-page Merge operations are performed. The total time required to read and write m pages of R is

$$2 * \{t[\text{access}] + m * t[\text{I/O}]\}$$

The time necessary to perform $m/2$ two-page Merge operations is

$$(m/2) * 2 * t * \{2 * t[s] + t[cpu] + t[mov]\} = m * t * \{2 * t[s] + t[cpu] + t[mov]\}$$

where $2 * t[s]$ accounts for the loading of two values into registers, $t[cpu]$ is the time for a comparison, and t[mov] is the time for moving one tuple in main memory. In the worst case, the number of comparisons required to perform the merge of two sorted lists of tuples of length t is $2 * t$.

The same number is required for moving tuples. The time required for the implementation of one merge-sort subphase is

$$t[merge\_sort\_pg, R] = 2 * \{t[access] + m * t[I/O]\} + m * t * \{2 * t[s] + t[cpu] + t[mov]\}$$

For $\log_4(m)$ subphases, the time necessary for sorting R is

$$\log_4(m) * t[merge\_sort\_pg, R]$$

Similarly, the time necessary for performing the merge-sort operation on pages of relation S is

$$\log_4(s) * t[merge\_sort\_pg, S]$$

where

$$t[merge\_sort\_pg, S] = 2 * \{t[access] + s * t[I/O]\} + s * t * \{2 * t[s] + t[cpu] + t[mov]\}$$

In the second phase of the algorithm, the sorted R and S are merged. There will be approximately $(m + s)/2$ two-page Merge operations. The time necessary for performing these operations is

$$(m + s)/2 * 2 * t * \{2 * t[s] + t[cpu] + t[mov]\} = (m + s) * t * \{2 * t[s] + t[cpu] + t[mov]\}$$

The sorted R and S relations need to be read back to the main memory for these operations. This involves $t[access] + m * t[I/O]$ time for reading R and $t[access] + s*t[I/O]$ time for reading S.

Also, the tuples of R and S need to be concatenated to form the output of Join if the join attribute values match during the Merge operation. The time required to form the concatenated tuple is $2 * t[mov]$. Given a join selectivity factor (jn_fac), the total number of output pages is

$$u = ceil(m * t * s * t * jn\_fac/(t/2))$$

Therefore, the amount of time required to form the resulting relation L is

$$t[form, L] = m * t * s * t * jn\_fac * 2 * t[mov]$$

The total time required to perform the actual Join-by-Merge operation is

$$t[merge] = (m + s) * t * \{2 * t[s] + t[cpu] + t[mov]\} + 2 * t[access] + (m + s) * t[I/O] + t[form, L]$$

Since the results of the Join operation is a relation L, which is to be established in the database on the secondary storage, all pages of L need to be written to the secondary storage. Here, it is assumed that there are the same number of L pages in the output buffer as in the nested-loop–join algorithm. The time required is

$$t[\text{I/O}, L] = u * t[\text{I/O}]$$

The total data processing time required is as follows:

$$t[\text{process}] = \log_4(m) * t[\text{merge\_sort\_pg}, R] +$$
$$\log_4(s) * t[\text{merge\_sort\_pg}, S] + t[\text{merge}] + t[\text{access}] + t[\text{I/O}, L]$$

The data collection time involves the reading of the pages of L from the secondary storage and the transfer of $u * t$ tuples to the user's terminal. Thus,

$$t[\text{data\_collect}] = t[\text{access}] + t[\text{I/O}, L] + u * (t/2) * 2 * t[\text{tp\_out}]$$

The total execution time required for this algorithm is

$$t[\text{join\_sort\_merge}] = t[\text{inst\_flow}] + t[\text{process}] + t[\text{data\_collect}]$$

2.3.3 Statistical Aggregation by Categorization

In statistical database management applications, the user often wants to perform some aggregation functions such as Count, Sum, Average, Maximum, and Minimum over a set of attribute values found in a relation. One very frequent statistical operation used in the field of statistics is called *aggregation by categorization*. The difference between this and the single-pass aggregation operations described in Section 2.3.1 is that here the tuples of a relation are divided into categories based on their attribute values (i.e., the tuples of each category have the identical values in some selected attributes called category attributes). A statistical function is then performed on each category over some numerical attribute called a summary attribute. The result is a relation containing aggregated values (summary data) for the various categories. For example, the relation STUDENT_STATISTICS in Figure 2.9 contains the counts and average grades of students categorized by state, county, sex, and age. The following aggregate statement will compute the new counts and average grades for students categorized by sex and age.

AGGREGATE STUDENT_STATISTICS **BY** (SEX, AGE)

The result of the Aggregate operation is the relation shown in Figure 2.20. The new counts and average grades shown in the figure are computed based on the values shown in Figure 2.9.

The following subsections describe two algorithms for statistical aggregation that are considered to be suitable for the conventional system model. They are the sort-merge algorithm and the hashing algorithm. In the sort-merge algorithm, the relation R is first sorted on the category attributes. Thus, all the tuples with the same category attribute values (i.e., tuples of the same category) are grouped

COUNT_GRADE_BY_SEX_AGE

SEX	AGE	COUNT	AVG_GRADE
M	22	3666	3.67
F	22	3631	2.94
M	23	3716	3.17
F	23	2927	3.05

FIGURE 2.20
Aggregation by sex and age.

together. The corresponding summary attribute values are used to compute the aggregate value and to form a new output tuple for the resulting relation. In the hashing algorithm, the category attribute values are hashed to entries of a hash table. The system will check for possible collisions and perform the Aggregate operation for each tuple to form temporary aggregated results. Thus, the final summary values for the tuples of the resulting relation (or categories) can be derived in one scan of relation R.

2.3.3.1 THE SORT-MERGE ALGORITHM. The instruction flow time is the same as that for the previous operations in the conventional system model, that is,

$$t[\text{inst\_flow}] = t[\text{comp}]$$

The data processing time is broken down into the time required to sort the relation R and the time required for aggregating the summary attribute values. The time required to sort the relation R has been shown to be

$$\log_4(m) * t[\text{merge\_sort\_pg}, R]$$

This was derived in the sort-merge algorithm for the Join operation. It is assumed that there are w partitions of tuples of R to be formed, where w is the number of distinct category attribute values. To compute the summary attribute values for these w categories, each of the $m * t$ tuples needs to be processed. The time for aggregating the summary attribute values is

$$m * t * \{t[\text{s}] + t[\text{cpu}]\} + w * t[\text{mov}]$$

Here, it is assumed that only one summary attribute is involved in this operation and that one $t[\text{s}]$ is used to load a summary attribute value. The equation $w * t[\text{mov}]$ accounts for the forming of the resulting relation L in the output buffer. The total processing time is therefore

$$t[\text{process}] = \log_4(m) * t[\text{merge\_sort\_pg}, R] + m * t * (t[\text{s}] + t[\text{cpu}]) + w * t[\text{mov}]$$

Since the result of this aggregation operation is a relation with w tuples, and w is generally small, it is assumed that the entire resulting relation can be stored in the main memory. The data collection time, therefore, involves the transfer of these tuples of the user's terminal. Thus,

$$t[\text{data\_collect}] = w * t[\text{tp\_out}]$$

The total execution time for this algorithm is

$$t[\text{aggregate\_sort\_merge}] = t[\text{inst\_flow}] + t[\text{process}] + t[\text{data\_collect}]$$

2.3.3.2 THE HASHING ALGORITHM. The instruction flow time for this algorithm is also

$$t[\text{inst\_flow}] = t[\text{comp}]$$

The processing time consists of the time costs for reading the tuples of R, hashing their category attribute values, checking for collisions, and performing aggregation operations over their corresponding summary attribute values. The time required to read the entire relation R is

$$t[\text{read}, R] = t[\text{access}] + m * t[\text{I/O}]$$

The time for hashing x category attribute values of $m * t$ tuples of R is

$$m * t * x * t[\text{hash}]$$

Since collision can occur in a hash scheme, a collision factor, c_fac, is introduced. Its value represents the average comparisons necessary when each category attribute value is hashed to an entry of the hash table. It will be a real value greater than 1. For example, c_fac = 2.5 would mean that 2.5 attribute values need to be compared on an average to determine if an attribute value is in the entry of the hash table. Thus, the time for collision checking of $m * t$ tuples of R is

$$m * t * c\_fac * \{2 * t[\text{s}] + t[\text{cpu}]\}$$

The computation time for the actual aggregate values is given by

$$m * t * \{t[\text{s}] + t[\text{cpu}]\}$$

Since w denotes the number of categories established in the operation, there will be w tuples in the resulting relation. The time to establish the relation L in the output buffer is approximated by $w * t[\text{mov}]$. The total processing time for this algorithm is therefore

$$t[\text{process}] = t[\text{read}, R] + m * t * \{x * t[\text{hash}] + c\_fac * \{2 * t[\text{s}] + t[\text{cpu}]\} + \{t[\text{s}] + t[\text{cpu}]\}\} + w * t[\text{mov}]$$

The data collection time is the same as the preceding algorithm, that is,

$$t[\text{data\_collect}] = w * t[\text{tp\_out}]$$

The total execution for this algorithm is

$$t[\text{Aggregate\_hash}] = t[\text{inst\_flow}] + t[\text{process}] + t[\text{data\_collect}]$$

2.3.4   Storage Operations

The fourth category contains storage operations such as updates, deletions, and insertions, which have performance characteristics that are different from the other categories. The update operation illustrates this point. It generally involves (1) searching the database for the data object(s) that is to be updated, (2) updating the data object(s), and (3) updating all other related data objects necessary to keep the database in a consistent state. For example, if the identification name of the course entitled 'Computer Organization' in the COURSE relation of Figure 2.9 is to be changed from CIS4121 to CIS4321, the following update statement will cause the DBMS to first search the COURSE relation for a tuple(s) whose CTITLE equals 'Computer Organization.' Then the corresponding CID value will be updated. Furthermore, the CIS4121 values in the relation STUDENT_COURSE of Figure 2.9 must also be updated in order to keep the database consistent. The update statement would be:

UPDATE COURSE **WHERE** (CTITLE = 'Computer Organization')
WITH (CID = 'CIS4321')

The amount of processing associated with an Update operation depends very much on the integrity rules associated with the data object(s) being updated. The rules may trigger the execution of other integrity rules to keep the database consistent. This integrity issue will be discussed further in Sections 2.4.4 and 2.4.6. The amount of processing also depends on the access path structures of the files used to implement the relations whose data objects are to be updated. The more complex the structures are, the more difficult it will be to carry out the Update operation.

The following analysis of the Update operation does not deal with the possible triggering of other operations due to an update, since this will involve another nontrivial database management function, namely integrity enforcement. For a simple Update operation, the algorithm is similar to that of the Select operation, although it differs from the Select operation in that all updated tuples are written back to the secondary storage.

The instruction flow time remains the same, that is,

$$t[\text{inst\_flow}] = t[\text{comp}]$$

The time for selecting a subset of tuples for updating can be adopted from the expressions derived for the selection algorithm. As in the Select, q pages of the relation R are read from a disk cylinder to the main memory. The tuples to be updated are then selected from these q pages. Necessary changes are made in the selected tuples, and the entire q pages are written back to the same cylinder without a disk head movement. Assuming there are x attributes referenced in the selection conditions, the time to read q pages and to select the tuples for updating is

$$q * \{t[\text{I/O}] + t * x * \{2 * t[s] + t[\text{cpu}]\}\}$$

The number of tuples selected for update from the q pages is

$$sel\_fac * q * t$$

The time for the actual Update operation is

$$sel\_fac * q * t * \{2 * t[s] + t[cpu]\}$$

where $\{2 * t[s] + t[cpu]\}$ is used to approximate the tuple update time. The time to write all q pages back to the same cylinder is

$$q * t[I/O]$$

Here, it is assumed that each page contains some tuples that have been updated. The total processing time for (m/q) cylinders of R is therefore

$$t[process] = 2 * t[access] + (m/q) * q * \{t[I/O] + t * x * \{2 * t[s] + t[cpu]\} + sel\_fac * t * \{2 * t[s] + t[cpu]\} + t[I/O]\}$$

Since there is no data collection time involved in this operation, the total time for executing the update algorithm is

$$t[update] = t[inst\_flow] + t[process]$$

2.4 THE ARCHITECTURE AND FUNCTIONS OF A DATABASE MANAGEMENT SYSTEM

Up to this point, this chapter has presented: (1) the general characteristics and applications of databases and database management systems (Section 2.1), (2) the semantic contents and levels of data representation of a database (Section 2.2), and (3) four general categories of database operations and algorithms (Section 2.3). This section details the software system that provides the retrieval and manipulation of databases, that is, the database management system. The architecture (or the general structural framework) of a database management system is presented, and some important database management functions are described and illustrated.

2.4.1 A Database Management System Architecture

Figure 2.21 illustrates the general architecture of a DBMS. It shows how the software of the DBMS is related to the user, the application programs, the system software, and the database. In a DBMS, a user or a user group can have his or her view of the database defined in an external schema. The user can then develop application programs in some high-level programming language such as COBOL, PL/1, or FORTRAN with some data manipulation statement embedded in them to process the user's own view of the database. Alternatively, the user can use an ad hoc query language (e.g., an interactive query language such as QBE or SQL) to process the database. The DBMS provides the DML facility and processes queries

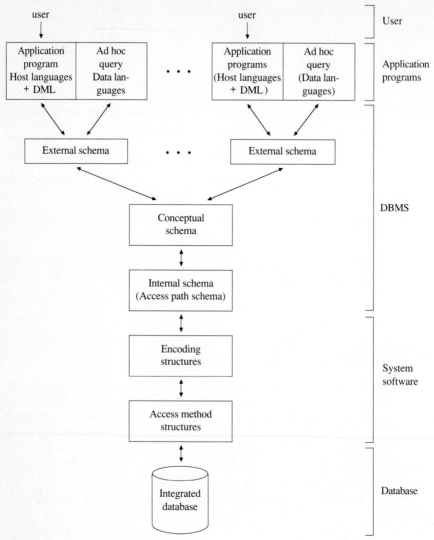

FIGURE 2.21
The architecture of a DBMS.

issued using the DML against the different views of the database defined by the various external schemata. The DBMS also takes care of the mappings between (1) the data represented by the external schemata and the data represented by the conceptual schema and (2) the conceptual schema and the internal schema, which defines the access path structures for efficient accesses to the database. The mapping processes are illustrated in Section 2.4.3.

The DBMS software makes use of the system software (i.e., the operating

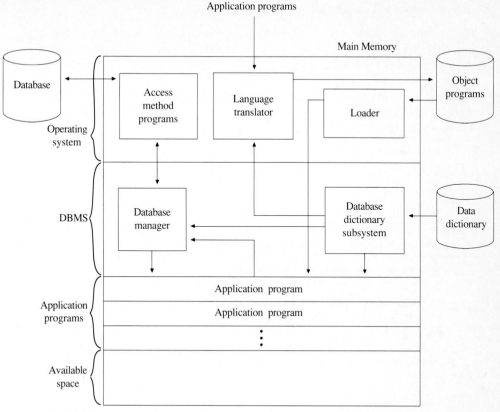

FIGURE 2.22
Storage allocation for application programs, databases, the DBMS, and related software systems.

system. and the compiler's translation facility) to access and manage the data stored both in the main memory and in the secondary storage devices.

Figure 2.22 is a simplified diagram showing the relationships and the memory layout of the DBMS software, application programs, and the system software at run time. As illustrated in the figure, application programs are generally compiled and stored in a secondary storage device in object code form. During the translation process, the external and conceptual schema information are used to relate program variables with the data objects defined in the schemata. Access to the data dictionary, which contains the schema information, is generally made through a data dictionary subsystem of a DBMS. At prerun time the object programs are loaded by the loader into the main memory. At run time, the DML commands embedded in the application programs are passed to the DBMS software system, which uses the access method programs of the operating system to access data from the secondary storage devices. The retrieved data are transformed by the DBMS software into structures that are suitable for use in the application programs.

2.4.2 Query Translation

One of the key functions of a DBMS is to translate high-level query language or DML statements into some internal command structure that is suitable for activating proper database manipulation routines to process the database. To illustrate this function, the query language SQL is used along with the external schema shown in Figure 2.10(*a*) and the relational algebra operations described in Section 2.3. The skeletons of the STUDENT and COURSE_STUDENT relations of Figure 2.10(*a*) are shown below:

>STUDENT (S#, SNAME, ADDRESS) KEY (S#)
>COURSE_STUDENT(CID, S#, CTITLE, PROF_NAME, GRADE_PT)
>KEY (CID, S#)

Assuming that a user is interested in retrieving the names of all those students who have taken a course taught by Professor T.B. Bronson, along with the course titles and grade points for these courses, the SQL query would be as follows:

>**SELECT** SNAME, CTITLE, GRADE_PT
>**FROM** STUDENT, COURSE_STUDENT
>**WHERE** STUDENT.S# = COURSE_STUDENT.S# AND
>COURSE_STUDENT.PROF_NAME = 'T.B. BRONSON'

A possible internal command structure for representing the translated result of this query is a hierarchical structure of relational algebraic operators shown in Figure 2.23.

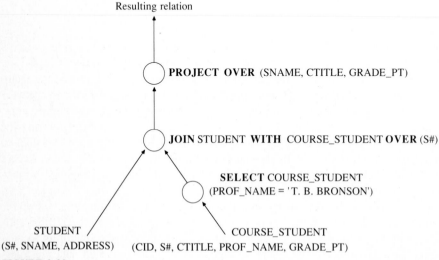

FIGURE 2.23
A hierarchical tree of relational algebraic operators.

2.4.3 Command and Data Mappings

The commands in the query tree of Figure 2.23 reference relations that have been defined only in the external schema. These relations do not have immediate physical correspondents in the conceptual schema or the internal schema. Thus, before these commands can be executed, the commands, along with their structures, must be mapped into commands and structures that make reference to data objects first defined in the conceptual scheme and then defined in the internal schema.

The relation STUDENT is the result of a projection on the STUDENT relation defined in the conceptual schema given in Figure 2.8, and the relation COURSE_STUDENT is the result of a Join operation between the COURSE and STUDENT_COURSE relations of Figure 2.8 followed by a Project operation. The derivation of these two relations from the relations defined in the conceptual schema can be explicitly stated by some mapping statements given in the external schema. Therefore, the DBMS can modify the original query tree of Figure 2.23 into the one shown in Figure 2.24 to account for the mapping.

The query tree of Figure 2.24 again needs to be mapped into a structure that operates on the data objects defined in the internal schema to take advantage of the efficient access paths. For example, the internal structure shown in Figure 2.12 has an index table for the attribute PROF_NAME. The index table can be used to provide a direct access to all the courses taught by T.B. Bronson. Thus, the query tree is modified to include the access to the index file PROF_INDEX for obtaining pointers to the COURSE tuples as illustrated in Figure 2.25. In the figure, the ACCESS and IDENTIFY commands are not relational algebraic commands. They are added to illustrate the operations on the access path structure defined by the internal schema.

Similar to the command mappings (from the external to the conceptual to the internal schemata), the data that are retrieved from the physical database also need to be transformed into the structures defined in the external schema. This is because the user's application programs expect data to be delivered in a certain format, which may not correspond to the internal structure. This transformation is carried out by the DBMS data manipulation programs in conjunction with the operating system's access method routines.

2.4.4 The Enforcement of Database Integrity and Security

Enforcing integrity and security in a database is an important feature of a DBMS. As discussed in Section 2.3.4, database integrity deals with maintaining the consistency and accuracy of data in a database [STO75, ESW75, and ZLO78]. Integrity constraints or rules are defined in the conceptual schema of a database and are used by the DBMS software to check for the accuracy and consistency of the database when the data are first loaded as well as when they are subsequently updated. Some typical examples of integrity constraints follow.

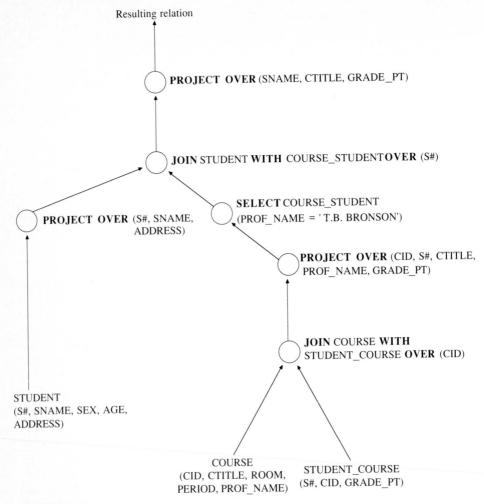

Resulting relation

PROJECT OVER (SNAME, CTITLE, GRADE_PT)

JOIN STUDENT **WITH** COURSE_STUDENT **OVER** (S#)

PROJECT OVER (S#, SNAME, ADDRESS)

SELECT COURSE_STUDENT (PROF_NAME = ' T.B. BRONSON')

PROJECT OVER (CID, S#, CTITLE, PROF_NAME, GRADE_PT)

JOIN COURSE **WITH** STUDENT_COURSE **OVER** (CID)

STUDENT
(S#, SNAME, SEX, AGE, ADDRESS)

COURSE
(CID, CTITLE, ROOM, PERIOD, PROF_NAME)

STUDENT_COURSE
(S#, CID, GRADE_PT)

FIGURE 2.24
A modified query tree to account for the external-to-conceptual mapping.

1. *Domain constraints.* For example, two domain constraints used in Figure 2.8 are: (1) student age must be greater than or equal to 16 and less than or equal to 70 and (2) class period must be greater than or equal to 1 and less than or equal to 7.

2. *Intratuple constraints.* For example, if the PROF_NAME of the COURSE relation in Figure 2.8 is equal to 'S.B. Jensen' then the PERIOD value cannot be equal to 1 since Professor Jensen is unwilling to teach a class in the first period.

3. *Intertuple constraints.* For example, if a course is taught by Professor N.T. Yong, the students' grades in the STUDENT_COURSE relation in Figure 2.8 cannot be equal to 4 since Professor Yong has never given and will never give a 4.0 to students in his course.

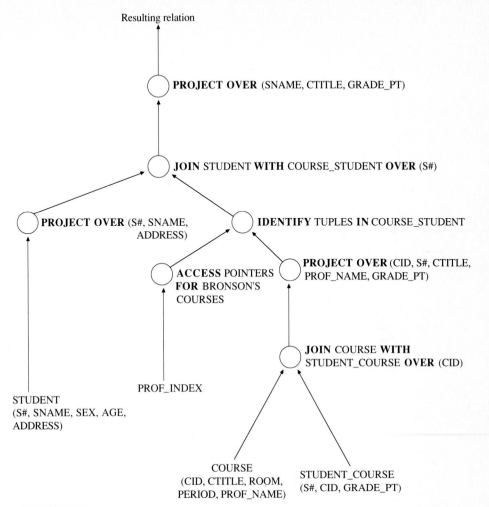

FIGURE 2.25
A modified query tree to account for the conceptual-to-internal mapping.

4. *Referential constraints.* For example, if a student is recorded as having taken a course in the relation STUDENT_COURSE, then the student must exist in the relation STUDENT. Similarly, the course should also exist in the relation COURSE of Figure 2.8.

Database security deals with the protection of the database from illegal accesses, alterations, and destruction [DEN79, DEN83, and FER81]. The use of external schemata to define different users' views of a database provides one level of protection since each user can only be allowed to access and manipulate the data objects defined by his or her external schema. In addition to using external schemata as a way of enforcing security, a DBMS needs to implement a number of security rules to protect the database at the data field, record or file level. Three general types of security rules or constraints follow.

1. *Data-independent rules.* For example, a user is not allowed to access students' grades no matter what grades the students received for the courses they took.
2. *Content-dependent rules.* For example, a user is not allowed to access students' grades unless the students received an A grade (4.0) and the instructor is Professor T.B. Bronson.
3. *Context-dependent rules.* For example, a user can retrieve students' names and grades independently. However, the user is not allowed to retrieve the data in such a way that the names and grades can be related.

Different DBMSs have different ways of enforcing the security constraints. For illustration purposes, the query modification approach proposed by Stonebraker [STO75] is used here as an example. As shown in Figure 2.26, if the user is subject to the previously mentioned data dependent rule, the DBMS can modify the query tree given in Figure 2.23 by adding a Select operation on top of the original query tree so that only the names of those students who have received a 4.0 grade in a course, along with the course titles, will be retrieved. The resulting query tree would resemble Figure 2.26. It is obvious that the resulting tree

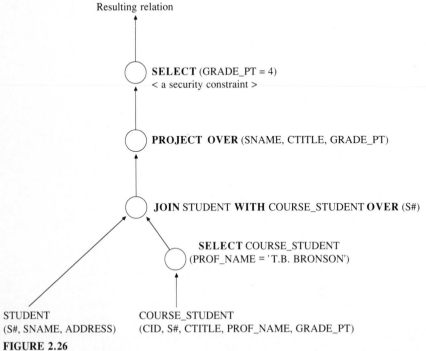

FIGURE 2.26
Query modification to account for a data dependent security rule.

structure is not an optimal one in terms of performance. A good DBMS would attempt to optimize the query tree before executing it.

2.4.5 Query Optimization

Query optimization is a process of analyzing and modifying a query before its execution so that the execution can be carried out more efficiently [SMI75, HAL76, WON76, AHO79, SEL79, YAO79, KIN81, MAK81, ROS82, JAR84, and KIM85]. The common approach taken by the existing DBMSs is to reduce the amount of data to be processed by the operators of the query tree by filtering out those data that do not contribute to the final results of the query. For example, the attribute ADDRESS in the relation STUDENT of Figure 2.26 is not used as the qualification condition of the query. Nor is it one of the attributes whose values are to be retrieved. The ADDRESS column can thus be deleted by a projection operation (as shown in Figure 2.27) so that the size of the STUDENT relation will be reduced before it is joined with the COURSE_STUDENT relation. In this particular case, only one column has been deleted and the amount of data reduction is small. However, if the relation contains many attributes and many columns of the relation can be deleted by the Project operation, the amount of time saved in executing the subsequent Join operation can be very significant. Reducing the amount of data involved in an operation also will save on the storage space required to store the relation produced by the operation.

Another obvious optimization possible in our example is to move the SELECT (GRADE_PT = 4) operation down as close to the leaves of the tree as possible since it reduces the number of rows (tuples) of the COURSE_STUDENT relation. As shown in Figure 2.27, the operation can be combined with the other Select operation so that only those COURSE_STUDENT tuples that satisfy the selection conditions (PROF_NAME = 'T.B. BRONSON' & GRADE_PT = 4) will be involved in the Join operation.

Query optimization is similar to program code optimization used in most high-level programming language compilers. For example, high-level language statements are first translated into assembly code, which, typically, is suboptimal. The optimizing component of a compiler would analyze this code and modify or re-arrange it to produce optimal code. Similarly, high-level DML statements are first translated by the DBMS into some internal representations (e.g., query trees in the example) and, subsequently, are modified to account for the different types of schema mappings and security constraints. These translated and modified representations, in turn, need to be optimized again by the DBMS.

2.4.6 Transaction Management

Transaction management is another important function provided by a DBMS [GRA81 and HAE83]. A *transaction* can be informally defined as a sequence of database operations that either must be executed to its entirety or should not be executed at all, so that the database can remain in a consistent state. If, after

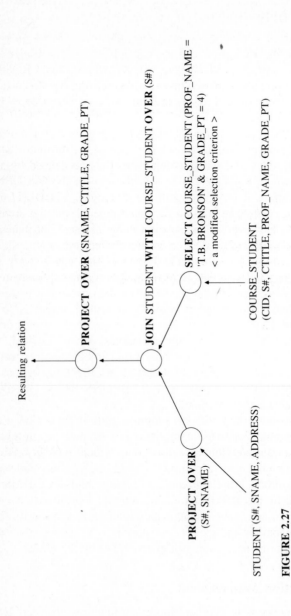

Resulting relation

PROJECT OVER (SNAME, CTITLE, GRADE_PT)

JOIN STUDENT **WITH** COURSE_STUDENT **OVER** (S#)

SELECT COURSE_STUDENT (PROF_NAME = 'T.B. BRONSON' & GRADE_PT = 4)
< a modified selection criterion >

COURSE_STUDENT
(CID, S#, CTITLE, PROF_NAME, GRADE_PT)

PROJECT OVER
(S#, SNAME)

STUDENT (S#, SNAME, ADDRESS)

FIGURE 2.27
An optimized query tree.

executing only some of the operations in the sequence, the DBMS finds out that it cannot or should not proceed further for reasons such as security/integrity violations or software/hardware errors, then the data that have been affected by the operations executed until now will have to be restored to their original state by the DBMS. The relations shown in Figure 2.9 will be used here as an example illustrating this DBMS function.

Suppose the grade of the student whose S# equals 17522 for the course EE5417 needs to be changed from 3.0 to 4.0. This change will not only affect the value in the STUDENT_COURSE relation, but it will also affect the statistics recorded in the STUDENT_STATISTICS relation. In order to keep the contents of the database consistent, it is necessary to change the AVG_GRADE of the proper student category to which this student belongs. Thus, there are two update operations involved, and they form a transaction that must be executed to its entirety or should not be executed at all. The constraints between the GRADE_PT of COURSE_STUDENT and the AVG_GRADE of STUDENT_STATISTICS is one type of so-called *interrelation constraint* and must be enforced by the DBMS.

Another example involves deletion operations. Suppose a user issues a deletion operation to delete the student's data (S# = 14256) from the STUDENT relation. In accordance with the referential constraint described in Section 2.4.4, the fact that this student took some courses (recorded in the STUDENT_COURSE relation shown in Figure 2.9) will have to be deleted also. This means that two deletion operations are involved; one triggers the deletion of the other, if the referential constraint is to be enforced. The transaction includes both deletions, and again either both or none should be executed if the database is to be left in a consistent state.

2.4.7 Recovery

Recovery is a database management system function that restores a database to a consistent and correct state after some failure has been detected by the DBMS [VER78]. The failure may be caused by an application program, the operating system, the operator, or the hardware itself. Such a failure may cause the database to be damaged or it may leave the database in a situation in which the integrity of the database cannot be guaranteed. In the former situation, the damaged database must be restored. This is generally accomplished by periodically dumping the entire database to an archival storage (e.g., a magnetic tape) and by recording the new value and the old value of each data item that has been modified and the new value (or old value) of an item that has been inserted (or deleted). These values are recorded in a special log maintained by the recovery manager. The database stored in the archival memory is then used to restore the damaged database when a failure occurs, and the log is used to redo all the operations that were completed before the failure occurred and after the last database dump. This redo process is often called *rollforward*.

In the second situation in which the integrity of the database cannot be ensured due to a failure, the recovery manager must undo all that has been done by transactions that were not completed when the failure occurred. This undo process is often called *rollback*. This is necessary so that all these transactions are either completed to their entirety or none of their operations have any effect on the database at all due to the rollback process. Therefore, a transaction is also called a *recoverable unit of a database operation*.

2.4.8 Concurrency Control

A DBMS allows multiple users to access and manipulate a common database simultaneously. The queries that are simultaneously executed by the DBMS on a time-sharing or multiprocessing system are called *concurrent queries*. Concurrent queries may produce different results or have different effects on the database depending on the order in which their operations are carried out. Such a dependence is, of course, not desirable. A mechanism is needed to ensure that the effect of a query will not be determined by the order in which the operations of the query are executed in relationship with those of other concurrent queries. In other words, the results produced by executing a set of queries in an interleaved fashion (i.e., the operations of different queries are interleaved) should be the same as that produced by a serial execution of these queries. The concurrent control software of a DBMS provides such a mechanism.

Some examples to illustrate the need for concurrency control are necessary. Several problems and solutions follow.

2.4.8.1 THE PROBLEM OF LOST UPDATE. Two concurrent queries are used to illustrate this problem. Suppose transactions A and B both want to update the student's (S# = 24010) grade for the course EE6967 shown in the STUDENT_COURSE relation of Figure 2.9. The reading and the updating operations of A and B occur at the time shown in Figure 2.28. At time t_2, transaction

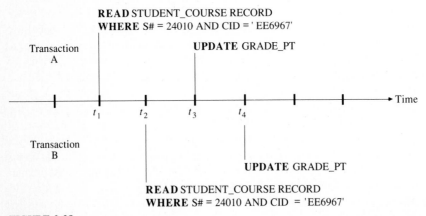

FIGURE 2.28
Two transactions update the same record.

B reads the student's record, thus the effect of transaction A's update at time t_3 is not recognized by transaction B. In effect, A's update is lost.

A popular solution to this type of problem is to use a locking mechanism that prevents other transactions from reading or updating (writing) a data object when a transaction is updating the data object. For example, as shown in Figure 2.29, transaction A would lock the student's record when it reads the record at time t_1 and unlock the record after it has made the update at time t_4. When transaction B attempts to read and lock the same record at t_2, it will find that the record has been locked and thus will be forced to wait until t_4, at which time the Read operation will be resumed. Transaction B proceeds to update the record at t_5 and unlock the record at t_6. This locking mechanism ensures that the result of executing transactions A and B in an interleaved fashion will be equal to some serial execution of these two transactions (i.e., executing A followed by B).

Concurrent transactions are said to be "serializable," if the result of executing them by interleaving is the same as some serial execution of these transactions. This property of serializability is used in many theoretical works on concurrency to prove that a proposed concurrency control mechanism is indeed correct [BER78, BER80, and KUN81].

2.4.8.2   THE PROBLEM OF TRANSACTION ROLLBACK. A transaction may read a data object updated by another transaction that is rolled back later due to some error. The data object contains erroneous data because the effect of the update is undone in the rollback process. For example, in Figure 2.30,

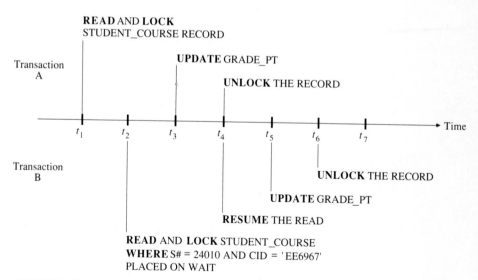

FIGURE 2.29
Transaction synchronization by locking.

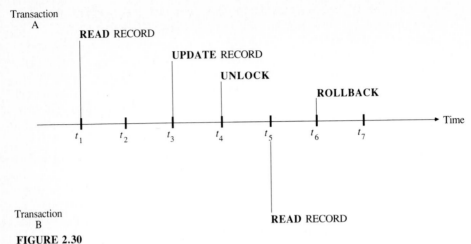

FIGURE 2.30
Transaction B reads the result of uncommitted update of transaction A.

transaction B's reading of the student record at time t_5 will get the grade updated by transaction A at t_3. However, at t_6, transaction A is rolled back due to some error. The Update operation at t_3 is undone, meaning that the original grade of the student is restored. In effect, transaction A has never been executed. The updated grade that B has read is no longer valid. This problem can again be solved if the data object remains locked until the transaction terminates normally and the update takes effect, or, in database terminology, is "committed."

In addition to the locking technique described and illustrated here, there are many other concurrency control techniques that have been proposed for both centralized and distributed DBMSs. The existing techniques fall into three general categories: locking techniques, time-stamping techniques, and optimistic techniques. The explanation of these techniques and their relative merits is beyond the scope of this book. Interested readers should refer to the literature on concurrency control techniques [GRA75, ESW76, GRA76, BER80, and KUN81].

2.5 SOME POSSIBLE PERFORMANCE IMPROVEMENTS TO DATABASE MANAGEMENT SYSTEMS

Having reviewed the principles, structural representations, and operations of databases, and the architecture and functions of a database management system, the text now illustrates the main performance bottlenecks of existing DBMSs and suggests areas where performance improvement can be made. Improving the efficiency of DBMS functions has been the main objective and motivation for the research and development of database computers. The principles, architectures, and techniques introduced by the database machines, to be presented in subsequent chapters, represent possible solutions to the following problems.

1. *Too many levels of command and data mappings.* In order to satisfy the requirements of data independence and high-level user interface, the existing DBMSs introduce many levels of data representations. Database management commands, as well as the data themselves, need to be translated several times during the retrieval or storage operations. This is one of the main causes of inefficiency. If the physical data can be stored in a structure very close to the structure seen by the user or application programs, and processed directly by the hardware, then much time can be saved.

2. *Software solutions to DBMS problems introduce overheads.* The existing DBMSs solve the efficiency problem by introducing complex data structures. These structures and their associated algorithms may solve the particular problems at hand effectively. However, they also introduce some side effects that are often time-consuming and difficult to handle. The use of indices and pointers for speeding up search operations is a good example. While they bring about search efficiency, indices also introduce great difficulties in database updates and require additional storage space. The search for hardware solutions is a reasonable alternative.

3. *I/O bottleneck.* The existing DBMSs use the conventional secondary storage devices to store their databases. The reading and writing of the data in and out of the main storage is the predominant time factor in all the database operations. Therefore, it is important to develop alternative storage devices or to use other architectural arrangements between storage devices and processors to eliminate or ease the I/O bottleneck. Solving the I/O inefficiency problem is the key to solving the problem of inefficient DBMSs.

4. *User's demand for more functionality.* The existing DBMSs attempt to meet the demands for more and more database processing functions or facilities (or functionality) by adding more and more layers of software to the existing systems. The systems themselves become very complex and costly to build and maintain. In view of the increase in software development cost and the decrease in hardware cost, the use of hardware to satisfy the demand for more functionality is a better solution.

5. *Primitive database operations are very time-consuming.* Section 2.3 described and illustrated a number of primitive operations that are needed for executing users' queries for the retrieval and manipulation of a database. Most of these primitives (e.g., Join, Duplicate_Elimination, Union, Intersection, Sort, etc.) are operations with an order of complexity of $n*m$ or $n*n$, where n and m are the number of data objects (e.g., records) involved in the operations. Improvements on these operations can be made to a certain extent by using better software algorithms. However, when the number of data objects involved is large, performance improvement can only be achieved by some form of parallel processing.

2.6 BIBLIOGRAPHY

[AHO79] Aho, A. V., Sagiv Y., and Ullman, J. D.: "Efficient Optimization of a Class of Relational Expressions," *ACM Transactions on Database Systems*, vol. 4, no. 4, Dec. 1979, pp. 435–454.

[ALL76] Allman, E., Stonebraker, M. R., and Held, G. D.: "Embedding a Relational Data Sublanguage in a General Purpose Programming Language," *Proceedings of the ACM SIGPLAN/SIGMOND Conference on Data: Abstraction, Definition, and Structure,* Salt Lake City, Utah, March 1976, pp. 25–35.

[ANS75] ANSI/X3/SPARC: Study Group on Data Base Management Systems, Interim Report, FDT (*ACM SIGMOD Bulletin*), vol. 7, no. 2, 1975.

[BER80] Bernstein, P. A., and Goodman, N.: "Timestamp-Based Algorithms for Concurrency Control in Distributed Database Systems," *Proceedings of the Sixth International Conference on Very Large Data Bases,* Montreal, Canada, Oct. 1980, pp. 285–300.

[BLA77] Blasgen, M. W., and Eswaran, K. P.: "Storage and Access in Relational Data Bases," *IBM System Journal,* vol. 16, no. 4, 1977.

[BRO81] Brodie, M. L.: "On Modeling Behavioral Semantics of Database," *Proceedings of the Seventh International Conference on Very Large Data Bases,* Cannes, France, 1981, pp. 32–41.

[BRO84] Brodie, M. L., Mylopoulos, J., and Schmidt, J. W. (eds.): *On Conceptual Modelling,* Springer-Verlag, New York, 1984.

[CHA74] Chamberlin, D. D., and Boyce, R. F.: "SEQUEL: A Structured English Query Language," *Proceedings of the 1974 ACM SIGMOD Workshop on Data Description, Access, and Control,* Ann Arbor, Mich., May 1974, pp. 249–269.

[CHA76] Chamberlin, D. D., et al.: "SEQUEL 2: A Unified Approach to Data Definition, Manipulation and Control," *IBM Journal of R&D,* vol. 20, no. 6, Nov. 1976.

[CHE76] Chen, P. P. S.: "The Entity-Relationship Model—Toward a Unified View of Data." *ACM Transactions on Database Systems,* vol. 6, no. 1, March 1976, pp. 9–36.

[COD70] Codd, E. F.: "A Relational Model of Data for Large Shared Data Banks," *Communications of the ACM,* vol. 13, no. 6, 1970, pp. 377–387.

[COD72a] Codd, E. F.: "Relational Completeness of Data Base Sublanguage," in *Data Base Systems,* Courant Computer Science Symposia Series, vol. 6, Prentice-Hall, Englewood Cliffs, N. J., 1972.

[COD72b] Codd, E. F.: "Further Normalization of the Data Base Relational Model," in Data Base Systems, Courant Computer Science Symposia Series, vol. 6, Prentice-Hall, Englewood Cliffs, N. J., 1972.

[COD79] Codd, E. F.: "Extending the Database Relational Model to Capture More Meaning," *ACM Transactions on Database Systems,* vol. 4, no. 4, Dec. 1979, pp. 397–434.

[DAT86] Date, C. J.: *An Introduction to Database Systems,* Addison-Wesley, Reading, Mass., 1986.

[DBT71] Data Base Task Group of CODASYL Programming Language Committee Report, April 1971.

[DEN79] Denning, D. E., and Denning, P. J.: "Data Security," *ACM Computing Surveys,* vol. 11, no. 3, Sept. 1979, pp. 227–249.

[DEN83] Denning, D. E.: *Cryptography and Data Security,* Addison-Wesley, Reading, Mass., 1983.

[DEW81] DeWitt, D., and Hawthorn, P.: "A Performance Evaluation of Database Machine Architectures," *Proceedings of the Seventh International Conference on Very Large Data Bases,* Cannes, France, Sept. 1981, pp. 199–213.

[DEW85] DeWitt, D. J., and Gerber, R.: "Multiprocessor Hash-Based Join Algorithms," *Proceedings of the Eleventh International Conference on Very Large Data Bases,* Stockholm, 1985, pp. 151–164.

[ESW75] Eswaran, K. P., Chamberlin, D. D.: "Functional Specifications of a Subsystem for Database Integrity," *Proceedings of the First International Conference on Very Large Data Bases,* Framingham, Mass., Sept. 1975, pp. 48–68.

[FER81] Fernandez, E. B., Summers, R. C., and Wood, C.: *Database Security and Integrity*, Reading, Mass, Addison-Wesley, 1981.

[GRA75] Gray, J. N., Lorie, R. A., and Putzolu, G. R.: "Granularity of Locks in a Large Shared Data Base," *Proceedings of the First International Conference on Very Large Data Bases*, Framingham, Mass., Sept. 1975, pp. 428–451.

[GRA76] Gray, J. N., Lorie, R. A., Putzolu, G. R., and Traiger, I. L.: "Granularity of Locks and Degrees of Consistency in a Shared Data Base," in G. M. Nijssen (ed.), *Proceedings of the IFIP TC-2 Working Conference on Modelling in Data Base Management Systems*, North Holland, New York, 1976.

[GRA81] Gray, J. N., "The Transaction Concept: Virtues and Limitations," *Proceedings of the Seventh International Conference on Very Large Data Bases*, Cannes, France, Sept. 1981, pp. 144–154.

[HAE83] Haerder, T., and Reuter, A.: "Principles of Transaction-Oriented Database Recovery," *ACM Computing Surveys*, vol. 15, no. 15, Dec. 1983, pp. 287–317.

[HAM78] Hammer, M. M., and McLeod, D. J.: "The Semantic Data Model: A Modeling Mechanism for Database Applications," *Proceedings of the 1978 ACM SIGMOD International Conference on Management of Data*, Austin, Tex., June 1978, pp. 26–34.

[HAM81] Hammer, M., and McLeod, D.: "Database Description with SDM: A Semantic Database Model, *ACM Transactions on Database Systems*, vol. 6, no. 3, Sept. 1981, pp. 351–386.

[HAL76] Hall, P. A. V.: "Optimization of a Single Relational Expression in a Relational Data Base System," *IBM Journal of R&D*, vol. 20, no. 3, May 1976.

[HEL75] Held, G. D., Stonebraker, M. R., and Wong, E.: "INGRES—A Relational Data Base System," *Proceedings of the National Computer Conference*, vol. 44, AFIP Press, Montvale, N.J., May 1975, pp. 409–416.

[HUL86] Hull, R., and King, R.: "Semantic Database Modelling: Survey, Application, and Research Issues," TR-86-201, Computer Science Department, University of Southern California, Los Angeles, Calif., April 1986.

[JAR84] Jarke, M., and Koch, J.: "Query Optimization in Database Systems," *ACM Computer Survey*, vol. 16, no. 2, June 1984, pp. 111–152.

[KAP78] Kapp, D., and Leben, J. F.: *IMS Programming Techniques: A Guide to Using DL/I*, Van Nostrand Reinhold, New York, 1978.

[KEN78] Kent, W.: *Data and Reality*, North Holland, Amsterdam, 1978.

[KIM85] Kim, W., Reiner, D., and Batory, D. (eds.): *Query Processing in Database Systems*, Springer-Verlag, New York, 1985.

[KIN81] King, J. J.: "QUIST: A System for Semantic Query Optimization in Relational Databases," *Proceedings of the Seventh International Conference on very Large Data Bases*, Cannes, France, Sept. 1981, 510–517.

[KNU75] Knuth, D. E.: *The Art of Computer Programming—Sorting and Searching*, Addison-Wesley, Reading, Mass., 1975.

[KUN81] Kung, H. T., and Robinson, J. T.: "On Optimistic Methods for Concurrency Control," *ACM Transactions on Database Systems*, vol. 6, no. 2, June 1981, pp. 213–226.

[MAK81] Makinouchi, A., Tezuka, M., Kitakami, H., and Adachi, S.: "The Optimization Strategy for Query Evaluation in RDB/V1," *Proceedings of the Seventh International Conference on Very Large Data Bases*, Cannes, France, Sept. 1981, pp. 518–529.

[MCG77] McGee, W. C.: "The IMS/VS System," *IBM System Journal*, vol. 16, no. 2, June 1977.

[ROS82] Rosenthal, A., and Reiner, D.: " An Architecture for Query Optimization," *Proceedings of the 1982 ACM SIGMOD International Conference on Management of Data*, Orlando, Fla., June 1982, pp. 246–255.

[SEL79] Selinger, P. G., Astrahan, M.M., Chamberlain, D.D., Lorie, R.A., and Price, T.G.: "Access Path Selection in a Relational Database System," *Proceedings of the 1979 ACM SIGMOD International Conference on Management of Data*, Boston, Mass., May 1979, pp. 23–34.

[SHI81] Shipman, D.: "The Functional Data Model and the Data Language DAPLEX," *ACM Transactions on Database Systems*, vol. 6, no. 1, March 1981, pp. 140–173.

[SMI75] Smith, J. M., and Chang, P. Y. T.: "Optimizing the Performance of a Relational Algebra Database Interface," *Communications of the Association of Computing Machinery,* vol. 18, no. 10, Oct. 1975, pp. 568–579.

[SMI77] Smith, J. M., and Smith, D. C. P.: "Database Abstractions: Aggregation and Generalization," *ACM Transactions on Database Systems,* vol. 2, no. 2, June 1977, pp. 105–133.

[STO75] Stonebraker, M. R.: "Implementation of Integrity Constraints and views by Query Modification," *Proceedings of the ACM SIGMOD International Conference on Management of Data,* May 1975, pp. 65–78.

[STO76] Stonebraker, M. R., Wong, E., Kreps, P., and Held, G. D.: "The Design and Implementation of INGRES," *ACM Transactions on Database Systems,* vol. 1, no. 3, Sept. 1976, pp. 189–222.

[SU79] Su, S. Y. W., and Lo, D. H.: "A Semantic Association Model for Conceptual Database Design," *Proceedings of the International Conference on the Entity-Relationship Approach to Systems Analysis and Design,* Dec. 1979.

[SU83] Su, S. Y. W.: "SAM∗: A Semantic Association Model for Corporate and Scientific-Statistical Databases," *Journal of Information Sciences,* vol. 29, 1983, pp. 151–199.

[SU86] Su, S. Y. W.: "Modeling Integrated Manufacturing Data Using a Semantic Association Model (SAM∗)," *IEEE COMPUTERS,* vol. 19, no. 1, Jan. 1986, pp. 34–49.

[TSI76] Tsichritzis, D. C., and Lochovsky, F. H.: "Hierarchical Data Base Management: A Survey," *ACM Computing Surveys,* vol. 8, no. 1, March 1976.

[VER78] Verhofstad, J. S. M.: "Recovery Techniques for Database Systems," *Association of Computing Machinery's Computing Survey,* vol. 10, no. 2, June 1978, pp. 167–195.

[WIE79] Wiederhold, G., and El-Masri, R.: "Structural Model for Database Design," *Proceedings of the International Conference on Entity Relationship Approach to Systems Analysis and Design,* Dec. 1979.

[WON76] Wong, E., and Youssefi, K.: "Decomposition—A Strategy for Query Processing," *ACM Transactions on Database Systems,* vol. 1, no. 3, Sept. 1976, pp. 223–241.

[YAO79] Yao, S. B.: "Optimization of Query Evaluation Algorithms," *ACM Transactions on Database Systems,* vol. 4, no. 2, June 1979, pp. 133–155.

[YOV81] Yovitz, M.C., Foulk, C.R., and Rose, L.L.: "Information Flow and Analysis: Theory, Simulation, and Experiments (I. Basic Theoretical and Conceptual Development)", *Journal of the American Society for Information Science,* John Wiley and Sons, Inc., New York, May 1981, pp. 188–202.

[ZLO75] Zloof, M. M.: "Query by Example," *Proceedings of the National Computer Conference,* vol. 44, AFIP Press, Montvale, N.J., May 1975.

[ZLO78] Zloof, M. M.: "Security and Integrity Within the Query-By-Example Data Base Management Language," *IBM Research Report RC 6982,* Feb. 1978.

INTELLIGENT SECONDARY STORAGE DEVICES

The size of a database in a real-world application is generally too large for the database to be stored in the main memory of a computer system. Therefore, it is stored in some secondary storage device. Traditional secondary memory devices have very limited processing capabilities. Data stored in these devices must be moved into the main memory before being examined by the central processor. Moving data between the main memory and the secondary storage is very time-consuming and is one of the main causes of inefficiency in the existing database systems. Intelligent secondary storage devices to be described in this chapter aim to alleviate this problem by building more processing capability into the storage devices so that data can be processed right on the devices. Processing efficiency is gained in these devices by parallel processing and by content and context addressing of the data. The general architecture and the characteristics of this category of data computers will be described as well as the specific designs and techniques used in several proposed systems.

3.1 CONVENTIONAL ROTATING MEMORY DEVICES: FEATURES AND LIMITATIONS

The cost and technical complexity involved in the development of high-speed, large-capacity main memories has traditionally forced most computer systems to use a variety of slower but less expensive secondary storage devices to store data and programs. These include devices such as magnetic tapes, disks, drums, mass memories, video disks, and so forth. Among these devices, the magnetic disks are the most widely used because of their low access time, high data transfer rate, direct access capability, and their overall cost-effectiveness. Their operating characteristics can be used to illustrate the limitations of the conventional memory devices.

A *magnetic disk* is a metal platter that has one or both sides coated with ferromagnetic particles that provide a data storage medium. A number of these platters are stacked on top of each other to form a *disk pack*. The surface of each platter is divided into a number of concentric bands called *tracks*. Each track is further divided into a number of areas called *sectors,* which are addressable storage units. Data are read from or written into a sector through a read/write head that floats above the surface as the disk rotates.

Two types of disks are commonly used: moving-head and fixed-head disks. In a moving-head disk, the read/write heads are attached on a movable arm to form a comblike assembly. All tracks under the read/write heads at a fixed position form a cylinder. When data are to be read into or written from a sector, the assembly is moved so that the heads are directly over the cylinder that contains the desired track. The proper head is then selected for the track that contains the desired sector. The time required to seek the track is called the *seek time.* The time for the proper sector to come under the read/write head is called the *latency time.* In a general input or output operation, a number of sectors will be read or written. The total time for transferring their contents is called the *transmission time.* Thus, the total time required for the completion of an I/O operation is the sum of the seek time, the latency time, and the transmission time. In most moving-head disk devices, the seek time is very significant in comparison to the transmission time. For example, the IBM 3300 disk drive has an average seek time of 30 msecs and a transmission rate of 806 characters per msec.

In a fixed-head disk, each track has its own read/write head. The selection of a proper track is done by electronically switching read/write heads rather than by mechanically moving the heads as in a moving-head disk. The seek time required for the moving-head disk is replaced in the fixed-head disk by a negligible amount of time for switching from one head to the other. This represents a considerable improvement over the operation of a moving-head disk as far as performance is concerned.

There are several serious limitations in the existing secondary memory devices of which the disk is a representation. The most serious one is the inability to process data at the place where data are stored (i.e., on the devices). The logic associated with the read/write mechanism is incapable of examining the contents of the storage devices. Consequently, all data relevant for a particular operation need to be moved to the main memory for processing by the CPU. A file is moved as often as it is used by application programs. Data transfer in and out of the secondary storage devices is slow, as mentioned, because the devices are mechanical and their mechanical speed is much less than the electronic speed of the CPU. Although the speed of secondary storage devices has improved considerably as a result of the progress made in secondary memory technology, it still cannot catch up with the speed improvements of processors. Thus, secondary storage–related operations remain the main bottleneck of a database system.

Another limitation is that data transmission can be done only one block (a disk sector or a physical block of a magnetic tape) at a time, even though a disk pack may have many read/write heads. This restriction results in the serial processing of the data files stored in the secondary storage devices.

The third limitation is that data must be located by their addresses rather than by their contents. To locate a block of data, the address of the disk sector needs to be computed and specified to the disk controller. When a data block has been moved from one place to another on the disk, the system must keep track of its physical address. Thus, conventional secondary storage devices must translate the user's search criteria, which are specified in terms of data contents, into addresses before the search can be carried out. The devices do not support the database management requirement that data be freely moved around to maximize the use of the storage space or to make the associated data physically adjacent for performance purposes.

3.2 CELLULAR-LOGIC DEVICES

The limitations discussed previously have motivated the design and development of several intelligent storage devices called *cellular-logic* (or CL) *devices* [SU79a]. These devices have characteristics that match well with the requirements of database applications. This section provides descriptions of the general architectural features, data organization, and database processing techniques of this category of database computers using several proposed systems as examples.

3.2.1 The Architecture of Cellular-Logic Devices

The general architecture of a cellular-logic device is shown in Figure 3.1. The device is controlled by a general-purpose computer that translates the high-level data manipulation requests into commands for the CL device, transfers commands to the device for execution, receives data transferred out of the device, and processes and outputs the data to the user. The CL device itself consists of the following four major components: M, P, C, and IO.

1. M is a set of circular memory elements (M_i's), each of which can be defined by a triplet (TG, DT, and SR). TG is the storage for tagging data items in order to distinguish different data types (e.g., character strings, numerical values, delimiter words, instruction words, etc.) or to delimit data items. DT is the storage space for the actual data and program instructions. Data as well as instructions can be recorded in a fixed-word format or a free format with delimiters and tags to separate them. SR is the storage space for the search results, which are used either for input/output purposes or as the context for further searches. SR can be a random access memory, a set of registers, or the same type of memory as DT. In the existing systems, disks, drums, CCD shift registers, and magnetic bubble memories have been used as the circular memories. Due to the circular

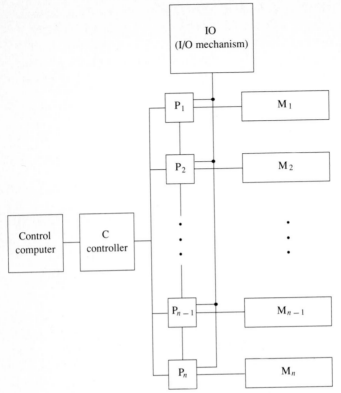

FIGURE 3.1
The general architecture of a cellular-logic device.

feature, the contents of TG, DT, and SR in each memory element can be scanned repeatedly by the associated processing elements to be described next.

2. P is a set of processing elements (P_i's), one for each M_i containing the logic for processing the contents of M_i. Each pair (P_i, M_i) forms a *cell*. The set of interconnected cells forms the main body of the device, which is thus called a cellular-logic device. The interconnecting structures of P_i's vary slightly from system to system, although they are all quite simple. Most systems allow processing elements to communicate directly with their immediate neighbors. The intercell communication feature of the CL devices distinguishes them from the so-called logic-per-track device proposed by Slotnick [SLO70]. The simplicity of the intercell interconnection also distinguishes CL systems from parallel systems such as ASP [SAV66 and SAV67], SOLOMON [SLO62], ILLIAC IV [SLO67], and OMEN [HIG72], which have more complex connections among processors.

Each processing element P_i consists of the following five categories of hardware facilities:

a. A set of registers or a buffer space (CP) for holding the comparands, which are data values to be matched against the data stored in the memory elements, and a set of registers or buffers to hold the data selected from M_i for comparison.

b. A mask control mechanism (MK) for selecting specific data fields or bit patterns from the data in storage.

c. An arithmetic and logic unit for performing arithmetic operations such as $=$, $>$, $\geq$, $<$, and $\leq$, and logical operations such as AND, OR, NOT, and XOR (exclusive OR).

d. Logic for calculating aggregation functions such as Sum, Average, Max, Min, Count, First Element, and so forth.

e. Logic for performing the primitive database operations such as Search, Mark, Modify, Delete, Insert, and Input and Output data.

3. The third component of a CL device is the controller, C. It controls simultaneous execution of the same instruction by all P_i's, against their corresponding memory elements. In CL systems, instructions are either fetched from one of the M_i's or fed by a front-end computer. Each instruction of a program is broadcast simultaneously to all the P_i's for execution and operates on different data streams stored in M_i's. Thus, CL systems have a single instruction stream and multiple data stream (SIMD) architecture.

4. The IO is the mechanism in a CL device used for moving data to and from M_i's. The input operation in a CL system is similar to that of a conventional system. Data are transferred into a selected M_i either starting at a location marked by a previous search operation or appending the new data at the end of M_i. The output process in CL systems is more complicated since data are searched and marked for output simultaneously. The order in which the data in different M_i's is to be output generally is based on either some priorities preassigned to the P_i's or on the order in which the data are scanned by P_i's.

When using CL devices for database management applications, one can partition data files horizontally into blocks of records and store them in the M_i's. Database queries or application programs that have been translated into sequences of commands can either be fed to the controller, which broadcasts one command at a time to the P_i's for execution, or can be stored in the M_i's, from where they are fetched later by the P_i's for execution.

The search command is used here to illustrate command execution in CL systems. The search is executed in parallel against the contents of M_i's. The hardware determines the type of words in the M_i's that should be examined using the tag information stored in TG space. Units of data (e.g., records that satisfy the search criterion) are marked by setting some bit in the SR space. The marked data can be used as the context for subsequent searches (see Section 3.4) or can be used by the I/O mechanism to transfer data to the control computer.

The main characteristics of CL devices can be summarized as follows:

1. CL systems avoid the problem of data staging by searching and processing data directly on the secondary storage.

2. CL systems gain search and processing speed by parallel processing of n segments of a database, where n is the number of processing elements. For some database operations, the processing time requires about $1/n$th the time necessary to process the n segments sequentially.

3. CL systems achieve economy in their implementation by using identical cells and conventional secondary storage devices.
4. CL systems avoid many levels of language mapping by hardware implementation of high-level database operations.
5. CL systems avoid the problem of data mapping by storing data in a form very similar to that seen by the user or the application program and by addressing the data by content and context.
6. CL systems achieve system reliablity and expandability by using a linear array of identical cells that are easy to maintain, replace, reduce, and expand.

In addition to this description of the general architecture and characteristics of CL devices, the architectures and features of some specific systems will be examined. Quite a few early computers were proposed for keyword retrieval of documents [HOL56, PAR71, and MIN72] and for character string manipulation [PAR72, HEA72, and HEA76]. These computers possess the general architecture and characteristics of CL devices and have had significant influence on the design of more recent systems as shown by Su [SU79a]. In this book, only the CL devices used for database management applications will be examined.

3.2.1.1 THE ARCHITECTURE OF CASSM. Context Addressed Segmented Sequential Memory (CASSM) is a research database computer designed and prototyped at the University of Florida during the period starting in 1972 to 1980 under the support of the National Science Foundation. The system contains a linear array of cells, each of which contains a processing element and a circular memory element as illustrated in Figure 3.2. Data as well as compiled programs are stored in the memory elements and are scanned and manipulated by the associated processing elements. The CASSM hardware is designed to support the high-level view of a database as a collection of sequential files. These files are stored serially starting from the first memory element to the nth element. Each file contains a set of hierarchically structured records that contain data and/or programs precompiled by the user-CASSM interface, a NOVA 800 computer. A file or a record can span more than one memory element. A hierarchical record is linearized in a top-down and left-to-right order (left list matrix) and is actually stored as a linear vector of 44-bit words in the memory elements (40-bit words were used in the early version of CASSM). Each file is partitioned into segments, each of which is stored in a memory element. The segments are simultaneously processed by n processing elements, thus reducing the task of processing the entire database into that of $1/n$th of the database.

Data or instructions are read by a read head of the circular memory element, processed by the processing element (a special-purpose processor) and written back to the memory by a separate write head as illustrated in Figure 3.2. The processing elements can communicate with their adjacent neighbors through three communication lines: a bottom priority line (BPR), a link (LINK), and a top priority line (TPR). Data are passed among the processing elements and the interface computer through a data bus and a serial tree adder whose functions, along with those of BPR, LINK, and TPR, will be dicussed later with applications.

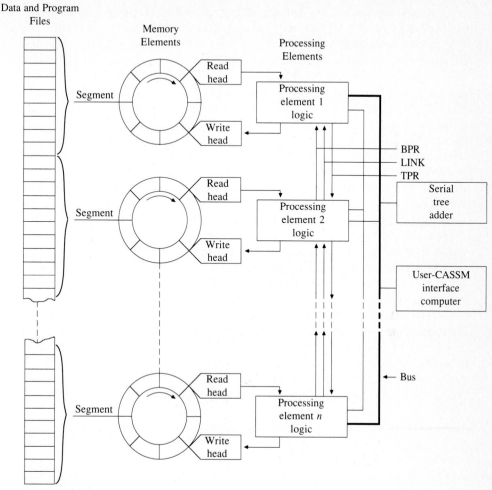

FIGURE 3.2
The overall architecture of CASSM. (*Source:* [SU79*b*] ©1979 IEEE)

A CASSM cycle may be loosely defined as one revolution of the memory elements. More precisely, it is the sum of a scan time and a gap time. The scan time is the time taken to scan the data on a memory element; the gap time, a design parameter, is at least the amount of time taken to synchronize the timing marks that start the memory elements. A global bit-time clock synchronizes the CASSM cells. During the gap time, a certain number of operations (e.g., the aggregate functions) may be performed, the time for which may depend on the organization of the data or the number of cells in the configuration.

   A processing element in CASSM consists of a number of parallel operating modules. Data and/or program instructions stored on each cell's rotating memory elements flow through a pipeline of modules as shown in Figure 3.3. The function of the read head is to pick up each word from the memory, adjust timing (through a FIFO), perform parity checking, and then pass it on to the Post processor. The previously active instruction and immediate operand (if the instruction had one) that were fetched in the preceding cycle are deactivated in the Post module. The Post module also takes care of some of the unfinished tasks of the instruction started during the last cycle. The next module on the pipeline is the Collection module, which shares part of the hardware of the Post. It checks for data words that might have been marked by the instruction executed in the previous cycle and transfers them out through the bus to the interface computer. Next, the Garbage Collection (GC) module, which also shares part of the Post module's hardware, tries to "absorb" any words with a tag that says "garbage word." Usually, garbage words are words that have been flagged for deletion either in Post or in Main. A garbage word is absorbed by the GC module by not passing it on to the Main module. The Main module executes the search part of the instruction fetched during the last cycle. Memory words that are output from the Main module are routed to both the Write and the Sel modules. The Write module updates words or status bits of those words in records that satisfied some search conditions and writes these words back to memory. The Sel module is responsible for fetching the instruction and operands for the next cycle.

While instructions to search and modify data are being executed by the processing element, supporting operations are being carried out concurrently by other modules. These operations are instruction fetch, operand recall, string-to-code word translation and input, data collection (output), and garbage collection. A simple example clarifies this concept of a concurrently operating pipeline of modules. Figure 3.4 shows the organizations of the M_i memory element at the beginning of the first and the second passes of this operation. Assume that the instruction I1 was fetched by the Sel module during the previous scan of the M_i,

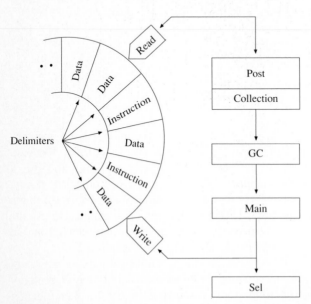

FIGURE 3.3
Parallel processing modules on a data pipeline.

and is passed to the Main module for execution during the current cycle. The instruction is a search command meant to pick all records containing the data word 'CD'. When such records are encountered, the processing element should mark the record delimiters associated with the records. The program instructions are also stored as ordinary data in a block delimited by the delimiter D10. This delimiter is set to '1' when an instruction in the block is being executed. By the time the Main module sees the first word of M_i, I1 would have been marked inactive (by setting its bit to '0') by the Post module, since I1 has been sent to Main for execution. When the word containing the characters CD reaches Main, the delimiter D40 has already passed it, hence Main cannot mark the delimiter D40 at this time. However, Main passes the number of the delimiter, 40 in this case, to the Post module. The Post module then counts each delimiter in the second pass and marks the fortieth delimiter, D40. Also, during the first cycle, Sel fetches the next active instruction from the active instruction block, that is, I2 at this time. As before, I2 is deactivated by the Post module and is broadcast to the Main modules of all the processing elements for execution during the second cycle. When Main encounters the record delimited by D40, it notes that the record has satisfied the previous search instruction. If I2 is now a delete instruction for deleting all marked records, then Main will set the tag bits associated with all the words of the record. Thus, all these words become garbage words to be collected by the GC module during the execution of the subsequent instructions.

3.2.1.2 THE ARCHITECTURE OF RAP. A CL system called the Relational Associative Processor (RAP) was designed and prototyped at the University of

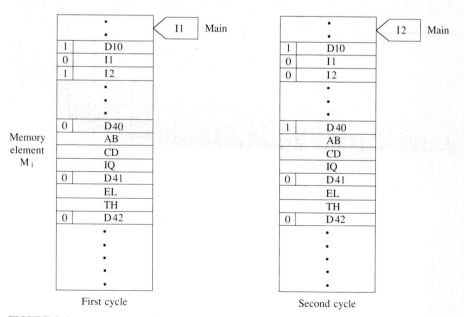

First cycle   Second cycle

FIGURE 3.4
Marking data and instruction words by parallel modules.

Toronto [OZK75, SCH76, and SCH78]. The architecture of RAP is shown in Figure 3.5. It consists of a controller, a set function unit, and a linear array of cells, each of which contains some cell logic (the processing element) and a memory element. RAP uses a general-purpose computer as its front-end processor to perform the following functions: (1) provide a data communication environment for database users, (2) compile users' queries expressed in a high-level query language into RAP primitives, (3) transfer compiled RAP primitives to the controller, (4) transfer data to the cell memories, (5) support a concurrent processing environment, (6) control database security and integrity, and (7) maintain encoding tables for relation names, domain names, and data.

The controller of RAP has a local memory to store a compiled query, which is in the form of a sequence of primitive database operations interpretable by the cells. It broadcasts primitive operations one at a time to all cells for execution and coordinates the cell activities. The set function unit is connected via a bus to the cells in the same way as the controller. The unit is controlled by the controller and can perform statistical computations on sets of values retrieved from the memory

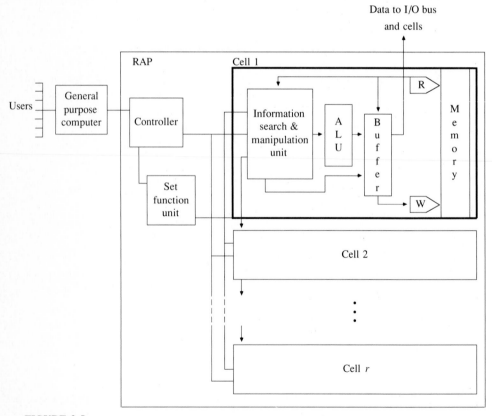

FIGURE 3.5
The architecture of RAP. (*Source:* [OZK75] copyright ©1975. AFIPS, reprinted by permission of AFIPS Press.)

elements. Aggregate functions such as Sum, Count, Maximum, Minimum, and Average are computed by this unit. In the second version of design, RAP.2 [SCH78], the set function unit is combined with the controller and the functions of both components are implemented using a minicomputer PDP 11/10. More recent work on RAP(RAP.3) is reported in [OZK86].

RAP has a linear array of identical cells. Each cell contains (1) an information search and manipulation unit (ISMU), (2) an arithmetic logic unit (ALU), (3) a buffer, (4) a pair of read and write heads, and (5) a memory. The ISMU handles the intercell communication, decodes the instructions from the controller, and evaluates the data search criteria. The ALU performs arithmetic computations, data modification operations, and intermediate set function calculations. The buffer is used to hold data read from the associated memory element for comparision against the search conditions specified in the search instructions. The original design system was designed with a 1024-bit RAM. The pair of separate read and write heads are used to read and write data stored in the memory element (a $5 \times 10**5$–bit disk track). Data are read from the memory element by the read head into the buffer, marked or modified based on the instruction being executed at the time, and written back to the memory element by the write head or deleted if they had been previously marked as garbage.

3.2.1.3 THE ARCHITECTURE OF RARES. The *R*otating *A*ssociative *RE*lational *S*tore (RARES) is an associative memory device designed at the University of Utah to support relational database management [LIN76]. Like CASSM and RAP, the content-addressing capability is added to an existing head-per-track disk. As shown in Figure 3.6, RARES consists of a general-purpose computer (GPC), a set of search modules (SM), a set of fixed read/write heads, an output buffer, an output arbiter, and a fixed-head disk used as the memory elements. The disk tracks in this system are divided into bands, each of which is formed by a set of physically adjacent tracks. Data are stored on these bands and are processed by their corresponding SMs. Thus, a band rather than a disk track forms a memory element, and an SM serves as the processing element in RARES.

The GPC serves as a front-end computer that accepts and translates relational queries issued by the users into query trees consisting of relational algebraic operators, optimizes the translated queries by modifying the query trees, and sends the Selection operations to RARES for execution. RARES is mainly designed to process the Selection operation and to support other operations that take advantage of the hardware selection capability (e.g., the sorting operation). The results of Selection operations are transferred from RARES to GPC for further processing.

Each search module in RARES is assigned 64 adjacent read/write heads that are mapped to 64 physical tracks that form a band. Search modules can move from band to band, and the track assignment to the search modules can overlap. Data recorded on the corresponding disk band are read by the read/write heads and transferred along 64 parallel lines to the search module (see Section 3.2.2.3 for details of RARES's data organization). The search module consists of a comparison circuit, a row queue, a response store, and a match result queue. Tuples are read from the disk band and transferred to the search module. Each

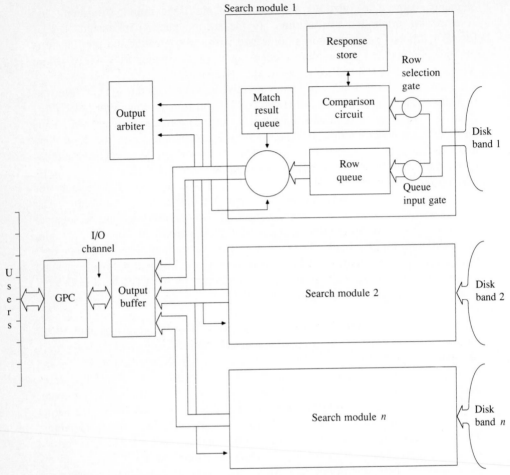

FIGURE 3.6
The architecture of RARES. (*Source:* [LIN76] copyright ©1976, Association for Computing Machinery, Inc., reprinted by permission)

tuple is directed simultaneously toward both the comparison circuit and the row queue. A tuple is folded on the disk band into "rows." The comparison circuit contains 64 one-byte comparators, which compare each row of a tuple against a search operand. The row queue holds the rows of tuples being compared. When the last row of a tuple has been compared, the queue input gate opens and new rows are shifted into the row queue. If the row match is successful, the result is accumulated for the tuple to which the row belongs. If all search conditions have been satisfied by a tuple, the accumulated result is placed in the match result queue shown in Figure 3.6. If the row match is successful and further matches are required on the tuple, a mark bit is placed in the response store. The output arbiter allows one search module at a time to transfer its tuples (those that have satisfied the search conditions) to the output buffer. Other modules ready to transfer data are instructed to place a mark in their response stores and wait for their turns. The accumulated tuples in the buffer are then transferred through the I/O channel to the GPC for further processing.

In RARES, the bands are variable in width. The output buffer has to be as wide as the maximal band width. If the band width is smaller than that of the buffer, the buffer is not fully utilized. The effective capacity of the output buffer reduces proportionally as the bands are reduced below the maximal width. The maximal band width also determines the size of the search operand register used for row comparison and the data lines connecting the search module and the output buffer.

3.2.2 Data Organizations of Cellular-Logic Devices

In cellular-logic devices, data can be physically stored in the memory elements, M_i's, in one of the following four ways: bit-parallel and word-serial, bit-parallel and word-parallel, bit-serial and word-serial, and bit-serial and word-parallel. In the case of bit-parallel and word-serial organization, data are stored in the fashion illustrated in Figure 3.7a. The bits of each character of a student name "Smith" are stored across eight memory elements and are accessed in parallel by the corresponding P_i's. The characters that form the word "Smith" are stored and accessed in a serial fashion. In the case of bit-parallel and word-parallel organization, data are arranged as illustrated in Figure 3.7b. Data words are stored one bit per memory element across the M_i's and are accessed by the corresponding P_i's in parallel. Figure 3.7c illustrates the bit-serial and word-serial organization in which data words are serially stored in every M and are accessed by the P_i's simultaneously in serial fashion. Thus, data access is parallel across M_i's and serial in each M. Figure 3.7d illustrates the bit-serial and word-parallel organization in which characters of data words are stored across M_i's and the bits of each character are stored serially.

The advantages and disadvantages of these four organizations are quite obvious. If bits or words are arranged in parallel fashion (Figures 3.7a, 3.7b, and 3.7d), the P_i's will have to be partitioned into groups to access the data in parallel. The timing for accessing the data by the involved P_i's must be synchronized perfectly in order for the bits or words to be fetched and compared against some search comparands properly. This requirement is hard to satisfy if a rotating disk is used as the storage device. However, the parallel organization does allow data to be transferred out to the control processor in parallel, if parallel lines for I/O are available. The serial organization, on the other hand, has fewer synchronization problems. However, data stored in each M must be transferred in and out of M in serial fashion. Nevertheless, if parallel I/O lines are available for the P_i's, data stored in the M_i's can be transferred in parallel to the control computer. It should be stressed here that both parallel and serial organizations have the same effect as far as the examination of the memory contents is concerned. In one rotation of the storage device, all the data words or bits can be examined by P_i's in both organizations.

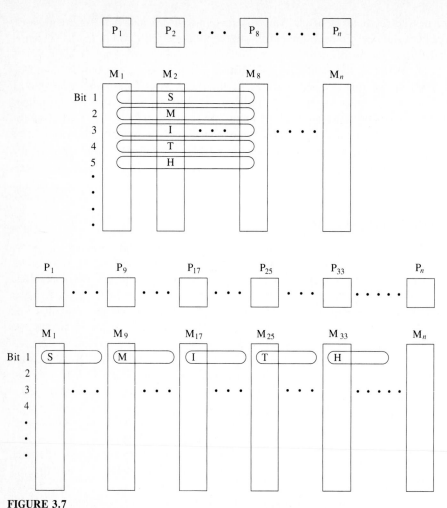

FIGURE 3.7
(*a*) Bit-parallel and word-serial organization and access. (*b*) Bit-parallel and word-parallel organization and access.

This discussion examined only the possible physical layout of data in the memory elements of CL devices. The actual structures used to store data fields, records, and files in the M_i's may vary from system to system. The following subsections describe the data organizations of CASSM, RAP, and RARES.

3.2.2.1 THE DATA ORGANIZATION OF CASSM. CASSM was designed to support the database operations of the three popular data models, namely, the relational model, the hierarchical model, and the network model. The underlying data structure of CASSM files is essentially hierarchical. This allows a relation in a relational model to be nested inside another relation in order, for example, to implement existence dependencies between the two relations. The concept of existence dependency may be explained with an example. The STUDENT relation

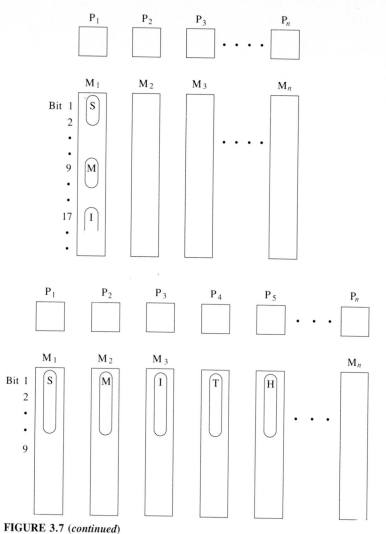

FIGURE 3.7 (*continued*)
(*c*) Bit-serial and word-serial organization and access. (*d*) Bit-serial and word parallel organization and access.

given in Chapter 2 is modified somewhat to illustrate CASSM's hierarchical structure and the dependency concept. As shown in Figure 3.8, if the students' address data are meaningful only when they are associated with the students, then they cannot be entered independently into the database without the presence of the students' unique identifiers (S# in Figure 3.8). In this situation, the address information is said to have an existence dependency relationship with the other student information. In CASSM, all student data are stored in a single file rather than in two separate files as they would be in a relational DBMS due to the normalization process required in the relational model. A normalized relation in a relational model is a special case of the hierarchical tree structure used in

CASSM. The network organization of the Data Base Task Group's (DBTG's) network model is also represented as a collection of hierarchical trees in CASSM. The rationale for using the hierarchical structure as a common structure to support the three popular data models is given by Su [SU78 and SU79b].

The data in CASSM are physically organized in a bit-serial and word-serial fashion. A hierarchically structured file is linearized in a top-down left-to-right order. As an example, the file in Figure 3.8 is represented as a four-level hierarchical tree shown in Figure 3.9 in which STUDENT and ADDRESS are followed by level numbers to delimit the file, the records, and the subrecords. The hierarchical tree of Figure 3.9 is linearized and physically stored in a sequence of 44-bit words in the memory as illustrated in Figure 3.10. In this figure, D's mark the delimiter words and N's mark the name-value pairs. All symbolic names (i.e., names of relations and attributes as well as character strings used as the values of the attributes) are stored as 16-bit code words. The brackets on the left side of the figure show the hierarchical structure of the records delimited by the delimiters. In Figure 3.11, a standard 44-bit word is divided into a 32-bit field for storing data or an instruction, a 3-bit field for status (i.e., M, H, and C), a 3-bit field for tags, a 1-bit field for parity (P), a 1-bit field for controlling data transfer (T), a 3-bit field for integrity and security control (U, Vt, and V-), and one unused bit not shown in the figure. The format of the 32-bit field is different depending upon the word type such as delimiter, name-value pair, and so forth. The three status bits are used to mark the word for collection (C), to indicate that the word satisfies a match (M), or to mark the hole for insertion (H). Five tag bits are used to mark different data types such as instruction word, name-value pair, delimiter, character string, pointer word, operand, and garbage word as shown in Figure 3.11.

The special word called "delimiter" is used to delimit a tree (file) or a subtree (record or subrecord). It contains a level number, a name, a 6-bit stack, a qualification bit Q, and a specification bit S. The level number and name are used to name a node of a tree. The Q bit is used to indicate whether the data associated with the node (tree or subtree) should be searched or not (i.e., whether they form the context of a search). Thus, selective nodes in the database can

STUDENT

S#	SNAME	SEX	AGE	ADDRESS				
				N#	STREET	CITY	STATE	ZCODE
14256	J.R. Jones	M	23	412	NW 5th St.	Gainesville	Fla.	32601
16242	J.C. Brown	F	21	1243	NE 10th Ave.	Newberry	Fla.	32401
.								.
.								.
.								.
.								.
24010	S.H. Smith	F	24	4236	SW 13th Ave.	Gainesville	Fla.	32611

FIGURE 3.8
A hierarchically structured file.

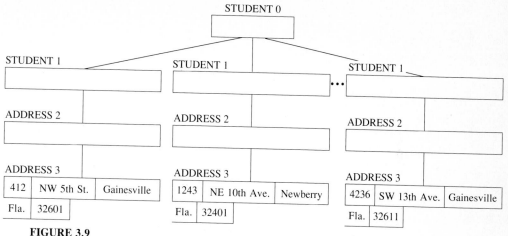

FIGURE 3.9
A hierarchical tree representation of the STUDENT file.

be operated upon by the search operation. The S bit is used to specify whether the node or its subordinates have satisfied the search. Since the S bits and Q bits associated with the delimiter words can be set at different nodes of a tree, a search can be accumulated at a record (with S bit set) when the subtrees at any level below it with Q bits set have satisfied a search condition. The temporary search results are stored in the bit stack, which allows complex Boolean expressions to be processed using stack operations.

The data organization described and illustrated in Figures 3.9 to 3.11 allows the CASSM hardware to access files, records, subrecords, and data items directly by contents since the level numbers and the file, record, and attribute names are stored explicitly. This organization eliminates the problems prevalent in the traditional implementation of hierarchical trees, where access to a node is generally through its ancestors. The way trees are linearized in CASSM ensures that the data of the subtrees of a given node are stored physically in adjacent order. This allows the CASSM hardware to search and mark trees and their subtrees in one revolution of the memory and allows related data to be output more easily.

In CASSM, attribute names are coded and stored along with every value of the attribute. Thus, the ordering of attribute-value pairs within a pair of delimiters is insignificant. The attribute-value pairs do not have to occupy consecutive storage space and can be mixed with other data or instruction words without losing their identity as elements of a record or subrecord. This property turns out to be very important because it is used to enforce integrity and security constraints as will be described in Section 3.2.6.

In CASSM, a file can occupy many tracks and the records of a file can span two adjacent tracks. The data organization also allows several small files to be stored on the same track. The data are essentially stored as a set of sequential records and files. This organization has the advantage of being very close to the application's view of a database as a set of sequential files. The mapping between

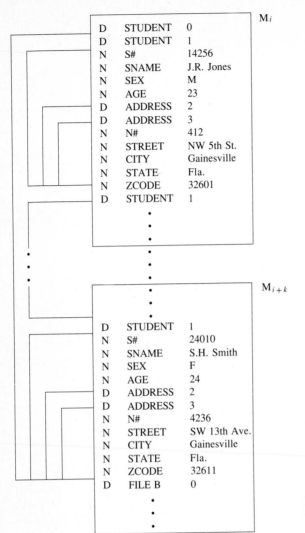

D	STUDENT	0	$\mathbf{M}_i$
D	STUDENT	1	
N	S#	14256	
N	SNAME	J.R. Jones	
N	SEX	M	
N	AGE	23	
D	ADDRESS	2	
D	ADDRESS	3	
N	N#	412	
N	STREET	NW 5th St.	
N	CITY	Gainesville	
N	STATE	Fla.	
N	ZCODE	32601	
D	STUDENT	1	

D	STUDENT	1	$\mathbf{M}_{i+k}$
N	S#	24010	
N	SNAME	S.H. Smith	
N	SEX	F	
N	AGE	24	
D	ADDRESS	2	
D	ADDRESS	3	
N	N#	4236	
N	STREET	SW 13th Ave.	
N	CITY	Gainesville	
N	STATE	Fla.	
N	ZCODE	32611	
D	FILE B	0	

FIGURE 3.10
CASSM's data organization on memory elements.

the application view and the physical structure is simple. However, a considerable amount of hardware is necessary to maintain the sequential nature of files and records during data insertions and deletions.

3.2.2.2 THE DATA ORGANIZATION OF RAP. RAP is designed to support a database management system based on the relational model. Data are stored in relations that are in the third normal form [COD7O]. The tuples of relations are stored sequentially on the disk tracks in the bit-serial and word-serial organization. Figure 3.12 shows how the STUDENT relation of Figure 2.9 is encoded and stored on a circular track. The beginning of a track is indicated by a timing marker (TM), which can be detected electronically by the disk hardware. This marker also serves to indicate the end of a track. The first two data blocks contain the

Mnemonics	Name	Tag								Status			Data				
D	Delimiter	U	V+	V−	T	P	O	O	O	M	H	C	Name	LEVEL	B-stack	S	Q
N	Name-value pairs	U	V+	V−	T	P	O	O	I	M	H	C	Name	VALUE			
P	Pointer	U	V+	V−	T	P	O	I	O	M	H	C	Name or L-pointer	R-pointer			
S	String	U	V+	V−	T	P	O	I	I	M	H	C	Byte	Byte	Byte	Byte	
I	Instruction	U	V+	V−	T	P	I	O	O	TYPE	IQ						
O	Operand	U	V+	V−	T	P	I	O	I	ON	F						
L	Protect lock	U	V+	V−	T	P	I	I	O	Status							
E	Erase (Garbage)	U	V+	V−	T	P	I	I	I	Status							

FIGURE 3.11
Word types and formats.

relation name and the attribute names, which are encoded to fixed-length words. Each of the succeeding blocks contains the concatenated attribute values in a tuple. They are again encoded to fixed-length words. The order of the encoded attribute names determines the order of the values in each tuple. The logical end of a track is indicated by a tuple block that contains a delimiting "track-end" (TKE) item.

All names, values, and delimiters are in the form of encoded bit patterns. The relation name block, attribute block, and tuple blocks of a relation are all of fixed size. However, the sizes of these blocks in different relations can be different. In RAP, unlike CASSM, a tuple cannot span two tracks, and two different relations cannot be stored in the same track. Names and values that are stored in the attribute and tuple blocks can be in a number of fixed sizes. Their lengths can be either 32, 16, or 8 bits. Each item is preceded by a two-bit code that gives four possible bit patterns. The first three patterns distinguish the three possible item lengths, and the fourth one is used to specify that the item is either a delimiter item (DL) or a track-end item (TKE). DL and TKE are distinguished from each other by another bit. Each tuple block contains the attribute values that form a tuple of the relation. The values are preceded by a one-bit deletion flag (DF) and four mark bits named A, B, C and D. The deletion flag indicates whether the tuple is marked for deletion or not, and the mark bits are used to indicate if the tuple satisfies a search condition. The mark bit can also be used to accumulate the results of various search conditions as will be shown in Section 3.2.3. The DF, A, B, C, and D bits of all the tuples of relations in the entire database form the SR storage discussed in the general architecture of CL devices (Section 3.2.1).

3.2.2.3 THE DATA ORGANIZATION OF RARES.

RARES, like RAP, is designed to support relational database management operations. Unlike CASSM and RAP, the data organization of RARES is in an orthogonal fashion (i.e., in the bit-serial and word-parallel organization). As illustrated in Figure 3.13, a relation R defined over the attributes A1, A2, and A3 is stored on one or more bands (a set of adjacent tracks). Each tuple of the relation is arranged on the row(s) of the band. The attribute values are stored across the tracks (word-parallel) and each eight-bit character of an attribute value is stored serially in a one-byte cell on the track (bit-serial). Different attributes can be of different lengths, but the values of an attribute are stored in a fixed-length field. For example, in Figure 3.13, the attribute A1 takes three cells, A2 three cells, and A3 four cells. All values associated with the same attribute have the same length.

The main advantage of the orthogonal layout is the increase in the access rate of tuples, since attribute values can be read and examined by the search modules (the processing elements) in parallel. The disadvantages of this organization are (1) the unused space in the last row occupied by a tuple constitutes a considerable waste of storage, (2) hardware control of variable-length fields and parallel reading of attribute values increase the buffer size and the amount of logic required in the search modules, and (3) additional circuits are required for the selection of variable-width bands on the disk surface.

Encoded STUDENT Relation

A1	A2	A3	A4	A5
V_{11}	V_{12}	V_{13}	V_{14}	V_{15}
V_{21}	V_{22}	V_{23}	V_{24}	V_{25}
·	·	·	·	·
·	·	·	·	·
·	·	·	·	·

Organization on Disk Track

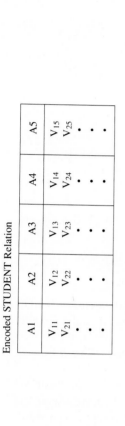
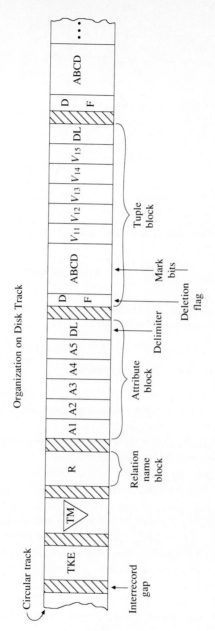

Name and Value Format

B1	B2		
	gw		
		hw	
			fw

B1	B2	
0	0	gw
0	1	hw
1	0	fw
1	1	DL or TKE

FIGURE 3.12

The data organization of RAP. (*Source*: [OZK75] copyright © 1975. AFIPS, reprinted by permission of AFIPS Press.)

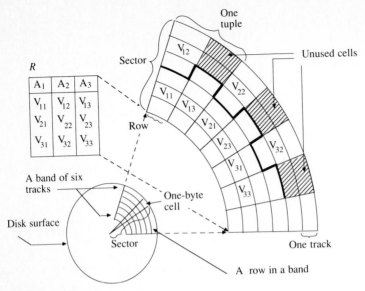

FIGURE 3.13
The orthogonal data organization of RARES. (*Source:* [LIN76] copyright ©1976, Association for Computing Machinery, Inc., reprinted by permission)

3.2.3 Content and Context Addressing

The techniques used in the cellular-logic devices to address data elements (data values, records, or files) are quite different from the conventional computer systems. Data elements are addressed by specifying their contents or the context in which the data elements occur rather than by their addresses. The following examples explain these two addressing techniques.

The content-addressing technique of the cellular-logic devices is illustrated by Figure 3.14. The figure shows n memory elements and their corresponding processing elements. Each row of a memory element may represent a data word, a record, or a data file. Here it will be referred to as a *word*. It has a mark bit (or a number of mark bits) that is used to indicate if the contents of the word satisfy a search condition. In this example, three characters are used to represent a word's contents. Each processing element contains a comparand register, a mask register, and a buffer. The comparand register holds the value(s) to be searched in all the memory elements. The mask register contains a bit pattern that is used to mask off that portion of the memory words the contents of which are not relevant to the search. The buffer contains the contents of the data word currently being scanned by the correponding processing element. In the example, the data value to be searched is the character string 'FB' in the second and third character positions of memory words, as specified by the mask with value 'OFF'. The contents of the mark bits shown in the figure flag the words that have satisfied the search condition after the processing elements have simultaneously examined the first three words in the memory elements. In this search, the contents of the memory

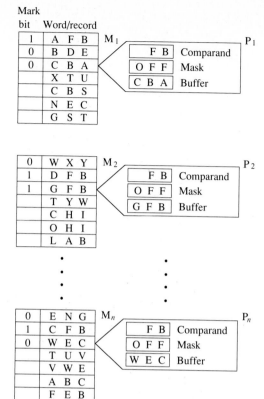

FIGURE 3.14
Content addressing in CL devices.

words are systematically examined. At the end of a complete scan, all words satisfying the search condition are marked with a '1' in their mark bits. Thus, data are searched by specifying the content of data 'FB', which corresponds exactly to the way a database user would request data from the database. Therefore, machine addresses are of no concern to the user.

The content-addressing technique used by the CL devices is different from the associative memory technique to be discussed in Chapter 5. The former uses one processing element for the content search of all the words in a memory element, whereas the latter uses one processing element for each word. Thus, the CL devices are sometimes called *pseudoassociative memories*.

The context-addressing technique of CL devices uses the content-addressing capability to first search and mark the words, records, or files that satisfy some search conditions. The marked words, records, or files are then used as the context for the next search. Context means only the marked words, records, or files that can possibly satisfy the second search. Figure 3.15 illustrates this technique.

In Figure 3.15, it is assumed that each row of the n memory elements represents a data record. The corresponding processing elements search the memory elements for those records that satisfy the search condition (A AND B) OR (NOT C). To perform this search one approach is to first use the content search capability to search for all records (rows) containing A in the first scan of the memory elements and to record the results in the mark bits as shown in the tables on the right side of the figure under the column labeled A. In the second scan, all records are searched for B and the results are logically ANDed with the contents of the mark bits, yielding the bit pattern shown under (A AND B) of the tables. In this second search operation, the marked records under column A serve as the context, since only those marked records under A can satisfy the condition (A AND B) even though the hardware sequentially searches every record anyway. The NOT C condition is searched next, and the results are logically ORed with the results under (A AND B) to obtain the final results shown under (A AND B) OR (NOT C). In order to carry out these Boolean operations, at least two sets of mark bits are necessary—one for recording the current results and the other to accumulate the search results in all the previous scans of the memory elements. The expression ((A AND B) OR (C AND D)) would require three sets of mark bits since the result of (A AND B) needs to be accumulated in one set of mark

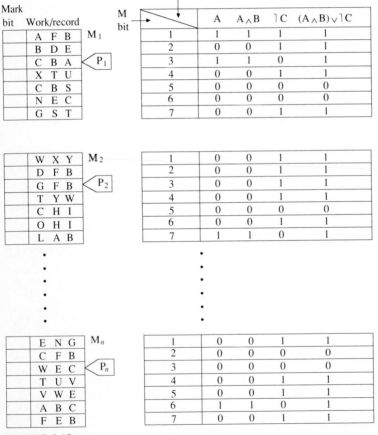

FIGURE 3.15
Context addressing in CL devices.

bits while the other two sets are used for evaluating (C AND D). If Boolean search expressions are normalized to a disjunctive or conjunctive normal form, a maximum of three sets of mark bits would be adequate.

In addition to this description of the general principles of the content and context search techniques, the specific search techniques used in CASSM and RAP will be examined in the following subsections.

3.2.3.1   CASSM'S DATA REPRESENTATION AND SEARCH TECHNIQUE.

As illustrated in Figure 3.10, CASSM allows data files to be hierarchically structured. The same example will be used to describe CASSM's search technique. As shown in Figure 3.16, the coded attributes and values of the STUDENT file are stored sequentially across k memory elements. Each record of the file is delimited by a delimiter word that contains (1) a word type D for delimiter, (2) a file name STUDENT, (3) a level number 1, which specifies the record level, (4) a six-bit stack for accumulating the search results, (5) an S bit, which marks the level where search results are to be accumulated, and (6) a Q bit, which marks the context where search is to be performed. Similar delimiter words are used to delimit the files and sub-records (e.g., ADDRESS is a subrecord of STUDENT). The table at the right side of the figure contains three copies of the top bit of the bit stack, the S bit, and the Q bit. These are used to illustrate how search contexts and results change during the execution of a retrieval query.

The retrieval query in this example is expressed in the CASDAL language (CASSM's data language) designed for the system [SU78]. The query shown below asks for the student numbers of those students who have the name J.R. Jones and live in a city called Gainesville.

IN STUDENT: IF CITY = 'GAINESVILLE' AND SNAME = 'J.R. JONES' THEN OUTPUT (S#)$

The query is translated into the CASSM's machine codes, which perform the following operations. CASSM first sets up the context for the search by setting the S and Q bits as shown under the column T1. The S bit of all student records are marked, since it is necessary to identify all those records that satisfy the search condition before the students' number can be output. The Q bits of all the STUDENT records and ADDRESS subrecords in the file are marked as the search context. In one memory scan, the condition CITY = 'GAINESVILLE' is searched and the results are stored on top of the bit stacks associated with the STUDENT records as shown in column T2. The next condition SNAME = 'J.R. JONES' is searched in the next scan of the memory elements, and the results are logically ANDed with the bit pattern stored in the bit stacks to produce the results shown in column T3. The next operation is to use the top bits of the bit stacks as the search context to set the collection bits associated with those marked records (not shown in the figure) to cause the proper student numbers to be collected by the collection modules of the processing elements (see Figure 3.3) for output to the user-CASSM interface computer.

This search technique allows a complex retrieval query with an arbitrary number of search conditions to be processed. The logic needed in the processing

Casdal query
IN STUDENT: IF CITY = 'GAINESVILLE' AND SNAME = 'J.R. JONES'; THEN OUTPUT (S#) $

M_i

Type		Contents	T1 Bit stack	T1 S	T1 Q	T2 Bit stack	T2 S	T2 Q	T3 Bit stack	T3 S	T3 Q
D	STUDENT	0	0	0	0	0	0	0	0	0	0
D	STUDENT	1	0	1	1	1	1	1	1	1	1
N	S#	14256									
N	SNAME	J.R. Jones									
N	SEX	M									
N	AGE	23									
D	ADDRESS	2	0	0	1	0	0	0	0	0	0
D	ADDRESS	3	0	0	1	0	0	1	0	0	1
N	N#	412									
N	STREET	NW 5th St.									
N	CITY	Gainesville									
N	STATE	Fla.									
N	ZCODE	32601									
D	STUDENT	1	0	1	1	0	1	1	0	1	1

M_{i+k}

Type		Contents	T1 Bit stack	T1 S	T1 Q	T2 Bit stack	T2 S	T2 Q	T3 Bit stack	T3 S	T3 Q
D	STUDENT	1	0	1	1	1	1	1	0	1	1
N	S#										
N	SNAME	S.H. Smith									
N	SEX	F									
N	AGE	24									
D	ADDRESS	2	0	0	1	0	0	0	0	0	0
D	ADDRESS	3	0	0	1	0	0	1	0	0	1
N	N#	4236									
N	STREET	SW 13th Ave.									
N	CITY	Gainesville									
N	STATE	Fla.									
N	ZCODE	32611									
D	FILE B	0	0	0	0	0	0	0	0	0	0

FIGURE 3.16
CASSM's data representation and search technique

elements is simple and limited since the hardware needs to process only one search condition per revolution of the memory. In this technique, the data must be processed on the fly at a speed comparable to that of the rotating memory device. If a larger unit of data (e.g., a record) needs to be processed against a number of search conditions in a single revolution of the memory, then a larger buffer space will be needed to store the data and a larger gap time (refer back to Section 3.2.1.1) will be necessary so that the processing can be done on the fly without missing some data units. The price paid for the generality and simplicity of the method is, of course, the need for many memory revolutions to execute a complex query. However, the number of revolutions is proportional to the number of search conditions in the query.

3.2.3.2 RAP'S DATA REPRESENTATION AND SEARCH TECHNIQUE. Using the previous STUDENT and ADDRESS example, the data in RAP is stored as two normalized relations (see Figure 3.17). The foreign key S# in the SADDRESS relation relates the student address information with the other student data stored in the STUDENT relation. To perform the same query given in the Section 3.2.3.1, RAP buffers a record at a time in its processing elements and processes a number of search conditions against each record in the buffer to determine if the search conditions are satisfied. For those records that satisfy the search conditions, the corresponding mark bits are set to mark the context for the subsequent searches or for output to the control computer.

The RAP's assembly program instructions for carrying out the query are given in Figure 3.17. The first instruction marks all the A bits of those records in the SADDRESS relation where CITY = 'GAINESVILLE'. The second instruction uses the student numbers of those A-marked records to "crossmark" those records in the STUDENT relation whose student numbers are equal. The results of this operation are stored in the C mark bits of the STUDENT records as shown in the figure. The crossmark operation is a time-consuming operation since it involves reading the student numbers of those A-marked records one by one and broadcasting each student number using the intercell communication facility of the ISMUs to all the cells that match the student numbers in the STUDENT records. The third instruction searches only those C-marked records for SNAME = 'J.R. JONES' and stores the results in the A mark bits. The fourth instruction outputs the student numbers of the A-marked STUDENT records to the work area named in the instruction.

RAP's data representation and search technique have several advantages over those of CASSM's. First, all data are represented in the form of normalized relations. The portion of the hardware for processing flat tables is most likely to be simpler than that for processing a hierarchical tree of many levels, which is a more complex data structure. Second, the entire record is read and buffered for processing against a number of search conditions. Complex searches in a relation can be carried out in a single revolution.

There are also a number of disadvantages associated with this data representation and search technique. First, the record size cannot exceed the buffer

Normalized relations

STUDENT (S#, SNAME, SEX, AGE) KEY (S#)
SADDRESS (S#, N#, STREET, CITY, STATE, ZCODE)
 KEY (S#, N#, STREET, CITY, STATE, ZCODE)

SADDRESS

Mark bits	S#	N#	STREET	CITY	STATE	ZCODE
(A) B C D	14256	412	NW 15th St.	Gainesville	Fla.	32601
(A) B C D	24010	4236	SW 13th Ave.	Gainesville	Fla.	32611

STUDENT

Mark bits	S#	SNAME	SEX	AGE
(A) B (C) D	14256	J.R. Jones	M	23
A B (C) D	24010	S.H. Smith	F	24

MARK (A) [SADDRESS : SADDRESS.CITY = 'GAINESVILLE']
CROSSMARK (C) [STUDENT: STUDENT.S # = SADDRESS.S#:
 SADDRESS: MKED (A)]
MARK (A) [STUDENT: STUDENT.SNAME = 'J.R. JONES':
 STUDENT: MKED (C)]
READ [STUDENT (S#): STUDENT.MKED (A)] [WORK, AREA]

FIGURE 3.17
RAP's data representation and search technique.

size unless some way of folding a large record is provided, but this will require added hardware. Second, the normalization of relations tends to break data into pieces, each of which is stored in a separate relation. During the retrieval process, many relations may have to be traversed by the Join or Semijoin operations to relate one piece of data with the other. For instance, the previous example shows that several revolutions of the memory are needed to satisfy the query.

3.2.4 Hardware Garbage Collection

In most database applications, the database is dynamic in the sense that data are constantly added into or deleted from the database. When data items or records are deleted, the physical storage space contains pockets of deleted data or garbage that needs to be collected by the system so that the space can be used to store useful information. Traditionally, the deleted space is collected together by some garbage collection software that chains the pockets of space to an available space list from which storage space can be obtained. Garbage collection by software is generally very time-consuming and therefore is not done at program run time. This causes the fragmentation of the memory space and often prevents programs from being run due to the lack of consecutive storage space, even though the sum of the fragmented spaces are enough for the programs. Ideally, the hardware should automatically collect these deleted spaces.

The architectural features, data organization, and processing strategies of CL devices allow hardware garbage collection to be built quite conveniently. Since data elements (words, records, or files) in each cell are sequentially read by the read head, routed through the processing element, and written back by the write head to the memory element, it is possible to trap those deleted data elements that have been marked for deletion (i.e., the garbage) by the processing element. These trapped elements are not written back to the memory element, and the elements following the trapped ones will occupy the physical positions of the trapped elements, in effect moving the good data up to fill the gaps. Two examples illustrate the hardware garbage collection process in a single cell and in multiple cells.

In Figure 3.18a, data elements that have been deleted in the previous operation are explicitly marked. In RAP, for example, the deleted records are marked by setting their deletion flags. In CASSM, deleted words are indicated by changing their tag bits to that of erase words (see Figure 3.11). In both cases, words or records are read and flow into some registers or buffer storage. The garbage words or records will not be passed on to the write head and thus will not be written back to the memory element. As illustrated in Figure 3.18a, a garbage word or record is trapped in the second shift register or buffer. The tap is set to bypass the trapped word or record.

Garbage collection in a single cell is easy. All garbage words or records can be collected in the same scan of the memory element. The collected space is pushed down toward the end of the memory element. In a CL device like CASSM in which all data words are to be maintained in strictly sequential order and records and files can run from one memory element into the other, the collection task is more involved. This is because when a garbage word is taken out of a cell, the entire database following the garbage word must be moved up by one space to keep the database in a strictly sequential order. The technique used is illustrated in Figure 3.18b. Before the collection operation, the memory element M_i contains a garbage word as shown under T1. During the first scan of the memory, all words before the word labeled G are read and written to the same space in M_i and all words in $M_i + 1$ are read and written to the same space in $M_i + 1$. However, all words following the G word in M_i are moved up by one position since the garbage word is taken out in the first scan. This leaves an empty space at the end of M_i, and the result is shown under T2. In the second scan of the memory, all memory elements below M_i would store their first words in the registers reserved for the garbage collection purpose. All the subsequent words

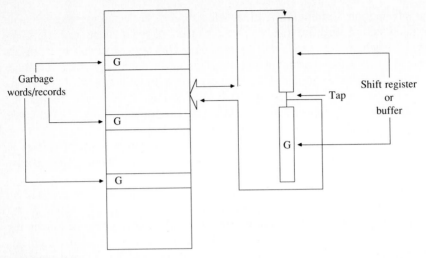

FIGURE 3.18a
Garbage collection in a single cell.

are moved up by one position. When the last words of the memory elements are being scanned by the processing elements, the contents of the register associated with $M_i + 1$ is used to fill the last word position of M_i, the contents of the register associated with $M_i + 2$ is used to fill the last word position of $M_i + 1$, and so forth. In effect, all data words in the sequential store following the G word have been moved up in the second scan of the memory. In order to keep the hardware simple, CASSM collects one garbage word at a time in the background while the other processing modules of the processing elements carry out their preassigned tasks. Although, the garbage collection process is slow, it overlaps with foreground data retrieval and manipulation operations. Uncollected garbage words are bypassed by the other modules; thus, they do not affect the results of the foreground operations.

3.2.5   Content/Pointer-to-Address Mapping

This is a technique introduced in CASSM for traversing the data in different files either by their contents or by pointers. To explain this technique, it is first necessary to describe how existing DBMSs use relational and network database models to represent the relationships or associations among data entities. Next, it is necessary to explain how the content/pointer-to-address mapping technique can be used to support the traversal of entities through their relationships or associations.

In the relational model, the relationships among entities are represented by explicitly storing the primary key values in the relations involved. The STUDENT and COURSE database shown in Figure 2.9 is used as an example to illustrate this point. Figure 3.19 is a skeleton of Figure 2.9, with columns rearranged to simplify the drawing. It shows that the relationship between STUDENT tuples and COURSE tuples are represented by the relation STUDENT_COURSE. In search-

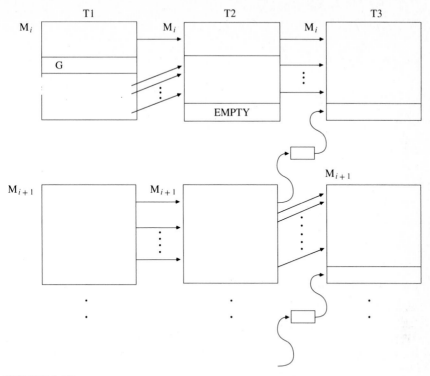

FIGURE 3.18*b*
Garbage collection in multiple cells.

ing the database, it is often necessary to match the values of S# in STUDENT relation with that of S# in STUDENT_COURSE and vice versa, or to match the values of CID in COURSE relation with that of CID in STUDENT_COURSE relation and vice versa. Value matching is a frequent, primitive operation in a relational system. It is used whenever a relational Join operation is performed.

In the CODASYL network model, the relationship between two entities (or record types) is represented by a CODASYL set, which connects two record types with one as the owner and the other as the member. Each occurrence of the set is formed by one occurrence of the owner record type and zero or more occurrences of the member record type. Figure 3.20 shows the STUDENT_COURSE set defined over STUDENT and COURSE record types together with some example occurrences. The member occurrences associated with an owner can either be chained together in a linked list or connected by a pointer array (i.e., a linear array of pointers). Pointer arrays are used in Figure 3.20. The use of pointers to locate the associated record occurrences is a frequent and essential operation in a network database. *Forward pointer transfer* is an operation that starts with a set of pointers and locates all the record occurrences to which they point. This operation is very useful and is well supported by the conventional systems since the pointers can be used to directly access the pointed occurrences. Another operation that is equally useful is called the *backward pointer transfer*. It starts with a record occurrence

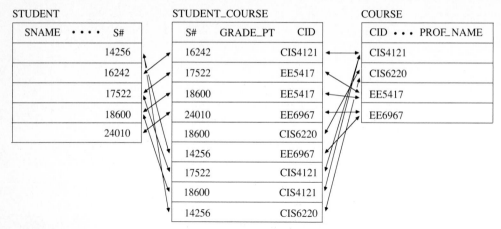

FIGURE 3.19
Pointers by content in relational systems.

and locates all the occurrences that contain pointers to it. This operation is not possible in a traditional system since it is impractical to search the entire database to examine all records to see if they contain the pointer to a given occurrence. For this reason, backward pointers are explicitly established in a traditional system to achieve the backward pointer transfer. In a CL device, this operation as well as the value matching and forward pointer transfer operations can be conveniently implemented without the backward pointers since all records in a database are searched by content in every memory scan.

The CASSM project has exploited the content/pointer-to-address technique to implement these three operations. The following subsections explain the technique used and the support provided to these three operations. The reader may want to refer back to the architecture and data organization of CASSM shown in Figures 3.2, 3.3, and 3.11.

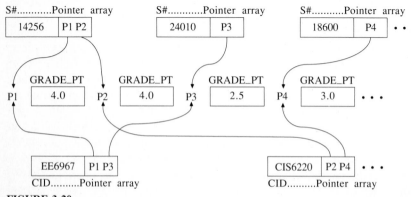

FIGURE 3.20
Pointers by location in network systems.

3.2.5.1 VALUE MATCHING. A search instruction is used to set the hardware T bits of some selected words (see Figure 3.21) whose values are to be used to match with those of the other files. These words are called *T words* for short. During the Transfer operation, the value part of each T word is interpreted as an address into a global random access memory (GRAM). This GRAM is formed by the concatenation of many one-bit wide random access memories (RAM's), one residing in each cell. There are at least as many bits in the RAM as there are words in the cell. In the Main module of each processing element (see Figure 3.3), there is a submodule called Address whose purpose is to access the GRAM, given the value part of a T word. The address in GRAM will hereafter be referred to as Gaddress. The presence of a T word is indicated by storing a 1 at the proper GRAM location, whose Gaddress is equal to the value of the T word. In one scan of the memory, all T word values are mapped to Gaddresses as illustrated in Figure 3.21a, which represents the first half of the value-matching operation. In the figure, four cells and their RAMs, which form the GRAM, are shown. The values 4, 5, and 6 are mapped to Gaddresses 4, 5, and 6, respectively. To achieve this content-to-address mapping, the Address submodules must compete with each other for access to the GRAM, since GRAM is common to all the cells. In the figure, cells *a* and *c* have found a name/value word whose T bit is set. Both cells will want to access GRAM at the same time. This conflict is resolved by giving the cell that appeared earlier in the sequential store, cell *a* in this case, the higher priority. Priorities among cells are determined in CASSM by the use of two priority lines TPR and BPR shown in Figure 3.2. Cell *c* will have to process its T word later, perhaps during the next memory cycle if no other conflict exists. After cell *a* gets control, it broadcasts the Gaddress (i.e., the value 6) bit-serially using the data bus shown in Figure 3.2. The physically topmost cell in CASSM, in this case cell *a*, uses the Gaddress as one of the inputs to a serial tree adder. The topmost tree adder input adds the Gaddress, and every other cell adds the negative of the number of RAM bits in its portion of GRAM. The first cell to see a negative result has the required address in its local RAM. It uses the control line LINK (see Figure 3.2) to inform the cell positioned immediately above it that it has the proper RAM bit. It then sets the RAM bit, and all the Address submodules compete again for the next GRAM access. The arrows in Figure 3.21a show how RAM *a* and RAM *b* are set according to the values of the T words.

The second half of the value-matching operation involves the use of Gaddresses to mark those words that are within the proper search context and whose values correspond to the Gaddresses. The M bits associated with the machine words are used for this purpose. Figure 3.21b illustrates the second half of the value-matching operation. As the contents of the memory elements are examined by the processing elements in parallel, GRAM is accessed by the processing elements. If the GRAM location inferred from the value part of a word contains '1', the M bit of the word is set. In our example, the M bits of the words with data values 4, 5, and 6 are set to '1' as shown in Figure 3.21b. It should be noted that conflicts between the Address modules still occur as illustrated by the

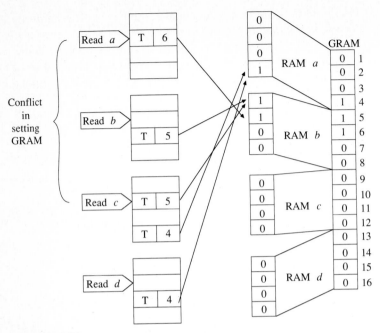

FIGURE 3.21a
First half of value matching. (*Source:* [SU79b] ©1979 IEEE)

read heads in the figure. Cells *b* and *d* pick up a Gaddress and need to look up GRAM at the same time. This conflict is again resolved by the TPR line. Thus cell *d* will have to yield its turn.

3.2.5.2 FORWARD POINTER TRANSFER. The forward pointer transfer operation is also accomplished in two stages. In the first half of the transfer, words with their T bits set are taken into consideration. The value part of each pointer word, or P word, contains a record number (RN). This number is used to access the GRAM. Access conflicts can arise as shown in Figure 3.22a. In this figure, D_i's are delimiter words. P5 denotes a pointer whose value part is 5. As shown, cells *b* and *d* are in conflict when accessing GRAM. This problem is again resolved by the TPR line, and the proper topmost P word is processed first. It should be emphasized that the Gaddress, as specified by the value part of the P word, is a global delimited number in the entire database, not in the particular memory element. Another important point is that unlike value matching, each cell contributes not all of its RAM bits but only as many as there are delimiters in its own memory element. In Figure 3.22a, RAM *a* contributes three bits to GRAM because there are three delimiters in cell *a*. The pointer words P3, P5, and P7 cause the third, fifth, and seventh bits of GRAM to be set.

In the second half of the transfer, the Post module in each cell accesses its own RAM bits, as illustrated in Figure 3.22b. If a bit in RAM is set, the S and Q bits of the corresponding delimiters are set and a bit operation is performed on the bit stacks associated with the delimiter words. As shown in

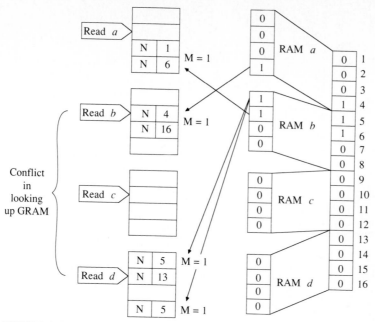

FIGURE 3.21*b*
Second half of value matching. (*Source:* [SU79*b*] ©1979 IEEE)

Figure 3.22*b*, the S and Q bits of the delimiters D3, D5, and D7 are set, thus the data elements (records, subrecords, or files) they delimit become the next search context. Subsequent instructions can then search the contents of these data elements. Since each RAM contributed as many bits as there are delimiters in the local memory element, there is no conflict in GRAM access for all the cells in the second half of the transfer operation.

3.2.5.3 BACKWARD POINTER TRANSFER. The backward pointer transfer operation is the reverse of the forward pointer transfer. It aims to identify all pointer words pointing to some selected data elements (e.g., records). Figures 3.23*a* and 3.23*b* illustrate this operation. Again all the RAMs contribute only as many bits as there are delimiters in the local memory element. A transfer instruction with the record number (RN) option initiates the first half of the transfer. The record numbers of the previously selected records are mapped onto GRAM. In Figure 3.23*a*, the delimiter numbers of D2, D3, D5, and D6 are used to set the second, third, fifth, and sixth bits of GRAM. In each cell, the Address submodule accesses the local RAM. The address used is the local record number of the delimiter marked at the end of the previous search operation.

The second half of the backward pointer transfer is quite simple. The search part of the instruction (including the checking of pointer words) is carried out for each word scanned. If the search is successful, its value part is used to address GRAM. If a '1' is found, then the M bit of the pointer word is set. The whole GRAM must be accessed by each cell because there is no assurance that the

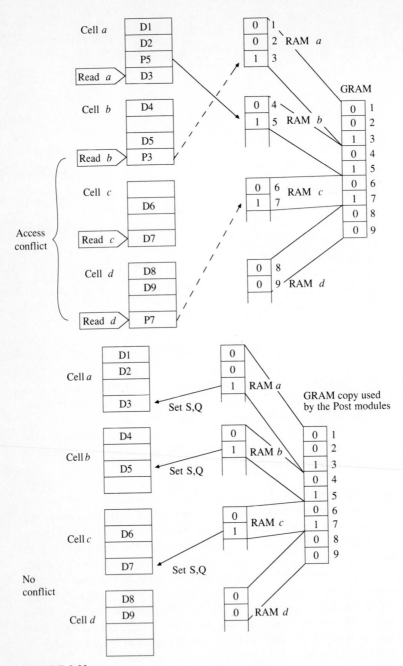

FIGURE 3.22
(a) First half of forward pointer transfer. *(b)* Second half of forward pointer transfer. (*Source:* [SU79*b*] ©1979 IEEE)

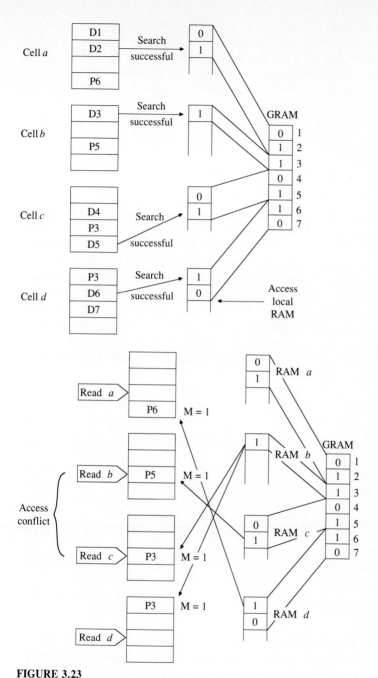

FIGURE 3.23
(*a*) First half of backward pointer transfer. (*b*) Second half of backward pointer transfer. (*Source:* [SU79*b*] ©1979 IEEE)

corresponding RAM bit is in the local RAM. This creates addressing conflicts between the cells, and the problem is again resolved by the TPR line. For example in Figure 3.23*b*, both cells *b* and *c* need to access GRAM, and cell *b* gets the priority. The pointer value is broadcast as a Gaddress. This address goes through the adder circuits as described in the value-matching section. Cell *c* finds the RAM bit that corresponds to the fifth bit in GRAM. That bit happens to be '1', and the pointer word in cell *b* is marked by setting M bit to '1'. In the same memory scan, the pointer words P6 in cell *a* and P3 in cell *d* are also marked.

3.2.6   Associative Programming and Its Applications to Integrity and Security Control

The concepts of associative memory and associative memory systems have been in existence for many years (see Chapter 5). Nevertheless, their use has been restricted to fast memory devices that search data by contents. They are not used as the main memory of a conventional computer in which instructions as well as data are stored and fetched for execution. In other words, the content-addressing capability and other features of the associative memory have not been used to support the selection and execution of program instructions. The CL devices are a type of associative memory implemented on secondary storage devices. Using this fact, the programming technique for associative memories has been studied in the CASSM project [SU77]. Its applications to database integrity and security control are reported in [HON81 and HON82].

The term *associative programming* is defined by Su [SU77] as the technique of programming an associative memory in which program activation and deactivation are based on high-level data conditions. Instructions are embedded in the structure of data and are selected for execution when the associated data have satisfied some search conditions during content and/or context searches. The instructions may further operate on the database to produce output or to further cause other instructions or programs to be activated for execution. This trigger effect has been shown to be very effective for enforcing integrity and security rules that are often dependent upon the run-time data values.

To explain this, the following section presents the way in which program instructions are fetched for execution by the processing elements of CASSM. The technique of embedding instructions with data and of activating instructions for execution is then described. The methods for enforcing integrity and security rules using the associative programming technique are then described and illustrated in Sections 3.2.6.3 and 3.2.6.4.

3.2.6.1   THE INSTRUCTION FETCHING TECHNIQUE. An instruction in CASSM is explicitly tagged with an instruction code (see Figure 3.11) and is distinguished from other types of words by the hardware. An instruction can either be active or inactive, labeled by the instruction queue (IQ) bit (see Figure 3.11). All inactive instructions are ignored by the processing modules when the contents of the memory are examined. Inactive instructions can be activated under program control and entered into the active (or queued) state awaiting their turn to be fetched for execution by the processing elements. As illustrated in Figure 3.24, when a current instruction is being executed by the Main modules of the processing elements, the Sel modules fetch the first active instructions in parallel from their corresponding memory elements. Each Sel module stores its first active instruction, if one is found, and its address in their respective buffers. It also flags the fact that an instruction has been found in the memory element. In the figure shown, cells b and c contain instructions. During the gap time, the priority circuit TPR, mentioned in the preceding section, is used. It gives the priority to the first cell in the sequential store that has found an active instruction, cell b in this case. The instruction is broadcast to all the Main modules of the processing elements for execution during the next memory cycle. The instruction address stored in the buffer is used by the Post module of cell b to set the IQ bit of the fetched instruction. This would make it inactive and disqualifies it for further fetching.

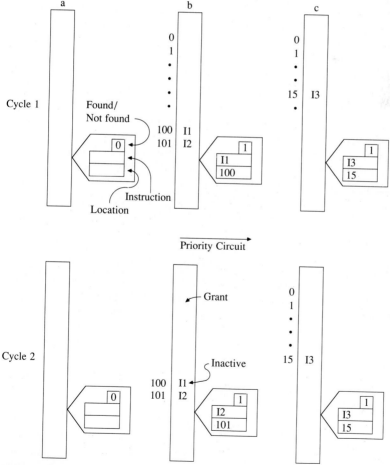

FIGURE 3.24
Instruction fetching.

Thus, in the next cycle when I1 is being executed, instruction I2 will be the one fetched. I3 will have its turn after both I1 and I2 have been executed and have become inactive.

3.2.6.2 ACTIVATION OF INSTRUCTION SEGMENTS BASED ON HIGH-LEVEL DATA CONDITIONS.

Section 3.2.3.1 (see Figure 3.16) described how data can be searched by content and context based on high-level data conditions in CASSM. If instructions that represent programs or procedures for handling error conditions, integrity rules, or security rules are embedded in the structures of different data elements such as files, records or subrecords, then the program segments associated with those data elements that have satisfied some search conditions can be activated through program control. These instruction segments will be put in the queue for execution by the processing elements according to the instruction fetching technique described. The instruction segment that comes early in the sequential store will be fetched first. However, if a later active segment needs to be executed before the earlier ones, programming techniques exist to allow the earlier segments to be temporarily deactivated and later reactivated after the later segment has been executed. These techniques are detailed by Su [SU77].

The execution of these segments may again change the database and cause other instruction segments to be executed. This ability of allowing instructions to be stored with the data for which the programs are written, and of triggering the execution of these programs when the associated data have certain contents, or appear in certain contexts, or are operated upon by certain operations, can be a very powerful way of enforcing integrity and security rules and expert rules as well [SU85]. It has been demonstrated in that the programming concepts of loops, subroutine calls, jumps, and so forth can also be implemented in the CASSM-like CL devices [SU77]. With these basic programming capabilities, complex programs can be implemented and run on the intelligent secondary storages.

3.2.6.3 ENFORCEMENT OF DATABASE INTEGRITY.

The problem of enforcing database integrity is to check if an operation that is to be executed or has been executed is valid and consistent with the integrity constraints defined for the database. Integrity is generally associated with the storage operations such as Deletion, Insertion, and Update. A major problem encountered by the conventional DBMSs in enforcing integrity rules is the high cost of moving large quantities of data from the mass storage to the main memory for integrity checking. Another problem is that many data dependent integrity rules can only be enforced at run-time since they depend on the run-time values of the attributes involved. Run-time checking of these rules can be costly since a considerable amount of overhead is involved.

Associative programming techniques can effectively solve these problems. The technique used is to store integrity rules as program procedures that are stored together with relevant data and are activated for execution when the associated data are operated upon by storage operations. A summary of integrity control scheme for CL devices proposed by Hong and Su [HON81] follows.

The most frequent integrity violations occur during update operations. The integrity control scheme for update operations is divided into five phases: modification, assertion-validation, backout, trigger, and replacement.

Modification phase. In this phase, the database operation is performed using content and context search techniques. Data items that satisfy the search conditions specified in the Update operation are marked for Update. Each data value to be updated is copied and the Update is performed on the copy. Here the data items in the old copy are called the old data items and the data items in the new copy are called the new data items. In order to distinguish the new data items, the old data items, and the data items that are not affected by the Update, two storage bits (see Figure 3.11) are introduced for each item. The bit $V+ = 1$ indicates a new data item, while the $V- = 1$ indicates an old data item. Items not affected by the Update will have $V+ = 0$ and $V- = 0$.

Assertion-validation phase. In this phase, integrity assertions related to the data being updated are first activated for execution. These assertions are initially translated into program procedures and are stored in the memory. The correctness of the Update operation is verified by these procedures. If the Update is found to violate any of the assertions, the backout phase is initiated. Otherwise, the trigger phase is entered. Since the old data items are not involved in the validation phase, they are made invisible by setting the no-access bits U of all the old data items to '1' before validation. After the validation, all U bits are set back to '0'. The data items with bits $U = 1$ are recognized by the processing elements and are automatically by-passed by the hardware during a memory scan.

Backout phase. When an Update violates some integrity rule, the backout phase is entered to ensure that the old data items are not modified. In this phase, the new data items are deleted by merely changing their associated tags to erase words (see Figure 3.11). The $V-$ bits of the old data items are reset to '0' so that the database is restored to the state before the operation.

Trigger phase. If the activated assertions in the validation phase are satisfied, then this phase is entered. This phase determines whether the current Update triggers some other Updates. A *trigger,* a term first used by Eswaran [ESW76], specifies the actions (i.e., predefined procedures) necessary for updating other related data if one portion of the database is modified. Triggers are activated for execution if their associated trigger conditions are satisfied.

Replacement phase. This phase is entered only if an update and all its associated triggered updates do not violate any integrity constraint. In this phase, the new data items should substitute the old data items. This is accomplished by changing the tags of old data items to erase words and by resetting the bits $V+$ of the new data items to '0'.

This five-phase scheme is implemented in CASSM using the technique described in the following example. Consider the relation EMPLOYEE (E#, SALARY, DEPARTMENT) KEY (E#),

Employee	E#	Salary	Department
	E1	23000	D6
	E4	24000	D3
	E8	30000	D6

and the query Q.

> Q: Increase the salaries of employees who work in the department D6 by 10 percent.

A possible organization of the relation and the procedure that implements the integrity constraint, "No employee's salary can be more than $100,000," are stored in the structure shown in Figure 3.25. In the figure, "D (relation name) 0" are delimiters of relations. The symbols W, X, and M are used to tag the work space, to mark the point for inserting the work space, and to mark the data item for update, respectively. The work space is a set of machine words (one for each record of a relation) initially reserved at the end of the corresponding records (see the column marked "Before update"). The abbreviated symbols are used for relation names and attributes to signify that coded words are used for all the character strings. To perform the Update operation, the following steps are taken. In step 1 of Figure 3.25, the data items to be updated are first searched and their associated bits $V-$ and X are set to '1'. In our example, the salaries of the first and third tuples satisfy the search and are marked with "x" and "v−" symbols. In step 2, the work spaces of the tuples that contain the old data items are shifted upward to the locations immediately following the old data items. This shifting can be done in a single memory revolution. Note that the X bit is erased immediately after the shifting. In step 3, the M bits of the data items whose $V- = 1$ are set to '1'. In step 4, the data items with $M = 1$ are fetched by the processing elements of the CL device, and the updated values are stored into the corresponding work spaces immediately following the old data items. The M bits of the old items are cleared immediately after the data items have been fetched, and their U bits are set. The $V+$ bits of these updated words of the new data items in the work space are set to '1' during Update. The procedure that implements the salary constraint and that is stored under the delimiter "D EMP 0" is activated for execution. This procedure searches in the same context to verify if the updated salary values violate the constraint. In this validation, the old data items are transparent to the search since their U bits are set. If the updated values do not violate the constraint, the old data items are tagged with W making them the work spaces, their corresponding bits X are set to '1', and the bits $V+$ and $V-$ are reset to '0' as shown in step 5. Otherwise, the new data items are tagged with W, their corresponding bits X are set to '1', and the bits $V+$ and $V-$ are reset to '0' as shown in step 5'. In this case, a violation message will be tagged for output. In either case, the work spaces W with X bits set to '1' are shifted down to the locations at the end of the records as shown in the final step.

Before update	Step 1	Step 2	Step 3
D EMP 0	D EMP 0	D EMP 0	D EMP 0
D EMP 1	D EMP 1	D EMP 1	D EMP 1
E = : E1	E = : E1	E = : E1	E = : E1
SAL: 23000	XV− SAL: 23000	V− SAL: 23000	MV− SAL: 23000
DEPT: D6	DEPT: D6	DEPT: D6	
W [ ]	W [ ]	W [ ]	DEPT: D6
D EMP 1	D EMP 1	D EMP 1	D EMP 1
E = : E4	E = : E4	E = : E4	E = : E4
SAL: 24000	SAL: 24000	SAL: 24000	SAL: 24000
DEPT: D3	DEPT: D3	DEPT: D3	DEPT: D3
W [ ]	W [ ]	W [ ]	W [ ]
D EMP 1	D EMP 1	D EMP 1	D EMP 1
E = : E8	E = : E8	E = : E8	E = : E8
SAL: 30000	XV− SAL: 30000	V− SAL: 30000	MV− SAL: 30000
DEPT: D6	DEPT: D6		
W [ ]	W [ ]	DEPT: D6	DEPT: D6
D XY O	D XY O	D XY P	D XY O

Step 4	Step 5	Step 5'	Final step
D EMP O	D EMP O	D EMP O	D EMP O
D EMP 1	D EMP 1	D EMP 1	D EMP 1
E = : E1	E = : E1	E = : E1	E = : E1
V− SAL: 23000	XW [ ]	SAL: 23000	SAL: 25300 or 23000
V+ [SAL: 25300]	SAL: 25300	XW [ ]	DEPT: D6
DEPT: D6	DEPT: D6	DEPT: D6	W [ ]
D EMP 1	D EMP 1	D EMP 1	D EMP 1
E = : E4	E = : E4	E = : E4	E = : E4
SAL: 24000	SAL: 24000	SAL: 24000	SAL: 24000
DEPT: D3	DEPT: D3	DEPT: D3	DEPT: D3
W [ ]	W [ ]	W [ ]	W [ ]
D EMP 1	D EMP 1	D EMP 1	D EMP 1
E = : E8	E = : E8	E = : E8	E = : E8
V− SAL: 30000	SAL: 30000	SAL: 30000	SAL: 33000 or 30000
V+ [SAL: 33000]	XW [ ]	XW [ ]	DEPT: D6
DEPT: D6	DEPT: D6	DEPT: D6	W [ ]
D XY O	D XY O	D XY O	D XY O

FIGURE 3.25
An example of an UPDATE operation.

Integrity validation for insertions and deletions is simpler and does not require a work space. New data items are inserted immediately following the insertion point located by a search, and the V + bits of the inserted data are set to '1'. Integrity rules relevant to the Insertion operation are invoked. If the Insertion is valid, the V + bits are reset; otherwise the inserted data items are tagged as garbage words and collected by the garbage collection modules. For deletions, the V − bits of the data to be deleted are set to '1', and the integrity rules relevant to this particular Deletion are applied. If valid, the V − words are tagged as garbage words; otherwise they are reset to '0' as if the Deletion had never taken place.

3.2.6.4 ENFORCEMENT OF DATABASE SECURITY. The protection of a database against unauthorized disclosure, alteration, or destruction is an important function of a DBMS. As discussed in Section 2.4.4, there are three basic types of security constraints: data independent (DI), content dependent (CD), and context dependent (CXT) constraints. The principal difficulty in evaluating database accesses with respect to a set of security constraints in conventional systems is the dependency of security verifications on the contents and contexts of database elements. Such dependency usually requires moving large quantities of data from secondary storage to main memory for verification even if the data are not actually involved in the user's request. For example, the security rule that prevents a user from seeing the salaries of employees who work in department D6 would require that the values of both salaries and department names be moved into the main memory for security verification, even though only the salaries are of interest to the user. It would be advantageous if the task of security checking can be offloaded to the storage device in which the data are stored. A technique for enforcing security rules in the CL device CASSM has been investigated and reported by Hong and Su [HON82]. This technique is described by the following example.

A general model of the user-database interaction in a CL device is given in Figure 3.26. Before the user issues a query or runs an application program, the user's identification and authenticity are checked (using standard methods such as checking identification numbers, passwords, etc.) to determine whether the user has the right to use the system. This represents the first level of security control. The user's query or program will be translated only after passing this level of control and checking. The translator (a compiler or an interpreter) would identify the operation type (Read, Write, Delete, Insert, or Update) and the associated attributes and relations (files) upon which they are operating. This information is used to construct a procedure called an *activator,* which is incorporated into the translated codes. During the execution of the program, the procedure searches the security file (to be described next) associated with the user and activates the proper security verification procedures based upon the operation and the operands of the query or program. The verification procedures, when executed, will mask the unauthorized portion of the database by setting the no-access bits (the U bits) of the protected data items or records. The bit setting forms a security window through which the user's query or program can only see the data that he or she has the right to see. All data elements marked by U bits are ignored by the hardware when the contents of the memory elements are examined. By dynamically creating security windows under program control, different types of security rules can be enforced by the CL device.

The security rules are implemented using a security file associated with each user or user group. It consists of several hierarchically structured subfiles as illustrated in Figure 3.27. In this figure, S_i represents the user's ID. One of the $(1,S_i)$ nodes, the one labeled DI, identifies the subfile containing all the data independent rules associated with this user. These rules are divided into groups depending on the operation types for which these rules should be applied; and

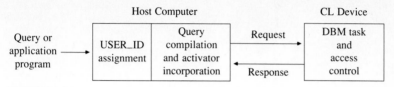

FIGURE 3.26
A general model of User-Database interaction in a CL device.

they are stored at the next level of the security file, that is, the $(2,S_i)$ nodes under the $(1,S_i)$ node labeled DI. All the content dependent rules are stored in a similar way in the subfile labeled CD, and the context dependent rules are stored in the subfiles labeled CXD. The structure of the CXD subfiles are different from those of the DI's and CD's. A detailed description of CXD structure is out of the scope of this book. Interested readers should refer to the original paper for details [HON82].

Figure 3.28 illustrates the general security file of Figure 3.27. The security file shown in this figure implements the following three security rules:

1. User S_i is not allowed to output the medical information stored in relation EMP of Figure 3.29.
2. User S_i is not allowed to update the salary values of the employees.
3. User S_i should not be allowed to output the salary information of those employees who work in department D1.

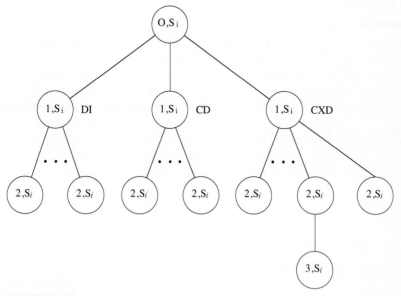

FIGURE 3.27
A hierarchically structured security file.

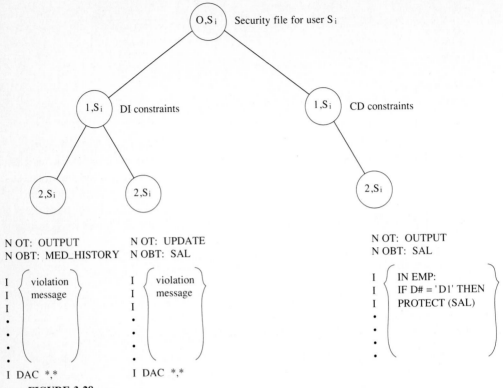

FIGURE 3.28
The security file of user S_i.

Each of these rules is implemented in the form of data words and instructions that are stored in the security file as shown in Figure 3.28. For example, the data words contain the operation type OT = OUTPUT and the object type OBT:MED_HISTORY (see the left-most $(2,S_i)$ node of the figure). They specify the conditions under which the instructions are to be activated. In the first two rules, if user S_i attempts to output employees' medical history information or to update the salary information, a violation message will be output by the procedure and the deactivation instruction (DAC *,*) will deactivate the program currently being executed (i.e., the program will be aborted). The instruction portion of rule

EMP

ENAME	SAL	DEPT#	MED_HISTORY
Carrol	36 000	D1	(Text 1)
Weber	30 000	D3	(Text 2)
Smith	25 000	D1	(Text 3)
Moore	40 000	D2	(Text 4)
Ford	31 000	D1	(Text 5)

FIGURE 3.29
The original relation EMP.

3 is a procedure that searches the EMP file for all the records whose D# equals 'D1' and sets the U bits associated with the attribute SAL to '1' so that salary values will be by-passed by the hardware during the execution of the operation.

Assume that user S_i submitted a program containing the following two queries expressed in CASDAL:

1. IN EMP: IF ENAME = 'MOORE' THEN OUTPUT (SAL, MED_HISTORY)
2. IN EMP: OUTPUT (ENAME,SAL)

The operation type and the relation name and attribute names will be extracted during the translation process. The translator will construct an activator for each query based on the extracted information and insert it into the translated codes as shown in Figure 3.30. An activator always precedes the program codes to create a security window, and the program codes are followed by an instruction to clear the U bits in case some security procedure is activated. During the execution of the program codes shown in Figure 3.30, the activator 1 would search the $(2,S_i)$ nodes of the security file for OT = 'OUTPUT' AND OBT = 'MED_HISTORY' and activate their associated instructions. In our example, the left-most $(2,S_i)$ node of Figure 3.28 satisfies the search condition. The activation of its instruction will cause a violation message to be output, and the rest of the program will be deactivated by the (DAC *,*) instruction. Assume that the search was not successful. The query 1 will then be executed without violating any security rule, and activator 2 will subsequently be executed. Its execution will activate the procedure that implements the CD rule shown in Figure 3.28. The security procedure will set the U bits of the salary fields in which the D# equals 'D1'. Thus the security window has been formed and is illustrated by Figure 3.31a in which the * signs indicate that some salary values have been masked out. The procedure that implements query 2 is then executed over the security window, and the retrieval result is shown in Figure 3.31b. The final instruction (CLS U) resets the U bits to '0'; thus the whole database becomes the context of the next program.

3.2.6.5 REMARKS ON ASSOCIATIVE PROGRAMMING.

Section 3.2.6 has described the associative programming technique investigated in the CASSM project for CL devices and its application to the enforcement of database integrity and security. Integrity control and protection of a database from unauthorized access and modification are two of the very important control functions of a DBMS. These two functions place a considerable burden on a mainframe computer and seriously drain the system resources. The hardware and software mechanisms described in this subsection offload these functions to a CL device on which data can be searched and manipulated and on which procedures can be searched and activated for execution using associative techniques. The associative programming technique allows different integrity and security procedures to be triggered and executed under different data conditions.

There are three distinct advantages to using the techniques presented. First, the problem of staging data in a main memory for the verification or validation of security and integrity rules can be eliminated because database integrity and secu-

Activator $\left\{ \begin{array}{l} \text{IN 2,}S_i : \\ \text{IF OT = 'OUTPUT' AND OBT = 'MED\_HISTORY'} \\ \text{THEN ACTIVATE (2,}S_i) \end{array} \right.$

Query 1 $\left\{ \begin{array}{l} \text{IN EMP:} \\ \text{IF ENAME = 'MOORE'} \\ \text{THEN OUTPUT (SAL, MED\_HISTORY)} \end{array} \right.$

Clear U bits $\left\{ \begin{array}{l} \text{CLS U} \end{array} \right.$

Activator 2 $\left\{ \begin{array}{l} \text{IN 2,}S_i : \\ \text{IF OT = 'OUTPUT' AND OBT = 'SAL'} \\ \text{THEN ACTIVATE (2,}S_i) \end{array} \right.$

Query 2 $\left\{ \begin{array}{l} \text{IN EMP:} \\ \text{OUTPUT (ENAME, SAL)} \end{array} \right.$

Clear U bits $\left\{ \begin{array}{l} \text{CLS U} \end{array} \right.$

FIGURE 3.30
The translated program.

rity are enforced where the data are stored. Second, offloading the integrity and security to the CL device would simplify the DBMS software of the mainframe. Third, the functions can be carried out much more efficiently in a CL device because (1) the enforcement of integrity and security rules generally requires the search of large quantities of data, and data search can be carried out very efficiently on an associative device, (2) different rules are needed to verify the operations on data with different contents and contexts, and the associative programming technique allows simultaneous activations of procedures to enforce

EMP

ENAME	SAL	D#	MED_HISTORY
Caroll	*	D1	(Text 1)
Weber	30 000	D3	(Text 2)
Smith	*	D1	(Text 3)
Moore	40 000	D2	(Text 4)
Ford	*	D1	(Text 5)

FIGURE 3.31*a*
The security window.

EMP

ENAME	SAL
Weber	30 000
Moore	40 000

FIGURE 3.31*b*
The retrieval result of query 2.

the rules, and (3) the concept of the security window and the integrity enforcement scheme using old and new copies of data can be carried out quite easily using the associative search and the marking and unmarking capabilities of a CL device. It would be worthwhile to investigate the possible use of the associative programming technique to implement knowledge rules in a knowledge-based system, since knowledge rules are similar to integrity and security rules in structure with IF and THEN conditions and since the capability of triggering rules is essential.

3.3 MAGNETIC BUBBLE MEMORY

Section 3.2 presented the principles, architectures, and techniques of several cellular-logic devices. This section describes another intelligent secondary storage device—a magnetic bubble memory (MBM) system. This section (1) gives a brief introduction to the magnetic bubble memory technology, (2) describes the major-minor loop architecture of MBM, which is prevalent in the existing commercial products, and (3) discusses and illustrates the architecture and techniques used in the MBM system designed at the IBM laboratory in Yorktown Heights.

3.3.1 Introduction to Magnetic Bubble Memory Technology

The concept of magnetic bubble devices was first introduced at Bell Laboratories in 1967 [TRI82]. The real debut of magnetic bubble devices occurred in 1969 when Bell Labs successfully constructed a shift register storage device using magnetic bubbles. It was not until 1977 that the Texas Instruments TBM 0103 MBM became the first known bubble memory to be used in a commercial product, the TI Silent 700 Model 763/765 Data Terminal.

A thin magnetic film, when not influenced by any magnetic fields, will have a random distribution of positive and negative areas. When this film is subject to a magnetic field, the areas of one polarity will shrink in size and the areas of the other polarity will expand. A strong magnetic field can reduce the size of one of the polarities to small cylinders. These cylinders look like bubbles when they are observed from the top. Thus, a magnetic bubble is a cylindrical magnetic domain with a polarization opposite that of the magnetic film. In order to keep the bubbles stable, it is necessary to apply a bias field to prevent the bubbles from stretching out and merging with their neighbors. The size of the bubbles can be manipulated by varying the bias field and the magnetization of the material. The type of materials that have been used for magnetic bubble devices are garnets, hexaferrites, orthoferrites, and amorphous materials.

Storage of binary information is indicated either by the presence or absence of a bubble in a specific location on the thin film. Since any data can be stored in a modern digital computer using a binary representation, magnetic bubble memory devices can be used as permanent storage devices. In order to use bubbles as a memory device, it is necessary to have a way of creating, moving, sensing, and destroying individual bubbles. As stated previously, a bubble can be created on a thin magnetic film by applying a strong localized magnetic field of opposite polarity to the film. Another way of creating a bubble is to spawn a new one by stretching an existing bubble and splitting it in two using an appropriate localized field. To destroy bubbles, the reverse process of these two methods can be applied.

Bubbles can be moved on the plane of the magnetic film by creating a gradient in the bias field, which is introduced by current-carrying conductors on the material. Bubbles move in the direction of the field. By creating the field in a different direction, bubbles can be moved in different directions. For example, Intel bubble memories [INT84] use a pair of coils that are perpendicular. By changing the polarity on the coils, fields can be created in four directions. In order for the bubbles to move in an orderly fashion and in a precise path, magnetic patterns called *chevrons* are embedded in the substrate. The bubbles move around a chevron when put under the influence of the magnetic field and can jump from chevron to chevron. Thus, the bubbles are steered by the chevrons, and their paths of movement are determined by the layout of the chevrons. The paths of the bubbles can be altered by a permalloy switch configuration, which is controlled by currents to the switch. The capability of changing the path of bubble movement is important for the implementation of the major-minor loop organization to be described in Section 3.3.2.

At present, Intel and Motorola of the United States and Hitachi and Fijitsu of Japan are the main manufacturers of magnetic bubble memory chips. The largest bubble memory device on the market is Intel's 4 megabit chip (7114), which has an average access time of 88 ms and can reach a maximum transfer rate of 200K bits per second. Current prices are between $200 to $300 per megabit. It is expected that the price will fall drastically in the near future. In terms of price and performance, magnetic bubble memories fill the gap between the traditional disks and semiconductor memories.

3.3.2   Major-Minor Loop Architecture

Magnetic bubble memories are inherently sequential devices due to the way bubbles are propagated throughout the material. The early architecture of bubble memories was a long shift register with one station to sense the bubbles and another to generate and annihilate them. A timing circuit is used to clock the shifting of the bubbles. This architecture is not desirable for two main reasons: low yield and slow speed. It gives low yield because a single flaw in the long shift register ruins the whole memory device. It is slow because the contents of the shift register must be shifted sequentially to the read port (the sensing station) before its contents can be examined. The access time is slow (half the memory size on average) if the shift register is very wide.

A popular architecture that has been used in Intel's products is the major-minor loop architecture (see Figure 3.32). In this architecture, a set of parallel, synchronized shift registers called *minor loops* are used to store data. Some of these minor loops can be inactive. For example, the Intel 1 megabit bubble chip (7110) has 320 minor loops, of which 272 loops are used for storing data and error correction codes and the rest are used as spares to increase the yield. A *boot loop* is used to store the map of the inactive loops and is the first one to be loaded to the controller when the bubble memory is initialized. A page of data consists of one bit from each of the active minor loops—each bit in the same relative position. Thus, there are as many pages as bits in a loop. Data in these minor loops can be accessed by first shifting a desired page to the transfer-out position and then transferring the page in parallel to another shift register called a *major loop*. The page in the major loop is then shifted serially past a detector, which reads its contents. Besides Read or Detect, the other basic operations of this memory architecture include Replicate, which copies bubbles, Annihilate, which destroys bubbles, Generate, which creates new bubbles, and Transfer, which moves data between minor and major loops. A controller is used to control the timing of these operations.

In early bubble devices [NAD76], transferring of a page from the minor loops to the major loop was destructive in the sense that it left a page of voids at the transfer-out position in the minor loops. The transferred page in the major loop is shifted through the replicator which reproduces a copy of the original page. The copy is shifted to the detector for reading and is subsequently annihilated by the annihilator. The original copy meanwhile continues to go around the major loop until it reaches the transfer-in position. At this time, a Transfer operation restores the page to its original position in the minor loops. In the Intel 7110, the data are copied from the minor loops rather than removed from them. Thus, a power failure in the middle of a Read operation will not corrupt the data.

To load data into the bubble memory, the generator creates a new page of serial bits in the major loop. The created page is then moved to the transfer-in position before it is transferred to the minor loops. The Write operation requires that the bubbles at the positions to be occupied by the new page be annihilated first.

The major-minor loop architecture is used in both of Intel's present products (the 1 megabit chip 7110 and the 4 megabit chip 7114). The one megabit chip appears to the user as consisting of 2048 pages, each of which is 64 bytes wide. Eight 7110s can be tied to a single controller and configured as 16K pages of 64 byte wide, 2K pages of 512 byte wide, or any other configurations. The 4 megabit chip is made up of 8 octets of 80 minor loops each. It appears to the user as containing 8192 pages of 64 bytes. Eight of these chips can be tied to a single controller.

3.3.3 Bubble Memory and Its Application to Database Management

There are several features of bubble memories that are desirable for database management applications. They are:

1. *Non-volatility*. Data are retained when power is down. Bubble memories are ideal permanent storage devices.

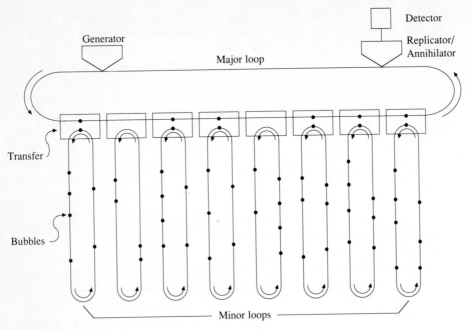

FIGURE 3.32
The major-minor loop architecture.

2. *Complete control of timing.* Bubbles in the major or minor loops can be shifted synchronously using a single time control. They allow synchronization on a page-by-page basis, which is difficult to achieve on conventional disk systems.

3. *Low power.* These devices inherently consume less power than existing devices. This is an important requirement in many special applications (e.g., military applications).

4. *High density.* Very high densities can be achieved using bubble technology. It is estimated that $10**9$ bits per square inch can be expected out of future products [CHA75b].

5. *Sequential storage.* The sequential nature of bubble memories match very closely with the sequential view of a database as a set of sequential files, a file as a set of sequential records, and a record as a set of sequential fields.

6. *Good access time.* Bubble memories can be used for secondary storage devices just like disk drives but with better access time. Units with the major-minor loop architecture may also have higher data rates than disks [INT84].

7. *Flexible chip organization.* Bubble chips can be grouped and configured to match the conceptual data structure of a high-level data model (e.g., the relational data model).

One major research effort on the use of magnetic bubble memories to implement a cellular-logic device was conducted at IBM Yorktown Heights [CHA75a and

CHA78a]. This system is based on the major-minor loop architecture but with some significant modification and extension. The cell architecture is shown in Figure 3.33. It consists of (1) a bubble memory chip, which serves as the memory element, (2) a bubble chip controller, which controls the input, output, and serial-to-parallel conversion for the bubble chip, and (3) a processing element called *logic cell,* which performs associative searches on the data transferred out of the bubble memory chip. The memory chip has two major loops, one for writing and one for reading. Similar to the other cellular-logic devices described in this chapter, the Read and Write mechanisms of this system are separated. Writing data into the minor loops is done first by generating bubbles in one of the major loops by the generator or destroying bubbles in that major loop by the annihilator. The contents of the major loop are then transferred into the minor loops as illustrated in the figure. Reading data out of the minor loops is done first by transfering data into the second major loop at the other end of the minor loops, and the data are shifted to the detector for reading. Two buffer loops are used to buffer the data that are soon to be read from or written into the minor loops. They are used to reduce the access time of the memory.

There are a number of off-chip marker loops, which are used as dynamic indexing loops, whose functions are (1) to mark those corresponding data elements in the minor loops that satisfy some search conditions, (2) to avoid reading out data elements that are not marked (i.e., that do not satisfy some previous search operation), and (3) to assist in linking data between different chips.

This bubble memory system is designed specifically for supporting relational database processing and management. A relation in this system is stored in bit-parallel word-parallel fashion. The minor loops on a bubble chip are partitioned into groups, each of which is used to store the values of an attribute of a relation (see Figure 3.33). Thus, a tuple of a relation is stored across the minor loops, each of which contributes one bit to store the bit pattern of the tuple. In one bit of time, a tuple can be transferred from the minor loops to the major loop. Its contents are then sequentially shifted to the detector for reading. Since data in the major loop are shifted sequentially, the time taken for data to be read by the detector is longer than the shifting time of the minor loops. Thus, when the data in the major loop have been read, it is most likely that the next batch of data elements would already have been loaded into the buffers from the minor loops.

The data read by the detector are routed to the logic cell processing element, which contains, among other things (1) a register, REG1, which holds the transferred data, (2) a register, REG2, to hold the data word to be compared against the data words transferred out of the major loop, 3) a one-bit wide comparator for matching the contents of these two registers, and (4) a number of marker loops, which can be used for a number of purposes. Since data coming out of the major loop are received by the logic cell one bit at a time, a one-bit wide comparator is sufficient and is suitable for matching variable length words. In processing a relation in a relational database, a tuple or some selected attribute value(s) of a tuple is examined by the logic cell to determine if the tuple or attribute value satisfies some prespecified conditions. The result is recorded by setting a bit on

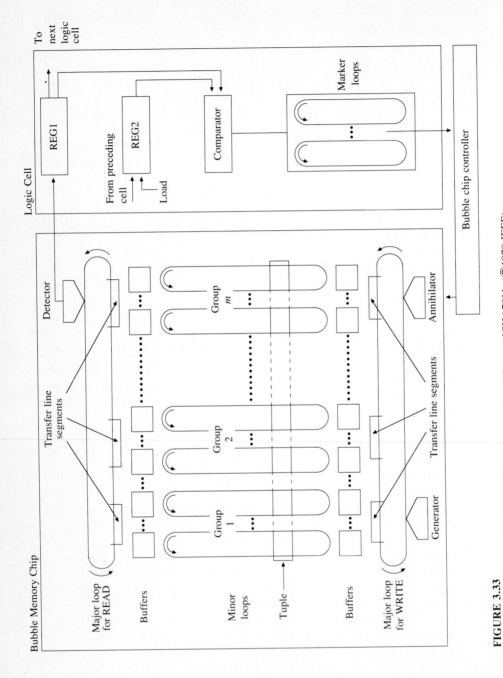

FIGURE 3.33
The cell architecture of Chang's bubble memory system. (*Source:* [CHA78b]) ©1978 IEEE)

a marker loop, the bit position of which corresponds to the tuple position in the minor loops.

A relation with many attributes can be accommodated by increasing the number of chips in the horizontal direction. A relation with many tuples can be accommodated by using several bubble chips in the vertical direction. If relations are small in width or depth, several ralations can be stored in a single chip. Attribute values can be independently accessed or written by selecting the proper groups of minor loops for data transfer. The transfer line segments (see Figure 3.33), which correspond to the groups and the marker loop(s), are used to define the boundaries of the various relations. This data organization is very flexible for storing relations with different sizes. It allows relations to be stored in a structure very close to the user's view of relations as flat tables.

The off-chip marker loops are the same size as the minor loops. They are kept in synchronization with the minor loops. Each bit position in a marker loop corresponds to a tuple stored on a chip. It can be used to mark tuples that satisfy a search condition. The marker loop in this case is used as an index loop that dynamically indexes the tuples. It can be used by the controller to selectively read out the attribute values of those marked tuples. Thus, only the appropriate attribute values for the given search context will be read and examined by the logic cell. If a search involves several qualification conditions to be operated on more than one relation, multiple marker loops can be used to accumulate the search results, which can then be logically manipulated to implement a complex Boolean expression in a retrieval query. This function of the marker loops is similar to the bit stacks of CASSM and the marker bits of RAP.

The following examples illustrate how the relational Selection and Semijoin operations can be carried out by using an off-chip marker loop (see the STUDENT database model shown in Figure 2.9). For the convenience of the reader, the example database model is repeated here:

STUDENT (S#, SNAME, SEX, AGE, ADDRESS) KEY (S#)
COURSE (CID, CTITLE, ROOM, PERIOD, PROF_NAME) KEY (CID)
STUDENT_COURSE (S#, CID, GRADE_PT) KEY (S#, CID)

The following query and the instructions proposed by Chang [CHA78b] illustrate the Selection operation.

Query: Print the titles of the courses that are taught in period 4 by Professor Jones.

Instruction	Command	Table	Column	Index	Test	Set Index
1	SELECT	COURSE	PERIOD	OFF	= 4	ON
2	SELECT	COURSE	PROF_NAME	ON	≠ JONES	OFF
3	READ	COURSE	CTITLE	ON		OFF

Instruction 1 will cause the values of the column PERIOD of the COURSE relation to be transferred out of the minor loops. Through the Read major loop and the detector, these values are compared one by one with the value 4, which is preloaded into register REG2 of the logic cell. All bits in the dynamic index loop (the marker loop) are initially off. The bits whose corresponding tuples contain the period value 4 are set to '1' by this instruction. Instruction 2 reads all the names under the column PROF_NAME if their tuples have been indexed, that is, the bits in the dynamic index loop that correspond to the tuples have been set by the previous instruction. These names are compared with the value 'JONES'. If they are not equal, the corresponding bits in the loop will be set to OFF. At this stage, the tuples whose corresponding bits remain ON would contain the course titles offered in period 4 by Professor Jones. Instruction 3 reads the names from the CTITLE column from the bubble chip for output. The corresponding bits in the dynamic index loop are set to OFF, thus returning the bit setting to the initial state.

To illustrate the Semijoin operation, the following query and instructions are used. This example also shows how the dynamic index loop can be used to link or relate two relations.

Query: Print all the names of male students who took CIS4032.

Instruction 1 sets the proper bits of the dynamic index loop whose corresponding tuples in the STUDENT_COURSE relation contain the CID value "CIS4032". A count for the number of these tuples is kept in a special register named IND_CNT.

Instruction	Command	Table	Column	Index	Test	Set Index
1	SELECT	STUDENT_ COURSE	CID		= CIS4032	ON
2	WHILE IND_CNT	STUDENT_ COURSE			≠ 0	
	DO[SELECT_NEXT	STUDENT_ COURSE	S#	ON		OFF
	REG2 (STUDENT) ←REG1 (STUDENT_ COURSE)	STUDENT STUDENT_ COURSE				
3	SELECT]	STUDENT	S#	OFF	= REG2	ON
4	SELECT	STUDENT	SEX	ON	≠ MALE	OFF
5	READ	STUDENT	SNAME	ON		OFF

Instruction 2 is a DO_WHILE instruction that repeats all commands in the loop enclosed by the pair of brackets until the value in IND_CNT has been decremented to zero. In the loop, the SELECT_NEXT command selects S# whose index bit is ON, and it resets the bit once selected. The command REG2(STUDENT)← REG1(STUDENT_COURSE) transfers the S# stored in REG2 of the bubble chip containing the STUDENT relation to REG1 of the bubble chip containing the

STUDENT_COURSE relation. Instruction 3, which is in the DO_WHILE loop, marks the bits of those tuples in the STUDENT relation that contain an S# equal to the S# transferred into REG1. After the DO_WHILE loop, all the student numbers from the STUDENT_COURSE relation would have been transferred to the STUDENT relation. Instruction 4 resets the marker bits of all those marked tuples whose SEX values are not equal to 'MALE'. The last instruction reads and outputs the student names of those tuples whose marker bits remain ON.

This bubble memory system is conceptually and architecturally similar to the other cellular-logic devices presented in this chapter. It nevertheless has a number of significant features and advantages over the others. First, the system allows selective reading of the contents of the minor loops. Not all the data stored in the memory element must be read and processed by the processing element (the logic cell). This feature can potentially save a lot of data transfer time. However, the speed of reading in this system is still limited to the sequential reading of data from the major loop. Second, the off-chip marker loops (i.e., marker loops that do not reside in the same memory chip) can be examined and processed by the system without having to access the memory elements (the bubble chips). Access to the data in these loops can be much faster. Third, bubble chips offer a very flexible way to configure and organize the data in relational format or other high-level data structures. This is advantageous since the hardware representation of data is very close to the application view of the data. The cost of mapping different data representations can be saved.

Unfortunately, these features and those of the bubble memories were not fully exploited and tested by prototyping or full-scaled implementation due to the untimely death of Dr. H. Chang in 1982.

3.4   ANALYSIS

In this section, an abstract model is used to analyze four representative database operations: Select, Join, Statistical Aggregation, and Update. Performance parameters for the algorithms of these operations will be identified, and cost formulas in terms of execution time of the algorithms will be derived.

3.4.1   An Abstract Model for Systems Using an Intelligent Secondary Storage Device

Figure 3.34 shows the abstract model of a system with an intelligent secondary storage device. It consists of a terminal, a host computer with main memory, an intelligent disk controller, a linear array of p processing elements (each of which corresponds to a track of a logic-per-track disk), and the disk. The user's query is issued at the terminal to the host computer, which translates the query to some internal representation. The translated query is then sent to the intelligent disk controller, which in turn broadcasts database commands, one at a time, to the processing elements. Each command is processed in parallel by the processing elements against the contents of all the disk tracks. Selected data are retrieved from the disk to the controller and then to the host computer. For some database commands such as join and statistical aggregation, the host computer is required to further process the retrieved data. The final results are then transferred to the user's terminal.

It is assumed that each of the p processing elements consists of a read head, comparison and modification logic, a write head, and a buffer to store x attribute values, which are specified in the selection command as search conditions and are compared with the contents of a disk track. Each processing element also has a buffer to store a tuple read from the track for comparison or for output. The disk controller has two output buffers for double buffering the tuples coming out of the processing elements. Each output buffer is able to store one page (t tuples) of the resulting relation L for output to the host computer. With the exception of the processing elements, the rest of the components in this model are the same as those in the conventional system model discussed in Chapter 2.

3.4.2 Analyses of Algorithms

The following analyses provide the cost formulas for the four representative database operations. Table 3.1 shows the parameters used in the following analyses.

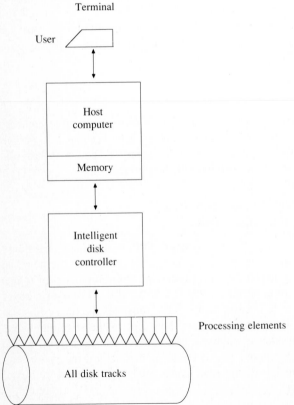

FIGURE 3.34

An abstract model for systems using an intelligent secondary storage device.

3.4.2.1. SELECT. The selection query is first translated by the host computer, and the translated query is then transferred to the intelligent disk controller. In this case, the translated query is a selection command that is broadcast to all the processing elements for execution. The instruction flow time is therefore

$$t[\text{inst\_flow}] = t[\text{comp}] + t[\text{tp\_xfer}] + t[\text{brcast}]$$

The referenced relation R is stored on the disk one page per track. Consistent with the capability of cellular-logic devices (e.g., RAP), it is assumed that in one revolution of the disk, all m pages of relation R can be searched and those tuples that satisfy the selection conditions can be marked for output in one disk revolution. Thus, the data processing time for the selection command is

$$t[\text{process\_select}] = t[\text{lat}] + t[\text{I/O}]$$

TABLE 3.1
Performance Parameters

Parameter	Definition
R	Name of a referenced relation
m	Number of pages in relation R
S	Name of the inner relation in a Join operation
s	Number of pages in relation S
L	Name of resulting relation of an operation
sel_fac	Selectivity factor for the Selection operation; that is, the ratio of the number of selected tuples of a referenced relation to the total number of tuples of that relation
t	Number of tuples per page of R or S
w	Number of distinct categories in statistical aggregation by categorization
x	Number of attributes involved in selection conditions
$t[\text{access}]$	Disk seek time plus latency time
$t[\text{brcast}]$	Time for broadcasting a command to all the processing elements
$t[\text{comp}]$	Compilation time for a simple query
$t[\text{cpu}]$	Time for comparing two values in registers or an arithmetic operation
$t[\text{I/O}]$	Track (page) read/write time
$t[\text{lat}]$	Disk latency time
$t[\text{mov}]$	Time for moving a tuple of R or S within memory
$t[\text{rev}]$	Disk revolution time; also used as the time for reading or writing a page in the analysis
$t[\text{s}]$	Time to load a value from the memory to a register
$t[\text{tp\_out}]$	Time for transferring a tuple to an output buffer associated with the user-interface device (e.g., a terminal).
$t[\text{xfer}]$	Time for transferring a page between two processors
$t[\text{tp\_xfer}]$	Time for transferring a tuple or an instruction between two processors

where $t[\text{lat}]$ is the disk latency time and $t[\text{I/O}]$ is the same as $t[\text{rev}]$, the disk revolution time.

Now, the marked tuples on the disk need to be collected for output to the user's terminal. First, they must be read from the disk by the processing elements. If two or more marked tuples are being read by the processing elements, only one can be transferred out to the disk controller. The rest must wait for the next disk revolution. Thus, in one revolution of the disk, at most t tuples can be transferred out to the controller. It can be less than t, if there is collision on the output or if none of the tuples being read by the p processing elements is marked. Therefore, the output time depends on the distribution of the marked tuples on the disk. Since R is stored in m consecutive disk tracks, the worst case is to read these tracks sequentially in $m * t[\text{I/O}]$ time to output all the marked tuples. The best case would be that all the marked tuples are in ceil(sel_fac $* m$) tracks. Taking the average of these two cases, the time to transfer the marked tuples to the disk controller is

$$t[\text{disk\_output}, R] = \text{ceil}(1/2 * (m + \text{ceil}(\text{sel\_fac} * m)))$$
$$* t[\text{I/O}] + t[\text{lat}]$$

where sel_fac is the selectivity factor and $t[\text{lat}]$ accounts for the latency time for the beginning of all tracks to come under the read/write heads. It is assumed that the transfer of the linear sequence of marked tuples to the controller overlaps with the reading of these tuples out of the disk. As the tuples are transferred to the disk controller, they are accumulated in an output buffer. As soon as a page of tuples has been accumulated, it is transferred to the host computer. From there, the tuples are output to the user's terminal. Thus, without considering possible time overlaps the total data collection time is

$$t[\text{data\_collect}] = t[\text{disk\_output}, R] + \text{ceil}(\text{sel\_fac} * m) * (t[\text{xfer}]$$
$$+ t * t[\text{tp\_out}])$$

The total execution time for this algorithm is

$$t[\text{Select}] = t[\text{inst\_flow}] + t[\text{process\_select}] + t[\text{data\_collect}]$$

3.4.2.2 JOIN. The Join operation considered here is the explicit join. Even though all the cellular-logic devices discussed in this chapter can perform the implicit join on the disk, the forming of the concatenated tuples of the resulting relation required by the explicit join cannot be done on the intelligent disk directly. It has to be accomplished by the host computer. For this reason, the algorithm used here for the Join operation is the nested-loop–join algorithm, which makes the best use of the selection capability of this model. In this algorithm, the smaller relation, say R, is first read from the disk, page by page, to the host computer. The join attribute value(s) in each R tuple is extracted and used as the selection conditions to select all the tuples of the relation S that satisfy the join condition. These tuples of S are transferred to the host computer, which joins them with the R tuple currently being processed to produce the tuples of the resulting relation L.

The instruction flow for this operation is

$$t[\text{inst\_flow}] = t[\text{comp}] + m * t * (t[\text{tp\_xfer}] + t[\text{brcast}])$$

since this algorithm involves issuing $m * t$ selection commands to the processing elements to retrieve the tuples of S.

The processing of the Join operation consists of the following time components: (1) the reading of R, (2) the selection operations on S to retrieve tuples of S, and (3) the joining of tuples of R with tuples of S to produce the relation L. Each time component will now be detailed.

The time for reading one page of R by the controller would take $t[\text{lat}]$ + $t[\text{I/O}]$. The page is transferred by the controller to the host computer in $t[\text{xfer}]$ time. For each tuple of R in a page, a selection command is issued to the processing elements. The time to retrieve all S tuples that satisfy the search conditions is similar to that derived for the selection algorithm, that is,

$$t[\text{retrieve}, S] = t[\text{process\_select}] + t[\text{disk\_out}, S]$$
$$+ \text{ceil}(\text{sel\_fac} * s) * t[\text{xfer}]$$

where $t[\text{disk\_out}, S] = 1/2 * (s + \text{ceil}(\text{sel\_fac} * s)) * t[\text{I/O}] * t[\text{lat}]$ is the average output time for transferring tuples of S out of the disk to the controller and is similar to $t[\text{disk\_out}, R]$, explained in the selection algorithm.

The retrieved pages of S need to be joined with the R tuple currently being processed. This will take the following time

$$t[\text{jn\_Rt\_Spg}] = \text{sel\_fac} * s * t * (2 * t[\text{mov}])$$

where $(2 * t[\text{mov}])$ accounts for the concatenation of two tuples to form a resulting tuple of L.

Taking the preceding reading time and transfer time for a page of R, the retrieval time of S for each tuple of R, and the preceding Join time into consideration, the time to join one page of R with S would be

$$t[\text{jn\_Rpg\_S}] = t[\text{lat}] + t[\text{I/O}] + t[\text{xfer}] + t * (t[\text{retrieve}, S]$$
$$+ t[\text{jn\_Rt\_Spg}])$$

Since R has m pages, the total Join time would be

$$t[\text{jn\_R\_S}] = m * t[\text{jn\_Rpg\_S}]$$

These pages of L need to be written back to the disk as they are produced, since the main memory of the host computer cannot store the entire result of the Join operation. The writing time for these L pages would be

$$t[\text{I/O}, L] = \text{ceil}(2 * m * t * \text{sel\_fac} * s) * (t[\text{xfer}] + t[\text{I/O}] + t[\text{lat}])$$

Here, only one $t[\text{lat}]$ is involved because it is assumed that the relation is written in consecutive disk tracks. Only the first read/write requires the latency time. The small amount of time for the switching of the read/write head is ignored.

The total processing time, including the output time of L for this algorithm, is

$$t[\text{process}] = t[\text{jn\_R\_S}] + t[\text{I/O}, L])$$

The collection time for transferring the result of the Join operation to the user consists of (1) reading the pages of L, which were written back to the disk, to the host computer and (2) transferring these pages from the output buffer to the user's terminal. Thus,

$$t[\text{data\_collect}] = t[\text{I/O}, L] + 2 * m * t * \text{sel\_fac} * s * t * t[\text{tp\_out}]$$

The total execution time for this algorithm is

$$t[\text{Join}] = t[\text{inst\_flow}] + t[\text{process}] + t[\text{data\_collect}]$$

3.4.2.3 STATISTICAL AGGREGATION.

The processing elements in the model for cellular-logic devices have rather low processing capability. They are not able to implement the sort-merge or hash-based algorithms used in the conventional system model of Chapter 2 to perform the aggregation operation. Thus, this operation needs to be performed by the host computer using the following algorithm.

Each page of the referenced relation R is read and transferred to the host computer. The category attribute values (assuming there are y such attributes involved in the operation) of each tuple are accessed and compared with a table of distinct categories established for this operation. The table is empty at the beginning. As the tuples of R are examined and compared with the entries of the table, new categories are gradually added to the table. It is assumed that there are w distinct categories formed by this operation. For each distinct category in the category table, an average of half the w table entries need to be searched. If the category represented by the category attribute values is already in the table, the computation of the intermediate aggregate value is performed for the summary attribute (assuming only one summary attribute is involved). If the category is not in the table, it is added as a new entry to the table. This process continues for each tuple of R until the last tuple has been processed. It is assumed that w is not a very large number and that the w tuples of the resulting relation L can be held in the main memory of the host computer. The instruction flow time is

$$t[\text{inst\_flow}] = t[\text{comp}] + t[\text{tp\_xfer}] + t[\text{brcast}]$$

The reading of a page of R and its transfer to the host computer is given by

$$t[\text{read\_pg}, R] = t[\text{lat}] + t[\text{I/O}] + t[\text{xfer}]$$

For each tuple of R in a page, a table search is performed to identify the category to which it belongs. Roughly, $w/2$ entries of the category table need to be examined. The comparison of y attribute values with each entry will take $y * (2 * t[s] + t[\text{cpu}])$. Processing each tuple involves a calculation of the aggregated summary value which will be approximated here by $(t[s] + t[\text{cpu}])$.

The total processing time for m pages of R is then,

$$t[\text{proc\_m\_pg}, R] = m * t[\text{read\_pg}, R] + m * t * (y * w/2$$
$$* (2 * t[s] + t[\text{cpu}]) + t[s] + t[\text{cpu}])$$

Since the resulting relation L is assumed to be stored in the main memory of the host computer, the data collection time involves only the transfer of the tuples of this relation to the user's terminal, that is,

$$t[\text{data\_collect}] = w * t[\text{tp\_out}]$$

Thus, the execution time of this algorithm is

$$t[\text{Aggregate}] = t[\text{inst\_flow}] + t[\text{process}] + t[\text{data\_collect}]$$

3.4.2.4   UPDATE. The Update operation in this model is performed by selecting all tuples of R that satisfy the update conditions (the same as the Selection operation) and, in the same revolution, modifying the selected tuples.

The instruction flow time is

$$t[\text{inst\_flow}] = t[\text{comp}] + t[\text{tp\_xfer}] + t[\text{brcast}]$$

where the last two terms account for the transfer of the selection command from the host computer to the controller and the broadcasting of the command to all the processing elements respectively.

It is assumed that the selection of the qualified tuples and the Update operation can be carried out in the same revolution of the disk, that is,

$$t[\text{process}] = t[\text{lat}] + t[\text{rev}]$$

Since no data collection is involved in an update operation, the execution time for this operation is

$$t[\text{Update}] = t[\text{inst\_flow}] + t[\text{process}]$$

The preceding analyses of Selection, Join, Statistical Aggregation, and Update operations and the derived cost formulas do not account for the possible overlaps between processing time and I/O time. Those readers who are interested in the performance of this model under a specific set of parameter values should make the necessary adjustment to the formulas to account for the overlaps. It is suggested that the values assigned to m, s, sel_fac, $t[\text{I/O}]$, $t[\text{xfer}]$, $t[\text{brcast}]$, and w be varied to determine their effects on the processing time of these algorithms. The performance of this model is particularly sensitive to the selectivity factor sel_fac, which determines the amount of data to be output from the intelligent disk, and the block transfer time $t[\text{xfer}]$.

3.5   SUMMARY AND DISCUSSION

In this chapter, the architectures and features of several cellular-logic devices have been described—they are, CASSM, RAP, RARES, and IBM's MBM. The techniques of data organization, content and context addressing, content/pointer-to-address mapping, hardware garbage collection, and integrity and security enforcement using an associative programming strategy have been described and illustrated by examples. The work in cellular-logic devices has demonstrated that it is feasible to off-load a considerable amount of frequent database management functions to the secondary storage devices where data are stored, thus relieving the load of a host computer. With their associative search capabilities, these devices can search large databases efficiently to filter out data that are not relevant to a retrieval request, thus relieving the I/O bottleneck between the secondary storage and the main memory.

Building intelligence into secondary storage devices for processing data where they are stored is perhaps the most important principle introduced by the work on cellular-logic devices. Since transferring large quantities of data in and out of the archival memory is still the main bottleneck of a computing system, the idea of pairing processing elements with memory elements to achieve parallel processing and associative search of data is important for removing or easing the bottleneck. Research and development work on intelligent secondary storage devices is not only worth pursuing, but it can be the key to a very powerful computing system.

There are, however, a number of problems that need to be solved before such devices can become practical for use in database management applications.

1. The idea of pairing a processing element with a disk track, which has been experimented in the CASSM and RAP projects, is conceptually sound. However, it is still not practical to build such a disk based on today's hardware cost. Although, head-per-track disks have been available for a long time, to expand the read/write heads to do the types of data manipulation operations suggested by the research work will require that these read/write heads be replaced by rather intelligent processors; something equivalent to today's microprocessors. Since the amount of data a disk track can hold is very limited, the cost of using a microprocessor for each track will be difficult to justify. One solution is to use a larger memory element for each processing element. For example, for those disks that have several read/write heads for each disk surface, consider the entire band of disk tracks associated with each read/write head to be a single memory element. The contents of each band of tracks can be sequentially scanned by the read/write head. Thus, a memory cycle of such a disk would be defined as the time to scan that band of tracks. In a moving-head disk system, consider the whole surface as a memory element. If there are k tracks in a surface, k revolutions of the disk will be needed for the processing element to scan the memory element. This will, of course, further prolong the memory cycle time of an intelligent disk.

2. There is a technical difficulty in keeping the multiple read/write heads aligned. For the cellular-logic device to work properly, all processing elements' operations must be synchronized. They must be able to read the words in their corresponding tracks at the same time. If a number of intelligent disks are used to store a large database, all the processing elements in these disks need to be aligned. This will certainly present an even greater difficulty than the single-disk situation. The technology for disk alignment may exist, but it will certainly increase the cost of building such disks considerably. Using other memory devices (e.g., magnetic bubble memories and charge-coupled devices) would be a solution to this alignment problem since these devices can be driven by a common clock and can operate synchronously with respect to the data they scan. However, the cost of these memory devices is considerably higher than disks.

3. Based on the analyses of algorithms for the four representative database operations presented in Section 3.4, it should be clear to the reader that the main advantage of the intelligent secondary storage devices is their selection capability. They are not able to perform Join and Statistical Aggregation operations directly; the host computer needs to be involved in carrying out those operations. This means that the data stored on an intelligent storage device need to be moved to the host computer's main memory before the operations can be performed. The results of these operations will have to be moved back to the intelligent storage device. Data movement between the intelligent storage device and the host computer is very time-consuming. Thus, the I/O bottleneck problem addressed in Chapter 1 may still exist in these systems when such operations are being performed.

4. Although an intelligent storage device can perform selection efficiently by scanning and marking tuples that satisfy some given data conditions, the marked tuples still need to be transferred out to the host computer. The transfer time is significant in this type of device unless a parallel output capability, which most of the existing secondary storage devices do not have, is provided.

These problems must be solved before the ideas and techniques introduced by the research work on intelligent secondary storage devices can be put to practical use.

3.6 BIBLIOGRAPHY

[BON77] Bonyhard, P. I., et al.: "High Performance Magnetic Bubble Replicate Gate Design," *IEEE Trans. on Magnetics,* Sept. 1977, pp. 1258–1260.

[BUS76] Bush, G. A., Lipovski, G. J., Watson, J. K., Su, S. Y. W., and Ackerman, S.: "Some Implementations of Segment Sequential Functions," *Proceedings of the Third Symposium on Computer Architecture,* Clearwater, Fla., 1976, pp. 178–185.

[CHA72] Chang, H.: "Bubble Domain Memory Chips," *IEEE Trans. on Magnetics,* Sept. 1972, pp. 564–568.

[CHA75a] Chang, H., and Lee, S. Y.: "Associative-Search Bubble Devices for Content-addressable Memories," *IBM Tech. Disclosure Bull.,* vol. 18, no. 2, July 1975, pp. 598–602.

[CHA75b] Chang, H.: "Magnetic Bubble Technology—Present and Future," *Proceedings of the Seventh Conference on Solid State Devices,* Tokyo, 1975.

[CHA78a] Chang, H.: "On Bubble Memories and Relational Data Base," *Proceedings of the Fourth International Conference on Very Large Data Bases,* Berlin, Sept. 13–15, 1978, pp. 207–229.

[CHA78b] Chang, H., and Nigam, A.: "Major-Minor Loop Chips Adapted for Associative Search in Relational Data Base," *IEEE Trans. on Magnetics,* Nov. 1978, pp. 1123–1128.

[CHE78] Chen, T. C., Lum, V. W., and Tung, C.: "The Rebound Sorter: An Efficient Sort Engine for Large Files," *Proceedings of the Fourth International Conference on Very Large Data Bases,* Sept. 13–15, 1978, pp. 312–315.

[COD70] Codd, E. F.: "A Relational Model of Data for Large Shared Data Banks," *CACM,* vol. 13, no. 6, 1970, pp. 377–387.

[COM82] *Computer Design,* Dec. 1982.

[COP73] Copeland, G. P., Lipovski, G. J., and Su, S. Y. W.: "The Architecture of CASSM: A Cellular System for Non-numeric Processing," *Proceedings of the First Annual Symposium on Computer Architecture,* Dec. 1973, pp. 121–128.

[COP74a] Copeland, G. P.: "A Cellular System for Non-Numeric Processing," Ph.D. dissertation, Department of Electrical Engineering, University of Florida, 1974.

[COP74b] Copeland, G. P., and Su, S. Y. W.: "A High-level Data Sub-language for a Context-Addressed Segment-Sequential Memory," *Proceedings of the ACM SIGFIDET Workshop on Data Translation, Access, and Control,* May 1974, pp. 265–275.

[DOT80] Doty, K. L., Greenblatt, J. D., and Su, S. Y. W.: "Magnetic Bubble Memory Architectures for Associative Searching of Relational Databases," *IEEE Trans. on Computers,* vol. C-29, no. 11, 1980, pp. 957–970.

[ESW76] Eswaran, K. P.: "Specification, Implementations, and Interactions of a Trigger Subsystem in an Integrated Database System," *IBM Res. Rep. RJ1820,* Nov. 1976.

[HEA72] Healy, L. D., Lipovski, G. J., and Doty, K. L.: "The Architecture of a Context Addressed Segment-Sequential Storage," *AFIPS Conference Proceedings,* vol. 41, 1972 FJCC, Anaheim, Cal., 1972, pp. 691–701.

[HEA76] Healy, L. D.: "A Character-Oriented Context-Addressed Segment-Sequential Storage," *Proceedings of the Third Annual Symposium on Computer Architecture,* Clearwater, Fla., Jan. 1976, pp. 172–177.

[HIG72] Higbie, L. C.: "The OMEN Computers: Associative Array Processors," *Digest of Papers,* COMPCON 1972, pp. 287–290.

[HOL56] Hollander, G. L.: "Quasi-Random Access Memory Systems," *AFIPS Conference Proceedings,* 1956, EJCC, New York, 1956, pp. 128–135.

[HON81] Hong, Y. C., and Su, S. Y. W.: "Associative Hardware and Software Techniques for Integrity Control," *ACM Trans. on Database Systems,* vol. 6, no. 3, Sept. 1981, pp. 416–440.

[HON82] Hong, Y. C., and Su, S. Y. W.: "A Protection Mechanism for Cellular Logic Devices," *IEEE Trans. on Software Engineering,* vol. SE-8, no. 6, Nov. 1982, pp. 583–596.

[INT84] Intel Corporation: *Intel Memory Components Handbook,* 1984.

[JUL76] Juliussen, J. E.: "Magnetic Bubble Systems Approach Practical Use," *Computer Design,* Oct. 1976, pp. 81–91.

[LIN76] Lin, C. S., Smith, D. C. P., and Smith, J. M.: "The Design of a Rotating Associative Memory for Relational Data Base Applications," *ACM Trans. on Database Systems,* vol. 1, no. 1, 1976, pp. 53–65.

[LIN77] Lin, C. S.: "Sorting with Associative Secondary Storage Devices," *Proceedings of the 1977 NCC,* Dallas, Tex., 1977, AFIP Press, Montvale, N.J., pp. 691–695.

[LIP75] Lipovski, G. J., and Su, S. Y. W.: "On Non-Numeric Processors," *Computer Architecture News,* vol. 4, no. 1, March 1975, pp. 14–19.

[LIP78] Lipovski, G. J.: "Architecture Features of CASSM: A Context Addressed Segment Sequential Memory," *Proceedings of the Fifth Annual Symposium on Computer Architecture,* Palo Alto, Calif., April 1987, pp. 31–38.

[MIN72] Minsky, N.: "Rotating Storage Devices as Partially Associative Memories," *AFIPS Conference Proceedings,* vol. 41, part 1, 1972 FJCC, Anaheim, Cal., 1972, pp. 587–596.

[NAD76] Naden, R. A., et al.: "Electrical Characterization of a Packaged 100K bit Major/Minor Loop Bubble Device," *IEEE Trans. on Magnetics.,* Nov. 1976, pp. 685–687.

[OZK75] Ozkarahan, E. A., Schuster, S. A., and Smith, K. C.: "RAP- An Associative Processor for Data Base Management," *AFIPS Conference Proceedings,* 1975 NCC, Anaheim, Cal., 1975, pp. 370–387.

[OZK77] Ozkarahan, E. A., and Sevcik, K. C.: "Analysis of Architectural Features for Enhancing the Performance of a Database Machine," *ACM Trans. on Database Systems,* vol. 4, no. 2, 1977, pp. 297–316.

[OZK86] Ozkarahan, E.: *Database Machines and Database Management,* Prentice-Hall, Englewood Cliffs, N.J., 1986.

[PAR72] Parhami, B.: "A Highly Parallel Computing System for Information Retrieval," *AFIPS Conference Proceedings,* vol. 41, part II, 1972 FJCC, Anaheim, Cal., 1972, pp. 681–690.

[PAR71] Parker, J. L.: "A Logic per Track Retrieval System," *Proceedings of the IFIP Congress 1971,* Ljubljara, Yugoslavia, 1971, pp. TA-4-146–TA-4-150.

[POH76] Pohm, A. V., et al.: "Bubble memories for Microcomputers and Minicomputers," *IEEE Trans. on Magnetics,* vol. 12, no. 6, Nov. 1976, pp. 636–638.

[SAV66] Savitt, D. A., Love, H. H., and Troop, R. E.: "Associative-Storing Processor Study," Defense Documentation Center, Document No. AD 488538, June 1966, p. 202.

[SAV67] Savitt, D. A., Love, H. H., and Troop, R. E.: "ASP: A New Concept in Language and

Machine Organization," *IFIPS Conference Proceedings,* vol. 31, 1976 SJCC, Freudenstadt, Germany, 1976, pp. 87–102.

[SCH76] Schuster, S. A., Ozkarahan, E. A., and Smith, K. C.: "A Virtual Memory System for a Relational Associative Processor," *AFIPS Conference Proceedings,* vol. 45, 1976 NCC, New York, 1976, pp. 855–862.

[SCH78] Schuster, S. A., Nguyen, H. B., Ozkarahan, E. A., and Smith, K. C.: "RAP 2— An Associative Processor for Data Bases," *Proceedings of the Fifth Annual Symposium on Computer Architecture,* Palo Alto, Cal., April 1978, pp. 52–59.

[SLO62] Slotnick, D. L., et al.: "The SOLOMON Computer," *AFIPS Conference Proceedings,* 1962 FJCC, Philadelphia, Pa., 1967, pp. 97–107.

[SLO67] Slotnick, D. L.: "Achieving Large Computing Capabilities through an Array Computer," *AFIPS Conference Proceedings,* 1967 SJCC, vol. 33, Atlantic City, N.J., 1967, pp. 471–475.

[SLO70] Slotnick, D. L.: "Logic per Track Devices," in J. Tou (ed), *Advances in Computers,* vol. 10, Academic Press, New York, 1970, pp. 291–296.

[SMI79] Smith, D. C. P., and Smith, J. M.: "Relational Data Base Machines," *COMPUTER,* vol. 12, no. 2, 1979, pp. 28–38.

[SU73] Su, S. Y. W., Copeland, G. P., and Lipovski, G. J.: "Retrieval Operations and Data Representations in a Context-Addressed Disc System," *Proceedings of the CAM SIGPLAN and SIGIR Interface Meeting,* Gaithersburg, Md., Nov. 1973, pp. 144–156.

[SU75] Su, S. Y. W., and Lipovski, G. J.: "CASSM: A Cellular System for Very Large Data Bases," *Proceedings of the International Conference on Very Large Data Bases,* Framingham, Mass., Sept. 1975, pp. 456–472.

[SU77] Su, S. Y. W.: "Associative Programming in CASSM and Its Applications," *Proceedings of the Third International Conference on Very Large Data Bases,* Tokyo, Oct. 6–8, 1977, pp. 213–228.

[SU78] Su, S. Y. W., and Emam, E.: "CASDAL: CASSM's Data Language," *ACM Trans. on Database Systems,* vol. 3, no. 1, March 1978, pp. 57–91.

[SU79a] Su, S. Y. W.: "On Cellular-logic Devices: Concepts and Applications," *IEEE COMPUTER,* vol. 12, no. 3, pp. 11–27.

[SU79b] Su, S. Y. W., Nguyen, L., Ahmed, E., and Lipovski, G.: "The Architectural Features and Implementation Techniques of Multicell CASSM," *IEEE Trans. on Computers,* vol. C-28, no. 6, June 1979, pp. 430–445.

[SU85] Su, S. Y. W., and Raschid, L.: "Incorporating Knowledge Rules in a Semantic Data Model: An Approach to Integrated Knowledge Management," *Artificial Intelligence Applications Conference,* Miami, Dec. 1985, pp. 250–256.

[TRI82] Triebel, W. A.: *Handbook of Semiconductor and Bubble Memories,* Prentice-Hall, Englewood Cliffs, N.J., 1982.

CHAPTER
4

DATABASE FILTERS

In conventional computer systems used for database management applications, large quantities of data are stored on secondary storage devices such as disks, magnetic tapes, video disks, and so forth, in the form of a set of files. Selected files are moved into the main memory of the computer system for retrieval and/or update purposes. Since the contents of a file can only be examined by the processor after the file has been staged in the main memory, the file may contain a lot of data that are not relevant to a particular retrieval and/or update. In this case, large quantities of data are transferred for no purpose. The time needed to transfer data between the secondary storage device and the main memory is determined by the speed of the secondary storage device and that of the data link between them. It is slow when compared with the processor's speed. This data staging time is the predominant time factor that limits the performance of a computer system and causes the so-called I/O bottleneck.

This chapter presents a category of database computers called *database filters*. These computers function as filters for trapping those irrelevant data when data are transferred between the secondary storage device and the main memory, thus reducing the amount of data transfer. They also serve as a data transformer that restructures the input file or correlates multiple input files to produce the output in a form useful to a host computer.

This chapter is divided into four sections. Section 4.1 details the three general approaches used to solve the I/O bottleneck problem. The concept of data filtering is elaborated on in Section 4.2. Section 4.3 illustrates the architectures and techniques used in several database filters, and Section 4.4 summarizes the discussion.

4.1 THREE GENERAL APPROACHES TO THE I/O BOTTLENECK PROBLEM

There are three general approaches to the solution of the I/O bottleneck problem. The first approach is to increase the communication bandwidth between the secondary storage device and the main memory so that data can be moved faster between these two storage devices. For example, using a fast communication line or using secondary storage devices with parallel read-out capability or using a direct memory access method (DMA) or multiported memory are possible approaches to relieve the bottleneck problem.

The second approach is to minimize the amount of data that needs to be moved into the memory by clustering data based on their semantic properties (e.g., common properties, frequency of being accessed together, etc.). Instead of storing the large file as a single entity in a database, one can partition the file either vertically or horizontally into a number of smaller files, each of which contains data records that are semantically related and are likely to be accessed together. Related files can be stored physically together on the same track or cylinder of a disk. Thus, a smaller quantity of data can be named and accessed independently and efficiently by different applications. This, of course, is the traditional data clustering approach used often in database management and information storage and retrieval.

The third approach to the I/O bottleneck problem is to use a hardware device to serve as a database filter for filtering out irrelevant data transferred out of the secondary storage devices. This last approach is explained further in the next section but note that all the above three approaches have been used in a number of existing database computers.

4.2 THE CONCEPT OF DATA FILTERING

In a traditional computer system, the operations of a secondary storage device are controlled by a controller, as illustrated in Figure 4.1. The controller receives input and output commands from the central processor and issues "orders" to the secondary storage device to perform the actual I/O operations. Data are

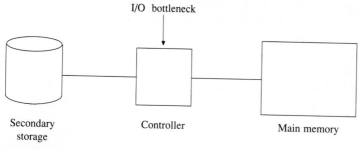

I/O bottleneck

Secondary storage   Controller   Main memory

FIGURE 4.1
I/O bottleneck in conventional systems.

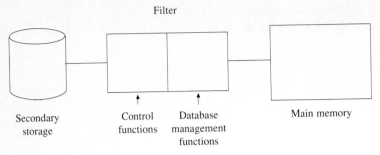

FIGURE 4.2
Database filter.

transferred between the secondary storage device and the main memory through the controller, which simply forwards the data without examining contents or modifying them. The concept of data filtering is to replace the controller with a more intelligent processor called a *database filter* or an *intelligent secondary storage controller*. This device not only performs the regular control functions to operate the secondary storage device but also carries out one or both of the following two types of data management functions: (1) data reduction and (2) data transformation (see Figure 4.2).

4.2.1 Data Reduction

In this case, the input to the database filter is a file containing a set of records. The filter uses either hardware or software means to examine the contents of these records when they are transferred from the secondary storage device to the main memory of a host computer. The function of the filter is to determine which of the records satisfy the search conditions given to the filter by the host computer and to trap those records that do not satisfy the search. The filter is capable of performing the Selection operation in this case. Thus, the output of the filter is a subset of the input records resulting in a reduction in the length of the original input. Similarly, a database filter can reduce the width of the input by filtering out some selected fields of each input record, that is, the Projection operation without the elimination of duplicates. This technique of data reduction is different from the traditional software indexing technique in that the former examines the contents of every record to do the Selection whereas the latter maintains an index to directly access a subset of records that have certain data properties.

The Selection and Projection operations can quite easily be carried out by a filter "on the fly" when input records are being read into the main memory. This is because in both operations input record contents can be quickly examined to determine if any output needs to be generated by the filter without relying on the contents of the other records.

4.2.2 Data Transformation

Another key database function that some of the proposed database filters can perform is the transformation of the structure and/or contents of the input data.

For example, a filter may perform a Sort operation on the input records to produce a sorted file, or it may merge, join, or take the difference of two input files to produce a new file as output. This data transformation function is much more difficult to perform than the reduction function. It may involve multiple scans of the input data before producing the output. One main challenge to the database filter designers is to design the right hardware and algorithms to perform these more complex database functions with minimal delay in producing the output results.

*   *   *

The term database filter is used in this text to refer to those hardware devices that perform one or both of these functions. There are several more elaborate systems that perform not only these two functions but also other database management functions such as query translation and optimization, integrity and security control, recovery, and so forth. They are called dedicated database computers and will be presented in Chapter 6.

4.3   ARCHITECTURES AND TECHNIQUES

The following subsections describe the architectures and implementation techniques of five database filters. Some of these filters are components of some more elaborate database computers. Nevertheless, they are presented here since the same concept of data filtering is used.

4.3.1   Architecture of CAFS and Content-to-Address Mapping Using Bit Arrays

The Content Addressable File Store (CAFS) is a special-purpose peripheral device designed principally to handle real-time transactions in a multiuser environment [BAB79]. The system was prototyped and manufactured by the International Computers Limited of England. The system reported by Babb [BAB79] uses 60 megabyte disk drives as the secondary storage devices. The instantaneous data scanning rate is about 4 megabytes per second, which typically results in a 2 megabytes per second rate visible to the user. Several such systems have been built and are in use.

4.3.1.1   BASIC ARCHITECTURE. The basic architecture of CAFS is shown in Figure 4.3. The hardware consists of an array of key registers and their corresponding latch comparators, a search evaluation unit, a retrieval unit, and a disk drive. Data stored in the form of relations are stored on the disk. To perform the Selection operation of Figure 4.3 on this system, the key words or attribute-value pairs found in the qualification conditions of a query are first loaded in the key registers as illustrated in the figure. Also, the relational operators ($=, \geq, \leq, <$, and $>$) associated with these attribute-value pairs are stored in the

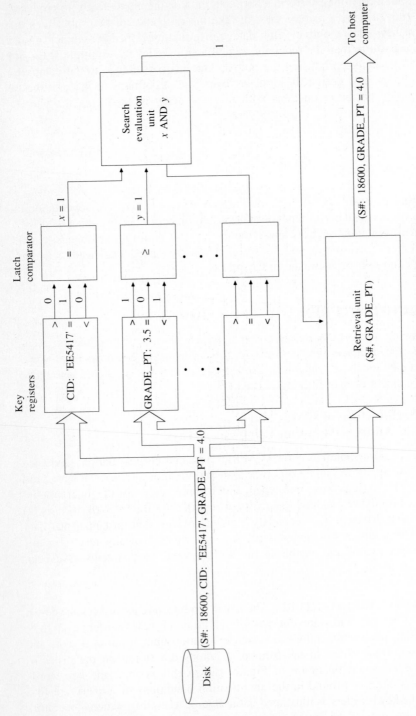

FIGURE 4.3
The basic architecture of CAFS. (*Source:* [BAB79])

SELECT STUDENT_COURSE (S#, GRAD_PT) **WHERE**
CID = EE4517' AND GRADE_PT ≥ 3.5

corresponding latch comparators. The tuples of the STUDENT_COURSE relation are then read from the disk in a multiplexed mode (up to 12 tracks multiplexed) and piped simultaneously to all the key registers and the retrieval unit. The key registers are in effect low-intelligence processors capable of comparing their key words against each tuple flowing from the disk. Each key register will set a latch if the value in a tuple is greater than, equal to, or less than the value preloaded in the register. The output of these latches goes to the latch comparators corresponding to the key registers. In these latch comparators, the preloaded relational operators are compared with the latch settings to determine their output. For example, the output labeled x and y is equal to 1 for the tuple currently being processed, since CID = 'EE5417' and GRADE_PT $\geq$ 3.5.

The Boolean AND condition of these two separate tests is verified by the search evaluation unit, and it is determined that the current tuple satisfies that AND condition. Thus, the output of the search evaluation unit is true. This fact signals the retrieval unit, which is holding the current tuple, to output the S# and GRADE_PT values.

The hardware allows multiple search conditions to be evaluated against the same input data stream. Therefore, it is a multiple instruction stream and single data stream (MISD) architecture. Figure 4.3 illustrates how the Selection and Projection operations are carried out in CAFS.

4.3.1.2 CAFS ARCHITECTURE WITH BIT ARRAYS. Extending this basic architecture, CAFS uses a number of single-bit array stores to achieve the content-to-address mapping technique described in Section 3.2.5. This mapping technique is used to support relational operations such as Join and Elimination of Duplicates following a Projection operation.

A bit array store in CAFS is a single-bit wide random access memory. To perform an Equi-Join operation between two relations over a common attribute, the system reads the first relation R1 and uses the values of the common attribute to address the bit store to set the addressed bits to '1'. It then reads the second relation R2 and uses the values of the common attribute to verify if the addressed bits have already been set. If so, this indicates that the values of the second relation match with those of the first relation. The corresponding tuples are then concatenated to form the tuples of the resulting relation. This simple approach will work only if the values of both relations fall in the limit of the bit array store. In other words, there is one-to-one mapping between all distinct attribute values and the addresses of the single-bit array store. This requirement cannot always be satisfied since the values of some attributes may be very large. An encoding scheme is therefore introduced in CAFS to assign a unique code to each distinct value of an attribute. The STUDENT_COURSE database of Figure 2.9 is used here as an example to illustrate the scheme. The attribute CID of STUDENT_COURSE relation has a data type, CHAR(7). To map a value of this attribute directly to a bit address of an array store would require that the array store be at least 2^{56} bits (7 characters times 8 bits per character) large. However, the number of distinct values (all course numbers) of this attribute is relatively small. If there are, for example, 200 distinct course numbers, the coded values

COURSE

CID	CTITLE	ROOM	PERIOD	PROF_NAME	ICID
CIS4121	Computer Organization	Larsen 210	2	T.B. Bronson	1
CIS6220	Compiler	Benton 211	4	S.B. Jensen	2
EE5417	Database Engineering	Weil 507	6	N.T. Yong	3
EE6967	Database Machine	Larsen 210	4	T.B. Bronson	4
⋮					

STUDENT_COURSE

S#	CID	GRADE_PT	ICID
16242	CIS4121	4.0	1
17522	EE5417	3.0	3
18600	EE5417	4.0	3
24010	EE6967	2.5	4
18600	CIS6220	3.0	2
14256	EE6967	4.0	4
17522	CIS4121	3.0	1
18600	CIS4121	3.0	1
14256	CIS6220	4.0	2

FIGURE 4.4
COURSE and STUDENT_COURSE relations with coupling indexes.

1 to 200 can be assigned to replace the original 7-character course numbers. It is proposed in CAFS that additional attributes called *coupling indexes* be added to relations and that Join operations be performed over these indexes. For example, Figure 4.4 shows the relations STUDENT_COURSE and COURSE of Figure 2.9 after two coupling indexes have been added to them. Each value of the coupling index named ICID is a coded value that uniquely identifies a CID number.

Figure 4.5 shows the architecture of CAFS with a bit array store. Figure 4.4 is used here to illustrate how the bit array store is used to perform the Join operation involved in the following query expressed in English:

Retrieve the student numbers and grade points of those students who take the courses offered in Larsen 210.

For the above retrieval query, CAFS reads the COURSE relation from the disk and selects those tuples with ROOM values equal to Larsen 210. In the example,

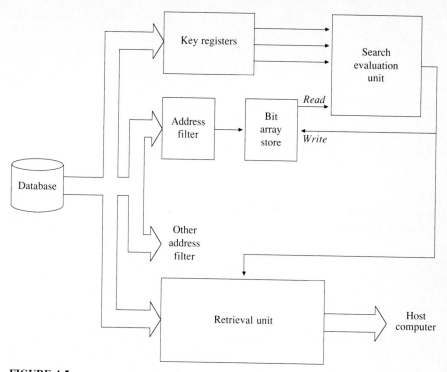

FIGURE 4.5

CAFS architecture with a bit array store. (*Source:* [BAB79] copyright ©1979, Association for Computing Machinery, Inc., reprinted by permission)

the tuples identified by CIS4121 and EE6967 are selected. CAFS then clears the contents of the bit array store and uses the corresponding ICID values (i.e., 1 and 4) to address and mark the first and fourth bits of the bit array store. Next, the STUDENT_COURSE relation is read from the disk, and the ICID column is examined. For each tuple examined, CAFS checks its ICID value to see if the bit array store addressed by that value has been marked. If so, the retrieval unit is signaled to output the S# and GRADE_PT of the current tuple to the host computer (see Figure 4.5). Otherwise, the next tuple of the STUDENT_COURSE relation is processed. In effect, the marking and checking of the bit array store implements the Join operation needed to respond to the query. This technique of processing allows the Join operation to be carried out in a single scan of the STUDENT and STUDENT_COURSE relations.

The processing technique, which was introduced independently in this work, is similar to that used in the CASSM system described in Section 3.2.5. However, the hardware implementation of the bit array store is rather different. In CASSM, the bit array is physically distributed in multiple cells. In CAFS, the bit array is a single RAM.

One serious drawback of this coupling index approach is the need to create a new column of data for every attribute, each of which can potentially be used as a join field. If coupling indexes are introduced for all attributes, the size of the database can be easily doubled. If only some selective attributes are chosen to establish the coupling indexes, CAFS will not be able to perform the Join operation on the fly over those attributes that are not indexed.

4.3.1.3   CAFS ARCHITECTURE WITH HASHED BIT ARRAY STORES. An-
other processing technique introduced in CAFS is the use of the traditional software hashing technique to transform the contents of a keyword to an address in a bit array store. The keyword in this case can be formed by a single attribute value or a composite of attribute values. The keyword K is used as the argument of a hashing function $H(k)$, which computes an address in the range of addresses of a bit array. One popular hash function is the division modulo b, which generates an address between 1 and b using $(K \bmod b) + 1$.

One difficulty associated with using hash coding is the problem of collision, that is, more than one key, when applying the same hash function on them, produce the same address. There are several standard ways of handling the collision problem in the data structure literature. All of them involve some added overhead for maintaining a list of all the keys that are mapped to the same address. The method of using hashed-bit array stores proposed in CAFS avoids the overhead of maintaining the key lists at the expense of allowing a small chance of error to occur when performing database operations using the bit array stores. As shown in Figure 4.6, the tuples of a relation are broadcast to the key registers, the address filter, and the retrieval unit. The value of the attribute over which a Selection or Join operation is to be performed is extracted. Each key value is transformed into three addresses by three separate hash coders (each implements a different hash function), and the addresses are used to mark the corresponding bit array store. The output of these three bit array stores are logically ANDed by the AND gate shown in the figure. If the output of the AND gate is '1', then the key K is considered to be in the bit array stores. Otherwise, the key has not been mapped to the bit array stores.

This approach reduces the chance of collision since it is not likely that two different keys will be mapped to an identical set of three addresses using three different hash functions. However, it still allows for the existence of spurious keys. Figure 4.7 illustrates the problem. Here, key K_1 is mapped to three addresses denoted by $M_1(H_1(K_1))$, $M_2(H_2(K_1))$ and $M_3(H_3(K_1))$. Key K_2 is mapped to $M_1(H_1(K_2))$, $M_2(H_2(K_2))$, and $M_3(H_3(K_2))$, where M_1, M_2, and M_3 are the bit array stores and H_1, H_2, and H_3 are the three hash functions. It is assumed that the addresses $M_2(H_2(K_1))$ and $M_2(H_2(K_2))$ are equal. Assume key K_3 is transformed by the same hash functions into three addresses as shown in the figure. Since the three addresses $M_1(H_1(K_3))$, $M_2(H_2(K_3))$, and $M_3(H_3(K_3))$ are all set to '1', due to the mapping of K_1 and K_2 into the bit array stores, CAFS will regard K_3 as a key that matches with what has been mapped to the stores. Nevertheless, it is a spurious key.

The procedure for performing an Equi-Join operation, Join A and B over T, is as follows:

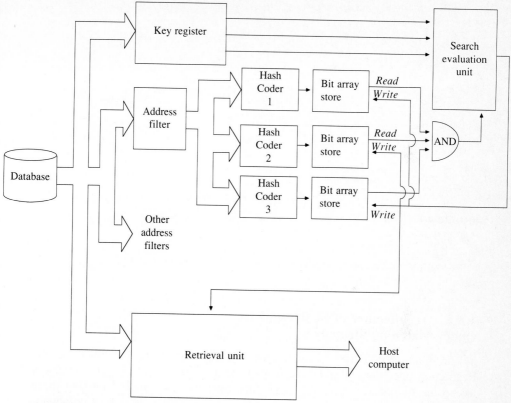

FIGURE 4.6
CAFS architecture with hashed-bit array stores. (*Source:* [BAB79] copyright ©1979, Association for Computing Machinery, Inc., reprinted by permission)

1. Clear the bit array stores.
2. Store the T values of A in the bit array stores as well as in a list P'.
3. Place all T values of B in a list P if the values have been stored in the bit array stores.
4. Eliminate from list P those T values that are not in P'. The list P contains all T values that satisfy the Equi-Join operation.
5. Scan the tuples of A and B. If the T value of a tuple is not in the list P, the tuple does not satisfy the Join operation and is ignored. Otherwise, the tuple is concatenated with the tuple of the other relation.

There are advantages associated with this approach. First, it requires no special coupling indices, which are needed for the single-bit array store described in Section 4.3.1.2. This eliminates the problem of keeping coupling index values consistent after updates. Second, it saves the storage space required for storing the indices. However, this method is not as fast as the single-bit array

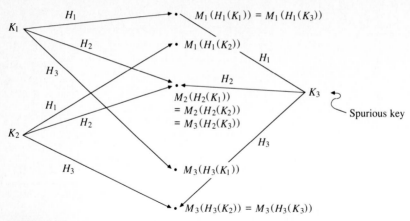

FIGURE 4.7
A spurious key.

store method since some overhead is involved in sorting out the ambiguities of keys.

4.3.2   Architecture of SURE and Its Query-Matching Strategy

SURE is a special-purpose search processor for performing the Selection and Restriction operations of database management systems [LEI78]. The processor is capable of linearly searching large files read from a disk and passing those records, which satisfy a selection or restriction condition, to a host computer, thus serving as a database filter. It was designed and prototyped at the Technical University of Braunschweig in West Germany under the support of the German Ministry of Defense and the Research Council. The research project started in 1974, and the prototype system was completed in 1979.

4.3.2.1   BASIC ARCHITECTURE.   The basic configuration of the search processor is shown in Figure 4.8. It consists of three components: a data memory, a search unit, and a control processor. The data memory is a Siemens 72 megabyte moving-head disk (type 3455) with nine surfaces. It was modified to allow parallel reading of the contents of a cylinder (nine tracks). A byte stream containing interleaved bytes from nine separate records is multiplexed to the search unit in which the record contents are examined. Data are transferred to the search unit at 137 nanosecond per byte data rate.

The search unit consists of a control and data manipulation component, 14 search modules, and a match word generator. The control and data manipulation component handles the multiplexing and buffering of data, detects errors in data transmission from the data memory, and recognizes special codes (e.g., field and record delimiters) in the data stream. Each of the 14 search modules contains a special hard-wired processing unit and a random access memory to

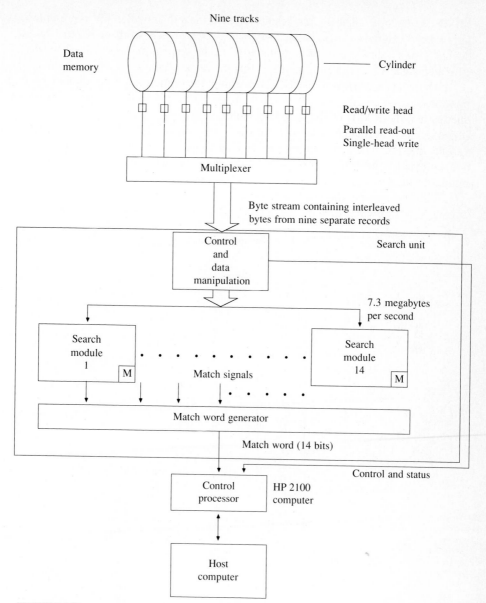

FIGURE 4.8
The architecture of SURE. (*Source:* [LEI78] ©1978 IEEE)

store the operators and operands of a translated query. Each module is capable of comparing the operands against the data items of the input records and performing logic evaluation to determine if an input record satisfies a Boolean expression. Thus, 14 separate queries can be simultaneously processed against the same data stream of records. Therefore, the basic architecture of this system is an

MISD architecture. The search results of these search modules are represented by 14 match signals. These signals are sent to the match word generator. This device allows a data record to be transferred to the control processor if any of the 14 match signals is on, which indicates that the record satisfies at least one query.

The control processor, an HP 2100 computer in the prototype implementation, manages the data records received from the search unit and preloads the queries into the RAMs of the search modules. It also uses the 14-bit match word (the output of the match word generator) to sort out the records that satisfy the various queries. The selection of proper data fields (i.e., the Project operation) is also done by the control processor before the projected data records are transmitted to the host computer.

The general operation of this system is as follows. A cylinder-full of records is read into the search unit in one revolution of the disk. While the records are

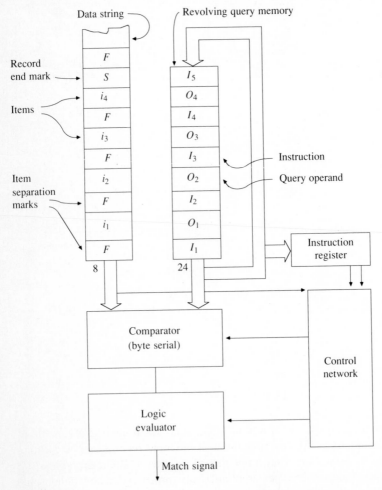

FIGURE 4.9
The configuration of a search module. (*Source:* [LEI78] ©1978 IEEE)

being read, they are evaluated by as many as 14 queries simultaneously. The results of the evaluation are used by the control processor to sort out which records have satisfied which queries. The records that have satisfied a specific query are then transferred to the host computer.

4.3.2.2 THE SEARCH MODULE WITH A REVOLVING QUERY MEMORY. The search module is the central component of this system. Figure 4.9 shows the key components of the search module. A revolving query memory is used to store the instructions and operands of a query. Each word in this query memory is 24 bits wide. The input data stream is a linear string of bytes with delimiters separating data fields (the *F* delimiter) and records (the *S* delimiter). Byte-by-byte the data records are shifted into a single byte comparator in which data bytes are compared serially against the operand bytes. The comparison operation ($\leq$, $\geq$, $<$, etc.) is determined by the instruction code shifted from the revolving query memory into the instruction register. The result of the comparison is evaluated by a logic evaluator, which determines if a record satisfies a Boolean expression. The Search operation described in the preceding section is controlled by the control network shown in the figure.

Instruction format

Instruction code (4)	Modification bits (5)	Operand address (11)

Instruction code		Definition	
ID	Compare operation	Identity (query operand = data item)	set F = '1' or '0'
GD	Compare operation	Greater than	set F = '1' or '0'
KD	Compare operation	Less than	set F = '1' or '0'
ME	Compare operation	Masked bit are all 1's	set F = '1' or '0'
MN	Compare operation	Masked bit are all 0's	set F = '1' or '0'
NL	Compare operation	No operation (no matter what data item is, the match is always satisfied, i.e., f = 1)	
KR		Skip rest of category	
KN		End of category (test for the condition)	
SR		Skip rest of record	
SN		End of record (test for the condition)	
LV		Load variable (load a data item and use it as an operand to compare with another data item in the same input record)	

Modification bits	Definition
FI	Invert item's match result (negate the match result)
BO	Boolean operation (AND/OR)
TE	Apply to second status level
WK	Repeat instruction within category
WB	Boolean operation when repeating

FIGURE 4.10
Instruction format and codes. (*Source:* [LEI78] ©1978 IEEE)

4.3.2.3 INSTRUCTION FORMAT AND OPERATION CODES. A word in the revolving query memory has 24 bits, as illustrated in Figure 4.10. Four of the 24 bits are used by the system for error correction codes. An instruction word occupies 20 bits (4 for the instruction code, 5 for modification bits, and 11 for the operand address). An explanation of the instruction codes and modification bits is given in the figure. In this system, an operand word is 10 bits wide, with 2 bits used for special codes and the remaining 8 bits used for storing one byte of the operand. Thus, two operand bytes fit into one word of the revolving query memory. The 2-bit special codes are used: (1) to mask out the associated operand byte so that the operand byte always matches with the corresponding byte of a data item in the data stream, (2) to mark the end of an operand, and (3) to indicate a skip to the end of an item in the input data stream (i.e., to ignore the remaining bytes of an item).

There are three mark bits used to store and accumulate the search results. An F bit is used to mark the result of the current comparison. When a comparison is satisfied, F is set to '1'. The result can be negated by using the FI modification code. In this case, F is set to '1' if the comparison fails. A Z bit is used to accumulate the intermediate results of a Boolean expression evaluation. By using the BO modification code of Figure 4.10, the result of the current comparison (the F value) can be logically ANDed or ORed with the old value of Z, and the result is stored in Z. An E bit is used to store the final result. By using the modification code TE, the result of a current comparison is stored in $Z (F \rightarrow Z)$ and Z is logically ANDed or ORed with E to produce the new E value.

4.3.2.4 A SELECTION EXAMPLE. A simple example illustrates how the Selection operation is carried out in SURE. Figure 4.11 shows the logical and physical layout of a COURSE table. Note that this system can process unnormalized relations. The attribute PROF_NAME takes multiple values and is called a *category*. The query, "Find all physics courses taught by Blake" is translated into a sequence of instructions and operands that are preloaded into the revolving query memory of one of the search modules, as illustrated in the figure. The first instruction, I1, is a NOOP, which causes the first data item in the input stream to be by-passed. This instruction always results in F = '1'. The second instruction, I2, specifies an identity match and results in F = '1' since the item Physics matches with the operand. The modification codes, TE and BO = '0', cause E to be set to '1', as shown in the figure. I3 is a NOOP that again is used to skip the next item, ROOM, in the input stream. I4 is an identity match instruction that compares the operand Blake against every data item in a category. The modification code WK causes the instruction to be repeated within the category, and the WB = '0' specifies a logical OR of each comparison in the category. The modification codes TE and BO = '1' causes a logical AND between the result of this instruction and the result of I2 previously stored in E. The result is again stored in E. I5 causes the rest of the record to be skipped (generally, there are other data items in the input stream). In this example, the first record of the input stream will result in E = '1', which will cause the match signal of the search module to be set to '1'.

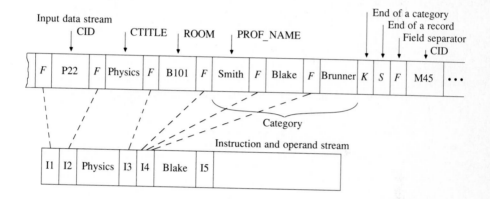

COURSE

CID	CTITLE	ROOM	PROF_NAME
P22	Physics	B101	Smith Blake Brunner
M45	• •	• •	• •

Instructions

    I1 = NL (no operation)
    I2 = ID (compare identity)
        TE and BO = '0' $(F \rightarrow Z; Z \vee E \rightarrow E)$
    I3 = NL (no operation)
    I4 = ID (compare identity)
        WK (repeat instruction within category)
        WB = '0' (logical OR when repeating)
        TE AND BO = '1' $(F \rightarrow Z; Z \wedge E \rightarrow E)$
    I5 = SR (skip rest of the record)

FIGURE 4.11
An example of a selection operation.

This system also supports the Restriction operation, which involves the comparison of two attribute values of the same record to determine if the record satisfies the restriction condition. The technique used in this system for implementing the Restriction operation involves moving the value of the first attribute value from the input data stream to the revolving query memory. The moved value is then compared against the second attribute value in the input data stream. This operation is performed by the instruction LV shown in Figure 4.10.

4.3.3 Architecture of VERSO and Its Query-Processing Strategy

VERSO is a relational database computer designed and prototyped using the concept of a database filter [BAN83]. It is a French project started by INRIA in early 1980. The key features of this system are: (1) the ability to perform both unary and binary database operations in linear time and (2) the use of a programmable automatonlike device as a filter for performing unary and binary operations. The second feature allows programs that drive the automaton to be compiled and loaded into the memory of the automaton to perform various filtering functions.

4.3.3.1 ARCHITECTURE. The architecture of VERSO is shown in Figure 4.12. VERSO serves as a back-end machine for a front-end computer, which in a prototype implementation uses a Motorola 68000 microprocessor named PILOT. It is connected to the front-end computer by a common bus. It consists of four main components: a controller (realized from AMD microprocessors), a RAM used as a data buffer for output to the disk, a disk controller (an SMD interface), and a filter. The functions of the controller are: (1) to interact with the frontend computer PILOT to receive search requests and to return search results, (2) to

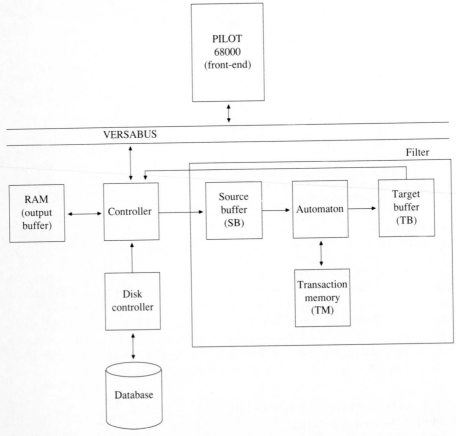

FIGURE 4.12
The architecture of VERSO. (*Source:* [BAN83] copyright ©1983. Prentice-Hall, Inc., reprinted by permission.)

issue I/O commands to the disk controller for all I/O operations, (3) to control the operations of the filter, (4) to perform internal sorting and data rearrangement of data blocks, and (5) to generate automaton programs for controlling the operations of the filter based on the operations to be performed and the structure of data files to be processed. The main functions of the disk controller are as follows: (1) to load prestored automaton programs into the transaction memory (TM) of the filter, (2) to handle disk I/O operations, (3) to perform data transfer between the disk (disk extension, if more permanent storage devices are needed) and a source buffer (SB), which is a 32K-byte RAM in the prototype implementation, and between the disk and a 512K-byte RAM used as a buffer memory for speeding up the unloading of filtered results from a target buffer (TB), a 32K-byte RAM, to the disk.

The key components of the filter are shown in more detail in Figure 4.13. For supporting binary operations such as Join, Union, and Intersection of two files, the SB is divided into two sections, SB_1 and SB_2, each of which is used to load a separate file and has a buffer address register (BAR) and a stack associated

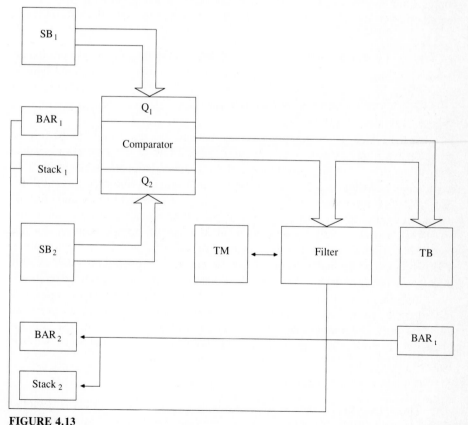

FIGURE 4.13
Components of the filter. (*Source:* [BAN83] copyright © 1983. Prentice-Hall, Inc., reprinted by permission.)

with it. The TB also has a buffer address register, that is BAR_t. The *automaton,* the special-purpose hardware that controls the operations of the filter, controls the update of BAR_1, BAR_2, and BAR_t to determine the addresses for reading from and writing into SB_1, SB_2, and TB. It is driven by automaton programs, which are the compiled codes of relational algebraic queries, preloaded into the TM by the controller.

The general operation of the filter is as follows. Before performing a binary operation, the involved relations are presorted by the controller, which moves the relations into SB_1 and SB_2, respectively. The data in these two buffer sections are fetched by the automaton using the addresses in BAR_1 and BAR_2 and are compared by the comparator. The controller and the automaton can have simultaneous access to the SB. The hardware is designed in such a way that the reading of data by the automaton will not be ahead of the loading of data by the controller. The automaton pops and pushes data or addresses from or into the stacks according to the operations specified in the automaton program under execution, and it moves the resulting data records to the target buffer TB. When TB is full, its contents are moved to the RAM. When the RAM is full, its contents are moved to the disk. Before detailing the query-processing operation of the automaton, the next section will describe the data representations in VERSO.

4.3.3.2 DATA REPRESENTATIONS. VERSO is a relational database computer. It processes normalized relations. For efficiency reasons to be explained later in this section, normalized relations are transformed into more compact structures for processing and storage. VERSO establishes three levels of data representation: logical, formatted, and physical.

At the logical level, relations are normalized and the operations performed on these relations are relational algebraic operations (e.g., Projection, Selection, Intersection, Union, Difference and Join) and relational Update operations (e.g., tuple insertion and deletion of tuples) that satisfy some search conditions. Normalized relations are conceptually appealing for their uniformity and simplicity in structure; they are necessary for avoiding the so-called storage anomalies [DAT75]. However, they are not practical in terms of storage requirement and processing efficiency since the primary keys of relations must be replicated often. This occupies additional storage, and time-consuming operations such as Join must be repeated frequently to relate data that are scattered in different relations.

In VERSO, normalized relations at the logical level are transformed into a more compact format according to the expected Retrieval and Update operations to be performed on the normalized relations. For example, the COURSE relation given in Figure 4.14a may have the following set of expected Retrieval and Update operations:

$$\{CID \rightarrow CTITLE, CID \rightarrow (ROOM, PERIOD), CID \rightarrow PROF\_NAME\}$$

This set represents the fact that retrievals and updates of CTITLE, ROOM, PERIOD, and PROF_NAME are always through the primary key CID. In this case, COURSE relation in Figure 4.14a can be transformed into a compact

COURSE

CID	CTITLE	ROOM	PERIOD	PROF_NAME
CIS4121	Computer Organization	Larsen 210	2	T.B. Bronson
CIS4121	Computer Organization	Benton 211	4	S.B. Jensen
EE5417	Database Engineering	Weil 507	6	N.T. Yong
EE5417	Database Engineering	Larsen 211	4	T.B. Bronson
· · ·				

COURSE

CID	CTITLE	ROOM	PERIOD	PROF_NAME
CIS4121	Computer Organization	Larsen 210	2	T.B. Bronson
		Benton 211	4	S.B. Jensen
EE5417	Database Engineering	Weil 507	6	N.T. Yong
		Larsen 211	4	T.B. Bronson
· · ·				

FIGURE 4.14
(*a*) Normalized COURSE relation. (*b*) Unnormalized COURSE relation.

structure as shown in Figure 4.14*b*. The compact structure can be abbreviated in the following regular expression:

COURSE((CID CTITLE (ROOM, PERIOD) * PROF_NAME *)*)

where * indicates the multiple occurrences of the item(s). Thus, the relation COURSE is represented by a file of records, each of which consists of a CID, a CTITLE followed by a sequence of ROOM-PERIOD pairs, and a sequence of PROF_NAMEs.

In order to allow a binary operation to be carried out in a single scan of the relations (i.e., at linear time), VERSO presorts the relations based on some selected attributes. Thus, the above compact format of COURSE is further transformed into a sorted relation at the formatted level based on major-minor keys represented by the following expression:

COURSE(*CID* CTITLE (*ROOM PERIOD*) * (*PROF_NAME*)*)

In this expression, key attributes are in italics.

At the physical level, sorted relations are partitioned into blocks, each of which corresponds to a disk track of 16K bytes (i.e., a disk page). A physical relation is represented by a four-tuple (R, CF, K, P), where R is a relation schema, CF a compaction format, K a sort key consisting of one or more key attributes, and P a list of disk page addresses. Records are stored in the disk pages. No record can be split over two pages.

4.3.3.3 PROCESSING RELATIONAL OPERATIONS.

In VERSO, it is assumed that the front-end computer of this filter (PILOT 68000) supports a relational DBMS. The user uses the relational algebraic language to query and update a database containing, in the user's conceptual view, normalized relations. Since VERSO represents these relations in a formatted (compact and sorted) structure, the relational algebraic operations on normalized relations are translated into operations on formatted relations. The execution of these operations is done by the filter hardware block-by-block on the physical relations.

The main component of VERSO is its programmable automaton, which is driven by programs to perform unary or binary operations. Programs are represented in the form of state diagrams, each of which consists of a set of transitions and output functions. The nodes of a diagram represent the states of the automaton, and the arcs represent the conditions and operations that take the automaton from the initial state through other states to the final state. The execution of Projection, Selection, Insertion, and Deletion operations are translated into block operations. Binary operations such as Intersection, Difference, and Union operations are performed first by sorting the tuples of the formatted relations and then merging the sorted relations. The Join operation between two relations is done by first sorting the relations and then carrying out a block-by-block Join operation. The merging of two blocks of tuples is used to illustrate how binary operations on formatted relations are performed in the filter. The example was taken from Bancilhon and Scholl [BAN83].

The merging of two formatted relations is carried out by merging one block of one relation with one block of the other relation and then by repeating the Block-Merge operation. In order to merge two blocks, three buffers are necessary: two source buffers for storing the two source blocks and one target buffer for storing the merged result. Associated with these buffers (SB_1, SB_2, and TB), there are registers (Q_1 and Q_2), buffer address registers (BAR_1, BAR_2 and BAR_t), and stacks ($STACK_1$, $STACK_2$, and $STACK_t$) as shown in Figure 4.13. The primitive operations of the filter involve the loading of data into SB_1 and SB_2, the storing of data into TB, the loading of data from SB_1 and SB_2 to Q_1 and Q_2, respectively, the comparison of data in Q_1 and Q_2, and the popping and pushing of data or addresses to the stacks as listed in Figure 4.15.

Figure 4.16 shows the finite state diagram that drives the filter to perform the merging operation. The automaton driven by the diagram performs the merging of two blocks whose record compact format is (course)$*$. At the initial state S1, it is assumed that both Q_1 and Q_2 contain the field delimiter denoted by the % sign. The % sign in Q_1 is first output to the target buffer (operation 10). The addresses

Operations

1. $Q_1 \leftarrow SB_1(BAR_1)$ and BAR_1 $BAR_1 + 1$
2. $Q_2 \leftarrow SB_2(BAR_2)$ and BAR_2 $BAR_2 + 1$
3. $Q_1 = Q_2$?
4. Push BAR_1 on $Stack_1$
5. Push BAR_2 on $Stack_2$
6. $BAR_1 \leftarrow$ Pop (S1)
7. $BAR_2 \leftarrow$ Pop (S2)
8. Pop ($Stack_1$)
9. Pop ($Stack_2$)
10. TB (BAR_t) $\leftarrow Q_1$ and $BAR_t \leftarrow BAR_t + 1$
11. TB (BAR_t) $\leftarrow Q_2$ and $BAR_t \leftarrow BAR_t + 1$
12. Push BAR_t on $Stack_t$
13. $BAR_t \leftarrow$ Pop ($Stack_t$) **FIGURE 4.15**
14. Pop ($Stack_t$) The primitive operations of the filter.

of these two % signs in the source buffers are stored in $STACK_1$ and $STACK_2$, respectively (operations 4 and 5). The next characters in SB_1 and SB_2 are read into Q_1 and Q_2 (operations 1 and 2) and compared (operation 3). This sequence of operations brings the automaton to the state S2. If Q_1 and Q_2 are equal, the character in Q_1 is output to TB and the next characters are compared (operations 1, 2 and 3). Thus, duplicates are eliminated in this merging process. If Q_1 is less than Q_2, $STACK_1$ is popped to get rid of the delimiter % (operation 8) and the content of Q_1 is output to TB (operation 10). In the state S4, all the subsequent

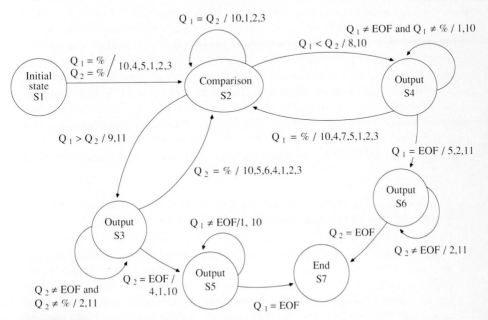

FIGURE 4.16
A finite state diagram for merging two blocks.

characters up to the next delimiter or end-of-file (EOF) in SB_1 are transferred to TB. At this time, the smaller element (data item or record) in the sorted SB_1 has been moved to the TB. The encountering of the next % sign in SB_1 signals the filter to start comparing the next element of SB_1 with the element in SB_2 that has been found to be larger. To reinitiate the comparison, the sequence of operations shown on the arc $S4 \rightarrow S2$ is executed. In this sequence, the effect of operations 5 and 7 is to restore BAR_2 to the beginning address of the element in SB_2 to allow the old SB_2 element to be compared with the next SB_1 element. While in state S4, the encountering of an end-of-file in SB_1 will cause the transfer of the current character of SB_2 loaded in Q_2 and the remaining characters in SB_2 (up to the EOF) to the TB in state S6. While in state S6, an EOF character in SB_2 will cause the automaton to enter the End state, S7.

If Q_1 is greater than Q_2 in the original comparison at S_2, the operations are symmetric to the operations of the above case.

The above example is only for illustrating the merging part of the operation. It is not complete. A testing of the end-of-block or end-of-file is necessary to bring the automaton to a termination state.

4.3.3.4 A SOFTWARE FILTERING APPROACH.

In conjunction with the design and implementation of the prototype VERSO, another approach to database filtering was also taken by researchers in INRIA and the University of Paris XI. The approach uses a general-purpose processor and software to replace the special-purpose hardware to achieve the effect of data filtering [GAM85]. In this approach, the hardware filter is replaced by an exchange module, or EM (see Figure 4.17), which is composed of (1) an 80186 processor for performing the filtering functions by software means and the loading and unloading of data blocks between the disk and the local memory (LM), (2) a DMA module that allows data blocks to be moved between the disk and the LM in a direct memory access mode, (3) an EPROM for storing the system kernel, which controls disk transfers and communication with the front-end computer, and (4) a 512K-byte dynamic RAM—the LM—which stores the program code for filtering functions and two pools of source and target buffers. The filtering functions (e.g., selection and projection) are carried out using three processes, two buffer pools, and two first-in, first-out queues (FIFOs), as illustrated in Figure 4.18. These three processes follow.

1. *Data loading*. The loader loads the sequence of disk blocks of a source relation block-by-block into a source buffer. The buffer address is entered into F_1, one of the FIFOs.

2. *Data filtering*. The filter performs the filtering function on the block of records and stores the resulting data records into a free target buffer. If the target buffer is full, its address is entered into F_2, the second FIFO, and another target buffer is allocated. When all records in the source buffer have been processed, the source buffer is returned to the source buffer pool and another source block is obtained by popping F_1. It is assumed that data loading and filtering can be carried out concurrently.

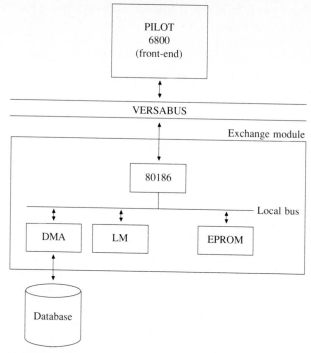

FIGURE 4.17
The architecture of a disk exchange module. (*Source:* [GAM85])

3. *Data unloading.* The unloader unloads the filled target buffer by writing its contents onto the disk or by sending the resulting records to the front-end computer. The buffer address is popped from F_2, and the buffer is returned to the target buffer pool.

These three processes operate in a pipeline fashion. The main difference between the hardware approach and the software approach is that the former uses

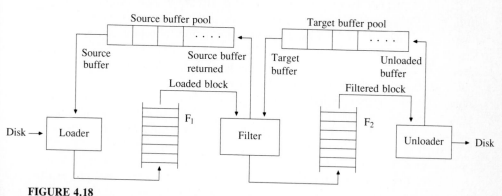

FIGURE 4.18
Three filtering processes. (*Source:* [GAM85])

the special-purpose automaton to perform filtering functions at very high speeds (approximately 400 ns per character) against all the characters of the source blocks, whereas the latter uses slower program codes (2.75 μs per character estimated) and software techniques to access selected disk blocks. A performance analysis study has been carried out to compare these two approaches. The results were reported by Gamerman and Scholl [GAM85] and are summarized as follows:

1. There is no question that the hardware approach is faster than the software approach. However, under the assumptions made in the study, the hardware approach does not perform three times faster than software filtering despite the fact that the hardware filter is much faster than the software code.
2. It is found that the hardware filter's speed is so high in relation to the speed of data transfers among the disk, the source buffer, the target buffer, and the RAM that it is idle more than half the time. A slower filter than VERSO will not degrade the performance of the overall system.
3. Although inferior to hardware filtering, software filtering provides an acceptable performance and has advantages in terms of flexibility in implementing different algorithms and ease of implementation and modification.

4.3.4   Architecture of DBC's Mass Memory and Its Filtering Technique

The Data Base Computer (DBC), designed at The Ohio State University, is an elaborate database computer consisting of a number of general-purpose and special-purpose machine components [BAN79]. One of the main components of the system is the mass memory, which uses a combination of software and hardware approaches to achieve the effect of data filtering [HSI76, and KAN78]. Only the design of the mass memory and its filtering technique will be described here. The DBC system itself will be described in Chapter 7.

4.3.4.1   ARCHITECTURE. The organization of the DBC's mass memory is shown in Figure 4.19. The mass memory consists of a mass memory controller (MMC), an I/O bus, and a mass memory information processor consisting of an array of track information processors (TIPs), a disk drive selector, a number of disk drive controllers, and a set of moving-head disks. Records of data files are clustered based on their common data properties and are stored together on the adjacent tracks of disk cylinders (i.e., related records are stored together in the same cylinder). An indexing scheme is used to allow direct access of cylinder contents. The layout of records on disk tracks is in a bit-serial and word-serial fashion. It is assumed that the disks have parallel read-out capability. If there are t tracks on a cylinder, t bits of data (one from each track) can be read in parallel by a selected disk drive controller. The disk drive selector activates a proper disk drive to transfer t streams of records out of a selected disk and deliver them

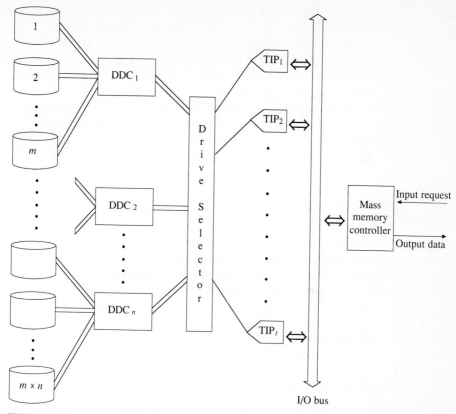

FIGURE 4.19
The mass memory organization of DBC. (*Source:* [HSI76] reprinted by permission of the author.)

to t track information processors in which the records in these data streams are processed.

A search command, in the form of a set of search predicates, is given to the MMC by a Data Base Command and Control Computer. The search predicates are simultaneously broadcast to the track information processors to be used to process against the t data streams. Each track information processor contains a record-length buffer to hold a record read from a bit stream. It processes a record at a time and outputs those records that satisfy the search predicates to MMC through the I/O bus. In turn, MMC passes the selected records to the computer, which issued the search request. Thus, the architecture of the mass memory is an SIMD architecture that provides content-addressing capabilities. It is the same as the cellular approach used in the intelligent secondary storage devices presented in Chapter 3 except that processing elements are dynamically associated with memory elements (the disk tracks) using moving-head disks.

4.3.4.2 TECHNIQUE. The mass memory design uses a combination of filtering techniques. First, the system uses a conventional clustering technique to place related data records together on disk cylinders and an indexing technique to allow only a selected number of cylinders to be accessed for processing by the track information processors. These are software techniques for reducing the amount of data to be fetched from the secondary storage, a great saving in secondary storage data transfer time. Second, the design allows parallel read-out of cylinder contents, which increases the bandwidth of the data channel between the disks and the track information processors. Finally, the array of information processors allows the filtering function (Selection) to be carried out in parallel over multiple streams of data records. The last two techniques are hardware techniques. Note that this design uses all three general approaches to the I/O bottleneck problem discussed in Section 4.1.

4.3.5 Architecture and Technique of DBM'S Data Filter

The Data Base Machine (DBM) designed by Yao, Tong, and Sheng [SHE81 and YAO81] at the University of Maryland is another example of a database computer that centers around the database filtering concept. Different from the database filters presented in the preceding sections, the filter components in this computer

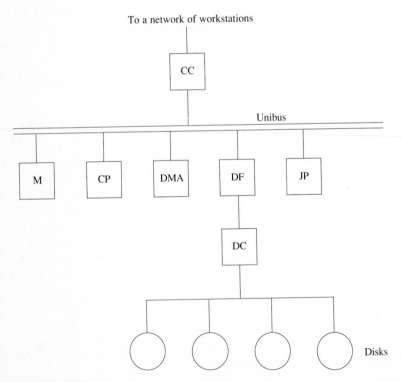

FIGURE 4.20
The organization of DBM. (*Source:* [YAO81] ©1981 IEEE)

are composed of a two-dimensional array of processors and the design is highly regular; thus, it is suitable for VLSI implementation.

4.3.5.1 ARCHITECTURE. The organization of DBM is shown in Figure 4.20. DBM is designed as a back-end computer that serves a network of workstations. Its main function is to retrieve and manipulate the data stored on the secondary storage in response to the queries issued to the workstations by users. A number of these DBMs can be used in the network, each of which can be assigned to a cluster of disks controlled by a disk controller (DC). The DBM itself consists of a main memory (M), a central processor (CP), a direct memory access controller (DMA), a filter named data filter (DF) for performing relational Select and Project operations, and another filter named join processor (JP) for performing relational Join operations. These components are connected together by a unibus to which the network communication controller (CC) is also connected. The components of interest are the two filters, which serve to reduce and transform, respectively, the data read from the disks to the CP.

The data filter is composed of a two-dimensional array of parallel comparators, as shown in Figure 4.21. These comparators are preloaded with the attributes and values specified in a selection operation. Data fetched from the secondary storage (the input stream) are broadcast to the comparators on the leftmost column of the array and are then passed sequentially to the comparators on

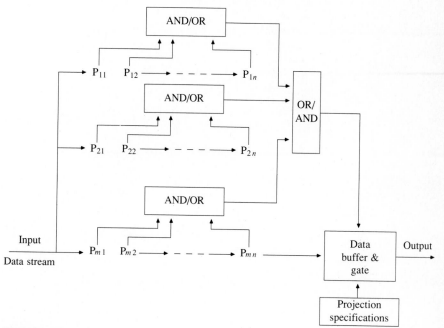

FIGURE 4.21
The selection processor array. (*Source:* [YAO81] ©1981 IEEE)

all the rows for data matching. The comparators on each row are connected to an AND/OR network, which evaluates the AND or the OR condition of the comparators' outputs. The results of all the AND/OR networks are again evaluated by an OR/AND network to determine the OR or AND condition of these results. These AND/OR and OR/AND networks are used to evaluate selection conditions expressed in disjunctive or conjunctive normal forms, as will be explained in Section 4.3.5.2.

The data buffer and gate component of Figure 4.21 holds the tuple read from the secondary storage. The projection specification and the output of the OR/AND network are used by this component to perform the Project operation over the selected tuples.

The join processor, which transforms data received from two inputs, is again a two-dimensional array of comparators, as shown in Figure 4.22. The processor array contains a number of buffers (labeled R and S in the figure) for storing the join values of two relations. Their contents are simultaneously broadcast to

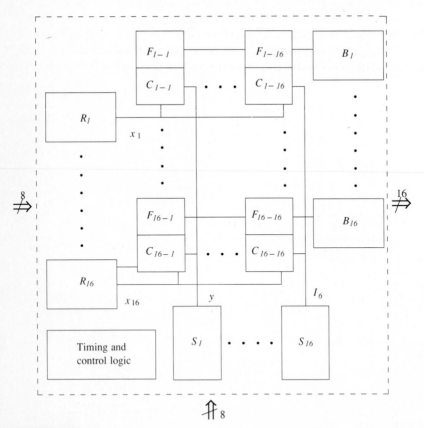

FIGURE 4.22
The system organization of the join processor array. (*Source:* [YAO81])

their corresponding rows and columns of comparators labeled as C. The output buffers, labeled as F, are used to store the addresses (or pointers) of the matched tuples. A set of bit matrix Bs are used to record if a value in an R buffer matches with a value in an S buffer. They are used to generate the join results. The operation of the join processor arrays is controlled by a timing and control logic unit.

4.3.5.2 TECHNIQUE. The Select operation issued against a relation is first transformed into a disjunctive (or conjunctive) normal form. Each clause of a disjunctive (conjunctive) normal form is a conjunction (disjunction) of predicates, each of which is composed of an attribute, a comparison operator, and an attribute value. The predicates of each clause are loaded in a row of comparators in the selection processor array. The relation that is to be searched forms a data stream and is transferred from the disk simultaneously to the first processors in all the rows. From there, the data are piped sequentially to all the processors in the rows (see Figure 4.21). As data pass by each processor, the processor evaluates the preloaded predicate against the data (to see if a tuple of a relation satisfies its comparison condition) and outputs a true or false value. The output of each row of comparators is sent to an AND/OR network, which evaluates the AND/OR condition of the results depending on whether the query is represented in disjunctive or conjunctive normal form. The results of all the rows are again evaluated by another OR/AND network to produce the final result. Thus, a complex search expression in disjunctive/conjunctive normal form can be processed in parallel against the tuples of a relation to select those that satisfy the expression. The Projection operation is performed on the selected tuples by suppressing the output of unprojected fields by the data buffer and gate component.

The Join operation is performed in the join processor array in the following manner. Assume that the two source relations are partitioned into x and y subrelations, respectively. The join values of these subrelations are projected out from the output of the selection processor array and are stored in x number of R buffers and y number of S buffers. The nested-loop algorithm is used to perform the Join operation. At the beginning of the operation, a set of x values from the R buffers is broadcast to x rows of comparators, while a set of y values is being broadcast to y columns of comparators in which these values are simultaneously compared. The results are recorded in the bit matrices. They, together with the addresses or pointers of the matched tuples stored in F buffers, are used by the central processor (CP of Figure 4.20) to generate the partial join results. After that, the next set of y values are broadcast to the comparators for comparison against the same set of x values. The process continues until all the values in S buffers have been compared. At this time, the next set of x values from the R buffers are transferred into the comparators, and the iteration through the values in the S buffers continues. The Join operation terminates after the last set of x values has been compared against the last set of y values.

4.4   ANALYSIS

This section analyzes the four representative database operations used throughout this book in the context of an abstract model for systems that use database filters. Cost formulas will be derived for some selected algorithms.

4.4.1   An Abstract Model for Systems with a Database Filter

The abstract model is shown in Figure 4.23. It consists of a terminal, a host computer, a database filter, and a number of disks. A user's query is submitted through the terminal to the host computer. It is translated into an internal representation, and a proper command is transferred to the database filter for processing. The data retrieved by the database filter are further processed by the host computer. The resulting relation is written to a disk and later collected for output to the user's terminal.

Assume that the database filter can perform a Selection operation on the fly as a referenced relation is being read from the disk to the filter's main memory. The tuples of a relation form a continuous stream of data that serves as the

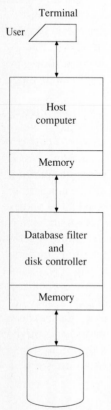

FIGURE 4.23
An abstract model for systems with a database filter.

input to the database filter. The filter contains a linear array of cells, each of which is loaded with a search predicate consisting of an attribute, a comparison operator, and a value. Each predicate forms a part of the search conditions of the Selection operation. The input stream of tuples are compared in parallel with the predicates loaded in the comparison cells. The output of these cells are evaluated to determine if the Boolean conditions of these predicates specified in the query are satisfied. Only those tuples that satisfy the search conditions are transferred into the filter's main memory. Also assume that the filter can perform the Join operation. This assumption is consistent with the designs of more advanced database filters such as VERSO.

4.4.2   Analyses of Algorithms

This section analyzes some algorithms for Select, Join, Statistical Aggregation, and Update operations. Table 4.1 shows the basic parameters used in the following analyses.

4.4.2.1   SELECT.   The instruction flow for this algorithm consists of the compilation of the selection query and the transfer of the selection command to the database filter for execution. Thus,

$$t[\text{inst\_flow}] = t[\text{comp}] + t[\text{tp\_xfer}]$$

The database filter reads m pages of the referenced relation R as a continuous stream of tuples. The input time is

$$t[\text{read, R}] = m * t[\text{I/O}]$$

Here, it is assumed that the relation R is stored in consecutive tracks and in consecutive cylinders. Only the first cylinder access involves the $t[\text{access}]$, which will be accounted for in the formula for $t[\text{process}]$ to be shown later. The small amount of time for the switching and intercylinder movements of read/write heads is ignored.

Since it is assumed that the filter can process data on the fly, the processing time for the Selection operation on the stream of tuples overlaps with the read time.

Assuming a selectivity factor of sel_fac, the number of output pages would be ceil(sel_fac $* m$). Since the resulting relation of a Selection operation may be too large to be stored in the database filter, it is assumed that the pages of the resulting relation L are written back to the disk as they are produced by the database filter. This assumption is a reasonable one, since the result of a Selection will generally be operated on by other relational operators; therefore, it needs to be established as a relation in the database. Consistent with the assumption made in the conventional system model described in Chapter 2, the time required to write the pages of L is

$$t[\text{I/O}, L] = \text{ceil}(\text{sel\_fac} * m) * t[\text{I/O}])$$

TABLE 4.1
Performance parameters

Parameter	Definition
R	Name of a referenced relation
m	Number of pages in relation R
S	Name of the inner relation in a Join operation
s	Number of pages in relation S
L	Name of the resulting relation of an operation
jn_fac	Join selectivity factor; that is, the ratio of the number of tuples of L to the number of tuples of the crossproduct between R and S
q	Number of tracks in a disk cylinder
sel_fac	Selectivity factor for the Selection operation; that is, the ratio of the number of selected tuples of a referenced relation to the number of tuples of that relation
t	Number of tuples per page of R or S
u	Total number of pages of L produced by joining relations R and S
w	Number of distinct categories in statistical aggregation
t[access]	Disk seek time plus latency
t[comp]	Compilation time for a simple query
t[cpu]	Time for comparing two values in registers or an arithmetic operation
t[I/O]	Track (page) read/write time
t[mov]	Time for moving a tuple of R or S
t[s]	Time to load a value from the memory to a register
t[tp_out]	Time for transferring a tuple to an output buffer associated with the user-interface device (e.g., a terminal)
t[xfer]	Time for transferring a page between two processors
t[tp_xfer]	Time for transferring a tuple or an instruction between two processors

Since the writing of L pages occurs while the system still needs to read and process the pages of R, relation L must be written to a separate disk from that of R. Therefore, the total processing time for this algorithm is

$$t[\text{process}] = 2*t[\text{access}] + t[\text{read}, R] + t[\text{I/O}, L]$$

The data collection for this algorithm consists of reading the pages of L back from the disk into the memory of the filter, transferring these pages to the host computer, and writing the tuples in these pages to the user's terminal. The collection time is

$$t[\text{data\_collect}] = t[\text{access}] + t[\text{I/O}, L] + \text{ceil}(\text{sel\_fac} * m)$$
$$* t[\text{xfer}] + \text{sel\_fac} * m * t * t[\text{tp\_out}]$$

The total execution time for this algorithm is

$$t[\text{Select}] = t[\text{inst\_flow}] + t[\text{process}] + t[\text{data\_collect}]$$

4.4.2.2 JOIN. In this algorithm, the join query is compiled by the host computer, and its internal representation (a join command and join attributes and join condition) is transferred to the filter for execution. The instruction flow time is

$$t[\text{inst\_flow}] = t[\text{comp}] + t[\text{tp\_xfer}]$$

The relations in this model are assumed to be presorted by some keys, just as in VERSO. If the join attributes are the same as the sort keys, the Join operation can be carried out by the filter by merging the two sorted relations. If they are not the sort keys, the relations are first sorted before they are merged to produce the join results. Here, assume that the relations R and S must be sorted first. The analysis of the sort-merge algorithm for the Join operation has been presented in Chapter 2. The result of the analysis is used here.

$$t[\text{process}] = \log_4(m) * t[\text{merge\_sort\_pg}, R]$$
$$+ \log_4(s) * t[\text{merge\_sort\_pg}, S]$$
$$+ t[\text{merge}] + t[\text{access}] + t[\text{I/O}, L]$$

The data collection time consists of reading those pages of L from disk, transferring these pages to the host computer, and outputting all the tuples of L to the user's terminal.

$$t[\text{data\_collect}] = t[\text{access}] + u * t[\text{I/O}] + t[\text{I/O}, L] + u * t * t[\text{tp\_out}]$$

For the explanations of the terms used in the expressions for $t[\text{process}]$ and $t[\text{data\_collect}]$, see Section 2.3.2.

The total execution time of this algorithm is

$$t[\text{Join}] = t[\text{inst\_flow}] + t[\text{process}] + t[\text{data\_collect}]$$

4.4.2.3 STATISTICAL AGGREGATION. Since the data filter in this model is assumed to have the sorting and merging capabilities, the sort-merge algorithm is used for this operation. The analysis is very similar to that presented for the conventional system model in Section 2.3.3.

The instruction flow time is

$$t[\text{inst\_flow}] = t[\text{comp}] + t[\text{tp\_xfer}]$$

The data processing time consists of two time components. First, the time to sort the relation R has been shown to be

$$\log_4(m) * t[\text{merge\_sort\_pg}, R]$$

Second, the time for aggregating the summary attribute values has been shown to be

$$m * t * (t[s] + t[\text{cpu}]) + w * t[\text{mov}]$$

Assuming that the resulting relation L containing w tuples is small enough to be kept in the filter's memory, the data processing time for this algorithm is

$$t[\text{process}] = \log_4(m) * t[\text{merge\_sort\_pg}, R] + m * t * (t[s] + t[\text{cpu}]) + w * t[\text{mov}]$$

The data collection time for this algorithm consists of transferring $\text{ceil}(w/t)$ pages of L to the host computer, and all tuples in these pages are output to the user's terminal.

$$t[\text{data\_collect}] = \text{ceil}(w/t) * t[\text{xfer}] + w * t[\text{tp\_out}]$$

The total execution time for this algorithm is

$$t[\text{Aggregate}] = t[\text{inst\_flow}] + t[\text{process}] + t[\text{data\_collect}]$$

4.4.2.4 UPDATE. In this algorithm, the tuples of the referenced relation R, which satisfy some selection conditions, are first retrieved by the host computer page by page. The selected tuples in each page are then updated and written back to a disk. The instruction flow time is

$$t[\text{inst\_flow}] = t[\text{comp}] + t[\text{tp\_xfer}]$$

where $t[\text{tp\_xfer}]$ accounts for the transfer of the selection command to the filter.

As in the analysis of the selection algorithm, the selection phase of the Update operation can be carried out during the time the relation R is being read from the disk. The processing time for the selection phase, including the time to transfer pages of selected tuples, is

$$t[\text{select}, R] = t[\text{access}] + m * t[\text{I/O}] + \text{ceil}(\text{sel\_fac} * m) * t[\text{xfer}]$$

As in Chapter 2, assume that the tuple update time is $(2 * t[s] * t[\text{cpu}])$. The time for updating all the selected tuples, page by page, and writing them back to disk is

$$\begin{aligned} t[\text{update\_write}, L] = {} & \text{sel\_fac} * m * t * (2 * t[s] + t[\text{cpu}]) \\ & + \text{ceil}(\text{sel\_fac} * m) * (t[\text{xfer}] + t[\text{I/O}]) \\ & + t[\text{access}] \end{aligned}$$

The total data processing time for this algorithm is

$$t[\text{process}] = t[\text{select}, R] + t[\text{update\_write}, L]$$

Since no output to the user's terminal is involved in an update operation, the total execution time would be

$$t[\text{Update}] = t[\text{inst\_flow}] + t[\text{process}]$$

The analyses and cost formulas presented here do not account for the possible overlaps between the processing time of the filter and the data transfer times between the secondary storage and the filter and between the filter and the host computer. Some changes to the formulas are necessary to account for the overlaps. Those readers who are interested in the performance of this model under a specific computing environment should assign the proper values to the parameters (shown in Table 4.1) that best represent the environment and vary, in particular, the values for m, s, sel_fac, $t[I/O]$, and $t[xfer]$ to determine their effects on the overall processing time of the algorithms. Similar to the model for intelligent secondary storage devices presented in Chapter 3, this model is particularly sensitive to the quantities of output data transferred from the secondary storage, to the filter, and to the host computer.

4.5 SUMMARY AND DISCUSSION

This chapter detailed the problem of the I/O bottleneck found in conventional computers and the general approaches useful for solving this problem. The concept of data filtering was then presented. The architectures and filtering techniques of five filters were described and illustrated. Based on an abstract model for systems with a database filter, analyses of algorithms for four representative database operations were presented and cost formulas for these algorithms were derived.

A database filter is a special-purpose processor placed between secondary storage devices and a front-end computer. Its main function is to reduce the amount of data to be transferred from the secondary storage to the front-end by filtering out those data that do not satisfy some search criterion. It can also restructure or combine files to produce data that are useful to the front-end computer.

Five different architectures were presented in this chapter. CAFS uses a number of parallel comparators or key registers, which independently verify if the records in a single data stream satisfy the various conditions assigned to these comparators. In SURE, an array of more sophisticated processors (as compared to the key registers of CAFS), that is, the search modules, are used. These search modules can execute separate queries against a single stream of records feeding into these modules. Although both CAFS and SURE have an MISD architecture, the former exploits intraquery concurrency by verifying multiple search conditions at the same time, whereas the latter exploits parallelism by executing multiple queries concurrently.

VERSO provides an example of the compilation approach, which uses compiled programs to drive a special-purpose automaton to perform unary and binary operations at a speed less than the ordinary disk transfer rate. It has an SISD architecture and offers great flexibility in modifying the operation of the automaton. The mass memory module of the DBC has an SIMD architecture. The parallel-processing power offered by the track information processors and the speed of data transfer provided by the parallel read-out capability of the disks allow the data filtering task to be carried out on the fly as selected cylinder contents are being read by a processor. The DBM uses two-dimensional arrays of parallel comparators to gain speed in performing the relational Selection, Projection, and Join operations.

Several points about the database filtering approach must be mentioned here. First, the time savings gained by using a database filter is not due to the savings in disk read time, since all records of a file need to be read into the filter from the secondary storage; rather, it is due to the reduction in the amount of data transferred between the filter and the host computer's main memory. From the host computer's viewpoint, the file it reads has been reduced or transformed by the database filter. Thus, the database filtering approach only eases the I/O bottleneck rather than eliminating it completely.

Second, hardware for performing some database operations, such as Selection and Projection without the removal of duplicates, are easy to implement and can operate at the speed of the disk. Hardware for supporting other types of operations, such as Join and Statistical Aggregation operations, are more difficult. Special-purpose hardware (e.g., a sorter and merger) need to be incorporated into a database filter to allow it to process these operations on the fly. As the capability of a filter is extended to do more complex database operations, it may soon reach the level of complexity close to a dedicated database computer (or called a back-end computer), to be described in Chapter 7. The original concept of a simple filtering device for data reduction and transformation may soon be lost.

Third, a database filter is usually used as a component of a larger database computer. It will be effective to pair a database filter with each disk (or other secondary storage device) in a multidisk system for data filtering purposes.

Lastly, quantitative evaluation and comparison of different approaches to database filtering is not available, and the hardware costs associated with these approaches are not known. The temptation for a designer is to increase the number and complexity of functions in a database filter. However, this may not justify the hardware cost.

4.6 BIBLIOGRAPHY

[BAB79] Babb, E.: "Implementing a Relational Database by Means of Specialized Hardware," *ACM Trans. on Database Systems,* vol. 4, no. 1, 1979, pp. 1–29.

[BAN80] Bancilhon, F., and Scholl, M.: "Design of a Backend Processor for a Data Base Machine," *Proceedings of ACM's SIGMOD 1980 International Conference on Management of Data,* May 1980, pp. 93–93g.

[BAN83] Bancilhon, F., Richard, P., and Scholl, M.: "VERSO: The Relational Database Machine," in D. Hsiao (ed.), *Advanced Database Machine Architecture,* Prentice-Hall, Englewood Cliffs, N.J., 1983, pp. 1–18.

[BAN79] Banerjee, J., and Hsiao, D. K.: "Concepts and Capabilities of a Database Computer," *ACM TODS,* vol. 4, no. 1, March 1979, pp. 1–29.

[DAT75] Date, C. J.: *An Introduction to Database Systems,* Addison-Wesley, Reading, Mass., 1975.

[GAM85] Gamerman, S., and Scholl, M.: "Hardware Versus Software Data Filtering: The VERSO Experience," *Proceedings of the Fourth International Workshop on Database Machines,* Grand Bahama Island, March 6–8, 1985, pp. 112–136.

[HSI76] Hsiao, D., and Kannon, K., "The Architecture of a Database Computer Part III: The Design of the Mass Memory and its Related Components," OSU-CISRC-76-3, Ohio State University, December 1976.

[KAN78] Kannon, K., "The Design of a Mass Memory for a Database Computer," *Proceedings of the Fifth Annual Symposium on Computer Architecture,* April 1978, pp. 44–51.

[KAR76] Karlowsky, I., Leilich, H. O., and Zeidler, H. C.: "Content Addressing in Data Base by Special Peripheral Hardware: A Proposal Called 'Search Processor,'" Informatik Fachberichte Nr. 4, Springer Verlag Berlin-Heidelberg, New York, 1976, pp. 113–131.

[LEI78] Leilich, H. O., Stiege, G., and Zeidler, H. C.: "A Search Processor for Data Base Management Systems," *Proceedings of the Fourth International Conference on Very Large Data Bases,* Sept. 15–18, 1978, pp. 280–287.

[SHE81] Sheng, Y. Z., Tong, F., and Yao, S. B.: "Data Filter—A Relational Selection Processor," Tech. Report, Database Research Lab., University of Maryland, College Park, Md., Oct. 1981.

[YAO81] Yao, S. B., Tong, F., and Sheng, Y. Z., "The System Architecture of a Data Base Machine (DBM)," *IEEE Database Engineering Bulletin,* vol. 4, no. 2, 1981, pp. 53–62.

CHAPTER

5

ASSOCIATIVE MEMORY SYSTEMS FOR DATABASE MANAGEMENT

Chapter 1 detailed some limitations of the main memory of conventional computer systems and noted that they contribute to the inefficiency of using conventional systems for database applications. These limitations are:

1. The size of the main memory is generally too small for storing large data files.
2. Data in the main memory must be located by addresses rather than by content or context.
3. Memory words are accessed and processed one at a time by a single processor.
4. Unless the addresses of some selected words are stored and maintained, the memory hardware is not able to locate the selected words directly.

The first limitation is due to the size of the memory address register or the bandwidth (i.e., the number of address lines) of the internal bus connecting the memory and the central processor of a computer system. It has been partially alleviated in large systems which use 128 megabyte memory or more. A large main memory allows large quantities of data to be paged from secondary storage devices into the memory for processing. It reduces the amount of I/O operations and thus the I/O time required to process large data files, since less overhead is involved when large quantities of data are transferred in each I/O operation.

The other three limitations can be removed by using more "intelligent" memory systems. This chapter will describe the architectures and techniques used in a number of associative memory systems that possess hardware features that can alleviate these limitations of the conventional main memory.

5.1 ARCHITECTURE AND FEATURES OF ASSOCIATIVE MEMORIES

An *associative memory* is a memory device that is content-addressable in that data stored in the memory can be accessed by specifying the contents of its memory words rather than by specifying their addresses. An *associative memory system* is a computer system that uses one or more than one associative memory as the main component of the system. Since processors are always paired with memory elements in all the designs and implementations of associative memories, the term *associative processor* is regarded as synonymous with *associative memory* in this chapter.

Research and development work in associative memories was very active during the late 1950s and early 1960s. Applications of this type of memory device in small-scale numeric and nonnumeric processing were extensively discussed in the literature during that time period. It was not until the 1970s that the use of associative memories for database management applications was investigated. Associative memories have been used in systems developed for signal processing, pattern recognition, information retrieval, database management, memory address translation, and so forth. This chapter details the systems for database management applications.

There are two main features of an associative memory that are very desirable for database management. First, the intelligence (or logic for processing data) is distributed among the memory elements, each of which may store a single bit, a byte, or larger quantity of data. In other words, each memory element is paired with a processing element, and the contents of all memory elements can be examined and manipulated simultaneously by their corresponding processing elements. It is this parallel-processing capability that offers tremendous computational power for processing large quantities of data efficiently.

Second, associative memories offer the content-addressing and context-addressing capabilities. Any data item or combination of data items to be searched in an associative memory is broadcast to all the processing elements. These elements simultaneously compare the data item (the search operand) stored in a comparand register against the contents of their associated memory elements. Those memory elements whose data satisfy the search condition are flagged by setting bits in a response store that contains one or several bits for each memory element. The contents of the response store can then be used as the context for the next content search or as the markers for controlling the output of the memory elements' contents. Boolean operations can be performed on the contents of the response store to determine if the memory elements contain bit or field patterns that satisfy a search request expressed in a Boolean expression. Content-addressing and context-addressing techniques have been explained and illustrated in Chapter 3. The intelligent secondary storage devices presented in that chapter are, in fact, one type of associative memory, as will be explained in the next section. The content and context capabilities allow data to be stored in a form that closely resembles how the user views it. They also offer great flexibility in data searches, since any data item can be searched as easily as any other item. In fact, all items are searched by content in each memory scan. This is not true in the existing DBMSs in which indexed data items can be searched much faster than nonindexed items.

Based on the degree of distribution of processing logic, that is, the amount of memory associated with each processing element, Yau and Fung [YAU77] classify associative processors/memories into the following four categories: (1) fully parallel associative memories, (2) bit-serial associative memories, (3) word-serial associative memories, and (4) block-oriented associative memories.

5.1.1 Fully Parallel Associative Memories

In a fully parallel associative memory, a file is treated as a two-dimensional array of bits or a single stream of bits with one row following the other. Each bit has a processing element, which contains logic for comparing the bit against a bit provided by a processor external to the associative memory, and a response store (a single bit) for recording the result of the comparison. The memory element and the processing element form a cell. Thus, all bits in the associative memory can be examined simultaneously. This architecture is illustrated by Figure 5.1a. In this figure, each square represents a memory element containing one bit and the symbol in the square represents a processing element. This architecture provides maximal parallelism since all bits and all words can be searched in parallel (bit-parallel and word-parallel). However, such a memory device would be very expensive to build since a very large number of cells would be necessary for storing and processing a practical database, and a complex interconnection of these cells would be necessary so that words, data items, or records in the bit array or string can be matched and recognized.

To reduce the number of cells, to simplify the interconnection, and to make it more economically feasible for data management applications, each memory element may be enlarged to store a whole data item or a simple pattern of data items instead of a single bit. In this case, all items or patterns of items can still be compared in parallel with an item or a pattern of items (i.e., the search operand) provided to the associative memory from an external source. The early associative memories proposed by Lee and Paull [LEE63] and Savitt, Love, and Troop [SAV67] used this approach. They can be considered as fully parallel associative memories. The architectures of these systems will be described in Sections 5.3.1 and 5.3.2.

5.1.2 Bit-Serial Associative Memories

In a bit-serial associative memory, a vector of processing elements is used to process a vertical bit slice of the memory words (see Figure 5.1b). The bit slices of the memory are processed serially by the same vector of processing elements,

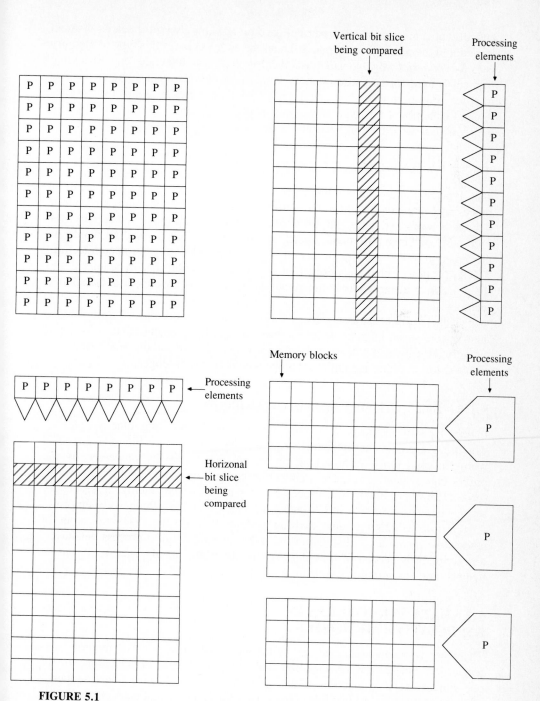

FIGURE 5.1
(*a*) Fully parallel associative memory. (*b*) Bit-serial associative memory. (*c*) Word-serial associative memory. (*d*) Block-oriented associative memory.

and all words are compared in parallel (one bit at a time) with the search operand loaded into the processing elements. Thus, the architecture of this type of memory is called *bit-serial word-parallel architecture*. In this architecture, one processing element is used for an entire memory word. It represents a considerable savings in processing logic when compared with the fully parallel associative memories. A good example of this type of memory is the STARAN [RUD72 and GOO75], which will be described in Section 5.3.3.

5.1.3   Word-Serial Associative Memories

This type of memory is similar to the bit-serial memory except the vector of processing elements has the same number of elements as the number of bits in a memory word and horizontal bit slices (i.e., words) are processed serially (see Figure 5.1c). Since all bits of a word are processed in parallel and all words are processed in serial, this type of memory has a bit-parallel word-serial architecture. STARAN allows either a horizontal bit slice or a vertical bit slice to be loaded into the processing elements for comparison. Therefore, it is a word-serial associative memory also.

If the width of an associative memory is narrow as compared to its length, then a word-serial memory requires fewer processing elements than a bit-serial memory. However, it will have less degree of parallelism and the processing time required for scanning the entire memory would be much longer.

5.1.4   Block-Oriented Associative Memories

In this type of memory, the entire memory is divided into blocks, each of which has a processing element to examine its contents (see Figure 5.1d). The words in each block form a long bit stream that is serially processed by the processing element. Thus, the architecture can be considered as bit-serial word-serial. However, blocks are processed in parallel. The intelligent secondary storage devices described in Chapter 3 are block-oriented associative memories.

Before examining some existing systems that use the first three types of associative memories and studying the techniques they use to process databases, a description is needed of how data and relationships among data items can be mapped and structured in associative memories.

5.2   DATA STRUCTURES IN ASSOCIATIVE MEMORIES

There are two data organizations commonly used in associative memory systems: one-dimensional organization and two-dimensional organization. In the one-dimensional organization, a data file can be considered a linear sequence of records. Each record is a linear sequence of characters, and each character is a linear sequence of bits. A linear array of processing elements can be assigned to some predetermined units of data. These can be individual bits, attribute values, composite values, records, or blocks of records. These data units are stored in the cell memory elements and are searched by content and processed in parallel by the processing element of each cell.

The data organization proposed by Lee and Paull [LEE63] provides an example of this organization. In this early associative memory system, the associative memory is composed of a linear array of cells, each of which contains a memory for storing a string of data elements and a processing element for examining the memory contents. The architecture of this system will be described in more detail in Section 5.3.1 . In each cell memory, when a string is to be stored, each component of the string is prefixed by a different tag, say #, followed by a number i to mark the beginning of the ith item and is postfixed by a unique tag, say $, to mark its end. Another special symbol, say &, is used to mark the beginning of a string. Thus, if a string of data elements denoted by $(x_1, x_2, x_3, x_4, x_5)$ is to be stored in a cell memory, it will take the following physical form:

$$(\&\#\_1x\_1\$\#\_2x\_2\$\#\_x\_3\$\#\_4x\_4\$\#\_5x\_5\$)$$

where $\#_i$'s are different tags for the components. The same tags can be used for other strings stored in the cell. Note that each component may contain an arbitrary number of symbols from an alphabet (e.g., CTITLE). If a search is to be made for a component x_4 in the entire associative memory so that all strings containing x_4 are to be output, the string $(\#_4x_4\$)$ would be broadcast to all the cells for content search against the cell memories. The cells that satisfy the search condition will be marked for output of their data. The number of components stored in a cell depends on the cell memory size and the amount of logic built into each processing element to compare the components against the contents of a search operand. The hardware architecture and techniques used to support this type of data organization will be described in the next section.

One problem with the use of special tags to separate data components is that a proper tag needs to be used to create the proper search operand. This implies that a directory needs to be maintained for associating tags with data components and a dictionary look-up is needed to determine the proper tag associated with each component.

In the two-dimensional organization, data are stored in a two-dimensional array, which is the physical organization of an associative memory. The records of a file are stored on separate rows (or words) of the array. If a record is too large to fit into a single row, it can be split into multiple sections, each of which has a different section tag (stored in the memory as a separate field) for distinguishing the sections and each of which contains the primary key field to facilitate content searches. If the file is too large to fit into the associative memory, a block or page of records can be moved into the array one at a time for content search or multiple memory modules can be used to store the records. If the files to be processed are small, multiple files can be stored in the same array, each of which is labeled by a separate tag. The tags can be used as a part of the search conditions to distinguish different files. Figure 5.2 shows one possible data layout of records from two files. It illustrates the possible data organization discussed here.

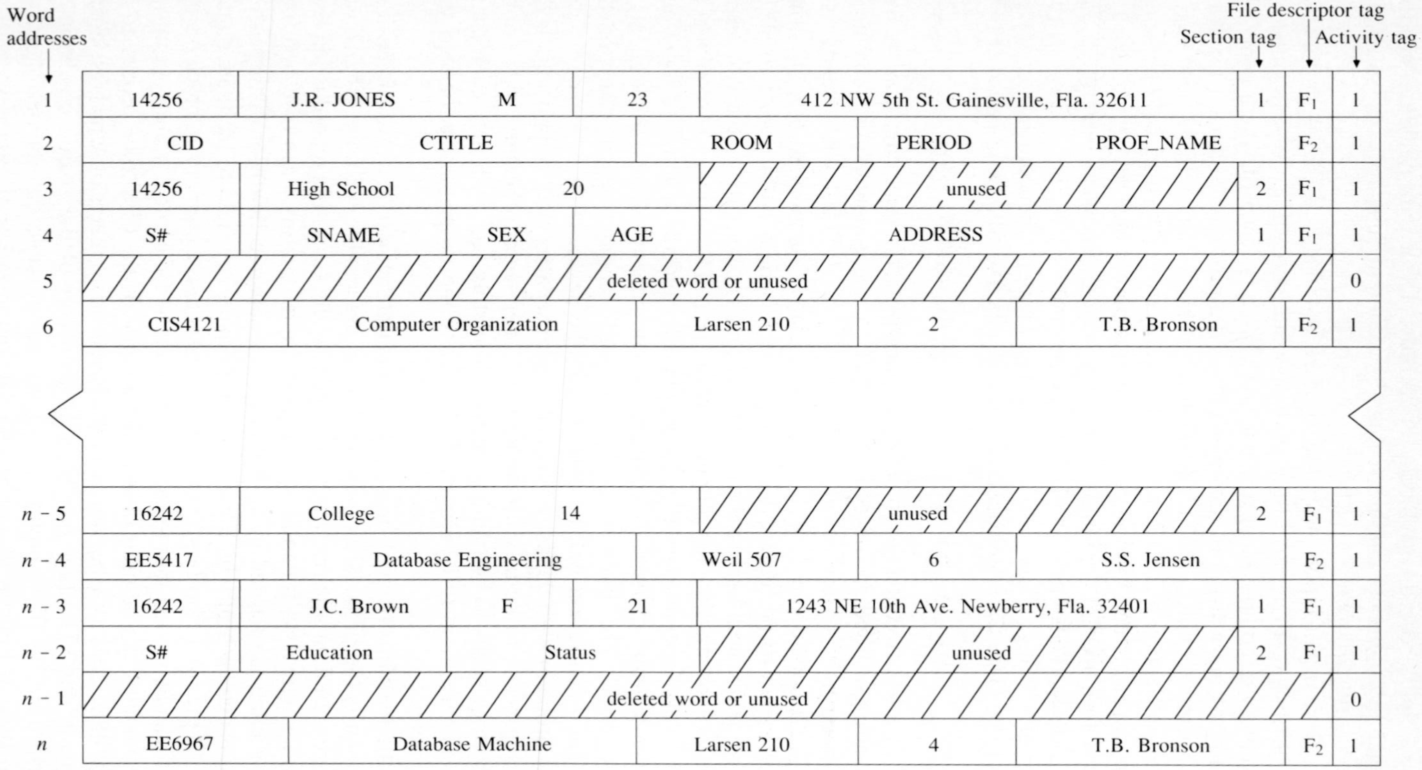

Word addresses →

Word address						Section tag	File descriptor tag	Activity tag
1	14256	J.R. JONES	M	23	412 NW 5th St. Gainesville, Fla. 32611	1	F_1	1
2	CID	CTITLE			PERIOD / ROOM / PROF_NAME		F_2	1
3	14256	High School	20	unused		2	F_1	1
4	S#	SNAME	SEX	AGE	ADDRESS	1	F_1	1
5	deleted word or unused							0
6	CIS4121	Computer Organization	Larsen 210	2	T.B. Bronson		F_2	1
⋮								
n − 5	16242	College	14	unused		2	F_1	1
n − 4	EE5417	Database Engineering	Weil 507	6	S.S. Jensen		F_2	1
n − 3	16242	J.C. Brown	F	21	1243 NE 10th Ave. Newberry, Fla. 32401	1	F_1	1
n − 2	S#	Education	Status		unused	2	F_1	1
n − 1	deleted word or unused							0
n	EE6967	Database Machine	Larsen 210	4	T.B. Bronson		F_2	1

FIGURE 5.2
Data organization in an associative array.

In Figure 5.2, the STUDENT and COURSE files are explicitly tagged by file descriptor F_1 and F_2, respectively. The STUDENT file is divided into two sections labeled by section tags 1 and 2. The activity tag can be one-bit wide. It is used to indicate if a word contains useful data (tag = '1') or has been deleted (tag = '0'). Notice that in this organization the sections of a record or the records of different files do not have to be stored in consecutive order. This is because they are searched by content rather than by address. Their physical locations in the memory are not important and their relationships (i.e., belonging to the same record or file) are identified by their common tags. This is a very significant characteristic of an associative memory, since the space occupied by deleted words can be reused for other records as long as the space is large enough. The system does not have to move the records around in order to keep them in consecutive order. However, it should be noted that since files stored in the secondary storage are stored in a sequential order, records of a file will normally be loaded into the associative memory in a consecutive order.

There are drawbacks in this organization that should be mentioned. First, the section and file descriptor tags can occupy a considerable amount of space, if the number of sections and files are large, since each tag may take many bits. More tag fields will be needed to store a hierarchically structured file by nesting sections within sections. Since associative memories are generally quite small due to their building cost, one should avoid using an excessive amount of space for implementing file or record structures.

Second, the data field formats of the sections or records can be different. In order to search the data by content, it is necessary to predetermine the formats of different fields so that a proper search operand and a mask can be constructed to pick up the proper field values for comparison. If special tags are used to separate the data fields, as are used in the one-dimensional organization, the same problem of deciding which tag to use in a search operand also exists in the two-dimensional case.

The first drawback does not have a good solution. If the structures of files in a database are complex, wider memory words would be beneficial since they would leave enough space for storing the actual data. The second drawback, however, can be removed if all data items are coded into a standard size so that all field boundaries are fixed in the memory. However, the translation of a variable-length item into a fixed-size value needs to be done frequently. This would involve a table look-up operation, which is a good candidate for associative processing. The system RELACS [OLI79] uses associative memories to store the translation table as well as the coded data. More details about this system will be given in the next section.

More complex data structures can also be implemented in an associative memory. For example, a hierarchically structured file F_1 (i.e., an unnormalized relation in the relational terminology) can be represented as follows:

$$F_1(A_1, A_2, A_3(A_{31}, A_{32}, A_{33}), A_4)$$

where A_1, A_2, and A_4 are attributes whose values are atomic and A_3 is an attribute whose values are nonatomic. Each value of A_3 is defined over attributes A_{31}, A_{32}, and A_{33}. The file can be transformed into what is called an Associative Normal Form (ANF) by DeFiore, Stillman, and Berra [DEF71] as follows:

$$F_1(A_1, A_2, A_4, \$)$$
$$A_3(A_{31}, A_{32}, A_{33}, \$)$$

where $\$$ is a special attribute whose atomic values are used to explicitly label the nesting relationship between the occurrences of F_1 and A_3. In effect, the introduction of this new attribute, $\$$, allows the hierarchical structure to be represented as normalized relations. The resulting relations can be stored in an associative memory, as illustrated in Figure 5.2. If the hierarchical structure of a record type contains many levels of nested record types, a level field can be introduced for each level of nesting to indicate the parentage of the record types. For example, as proposed by Moulder [MOU73], a three-level nesting of record types represented by

$$F_1(A_1, A_2, F_2, (B_1, B_2, F_3(C_1, C_2), B_3), A_3)$$

is stored in an associative memory as the following set of normalized record types:

$$F_1(A_1, A_2, A_3, L_1, L_2, L_3)$$
$$F_2(B_1, B_2, B_3, L_1, L_2, L_3)$$
$$F_3(C_1, C_2, L_1, L_2, L_3)$$

where L_1, L_2, and L_3 are the three-level fields introduced to explicitly label the nesting relationship among the record types. Thus, an occurrence of F_3 may have $L_1 = 4$, $L_2 = 2$, and $L_3 = 5$ to indicate that the occurrence belongs to the fourth record occurrence of F_1, the second occurrence of F_2 nested in the F_1 occurrence, and the fifth occurrence of F_3 nested in the F_2 occurrence.

A semantic net structure can also be mapped into an associative array. For example, as proposed by Savitt, Love, and Troop [SAV67], complex semantic information can be represented by a network structure of relations. A *relation* in this context can be represented by a triplet (A, R, B), where A and B are data items related by a link R. It can also be represented by a directed graph (see Figure 5.3a). An item in a relation may itself be a relation, as shown graphically in Figure 5.3b. An item in a semantic net can be linked to any number of items or relations. It can also be pointed to by any number of items and relations. An example of such a graph is shown in Figure 5.4, which contains some student

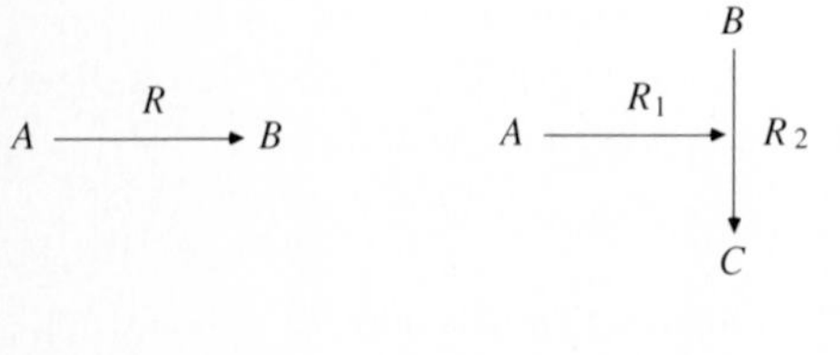

FIGURE 5.3
(*a*) A relation. (*b*) A relation with a compound item.

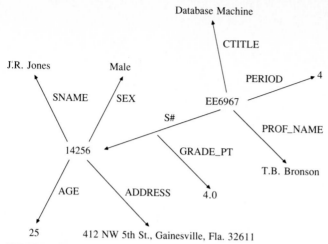

FIGURE 5.4
Some STUDENT and COURSE data in graphic form.

and course data from Figure 2.9. This graph can be stored in a two-dimensional array of cells (see Figure 5.5) in which data items, links, and relations are stored in separate cells. A relation is stored in a cell by the cell addresses of its data items and link. For example, the cell addressed by row 4 and column 2 contains a relation represented by three addresses: (1,1) is the address of the student number 14256; (1,2) is the address of the link SNAME; and (6,4) is the address of the student's name J. R. JONES. The hardware of the association-storing processor (ASP) proposed by Savitt, Love, and Troop [SAV67] supports the processing of this data structure. The hardware system will be described in the next section.

It should be obvious from this description of data structures and their mappings into associative memories that any complex data structure can be transformed into a structure that can be processed by an associative memory. However, this does not mean that the transformed structure would necessarily be efficient for the associative memory. The structure must match the capability of the hardware system. This explains why different associative memories use different structures to store their data.

5.3   ARCHITECTURES AND PROCESSING TECHNIQUES OF ASSOCIATIVE MEMORY SYSTEMS

This section examines the architectures and techniques of some selected systems. In several instances, the architectural features of these systems are highlighted while their detailed hardware designs are not. For more detail, interested readers should examine the references provided in this section.

	1	2	3	4	5
1	14256	SNAME	PERIOD	CTITLE	Database Machine
2	4.0	AGE	4		EE6967
3	ADDRESS	PROF_NAME	(1,1) (2,2) (6,5)	T.B. Bronson	(5,4) (6,1) (2,1)
4	(1,1) (3,1) (4,4)	(1,1) (1,2) (6,4)	SEX	412 NW • • • • • •	(2,5) (3,2) (3,4)
5		(1,1) (4,3) (5,5)	S#	(2,5) (5,3) (1,1)	Male
6	GRADE_PT	(2,5) (1,3) (2,3)	(2,5) (1,4) (1,5)	J.R. Jones	23

FIGURE 5.5
Data organization in an associative array.

5.3.1   A Content-Addressable Distributed Logic Memory

The content-addressable distributed logic memory proposed by Lee and Paull [LEE63] is one of the early associative systems designed specifically for information retrieval applications. It is composed of a linear array of identical sequential machines called *cells*. These cells are interconnected by a bus consisting of control and data lines, (see Figure 5.6). Through these control and data lines, a control computer controls the operations of this distributed logic memory. Each cell contains circuits for inputting and outputting data from and to the control

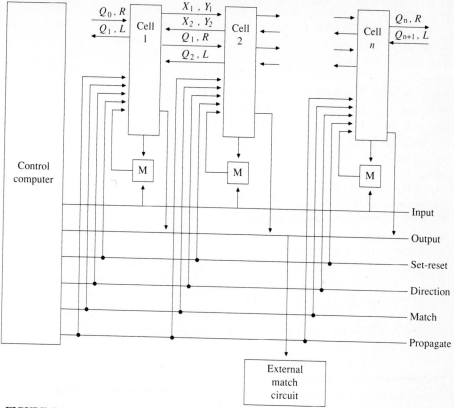

FIGURE 5.6

The architecture of a content-addressable distributed logic memory. (*Source:* [LEE63] ©1963 IEEE)

computer, matching data stored in the cell memory elements against some search operand provided by the control computer, and propagating status and signals to the left or right in the linear array of cells. The memory elements of these cells are formed by bi-stable devices such as relays and flip-flops. Each memory element of a cell contains two "activity" flip-flops named X and Y. It also contains n "symbol" flip-flops for holding n symbols from an alphabet (e.g., n characters of an attribute value), where n is a design parameter that determines the size of a memory element. Thus, the state and symbol of a cell represent the contents of the cell.

The *input* line in the figure represents a number of control and data lines through which data can be transferred into the cell memory. The Input operation is controlled by an input circuit. Similarly, the *output* line in the figure represents a set of output lines for the cells to output data to the control computer. The *set-reset* lines allow the control computer to set or reset the activity flip-flops.

The *match* line is used by the control computer to activate a Match operation. It resets a match flip-flop (external to the cell memory; not shown in the figure) before the Match operation. At the end of a Match operation, the match flip-flop signals if a match is found in the cell memory. Two *direction* lines control the direction of propagating the activity signals to the left or right neighbor(s). A propagation is activated by setting the *propagation* line and by selecting a direction. The activity signals are transferred through the X and Y lines connecting the cells. In addition to the activity lines, a set of *step-propagation* lines, which are designated by a Q in the figure and controlled by a propagation circuit, allows the propagation signals to travel from cell to cell. The purpose of propagating X and Y activities will be given in an example later.

Since the Match operation is the main operation of an associative memory, the match circuit proposed by Lee and Paull [LEE63] will be explained here. Figure 5.7 shows the match circuit of the ith cell and the associated control and data lines. X_i and Y_i are the activity flip-flops, and $a_1(i),...a_n(i)$ holds the symbol stored in the ith cell. The control line M is made active during matching, and the content of every cell is compared against the bit pattern of $X, X', Y, Y', a_1, a_2', ...a_n, a_n'$ provided by the control computer on the bus. If the match is successful in a cell, the output of the right-most AND gate (see Figure 5.7) will be '1'. The match signal is collected at the match output signal (MOS) line and proceeds to a threshold circuit that determines whether there is no match, one match, or a multiple match.

The following example illustrates the matching operation in this system and describes a sample of primitive instructions. As explained in Section 5.2, the data structure of a file in this system is a linear string of records, attribute names, and values separated by special symbols that serve as delimiters. For example, the COURSE relation would be mapped into a string of symbols containing a substring is

$$.......\%\#_1 CID\$\#_2 CTITLE\$\#_3 ROOM\$\#_4 PERIOD\$\#_5 PROF\_NAME\$\%....$$

where a % marks the beginning of a record, a # indicates the beginning of attribute names CID, CTITLE, ROOM, PERIOD, and PROF_NAME, and a $ marks the end of these attribute names. The symbols in the string are stored in a distributed fashion in the cells, each of which contains a segment of the string. Assume that some segments prefixed by the symbol % are stored in a cell. The retrieval problem is to find all the cells that contain the substring #2CTITLE$ and to have the cells output the entire string between two % signs including the prefix (i.e., the left % sign). Figure 5.8 shows the program that does the retrieval.

The instructions shown in the table are divided into the following fields: the symbolic address of an instruction, the command or operation to be performed, the propagation direction, the activity flip-flop(s) involved, the cell content, and the next instruction to be executed. The match-propagate and kill activity (MKA) command causes every cell that has the content shown in the content column to propagate its X activity to its R (right) neighbor. The X activities of all the

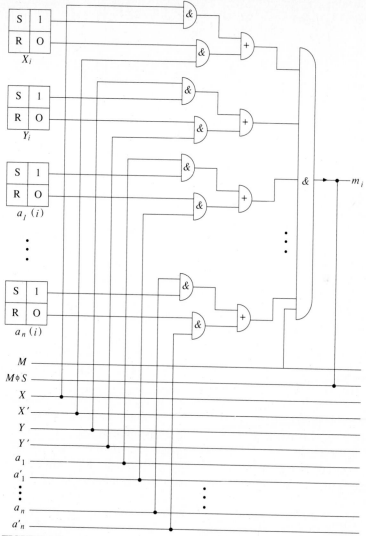

FIGURE 5.7
Cell i's match circuit. (*Source:* [LEE63] ©1963 IEEE)

cells are then killed except those that have just received the propagated X activity. The effect of the first eight MKA instructions is to set the X activity flip-flops of all the cells that contain the substring #2CTITLE$. The next instruction (TNM) will cause the program execution to branch to the end of the program if the match fails (i.e., no cell contains the substring).

The propagate and reset activity (PRA) command causes all cells to propagate the activity (X) in the direction (L) shown in the instruction and reset their

Address	Command	Direction	Activity	Cell content	Goto
	MKA	R	X	#Z, $X = 0$, $Y = 0$	
	MKA	R	X	C, $X = 1$, $Y = 0$	
	MKA	R	X	T, $X = 1$, $Y = 0$	
	MKA	R	X	I, $X = 1$, $Y = 0$	
	MKA	R	X	T, $X = 1$, $Y = 0$	
	MKA	R	X	L, $X = 1$, $Y = 0$	
	MKA	R	X	E, $X = 1$, $Y = 0$	
	MKA	R	X	$, $X = 1$, $Y = 0$	
	TNM				END
$A1$	PRA	L	X		
	R		X		
	XM			%	
	TNM				$A1$
$A2$	PRA	R	X		
	R(P)		X		
	XM			%	
	TNM				$A2$
	KA			X	
END	H				

FIGURE 5.8
A retrieval program.

own X activity. The instruction R retrieves the contents of any cell, which is X active, to an output buffer. The external match (XM) command causes the contents of the output buffer to be matched against the immediate operand % given in the instruction. If the match fails, the program loops back to the PRA command at $A1$. The propagation and the search continue until the symbol % (the beginning of a record) is found. The next four instructions starting from $A2$ propagate right, retrieve, and output symbols (the R(P) instruction) until the next % symbol in the string is encountered. The next instruction, KA, kills the X activity (i.e., resets the X flip-flop), and the last instruction halts the program.

5.3.2 Association-Storing Processor

The association-storing processor (ASP) is an associative memory system designed by the Hughes Aircraft Company under the support of the Rome Air Development Center for directly processing the instructions of a high-level programming language in hardware [SAV67]. The language is designed to retrieve and manipulate data stored in a network of relations described in Section 5.2. It is a high-level user interface for a wide range of database management and information retrieval applications.

The organization of the ASP machine is shown in Figure 5.9. The context-addressable memory is used for storing data and programs. It is capable of accessing data by specifying the context in which the data occur, that is, the relations with other data items. A microprogram memory (a small read-only

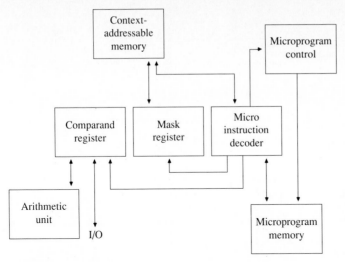

FIGURE 5.9
The organization of the ASP machine. (*Source:* [SAV67] copyright ©1967. AFIPS, reprinted by permission of AFIPS Press.)

memory) is used to store a microprogram. When the microprogram is executed by the microinstruction decoder and the microprogram control unit, it retrieves the ASP program instructions stored in the context-addressed memory against the data stored in the same memory. There are two registers associated with the context-addressed memory—a comparand register and a mask register. The comparand register holds the data word for search in the memory, and the mask register holds a bit pattern for masking specified bit positions of the memory words so that they can be searched by content. The arithmetic unit performs some built-in functions (e.g., Sum, Count, etc.), and the I/O facility provides communication between the ASP machine and the external world (e.g., a host computer).

The context-addressable memory consists of a two-dimensional array of identical cells that are interconnected both locally and globally (see Figure 5.10). Locally, each cell is connected to its north and west neighbors. The cell on the top of each column is connected to the cell at the bottom of the column, and the cell at the west end of each row is connected to the cell at the east end of the same row. The signals generated by the cells travel in the north and west directions. Any cell can communicate with any other cell in the array by first traveling north to the right row of the destination cell and then traveling west to reach the destination. Globally, each cell is connected to the comparand register, the mask register, and the microinstruction decoder. Thus, data words stored in the comparand register can be broadcast simultaneously to all the cells for comparison.

Each cell consists of a cell memory or memory element and a cell logic or processing element. The cell memory contains five fields of equal length. Three of them are used to store instruction, data items, or coded representation of relations. The other two fields are used as tags that mark data items or relations satisfying

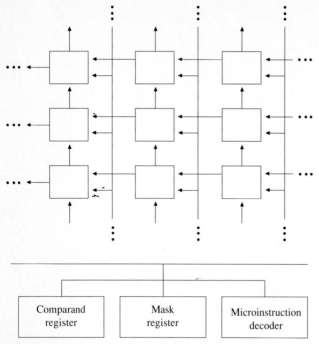

FIGURE 5.10
Cell interconnection.

a search condition. The cell logic performs comparison operations and generates and propagates intercell communication signals. It also records the results of a comparison in the match flip-flops associated with the cells and performs Boolean operations on the results of successive comparisons, which are recorded in another flip-flop to obtain the final result of a complex Boolean expression.

In the context-addressable memory, each cell has a built-in address consisting of a row number and a column number of the cell in the memory array. The message format of an intercell communication consists of address signals of the destination cell; it may also consist of some message, the content of which depends on the function executed. Signals for intercell communication are initially generated as a result of some global operation responded to by all cells having a particular tag. These cells would simultaneously send out the addresses of other cells stored in their memory (e.g., the addresses of two items and a link, which form a relation). The addresses and messages would propagate northward simultaneously and in synchronism until the proper row numbers have been reached. At that point, the signals turn westward until they reach cells with the matching built-in addresses. The match flip-flops of these destination cells are set. This intercell communication scheme allows data items or relations stored in the cell memory, which enter into some relations with other data items and relations, to be searched and marked in parallel. The marked items and relations can then be used to propagate to other items and relations.

The following examples, which demonstrate the power of the ASP machine and its instructions in performing pattern matching in a network of relations, use the data organization given in Figure 5.5.

Example 1. Find the value(s) of X in the relation (EE6967, PROF_NAME, X) or the name(s) of the professor(s) who teaches EE6967. The following three operations are necessary to perform the search:

(a) Search for the relation ((2,5), (3,2), D/C) where (2,5) and (3,2) are the addresses of the cells containing EE6967 and PROF_NAME, respectively. D/C stands for the 'do not care' symbol. The match flip-flops of those cells that contain the pattern will be set. In this example, the match flip-flop for cell (4,5) is set.

(b) Set the transmission tags and indicators of the third data field of those cells that have a match in step (a). In this example, the transmission tag and the indicator of the third data field, that is, (3,4) of cell (4,5), are set.

(c) The content address function makes the cells with their transmission tags set in step (b) send out the third data field. The cells that are addressed by the third data field will set their match flip-flops. In this example, the match flip-flop of cell (3,4) is set.

(d) The matched cell(s) in step (c) can then be output or used as the context for a subsequent search.

Example 2. Find all values of X and Y such that the relation (X, R_2, Y) appears in the context of the structure represented by the relations (A, R_1, X), (X, R_2, Y) and (B, R_3, Y). Here, X and Y are variables. For this query, the following operations must be performed:

(a) Perform the same set of operations as in the previous example to find a set of cells containing the values of X in the relation (A, R_1, X). These cells are marked.

(b) Do the same for the values of Y in the relation (B, R_3, Y). The Y values are marked.

(c) These two sets of X and Y values may not all enter into a relation through the R_2 link. A "boxcar" function is available in ASP to handle this two-variable situation. Before the function is executed, all cells containing (D/C, R_2, D/C) are tagged as transmission cells by setting their transmission tags. Their left data field indicators are also set. When the boxcar function is executed, it makes all the transmission cells send out the addresses of the left field (the locomotive). Each address is followed by the address of the transmission cell (i.e., the boxcar of the locomotive). Those cells that were marked in step (a) will respond to the transmission by sending back the boxcar addresses to the transmitter if their built-in addresses match the addresses (the locomotive) just transmitted. Otherwise, they simply ignore the transmission. This causes only a subset of the original transmitters to remain marked. This subset of cells would contain all relations having the pattern $(X, R_2, D/C)$ and appearing in the context of the structure (A, R_1, X) and $(X, R_2, D/C)$.

(d) Mark this subset as the transmission cells and set their right data field indicators. The boxcar function is again executed. This time, only the cells marked in step (b), whose built-in addresses match with the transmitted addresses, would respond by sending back the boxcar addresses to the transmitters. This causes a subset of the original transmitters to remain marked. This subset would contain the relations (X, R_2, Y), which appear in the context of the structure given in the query. The addresses of X and Y in these relations can then be used to locate the values of X and Y.

An associative system called SNAP, which is similar in architecture to ASP, has been proposed by Moldovan and Tung [MOL85] for knowledge-based applications. It uses the same data or knowledge representation as ASP, that is, the data/knowledge base is represented by a network of ASP-type relations. However, the cells in this system are locally connected to all four neighbors. The physical organization of the cell memory is more compact than ASP. The work reported by Moldovan and Tung [MOL85] shows that this type of associative memory is capable of performing a wide range of artificial intelligence functions (e.g., logic inference, complex search functions, etc.) in addition to database management and information retrieval functions.

5.3.3 STARAN

STARAN is an associative memory system designed and developed under the support of the United States Air Force. Several versions of the system have been developed. According to Rudolph [RUD72], the first working model was built by the Goodyear Aerospace Corporation in 1969. A more powerful version was tested by the Federal Aviation Administration in 1971 for collision detection in a live air traffic control environment at Knoxville, Tennessee. This test demonstrated the parallel-processing capability of the associative memory and its suitability for real-time processing of air traffic data. The success of this test apparently led to the development of STARAN S system, which became commercially available in 1972. Since then, a number of associative memory systems have been built around the STARAN for database management applications. In this subsection and Section 5.4, some of these works will be examined.

Figure 5.11 shows an overall organization of the STARAN system. It consists of three main components: the control memory, the control logic, and the associative arrays.

1. *Control memory.* Two types of memories are used for storing the data and programs of this system—a bulk core memory and a high-speed semiconductor memory. The application programs are stored in the core memory, which is a 16K-word (32 bits each), nonvolatile memory and can be expanded to 32K words. The core memory can also be used for low-speed data buffering. The high-speed memory consists of four memory pages, each of which has 512 32-bit words. The memory uses bipolar semiconductors with a 200 ns access time [MIN72]. Page

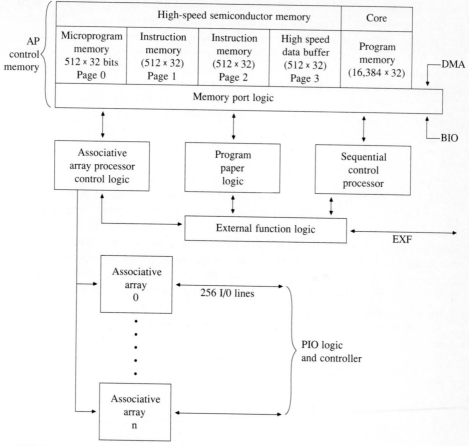

FIGURE 5.11
Block diagram of the STARAN system. (*Source:* [RUD72] copyright ©1972. AFIPS, reprinted by permission of AFIPS Press.)

0 is used to store a microprogram library. The microprograms provide system control during the execution of application programs. Pages 1 and 2 are used as cache memories for program instruction loaded from the core memory. While the program instructions in one page are being executed, the other page is used for program loading from the core memory. Page 3 is used as a high-speed data buffer that stores instructions and data that must be accessed at a high speed. Both types of control memories are sequentially accessed by STARAN.

　　2. *Control logic.* The control logic of STARAN consists of four modules, as shown in Figure 5.11. The associative processor control logic loads data into the associative arrays, broadcasts instructions to their processing elements, and controls the search operations carried out in the arrays. The program pager controls the loading and unloading of the high-speed control memory. The external function logic enables the AP control, sequential control, or an external

device to control the STARAN operations. By issuing external function codes to this control logic, one control element can interrogate and control the status of the other control element. The sequential control processor is a small control computer (a PDP-11 with an 8K 16-bit memory) that allows STARAN to operate as a stand-alone system. This processor is used for processing system software such as assembler, operating system software, and so forth.

3. *Associative arrays.*   The associative array of STARAN is composed of 256 × 256 cells arranged in a two-dimensional array (see Figure 5.12). It has 256 processing elements for processing a bit slice taken either from a column or from a row. Thus, it is capable of accessing an array load of data in both bit-serial word-parallel or bit-parallel word-serial modes, as discussed in Section 5.2. There is a comparand register for storing the data word to be searched in the array. A mask register is used to select the proper bit pattern from each bit slice from the array for comparison with the comparand register. The result of a parallel comparison by 256 processing elements can be recorded in one of the three response stores available in each processing element. Boolean operations can be performed on the contents of these response stores to implement Boolean expressions found in retrieval queries. The contents of a response store can also be used to serve as a mask for masking out rows or columns that will not participate in the next instruction execution.

A maximum of 32 arrays can be connected to STARAN. Any subset of these arrays can be selected for program execution.

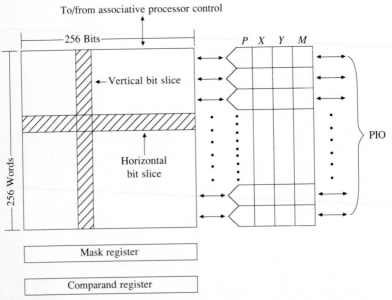

FIGURE 5.12
STARAN associative array.

Input and output speed is an important design consideration in an associative memory system since the speed of loading and emptying the associative memory would determine how fast large quantities of data can be searched and, thus, determine the overall performance of the system. STARAN has four different interface methods: direct memory access (DMA), buffer input/output (BIO), parallel input/output (PIO), and the external function logic, which provides STARAN with communication channels to the sequential controller and secondary storage devices. DMA and BIO are used in STARAN to load the control memory from external devices. Access to the control memory is provided through calls to the external function logic. The PIO allows parallel loading and emptying of the associative arrays. It can transfer 1024 words at a rate of 3 megacycles per second.

STARAN has four addressing modes: word addressing, immediate addressing, indirect addressing, and array addressing. Word addressing instructions get operands from the high-speed data buffer, DMA, or the core memory. Instructions using immediate operands get their operands from the currently active instruction memory. Indirect addressing is supported by a data pointer register. This register contains the address of data stored in the high-speed data buffer, core memory, or data accessible through DMA. Array addressing can be either immediate or indirect through some field pointer registers used to store the bit slice number or the word number of the operand stored in an associative array.

The Associative Processor Programming LanguagE) (APPLE) is an assembly language that was developed to handle features unique to the parallel organization of STARAN [DAV74]. It provides six groups of instructions: assembler directives, branch instructions, register load and store, array instructions, control and test instructions, and I/O instructions. Since all but the array instructions resemble those of the traditional computers, only the array instructions will be described here. The array instructions deal with operations on the associative arrays and the registers in the processing elements. They operate on arrays enabled by an array select register and on variable-length fields in each array word defined by some field counters and length counters. To support these operations, a common register in the associative array control logic is used to store the operand used in common by all the selected array words.

The array operations are classified into five subgroups: Loads, Stores, Associative Searches, Parallel Moves, and Parallel Arithmetic operations. The Load instructions load the registers of the processing elements or the common register with data fetched from arrays. Logical operations can be performed between the registers of the processing elements (PEs) and the array data, and a field pointer can be incremented or decremented as part of the Load instructions. The Store instructions are used to move data stored in the registers of the processing elements (PEs) or the common register into those mask-enabled array words. The Load instructions, logical operations, and operations that change field pointer contents can be specified as a part of these Store instructions. The Associative Search instructions search for some specified conditions in those array words enabled by the mask register. The Parallel Move instructions move an array memory field to another field within the same word. Only those words enabled by the mask register will participate in the operation. The Parallel Arithmetic instructions perform parallel operations in the arrays. For example, an arithmetic operation can be performed between a value in the common register and a value in a field of all array words in parallel, or it can be performed between a field with another field of the same record in all the array words. Arithmetic operations in APPLE are Add, Subtract, Multiply, Divide, and Square Root.

Now consider how the relational Selection, Projection, and Join operations can be performed in STARAN. The Selection operation is very straightforward. Records of a data file stored in secondary storage devices are loaded into the associative arrays. In general, a Selection involves a Boolean expression of predicates, each of which consists of an attribute, a comparison operator (e.g., the equality operator), and a search value. These predicates are processed one at a time. STARAN can load the comparand register with the search value of a predicate, and it can load the field pointer register with the field number of the attribute involved. A field match is performed. Any record that satisfies the condition will set its response bit. The setting of a response store for one predicate is then logically combined (AND, OR, and NOT) with the results of the next predicate verification, and the results are again stored in the response store. This process continues until all the predicates of a query are processed. The contents of the final response store mark those records that satisfy the Selection operation.

The Join and Projection with elimination of duplicates operations can be performed in this system by a sequence of selections. In the case of the Join operation, the join field and its value in the shorter relation can be used as search predicates. The comparand register is loaded with a search value and is used to perform a content search of the longer relation loaded into the associative arrays. The matched records can then be retrieved and concatenated with the record of the shorter relation, which contains the current search value. In the case of the Projection operation, the attributes over which the Projection is to be made are used in a series of Selection operations. Each tuple of the relation to be projected is processed in turn. The values of the projection attributes in each tuple are used to search all the other tuples of the same relation loaded in the associative arrays. All the tuples that contain the same values are duplicates and are deleted from the arrays. The process continues until all the duplicates have been deleted from the file.

5.4 INPUT AND OUTPUT PROBLEMS IN ASSOCIATIVE MEMORIES

Although the content- and context-addressing capabilities, and parallel-processing capabilities of associative memories offer great speed and flexibility in searching data stored in these memory devices, there are two main disadvantages—the hardware cost and the input/output problems associated with them. Due to their cost, the early associative memories were rather small. Thus, the amount of data that could be loaded and processed in these memories was extremely limited.

Although recent advances in memory technology allow much larger associative memory devices to be built at a much lower cost for database management applications, one still cannot assume that all data can be stored in this type of memory device. Data still must be stored in some archival memory (e.g., disks or magnetic bubble memory devices) and must be moved into associative memory modules one load at a time in a sequential fashion. Since data search and processing time in an associative memory is insignificant when compared with data loading time and since the latter is restricted by the speed of the archival memory, input or staging data in an associative memory is a serious problem.

Outputting data from an associative memory presents some difficulties also. In this type of memory, words that satisfy a search are marked by setting bits in their corresponding response stores. These marked words still must be transferred out of the memory to a control processor or an auxiliary memory. The output speed would depend on the bandwidth of the data path between the associative memory and the other processor or memory device.

In order to really take advantage of the search and processing speed of associative memories, the I/O problems must be solved. Fortunately, these problems are similar to the size limitation of the main memory in a conventional computer. Some solutions found in a conventional system can also be used in an associative memory system. In addition to these, the other database computer approaches can also be combined with the associative memory approach to ease the input and output problems. The following memory organizations and techniques have been used in several more recent associative memory systems:

1. *Parallel data movement between memory devices.* An associative memory can be used together with other kinds of memory devices to form a memory system in which data can be moved between these devices in parallel, thus speeding up the data staging and emptying processes.

2. *High-speed auxiliary memory and memory caching.* A large high-speed auxiliary memory can be used as the permanent storage for a database to ease the I/O problems. Alternatively, an associative memory can be used as a part of a memory hierarchy consisting of memories of different speeds and costs. Just like the control memory of STARAN, a cache memory can be used to buffer data transferred from a secondary storage to an associative memory, thus increasing the effective speed of the secondary storage.

3. *Data reduction.* The amount of data that needs to be loaded into the associative memory for processing can be reduced by using either a hardware approach or a combination of software and hardware approaches. In the hardware approach, an intelligent secondary storage device or a database filter (described in Chapters 3 and 4) can be used to filter out the irrelevant data so that only a small quantity of data needs to be staged for associative searches. Traditional software approaches (e.g., indexing approaches), can also be used to locate the relevant data blocks in a secondary storage for loading into an associative memory. Multiple associative memories can be used to support the software techniques used.

The following subsections use some proposed associative memory systems as examples to explain these approaches. Some of these systems use a combination of these approaches. In this case, the subsection in which each is presented has no particular significance.

5.4.1 Parallel Data Movement between Memory Devices

An example of this approach is found in the Associative Processor Computer System (APCS), which was designed and developed by the Systems Development Corporation in Santa Monica, California for the United States Air Force's Tactical Air Control Center [LIN73]. The memory system is used in the Tactical Air Control System (TACS) for real-time processing of surveillance data used for air support in combat areas. It is an integrated associative computer system, rather than a so-called hybrid system, with an interconnection of serial and associative processors. The system block diagram of APCS is shown in Figure 5.13.

The central processor of APCS is an integration of three types of processors: two associative processing units (APUs), a sequential processing unit (SPU), and an input/output processor (IOP). The APUs, each of which contains $2K \times 256$ bits of associative store, provide the content-addressing and context-addressing capabilities. The SPU executes user programs. The IOP controls the I/O oper-

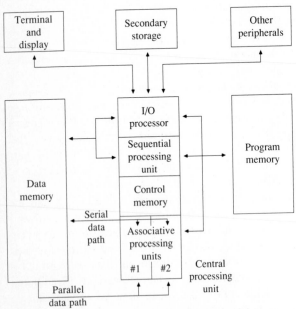

FIGURE 5.13

Block diagram of APCS. (*Source:* [LIN73] copyright ©1973. AFIPS, reprinted by permission of AFIPS Press.)

ations of terminals, displays, secondary storage devices, and other peripherals. The memory system of APCS consists of three units: microprogrammed control memory (MCM), secondary memory, and primary memory. The MCM stores the microprograms that control the parallel operations of the other control units of the system. The secondary memory stores the database. The primary memory is divided into a program memory, which stores user programs, data management functions, and executive routines, and a data memory, which stores the database directory and several current active data files.

The key feature of this system is that the three types of processors can operate independently on their corresponding memory units, thus overlapping most of their operations. For example, the IOP can be filling or emptying data and programs into or out of the data and program memories, while the SPU is interpreting microcodes stored in the control memory and the associative memory units are processing their data in parallel. Thus, speed is gained by parallel operations of processors and memory units.

An additional feature of this system is that data in secondary storage can be prestaged in the data memory, a faster memory than the secondary storage, and loaded into the associative memory modules either serially, via a serial data path, or in parallel, via a 512-bit parallel data path. This memory organization greatly eases the I/O problems discussed previously.

Another example of using the parallel data movement approach is found in the STARAN Evaluation and Training Facility (SETF) reported by Moulder [MOU73]. The configuration of SETF is shown in Figure 5.14. The main feature of this system is the coupling of a four-array STARAN with a parallel head-

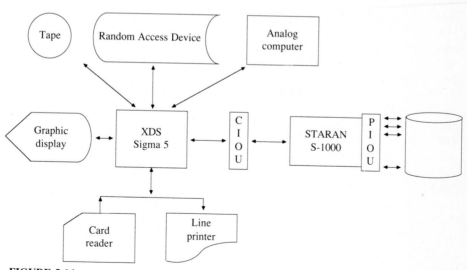

FIGURE 5.14
STARAN evaluation and training facility. (*Source:* [MOU73] copyright ©1973. AFIPS, reprinted by permission of AFIPS Press.)

per-track disk (PHD). The disk has one surface that is divided into 384 sectors and contains 72 tracks. Of these 72 tracks, 64 are tied to STARAN. Each track has 256 bits in each sector. The disk is connected to a parallel I/O unit (PIOU), which is a part of a custom input/output unit (CIOU). The PIOU allows data to be transferred between the associative arrays and PHD through 64 parallel channels. The switching capability of the CIOU allows these channels to be time-shared among the STARAN arrays. Since the associative array contains 256 × 256 bits, the 64 parallel channels allow 64 256-bit words to be loaded from the disk at one time. The disk has a rotating speed of 39 msecs. It takes approximately 100 μsecs for a sector to pass the disk heads. If data are physically arranged on every other sector on the disk track, this will allow 100 μsecs for performing complex or multiple searches between data loading.

An XDS Sigma 5 computer is used as the control computer in this system. The configuration also includes an analog computer, EAI7800, and a full complement of peripherals.

5.4.2   High-Speed Auxiliary Memory and Memory Caching

The I/O problems of associative memories can be reduced or eliminated by increasing either the physical speed of the auxiliary database storage, using faster memory devices, or the effective speed of the database storage, using the traditional memory-caching technique. System organizations that use these two techniques will be examined.

In their study, Farnsworth, Hoffman, and Shutt [FAR76] use a mass memory in place of disks. The study uses the STARAN as the basic configuration. It is assumed that four associative array modules, each of which contains 256 × 256 bits are used. Four mass storage modules (4096 × 256 × 256 each) are used as the database storage. They are connected to the associative arrays through a custom I/O interface as shown in Figure 5.15. The interface has intelligence to perform various database functions. The 1024 parallel lines allow the four arrays to be loaded by 256-bit serial transfers in approximately 165 μsec (a transfer rate of 300 to 450 nsecs per bit slice is assumed). This memory organization with an expanded array size (1024 × 256 bits per array) is used in Berra and Oliver [BER79] to calculate the retrieval speed from a database greater than 10^9 bits. It is assumed that an associative array holds eight pages of data, with each page containing 128 × 256 bits. Each of the four mass memory modules contains 8K pages, i.e., 32 megabytes per module, and four modules contain 32K pages. Following Farnsworth's estimate, the overhead time for locating data pages on the mass memory is 50 μsecs, and the loading time of all four associative arrays is 115 μsecs. If the search produces 10 responding records, and the retrieval of these 10 responders is 300 μsecs, then it will only take 2 seconds ((500 μsecs/8 pages) × 32K pages) to search the entire mass memory.

Another configuration considered by Berra and Oliver [BER79] is to use a fast buffer memory as a cache between the associative arrays and the secondary

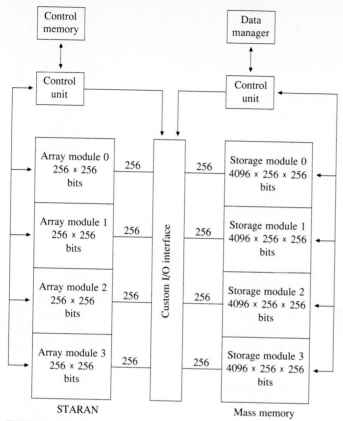

FIGURE 5.15
STARAN/mass memory interface. (*Source:* [BER79] ©1979 IEEE)

storage. Figure 5.16 shows the fast buffer memory and its interface to disks. The buffer memory is divided into 10 partitions, each of which contains 80 pages of data. All together there are 100 disks, which are divided into 10 banks of 10 disks each. It is assumed that each disk has 20 heads and 20 surfaces with 100 tracks per surface. Each track is capable of holding one array load of data, that is, 32K bytes. It is further assumed that a disk revolution takes 20 msecs and positioning of the read/write head takes a maximum of 20 msecs. Allowing a maximum of one revolution to locate the data and another revolution to read the data, it will take 40 msecs to fill one partition of the buffer memory from the disks. The interface between the fast buffer memory and the disks allows data to be transferred between these memory devices in parallel.

The data movement during a search operation will be as follows. Data stored in the disks will be moved across the disk interface in parallel to fill the 10 partitions of the buffer memory during the initial loading. This will involve 60 msecs—20 msecs for moving the heads (the seek time), 20 msecs for waiting for the right block to come under the heads (the worst-case latency time), and 20

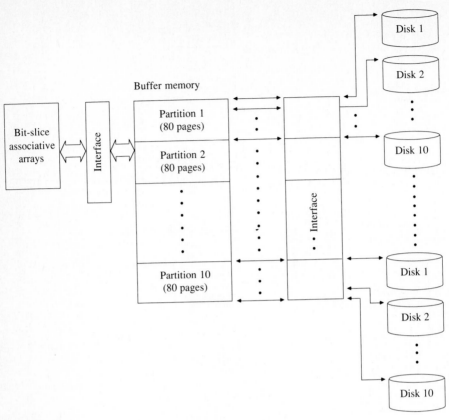

FIGURE 5.16
A fast buffer memory and its interface to disks. (*Source:* [BER79] ©1979 IEEE)

msecs for reading the data from the disks to all partitions in parallel. The data in partition 1 will be moved to the associative arrays, 8 pages at a time, to fill the arrays. The data will then be searched and the results retrieved. Based on a previous calculation, one array load of data can be searched in 500 μsecs. Since there are 10 array loads worth of data in each partition, 5 msecs will be required to search a partition. After partition 1 is searched, partition 2 will be loaded and searched in the arrays in the same manner. At the same time, partition 1 will be refilled with data from the disks. The process will continue until all the data involved in a retrieval operation are fully staged in the associative arrays and searched.

If 5 msecs is required to search a partition, 50 msecs will be required to search the entire buffer memory. Since the buffer memory can be loaded 20 times before incurring a time penalty for moving the disk read/write heads to another cylinder, the quantity of data that can be searched without moving the disk arm is

20 tracks per disk $\times$ 100 $\times$ 8 pages per track
= 16,000 pages
= 16,000 pages $\times$ 4K bytes per page
= 64 megabytes.

The time required for searching 64 megabytes of data associatively is

20 buffer memory loads $\times$ 50 msec per load
= 1 second.

It was estimated by Berra and Oliver [BER79] that the entire 100 disks which contain 6.4×10^9 bytes can be searched in approximately 100 seconds. This study shows that the I/O problems of associative memory can be solved, for some applications at least, by using a fast buffer memory as a cache in a memory hierarchy involving associative memory arrays.

5.4.3 Data Reduction Approaches

This section examines hardware approaches to reduce the amount of data to be loaded into an associative memory. Shaw [SHA79 and SHA80] proposes an architecture for processing relational databases that consists of two types of associative memories: (1) a cellular-logic device such as CASSM or RAP as a secondary associative memory (SAM) and (2) a STARAN-like memory as the primary associative memory (PAM). SAM is a larger but slower content-addressable device with a capacity of between 1 and 100M bytes and an operation time of between 1 and 100 msecs. PAM is a smaller but faster device with a capacity of between 10K bytes and 1M bytes and an operation time of between 100 nsecs and 10 msecs. The speeds of these two devices are chosen in such a way that a quantity of data sufficient to fill PAM can be transferred from SAM to PAM in a single revolution of SAM. Since SAM has the capability of processing data right where they are stored, relational selection operations can be performed on SAM to select only those tuples that are relevant for further processing in PAM. The selected tuples are then loaded into PAM for subsequent associative searches. This approach reduces the amount of data that needs to be loaded into PAM, thus easing the input problem discussed previously.

Another hardware approach is proposed by Hurson [HUR80 and HUR81]. The associative memory system called Associative Search Language Machine (ASLM) is shown in Figure 5.17. Like most database machines, it is a back-end to a general-purpose computer. It performs query translation, output genera-tion, and other DBMS functions. The associative hardware consists of four main components: a controller, an index processor, a secondary storage inter-face, and a nonnumeric processor. The controller is a microprogrammable con-trol unit that stores the microinstructions, of a translated program written in a high-level language, decodes the microinstructions, and propagates the control sequences to the various modules of ASLM. The index processor is composed of an associative memory for storing the names of relations and attributes, a

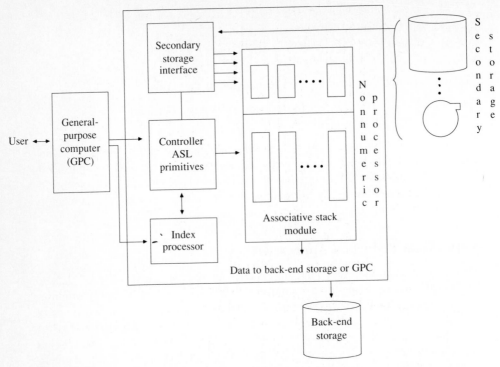

FIGURE 5.17
The organization of ASLM. (*Source:* [HUR80] reprinted by permission of the author.)

small processing unit with a random access memory for processing and storing the descriptions of relation names and attributes (i.e., the attributes contained in a relation, the domain names, domain types and maximum length of
domains associated with the attributes, disk addresses of relations, etc.), and a
hard-wired control unit. The index processor isolates the user from the internal
data structures used in ASLM. The secondary storage interface provides access
to the data stored in secondary storage devices and transfers data to the nonnumeric processor. An assembly of registers is available in the interface to buffer
the data to be passed between the secondary storage and the nonnumeric processor.

The nonnumeric processor is the key component of this system. It consists
of a number of cells and associative stacks. The cells contain processing logic
capable of performing relational selections and projections without duplicate
elimination. They serve as database filters, reducing the width and length of a
relation when it is being transferred into the associative stacks. The associative
stacks are associative memory modules augmented by a top-of-stack register for
each stack. These stacks can be used for content search as well as for stack
processing of data. ASLM couples an associative memory and database filters to
ease the input problem of the associative memory.

A combined software and hardware approach for achieving data reduction and other functions will now be examined. One traditional software approach to avoid searching a large quantity of data stored in the secondary storage is to build a directory that contains the names of relations or attributes and the addresses of their tuples and/or their descriptive information stored in the secondary storage. By looking up this directory, relevant data can be directly accessed from the secondary storage. This scheme can also be used in an associative memory system to selectively load the data stored in a secondary storage into an associative memory for content searches, thus easing the input problem. However, the maintenance and processing of data in a directory can be rather time-consuming. Fortunately, associative memories can be used to process the directory data as well as the raw data of a database. The following system contains this capability as well as other features.

The design of a multiassociative memory system called the Relational Associative Computer System (RELACS) is reported by Oliver [OLI79]. It is based on STARAN-type associative memory arrays. RELACS consists of five functional components (see Figure 5.18): a dictionary/directory processor (DDP), an associative query translator (AQT), two associative arrays (AU$_0$ and AU$_1$), a mass storage device (MSD), and an output buffer (OB). RELACS serves as a back-end to a host computer.

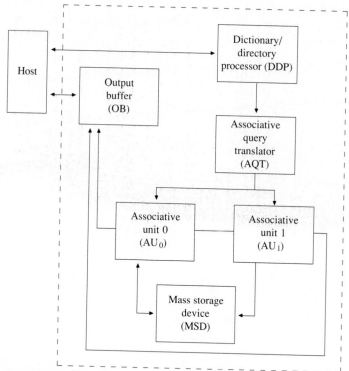

FIGURE 5.18
The organization of RELACS. (*Source:* [OLI79] reprinted by permission of the author.)

In an associative array, it is advantageous to shorten and standardize the size of relation and attribute names so that they will occupy less space in the associative store. This scheme will also make it easier to pick up the proper data fields for comparison. For this type of data organization, a dictionary/directory is necessary to map the external names to their internal representations and to relate attribute names to their relations. In RELACS, the location on the MSD of every relation is contained in the dictionary. Every attribute is described by its access code and whether it is a primary key for a relation. The DDP of RELACS maintains and processes the dictionary/directory. It transforms relation and attribute names into their shortened names and vice versa and supplies the sizes of the attributes and relations. DDP performs its functions by using the associative arrays shown in Figure 5.19.

AM_1 contains the external attribute names, and AM_2 contains the internal attribute names, that is, the shortened names. Each word of AM_1 is connected to its internal name in AM_2 through array I. A search in AM_1 will reveal the internal name of any attribute by setting the response bit in AM_2. Synonyms of an attribute are connected from different words in AM_1 to the same word in AM_2. AM_3 contains the external names of relations, and AM_4 stores the shortened names of the relations, relation length, and their locations in the MSD. The function of array IV for AM_3 and AM_4 is the same as that of array I for AM_1 and AM_2.

Array III connects the internal attribute names of AM_2 to the relation names in AM_3. It is a bit map relating one attribute name to a relation name. AM_5 contains the descriptions of attributes, that is, their data types, uniqueness,

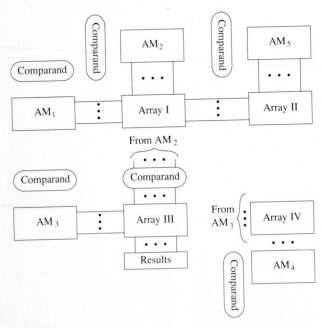

FIGURE 5.19
The associative arrays used by the dictionary/directory processor. (*Source:* [OLI79] reprinted by permission of the author.)

security levels, read/write privileges, and so forth. Array II is also a bit map that relates each attribute to its description. The matching performed by array II is between AM_1 and AM_5.

When a query is given to RELACS by the host computer, the DDP transforms all the relation and attribute names referenced in the query into their internal names. It also fetches information related to the attributes and relations. The amended query and the fetched information are passed to the AQT for translation.

The AQT consists of three components (see in Figure 5.20). The microprogrammed controller generates control signals to operate both the query/data memory and the job queue buffer to carry out the translation task. It contains a control store for storing microprogrammed sequences of instructions for performing retrieval, deletion, and modification operations. It also contains a number of general-purpose registers and a memory to store a memory management software which supports virtual memory management of the query/data memories.

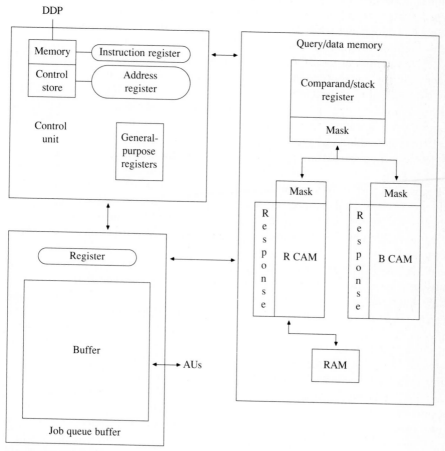

FIGURE 5.20

The components of the associative query translator in RELACS. (*Source:* [OLI79] reprinted by permission of the author.)

The query/data memory module has four functional units: a comparand/stack register, a relation content-addressable memory (RCAM), a Boolean content-addressable memory (BCAM), and a relation descriptor memory (RAM). The comparand/stack register is a stack of registers that are used to store the search conditions of the amended query—the output of the DDP. Each of these conditions is popped from the stack and loaded into the comparand register of RCAM or BCAM, where the translation takes place. When the stack is empty, the translation will be complete. The mask register associated with the stack is used to select the proper values or names in the comparand/stack registers as comparand arguments as directed by the translation program.

The function of the RCAM is to store and search the relation descriptor data required to process the query. The descriptor data are provided by the DDP and are initially stored in the RAM. They include the names of relations and their addresses as well as the attribute names associated with the relations and their column positions in a tuple. These data are moved from the RAM to the RCAM for associative searches. The staging of these data is done automatically by the memory management software of the control unit when the data required by the query are not currently residing in the RCAM.

The function of the BCAM and its structure is similar to that of the RCAM. It contains comparison operators (e.g., $=$, $>$, $<$, etc.), Boolean operators, and the addresses of the microprograms stored in the associative units, which perform the corresponding operations. During the translation process, an operator found in the comparand/stack register is used to associatively search the BCAM. The corresponding address of the microprogram is returned.

The job queue buffer (JQB) is used to store the translated instructions of a query that are to be used to control the operations of the associative units (AUs). When an AU is free, it is given the address of a block of instructions in the JQB. The instructions are then accessed and processed by the AU independently of the other AU. The register shown in the figure is for holding an instruction that is being assembled by the query translator. The assembled instruction is then stored in the JQB.

The two AUs of RELACS are identical. They are used to process the translated query to carry out associative searches on the data loaded in these units. Each unit is composed of four systems (see Figure 5.21). The associative system performs data searches and manipulations. The I/O system loads and unloads the array memory. The control system controls the operations of the array during instruction execution. The control memory is used for communications between the AUs and the other components of the RELACS. It also contains the subroutines needed to perform various database management functions. The AUs are similar to the associative arrays of STARAN in *functions* but with some significant differences in *structures*. They are larger in design (1024 × 1024) and are expandable. RELACS has an array of comparand registers instead of a single register; thus, multiple words can be tested for matching simultaneously. Furthermore, there is an array of response store associated with the comparand array to record the results of the multiple-word matching. Each word in the comparand array has a corresponding column in the response array. Each row in

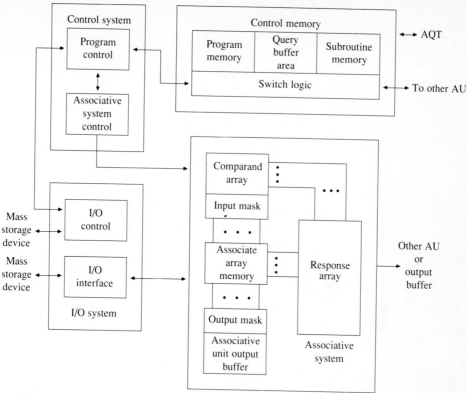

FIGURE 5.21

Block diagram of an associative unit in RELACS. (*Source:* [OLI79] reprinted by permission of the author.)

the response array records the response of an array word as it is matched against all the comparands. The AU is controlled by two mask registers instead of one in STARAN. The input mask register is used to mask fields during search operations. The masked fields will not participate in searches. The output mask register is used to perform the Projection operation. Setting the output mask prevents certain bit-slices from entering the output buffer. The projected tuples are passed to the other AU for duplicate elimination.

The matching process in RELACS is divided into as many steps as the width of the comparand. Each step represents the comparison of a bit-slice of the comparand array and a bit-slice of the associative array. Each step of the comparison consists of two phases. Before the matching process starts, the response array elements are initialized to '1'. During the first phase of each step, all comparand words with a '0' and their associated response registers are activated. A position in the activated response registers is marked if the comparand word for the column contains a '0' bit, and the array word for the row has a matching '0'. During the second phase, the comparand words with a '1' are activated. The same matching process takes place. An example of this matching algorithm is shown in Figure 5.22.

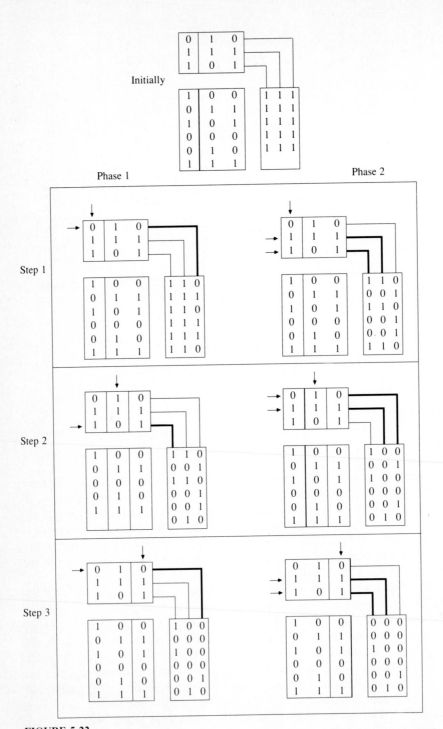

FIGURE 5.22
An equal-to-comparand search using multiple comparands. (*Source:* [OLI79] reprinted by permission of the author.)

In the figure, the arrows point to the element(s) in a bit-slice which contains a '0' in phase 1 and a '1' in phase 2. The darker lines connecting the comparand and response arrays show the comparands and response registers activated in each step. The response array resulting from phase 2 of step 3 shows that the first comparand matches with the fifth array word, the second comparand with the last array word, and the third comparand with the third array word.

The key features of the RELACS system are:

1. Associative memories are used to store and process directories/dictionaries that contain information for transforming the long external relation and attribute names to shorter internal names, locating relations and tuples, accessing the descriptors of relations and attributes, and so forth.
2. The query translation process is also aided by the use of associative memories that provide fast look-ups of relation and attribute descriptors as well as routines for code generation.
3. The use of an array of comparands allows multiple comparands to be associatively processed against the contents of an associative array in an efficient manner.

These desirable features are produced by using a number of quite elaborate hardware subsystems.

5.5 ANALYSIS

This section introduces an abstract model for associative memory systems and analyzes the instruction and data flow in this model. Algorithms for the four representative database operations will be introduced and analyzed. Cost formulas for these algorithms will be derived.

5.5.1 An Abstract Model for Associative Memory Systems

The abstract model is shown in Figure 5.23. It consists of a terminal, a host computer, an associative memory system, a disk controller, and a disk. The user's query is compiled by the host computer, which issues a data loading command to the disk controller to load the pages of a referenced relation into the associative memory. A search command is then sent to the associative memory for processing against its contents. Data that satisfy the search are marked and transferred to the main memory of the host computer for output to the disk or to the user's terminal.

Assume that the associative memory is two-dimensional, similar to that of the STARAN. Each row of the associative memory is able to store a tuple of a referenced relation. The memory can hold q pages of the relation R or S.

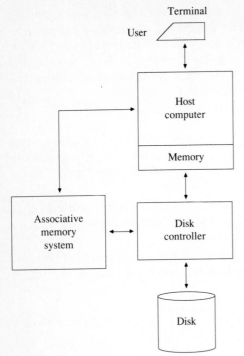

FIGURE 5.23
An abstract model for associative
memory systems.

5.5.2 Analyses of Algorithms

This section provides analyses of four database operations: Select, Join, Statistical
Aggregation, and Update. The performance parameters used in these analyses are
given in Table 5.1.

5.5.2.1 SELECT. The associative memory is best suited for the Selection
operation. The pages of a referenced relation can be loaded into the associative
memory and searched in an associative manner to identify those tuples that satisfy
the conditions of the search. All these tuples can be marked in one memory cycle
and moved to the main memory of the host computer. The result of a selection
is a relation that needs to be established in the database and stored on disk for
subsequent processing. Thus, the pages of the resulting relation L are written
to the disk as they are produced. The process of loading the associative memory, searching its contents, transferring data to the host computer's memory, and
writing data to the disk is repeated until the last load of pages of R has been
processed.

   Like the other abstract models and analyses presented in this book, it is
assumed that there is no conflict in reading and writing data from and to the disk,
since, in general, there is more than one disk drive. Thus, the system can read
from one disk drive and write to another.

TABLE 5.1
Performance Parameters

Parameter	Definition
R	Name of a referenced relation
m	Number of pages in relation R
S	Name of the inner relation in a join operation
s	Number of pages in relation S
L	Resulting relation of an operation
b	Number of pages in an input buffer large enough to store all the tuples in R that have the same join attribute value
k	Number of distinct values of a join attribute in relation R
q	Number of tracks in a disk cylinder
sel_fac	Selectivity factor for the Selection operation; that is, the ratio of the number of selected tuples of a referenced relation to the number of tuples of that relation
t	Number of tuples per page of R or S
u	Total number of pages of L produced by joining $(m * t)/k$ tuples of R with the tuples of S
w	Number of distinct categories in statistical aggregation
t[access]	Disk seek time plus latency
t[comp]	Compilation time for a simple query
t[cpu]	Time for comparing two values in registers or an arithmetic operation
t[am_cycl]	Time to content search the associative memory
t[I/O]	Track (page) read/write time
t[mov]	Time for moving a tuple of R or S within the memory
t[s]	Time to load a value from the memory to a register
t[tp_mov]	Time to move a tuple from the associative memory to the host computer's main memory
t[tp_out]	Time for transferring one tuple to a terminal
t[xfer]	Time for transferring a page between two processors
t[tp_xfer]	Time for transferring a tuple or an instruction between two processors

The selection query is compiled by the host computer and then transferred to the associative memory system for execution. The instruction flow time in this model is

$$t \text{ [inst\_flow]} = t \text{ [comp]} + t \text{ [tp\_xfer]}$$

The host computer determines the relation referenced in the selection command and instructs the disk controller to stage q pages of data in the associative memory.

The time for loading these pages has been established as

$$t \text{ [read\_q\_pg, } R \text{]} = q * t \text{ [I/O]}$$

The memory cycle time of the associative memory is denoted by t [am_cycl], which is the time to associatively search the memory contents. The marked tuples in the associative memory are then transferred to the host computer's main memory. It is assumed here that the associative memory has parallel read-out capability, that is, a tuple can be transferred through parallel lines into the main memory of the host computer. However, the marked tuples still need to be serially transferred to the host memory. The tuple transfer time is represented by t [tp_mov]. The time to unload the marked tuples in q pages is

$$t \text{ [am\_unload]} = \text{ sel\_fac} * q * t * t \text{ [tp\_mov]}$$

The tuples received from the associative memory are tuples of the resulting relation L. The pages of L need to be written to the disk as they are produced. Out of the m pages of R searched, there are ceil(sel_fac $* m$) pages that have satisfied the search. Based on the analysis in Chapter 2, the time to write these pages to the disk is

$$t[\text{I/O}, L] = \text{ceil}(m * \text{sel\_fac}) * t[\text{I/O}]$$

Taking these time components into consideration, the total data processing time for this algorithm would be

$$\begin{aligned} t \text{ [process]} = (m/q) * \{ & t \text{ [read\_q\_pg, } R] + t \text{ [am\_cycl]} \\ & + t \text{ [am\_unload]} \} + t[\text{I/O}, L] \\ & + 2 * t \text{ [access]} \end{aligned}$$

where the last term accounts for two seek and latency times needed to sequentially read the relation R and to sequentially write the relation L.

The data collection consists of reading the pages of relation L sequentially from the disk and outputting the tuples to the user's terminal. Thus,

$$\begin{aligned} t \text{ [data\_collect]} = & t \text{ [access]} + t[\text{I/O}, L] \\ & + m * t * \text{ sel\_fac} * t \text{ [tp\_out]} \end{aligned}$$

The total execution time for this algorithm is therefore

$$t \text{ [Select]} = t \text{ [inst\_flow]} + t \text{ [process]} + t \text{ [data\_collect]}$$

5.5.2.2 JOIN. The associative memory does not have the capability of performing the explicit join operation directly. One method for executing a join is to make use of the selection capability of the associative memory in the following way. The smaller relation, say R, is first sorted over the join attribute(s). The pages of the sorted relation R are then read by the host computer into its main memory— b pages at a time. Assume that $b * t$ is the maximum number of tuples having the same join attribute value in relation R. The distinct join attribute values in the sorted relation R are then extracted one at a time and used to form selection commands to search the relation S, which is to be staged in the associative memory.

Each execution of a selection command will produce a number of S tuples that have satisfied the join condition. These tuples of S are read by the host computer from the associative memory and are joined with the set of R tuples that has the same join attribute value. The results of Join (i.e., the tuples of L) are accumulated in a one-page output buffer and transferred to the disk when the buffer is filled. This process continues until all the distinct join attribute values found in R have been searched against the S relation and their corresponding tuples have been joined with the retrieved tuples of S.

The total instruction flow time for the above algorithm is

$$t \text{ [inst\_flow]} = t \text{ [comp]} + k * t \text{ [tp\_xfer]}$$

where k denotes the number of distinct join attribute values in R and $k * t[\text{tp\_xfer}]$ accounts for the transfer of the k selection commands to the associative memory.

It has been shown in Chapter 2 that, by using a four-way external merge sort algorithm, the sorting of relation R will take

$$t \text{ [sort, } R] = \log_4(m) * t \text{ [merge\_sort\_pg, } R]$$

The reading of the sorted relation R from the disk, b pages at a time, is

$$t \text{ [read\_b\_pg, } R] = b * t \text{ [I/O]}$$

Now consider how many such reads are necessary to find the k distinct join attribute values and, at the same time, to keep all the R tuples, which have the same join attribute value, in the input buffer so that they can be joined with S tuples. Since there are k distinct join attribute values in R and there are $m * t$ tuples of R, there will be $(m * t)/k$ tuples, on an average, associated with each distinct join attribute value. It is assumed here that these tuples can fit into the b-page input buffer for the relation R, that is, $(m * t)/k \leq b * t$. The number of complete sets of R tuples having the same join attribute values in b pages will be

$$n = \text{floor } ((b * t)/((m * t)/k))$$

where floor is a function that rounds a fraction number down to the closest integer value. The total number of times to perform the b-page read of R is $\text{ceil}(k/n)$. Note that some pages of R may have to be read twice in order for a complete set of tuples, which have the same join attribute value, to be in the host computer's main memory at the same time. Therefore, the total time for reading the sorted R in this algorithm is

$$t \text{ [read, } R] = \text{ceil}(k/n) * t \text{ [read\_b\_pg, } R] + t \text{ [access]}$$

For each distinct join attribute value in R, a selection command is issued to the associative memory to select the tuples of S that have the same attribute value. Using the analysis result derived for relation R and given in the selection algorithm, the processing of relation S for each selection operation will take the following time:

$$t \text{ [process, } S] = t \text{ [access]} + (s/q) * \{t \text{ [read\_q\_pg, } S]$$
$$+ t \text{ [am\_cycl]}\}$$
$$+ \text{sel\_fac} * s * t * t \text{ [tp\_mov]}$$

The preceding terms have the same expressions as those given in the selection algorithm except that relation S, instead of relation R, is involved. There are sel_fac $* s * t$ tuples of S that satisfy the selection conditions. The function of sel_fac is to account for an average number of tuples of S that can join with the current tuple of R. The use of sel_fac in place of join selectivity factor has been explained in Section 3.4.2. These tuples need to be joined with the set of $(m * t)/k$ tuples of R that have the same join attribute value. The join time would be

$$t \text{ [jn\_Rm} * t/k\_S] = (m * t)/k * \text{sel\_fac} * s * t * \{2 * t \text{ [mov]}\}$$

where $\{2 * t \text{ [mov]}\}$ accounts for the moving of two tuples to form a tuple of L in the output buffer.

The number of pages produced by this Join operation is

$$u = \text{ceil}((m * t)/k * \text{sel\_fac} * s * t)/(t/2))$$

Here, the division by $t/2$ is to account for the fact that a tuple of L is roughly twice the size of a tuple of R or S. These u pages form a part of the resulting relation L. They need to be written to the disk. The writing time is

$$t \text{ [write\_u\_pg, } L] = u * t \text{ [I/O]}$$

The total processing time for joining k sets of R tuples with the tuples of S is

$$t \text{ [process]} = t \text{ [sort, } R] + t \text{ [read, } R] + t \text{ [access]} + k$$
$$* \{t \text{ [process, } S]$$
$$+ t \text{ [jn\_Rm} * t/k\_S]\} + t \text{ [write\_u\_pg, } L]\}$$

The data collection in this algorithm consists of reading all $k * u$ pages of L from the disk to the host computer's main memory and transferring their tuples to the user's terminal. Thus,

$$t \text{ [data\_collect]} = k * u * t \text{ [I/O]} + t \text{ [access]} + k * \text{sel\_fac} * s * t * t \text{ [tp\_out]}$$

The total execution time for this algorithm is

$$t \text{ [Join]} = t \text{ [inst\_flow]} + t \text{ [process]} + t \text{ [data\_collect]}$$

5.5.2.3 STATISTICAL AGGREGATION.

The associative search capability cannot be exploited in performing the Statistical Aggregation operation. Nevertheless, two possible algorithms have been devised here for this operation. In the first algorithm, the host computer reads the referenced relation R and examines all the tuples to identify the distinct category attribute values. When a new category is identified, it is used to search all the tuples of R and to pick those that fall in that category. This associative search is carried out in a manner similar to the Selection operation. The retrieved tuples are then aggregated to produce a tuple of the resulting relation. The process continues until all the distinct categories found in the initial reading of R have been processed. This algorithm requires that the relation R be transferred once to the host computer and w times to the associative memory, where w is the number of distinct categories formed in this operation. To identify new categories requires that each tuple of R be compared with the previously identified categories. Due to the significant I/O and category identification times, this algorithm is obviously less efficient than the one described in the conventional system model of Chapter 2 in which the host computer does the Statistical Aggregation operation without the use of the associative memory.

In the second algorithm, the pages of relation R are loaded into the associative memory and the distinct category attribute values are fetched directly by the control mechanism of the associative memory. The distinct category attribute values are then used to search the entire relation in the associative memory for those tuples that belong to the same category. These tuples are then transferred to the host computer, which aggregates the summary attribute values. This method is very similar to the first one. It requires repeated scans and readings of the relation R and is obviously not very efficient.

Based on the considerations given in these two approaches, one can conclude that the features of associative memories cannot be used to improve the performance of the Statistical Aggregation operation.

5.5.2.4 UPDATE.

An Update operation consists of a selection phase and a tuple modification phase. The selection phase can take advantage of the content search capability of the associative memory, whereas, the tuple modification phase can be carried out by the host computer.

The instruction flow time is

$$t \text{ [inst\_flow]} = t \text{ [comp]} + t \text{ [tp\_xfer]}$$

The time for retrieving all the tuples, which satisfy the selection conditions, from the associative memory to the host computer has been shown in the selection algorithm to be

$$(m/q) * \{t \text{ [read\_q\_pg, } R] + t \text{ [am\_cycl]} + t \text{ [am\_unload]}\}$$

The time to update the selected tuples is

$$\text{sel\_fac} * m * t * (2 * t \text{ [s]} + t \text{ [cpu]})$$

Assuming that all the pages of R contain at least one updated tuple, the time to write the updated relation back to the disk is

$$m * t \text{ [I/O]}$$

Therefore, the total processing time for this operation is

$$
\begin{aligned}
t \text{ [process]} = {} &(m/q) * \{t \text{ [read\_q\_pg, } R] + t \text{ [am\_cycl]} \\
&+ t \text{ [am\_unload]}\} + \text{sel\_fac} * m * t \\
&* (2 * t \text{ [s]} + t \text{ [cpu]}) \\
&+ m * t \text{ [I/O]} + 2 * t \text{ [access]}
\end{aligned}
$$

The total execution time for update would be

$$t \text{ [Update]} = t \text{ [inst\_flow]} + t \text{ [process]}$$

5.6 SUMMARY AND DISCUSSION

This chapter has defined the terms *associative memory* and *associative memory system* and has described the architectural features of associative memories. It has shown that the content and context searches and the parallel-processing capabilities of these memory devices are ideally suited for database management applications. Although the data organizations in these memories are limited to one-dimensional bit strings and two-dimensional bit arrays, more complex data structures (e.g., trees and networks) can be implemented in associative memories at the expense of some associative storage space for storing explicit pointers and labels that define the structures.

The architecture and techniques used in some selected associative memory systems have also been described and illustrated. While associative memories offer fast data searches, the speed of staging data into these memory devices and of transferring data out of them presents a potential problem to the practical use of these devices for large database applications. This chapter has described a number of associative memory systems that employ various hardware and software techniques to alleviate the input and output problem. Associative memories can be used in conjunction with other database computer approaches and conventional memory management techniques to ease the I/O problem. However, the additional hardware and software complicates an associative memory system and increases its cost. The best use of an associative memory is to store small data structures (e.g., a directory or an index table) permanently in the memory. The data then can be searched at a very high speed without paying the cost of data staging.

From the analysis presented in Section 5.5, it should be clear to the reader that the power of an associative memory system lies in its fast selection and update capabilities. It cannot perform operations such as Join and Statistical Aggregation without the help of a conventional host computer. For these operations, large quantities of data need to be moved into and out of the associative memory. It may be faster to perform these operations directly by the host computer. The reader can assign different values to the parameters given in the cost formulas to determine the conditions under which the Join and Statistical Aggregation operations, using the algorithms suggested in Section 5.5.2, perform faster or slower than on a conventional computer.

5.7 BIBLIOGRAPHY

[AND76] Anderson, G. A., and Kain, R. Y.: "A Content-Addressed Memory Designed for Data Base Applications," *Proceedings of the 1976 International Conference on Parallel Processing,* Waldenwoods, Mich., 1976, pp. 191–195.

[BAT77] Batcher, K. E.: "STARAN Series E," *Proceedings of the 1977 International Conference on Parallel Processing,* Bellain, Mich., Aug. 1977, pp. 140–143.

[BER74] Berra, P. B.: "Some Problems in Associative Processing Applications to Data Base Management," *AFIPS Conference Proceedings,* vol. 43, 1974 NCC, Chicago, Ill., 1974, pp. 1–5.

[BER76] Berra, P. B., and Singhania, A.: "A Multiple Associative Organization for Pipelining a Directory to a Very Large Data Base," *Digest of Papers,* COMPCON 1976, pp. 109–112.

[BER79] Berra, P. B., and Oliver, E.: "The Role of Associative Array Processors in Data Base Machine Architecture," *IEEE COMPUTER,* vol. 12, no. 3, 1979, pp. 53–61.

[DAV74] Davis, E.: "STARAN Parallel Processor System Software," *AFIPS Conference Proceedings,* vol. 43, 1974 NCC, Chicago, Il., 1974, pp. 17–22.

[DEF71] DeFiore C., Stillman, N., and Berra, P. B.: "Associative Techniques in the Solution of Data Management Problems," *Proceedings of the ACM National Conference,* Chicago, Ill., 1971, pp. 28–36.

[DEF73] DeFiore, N., and Berra, P. B.: "A Data Management System Utilizing an Associative Memory," *AFIPS Conference Proceedings,* vol. 42, 1973 NCC, New York, 1973, pp. 181–185.

[DEF74] DeFiore, N., and Berra, P. B.: "A Quantitative Analysis of the Utilization of Associative Memories in Data Base Management," *IEEE Trans. on Computers,* vol. C-23, no. 2, Feb. 1974, pp. 121–123.

[FAR76] Farnsworth, D. L., Hoffman, C. P., and Shutt, J. J.: "Mass Memory Organization Study," Rome Development Center, TR-76-254, Sept. 1976.

[GOO75] Goodyear Aerospace Corporation: *STARAN Reference Manual,* revision 2, GER-15636B, Akron, Ohio, June 1975.

[HUR80] Hurson, A.: "An Associative Backend Machine for Data Base Management," Ph.D. dissertation, University of Central Florida, Orlando, Fla., 1980.

[HUR81] Hurson, A. R.: "An Associative Backend Machine for Data Base Management," *IEEE Workshop on Computer Architecture for Pattern Analysis and Image Data Base Management,* Virginia, Nov. 1981, 225–230.

[KER79] Kerr, D.: "Data Base Machines with Large Content Addressable Block and Structural Information Processors," *IEEE COMPUTER,* vol. 12, no. 3, March 1979, pp. 64–79.

[LEE63] Lee, C. Y., and Paull, M. C.: "A Content Addressable Distributed Logic Memory with Applications to Information Retrieval," *Proceedings of the IEEE,* vol. 51, no. 6 June 1963, pp. 921–932.

[LIN73] Linde, R., Gates, R., and Peng, T.: "Associative Processor Applications to Real-Time Data Management," *AFIPS Conference Proceedings,* vol. 42, 1973 NCC, New York, 1973, pp. 187–195.

[LOV73] Love, H. H. Jr.: "An Efficient Associative Processor Using Bulk Storage," *1973 Sagamore Computer Conference on Parallel Processing,* Sagamore, N.Y., Aug. 1973, pp. 103–112.

[MIN72] Minker, J.: "Associative Memories and Processors: A Description and Appraisal," Technical Report TR-195, University of Maryland, July, 1972.

[MOL85] Moldovan, D. I., and Tung, Y. W.: "SNAP: A VLSI Architecture for Artificial Intelligence Processing," *Journal of Parallel and Distributed Computing,* vol. 2, 1985, pp. 109–131.

[MOU73] Moulder, R.: "An Implementation of a Data Management System on an Associative Processor," *AFIPS Conference Proceedings,* vol. 42, 1973 NCC, New York, 1973, pp. 171–176.

[OLI79] Oliver, E. J.: "RELACS, An Associative Computer Architecture to Support a Relational Data Model," Ph.D. dissertation, Syracuse University, Syracuse, N.Y., 1979.

[RUD72] Rudolph, J. A.: "A Production Implementation of an Associative Array Processor-STARAN," *Proceedings of the Fall Joint Computer Conference,* Las Vegas, Nev., Nov. 1972, pp. 229–241.

[SAV67] Savitt, D. A., Love, H. H. Jr., and Troop, R. E.: "ASP: A New Concept in Language and Machine Organization," *Proceedings of the Spring Joint Computer Conference,* San Francisco, Calif., 1976, pp. 87–102.

[SHA79] Shaw, D. E.: "A Hierarchical Associative Architecture for the Parallel Evaluation of Relational Algebraic Database Primitives," Stanford Computer Science Department Report STAN-CS-79-778, October 1979.

[SHA80] Shaw, D. E.: "A Relational Database Machine Architecture," *Proceedings of the Fifth Workshop on Computer Architecture for Non-Numeric Processing,* Pacific Grove, Calif., March 1980, pp. 84–95.

[YAU77] Yau S. S., and Fung, H. S.: "Associative Processor Architecture—A Survey," *Computing Surveys,* vol. 9, no. 1, March 1977, pp. 3–28.

CHAPTER

6

MULTIPROCESSOR DATABASE COMPUTERS: SYSTEMS WITH REPLICATION OF FUNCTIONS

Chapters 6 and 7 describe the architecture and techniques used in a number of multiprocessor database computers that have been designed (and some implemented) to relieve the execution bottleneck of conventional Von Neumann processors. As discussed in Chapter 1, the so-called Von Neumann bottleneck is caused mainly by the pairing of a single processor with a single main memory, which restricts the execution of programs to one instruction at a time. These two chapters examine various approaches of using a number of cooperating processors or complete computer systems, each with its own processor, memory, and secondary storage device, to achieve the parallel execution of database management functions. In some of the systems to be described, special-purpose functional processors are used for performing special database operations efficiently. Thus, processing speed is gained both by parallel processing and functional specialization.

This chapter is organized as follows. The need for parallel processing and functional specialization is discussed in Section 6.1. A classification of multiprocessor database computers is given in Section 6.2. Two categories of multiprocessor database computers are established: systems with replication of functions and systems with distribution of functions. Each of these categories is further divided into two subcategories. The hardware and software architectures and processing techniques of the two subcategories in the first main category are described and illustrated in Sections 6.3 and 6.4. The systems in the second main category are described in Chapter 7. Section 6.5 contains an analysis of two abstract models for the two subcategories of the first main category. The summary and discussion for Chapter 6 is found at the end of Chapter 7, after the systems in the second main category have been presented.

6.1   PARALLEL PROCESSING AND FUNCTIONAL SPECIALIZATION

A conventional computer has a single central processor to perform arithmetic and logic operations. It works fairly well for database management applications in which database management functions are not so complex and databases are not very large. However, when the functional complexity and the database size increase, as in most database applications, the performance of a computer system decreases rapidly. There are two obvious solutions to this problem: (1) parallel processing and (2) functional specialization. Both of these require more and better hardware to achieve faster computations.

The idea of parallel processing is straightforward. Suppose that a computational task takes a single processor x units of time to complete and that the task can be decomposed into n parallel subtasks with an equal computational complexity. These subtasks can then be assigned to n processors, which can execute all the subtasks in parallel. Theoretically, the original computational task can be carried out in x/n time. However, in practice, the subtasks may take different amounts of time to process and there is usually an overhead associated with the original task decomposition, processor assignment, and synchronization and communication among processors. Thus, the computation time using the parallel processing approach will fall short of the theoretical optimum.

There are two general approaches to achieving parallel processing: (1) reduction (or decomposition) and (2) pipelining. As explained previously, a complex computational task can be reduced or decomposed into a number of parallel subtasks. This approach exploits the *horizontal parallelism* inherent in most complex computational problems. For example, in a database management system, a complex query can be decomposed into a tree structure of primitive database operations such as Selection, Projection, and Join in a relational database. The primitive operations on the same horizontal level of the tree can be executed by different processors simultaneously, thus achieving the *horizontal concurrency*.

The second approach—pipelining—uses a linear array of processors to perform different functions required to complete a computational task. A portion of the data required by the task is given to the first processor in the pipeline. It transforms the data in some way and passes the result to the next processor. While the first processor is processing the next portion of its input data, the second processor processes the data it has received from the first processor and passes its result to the third processor. This process continues until the last processor generates its first output. At this time, the pipeline is full. All processors work simultaneously on their own assigned tasks on different portions of the data they received (which forms the data pipeline); at every step of computation, some final result is produced by the last processor. Using the pipelining approach, a query tree would start its execution at the leaf nodes. As soon as a unit of output data (e.g., a record or a block of records) is produced by a leaf node, it is passed on to its parent node for processing. The final result would be produced by the root of the query tree. The processors that are assigned to the primitive operations beginning from a leaf to the root of a query tree form a vertical line. This parallel-processing approach is therefore said to exploit the *vertical concurrency*. A combined processing technique using both horizontal and vertical concurrencies is desirable since it takes advantage of both the corresponding concurrencies offered by a multiprocessor system.

It should be noted that this pipelining approach for data processing is the same in concept as the pipelining approach used in many large-scale computers for speeding up the central processors by overlapping the operations of their components. The only difference is in the granularity of the data being processed. In database management, a data pipeline is formed by data blocks that may correspond to the contents of disk tracks, for example. In conventional computer architecture, however, a pipeline contains machine words that may be data or instruction words.

Besides using parallel-processing techniques to gain speed in carrying out database management functions, a multiprocessor database computer can use a number of dedicated processors to carry out specific database management functions. These processors can be implemented either on conventional general-purpose hardware with specialized software to perform the functions or on special-purpose hardware designed for these functions. Special-purpose software and hardware can perform efficiently since they are tailored to perform the specific functions. New hardware technologies such as large-scale integration (LSI) and very large scale integration (VLSI) can be exploited. The approach of hardware functional specialization is generally cost-efficient and cost-effective since the speed of hardware has dramatically increased and the cost of hardware has drastically decreased in recent years.

6.2   A CLASSIFICATION OF MULTIPROCESSOR DATABASE COMPUTERS

There is obviously more than one way to classify a set of multiprocessor database computers. The classification of this category of database computers used here is a problem-oriented classification, which is consistent with the way the major categories of database computers have been classified in Chapter 1. In designing a multiprocessor system, a major consideration is to determine how database management functions are to be assigned to the processors and how data memories are interconnected with the processors to achieve a maximal degree of parallelism. Therefore, the assignment of functions and the interconnection of processors and data memories is used here as the guideline in this classification.

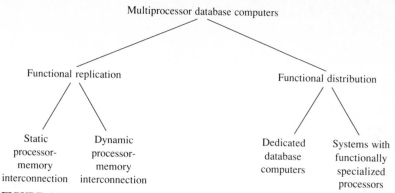

FIGURE 6.1
A classification of multiprocessor database computers.

Multiprocessor database computers are broadly divided into two categories: (1) systems with replicated functions and (2) systems with distributed functions (see Figure 6.1). In the first category, the processors used in these systems are general-purpose, Von Neumann processors, each of which is programmed to perform all or most of the essential database functions. Thus, the functions are replicated in all the processors that are assigned to do different functions at different times. This category is further divided into two groups based on how the processors and memories are interconnected: (1) systems with static processor-memory interconnection and (2) systems with dynamic processor-memory interconnection. Examples of the first group include MICRONET, MDBS, DBC/1012, EDC, GAMMA, HYPERTREE, REPT, NON-VON, and the University of Michigan's Boolean Cube-connected Multicomputer. Examples of the second group include DIRECT, GRACE, DBMAC, and SM3. Section 6.3 will describe the architectures, data organizations, and hardware and software techniques used by these two groups of multiprocessor systems.

In the second category, database management functions are distributed among a number of general-purpose or special-purpose processors. Each processor, when called upon, will execute its preassigned function(s). This category is further divided into two groups based on the way the functions are distributed: (1) dedicated database computers and (2) systems with functionally specialized processors. Examples of the first group include IDM, iDBP, and IQC. Examples of the second group include DBC, SABRE, RDBM, DELTA, DDM, CADAM, Systolic arrays, and VLSI tree machines. These systems will be described in Chapter 7.

6.3 MULTIPROCESSOR SYSTEMS WITH REPLICATION OF FUNCTIONS: STATIC PROCESSOR-MEMORY INTERCONNECTION

A database machine in this category is formed by a number of general-purpose microcomputers or minicomputers interconnected in some architectural structure.

Since the component systems use conventional general-purpose processors, they can be programmed to perform any database management function just as in conventional systems. Thus, database management functions can be replicated in these component systems and can be executed by sending proper commands to them. The replication of database management functions offers several advantages: reliability, availability, flexibility, and high performance. Reliability and availability are achieved by the redundant systems with the same functionality. A failed component can be easily replaced by another to carry out its functions. System flexibility is due to the ease in adding or reducing the number of component systems to meet different application needs. High performance can be achieved by assigning a subset or the entire set of component systems to simultaneously perform a specified function on different portions of a data file (SIMD processing) or by assigning different subsets of processors to work on different data streams (MIMD processing).

In order to fully exploit the parallel-processing potential of a multiprocessor system, it is necessary to pair a memory module with each processor so that all processors can simultaneously access and process the data stored in their own memory modules. There are two general ways of interconnecting processors and memory modules in this category of systems. They are (1) static processor-memory interconnection and (2) dynamic processor-memory interconnection. This section describes the systems that use the first approach. Section 6.4 will cover the systems that use the second approach.

In systems with static processor-memory interconnection, each processor has its own private memory module(s) and, in most cases, has its own secondary storage device(s). A private memory can only be accessed by the processor to which it is statically connected. In these systems, data files can either be horizontally or vertically partitioned into subfiles which are stored in a distributed fashion in the secondary storage devices. Different portions of these subfiles are preloaded into the private memory modules from the secondary storage devices and are simultaneously accessed and processed by the corresponding processors.

The main advantages of this interconnection method are: (1) accesses to the private memory modules are concurrent and free of memory contentions and (2) input/output of data from/to the secondary storage devices can be carried out in parallel if processors also have their own private secondary storage devices. However, this method is not without its disadvantages. Each processor is restricted to the size of its own private memory module for storing programs and data, since the private memory modules cannot be shared. Furthermore, several frequent database operations, such as Sort, Join, Duplicate Elimination, Set Intersection, Set Union, and so forth, require that the data produced by one processor be transferred to other processors. Sizeable data may have to be moved around or exchanged among the processors. Thus, the advantages of having private main memory and secondary storage for parallel processing and I/O do not apply to all database functions.

There are three predominant architectural structures used by this category of systems: bus, tree, and cube. Descriptions of the architectural features, data organization, and implementation techniques of these subcategories of machines follow.

6.3.1 Bus-Structured Systems

Several database machines have been designed and implemented using bus architecture. Some examples are the MICRONET of the University of Florida [SU78, BRO80, GEN82, SU82, and SU83], the EDC of the Electrotechnical Laboratory of Japan [UEM80], the MDBS of The Ohio State University [HSI81a, HSI81b, HE83, HSI83a, HSI83b, HSI83c, and BOY83], the commercial system, Teradata's DBC/1012 [TER84], and the GAMMA of the University of Wisconsin [DEW86]. Although, they are different in architectural details and implementation techniques in many aspects, they are quite similar in overall architectural concept and design objectives. The following subsections describe some common as well as distinct features and techniques of these systems.

6.3.1.1 ARCHITECTURE OF MICRONET, EDC, MDBS, DBC/1012, AND GAMMA.
The general organization of a bus-structured multiprocessor system is shown in Figure 6.2. The component systems are connected by a common bus or a ring bus through which database commands and data travel from one system to another. One of the component systems serves as a control computer, which, among other functions, translates high-level data manipulation queries into low-level database primitives, maintains the global data dictionary, dispatches database primitives to the other component systems (the data processors) for execution, manages transaction execution and other database management functions (e.g., concurrency control), and collects retrieval results from the data processors. The data processors handle I/O between the private main memories and secondary storage devices, perform the specified database operations, and assemble and deliver results.

The implementation techniques of the general architecture described previously are different from system to system. Descriptions of some of these follow.

MICRONET. MICRONET is a multiprocessor system designed and prototyped at the University of Florida during 1976 to 1982. It consists of a set of identical microcomputer systems (PDP 1103s were used in the prototype implementation), each of which consists of a processor, main memory, secondary storage medium, and standard I/O devices. MICRONET has the general architecture shown in Figure 6.3. All the computers in this system are connected to a custom-built bus called the MICRONET bus through custom-built interface units. Since all component systems are identical, any one of them can be dynamically designated as the control computer, the software of which is different from that of the rest of the component systems called *data computers*. The system operates in two modes: local and global. In local mode, each component computer can receive queries from the user. The queries are executed by the computer on its local database, and the results are returned to the user. In this mode, each computer

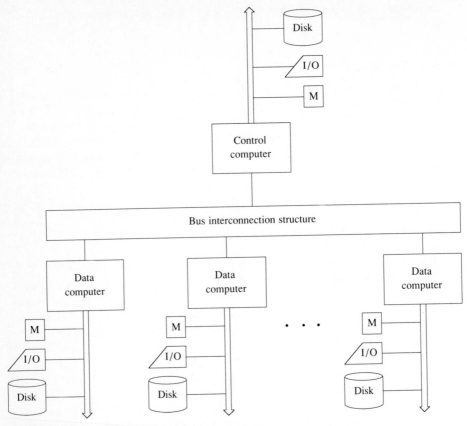

FIGURE 6.2
A general architecture of bus-structured systems.

serves as the control computer overseeing the execution of its local queries. In the global mode, queries are processed by all the component computers on the global database, which is physically distributed among the component systems. The execution of each query is controlled by the computer through which the query is submitted.

MICRONET can operate either as an independent microcomputer network or as a back-end multiprocessor system to a host computer. The design also achieves the goals of system reliability and availability since any component systems can be replaced by another, including the control computer. Also, removable disk packs can be moved from one system to another or exchanged between systems without affecting the result of a database request. This feature is achieved by addressing data files by names rather than by their physical disk units. The system can also be expanded easily. More interface units and component systems can be added by simply connecting them to the MICRONET bus. The number of disk units in each component system can be increased to accommodate large databases.

The key features of the MICRONET hardware are its custom-built bus and interfaces. These are specially designed to support the frequent database

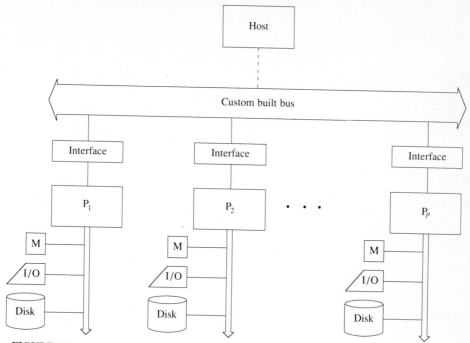

FIGURE 6.3
Architecture of the MICRONET.

operations such as Selection, Join, Projection, Sort and concurrency control operations. They provide simple hardware facilities to (1) perform interprocessor communication, synchronization, and control, (2) resolve bus access contention, and (3) broadcast data and commands. These facilities are essential in a multi-processor system with distributed databases.

The MICRONET bus is a flat cable consisting of 32 lines, 16 of which are used for address and data purposes; 12 of the other 16 lines are used for control purposes, and the other 4 lines are used for parity and error checking. The 12 control lines include:

1. Three lines associated with the clock circuit, which are used to grant the "sender" status to a "requesting" computer.
2. Two lines, a sender ready (SR) and a receiver ready (RR), which are used for hardware-handshaking purposes.
3. Five global acknowledge (GA) lines, which are used for communication and synchronization during parallel-processing operations.
4. Two lines, a global interrupt request (GINTR) line and a global interrupt acknowledge (GINTA) line, which are used to request and acknowledge interrupts issued by the computers, respectively.

The block diagram of the MICRONET interface is shown in Figure 6.4. It consists of six main modules:

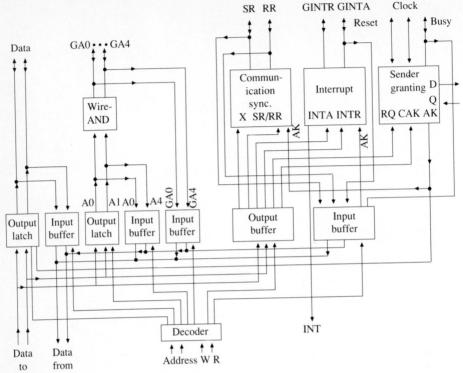

FIGURE 6.4

Block diagram of the MICRONET interface. (*Source:* [SU83] copyright © 1983. Computer Science Press, Inc., reprinted by permission.)

1. *Input and output buffers* temporarily store data transferred between computers.
2. A *decoder* selects the particular I/O buffer being read from or written to by the computer connected to this network interface.
3. A *global wire-AND circuit* is used to perform interprocess synchronization in the following way. The five local lines (A0 to A4) in the interface can be set or sensed by the computer connected to the interface. These lines are globally ANDed with the corresponding local lines in other interface units, and the resulting conditions (represented by GA0 to GA4) can be sensed by all computers. To illustrate how these lines can be used, assume that a computer has issued a retrieval request by broadcasting a command through the bus to all the computers, including itself. All the computers simultaneously carry out the command on the partitioned databases residing in their private secondary storage devices. Each receiver computer sets a predetermined local line upon its completion of the task. A computer to which the command does not apply (e.g., say, a computer that does not contain the right data) also sets its local line. When the last computer has set its local line, the corresponding global line becomes active. If the sender computer wants to know the completion of a task carried out by all the computers, it simply senses the global line. Processing can then be synchronized.

4. A *sender-granting circuit* resolves the possible contention in accessing the network bus by the processors. This circuit is a distributed, ring-structured circuit as shown in Figure 6.5. A flip-flop is available in each computer's network interface and is connected serially to the flip-flop of the next adjacent interface board. The flip-flop of the last interface board is connected to that of the first interface board to form a distributed, ring-structured shift register. Only one flip-flop is set after a reset signal. The shifting of the '1' in the ring is controlled by a clock. When the clock is enabled, the bit is shifted around the ring register. A computer that wishes to use the bus sets its request line, RQ. Any number of computers may make the same request simultaneously. The one with its flip-flop set receives access to the bus. It then sets the flip-flop B shown in the figure to disable the clock and sets the AK and BUSY lines. After its use of the bus, it sets the clear acknowledge line CAK to clear flip-flop B and starts the ring register rotating again. The hardware just described, in effect, implements a round-robin algorithm to schedule the use of the bus.

5. An *interrupt circuit* allows a computer to interrupt all other computers. The global interrupt request line, GINTR, is used to send the interrupt signal to all other computers; the global interrupt acknowledge line, GINTA, in turn is set when all computers have been interrupted.

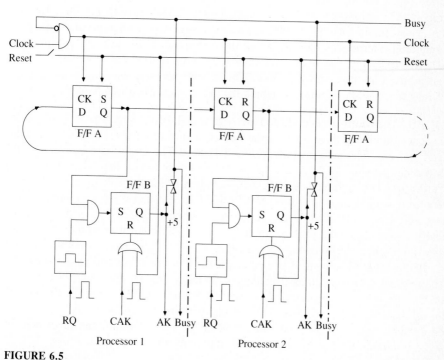

FIGURE 6.5
Sender-granting circuit. (*Source:* [SU83] copyright ©1983. Computer Science Press, Inc., reprinted by permission.)

6. A *communication synchronization circuit* performs hardware handshaking during interprocessor communication and data transfer. In MICRONET, a single bus, which contains control and address lines, is used. Only two control lines (SR and RR of Figure 6.4) are used to perform synchronization functions. These two lines are globally wire-ANDed and are used in the following manner. A sender computer issues an interrupt to all other processors via the GINTR line and waits for an acknowledgement via GINTA. After the acknowledgement is received, indicating that all the receiver computers are ready to receive data, the sender outputs a word on the data lines and sets the SR line. All receivers sense the SR line to see if data are ready. If so, all receivers read the data simultaneously and set their own local RR lines. When all local RR lines are set, the global RR line is set automatically. It tells the sender that all receivers are ready to receive another piece of data. The process continues until all the data have been broadcast.

EDC. EDC stands for *E*lectronic-disk Oriented *D*atabase *C*omplex. It is a multiprocessor system designed and prototyped by the Electrotechnic Laboratory of Japan in the late 1970s. The main architectural feature of this system is its use of magnetic bubble memories as the private secondary storage devices for storing partitioned data files (see Figure 6.6). Each bubble memory is composed of major-minor loop magnetic-bubble memory chips. In the prototype implementation, each bubble memory contains 128K bytes (16 64K-bit chips). A larger chip set (32 chips) was used in a later version, EDC II, built in 1980. Besides the private main memory module, each processor has a microprogram memory containing microcodes for controlling the operations of the processor. Similar to MICRONET, any one of the component systems (called data module in EDC) can be used as the control module. This design takes advantage of the features of magnetic bubble memories, which have been described in Chapter 3.

MDBS. The Multi-backend Database System (MDBS) is a multiprocessor system designed and being developed by the same group of researchers who designed the DBC system. The project started around 1980 at The Ohio State University and is presently being implemented at the Naval Postgraduate School in Monterey, California. The architecture of MDBS is shown in Figure 6.7. Its general architecture is very similar to that of MICRONET except that it uses a commercially available bus, ETHERNET, and the control computer is fixed rather than dynamically assigned. In the present implementation, the control computer is a VAX 780 running the UNIX operating system and the data processors are implemented on PDP 11/44s. The control computer (or the host) receives and passes database queries and spreads database management tasks among the multiple back-end processors (the data processors). A special feature of this system is the use of an attribute-based data model and a data-clustering technique. This system will be detailed further in the next subsection on data organization and placement in static (common bus) processor-memory interconnection multiprocessors.

DBC/1012. The DBC/1012 database computer marketed by the Teradata Corporation is the only commercially available system in this category. Its system

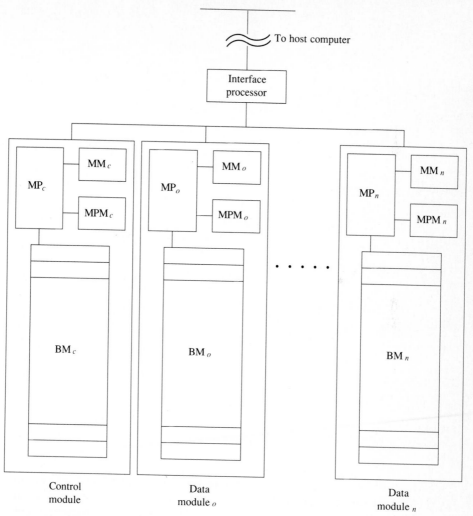

To host computer

MP: Module Processor
MM: Main Memory
MPM: Microprogram Memory
BM: Bubble Memory

FIGURE 6.6

Architecture of EDC. (*Source:* [UEM80] copyright ©1980. Elsevier Science Publishing Co., reprinted by permission.)

architecture is shown in Figure 6.8. DBC/1012 is designed to serve as a back-end processor to one or more host computers. It consists of one or, optionally, several control processors called interface processors (IFPs), two interprocessor buses called Ynets, a number of database processors called access module processors (AMPs), and disk storage units (DSUs).

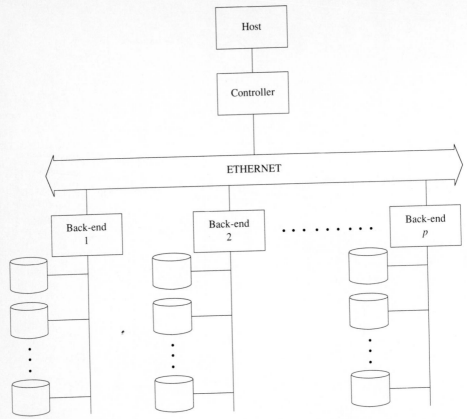

FIGURE 6.7
Architecture of MDBS. (*Source:* [HSI83*a*] copyright ©1983. Prentice-Hall, Inc., reprinted by permission.)

The IFP's main functions are (1) to manage the commands and data passed between a host computer and the DBC/1012, (2) to translate queries from a host computer into internal commands, (3) to pass the commands over the Ynets to the AMPs for execution, and (4) to collect the results generated by the AMPs. The hardware organization of an IFP is shown in Figure 6.9. It consists of:

1. A controller that is built using the Intel 8086 family of microprocessor components, including the 8087 Numeric Data Processor and a channel interface to the host computer using the Intel 8089 Input/Output Processor for managing the interface to an IBM block multiplexer channel. More recent systems use Intel 80286 and 80287 processors, which are two and one-half times faster than 8086.

2. A memory that contains 1M byte of RAM with error-checking and error-correction (ECC) capability and 64K bytes of erasable programmable read-only memory (EPROM).

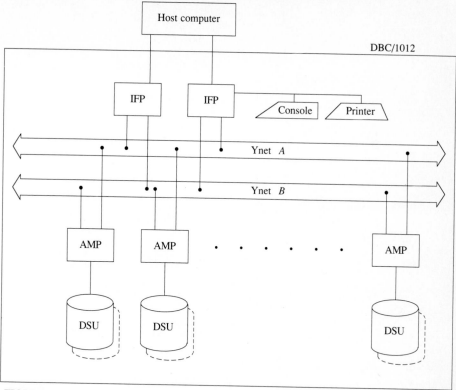

FIGURE 6.8

Architecture of DBC/1012. (*Source:* [TER84] reprinted by permission of Teradata Corporation.)

3. Two Ynet interface units, each of which contains the interface logic and 32K bytes of high-speed random access memory (HSRAM) for buffering the message blocks read from or written to the Ynets.

4. A processor module bus that connects these modules.

The AMPs are responsible for carrying out the execution of database operations. They receive commands from the IFPs and return the appropriate responses to them through the Ynets. The hardware organization of an AMP is shown in Figure 6.10. The AMPs use the same basic circuit boards as the IFPs. The only difference is that they use a Signetics 8X300 microprocessor for managing the industry standard SMD interface to the disk storage units (DSUs).

The DSUs are storage devices across which data files are evenly distributed. More than one DSU can be connected to a single AMP. The DSU used in DBC/1012 is a 474M-byte, Winchester-type, random-access device. It uses a fixed, sealed module as the storage medium with an average seek time of 18 msecs and a transfer rate of 1.9M bytes per second.

The Ynets are independent, intelligent buses that incorporate hardware mechanisms to perform many tasks associated with interprocessor communication,

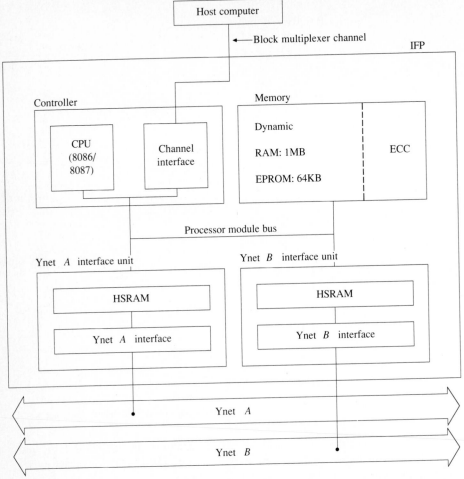

FIGURE 6.9
The hardware organization of IFP. (*Source:* [TER84] reprinted by permission of Teradata Corporation.)

synchronization, and control. They represent a very special feature of this system. A conventional bus is passive in the sense that it functions only as a medium through which data or messages travel. It does not contain any logic to transform these data or messages. Each Ynet, on the other hand, contains an array of active logic that provides a switching mechanism in the system. The Ynet not only passes messages or data blocks to and from IFPs and AMPs, but it also performs selection and sorting functions. A later section in this chapter will detail how these special-purpose buses are used to support some of the primitive database operations.

The basic Ynet configuration, called a *node module*, is shown in Figure

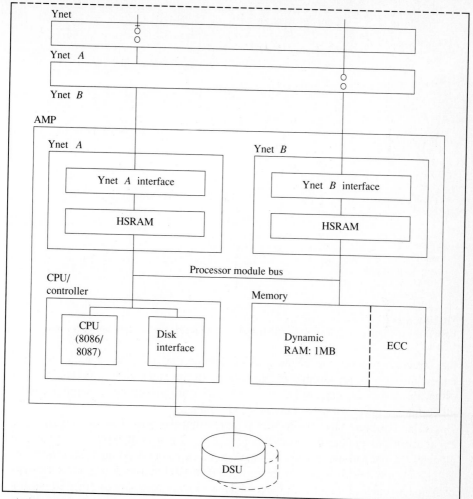

FIGURE 6.10

The hardware configuration of AMP. (*Source:* [TER84] reprinted by permission of Teradata Corporation.)

6.11. It is a hierarchical network of nodes. One set of the Ynet interface units for AMPs and IFPs are connected to the leaf nodes of one of the two Ynets, as illustrated in the figure. The other set, not shown in the figure, is connected to the other Ynet. A database request from an IFP would travel first up the node module hierarchy and then down either toward a single AMP (in case of a one-to-one communication between an IFP and an AMP) or toward a number or all of the AMPs (in case of a one-to-many communication). In the upward direction, if more than one IFP or AMP attempts to send data or requests simultaneously, then a hardware contention logic is available to resolve the contention. The two-

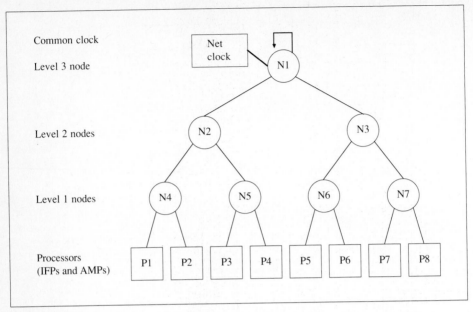

FIGURE 6.11
Basic Ynet configuration. (*Source:* [TER84] reprinted by permission of Teradata Corporation.)

bus structure reduces the chances of contention and provides a more effective bandwidth to a larger number of processors. In the downward direction, the bus offers the broadcast capability. Since all nodes are driven by a common clock, all communication within a Ynet is synchronous.

This common-bus architecture requires that the node module hierarchy be expanded if the number of processors increases. The system expansion is handled elegantly in the following way. A Ynet can be expanded beyond eight processors by using a number of node expansion modules. Each expansion module consists of 3 nodes, each of which can be connected to node modules or other expansion modules. Figure 6.12 illustrates how 64 processors can be connected to 2 Ynets using 16 node modules and 6 node expansion modules.

GAMMA. This is a multiprocessor system being developed at the University of Wisconsin by the same research group that developed the prototype DIRECT, a multiprocessor system with a dynamic processor-memory interconnection to be described in Section 6.4.1. The architecture of GAMMA is shown in Figure 6.13. It consists of a set of identical data computers (20 VAX 11/750s in the current implementation), each of which has its local main memory and secondary storage. These computers are interconnected by a ring bus (an 80M bits-per-second token ring developed by Proteon Associates). Another VAX computer running Berkeley UNIX is used as the host computer. Some of these data computers (8 of them in present implementaion) have disks as their secondary storage devices.

*   *   *

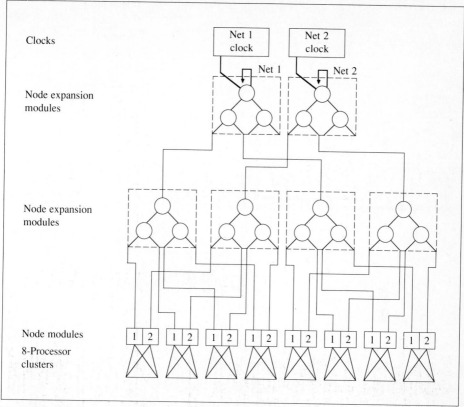

FIGURE 6.12

A multilevel network configuration. (*Source:* [TER84] reprinted by permission of Teradata Corporation.)

The architecture of these five systems have the following common features: (1) the pairing of processors and memory devices, (2) the parallel I/O capability, (3) the ease in expanding the computational power of these systems by increasing the number of component systems, (4) the use of general-purpose computers to allow flexible implementation of system and application software, and (5) the broadcasting capability (with the exception of the GAMMA, which can route data through the token ring).

The potential problems with the bus-structured systems are: (1) concurrent processes may simultaneously access the common bus or the token ring, generating a lot of bus access contentions (DBC/1012 uses two Ynets to avoid this problem), and (2) in a broadcasting system such as MICRONET, EDC, and MBDS, data processors not involved in an operation may be interrupted unnecessarily when data are broadcast through the bus.

6.3.1.2 DATA ORGANIZATION AND PLACEMENT. The file structure(s) used to organize data and the methods for partitioning and placing data in the compo-

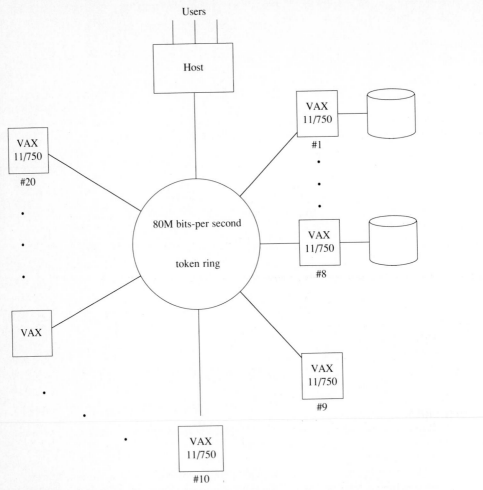

FIGURE 6.13
Architecture of GAMMA. (*Source:* [DEW86] copyright © 1986. Morgan Kaufmann Publisher, Inc., reprinted by permission.)

nent systems of a multiprocessor system play an important role in determining the efficiency of the system. These factors determine, to a great extent, the speed with which data can be accessed and manipulated and the amount of I/O and intercomponent data transfers required to carry out a database function. Several principles and techniques related to data organization and placement can be followed to increase the efficiency of a bus-structured system:

1. *Parallel processing.* If a data file is large, it can be divided either horizontally into subsets of records or vertically into subsets of attributes and values. These subsets can be stored in the local memory or secondary storage of the component systems. They can then be independently processed in parallel by the processors. Data can also be read from and written into disks simultaneously.

2. *Load balancing*. If data are evenly distributed among all the component systems, an identical operation to be carried out by each component system will take roughly the same amount of time (some difference may result due to different data contents) so that a maximal amount of concurrency can be achieved.

3. *Bus traffic reduction*. In a common-bus system, all messages and data that need to be passed among processors are transferred through the bus. To avoid bus contention and excessive waiting for the bus to be freed, it is important to reduce the amount and frequency of messages and data transfers. This can be achieved in many ways. One way is to place related data in the same component system so that data need not be fetched from another component system too frequently. Another way is to use an algorithm that requires the least amount of messages and data transfers through the bus. Still another way is to use hardware to reduce the number of transfers, resolve bus access contentions, and/or increase the speed of transfers.

The remainder of this section examines the data organization and placement strategies used in some of the bus-structured multiprocessor computers to show how these principles and techniques are applied.

In all the systems described in Section 6.3.1.1, the technique of horizontal partitioning of data files is used. Thus, subsets of records are distributed in different component systems, but all attribute values of a single record are stored in the same processor. This method of data partitioning is particularly suitable for relational database processing since a tuple (or record) of a relation is considered a basic data unit and a tuple or a set of tuples are processed one at a time by primitive relational operations. The systems in this subcategory use different data distribution strategies. The data structures used to store subsets of records in the component systems are also different. Descriptions of some of these follow.

MICRONET. The tuples of a relation in the MICRONET are naturally distributed among the component systems based on the need for supporting local applications. The number of tuples in one component system may be different from the others. However, for achieving a higher degree of parallelism in data processing, tuples can be moved around among the component systems to achieve an even distribution. The data organization of each segment of a relation is based on the fully inverted file concept. As shown in Figure 6.14, a base relation directory (BRD) contains an entry for each base relation in the database. The entry contains the relation name (R), the number of domains (ND), the relation size (RS) in terms of the number of tuples, and a pointer to an information block that stores the key domain name and a domain name table for converting domain names into unique domain numbers. Symbolic names in queries are replaced by domain numbers during query translation. The base relation segment directory (BRSD) in each data processor contains an entry for each relation segment stored in the processor. Each entry contains the name of the relation (R), the number of domains (ND), the number of valid tuples (NVT), the length of the condensed master table (LCMT), and a pointer to a data block describing the relation

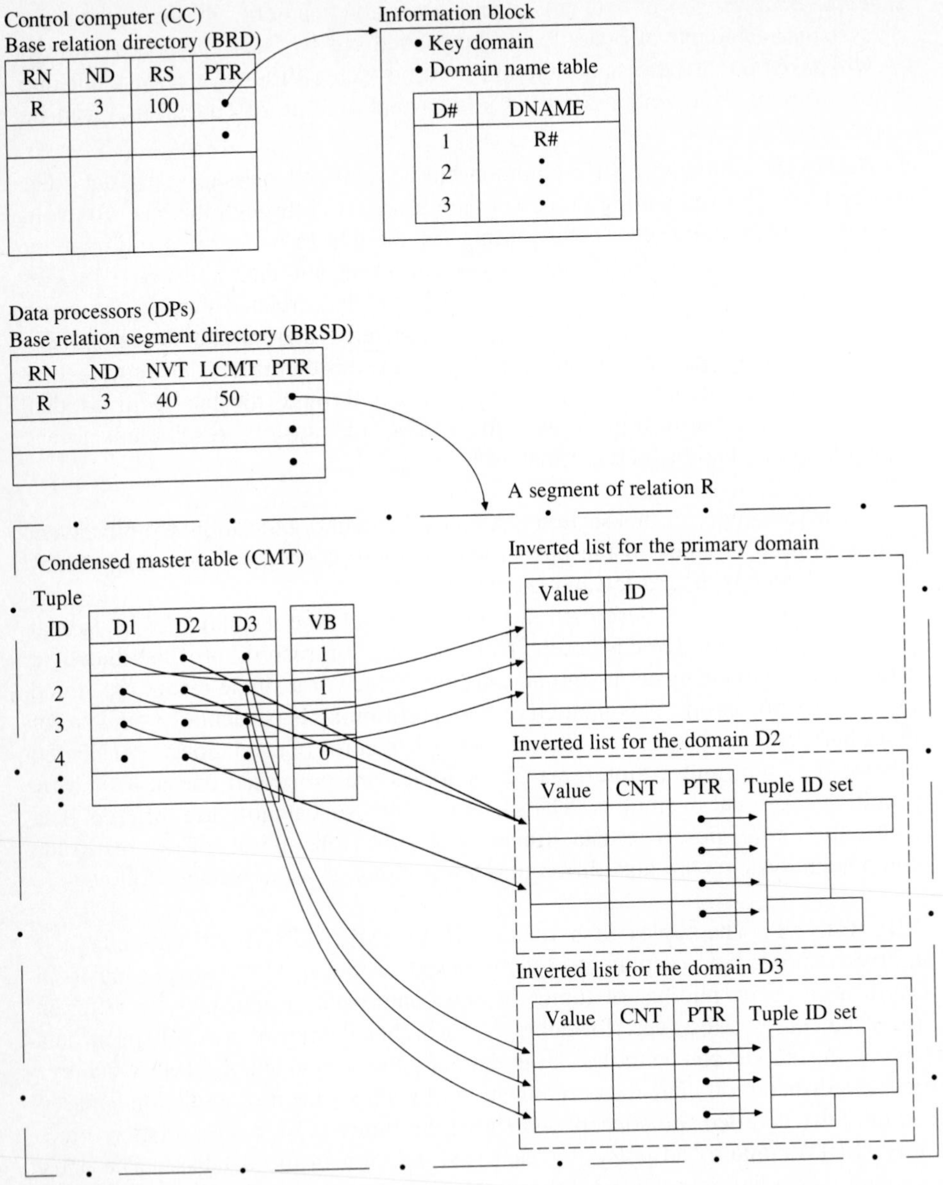

Control computer (CC)
Base relation directory (BRD)

RN	ND	RS	PTR
R	3	100	•
			•

Information block
• Key domain
• Domain name table

D#	DNAME
1	R#
2	•
3	•

Data processors (DPs)
Base relation segment directory (BRSD)

RN	ND	NVT	LCMT	PTR
R	3	40	50	•
				•
				•

A segment of relation R

Condensed master table (CMT)

Inverted list for the primary domain

	Value	ID

Tuple

ID	D1	D2	D3	VB
1				1
2				1
3				1
4				0

Inverted list for the domain D2

Value	CNT	PTR	Tuple ID set
		•	
		•	
		•	
		•	

Inverted list for the domain D3

Value	CNT	PTR	Tuple ID set
		•	
		•	
		•	

FIGURE 6.14
Base relation directories in the control computer and data processors. (*Source:* [SU83] copyright
©1983. Computer Science Press, Inc., reprinted by permission.)

segment. The data block contains a condensed master table (CMT) and inverted
lists (one for each domain of the relation). Each entry of the CMT corresponds to
a tuple in the original relation segment. Thus, the entry number is the same as the
tuple number. However, the values in the entry are pointers to the inverted lists
established for the domains of the original relation segment. Each column in the

CMT specifies the entries in an inverted head table where the actual values of a domain in the original relation segment can be found. In the inverted head table, all domain values are hashed by an order-preserving function (different functions can be used for different domains) and are stored at the hash addresses. A count (CNT) field specifies the number of times a value occurs in the column. It can be omitted for candidate key domains since the value is always 1. Another field contains a pointer to a set of tuple numbers that identifies the tuples containing the domain value. For key domains, the pointer field stores the tuple number.

Thus, the base relation segments are fully inverted. There are no master files for the original relation segments. They are replaced by the condensed master tables. A bit (VB) is used for each entry of the CMT to indicate if a tuple has been deleted (0) or not (1). Thus, the NVT field of the BRSD entry specifies the number of valid (undeleted) tuples, and the LCMT field specifies the total number of tuples.

STUDENT

S#	SNAME	SEX	AGE
14256	J.R. Jones	M	23
16242	J.C. Brown	F	21
17522	T.S. Larsen	M	26

COURSE

CID	CTITLE	PERIOD	PROF_NAME
CIS4121	Computer Organization	2	T.B. Bronson
CIS6220	Compiler	4	S.B. Jensen
EE5417	Database Engineering	6	N.T. Yong
EE6967	Database Machine	4	T.B. Bronson

STUDENT_COURSE

S#	CID	GRADE_PT
16242	CIS4121	4.0
16242	EE5417	2.5
17522	EE5417	3.0
14256	EE5417	3.0
14256	EE6967	4.0
17522	EE6220	3.5
17522	EE6967	2.0

FIGURE 6.15
Example relations.

As an example, Figure 6.15 shows three relation segments of our example education database. The content of the BRD in the control processor is given in Figure 6.16. The data organization of these three segments is shown in Figure 6.17.

The order-preserving characteristics of hash functions allow data comparison operators such as <, ≤, >, and ≥ to be carried out using the order of the inverted head table. The CMT is used to avoid storing the original domain values twice (once in a master file and once in an inverted file). During output time, data values must be fetched indirectly through the CMT. Thus, storage saving is achieved at the expense of longer output time. However, since output is the last step of a lengthy processing cycle and since output processing in MICRONET is also done in parallel fashion, the use of a condensed master table is felt to be justifiable. The fully inverted organization allows data to be retrieved at high speed. However, it has the well-known disadvantage associated with data updates. The disadvantage in this case is not as serious as a centralized system since data

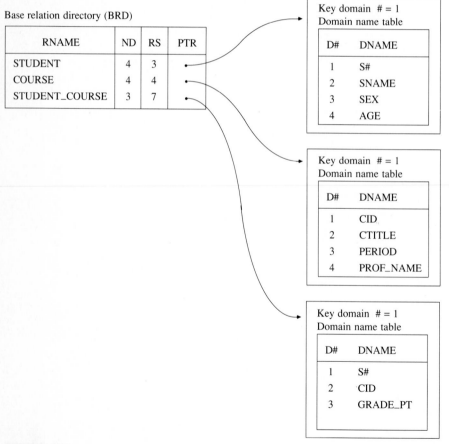

FIGURE 6.16
Base relation directory in the control computer.

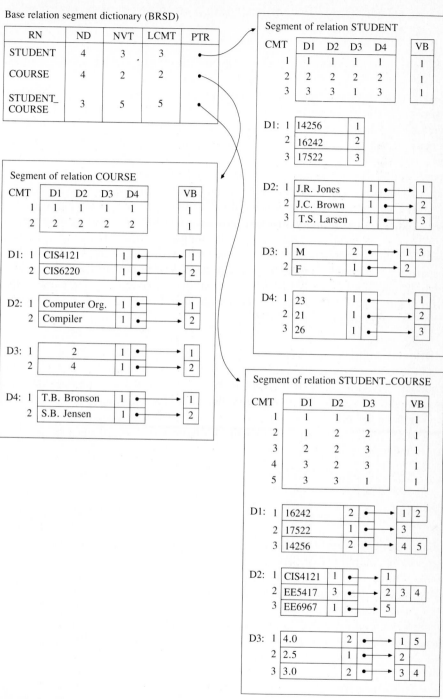

Base relation segment dictionary (BRSD)

RN	ND	NVT	LCMT	PTR
STUDENT	4	3	3	•
COURSE	4	2	2	•
STUDENT_COURSE	3	5	5	•

Segment of relation STUDENT

CMT	D1	D2	D3	D4		VB
1	1	1	1	1		1
2	2	2	2	2		1
3	3	3	1	3		1

D1: 1 | 14256 | 1
2 | 16242 | 2
3 | 17522 | 3

D2: 1 | J.R. Jones | 1 | • | → | 1
2 | J.C. Brown | 1 | • | → | 2
3 | T.S. Larsen | 1 | • | → | 3

D3: 1 | M | 2 | • | → | 1 | 3
2 | F | 1 | • | → | 2

D4: 1 | 23 | 1 | • | → | 1
2 | 21 | 1 | • | → | 2
3 | 26 | 1 | • | → | 3

Segment of relation COURSE

CMT	D1	D2	D3	D4		VB
1	1	1	1	1		1
2	2	2	2	2		1

D1: 1 | CIS4121 | 1 | • | → | 1
2 | CIS6220 | 1 | • | → | 2

D2: 1 | Computer Org. | 1 | • | → | 1
2 | Compiler | 1 | • | → | 2

D3: 1 | 2 | 1 | • | → | 1
2 | 4 | 1 | • | → | 2

D4: 1 | T.B. Bronson | 1 | • | → | 1
2 | S.B. Jensen | 1 | • | → | 2

Segment of relation STUDENT_COURSE

CMT	D1	D2	D3		VB
1	1	1	1		1
2	1	2	2		1
3	2	2	3		1
4	3	2	3		1
5	3	3	1		1

D1: 1 | 16242 | 2 | • | → | 1 | 2
2 | 17522 | 1 | • | → | 3
3 | 14256 | 2 | • | → | 4 | 5

D2: 1 | CIS4121 | 1 | • | → | 1
2 | EE5417 | 3 | • | → | 2 | 3 | 4
3 | EE6967 | 1 | • | → | 5

D3: 1 | 4.0 | 2 | • | → | 1 | 5
2 | 2.5 | 1 | • | → | 2
3 | 3.0 | 2 | • | → | 3 | 4

FIGURE 6.17
Base relation segments in a data processor.

updates and adjustment of pointers in this data organization can be performed in parallel by the data processors.

DBC/1012. In this system, selected attributes of a relation can be designated as the primary and secondary indices when a relation is created. An index table is created in which each value of an indexed attribute has a number of pointers associated with it. These pointers specify the disk addresses of all tuples containing that value. Thus, index tables for the indexed attributes can be used to directly access the associated tuples during retrieval operations. Data accesses through indexed attributes can be done very efficiently. DBC/1012 allows secondary indices to be created at run-time by a CREATE INDEX statement in its data manipulation language called *TE*radata *QUE*ry *L*anguage, or TEQUEL.

The tuples of a relation are initially distributed among AMPs based on the hash values of the primary indexed attribute. During data loading time, each processor is assigned a value range. The tuples whose hash values fall in a specific range are stored together in the secondary storage of an AMP. The data distribution task is aided by the hardware of the Ynets. Using this hashing scheme, relations may not be evenly distributed among the component systems unless the distribution of hash values can be predetermined and the sizes of the value ranges are properly adjusted for the AMPs.

MDBS. In MDBS, an attribute-based data model is used. In this model, the smallest unit of data is called a *keyword,* which is an attribute-value pair. For example, (SNAME, J. C. BROWN), (CTITLE, COMPILER), and (GRADE, A) are examples of keywords. A *record* in this model is comprised of a collection of keywords and a record body. The *record body* consists of a character string that is not used for search purposes. All the keywords of a record must be distinct. An example record is shown below:

((S#, 14256), (SNAME, J.R. Jones), (SEX, M), (AGE, 23),
(ADDRESS, 412 NW 5TH St. Gainesville, FLA. 32601))

In MDBS, a *file* contains a set of records, each of which is represented by a set of keywords. In order to facilitate fast access of records from secondary storage devices in response to search queries, MDBS clusters records based on the semantic similarity of their contents. Clusters of records become the logical units of a database. Records of a cluster are evenly distributed among the set of back-end computers. In each back-end computer, the set of the records belonging to a cluster are physically close together on a disk so that they can be accessed together with minimal disk access delays. The method used for record clustering is adopted from the earlier work on the DBC system, the data filtering aspect of which has been discussed in Chapter 4. A description of the clustering technique follows.

First, we define some terms. A *keyword predicate* is a construct of the form:

Attribute—Relational Operator—Value

where a relational operator can be one of the set $(=, \neq, >, <, \geq, \leq)$. A *descriptor* can be one of the following three types:

1. A conjuction of less-than-or-equal-to predicate and a greater-than-or-equal-to predicate, such that the same attribute appears in both predicates. An example of this type is: (AGE $\geq$ 23) and (AGE $\leq$ 35), which can be expressed in the form of a range specification, $23 \leq$ AGE ≤ 35.
2. An equality predicate such as S# = 14256.
3. A single attribute that is automatically paired with all the possible values of the attribute to form a set of descriptors of the second type. For example, if the attribute used is SEX, then two equality predicates are used to form two SEX descriptors: SEX = M and SEX = F.

   Descriptors are defined by a database creator. They represent semantic properties of records based on which records are to be grouped into clusters. Descriptors do not overlap in the sense that each specifies a single or a unique set of values. Thus, the descriptors ($20 \leq$ AGE ≤ 35) and ($30 \leq$ AGE ≤ 40) overlap each other and should not both be defined for a database.

   A *cluster* is a grouping of records of a file, the contents of which satisfy the conditions specified by a set of descriptors of the types described here. As an example of cluster formation, consider the following two data files with record numbers assigned to them to uniquely identify their records:

STUDENT file	RECORD #
((S#, 14256), (SNAME, J.R. Jones), (AGE, 23))	1
((S#, 16242), (SNAME, J.C. Brown), AGE, 21))	2
((S#, 17522), (SNAME, T.S. Larsen), (AGE, 26))	3

STUDENT_COURSE file	RECORD #
((S#, 14256), (CID, EE6967), (GRADE_PT, 4.0))	4
((S#, 16242), (CID, CIS4121), (GRADE_PT, 4.0))	5
((S#, 17522), (CID, EE5417), (GRADE_PT, 3.0))	6

   Assume that the creator of these two data files (e.g., the database administrator) specifies the following descriptors:

$20 \leq$ AGE ≤ 25
$26 \leq$ AGE ≤ 30
GRADE_PT

The set of descriptors generated by this specification is shown in Figure 6.18 in which a unique descriptor number is assigned to each descriptor. Here, it is

Descriptor	Descriptor ID
$20 \leq AGE \leq 25$	D1
$26 \leq AGE \leq 30$	D2
GRADE_PT = 4.0	D3
GRADE_PT = 3.0	D4

FIGURE 6.18
Descriptor table.

assumed that there are only two grade points, 4.0 and 3.0, associated with the attribute GRADE_PT in the database. These descriptors can be used to form a number of descriptor sets as shown in the second column of Figure 6.19. The set of records that satisfies the data condition(s) of each descriptor set forms a cluster. The descriptor sets that define clusters may overlap, that is, contain the same descriptor. However, each record of a file may belong to only a single cluster since the value(s) associated with different descriptors do not overlap, as explained previously.

The cluster definition table shown in Figure 6.19 contains cluster numbers, descriptor sets, and the disk addresses (track addresses) of the records that form the clusters. In this table, A1 means the address of record 1. The previous example, though simple, shows that the grouping of the records of a file to form a cluster can be based on not only the contents of the records but also their relationships with the records of other files. In fact, any complex relationship can be specified by the use of a set of descriptors to define a cluster of records. A cluster represents a set of semantically related records that is stored and accessed together as a logical unit of data. In MDBS, the records of a cluster are evenly distributed across the back-end computers. Thus, horizontal partitions of these records are stored in the disks of these back-end computers and processed simultaneously by them.

In MDBS, a high-level query is first parsed by the control computer (the host computer) and the parsed query is broadcast to all the data processors. The parsed query is represented by a disjunctive normal form of keyword predicates (i.e., disjunction of conjunctive expressions of predicates). The broadcast query is placed in a FIFO queue at each of the data processors, which executes the queries in its queue sequentially. In processing a query, each data processor examines its own descriptor table to determine a set of descriptors that matches with the search condition specified by each predicate in each conjunction. For each

Cluster #	Set of descriptors	Record addresses on disk
C1	{D1, D3}	{A1, A2}
C2	{D2, D4}	{A3}
C3	D3	{A4, A5}
C4	D4	{A6}

FIGURE 6.19
Cluster definition table.

conjunction of a query, a set of descriptor sets will be formed. A crossproduct of these descriptor sets is taken to produce a new set of descriptor sets. This set represents all the possible clusters that could have been formed during the cluster formation time. These clusters would contain records that may satisfy the conjunctive expression. The identified descriptor sets are used to search the entries in the cluster definition table to determine those clusters whose records need to be accessed for the conjunction. The same process is followed for all other conjuntions in the query. The result is a set of cluster sets whose union determines the final set of clusters that need to be accessed from the secondary storage for processing. From the cluster definition table, the addresses of those records in these clusters are readily available; thus, records can be directly accessed. This is an effective method to solve the I/O bottleneck problem addressed previously.

The advantage of the described data organization and query-processing strategy is that clusters of records that are relevant to a search query can be quickly located and retrieved from disks. Since each partition of the records belonging to the same cluster are stored together or nearby on a disk, secondary storage access overhead is greatly reduced. Furthermore, the descriptor table and cluster definition table can be used as index tables to access records directly. Only a relatively small amount of data needs to be accessed from the slow secondary storage.

The advantages of a data organization are also accompanied by some disadvantages. This organization has the following disadvantages. First, the clusters are predefined and represent the file creator's expectation of what kinds of queries are to be issued by users. If a query contains search conditions that do not match with the predefined descriptors, it will not have the same access speed advantage as those that do. This problem is the same as that of index-based data organizations. Second, in order to avoid storing records redundantly in secondary storage, which complicates the enforcement of data consistency, all clusters must be nonoverlapping, that is, a record can belong to only one cluster. This condition may increase the number of descriptors and clusters needed in the system and, thus, may increase the number of cluster accesses. For example, the users of the example education database often access student records in which the students' ages fall in two overlapping ranges: $20 \leq AGE \leq 30$ and $25 \leq AGE \leq 35$. They cannot be used as the descriptors since the clusters formed by these descriptors will contain common records. In this case, three nonoverlapping descriptors should be defined: $20 \leq AGE \leq 24$, $25 \leq AGE \leq 30$, and $31 \leq AGE \leq 35$. They can then be used to define three nonoverlapping clusters. If a query asks for student records with age values in the range $20 \leq AGE \leq 30$, two clusters of records corresponding to the first two nonoverlapping descriptors will be accessed from separate disk locations. Another related problem is that should the descriptors be changed to suit the users' changing needs, clusters may have to be redefined and the database physically reorganized. However, cluster re-formation and database reorganization can be done concurrently by the data processors in this distributed system. Lastly, the Crossproduct and Set Union operations required in query processing to find the proper clusters are rather time-consuming operations. The advantages of data clustering need to be weighed against these disadvantages.

Three data distribution strategies have been studied in the MDBS project.

1. *Exact division*. The records of a file are evenly divided among the disk drives of the data processors (see Figure 6.20a).
2. *Track splitting with placement from the first data processor*. Track-size data are evenly distributed among the disk drives of the data processors, and the extra records are stored starting from the first processor on (see Figure 6.20b).
3. *Track splitting with random placement*. This strategy is similar to the second one in that the division of the records is at the track boundary. However, the leftover data are stored in the disk drives selected at random (see Figure 6.20c).

A simulation model for the three strategies was developed and implemented. It was reported that a variation of the third strategy, (i.e., even distribution of track-size data and the assignment of leftovers to the disk drives of consecutive data processors starting from one selected at random) gives the best response time in data access and the highest storage utilization when there is a high sequentiality of the records [HSI81a and HSI81b].

GAMMA. Four tuple distribution strategies are used in GAMMA: (1) round-robin, (2) hashed, (3) range-partitioned with user-specified placement by key values, and (4) range-partitioned with uniform distribution. The round-robin strategy distributes tuples to the data processors in turn. Some of the data processors will get the leftover ones if the number of processors does not evenly divide the number of tuples. This strategy is the same as the one used in MBDS [DEM84]. The hashed strategy is the same as the one used in DBC/1012 described previously. The third strategy allows the user to specify ranges of primary index values for the data processors. The fourth strategy loads a relation in a round-robin fashion initially. The relation is then sorted using a sort-merge algorithm before it is redistributed, as evenly as possible, among the data processors.

After the distribution of a relation using one of these strategies, the segments of the relation are stored in the disks of the data processors. Similar to DBC/1012, primary and secondary indices are created for these segments. These indices are used for direct accesses to the tuples.

6.3.1.3 DATA PROCESSING STRATEGIES AND ALGORITHMS. This section examines the general algorithms for some database primitive operations that can be used in a common-bus multiprocessor system and shows how the execution of these algorithms can be supported by the hardware facilities provided by some of the systems in this category.

Since the components of this type of system are conventional computers, algorithms for implementing database functions can be any known software algorithms used in a conventional computer. More than one algorithm can be used by the processors to perform a function dependent on some algorithm selection criteria. Although it is possible for different processors to use different algorithms

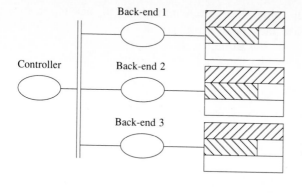

FIGURE 6.20a
Data placement strategy A—Exact division of data by the number of back-ends for placement. (*Source:* [HSI81a])

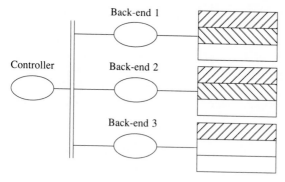

FIGURE 6.20b
Data placement strategy B—Back-ends accommodating only track-size data with the first back-ends accommodating the extra ones. (*Source:* [HSI81a])

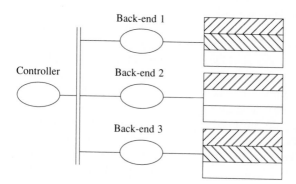

FIGURE 6.20c
Data placement strategy C—Back-ends accommodating only track-size data with arbitrary back-ends picking up the extra ones. (*Source:* [HSI81a])

to carry out a database function, the same algorithm is generally used by all processors in order to achieve approximately the same completion time in all processors. The programs that implement the algorithms are simply duplicated in all the processors and are activated according to the commands received by the processors.

The algorithms used for executing database primitive operations such as

Selection and Join can be very similar or different in different bus-structured systems, depending on whether they take advantage of specific architectural features available in each system. For example, the systems mentioned in this category perform Selection using the same general algorithm. The algorithm involves the following steps:

1. The control computer broadcasts the selection command to all the data processors.
2. The data processors fetch the relevant data from their corresponding secondary storage devices in parallel using the storage structure (e.g., indices, inverted lists) available in a particular system.
3. The data processors simultaneously examine the fetched records to determine if they satisfy the search condition(s) of the Selection operation.
4. The selected records are either transferred to the control computer through the common bus or the token ring or are stored in the processors for subsequent processing. In the former case, the control computer would forward the result to the user. In the latter case, the result of the Selection operation is a distributed file, the records of which are scattered in the secondary storage devices of these processors.

The specific methods for carrying out step 3 are different from system to system depending on the storage structures. For example, in MICRONET, data are inverted (see Figure 6.14). The attributes and values specified as search conditions in the selection command are used to access sets of tuple numbers of those tuples that satisfy different search conditions. A set intersection operation is performed over these sets to determine the set of tuples that satisfies all the search conditions. In DBC/1012 and GAMMA, selected attributes of a relation are specified as primary and secondary indices at the data definition time. If a search condition in a selection command makes reference to one of these indices, it is used to access the proper index table through which the tuples, which satisfy the indexed attribute and value, are retrieved. These tuples are further examined to determine if they satisfy those nonindexed attributes and values that form the other search conditions. The Ynet of DBC/1012 is used to aid the selection process in the following way. The tuples of a relation are distributed among the AMPs based on the hash values of the primary index. Each AMP has, in its secondary storage, those tuples whose hashed index values fall in a prespecified range. During the selection time, the search conditions are sent by the IFP, which controls the execution of the selection command, to the Ynet. If one of the selection conditions refers to the primary index, the hardware of the Ynet can automatically direct the search conditions to the AMP that contains the tuple (in the case of a unique primary index) or tuples (in the case of a nonunique primary index) that may satisfy the rest of the search conditions. Otherwise, the search conditions are given to all the AMPs, which carry out the Selection operation in parallel.

In the case of the Join operation, different systems may adopt different algorithms that are deemed suitable to the particular hardware features they have. Since the data processors used in this category of database machines are conventional processors, they can implement any of the known software algorithms. The selection of a proper algorithm for an operation is based on some optimization criteria. For example, DBC/1012 uses a number of distributed join algorithms: nested-loop, sort-merge, and hash-join algorithms. In this system, relations are horizontally partitioned based on the hash values of the primary indexed attribute and stored in a distributed fashion on the secondary storage devices of AMPs. If none of the join attributes of the two relations involved in a join operation is a primary index, the smaller of the two operand relations is broadcast through the Ynet to all the AMPs containing the larger relation. In parallel, all the AMPs perform the Join operation between the received relation and their corresponding segments of the larger relation. This join step can be carried out by a nested-loop algorithm or a sort-merge algorithm. In the latter case, relation segments need to be sorted first before a join-by-merging operation can be performed. In any case, each AMP produces a segment of the resulting relation. The results of this Join operation, that is, the segments of the resulting relation, can be left in these AMPs for subsequent operations or can be collected to the controlling IFP.

If the join attribute is a unique or nonunique primary indexed attribute for one of the two operand relations, say R, then the tuples of R would have been partitioned and distributed in the disks of AMPs based on the hash values of the primary index. In this case, the tuples of the other relation, S, are transmitted through the Ynet, which uses the hash values of the join attribute to determine the AMPs to which the tuples of S should be delivered. Since the same hash function is used for distributing the tuples of S as for distributing the tuples of R originally, the tuples of R and S are guaranteed to fall into the proper nonintersecting buckets. All AMPs containing the tuples of R and S can, therefore, simultaneously and independently carry out the Join operation on their corresponding relation segments to produce the distributed segments of the resulting relation.

During the collection of the resulting relation in this or other operations, the resulting relation can be sorted by the Ynet as the tuples are sent from the AMPs to the IFP through the binary-structured processing nodes of the Ynet. The logic in each node of the Ynet compares the two values of the join attribute received from the descendant nodes and allows the tuple with the smaller value (in the case of sorting in ascending order) to be forwarded up the binary tree. The sorted tuples coming out of the root of the tree are transferred to the IFP.*

GAMMA uses the same general hash-join algorithm as used in DBC/1012. However, the implementation details of this algorithm are different. In GAMMA,

---

*The author would like to acknowledge that the preceding description of the techniques and algorithms used in DBC/1012 is based on private correspondence with Dr. Philip M. Neches of the Teradata Corporation and discussions with Professor Alex Papachristidis, a former employee of the Teradata Corporation.

the tuples of the first operand relation, say R, are processed simultaneously by the processors that contain the segments of the relation R. During this first phase of processing, called the *building phase,* each involved processor builds an in-memory hash table and a local bit vector. It reads from the local stream of tuples of R and adds tuples to the hash table that is being constructed. For each tuple processed, its join attribute value is hashed and the hashed value is used to set a bit in the local bit vector using the content-to-address mapping technique described in Chapter 3. The tuples of relation R are partitioned based on the ranges of hash values of the join attribute. There are as many partitions established as there are processors involved in the Join operation. They are transferred to these processors. The second phase, called the *probing phase,* is then started. In this phase, the bit vectors are given to the processors that contain the second operand relation, say S. These processors check for those tuples of S whose join attribute values map to those positions of the bit vectors that have been set. These tuples will satisfy the join condition with the tuples of R and, therefore, are transmitted to the processors that hold the partitioned segments of R. The bit vectors are used in this manner to filter out the irrelevant tuples of S. Thus, the amount of data transmission in the network can be reduced. When the processors containing the partitioned segments of R receive the partitioned segments of S, they simultaneously probe their hash tables for matching tuples from the relation R. The matched tuples are joined to produce the distributed segments of the output relation. Therefore, the time for joining two large relations is reduced to the time for simultaneously joining many small partitions of these two relations.

6.3.2   Tree-Structured Systems

This section details the architectures, data processing strategies, and algorithms of three multiprocessor systems that use a tree structure as their basic processor interconnection scheme. The processors of these systems have their own local memory and have considerable processing power to perform database operations. They are HYPERTREE, which employs an enhanced binary tree interconnection, REPT, which uses a straight binary tree interconnection, and NON-VON, which is based on a binary tree of "large processing elements" and "small processing elements."

6.3.2.1 ARCHITECTURE OF HYPERTREE, REPT, AND NON-VON. When a set of processors are to be connected to form a network, the selection of an interconnection structure is based on a number of considerations. Four properties that are used as the design guide of the HYPERTREE system [GOO80a and GOO80b] are:

1. *The average path length between processor nodes.* The speed at which a processor in a network can communicate with another processor is dependent upon the number of links between them. Assuming that every processor in the network needs to communicate with all other processors, the performance

of the entire network can be improved if the average path length between processor nodes is minimized.

2. *The message density.* It is inefficient to burden a small number of processors in a network with the task of handling most of the communications (e.g., transferring or passing data and messages) while the others are idling. Communication tasks should be distributed and performed by as large a number of processors as possible.

3. *Expandability.* A network should be easily expandable. This is particularly required in database applications since processors often need to be added to handle the growing databases. If new processors and their communication links can be added without requiring the modification of the entire network, then the cost of expansion is minimized.

4. *Fault tolerance.* A network should not cease to function due to a break-down of a communication link. In order to achieve a reliable, fault-tolerant network, it is necessary to have redundant paths between each pair of nodes.

These four properties should be considered as the design goals of any network. However, they are conflicting goals. A network design usually must find a balance among them. The HYPERTREE is a good example of a system that attempts to achieve these goals.

The architecture of HYPERTREE. The application of the HYPERTREE system to database management was studied by Goodman at the University of California, Berkeley. The project is an extension of the X-Tree project reported by Sequine, Despain, and Patterson [DES78 and SEQ78]. The architecture of HYPERTREE is a combination of two interconnection structures: balanced binary tree and N-Hypercube. In a balanced binary tree network, each node has three ports. There are two successor nodes per parent node. The ith level of the tree has 2^i nodes, $i \geq 0$. In an N-Hypercube network, the nodes are placed at the vertices of an N-dimensional hypercube and the cube edges form the links between nodes.

The structure of HYPERTREE is shown in Figure 6.21. It is a balanced binary tree with some N-cube connections added between certain nodes at the same level of the tree. It is a partial N-cube; not all N-cube links are used. The locations of the N-cube links are determined by the chart shown in Figure 6.22. For each level, all those nodes that are a circled distance apart (see Figure 6.22) are connected by an N-cube link. For example, the circled distance for level 1 is 2. Nodes 2 and 3 in Figure 6.21 are thus connected by an N-cube link, since the distance between node 2 to node 3 through the root in the original binary tree is 2. In another example, the circled distance for level 3 shown in Figure 6.22 is 4. Therefore, N-cube links are added to connect the following pairs of nodes shown in Figure 6.21: (8, 10), (9, 11), (12, 14), and (13, 15). The distance between each pair through node 2 or node 3 of Figure 6.21 is 4.

In this system, the nodes are X-Tree processors having considerable processing capabilities and local memory space. The number of processors at the leaf

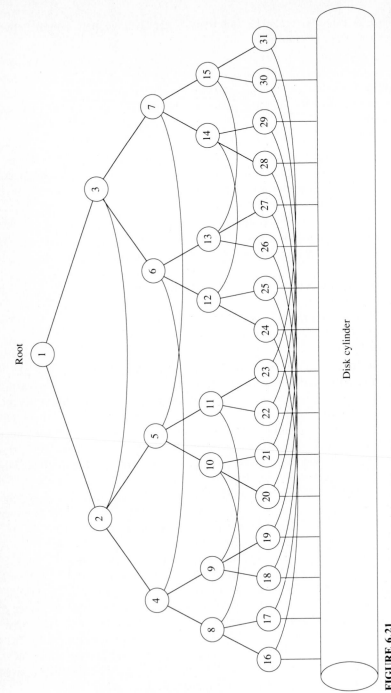

Root

Disk cylinder

FIGURE 6.21
Architecture of HYPERTREE. (*Source:* [GOO81] © 1981 IEEE)

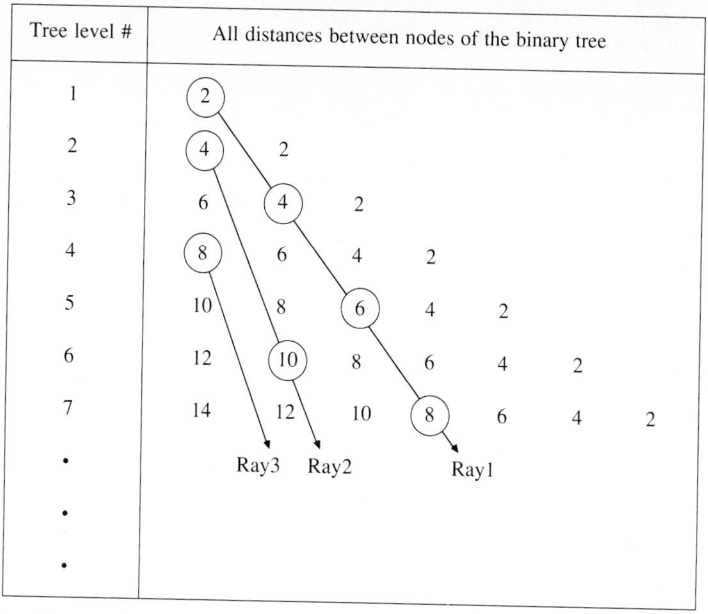

Tree level #	All distances between nodes of the binary tree
1	
2	
3	
4	
5	
6	
7	
•	
•	
•	

FIGURE 6.22

The node distance chart. (*Source:* [GOO81] ©1981 IEEE)

nodes determines the number of levels of the HYPERTREE. No internal node of the tree has its own secondary storage. Only the leaf nodes are connected to the read heads of a moving-head disk, one per head. Thus, they are able to access a cylinder-full of data in one revolution of the disk. This system assumes that the disk has parallel read-out capability. The local main memory associated with these processors is used to store the data. Data as well as messages are transmitted through the binary tree links or the N-cube links based on some efficient routing algorithm that finds the shortest path between two nodes.

Some of the nodes of HYPERTREE serve as the interface nodes to the users and accept user queries. The system executes the primitives and returns results to the proper user interface nodes from which data are transmitted to the users.

The architecture of REPT. REPT is a relational database machine designed by Shultz and Zingg at Iowa State University [SHU81 and SHU84]. The architecture is shown in Figure 6.23. It is a back-end database machine consisting of a number of identical processors with a binary tree interconnection. The root node is interfaced to a host computer and secondary storage devices that contain all the data files. All processors in the binary tree are able to perform database operations and have local memory to store both the data transmitted to them and the intermediate results they produce.

The general query-processing strategy used in this system is as follows. User queries are first submitted to the host computer. Queries expressed using relational algebraic operations, which can be the result of translation from some high-level

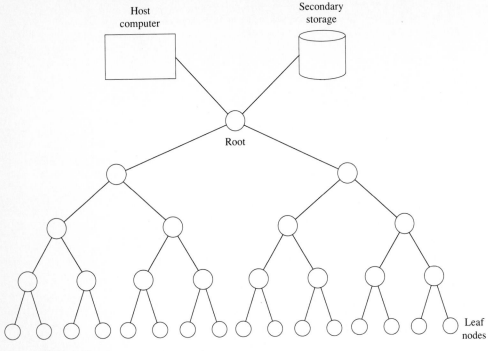

Host computer

Secondary storage

Root

Leaf nodes

FIGURE 6.23
Architecture of REPT. (*Source:* [SHU84] ©1984, Association for Computing Machinery, Inc., reprinted by permission)

query language, are sent via the root to all the processors. If the relations to be processed are not already in the processors' local memory, then the root processor will issue requests to the secondary storage device to fetch the relations. If the relations are already in the processors' local memory, then the operations will be concurrently performed on the data. The results generated by the processors are collected by the root, which forwards them to the host computer for output to the users.

Commands, messages, status, and data are transmitted serially up or down the binary tree through the tree links. Nodes can transmit data to their respective descendants in parallel. Thus, it takes a maximum of n steps to transfer any data from the root to the leaf nodes, where n is the depth of the tree. In this system, it is assumed that (1) the input and output of data and the processing of an assigned operation at each node overlap, and (2) the nodes can transmit tuples at the same rate that they arrive from the secondary storage; thus, tuple transmission time overlaps with secondary storage I/O time.

The architecture of NON-VON. NON-VON is a massively parallel supercomputer being built at Columbia University under the support of the Defense Advanced Research Projects Agency [SHA82 and HIL86]. This is a different

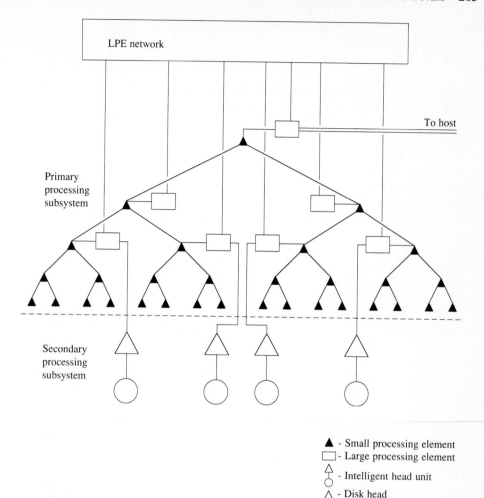

FIGURE 6.24
Architecture of NON-VON. (*Source:* [HIL86] ©1986 IEEE)

NON-VON from the original NON-VON designed by Professor Shaw (the same designer of the new NON-VON), which has been covered in Chapter 5.

The architecture of this system is shown in Figure 6.24. It consists of a binary tree of a large number of *small processing elements* (SPEs). Each SPE contains an 8-bit arithmetic and logic unit (ALU), a small RAM (64 bytes in the current implementation), and communication connections to three neighboring SPEs called the *parent, left child,* and *right child.* Additionally, each SPE is connected directly to two other SPEs, called *left neighbor* and *right neighbor,* which are the predecessor and successor in an in-order traversal of the binary tree. (Strictly speaking, these two connections do not make NON-VON a tree-structured system.) The SPEs do not store programs locally. Instructions executed by these processors are broadcast to them by some other processors called *large processing elements* (LPEs), which are connected to the top few levels (5 to 10) of the SPE tree.

The LPEs are microcomputers that are interconnected by an LPE network, as shown in the figure. The network allows data and commands to be transferred to and from the large processing elements. Each LPE is a general-purpose microcomputer and can be configured to contain a few megabytes of RAM. Programs are stored locally in the LPEs and can be independently and asynchronously executed by them. Different instruction sequences can be broadcast to their corresponding SPE subtrees for execution, giving NON-VON the capability of multiple-SIMD processing. The LPE, which issues an instruction sequence to a SPE subtree, serves as the control processor for the sequence. The root LPE of the binary tree is connected to a host computer, which serves as the front-end computer and an interface to the users.

The primary processing subsystem is currently under construction. It consists of a single LPE and 8,191 SPEs. A VAX 11/750 is used as the host computer. At the time of writing, 8 SPEs have been implemented on a single VLSI chip using an nMOS process with 3 micron feature size.

The secondary processing subsystem consists of a substantial number of disk drives (32 to 256 drives as envisioned). Each drive is connected via an *intelligent head unit* to an LPE. This interconnection provides a parallel I/O capability to the system. The disk heads are assumed to have data-filtering capabilities. They can perform simple operations (e.g., selection and partial match) on the fly when data are transferred from the disks to the LPEs.

6.3.2.2. DATA PROCESSING STRATEGIES AND ALGORITHMS.

Since the base data (i.e., the relations stored in the secondary storage) of the systems discussed in this section are input into the tree network from opposite ends—HYPERTREE and NON-VON from the leaf nodes and REPT from the root—the strategies and algorithms for performing database operations are different in these three systems. The Selection and Join operations are used as examples to show the different strategies and algorithms. A detailed analysis of the algorithms used in these three systems is provided by Shultz and Zingg [SHU84] and Hilyer, Shaw, and Nigram [HIL86].

Selection operation. In HYPERTREE, selection conditions are transmitted from a user-interface node, which originates a query, to all the leaf nodes. These selection conditions are represented as Boolean expressions. The tuples of relations are stored in a bit-serial word-serial fashion on the disk tracks. All leaf nodes can access all the tracks of a cylinder in parallel. Thus, tuples are processed one cylinder at a time. Leaf nodes can carry out the Selection operation on a track-full of tuples at a time. Tuples satisfying the search conditions are routed to the user-interface node. The key time components of this operation are the transmission of the selection command to the leaf nodes, the input of data from the disk, the Selection operation on segments of the relation, and the transmission of the selected tuples to the user-interface node. HYPERTREE can support Selection efficiently by (1) the use of the balanced binary tree links and the N-cube links to affect fast transmission of data and commands, (2) the parallel secondary storage I/O capability, and (3) the parallel selection capability of the leaf nodes.

In REPT, two cases of the Selection operation are considered. In the first case, the input relation is in secondary storage and, in the second case, the relation is already distributed across the leaf nodes. In the first case, the root node accesses the relation and performs the Selection as the tuples are read from the disk. The selected tuples are transferred to the host computer, where the query originated. The Selection is thus done by a single processor in a sequential fashion. In the second case, the relation is already evenly distributed across the leaf nodes by transferring tuples, starting from the root, to alternate descendant nodes. The selection command is transmitted to the leaves, which simultaneously perform the operation on their corresponding relation segments. The selected tuples are transferred up to the root for forwarding to the host.

In NON-VON, the secondary processing subsystem can perform the data-filtering functions. Two cases are considered for the Selection operation. In the first case, the source relation is stored on disks in a distributed fashion. The selection command and search conditions are given to the secondary processing subsystem. The intelligent head units read and examine the tuples residing in their corresponding disks in the same way as the database filters (see Chapter 4). The tuples, which satisfy the search, are collected to the host computer. In the second case, the source relation is already in the primary processing subsystem. In this case, the tuples of this relation are stored in an SPE subtree associated with an LPE, which serves as the control processor. The control processor broadcasts the search conditions at the rate of one byte per clock cycle to the SPEs. Each SPE associatively compares the incoming byte stream with the contents of its RAM to select the qualified tuples, which are then collected to the host computer.

Join operation. HYPERTREE adopts the technique of hashing words to a bit array, as used in CAFS [BAB79] to perform the Join operation. First, one of the base relations, say R, is read from the disk by the leaf nodes. Each leaf node keeps a bit array for marking those bits whose positions are the hashed values of the join field read by each node. After all the leaf nodes complete their processing of the join field values of R, the bit arrays are transmitted simultaneously to the parent nodes, which combine the arrays by performing a logical OR between pairs of descendant bit arrays. This process is carried out at each level of the tree until the root forms the final bit array for the relation R.

The same procedure is carried out for the second relation S to produce another bit array at the root. The root processor then performs a logical AND between the two bit arrays. The resulting array will contain the bit setting for those hash values whose corresponding join field values are found in both relations, R and S. The combined bit array is transmitted to all the leaf nodes that re-read their corresponding tuples of each relation. If the join field value of a tuple hashes to a location in the combined bit array that has been set to '1', then the tuple is sent to a chosen node. Otherwise, the tuple is ignored. A distributed routing algorithm is used to ensure that the tuples of both relations R and S whose join field values match are sent to the same processor and that R and S tuples are evenly distributed among a set of chosen processors. These processors will then perform the final Join operation by concatenating the tuples that have been transmitted to their local memory. This last step produces a relation, the result of the Join operation, which is distributed among the processors. The result relation is then collected at the user-interface node at which the Join operation was issued.

In this Join procedure, the construction of the local bit arrays is carried out in parallel by the leaf nodes. The logical OR of local bit arrays is done in parallel at each level of the tree. The broadcasting of the logically ORed final array is done in n steps of transmission starting from the root to the leaves (n is the number of levels of the tree). The redistribution of the actual tuples of S and R that have been found to satisfy the join condition is done in parallel. The final explicit join operation is done in parallel, but the collection of the join results by the user-interface node is done sequentially.

The Join operation in REPT is implemented in the following manner. Assuming that both relations R and S are stored in the secondary store and S is a smaller relation (i.e., contains less tuples), the first step of the Join is to distribute the tuples of S evenly among the leaf nodes. The leaf nodes sort the S segments received in parallel over the join field. The relation R is then read by the root and transmitted to all the leaf nodes where the Join operation is carried out in each node between the sorted segment of S and the entire R relation. The resulting relation is distributed among the leaf nodes and is collected by the root, which forwards the relation to the host.

In the event that relation S is too large for all the leaf nodes' memories to hold, a part of relation S is distributed among the leaf nodes and joined with relation R. After that, the remaining part of the S relation is distributed and joined with relation R. The process is repeated for each subset of S tuples.

In the above join procedure, the initial reading and distribution of S and R relations is done sequentially. The actual Join operation is carried out by the leaf nodes in parallel. The transmission of the join results can be done in parallel along the parallel tree links, but the collection of results by each parent node from the two descendants must be done one at a time.

NON-VON carries out the Join operation in the following manner. First, one of the operand relations, say R, is read from the disks by the control processor that issues the query. The intelligent head units of the secondary processing subsystem perform the Selection or Projection operations on R if such operations can precede the Join operation. It is assumed that R is the smaller relation and its tuples can fit the control processor's memory. Second, the second operand relation, S, is loaded in parallel via multiple LPEs into the SPEs of the SPE subtree rooted at the control processor. During this parallel loading operation from the disks, the corresponding intelligent head units can also perform the Selection or Projection operation to reduce the size of S, thus reducing the amount of data to be loaded into the SPE subtree. The tuples of S are stored in the SPEs, one tuple per SPE.

The loading operation will be interrupted when the subtree is full and resumed after the primary processing subsystem finishes the Join operation on that batch of data. The secondary processing subsystem continues to supply the SPEs with the next batch of data. Third, the Join operation is carried out by broadcasting the tuples of relation R to the SPEs, which perform associative matching between tuples of R and S. These SPEs report to the control processor the matched tuples of S. These tuples of S are then concatenated with the tuples of R by the control processor to produce the join result. The second and third steps are repeated for every batch of tuples of R loaded into the SPE subtree.

The key time components involved in both the Selection and Join operations described here are quite similar in HYPERTREE, REPT, and NON-VON systems. However, in REPT, inputting data from the disk is implemented in a serial fashion. HYPERTREE and NON-VON, on the other hand, have a parallel disk I/O capability. In REPT, the selected tuples and join results are always sent to the root. The path length of each transmission is n, where n is the depth (or number of levels) of the tree. In HYPERTREE, the collection operation is done by the user-interface node, which can be any node in the network. Also data transmission can be supported more efficiently by taking advantage of the N-cube links. Unlike HYPERTREE and NON-VON, the structure of REPT is a pure, binary tree and the root is responsible for disk I/O as well as communication with the host computer. Thus, the message density at the root is quite high and is a potential bottleneck in the system. As expected, the analysis reported by Shultz and Zingg [SHU84] shows that HYPERTREE has better performance than REPT in most of the cases examined. In NON-VON, data to be collected from either the secondary processing subsystem or the SPE subtrees can be transferred first to the control processors and then through the LPE network to the root LPE before they are forwarded to the host computer.

6.3.3 Cube-Structured Systems

In a multiprocessor system in which a number of processors are assigned to perform the same task over their corresponding segments of data, it is advantageous to keep the segments as close to the same size as possible so that the computation task can be completed by these processors at about the same time. Although it is easy to make the initial distribution of data segments as evenly as possible across disk drives, it is not possible to ensure that a distributed operation will produce evenly distributed data segments. As a result, further processing of the intermediate data by a number of processors will take different amounts of time, and the total execution time of this operation will be as long as the processing of the largest segment. In order to reduce the total execution time of a database operation under this situation, it is advantageous to redistribute the intermediate results of an operation to achieve an even distribution of data. Redistribution of data, while advantageous for a subsequent operation, can be itself rather time-consuming unless the degree of connectivity among processors is high and parallel paths for transferring data among processors are available. The interconnection schemes such as common-bus, ring, or tree interconnections used in the systems described previously have a limited connectivity. The following subsection describes a cube interconnection scheme for supporting data redistribution.

6.3.3.1 ARCHITECTURE OF A BOOLEAN CUBE-CONNECTED MULTICOMPUTER.

This is a multicomputer system being investigated at the University of Michigan [BAR87]. It incorporates data redistribution steps in the algorithms designed for database operations. The cube architecture consists of a set of N nodes, each of which is connected to $n = \log_2 N$ neighbors, where N is a power of two. Figure 6.25 shows a Boolean three-cube architecture with $N = 8$ nodes, each of which is labeled by a binary address. Each node consists of a processor, a main memory, and a secondary storage. It also contains the following hardware facilities to enhance performance in algorithm executions. Each node contains $\log_2 N$ message/packet buffers, one for each of its neighbors, and two independent communication processors capable of simultaneously receiving/transmitting messages or data along two separate links. It also has two special registers called tuple count registers (TCRs), the contents of which can be simultaneously read by any two of its neighbors. Data are exchanged among nodes by transmitting variable size packets through the links in parallel.

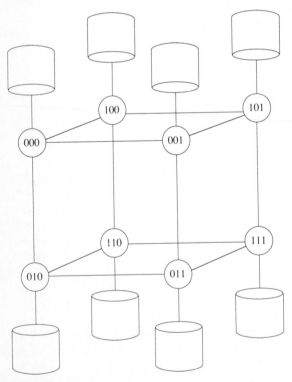

FIGURE 6.25
A Boolean three-cube architecture. (*Source:* [BAR87] ©1987 IEEE)

6.3.3.2 DATA PROCESSING STRATEGIES AND ALGORITHMS.

The Selection and Join algorithms used in this system illustrate the processing strategies in the cube architecture. Analyses of these and other relational operations are given by Baru and Frieder [BAR87].

In relational query processing, selection operations in a query tree are generally moved down to the leaves in order to reduce the amount of data to be processed by the operators at the higher levels of the tree. Therefore, it is assumed here that the selection command operates on a base relation that has been uniformly distributed across the nodes in a cube. The selection command can be entered through any node called the *host node*. It needs to be broadcast to all other nodes for performing the Selection operation in parallel.

The broadcasting task can be completed in $n = \log_2 N$ steps in the following way. In the first step, the host node sends the broadcast message to one of its n neighbors. The receiver of the message performs an exclusive OR between its binary address and the address of the sender to produce an n-bit number with a 1 in the jth bit position, for example. The receiver then transmits the message to its neighbors in $k = (n - j)$ steps, while the host continues to transmit the message to the other neighbors. In each k step, the original receiver, now the sender, transmits the message to its neighbor, whose address differs from its own in the $(j + 1)$th bit position first, and then in the $(j + 2)$th bit position next, and finally in the nth bit position. In general, in the kth step of broadcast ($1 \leq k \leq n$), there will be $2^{(k-1)}$ nodes that simultaneously transmit messages to $2^{(k-1)}$ other nodes in the cube. Figure 6.26 illustrates the broadcasting of a message by the host processor 010 in three steps.

Once the message has been broadcast, all nodes carry out the Selection operation against their corresponding relation segments in parallel. The result can either be left in these nodes for subsequent operations or be collected to the host processor for output to the user. The collection process can either be done serially or by "merging" and "cycling" operations, which will be described later in this chapter, with the Join operation.

In this selection algorithm, the command broadcasting step takes advantage of the parallel transmission paths existing in the cube. The actual Selection operation is also carried out in parallel.

A join operation is implemented in this system by a parallel nested-loop algorithm. The algorithm involves three phases: tuple balancing, merging, and join.

Tuple-balancing phase. A binary join operation operates on two intermediate relations produced by some preceding operations in a query tree. These intermediate relations are not necessarily evenly distributed across the nodes. *Tuple balancing* is the process of redistributing the tuples of a relation so that they are more evenly distributed among the nodes. It makes use of the two tuple count registers at each node to determine the number of tuples to be moved between neighboring processors and the two commmunication processors, which can simultaneously access the TCRs of two different neighbors. Tuple balancing proceeds in j stages

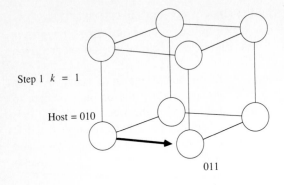

Step 1 $k = 1$

Host = 010

011

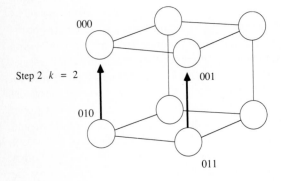

Step 2 $k = 2$

000

001

010

011

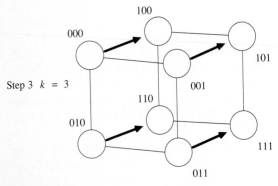

Step 3 $k = 3$

100

000

101

001

110

010

111

011

FIGURE 6.26
Broadcast of message from node 010. (*Source:* [BAR87] ©1987 IEEE)

where $1 \leq j \leq \log_2 N$. In each stage, nodes that differ in address in the jth bit balance the tuples of one relation R, and, simultaneously, nodes that differ in address in the $(n - j + 1)$th bit balance the tuples of the other relation, S. Figure 6.27 shows an example of tuple distribution in a two-cube having 4 nodes, each of which is labeled by an n-bit ($n = \log_2 N$) address. The initial distribution of R is represented by the numbers (5, 3, 2, 1) outside of the two-cube, and the initial

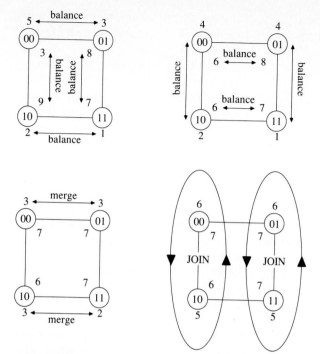

FIGURE 6.27
Tuple-balancing phase—step 1. (*Source:* [BAR87] ©1987 IEEE)

distribution of S is represented by the numbers (3, 8, 9, 7) inside of the cube. $R(i)$ and $S(i)$ will be the number of tuples of R and S at node i, respectively, where $0 \le i \le 3$. The tuple counts are stored in the TCRs of each node. In the first stage, one of the communication processors of node 0 reads TCR1 of node 1 and determines that it must transfer 1 tuple of R to node 1 so that both $R(0)$ and $R(1)$ have the value 4. The other communication processor reads TCR2 of node 2 and determines that it should receive three tuples of S from node 2 to balance $S(0)$ and $S(2)$ (both have the value 6). At the same time, node 3 balances its R and S tuples with nodes 1 and 2 in the same manner. Figures 6.27*b* and 6.27*c* show the distributions after the first and second stages of operation, respectively.

Merging phase. The tuple-balancing phase ensures that the number of tuples for both R and S in each processor is about the same as t5he other processors. The next phase in the nested-loop algorithm is to broadcast the smaller realtion, say R, to all the processors where the actual join operations (the third phase) take place. In order to increase the degree of parallelism in the third phase, which is a rather time-consuming step, the tuples of R in two adjacent processors can be merged so that both contain the same set of tuples and so that sub-cubes can be formed to cary out the third phase in parallel. For example, if the tuples of R in node 0 are merged with those in node 1 and those in node 2 are merged with those in node 11 (see Figure 6.27c), then two subcubes can be formed to carry out the join phase simultaneously (see Figure 6.27d). Note that the nodes in each subcube contain a distinct subset of the tuples of S.

It is suggested by Baru and Freider [BAR87] that this same merge process can also be carried out on the larger relation S for the following reason. If the number of tuples of S in each node is small, the computation time for the third phase may be very short in comparison with the time for transmitting packets containing the tuples of R. In this case, the processor will have to wait for the arrival of R packets. In order to balance the CPU and packet transmission times, it would be advantageous to merge the tuples of S in adjacent processors so that the number of tuples of S can be increased and the size of the subcubes can be reduced, that is, those processors that contain duplicates tuples of S do not have to participate in the third phase.

The same algorithm is used to merge the tuples of the smaller and the larger relations. Merging takes a maximum of n stages. In the jth stage ($1 \leq j \leq n$), nodes that differ in address in the jth bit are paired and the tuples of these pairs are merged simultaneously. The merging process stops when either the union of the tuples in each pair exceeds the maximal packet size (in this case, the value of j is denoted as k) or the entire relation has been replicated in each node (in this case, $j = n$).

Since the tuples of R and S are uniformly distributed after the tuple-balancing phase, individual processors can use their tuple counts to determine which of R and S is smaller and needs to be broadcast. If these two relations are about the same size, and their tuples are not evenly distributed after the tuple-balancing phase, this decision cannot be made independently by the processors. In this case, either a software or a hardware method can be used to decide the relative size of these two relations. A hardware technique using the global control line concept introduced in MICRONET is used by Baru and Frieder [BAR87] for this purpose.

Join phase. This last phase is performed by forming rings of processors and sending tuples of the smaller relation around the rings. This process is called *cycling,* which is also used to collect tuples of a resulting relation after merging its distributed segments. After the merging phase, the value of k, which indicates the point at which merging stopped, is used to form rings. Rings are formed based on the $n - k$ most significant bits of the addresses of the nodes in the cube. There are 2^k rings formed. Each ring contains $2^{(n-k)}$ nodes and has a full copy of R. If no merging was done in the preceding phase, that is, $j = k = 0$, a single ring containing all N nodes is formed. If $j = k = n$, then each node in the original cube has a copy of R and maximum parallelism is achieved in the join phase. In each ring, or subcube, packets of relation R are transmitted serially through the processors, which perform the Join operation with their local tuples of S. When a packet finally reaches the sender after cycling through the processors, it is destroyed.

From this description of the Selection and Join algorithms used in this system, it should be obvious that other primitive database operations can also take advantage of the high connectivity of this system to transmit commands, status, and data via parallel paths among the processing nodes. Data redistribution techniques introduced in this system can better balance the computation loads of the processing nodes, thus achieving a better execution time for a query. However, the price paid in this system is the cost of more complex interconnection and the additional hardware needed in each node to support tuple-balancing, merging, and cycling processes. More complex interconnection in a multiprocessor system also means it is more difficult to maintain reliable network communication and to perform error recovery. In this system, the performance is very sensitive to the data placement in the cube. For example, if two relations to be joined are in two nonadjacent subcubes, one of the relations must be moved from one subcube to the other before the join algorithm can be started.

6.4 MULTIPROCESSOR SYSTEMS WITH REPLICATION OF FUNCTIONS: SYSTEMS WITH DYNAMIC PROCESSOR-MEMORY INTERCONNECTION

From the preceding section on systems with static processor-memory interconnection, one can observe several characteristics related to data distribution and movement on such systems. First, the processors in these systems have their own main memory modules and, in some cases, their own secondary storage devices. The data are initially stored locally by the processors or are distributed to processors by a control computer. Second, since data are distributed among the processors, local data may have to be exchanged among the processors to carry out an operation (e.g., Join). Third, the results of an operation are distributed among the processors and need to be collected to the processor that made the original database request. The initial distribution, the data movement, and the result collection can be very time-consuming, especially if the quantity of data involved is large. It would be desirable to establish a dynamic interconnection between the processors and memories during the course of executing database operations to allow data to be read/written by processors from/to different memory modules. This subsection examines several database computers that have this dynamic interconnection feature. Their interconnection and data delivery schemes, data organizations, and database processing strategies are described.

6.4.1 Processor-Memory Interconnection and Data Delivery Schemes

There are two basic types of memories involved: the main memory modules and the secondary storage devices (e.g., disks). The interconnections between the processors and these two types of memories may take different structures. Also, a combination of static and dynamic interconnection schemes may be used to take advantage of the features of both schemes. The following database computers will be used as examples to describe the various processor-memory interconnections and data delivery schemes: DIRECT, GRACE, DBMAC, and SM3.

6.4.1.1 SHARED CACHE MEMORY SCHEME OF DIRECT AND GRACE. In many conventional large computer systems, fast semiconductor memory modules are used as "cache" for staging data and programs, which are originally stored in the slower secondary stores, to effectively achieve a high memory speed. The idea of cache memory for database applications was first used in the database computer DIRECT to speed up database accesses of a set of processors. A similar concept is used in the GRACE system for data staging. In both systems, data are first moved from the disk storage devices to a set of fast memory modules from which they are accessed by the processors. The cache memory modules are connected in such a way that they can be accessed (or shared) by any of the processors in these systems.

Architecture of DIRECT. DIRECT was designed and prototyped at the University of Wisconsin in the late 1970s [DEW79a, DEW79b, and BOR82]. Its overall objective is to support highly parallel processing of a set of relational queries, which access a common relational database. The system has an MIMD architecture and is capable of executing multiple queries simultaneously as well as processing the subtasks of a single query in parallel. The overall system architecture is shown in Figure 6.28. It consists of a host computer (a PDP 11/45 with the INGRES database management system), a back-end controller (a PDP 11/40), a set of query processors (PDP 11/03's), a set of charge-coupled device (CCD) memory modules used as the cache memory, and a set of mass storage devices (i.e., disks). The CCD memory modules, mass storage devices, and query processors are interconnected by a novel crossbar switch.

The host computer runs a version of the database management system INGRES, which accepts user queries and compiles them into a sequence of machine instructions containing relational algebra operations. The sequences of instructions form what are called *query packets,* which are sent to the back-end controller. The back-end controller allocates query processors to execute the instructions found in a query packet. Relations are stored in mass storage devices. Each relation is horizontally partitioned into "pages," each of which contains 16K bytes of tuples. Some of these pages are staged in the CCD memory modules when relations are referenced during the course of executing query packets. In case a page needed by a query processor is not in the CCD memory modules, the back-end controller will automatically fetch it from the mass storage. The pages needed for the execution of a relational operation are moved to the query processor's local memory modules (the static memory modules) from the CCD and are operated on by the query processors. The results of operations, in the form of pages of resulting relations, are stored in the CCD memory modules. They can be used as intermediate results for subsequent operations or moved to the mass storage as permanent relations.

DIRECT has a novel design for the interconnection matrix. A two-by-four matrix is shown in Figure 6.29. Each CCD module has data lines running to all query processors (QPs). Unlike the conventional crossbar interconnection in which the processors play an active role and the memory modules play a passive role in sending and receiving data, the roles are reversed in DIRECT. All CCD

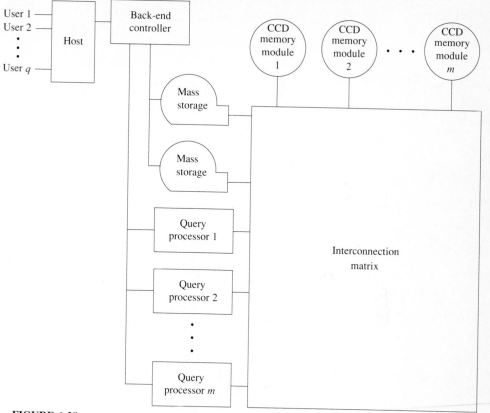

FIGURE 6.28
DIRECT system architecture. (*Source:* [DEW79a] ©1979 IEEE)

modules continuously broadcast their data (i.e., pages of tuples) by presenting them on their output lines running to each QP. Data from each CCD are loaded into a shift register eight bits at a time and are shifted out as a serial bit string. One or more QPs needing a particular page of data can "listen" for the data by selecting the proper line whose address is provided by the back-end controller. The serial bit string is converted into an eight-bit word string using a shift register before moving into the query processor's local memory. The same word-to-bit string conversion takes place when data are returned from QPs to CCDs. This interconnection scheme allows the following data accesses:

1. Each QP can rapidly switch between CCD modules that contain pages of the same or different relation, thus requiring minimal seek time.
2. All QPs can read the same page of a relation, thus providing the broadcast capability.
3. All QPs can simultaneously access different pages of the same or different relations, thus providing MIMD-processing capability.

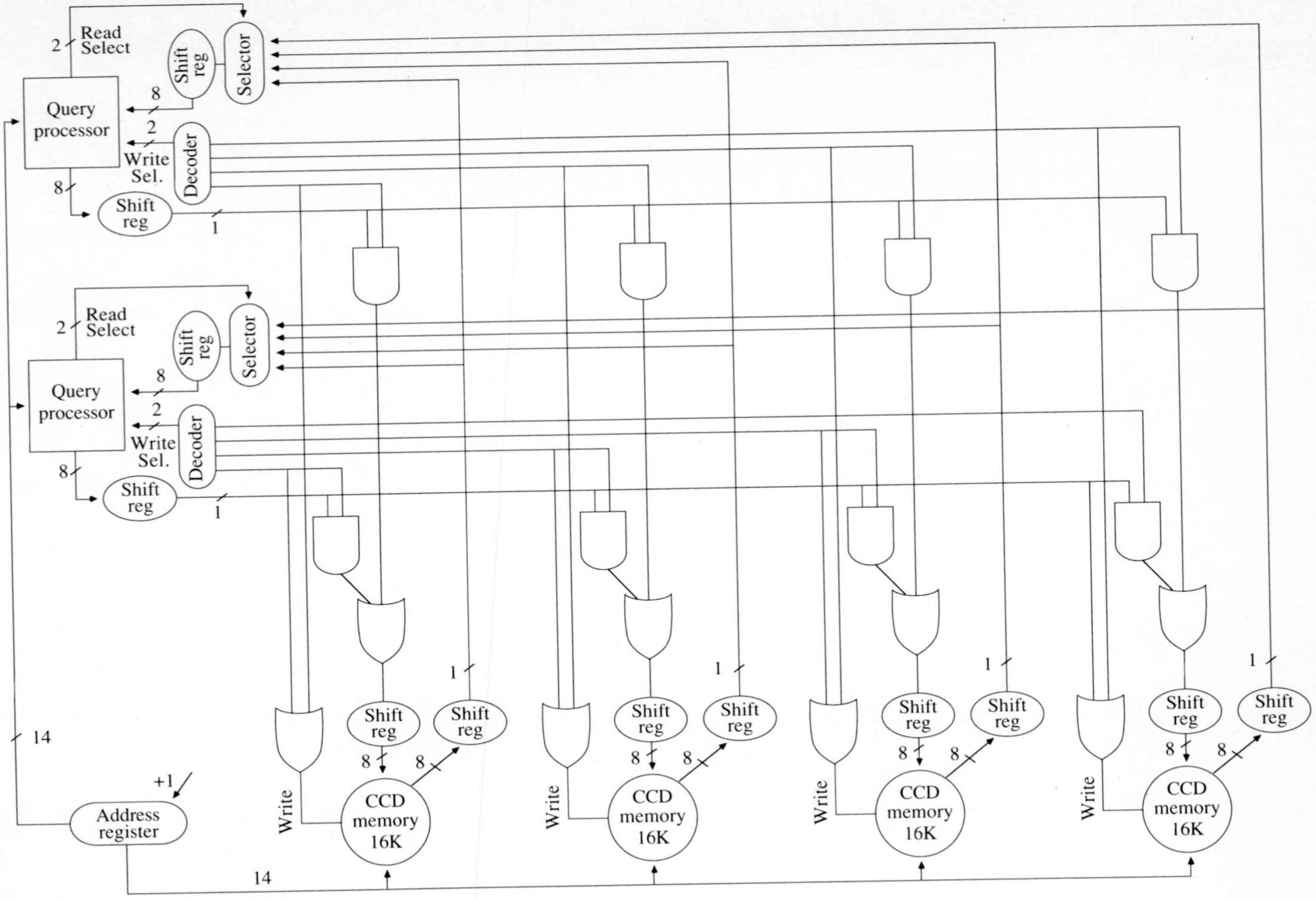

FIGURE 6.29

A 2×4 DIRECT configuration. (*Source:* [DEW79a] ©1979 IEEE)

4. QPs need not wait for the beginning of the page to start reading data; they can start reading data at any tuple boundary and can read the entire page as the CCD continues to shift its contents in a circular fashion, thus involving almost no latency time.

These access features are important for supporting concurrent processing of multiple query packets as well as simultaneous processing of multiple operations in a single packet. The delay involved in switch connection is minimal when compared to the relation search time. It does not degrade system performance. A weak point in this architecture, which is revealed in the analysis work reported by Shultz and Zingg [SHU84], is that relation pages must be moved very frequently between mass storage devices, CCD modules, and local main memory of QPs during the execution of database operations. Data movement time in this system cannot always overlap with the execution time of the processors. Also, since a single interconnection matrix is used, the data movement between the mass storage and the CCDs and between the CCDs and the main memory of the QPs can produce memory contention.

Architecture of GRACE. GRACE is one of several relational database machine efforts conducted in Japan. It has been researched and prototyped at the University of Tokyo [KIT81, KIT83a and b, KIT84, and KIT85]. Similar to DIRECT, it uses the shared cache memory scheme for staging data, but it has rather different hardware features. The hardware architecture of GRACE is shown in Figure 6.30. It consists of four types of modules: processing module (PM), memory module (MM), disk module (DM), and control module (CM). The processing and memory modules are connected by a multichannel ring bus called the *processing network*. The memory modules and the disk modules are connected by a second ring bus called the *staging network*. The operations in both rings are controlled by some control modules, which are also connected to the rings. Relations, which are stored in the disk modules, are first staged in the memory modules through the staging network before being accessed and processed by the processing modules through the processing network. This double-ring structure aims to reduce the potential memory access contentions caused by transferring data between DMs and MMs, and between MMs and PMs.

The architecture of GRACE is built around the techniques of hashing and sorting for implementing relational algebraic operations. The details of how these two techniques are used to improve performance will be given in a later section. Note, however, that the hashing scheme is used to partition data into buckets of tuples that can be independently processed by the PMs, and the sorting scheme is used to order the tuples of a relation so that some relational operations can be carried out more efficiently. GRACE contains hardware facilities to support these two techniques. Descriptions of the organizations of the PM, MM, and DM follow.

Processing module (PM). The organization of the processing module is shown in Figure 6.31. The functions of its component units will be described based on

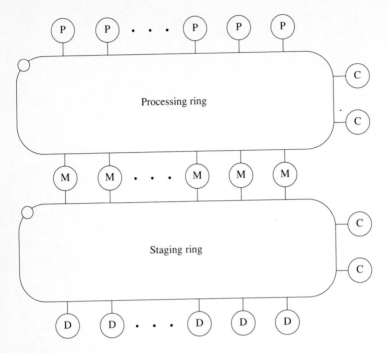

P: Processing module
M: Memory module
C: Control module
D: Disk module

FIGURE 6.30
Architecture of GRACE. (*Source:* [KIT84] ©1984 IEEE)

control and data flow. A database command is provided by a control module to a processing module. The control unit of the PM interprets the command and controls its execution. The ring bus interface unit performs data transmission to and from the MMs through the processing network. The received data, generally a hashed bucket, are first sorted by a hardware sorting unit, which implements a pipelined merge-sort algorithm using VLSI technology (see reference [KIT83c] for details about the sorter). The sorted tuples are then operated on by the tuple manipulation unit, which actually carries out the database command and rearranges attribute values if necessary. The resulting tuples are hashed into nonintersecting buckets based on attribute values for use by the next operation. The tuples are then transmitted to the MMs through the ring bus interface unit.

Memory module (MM). Figure 6.32 shows the organization of the memory module. The main functions of the memory module are (1) to store and provide a bucket-serial data stream to the PMs or DMs and (2) to store intermediate relations as they are produced. The storage medium used in the memory module can be semiconductor RAM or bubble memory. The prototype system uses bubble memory. Unlike the conventional major-minor loop organization, the bubble memory used

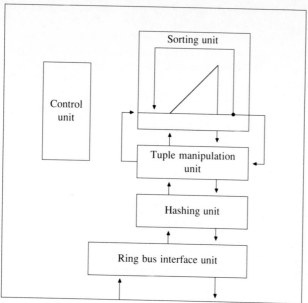

FIGURE 6.31
The organization of the processing module. (*Source:* [KIT84] ©1984 IEEE)

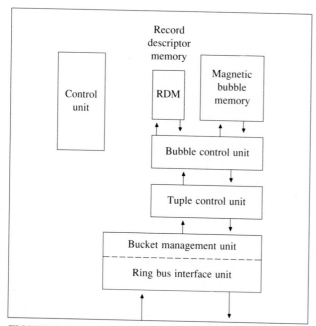

FIGURE 6.32
The organization of the memory module. (*Source:* [KIT84] ©1987 IEEE)

in GRACE has an on-chip hierarchy in which the minor loops are segmented into buffer loops and main loops in addition to the major loop. The bubble memory system uses 16 1-Mbit bubble memory chips with 4096-bit main loops and 128-bit buffer loops. The bubble control unit controls the operation of these chips to ensure a continuous flow of data from the bubble memory. The bubble memory is content addressable, thus, all relational tuples are accessed by content rather than by address. This is accomplished by the use of a record descriptor memory (RDM), which contains the hashed values of the tuples and some memory management tags. To store data into the memory, an arbitrary empty block denoted by an entry in the RDM is used. To fetch data from the memory, the RDM, which is synchronized with the rotation of the bubble memory, is used to address the tuples associatively. Tuples with the same hashed value that belong to a bucket are moved to the buffer loops continuously to produce a bucket-serial data stream with minimal interrecord gap time.

The tuple control unit of Figure 6.32 sets the operational modes of the bubble control unit and provides it with bucket identifiers for outputting the buckets. The bucket management unit maintains the number of tuples of each bucket and schedules their output. The control unit receives and interprets commands from the control modules of both ring networks to carry out the memory functions. The ring bus interface unit controls data transfers.

Disk module (DM). The function of the disk module is to store the base relations and temporary relations generated during query processing. It is also used to perform filtering and hashing functions. Data are stored on a conventional disk, which is controlled by a disk controller (see Figure 6.33). Data transferred out of the disk

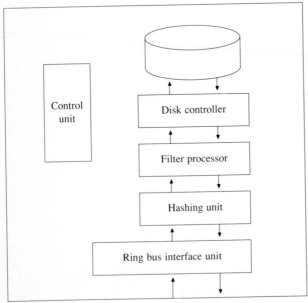

FIGURE 6.33
The organization of the disk module. (*Source:* [KIT84] ©1987 IEEE)

would pass a filter processor. This processor performs selection and projection functions over the tuples that are being transferred. The filter can filter out those tuples of relations that do not satisfy the selection condition and rearrange and/or delete attributes and their corresponding values (i.e., projection), if necessary, before passing the resulting tuples to a hashing unit. The function of the hashing unit is the same as that of the processing module described previously. It partitions the selected tuples into buckets that can be independently processed for the Join operation. GRACE uses the filtering concept introduced by several earlier database computers described in Chapter 4 to reduce the amount of data that need to be staged in the memory modules.

Control module (CM). The control modules activate and control the operations of all the memory, processing, and disk modules. Their main functions are to pass commands and processing information (e.g., qualification conditions, join fields, etc.) to some dynamically allocated modules and to oversee the orderly execution of the commands. For example, a control processor would pass information such as the identification name of a relation, the selection conditions, and the attributes to be projected to the memory module containing the relation. This will allow the selected and projected tuples to be staged in the selected main memory modules. To process these tuples, a control module would activate memory modules that hold the source and target relations as well as an adequate number of processing modules (depending on the processing power needed and the availability of processing modules) to carry out the operation. The query-processing strategy of GRACE will be described in Section 6.4.2.

The main architectural features of GRACE can be summarized below:

1. The separation of the processing network and the staging network, which allows the overlapping of data staging and processing operations.
2. The use of database filters to reduce the amount of data staged in the fast memory modules.
3. The use of hardware hashing and sorting to achieve a high degree of parallelism.
4. The dynamic resource allocation capability, which allows for maximum resource utilization.

Note here that the function of GRACE's memory modules is similar to DIRECT's CCD memory modules. However, different from DIRECT, the memory hierarchy of GRACE consists of two instead of three levels of memories. In DIRECT, the secondary storage, CCD memories, and the private memory of each processing module form the three levels of memory hierarchy. In GRACE, the processing modules do not have the private main memory modules used in DIRECT. Instead, data stored in the memory modules are transferred in the form of a pipeline of buckets through the component units of the processing module(s). The bucket-serial data stream is processed by the processing module(s), and the resulting bucket stream returns to the memory modules. This architecture avoids the step of moving data to some private memory before processing. However, it increases the traffic on the processing ring during an operation. When multiple processing modules are simultaneously executing different bucket streams, the possible contention in using the ring network may affect the performance.

6.4.1.2 GLOBAL SHARED MEMORY SCHEME OF DBMAC. DBMAC is a relational database machine designed and evaluated by a project sponsored by the Italian Applied Program for Informatics. The project started in 1979, and the results of this research have been documented [MIS81, MIS82, CES81, CES83, MIS83].

The architecture of DBMAC is shown in Figure 6.34. It uses a combination of static and dynamic memory-processor connections. The processing units (PUs) in this system are single-board computers, each of which has its own main memory modules. They are connected by a multibus (named G-bus) similar to the static systems described in Section 6.3. To facilitate the communication or message passing among these processing units, a global shared memory, G-RAM, is used. It is also connected to the G-bus and is used as a blackboard for the

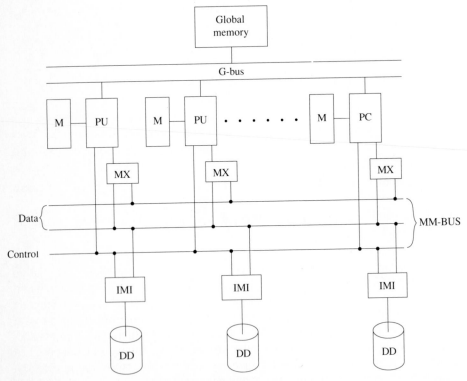

FIGURE 6.34
Architecture of DBMAC. (*Source:* [MIS83] copyright ©1983. Prentice-Hall, Inc., reprinted by permission.)

processing units to read and write messages. The PUs, global shared memory, and G-bus form what is called the physical "high" system.

The physical "low" system consists of the PUs and the disk devices (DDs), are connected by a mass memory bus (MM-bus). All PUs and DDs are connected to a control bus through which control information such as commands, handshaking packets, and disk addresses are transferred. The communication between PUs and DDs are carried out in a serial fashion. Data read from a disk device are bused to all the PUs through a dedicated data line selected for the transmission. Any number of PUs can receive the data, thus the system has broadcast capability. The data bus multiplexing logic (MXs) allows different sets of PUs to transfer data to and from different DDs simultaneously through different data lines. Each processing unit can access data from every disk device. Thus, the low system of DBMAC has a dynamic processor-memory interconnection.

There is an intelligent mass-memory interface (IMI) associated with each disk device. It handles the communication protocol for the DD and performs selections and intersections (two frequently employed operations in this system) on the fly when data are being transferred from a DD to PUs.

The software architecture of DBMAC support a domain-based model of data representation that will be discussed in a later section.

6.4.1.3 MEMORY SWITCHING SCHEME OF SM3.

SM3 is a dynamically partitionable multicomputer system designed and evaluated at the University of Florida for both nonnumeric (database) and numeric computations. It is a continuation and extension of the work on MICRONET conducted by the same group. The project on SM3 was started around 1982 as a system for supporting database processing [FEI84, SU84, BAR84, and BAR86]. It has been extended to provide architectural support for the efficient processing of numeric algorithms [BAR85 and THA87].

The main architectural features of SM3 are as follows. First, it provides fast network data movement and exchange by switching main memory modules between processors. Second, it uses a number of control lines to allow fast interprocessor communication and synchronization, a scheme adopted from the MICRONET system. Third, it uses a physically partitionable bus to allow the formation of a number of common-bus subnetworks for parallel execution of concurrent processes to achieve interquery and intraquery concurrencies (i.e., MIMD processing).

In a multiprocessor/multicomputer system, data files are generally stored in a distributed fashion among many processors so that they can be operated upon simultaneously. In performing many common database operations (e.g., Join, Intersection, Elimination of Duplicates, etc.), large quantities of data must be moved among these processors so that the local data of one processor can be compared with those of the other processors. The amount of data communication among processors increases as the number of processors increases. The conventional approach of moving data is through a data link (e.g., a data bus). This requires many levels of communication protocols and thus represents a considerable overhead. This approach also ties up the data and control lines and the processors involved in the transfer. The transfer time can become very significant when large amounts of data are transferred. The approach taken by SM3 is to use main memory switching as a means of data transfer between computers (see Figure 6.35). Two computers, each with its own main memory, share a memory module of a certain size. A switch is used to control access to the memory. When the switch is set to the left-hand side, the switchable module becomes a part of the main memory space of Processor A. The address space of the switchable module is contiguous to Processor A's local memory space. The contents of the switchable module can be randomly accessed by the processor at the memory access rate, similar to any local memory word. When the switch is set to the right-hand side, Processor B will have access to the module. Thus, a processor can store data into a switchable memory module and, at the memory switching time, transfer the entire module's contents to another processor. This concept of memory switching is different, for example, from the globally shared memory used in DBMAC and other multiprocessor systems [SWA77 and AHU82]. Here, the main memory modules are physically switched between processors and, once switched, are accessed exclusively by different processors without the usual memory contention problem.

In a multiprocessor/multicomputer system, a database query is decomposed into a query tree of primitive database operations and their associated information (e.g., data conditions). Operations on the same level of the tree can be assigned to different processors for execution to achieve intraquery parallelism. Different query trees can also be assigned to different processors to achieve interquery parallelism. During the execution of concurrent processes, two types of network operations are necessary: (1) communication among the cooperating processors to transmit messages, status, and commands and (2) network synchronization among the parallel processes to ensure orderly and meaningful computations.

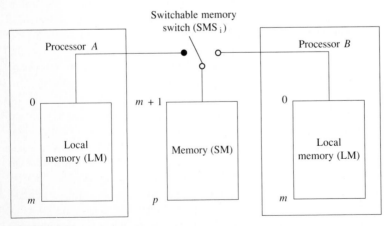

FIGURE 6.35
Switching of a main memory module.

Two popular methods used to achieve these network operations are: message passing and shared memory. In packet-switched systems, network communication and synchronization is achieved by forming packets of messages in the source processors and routing them to the proper destination processors. This is rather time-consuming since it involves not only packet transfer, routing, and interrupt processing, but also the detection of errors in transmission and possible retransmissions. In systems that use shared global memory, bus and memory contention is always a problem that degrades the performance. SM3 uses the control lines of the MICRONET bus, which has been described in Section 6.3.1.1, to achieve the functions required in network communication and synchronization.

The partitionable bus of SM3 is designed to support MIMD processing using a common-bus architecture. A common-bus system has several advantages. It is simple, reliable, less expensive to build, and easy to expand. However, a common concern of this type of system is its bus contentions and delays in data communication. This problem is even more severe if a large number of concurrent processes are executing in the system and large quantities of distributed data need to be exchanged among them. To avoid this problem and, at the same time, to retain the advantages of a common-bus system, SM3 supports a partitionable commonbus. The bus can be "physically" partitioned into a number of common-bus subnetworks, each containing a number of adjacent computers of the original network, and can operate independently on an assigned database task. The hardware technique used to achieve this is illustrated in Figure 6.36. The opening and closing of the switches on the original common bus can physically partition the bus into a number of segments. The computers connected to each

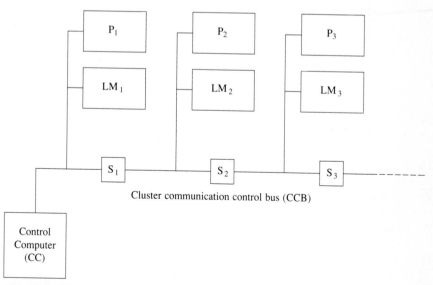

FIGURE 6.36
A partitionable bus.

segment would form a cluster (or a subnetwork). In Figure 6.36, Processors P1 and P2 form a cluster and the rest of the processors form another cluster. A control computer manages and manipulates the switches to dynamically create and combine clusters to meet the need of concurrent queries. The formation of clusters is based on the data distribution, processing power needed, file size, and other criteria. The dynamic reconfiguration capability of SM3 has been shown by analysis and simulation to be very effective in supporting different database processing algorithms.

Note that the technique of "dynamic, physical partitioning" of processors here is different from the "logical partitioning and dynamic allocation of processors" used in DIRECT, GRACE, and DBMAC. Physical isolation of processors in SM3 reduces interference and interruption among subnetworks, thereby increasing throughput, security, and reliability.

One additional feature of SM3 is its use of private secondary storage devices for the component computers, a feature present in most systems with static processor-memory interconnections. Unlike the three systems discussed in this subsection, the secondary storage devices in the SM3 are not shared by all the processors. The advantage of this structure is that I/O operations from/to secondary storage can be carried out in parallel without any contention. A potential disadvantage is that a processor cannot directly access the contents of other secondary storage devices, except those of its own. However, since SM3 can move data efficiently by memory switching, this is not considered to be a problem. Also, operations that require data exchange (e.g., Join) are often preceded by operations that do not (e.g., Selection and Projection). The Selection and Projection operations will bring the filtered data to the main memory ready for memory switching. Therefore, the need for moving data around is not considered a real problem by the designers of SM3.

The architecture of SM3 is shown in Figure 6.37. It consists of a control computer (CC) and a linear array of identical data computers (P_1, P_2, ...P_n). Each data computer is a complete computer system with a processor, local main memory, secondary storage device(s) and their corresponding device controller(s), and other peripheral devices that are connected by some internal bus. Additionally, each data computer has two switchable main memory modules serving as a pair of switching buffers for data transfer. The CC and P_i's are connected by two buses: a switchable memory bus (SMB) and a cluster control bus (CCB). The CCB is partitionable via the Si switches. For example, the setting of the Si switches as shown in the figure results in the formation of three clusters (or subnetworks): P_1-P_2-P_3, P_4-P_5, and P_6-P_n. In each cluster, one of the Pi's is designated as the cluster control processor (CCP). The CCP oversees the execution of the database task assigned to it by the CC.

In addition to the Si switches, there are two other sets of switches in the system, $CCPS_i$'s and SMS_i's, as shown in the figure. The CCP switches are used to select the cluster controllers in different clusters. When closed, a CCP switch specifies that the associated processor is designated as the cluster controller. The designation of cluster controller can be passed from one processor to another in

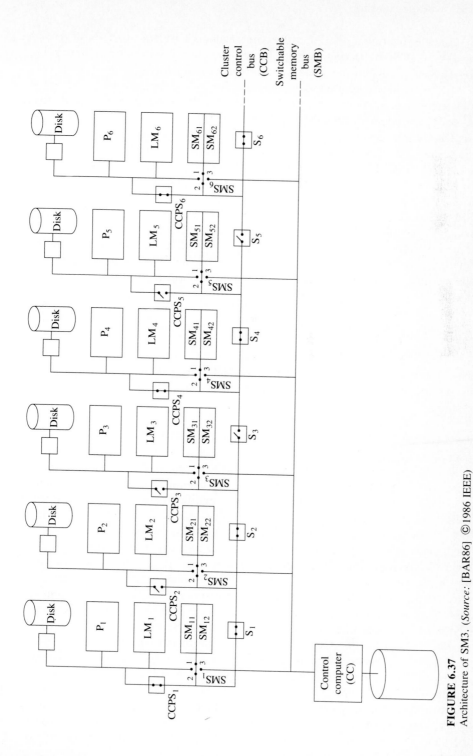

FIGURE 6.37
Architecture of SM3. (*Source:* [BAR86] ©1986 IEEE)

a cluster. In the figure, P_1, P_4, and P_6 are cluster controllers. A CCP can set and reset the $CCPS_i$ and SMS_i switches to pass the control status and to control the use of SMs to support the operation assigned to the cluster.

SMS switches are used to determine which processor can have access to the switchable main memory modules. Each switch is shown to have three positions. A switchable memory module can be connected to either Pi, CCP, or CC. At the Pi position (position 1), it is used by Pi to read data from it or to fill it with the result of a computation. At the CCP position (position 2), it is regarded as a part of the CCP's main memory. The CCP can fetch data from it, copy its contents to the SM of another processor, or broadcast the contents of the SM to all the processors in the same cluster. At the CCP position (position 3), the SM becomes a part of the CC's main memory. Since there are three positions and two SM modules, the switch is two out of three multiplexed. Two out of three processors can independently access the two SMs. In typical use, the Pi fills one SM while the other is being emptied by the CC. The next section describes how these hardware features are used to support the frequent database primitives.

6.4.2   Data Organization and Processing Techniques

This section examines the data organization and query-processing techniques used in the systems whose architectures have just been described in the preceding section.

6.4.2.1 DATA ORGANIZATION OF DIRECT.

In DIRECT, each tuple of a relation is of fixed length and the attributes of a relation are assigned maximal field width to accommodate the largest or widest values. This restriction wastes some space but eliminates the need for using delimiters or field width counts to separate variable-length fields and also simplifies data access and garbage collection tasks. Relations are divided into pages, each of which has 16K bytes, and are stored on mass storage devices as flat files. No auxiliary structure is used. Each physical page is the size of a CCD memory module. The back-end controller manages the CCD memory modules and is responsible for moving physical pages between the CCDs and the mass memory devices in responding to page access requests made by the query processors (QPs). When a QP wants to perform an operation on a relation, a request for a page of the relation is made. The back-end controller brings in the page from the mass storage to a CCD module and assigns the CCD page frame to the requesting QP. The QP reads the page contents into its input data buffer in its local main memory, performs the assigned operation on the data, and copies appropriate tuples into its output buffer. When the output buffer is full, a request is again made to the back-end controller for an available CCD page frame for storing the output page, which forms a part of a temporary relation. The back-end controller transfers the temporary relation to the host computer if it is the answer to the query; it transfers the relation to the mass memory if the relation is to be made permanent.

Figure 6.38 shows a number of tables maintained by the back-end controller to keep track of relations and their pages. Associated with each relation are three tables: the relation descriptor table, the page table, and the attribute catalog table. The meaning of the fields in these tables should be self-explanatory.

6.4.2.2 QUERY PROCESSING TECHNIQUES OF DIRECT. It is assumed in DIRECT that high-level query statements submitted by the users to the system are translated by the host into query packets. Two classes of query packets are distinguished. The first deals with database utility routines for creating a database, creating or destroying relations, and so forth. These are generated by the INGRES software running on the host, and they are executed by the back-end controller. The second contains regular user queries represented in the form of query trees. The nodes of these trees are relational operators such as select, join, and project, and the leaf nodes take relations as input. This type of query packet is assigned to the QPs by the back-end for execution.

In DIRECT, the QPs are assigned dynamically to query packets (QPKTs). When a compiled QPKT is received at the back-end controller, it is entered into a queue ordered by priority (see Figure 6.39). A list of all executing QPKTs is stored in a table called QPKTX. Three QP allocation strategies have been considered by the researchers of DIRECT: packet-level strategy, instruction-level strategy, and data flow strategy.

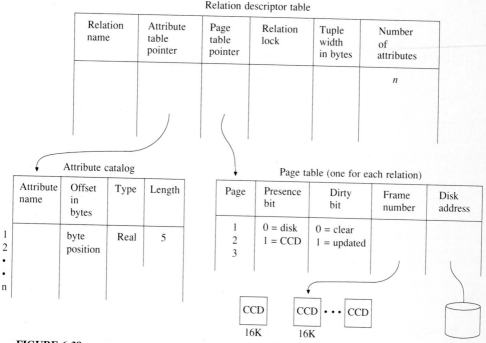

FIGURE 6.38
Tables for maintaining relations and pages. (*Source:* [DEW79a] ©1979 IEEE)

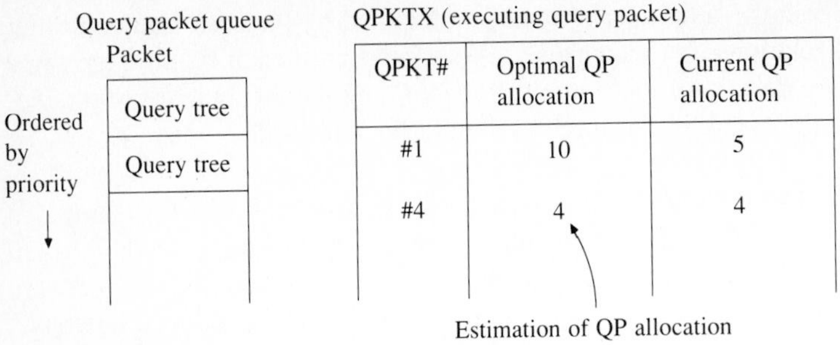

Query packet queue

Packet

Ordered by priority

| Query tree |
| Query tree |

QPKTX (executing query packet)

QPKT#	Optimal QP allocation	Current QP allocation
#1	10	5
#4	4	4

Estimation of QP allocation

FIGURE 6.39
Table for supporting processor relocation. (*Source:* [DEW79a] ©1979 IEEE)

1. *Packet-level strategy.* The optimal number of QPs assigned to a packet is calculated based on some heuristics, and the number is entered into the QPKTX table. Optimal allocation means that adding more QPs to a given packet will not decrease its execution time. It is difficult to determine the optimal number since many parameters that can affect the performance of a query are dependent on the nature of data (e.g., the selectivity factor of a selection or a join operation). Thus, heuristic methods are use in DIRECT to derive this number. The back-end controller attempts to allocate this number of QPs to a packet. If the optimal number of QPs are not available at the time of processor allocation, then the back-end controller assigns the maximal number of available QPs and records the present level of QPs in the QPKTX (see Figure 6.39). Whenever QPs become available as a result of, say, the completion of some other packets, the back-end controller assigns them to a packet that has less than its optimal number of QPs. The QP level of each packet is continuously monitored. Only when no packet is at a less-than-optimal level is a new packet assigned QPs. Once a QP is allocated to a packet, it cannot be taken away from it until it completes its execution.

2. *Instruction-level strategy.* This strategy is similar to the packet-level strategy, except that the optimal number is calculated for each primitive operation in a query packet instead of the whole packet. Its advantages are (a) the estimation of the optimal number can be more accurate since only a single operation and its input need to be considered and (b) QP utilization is improved since a near optimal number of QPs are used at every stage of packet execution. The penalty is, of course, the extra overhead involved in QP allocation.

3. *Data flow strategy.* In this method, QPs are assigned to process each node of a packet. As soon as a page is produced by the QPs that have been assigned to a node, the page is sent to its parent node in the query tree. When a page is available in each of its input node(s), the QPs assigned to that node will start their execution. This is in contrast to the earlier strategies in which the entire relation must be available before the execution of any stage of the query tree can start. In the data flow method, pages of relations form a number of data pipelines that flow through operators of the query tree. The QPs assigned to the operators take data pages from a pipeline(s), process the data, and put its output

data into its output pipeline. The execution of an operation is triggered by the availability of its input data. One obvious advantage of this strategy is that the response time of a query can be better than the other two strategies since the root of a query tree will receive and produce data much earlier. Another advantage is that page traffic between the CCDs and mass memory can be reduced since pages of intermediate relations can be immediately consumed by the subsequent operators (i.e., their QPs).

All these strategies allocate multiple QPs to a primitive database operation. These QPs process the pages of a relation in parallel. Some mechanism is necessary to prevent a page from being processed by more than one QP. DIRECT manages this by the use of the NEXT PAGE and GET PAGE operators. QPs do not explicitly ask for a page of a relation except when performing a join operation. They ask the back-end controller for the NEXT page. The back-end controller maintains a table that records each instance of a relation referenced by each executing query. A currency pointer in the table specifies the last page of a relation referenced by any QP that has been assigned to the packet. When the NEXT PAGE or GET PAGE request is received, the table is accessed to determine the next page that needs to be processed.

6.4.2.3 DATA ORGANIZATION AND PROCESSING TECHNIQUES OF GRACE.
As mentioned in a previous section, the architecture of GRACE is built around the ideas of hashing and sorting tuples of relations so that relational operations can be performed more efficiently on hashed and sorted relations. The purpose of hashing relational tuples is to partition the tuples into buckets based on the hash values of some selected attribute(s), for example, the join attribute(s). Each bucket will contain tuples having the same hash value. If two operand relations of a join operation are hashed in this manner, a pair of buckets, one from each relation, will be generated for each distinct hash value (or a range of hash values) of the join attribute. These pairs of buckets can then be assigned to different processors for performing the Join operation independently, that is, no interprocessor communication or data exchange will be reqired during the operation. Besides using this hashing scheme, GRACE uses a special sorting machine in each processing module to sort the buckets and then to perform the Join operation on the sorted buckets.

Query execution in GRACE involves two phases: the staging phase and the processing phase. During the staging phase, the tuples of a relation, which are stored across disk modules, are fetched in parallel from the disk modules. They form data streams that pass the filter processors and hashing units associated with the disk modules (see Figure 6.40). The filter processors filter out the unnecessary tuples, and the remaining tuples are hashed to form buckets that are evenly distributed across the memory modules through the staging network. The filtering and hashing operations are carried out on the fly as tuples are staged in the memory modules.

The processing phase begins after the data have been staged in the memory modules. The processing of a relational algebraic operation is carried out in the

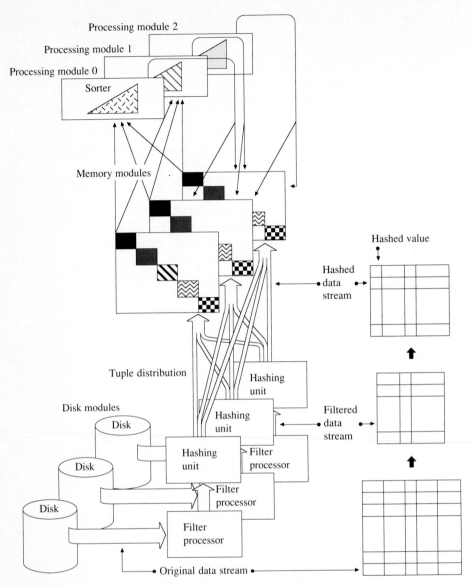

FIGURE 6.40
Conceptual view of staging and processing phases. (*Source:* [KIT84] ©1984 IEEE)

processing modules. The memory modules generate bucket-serial data streams that are sent to the processing modules. Similar to the CCDs in DIRECT, the memory modules play an active role in generating and transferring the data to processing modules. In the case of a unary operation, one processing module is assigned to process one bucket. The segments of a bucket are transferred in a pipeline fashion to the processing module. In the case of a binary operation, two buckets belonging to two different relations are pipelined to a processing module. The hardware sorter in the processing module takes the input data stream to produce a sorted data stream. The hardware sorter is able to sort data faster than the input time. The actual relational operation is then carried out on the sorted data stream, and the results are hashed over the attribute(s) involved in the next operation as they are produced. The hashed results are sent back to the memory modules for subsequent processing.

6.4.2.4 DATA ORGANIZATION OF DBMAC. The architecture of DBMAC is designed to support a domain-based internal schema rather than a relation-based one. Domains are obtained from relations by vertically partitioning the distinct attributes of all relations in the database followed by the elimination of the duplicates inside the partitions. Each domain contains the distinct values of an attribute, and there are as many domains as there are distinct attributes in the entire database. If an attribute is used in more than one relation, then the values of this attribute in these relations form the same domain. Instead of storing relations in the form of a set of files, each of which consists of a set of tuples or records, DBMAC organizes the relations by their domains in an inverted structure. As illustrated in Figure 6.41, a domain is conceptually the root (level 0) of a tree structure data organization. It branches at the next level (level 1) to all the distinct attribute values that form the domain. Each value at level 1 of the tree branches out to all the relations containing the same attribute that forms the domain. Each relation at level 2 is associated with the tuple identifications (TIDs) at level 3, which correspond to the tuples of the original relation containing that attribute value. Using this organization, an attribute value in a particular tuple of a relation

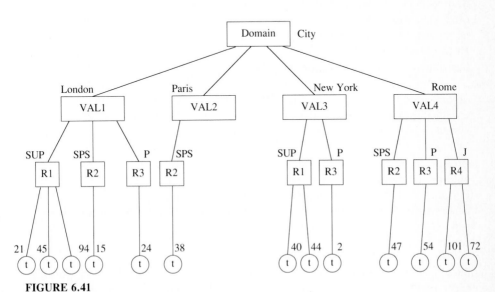

FIGURE 6.41
The conceptual view of a domain-based data organization.

VAL1	R1	t21	t45	t94	R2	t15	R3	A24	VAL2	R2	• • • • •

FIGURE 6.42
The physical organization of a file.

can be traced via a distinct path in the tree. At the physical level, each domain is maintained as a file of variable-length records. Each record implements a value subtree. As shown in Figure 6.42, an attribute value is followed by repeated occurrences of a relation name followed by a set of TIDs. Each file is stored sequentially on the disk tracks.

This data organization has three advantages. First, since data are organized by domains, the tuples of all the relations in the entire database containing a given attribute value can be easily accessed. Furthermore, if the qualification condition of a selection operation involves several attributes, the searches for the tuples associated with these attributes can be carried out simultaneously by the processing units (PUs). The next subsection examines the processing techniques for selection more closely.

Second, since the relation names and TIDs of all the relations containing the same attribute are stored together with attribute values, joining two relations over a common attribute can be easily done by taking the cross-product over two sets of TIDs. In a sense, this data organization has prejoined all those relations that can be joined.

The third advantage, which depends on the characteristics of the data, is the potential saving of storage space. In this data organization, each attribute value in a domain is stored only once. TIDs are used for reconstructing the original tuples of a relation instead of storing attribute values repeatedly. If attribute values are often repeated in the original relations and the widths of the attribute fields are large, then this organization can dramatically reduce the storage requirement. However, if the database does not possess the characteristics just described, then the domain-based organization may not have the space advantage.

This organization is not without disadvantages. Just like all the inverted organizations (e.g., those used in MICRONET and MDBS), any update made in the database would require that some inverted lists of TIDs (or pointers in other systems) be modified. Another equally serious problem is the reconstruction of relations for output to the user. Since the original relations are not explicitly stored and the resulting relation of any operation is represented by a set of TIDs, an output relation needs to be constructed by searching the database using the TIDs. Fortunately, in a transaction-oriented application, many database operations are performed before generating results for output to the user. The speed gained in processing the database using this data organization should outweigh the relation construction cost.

6.4.2.5 PROCESSING TECHNIQUES OF DBMAC. Cesarini, DeLuca Cardillo, and Soda [CES83] introduce two methods for performing parallel selection operations: a pipeline execution approach and a parallel execution approach. If a query contains a selection operation involving four attributes (A_1, A_2, A_3, and A_4) and a projection over a single attribute (A_5), the pipeline approach will involve operations shown in Figure 6.43. In this approach, a processing unit will be assigned to perform a DPSEL operation based on the attribute A_1. This operation searches the data associated with A_1 for the TIDs of tuples that satisfy the search condition associated with A_1. The TID list is passed to the next processing unit, which is assigned to perform the TLSEL operation. This operation takes the output tuple list of the first processing unit and intersects with the list obtained based on the A_2 condition. The process continues in a pipeline fashion for the A_3 and A_4 conditions. The last processing unit in the pipeline performs the TLVAL operation, which searches the data pool associated with the intended attribute (A_5) for the values corresponding to the TIDs of an input TID list, to produce the final result for the query.

The parallel execution approach is illustrated in Figure 6.44. In this approach, four DPSEL operations can be carried out in parallel by four processing units. Each DPSEL operation searches the data pool associated with the intended attribute for the TIDs of tuples satisfying the selection condition. The results (TID lists) produced by the DPSEL operations are intersected (by the INTID operation) in a binary tree structure to produce the TID list for the last processing unit, which performs the Projection operation.

Unlike the relation-based organization, in which the qualification conditions associated with all attributes are verified against tuples of a relation by a single

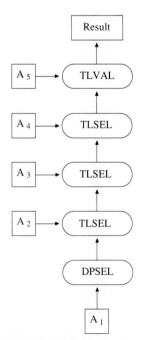

FIGURE 6.43
Pipeline execution of a selection on four attributes. (*Source:* [CES83] copyright ©1983. Prentice-Hall, Inc., reprinted by permission.)

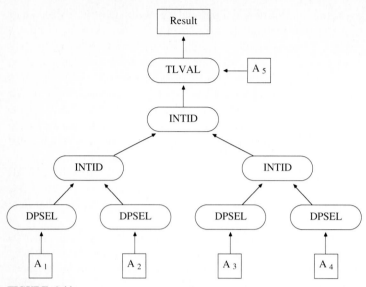

FIGURE 6.44
Parallel execution of a selection on four attributes. (*Source:* [CES83] copyright © 1983. Prentice-Hall, Inc., reprinted by permission.)

processor, the approaches described here exploit the domain-based organization by assigning the qualification conditions to different processors, thus increasing the degree of parallelism.

The relational join operation can be carried out very efficiently in this system. Joining two relations, $R1$ and $R2$, over an attribute A can be carried out as follows. For each distinct value of A, search the physical storage for the record containing all relation names and TIDs of tuples having that attribute value (refer back to Figure 6.41). If $R1$ and $R2$ are included in this set of relation names, extract the two sets of TIDs associated with these two relations and perform a Cartesian product operation over them to produce a set of TID pairs, which represents the result of the Join.

DBMAC uses two primitive operations very frequently: the selection and the intersection of TIDs. For this reason, the intelligent mass-memory interface is designed to perform these operations on the fly as data are transferred from disk devices to the main memory modules.

6.4.2.6 DATA ORGANIZATION AND PROCESSING TECHNIQUES OF SM3. In SM3, data files are horizontally partitioned and stored in a distributed fashion in the secondary storage devices of a number of adjacent data computers. Therefore, each data computer may have in its secondary storage some partitions of a file (or a relation). Database queries can be entered through the data computers or the control computer (CC), but they are translated by the CC. The transactions formed by these queries are managed by the CC. The CC forms clusters of adjacent data processors and assigns these clusters the tasks of performing the database operations in the transactions. The formation of clusters is based on two considerations: (1) the location of the data and (2) the processing power (in terms of the number of processors) needed to process the database operations. A cluster must contain the data to be processed by the operation assigned to it. Therefore, it is sometimes necessary to move data around by the memory-switching technique so that the data are physically residing in the adjacent processors, which form the cluster. Once a cluster is formed by the CC, one of the data computers is designated as the cluster control processor (CCP) and is given a database command. The CCP broadcasts the command to all the processors in the cluster and controls the execution of the command by all the data computers and the CCP itself.

All processors in a cluster execute a prestored program suitable for the command and generate the results that are stored in their local memory or secondary storage devices. The execution of the command can either be done independently (e.g., Selection operation) or cooperatively (e.g., Join operation) by the processors. The resulting data can be stored in a distributed fashion and used for subsequent operations or can be collected by the CC for output to the user. The collection process can be aided by the use of the memory-switching technique and is usually overlapped with secondary storage I/O and processing times. A description of a Selection algorithm and a Join algorithm follows. Other algorithms for these and other database operations can be similarly formulated for the SM3.

The general procedure followed for selection is as follows. A query is directed to the CC, which translates it into a query tree. Suppose a selection operation in the query tree is to be processed. The CC performs a directory lookup to determine which data computers contain the data file (or relation) to be processed. A second table lookup is performed to ensure that all the required computers are free to perform the operation. The CC forms a cluster and designates a CCP. The command is sent to the CCP, which broadcasts it to all its data computers via the cluster control bus (CCB). All the computers begin execution after receiving the command. Each data computer reads its local segment of the source relation A from secondary storage into one of its I/O buffers and does a simple scan of each block in order to perform the selection. While the block in the first buffer is being processed, the I/O controller goes ahead to read the next block into the second I/O buffer. Hence, there is an overlap between the I/O and processing activities. The tuples satisfying the selection condition are written to a switchable memory module, from which they are transferred to the CC. Since there are two switchable modules associated with each data computer, a data computer can be writing data into one module while the CC is reading out of the other module. Hence, CPU and data transfer operations are also overlapped. The result of the Selection operation may either be required as intermediate data for use in a later operation or may be the final output. In the first case, each data computer determines the response set and sets a local control line on completion. The Selection is complete when the corresponding global line is set. The results of the Selection are distributed in the data computers. In the second case, the processors write their output into the respective switchable memory modules (SMs). If the Selection operation in a data computer finishes before an SM is full, a data computer would set its local control line and interrupt the CC. The CC can then switch the SM to itself and read the result. If the SM fills up before the Selection finishes, the data computer would interrupt the CC without setting the local line and proceed with the operation using the second SM module. The results of the Selection are collected by the CC.

Many Join algorithms have been proposed for multiprocessor systems, all of which can be implemented in the SM3 system. Only the nested-loop algorithm will be described here. Assume that a join is to be performed between a larger relation A and a smaller relation B. A cluster containing both A and B relations is formed by the CC. The join is performed by fully broadcasting the smaller relation B while leaving the other relation in place. Each data computer in the cluster reads in a block of relation A. The CCP does a block-by-block broadcast of its local segment of relation B. As each block of B is broadcast, the data computers (including CCP) join this block with their local segments of relation A. The Join operation involves comparisons between every tuple of the B block and every tuple of an A block, concatenation of tuples to form the resulting tuples if they satisfy the join condition, and moving the result tuples into the SMs if the results are to be collected by the CC. After broadcasting all its blocks of relation B, the CCP passes on its CCP status to the next data computer in the cluster. The new CCP repeats the entire process of broadcasting its B blocks. The Join operation is complete when all the blocks of relation B have been broadcast and joined with the segments of relation A.

The operation is accelerated in the SM3 system by the use of the dual I/O buffers and dual switchable memories, which make I/O and data transfer operations transparent. For example, the time required for reading all the B blocks except the first one is transparent since, as one block is being processed, the I/O controller independently reads in the next block. Also, if the entire relation A does not fit in the I/O buffers in one parallel read by the data computers, subsequent segments of A can also be read in while the Join operation on data blocks is under way. The collection of the join results by the CC can be carried out in parallel to the processing of data blocks using the dual switchable memory modules. The process is similar to the collection of selection results already described. Similar to the Selection operation, the results of join can either be left in the data computers as a temporary relation for subsequent processing or collected by the CC for output to the user.

6.5   ANALYSIS

This section provides an analysis of four representative database operations based on the abstract models for multiprocessor systems with static and dynamic processor-memory interconnections. Important performance parameters for some selected algorithms will be identified, and cost formulas in terms of execution time will be derived. Table 6.1 lists the parameters used in the analyses. General assumptions made for the analysis in Chapter 2 are used in this chapter.

TABLE 6.1
Performance parameters

Parameter	Definition
R	Name of a referenced relation
m	Number of pages in relation R
S	Name of the inner relation in a Join operation
s	Number of pages in relation S
L	The resulting relation of an operation
b	Buffer capacity in pages
c_fac	Collision factor; a value greater than 1 to account for the extra processing needed due to collisions in hashing
$f1$	Cache hit ratio; i.e., probability of a page being in the cache memory
$f2$	Probability of having room for a page in the cache memory
jn_fac	Join selectivity factor; i.e., the ratio of the number of tuples of L to the number of tuples of the cross-product between R and S
$n1$	Number of two-page operations
p	Number of data processors
q	Number of tracks in a disk cylinder
sel_fac	Selectivity factor for the Selection operation; i.e., the ratio of the number of selected tuples of a referenced relation to the number of tuples of that relation
r_fac	A reduction factor that determines the number of w categories formed in each data processor
t	Number of tuples per page of R or S
u	Total number of pages of L produced by joining the fragments of relations R and S in a data processor
$u1$	Number of output pages of a selection operation in a data processor
$u2$	Total number of output pages, i.e., the number of pages of L
$u3$	Total number of output pages of a parallel binary merge operation
v	The sum of the number of tuple movements
w	Number of distinct categories in a statistical aggregation operation
x	Number of attributes involved in selection conditions

TABLE 6.1
Performance parameters *(continued)*

y	Number of category attributes in each tuple
$t[access]$	Disk seek time plus latency
$t[brcast]$	Time for broadcasting a page to data processors
$t[comp]$	Compilation time for a simple query
$t[cpu]$	Time for comparing two values in registers or an arithmetic operation
$t[hash]$	Time for performing a hash function over an attribute or value
$t[I/O]$	Track (page) read/write time
$t[mov]$	Time for moving a tuple of R or S within main memory
$t[msg]$	Time for transferring a short message between two processors
$t[s]$	Time to load a value from the memory to a register
$t[syn]$	Time for the synchronization of a process among data processors
$t[tp\_out]$	Time for transferring one tuple to a terminal
$t[tp\_xfer]$	Time for transferring a tuple or an instruction between two processors
$t[trans]$	Time for transforming a compiled query or a data page to suit a target system
$txfer]$	Time for transferring a page between two processors

6.5.1   An Abstract Model for Multiprocessor Systems with Static Processor-Memory Interconnection

The abstract model for this category of database machines is shown in Figure 6.45. In this model, it is assumed that each data processor has its own main memory and secondary storage devices. The processors in this model are conventional Von Neumann processors. Thus, the time parameters associated with local operations in these processors are similar to those used in the analyses of database operations in the conventional system model presented in Section 2.3. Each data file (or relation) is horizontally partitioned and evenly distributed in the storage devices of the data processors. The control processor and data processors are connected through an interconnection network that can be a common bus, a ring, a tree network, or any other network interconnection structure. It is further assumed that the interconnection network provides the broadcasting capability—that is, data, messages, control commands, and status can be transmitted from one processor to all the others simultaneously. The control processor issues database commands and collects the results of retrieval operations.

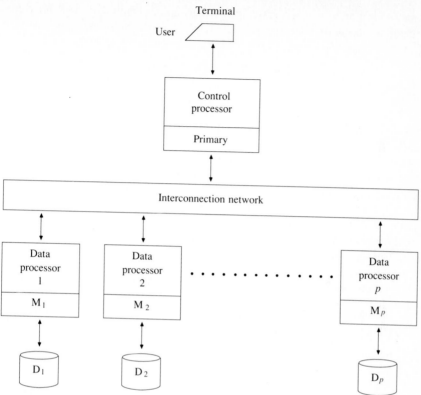

FIGURE 6.45
Abstract model for multiprocessor systems with static processor-memory interconnection.

6.5.2   Analyses of Algorithms

The following analyses of Select, Join, Statistical Aggregation, and Update operations, do not consider the possible overlaps among the time components in the derived formulas. The reader should adjust the formulas to fit the specific multiprocessor systems being evaluated, if overlaps are possible.

6.5.2.1   SELECT. The query is compiled by the control processor and broadcast to all the data processors. The instruction flow time is

$$t[\text{inst\_flow}] = t[\text{comp}] + t[\text{brcast}]$$

Assuming the tuples of relation R are evenly distributed among the p data processors, the number of pages stored in the secondary storage device of each data processor will be equal to $\text{ceil}(m/p)$. Each data processor will perform the Select operation over its own pages of R, and the operation is carried out in parallel with those of the other data processors. Thus, the data processing time of the whole network is equal to that of a single processor operating on $\text{ceil}(m/p)$ pages plus the time for synchronization after all data processors completed their operations. Since the data processors are conventional processors, the formula for the Select operation is similar to the one given in Section 2.3.1. Parameters will have the same meaning unless they are redefined. Table 6.1 shows some basic parameters used in the analyses presented in this chapter.

$$t[\text{process}] = \text{ceil}(m/p)/q * \{t[\text{Read\_q\_pg}, R] + \\ t[\text{process\_q\_pg}, R]\} + u1 * t[\text{I/O}] + \\ 2 * t[\text{access}] + t[\text{syn}]$$

where $u1 = \text{ceil}(\text{ceil}(m/p) * \text{selfac})$ is the number of output pages produced by each data processor.

The results of selection are distributed in the p processors. They need to be collected to the control processor for output to the user's terminal. The time for transferring a page from a data processor to the control processor is denoted as $t[\text{xfer}]$. At the end of the Selection operation carried out by the data processors, $u1$ pages of the selection results will have been written to the secondary storage. They need to be read back in parallel to the main memory for transfer in serial to the control processor. Once all the output pages of L have been received by the control processor, all $m * t * \text{sel\_fac}$ tuples in these pages need to be transferred to the user's terminal. Therefore, the total data collection time is

$$t[\text{data\_collect}] = p * u1 * t[\text{xfer}] + u1 * t[\text{I/O}] \\ + t[\text{access}] + m * t * \text{sel\_fac} * t[\text{tp\_out}]$$

The total execution time for this algorithm is

$$t[\text{Select}] = t[\text{inst\_flow}] + t[\text{process}] + t[\text{data\_collect}]$$

6.5.2.2 JOIN. The join algorithm that follows resembles the nested-loop algorithm used by Su and Mikkilineni [SU82 and SU83]. The instruction flow time is the same as that for the Selection operation.

$$t[\text{inst\_flow}] = t[\text{comp}] + t[\text{brcast}]$$

Since relations are horizontally partitioned and evenly distributed in the secondary storage devices, each data processor is assumed to contain $\text{ceil}(m/p)$ pages of relation R and $\text{ceil}(s/p)$ pages of relation S. In the nested-loop–join algorithm, the pages of the relation R (assuming that R is smaller than S) are broadcast from each data processor to all the others one at a time. Each page will be joined with all the pages of S simultaneously in the data processors. The time to read and broadcast an R page is

$$t[\text{brcast\_pg}, R] = t[\text{access}] + t[\text{I/O}] + t[\text{xfer}]$$

The time to join one page of R with $\text{ceil}(s/p)$ pages of S is similar to the expression given in Section 2.3.2. The reader should refer back to the expressions presented in that section for explanation of the following terms.

$$t[\text{jn\_pg}, R] = \text{ceil}(s/p)/q * \{t[\text{read\_q\_pg}, S] \\ + t[\text{jn\_Rpg\_Sq}]\}$$

The time for processing one page of R, including the broadcast time for the page and the synchronization time, is

$$t[\text{proc\_pg}, R] = t[\text{jn\_pg}, R] + t[\text{brcast\_pg}, R] + t[\text{syn}]$$

The number of pages produced by joining ceil(m/p) pages of R with ceil(s/p) pages of S in each data processor is

$$u = \text{ceil}(\text{jn\_fac} * \text{ceil}(m/p) * t * \text{ceil}(s/p) * t)/(t/2))$$

The time required to write these u pages to the secondary storage is then

$$t[\text{I/O}, L/p] = u * t[\text{I/O}]$$

The total time for processing ceil(m/p) pages of R including the output time is

$$t[\text{process}] = (2 + \text{ceil}(m/p)) * t[\text{access}]$$
$$+ \text{ceil}(m/p) * t[\text{proc\_pg}, R]$$
$$+ t[\text{I/O}, L/p]$$

where $(2 + \text{ceil}(m/p)) * t[\text{access}]$ accounts for the seek and latency times involved in the reading of the fragment of R, the reading of the fragment of S (ceil(m/p) times), and the writing of the Join result in each data processor.

The data collection time for this operation is similar to that of the Select operation. There are $m * t * s * t * \text{jn\_fac}$ tuples to be transferred to the user's terminal. They are collected from the data processors that hold the join results. The collection would involve reading u pages of the resulting relation L from the secondary storage by all data processors in parallel and transferring all the pages of L to the control processor. The transfer of L pages to the control processor by the p data processors is carried out in a sequential manner since all the data must be transmitted through the same interconnection network. Therefore, the data collection time is

$$t[\text{data\_collect}] = m * t * s * t * \text{jn\_fac} * 2 * t[\text{tp\_out}]$$
$$+ t[\text{I/O}, L/p]$$
$$+ p * u * t[\text{xfer}]$$
$$+ t[\text{access}]$$

The total execution time for this algorithm is

$$t[\text{Join}] = t[\text{inst\_flow}] + t[\text{process}] + t[\text{data\_collect}]$$

6.5.2.3 STATISTICAL AGGREGATION.

A merge-sort algorithm will be used here for this operation. The instruction flow for this operation is the same as that for the previous operations.

$$t[\text{inst\_flow}] = t[\text{comp}] + t[\text{brcast}]$$

For ceil(m/p) pages of the relation R residing in each data processor, the time to sort these pages using the four-way external merge-sort algorithm, which has been analyzed in Section 2.3.3, is

$$t[\text{sort\_p}, R] = \log_4(m/p) * t[\text{merge\_sort\_pg}, R]$$

The time necessary to perform the local aggregation operation is

$$\text{ceil}(m/p) * t * \{t[\text{s}] + t[\text{cpu}]\}$$

Assuming that there are $w * \text{r\_fac}(i)$ distinct categories (or partitions) formed in each data processor, DPi, $w * \text{r\_fac}(i)$ number of tuples will be formed in each data processor as a part of the result of the local aggregation operation. (Here, w is the number of distinct categories of tuples formed by the aggregation operation; and $\text{r\_fac}(i)$, whose value is less than or equal to 1 and greater than $1/w$, is a reduction factor that determines the number of categories formed in the ith data processor.) These tuples need to be transferred in pages to the control processor, which will perform the final aggregation over the tuples received from all the data processors. The time necessary to transfer the pages of the locally aggregated tuples to the control processor is

$$\sum_{i=1}^{p} \text{ceil}(w * \text{r\_fact}(i)/t) * t[\text{xfer}]$$

The final aggregation operation carried out by the control processor will take the following amount of time:

$$\sum_{i=1}^{p} \text{ceil}(w * \text{r\_fac}(i)) * \{t[\text{s}] + t[\text{cpu}]\}$$

Accounting for the synchronization required at the end of sorting and local aggregation phases, the total time for this operation is

$$\begin{aligned}
t[\text{process}] = {}& t[\text{sort\_p}, R] + \text{ceil}(m/p) * t * \{t[\text{s}] + \\
& t[\text{cpu}]\} + 2 * t[\text{syn}] \\
& + \sum_{i=1}^{p} \{\text{ceil}(w * \text{r\_fac}(i)/t) * t[\text{xfer}] + \\
& \text{ceil}(w * \text{r\_fac}(i) * \{t[\text{s}] + t[\text{cpu}]\}\}
\end{aligned}$$

The final aggregated values and the resulting relation are now in the control processor. They are to be transferred to the user's terminal. The data collection time is

$$t[\text{data\_collect}] = w * t[\text{tp\_out}]$$

Therefore, the total execution time is

$$t[\text{Aggregate}] = t[\text{inst\_flow}] + t[\text{process}] + t[\text{data\_collect}]$$

6.5.2.4 UPDATE. The instruction flow time remains the same. To perform the Update operation, q pages of the relation R are read by each data processor from its own secondary storage. The time for this is $t[\text{read\_q\_pg}, R]$ as in the Selection operation. The time required to select those tuples in the q pages for update, assuming x attribute values are involved in the search conditions, is

$$q * t * x * \{2 * t[\text{s}] + t[\text{cpu}]\}$$

The time to update the values of the selected tuples is

$$\text{sel\_fac} * q * t * \{2 * t[s] + t[\text{cpu}]\}$$

where sel_fac is the selectivity factor and $\{2 * t[s] + t[\text{cpu}]\}$ is used to approximate the time for updating a tuple.

After the Update operation, the updated pages need to be written back to the secondary storage. Assuming all $\text{ceil}(m/p)$ pages in a data processor have been updated, the time necessary to write them back is $t[\text{access}] + \text{ceil}(m/p) * t[\text{I/O}]$. For a total of $\text{ceil}((m/p)/q)$ cylinders of data pages in each data processor's secondary storage, the processing time in each data processor is

$$\begin{aligned}
t[\text{proc}/p] = \; & \text{ceil}(m/p)/q * \{t[\text{read\_q\_pg}, R] \\
& + q * t * x * \{2 * t[s] + t[\text{cpu}]\} \\
& + q * t * \text{sel\_fac} * \{2 * t[s] + t[\text{cpu}]\}\} \\
& + t[\text{access}] + \text{ceil}(m/p) * t[\text{I/O}]
\end{aligned}$$

Since all the data processors operate in parallel, the data processing time for this algorithm is $t[\text{proc}/p]$ plus the time for performing one synchronization at the end of updates by the data processors. Thus,

$$t[\text{process}] = t[\text{proc/p}] + t[\text{syn}]$$

There is no data collection time in this operation. Thus,

$$t[\text{Update}] = t[\text{inst\_flow}] + t[\text{process}]$$

6.5.3 An Abstract Model for Multiprocessor Systems with Dynamic Processor-Memory Interconnection

The abstract model is shown in Figure 6.46. It consists of a host processor, a back-end controller, a set of data processors, a set of cache memory modules, an interconnection network between the data processors and the cache memory modules, a set of disks, and an interconnection network between the cache memory modules and the disks. The data processors have their own local main memory for storing input data transmitted from the cache and for buffering the processed data.

The general sequence of operations in this model is as follows. The host processor receives the queries from the user at a terminal device and performs the usual query translation task. A translated query is transferred to the back-end controller in the form of a sequence of relational algebraic commands. The back-end controller is responsible for checking if the pages of the relation referenced by a command are already in the cache memory and for assigning a set of data processors to execute the command. If a page needed for processing is not in the cache memory, the back-end controller would instruct the loading of the page from the secondary storage to the cache memory. The data processors have access to any set of cache memory modules for data needed for their assigned commands.

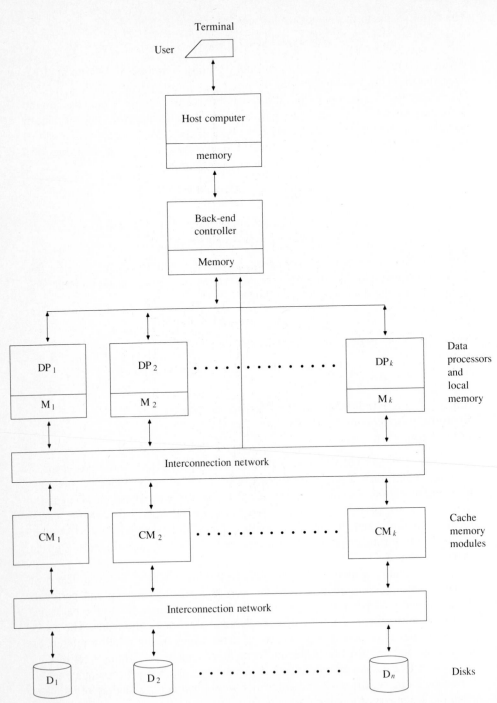

FIGURE 6.46
Abstract model for multiprocessor systems with dynamic processor-memory interconnection.

They also can write data to any of the cache memory modules or broadcast data to any set of the cache memory modules. The data needed for processing are first loaded into the local memory of the data processor. The local memory also contains an output buffer for storing the results of the operation. When the output buffer is full, the data are transferred to the cache memory and then moved to the secondary storage.

6.5.4 Analyses of Algorithms

In the following analyses, it is assumed that the data processors are conventional computers. Therefore, the time parameters for command execution will be similar to those derived for the conventional system model presented in Chapter 2. Assume that there are k data processors and k cache memory modules. These processors and cache memory modules are dynamically assigned to a set of concurrent queries. Also assume that p processors and p memory modules have been assigned to each of the operations to be analyzed and that each cache memory module can hold one page of data, which is the size of a disk track. A new parameter, a probability factor f, is introduced for this model to account for the probability of a referenced page being already in the cache memory. This parameter is used to obtain a more accurate page read time. Similar to other analyses presented in this book, possible overlaps among the time components in the cost formulas will not be considered. The reader should adjust the expressions to account for the overlaps achievable in a specific system.

6.5.4.1 SELECT.
The query for the Selection operation is received by the host computer, which translates it and then passes it on to the back-end controller. The controller schedules the execution of the select command and broadcasts the command to the data processors. The instruction flow time is

$$t[\text{inst\_flow}] = t[\text{comp}] + t[\text{tp\_xfer}] + t[\text{brcast}]$$

The data processing time consists of the time to simultaneously stage pages of the relation R into the data processors' local main memories, perform the Selection operation in parallel on the pages, and write back the results or output pages to the cache memory or the secondary storage. The probability of a page of R being already in the cache memory is considered to be $f1$. The expected time to stage an arbitrary page of R in the local memory of a data processor is

$$t[\text{read\_pg}, R] = f1 * t[\text{xfer}] + (1 - f1) * \{t[\text{access}] + t[\text{I/O}] + t[\text{xfer}]\}$$

Assume that the interconnection network between the data processors and the cache memory modules allows p pages of R to be loaded simultaneously into the data processors' local memory (one page per processor). After p pages have been loaded into the p data processors, the time to perform the Selection operation over the p pages in parallel is the sum of (1) the time to load x number of attribute values specified in the selection conditions to the processors' registers, (2) the time to perform the comparison operations to verify the search conditions, and (3) the time to write the selected tuples to the output buffers. The number of output tuples from each page is sel_fac $*$ t. Therefore, the time for processing p pages of R in parallel is the same as that for processing one page, which is

$$t[\text{proc\_pg}, R] = t * x * \{2 * t[\text{s}] + t[\text{cpu}]\} + \text{sel\_fac} * t * t[\text{mov}]$$

Including the page read time and the time for processor synchronization after the processing of p pages in parallel, the time for performing the Selection operation over p pages of R is

$$t[\text{proc\_p\_pg}, R] = t[\text{read\_pg}, R] + t[\text{proc\_pg}, R] + t[\text{syn}]$$

The output of the selection, that is, the pages of the resulting relation L, need to be written back either to the cache memory or to the secondary storage, if there is no room in the cache memory. If the probability of having room in the cache memory is $f2$, then the expected time to write an output page into the cache or the secondary storage is

$$t[\text{write\_pg}, L] = f2 * t[\text{xfer}] + (1 - f2) * (t[\text{access}] + t[\text{I/O}] + t[\text{xfer}])$$

The value of $f2$ depends on the page relacement algorithm used and the number and page access requirements of queries being executed by the system at the time.

Since there are m pages of R, ceil(m/p) is the number of times pages must be staged in the data processors for processing; ceil(m/p) is also the number of pages each data processor receives. The number of output pages each data processor produces is ceil(ceil(m/p) $*$ sel_fac). Again, assume that the interconnection network in this model allows the output pages of the data processors to be written to either the cache memory or the secondary storage in parallel. The total processing time for the Selection operation is

$$t[\text{process}] = \text{ceil}(m/p) * \{ t[\text{proc\_p\_pg}, R] + \text{ceil}(\text{ceil}(m/p) * \text{sel\_fac}) * t[\text{write\_pg}, L] \}$$

The data collection time for this operation consists of the time necessary to read a total of m $*$sel_fac output pages of L from the cache memory or the secondary storage to the back-end controller and from there to the host computer for output to the user's terminal.

$$t[\text{data\_collect}] = p * \text{ceil}(\text{ceil}(m/p) * \text{sel\_fac}) * \{ t[\text{read\_pt}, R] + t[\text{xfer}] \} + m * t * \text{sel\_fac} * t[\text{tp\_out}]$$

Therefore, the total execution time of this algorithm is

$$t[\text{Select}] = t[\text{inst\_flow}] + t[\text{process}] + t[\text{data\_collect}]$$

6.5.4.2   JOIN. Two algorithms for implementing the Join operation are considered here. They are the nested-loop–join algorithm and the sort-merge–join algorithm, which have been described by Bitton, Boral, DeWitt, and Wilkinson and by Valduriez and Gardarin [BIT83 and VAL84].

Nested-loop–join algorithm. The instruction flow time for this algorithm is the same as the time for Select.

$$t[\text{inst\_flow}] = t[\text{comp}] + t[\text{tp\_xfer}] + t[\text{brcast}]$$

Assume that each data processor has $b + 1$ pages of local main memory. To perform the Join operation, $b - 1$ pages of the outer relation R are loaded into the local memory of each data processor. One page of the inner relation S is then broadcast to all the data processors, which carry out the operation in parallel and produce results in a one-page output buffer. The results of Join, that is, the pages of relation L, are written back to the cache or to the secondary storage as they are produced. After the $b - 1$ pages of R have been joined with one page of S, another S page will be broadcast and joined. This process continues until the entire S relation has been joined. At this time, the system starts another cycle by loading $b - 1$ pages of R to join with the pages of S. The algorithm terminates after the last $b - 1$ pages of R have been joined with all the pages of S. The total number of cycles required is $(m/(p * (b - 1)))$.

In each processing cycle, there are $p * (b - 1)$ pages of R loaded into the data processors. The time required to read $b - 1$ pages is

$$t[\text{read\_}(b - 1)\_\text{pg}, R] = (b - 1) * t[\text{read\_pg}, R]$$

where $t[\text{read\_pg}, R]$ is as defined in the Select algorithm presented for this model.
The time to broadcast s pages of S is

$$t[\text{brcast}, S] = s * t[\text{read\_pg}, S]$$

where $t[\text{read\_pg}, S]$ can be derived by replacing m with s in the expression for $t[\text{read\_pg}, R]$.

The actual Join between $b - 1$ pages of R and one page of S, including the time to move the joined tuples to the output buffer, is

$$t[\text{jn\_Rb-1\_S1}] = t * (b - 1) * t * \{2 * t[s] + t[\text{cpu}]\} + \text{jn\_fac} * t \\ * (b - 1) * t * t[\text{mov}]$$

The time to join $b - 1$ pages of R with s pages of S including the time for processor synchronization after each block of S, is

$$t[\text{jn\_Rb-1\_Ss}] = s * \{t[\text{jn\_pg}, S] + t[\text{syn}]\}$$

This is also the time for joining $p * (b - 1)$ pages of R with s pages of S, since all data processors operate in parallel.

The time for writing the resulting pages of L back to the cache or the secondary storage will now be considered. There are a total of $u2 = \text{ceil}((m * t * s * t * jn\_fac)/(t/2))$ pages of L. Therefore, the writing time is

$$t[\text{write\_u\_pg}, L) = u2 * t[\text{write\_pg}, L]$$

where $t[\text{write\_pg}, L]$ is as given in the Select algorithm.
The total data processing time for this algorithm is

$$t[\text{process}] = (m/(p * (b - 1))) * \{t[\text{read\_(b-1)\_pg},R]$$
$$+ t[\text{brcast}, S] + t[\text{jn\_Rb-1\_Ss}]\}$$
$$+ t[\text{write\_u2\_pg}, L]$$

The data collection time involves the reading of the u output pages by the controller from either the cache memory or the secondary storage and the transmission of these pages to the host computer for output to the user's terminal. Thus,

$$t[\text{data\_collect}] = u2 * \{f1 * t[\text{xfer}] + (1 - f1) * \{t[\text{I/O}] +$$
$$t[\text{xfer}]\} + t[\text{xfer}] + t * 2 * t[\text{tp\_out}]\}$$

The total execution time for this algorithm is

$$t[\text{Join, nested}] = t[\text{inst\_flow}] + t[\text{process}] + t[\text{data\_collect}]$$

Sort-merge join algorithm. We adopt the b-way merge-sort algorithm described by Valduriez and Gardarin [VAL84] to implement the sort-merge–join algorithm. This sorting algorithm iteratively merges b runs of $b**(i - 1)$ pages into a sorted run of $b**i$ pages starting from $i = 1$. A *run* is an ordered sequence of sorted pages. The value of i is incremented for each successive iteration until all elements residing in each processor have been processed and included in the b runs formed by that processor. The process up to this stage is called "suboptimal stage" by Bitton, Boral, DeWitt, and Wilkinson [BIT83]. During the suboptimal stage, the merge of b runs is carried out by successively reading one page of each run into b input buffers. When a page is read for the first time, it is sorted using an internal sort algorithm. The ordered tuples in the input buffers are moved to the ouput buffer, which is emptied to the cache memory when full. In each iteration, the number of runs in each processor is divided by b, while the size of each is multipled by b. On the completion of this stage, each processor has b runs of $m/(p * b)$ pages that must be merged to form a single run at the next stage of processing, which is called "optimal stage." Here, it is assumed that p evenly divides m. All processors carry out the merge operation in parallel at this stage to produce p runs of m/p pages each. The algorithm then goes through another stage of processing, called a "postoptimal stage," to complete the sorting operation. At this last stage, if p equals b, a single processor is used to merge these p runs to produce the final sorted relation. If p is greater than b, the processors are arranged into a tree of order b and the p runs are merged by the tree of processors. In this tree merging, the number of processors is divided by b at each level and there are $\log_b p$ levels of processing. At the root level, one processor merges b runs to produce the final sorted relation.

This sorting process is applied on both relations R and S. The sorted relations are then joined by merging them in a single processor.

The derivation of the cost formulas for the sorting algorithm described here is quite involved. It is presented in detail by Valduriez and Gardarin [VAL84]. The formulas that follow use the notations described in this book. Interested readers should read the paper [VAL84] for details.

The time for sorting m pages of R is

$$t[\text{sort}, R] = m/p\{t[\text{sort\_page}] + t[\text{merge\_b\_page}] * \log_b(m/p) \\ + t[\text{merge\_b\_page}] * \{1 - b * * \log_b p\}/(b - 1)\}$$

and the time for sorting s pages of S is

$$t[\text{sort}, S] = s/p\{t[\text{sort\_page}] + t[\text{merge\_b\_page}] * \log\_b(s/p) \\ + t[\text{merge\_b\_page}] * \{1 - b * * \log\_bp\}/(b - 1)$$

where

$$t[\text{sort\_page}] = (t[\text{cpu}] + t[\text{mov}]) * t * \log_2 t$$

is the time for internally sorting a page of t tuples, and

$$t[\text{merge\_b\_page}] = \{b * (b - 1) * t * t[\text{cpu}]\} + \{b * t * t[\text{mov}]\} \\ + \{b * (t[\text{read\_pg}] + t[\text{write\_pg}])\}$$

is the time for merging b pages. In this formula, $t[\text{read\_pg}]$ and $t[\text{write\_pg}]$ are the same as $t[\text{read\_pg}, R]$ and $t[\text{write\_pg}, L]$ derived in the selection algorithm, respectively.

The time to join the sorted relations R and S by merging is

$$t[\text{merge}] = (m + s) * t[\text{read\_pg}] + \text{Max}(m, s) * (2 * t * t[\text{cpu}]) \\ + m * s * \text{jn\_fac} * t[\text{write\_pg}]$$

The total processing time for the sort-merge algorithm is

$$t[\text{process}] = t[\text{sort}, R] + t[\text{sort}, S] + t[\text{merge}]$$

The data collection time is the same as that derived for the nested join algorithm given above.

$$t[\text{data\_collect}] = u2 * \{f1 * t[\text{xfer}] + (1 - f1) * \\ \{t[\text{access}] + t[\text{I/O}] + t[\text{xfer}]\} \\ + t[\text{xfer}] + t * 2 * t[\text{tp\_out}]\}$$

The total execution time of this algorithm is

$$t[\text{join}, \text{sort-merge}] = t[\text{inst\_flow}] + t[\text{process}] + t[\text{data\_collect}]$$

6.5.4.3 STATISTICAL AGGREGATION.
Two algorithms for this operation have been analyzed by Baru and Su [BAR84]. The parallel-merge–aggregate algorithm will be used here, although with some modifications to make it consistent with our other analyses.

Parallel-merge–aggregate algorithm. In this algorithm, the relation R is first evenly distributed to all the data processors. Each processor partitions the tuples received based on the values of the category attributes and computes the aggregate value for each partition. The partial results of aggregate values produced for different categories in the data processors are then combined by a parallel merge of the output pages. This algorithm is suitable for a relation that has a small number of categories but has a large number of tuples.

The instruction flow time remains the same.

$$t[\text{inst\_flow}] = t[\text{comp}] + t[\text{tp\_xfer}] + t[\text{brcast}]$$

As previously shown, the time necessary to read a page into each processor is $t[\text{read\_pg}, R]$. Since there are w categories in total, assume that each data processor receives tuples that fall in $w * \text{r\_fac}$ categories, where r_fac is a reduction factor whose value is greater than or equal to $1/w$ but less than or equal to 1. Besides the reading time, the processing of a page of R also contains the time to (1) read each tuple's category attributes (assuming y of them), (2) compare them with the values that define the categories already established in each processor to determine the category to which the tuple belongs, and (3) compute the intermediate summary attribute value for that category. Since the number of categories continues to increase as the tuples are processed, the number of comparisons in the second step increases with the number of categories. It is assumed that, on an average, $w * \text{r\_fac}/2$ of comparisons are needed for each tuple. The time for processing a page of the R relation is

$$t[\text{proc\_pg}, R] = t[\text{read\_pg}, R] + t * \{y * \{t[s] + \{w * \\ \text{r\_fac}\}/2 * \{2 * t[s] + t[\text{cpu}]\}\} + t[\text{cpu}]\}$$

Since all data processors operate in parallel, this time component is also the time for processing p pages. The time to process m pages of R is

$$t[\text{proc\_m\_pg}, R] = \text{ceil}(m/p) * t[\text{proc\_pg}, R]$$

During this aggregation operation, each processor would produce $(w * \text{r\_fac})/t$ output pages containing tuples with intermediate summary attribute values. These pages must be merged first to form a larger set of ouput tuples. This set is then merged with the other sets of output tuples produced by the other data processors. In order to facilitate the merges, it is desirable to produce the output pages in a sorted order. The sorting can be done in the following manner. For every new partition encountered during the aggregation phase, the data processor is required to add a new tuple to the output. In order to keep the output in sorted order, the new tuple needs to be inserted into the proper place in the sorted output page. This would require, on the average, the moving down of one-half of the tuples already produced. Therefore, for $w * \text{r\_fac}$ output tuples generated by each data processor, the sum of the number of tuple movements, v, can be represented by a finite arithmetic series as follows:

$$v = 1/2 + 2/2 + 3/2 + \dots\dots + \{w * \text{r\_fac} - 1\}/2$$

This can be rewritten as

$$\begin{aligned} v &= (1/2) * \{1 + 2 + 3 + \dots\dots + (w * \text{r\_fac} - 1)\} \\ &= (1/2) * \{(w * \text{r\_fac}) * (w * \text{r\_fac} - 1))/2 \\ &= \{(w * \text{r\_fac}) * (w * \text{r\_fac} - 1)\}/4 \end{aligned}$$

Therefore, the total time to sort and write the output pages at each processor is

$$t[\text{sort\_write\_p}, R] = v * t[\text{mov}] + \{(w * \text{r\_fac})/t\} * t[\text{write\_pg}, R]$$

The next phase of the operation is a parallel-merge process that combines two output pages to form one larger output page. The time for this two-page operation consists of reading two sorted pages, merging them, and writing the resulting two sorted pages. This time is

$$t[\text{2pg\_sort\_merge}] = 2 * \{t[\text{read\_pg}, R] + t * \{2 * t[s] \\ + t[\text{cpu}] + t[\text{mov}]\} + t[\text{write\_pg}, R]\}$$

Since each data processor produces $\text{ceil}((w * \text{r\_fac})/t)$ output pages, the number of two-page operations in this merge-sort method is

$$n1 = \text{ceil}((w * \text{r\_fac})/(2 * t)) * \log_2\{\text{ceil}((w * \text{r\_fac})/(2 * t))\}$$

The total time of the merge operation is therefore

$$t[\text{merge}] = n1 * t[\text{2pg\_sort\_merge}]$$

Now the output of all the data processors need to be merged. The p processors implement a parallel-binary-merge to combine p runs of $\text{ceil}(w * \text{r\_fac}/t)$ pages through a total of $\log_2 p$ intermediate stages. The basic operation in this parallel-binary-merge method is for each processor to read two pages with a time of

$$2 * t[\text{read\_pg}, R]$$

and merge them with a time of

$$t[\text{merge\_2pg}] = 2 * t * \{2 * t[s] + t[\text{cpu}] + t[\text{mov}]\}$$

The time to perform the parallel binary merge operation is

$$t[\text{par\_merge}] = \{\text{ceil}(w * \text{r\_fac}/t) + \log_2(p)\} * \{2 * t[\text{read\_pg}, R] \\ + t[\text{merge\_2pg}]\}$$

The total number of output pages of this merge operation is $u3 = \text{ceil}(w/t)$. The time to write these pages back into the cache or the secondary storage is

$$t[\text{write\_u3\_pg}, L] = u3 * t[\text{write\_pg}, L]$$

Therefore, the total data processing time is

$$t[\text{process}] = t[\text{proc\_m\_pg}, R] + t[\text{sort\_write\_p}, R] \\ + t[\text{merge}] + t[\text{par\_merge}] + t[\text{write\_u3\_pg}, L]$$

The data collection time for this operation consists of the time to read u pages from the cache and the secondary storage, transfer them to the back-end controller and then to the host computer, and output the tuples to the user's terminal. The collection time is

$$t[\text{data\_collect}] = u3 * \{f * t[\text{xfer}] + (1 - f) * \{t[\text{I/O}] \\ + t[\text{xfer}]\} + t[\text{xfer}] + t * t[\text{tp\_out}]\}$$

The total execution time for this algorithm is

$$t[\text{Agg\_par\_merge}] = t[\text{inst\_flow}] + t[\text{process}] + t[\text{data\_collect}]$$

6.5.4.4 UPDATE. The instruction flow time remains the same.

$$t[\text{inst\_flow}] = t[\text{comp}] + t[\text{tp\_xfer}] + t[\text{brcast}]$$

The data processing time of this operation consists of the following three steps. First, each data processor loads $b + 1$ pages of the referenced relation R into its local memory. Here, it is assumed, as it is in the join algorithm presented previously, that $(b + 1)$ pages can fit into the local memory of each data processor. Since the loading can be done simultaneously among all data processors, $(b + 1) * p$ pages are staged at the local memories in one staging process. The cost for loading $(b + 1) * p$ pages is

$$t[\text{read\_b} + 1\_\text{pg}, R] = (b + 1) * t[\text{read\_pg}, R]$$

Second, a selection operation is performed on all data processors simultaneously on their corresponding tuples to determine the tuples that must be updated. The following equation shows the time necessary (1) to load x attribute values from each of the $(b + 1)*t$ tuples into the register for comparison against the x attribute values used as the search conditions, (2) to compare the values to select the tuples to be modified, (3) to perform the actual update of the selected tuples, and (4) to synchronize the operation at the end of processing $b + 1$ pages.

$$\begin{aligned} t[\text{proc\_b} + 1, R] = & (b + 1) * t * x * \{2 * t[s] + t[\text{cpu}]\} \\ & + \text{sel\_fac} * (b + 1) * t * \{2 * t[s] + t[\text{cpu}]\} \\ & + t[\text{syn}] \end{aligned}$$

Third, the updated pages need to be written back to the cache memory or the secondary storage. Assuming each page has an update, the time cost involved is

$$t[\text{write\_b} + 1\_\text{pg}, R] = (b + 1) * t[\text{write\_pg}, R]$$

For a total of $(m/((b + 1) * p))$ such staging cycles, each of which involves the preceding three steps, the total data processing time is

$$\begin{aligned} t[\text{process}] = & (m/((b + 1) * p)) * \{t[\text{read\_b} + 1, R] + t[\text{proc\_b} + 1, R] \\ & + t[\text{write\_b} + 1\_\text{pg}, R]\} \end{aligned}$$

Since the Update operation does not involve a data collection process, the total execution time for this algorithm is

$$t[\text{Update}] = t[\text{inst\_flow}] + t[\text{process}]$$

6.6 BIBLIOGRAPHY

[AHU82] Ahuja, S. R., and Asthana, A.: "A Multi-Microprocessor Architecture with Hardware Support for Communication and Scheduling," *Proceedings of Architectural Support for Programming Language and Operating Systems,* Palo Alto, Calif., March 1982, pp. 205–209.

[AUE81] Auer, H., Hell, W., Leilich, H. O., Schweppe, H., Stiege, G., Seehusen, S., Lie, J. S.,

Zeidler, H., Teich, W.: "RDBM—A Relational Database Machine," *Information Systems,* vol. 6, no. 2, 1981, pp. 91–100.

[BAB79] Babb, E.: "Implementing a Relational Database by Means of Specialized Hardware," *ACM Transactions on Database Systems,* vol. 4, no. 1, 1979, pp. 1–29.

[BAE81] Baer, J. L., Gardarin, G., Girault, C., and Roucairol, G.: "The Two-Step Commitment Protocol: Modeling Specification and Proof Methodology," *Fifth International Conference on Software Engineering,* San Diego, Calif., 1981, pp. 363–373.

[BAN78] Banerjee, J., Baum, R. I., and Hsiao, D. K.: "Concepts and Capabilities of a Database Computer," *ACM Transactions on Database Systems,* vol. 3, Dec. 1978, pp. 347–384.

[BAN78a] Banerjee, J., Hsiao, D. K., and Ng, F. K.: "Data Network—A Computer Network of General-purpose Front-end Computers and Special-purpose Back-end Database Machines," in *Proceedings of the International Symposium on Computer Network Protocols,* A. Danthine, ed., Liege, Belgium, Feb. 1978, pp. D6-1–D6-12.

[BAN78b] Banerjee, J., and Hsiao, D. K.: "Performance Evaluation of a Database Computer in Supporting Relational Databases," in *Proceedings of the Fourth International Conference on Very Large Data Bases,* Berlin, Germany, Sept. 13–15, 1978, pp. 319–329.

[BAN78c] Banerjee, J., and Hsiao, D. K.: "A Methodology for Supporting Existing CODASYL Databases with New Database Machines," *Proceedings of the ACM '78 Conference,* Washington D.C., Dec. 1978, pp. 925–936.

[BAN79] Banerjee, J., Hsiao D. K., and Kannan, K.: "DBC—A Database Computer for Very Large Databases," *IEEE Transactions on Computers,* vol. C-28, no. 6, June 1979, pp. 414–429.

[BAN80] Banerjee, J., Hsiao, D. K., and Ng, F. K.: "Database Transformation, Query Translation and Performance Analysis of a New Database Computer in Supporting Hierarchical Database Management," *IEEE Transactions on Software Engineering,* SE-6, no. 1, Jan. 1980, pp. 91–108.

[BAR84] Baru, C. K., and Su, S. Y. W.: "Performance of Statistical Aggregation Operations in the SM3 System," *Proceedings of the ACM/SIGMOD International Conference on Management of Data,* Boston, Mass., June 1984, pp. 77–89.

[BAR85] Baru, C. K., Thakore, A. K., and Su, S. Y. W.: "Matrix Multiplication on a Multicomputer System with Switchable Main Memory Modules," *IEEE First International Conference on Supercomputing Systems,* Tarpon Springs, Fla., Dec. 1985, pp. 650–659.

[BAR86] Baru, C. K., and Su, S. Y. W.: "The Architecture of SM3: A Dynamically Partitionable Multicomputer System," *IEEE Transactions on Computers,* vol. c-35, no. 9, Sept. 1986, pp. 790–802.

[BAR87] Baru, C. K., and Frieder, O.: "Implementing Relational Database Operations in a Cube-connected Multicomputer," *Proceedings of the International Conference on Data Engineering,* Los Angeles, Calif. Feb. 1987.

[BIT83] Bitton, D., Boral, H., DeWitt, D.J., and Wilkinson, W.K.: "Parallel Algorithms for the Execution of Relational Database Operations," *ACM Transactions on Database Systems*, vol. 8, no. 3, September 1983, pp. 324–353.

[BOR81] Boral, H., and DeWitt, D. J.: "Processor Allocation Strategies for Multiprocessor Database Machines," *ACM TODS,* vol. 6, June 1981.

[BOR82] Boral, H., DeWitt, D. J., Friedland, D., Jarrell, N. F., and Wilkinson, W. K.: "Implementation of the Database Machine DIRECT," *IEEE's Transactions on Software Engineering,* vol. SE-8, no. 6, Nov. 1982, pp. 533–543.

[BOY83] Boyne, R. D., Demurjian, S. A., Hsiao, D. K., Kerr, D. S., and Orooji, A., "The Implementation of a Multi-Backend Database System (MDBS): Part III—The Message-oriented Version with Concurrency Control and Secondary Memory-based Directory Management," *Technical Report NPS52-83-003,* Naval Postgraduate School, Monterey, California, March 1983.

[BRI81] Britton Lee, Inc., "IDM 500: Intelligent Database Machine Product Description," Britton Lee, Inc., 1981.

[BRO80] Brownsmith, J. D., and Su, S. Y. W.: "Performance Analysis of the EQUI-JOIN Operation in the MICRONET Computer System," *Proceedings of the ICCC Conference,* IEEE, Oct. 1980, pp. 264–268.

[CES81] Cesarini, F., De Luca Cardillo, D., and Soda, G., "An Approach to DBMAC Query Processing Simulation," Workshop on Database Machines, Florence, Italy, Sept. 1981.

[CES83] Cesarini, F., De Luca Cardillo, D., and Soda, G., "An Assessment of the Query-Processing Capability of DBMAC," in *Advanced Database Machine Architecture*, David K. Hsiao, (ed.), Prentice-Hall, Englewood Cliffs, N.J. 1983, pp. 109–129.

[DEM84] Demurjian, S. A., Hsiao, D. K., Kerr, D. S., and Orooji, A., "The Implementation of Multi-backend Database System (MDBS): Part IV—The Revised Concurrency Control and Directory Management Processes and the Revised Definitions of Inter-Process and Inter-Computer Messages," *Technical Report NPS52-84-005*, Naval Postgraduate School, Monterey, California, Feb. 1984.

[DES78] Despain, A. M., and Patterson, D. A.,: "X-Tree: A Tree Structured Multi-processor Computer Architecture," *Proceedings of the Fifth Symposium on Computer Architecture*, Palo Alto, Calif., April 1978, pp. 144–150.

[DEW79a] DeWitt, D. J.: "DIRECT—A Multiprocessor Organization for Supporting Relational Database Management Systems," *IEEE Transactions on Computers*, vol. C-28, June 1979, pp. 395–406.

[DEW79b] DeWitt, D. J.: "Query Execution in DIRECT," *Proceedings of the ACM SIGMOD 1979 International Conference on Management of Data*, Boston, Mass., May 1979, pp. 13–22.

[DEW86] DeWitt, D. J., Gerber, R. H., Graefe, G., Heytens, M. L., Kumar, K. B., and Muralikrishna, M.: "GAMMA: A Performance Dataflow Database Machine," *Proceedings of the Twelfth International Conference on Very Large Data Bases*, Kyoto, Japan, Aug. 26–29, 1986, pp. 228–237.

[FAG79] Fagin, R., Nievergelt, J., Pippenger, N., and Strong, H. R.: "Extendible Hashing—A Fast Access Method for Dynamic Files," *ACM Transactions on Database Systems*, vol. 4, no. 3, 1979, pp. 315–344.

[FEI84] Fei, T., Baru, C. K., and Su, S. Y. W.: "SM3: A Dynamically Partitionable Multicomputer System with Switchable Main Memory Modules," *Proceedings of the International Conference on Computer Data Engineering*, Los Angeles, April 1984, pp. 42–49.

[GAR81] Gardarin, G.: "An Introduction to SABRE: A Multi-Microprocessor Database Machine," *Sixth Workshop on Computer Architecture for Non-Numeric Processing*, Hyeres, France, June 1981.

[GAR83] Gardarin, G., Bernadat, P., Temmerman, N., Valduriez, P., and Viemont, Y.: "SABRE: A Relational Database System for a Multimicroprocessor Machine," in *Advanced Database Machine Architecture*, D. K. Hsiao (ed.), Prentice-Hall, Englewood Cliffs, N.J. 1983, pp. 19–35.

[GEN82] Genduso, T. B., and Su, S. Y. W.: "An Analytical Model of the MICRONET Distributed Database Management System," *Proceedings of the Third International Conference on Distributed Computing Systems*, Miami/Ft. Lauderdale, Fl., Oct. 1982, pp. 232–239.

[GOO80a] Goodman, J. R.: "An Investigation of Multiprocessor Structures and Algorithms for Data Base Management," Ph.D. dissertation, Computer Science Division, University of California at Berkeley, 1980.

[GOO80b] Goodman, J. R., and Despain, A. M.: "A Study of Interconnection of Multiple Processors in a Data Base Environment," *Proceedings of the International Conference on Parallel Processing*, IEEE, Harber Springs, Mich., Aug. 1980, pp. 269–278.

[GOO81] Goodman, J. R., and Sequin, C. H.: "Hypertree: A Multiprocessor Interconnection Topoloty," *IEEE Transactions on Computers*, vol. C-30, no. 12, 1981, pp. 923–933.

[HAK77] Hakozaki, K., et al.: "A Conceptual Design of a Generalized Database Subsystem," *Proceedings of the Third International Conference on Very Large Data Bases*, Tokyo, Japan, 1977, pp. 246–253.

[HE83] He, X. G., Higashida, M., Kerr, D. S., Orooji, A., Shi, Z. Z., Strawser, P. R., and Hsiao, D. K., "The Implementation of a Multi-Backend Database System (MDBS): Part II—The First Prototype MDBS and the Software Engineering Experience," in *Advanced Database Machine Architectures*, D. K. Hsiao (ed.), Prentice Hall, Englewood Cliffs, N.J., 1983, pp. 327–385.

[HEL81] Hell, W.: "RDBM—A Relational Database Machine Architecture and Hardware Design," *Proceedings of the Sixth Workshop on Computer Architecture for Non-numerical Processing,* Hyeres, France, June 1981.

[HIK81] Hikita, S., Yamazaki, H., Hasegawa, K., and Mitsushita, Y.: "Optimization of the File Access Method in Content-Addressable Database Machine (CADAM), *NCC Proceedings AFIPS,* Chicago, Ill., 1981, pp. 507–513.

[HIL86] Hillyer, B. K., Shaw, D. E., and Nigram A.: "NON-VON's Performance on Certain Database Benchmarks," *IEEE Transaction on Software Engineering,* April, 1986, pp. 577–583.

[HSI78] Hsiao, D. K., and Kannan, K.: "Simulation Studies of the Database Computer (DBC)," *Technical Report OSU-CISRC-TR-78-1,* The Ohio State University, Feb. 1978.

[HSI80] Hsiao, D. K. (ed.): *Collected Readings on a Database Computer (DBC),* The Ohio State University Press, Columbus, Ohio, 2nd ed., 1980.

[HSI81a] Hsiao, D. K., and Menon, M. J.: "Design and Analysis of a Multi-Backend Database System for Performance Improvement, Functionality Expansion and Capacity Growth (Part I)," *Technical Report, OSU-CISRC-TR-81-7,* The Ohio State University, Columbus, Ohio, July 1981.

[HSI81b] Hsiao, D. K., and Menon, M. J.: "Design and Analysis of a Multi-Backend Database System for Performance Improvement, Functionality Expansion and Capacity Growth (Part II)," *Technical Report, OSU-CISRC-TR-81-8,* The Ohio State University, Columbus, Ohio, August 1981.

[HSI83a] Hsiao, D. K., et al.: "The Implementation of a Multi-backend Database System (MDB-S): Part I—An Exercise in Database Software Engineering," *Advanced Database Machine Architecture,* D. K. Hsiao (ed.), Prentice-Hall, Englewood Cliffs, N.J., 1983, pp. 300–326.

[HSI83b] Hsiao, D. K., and Menon, M. J.: "Design and Analysis of a Multi-backend Database System for Performance Improvement, Functionality Expansion and Capacity Growth (Part I)," *Technical Report NPS52-83-006,* Naval Postgraduate School, Monterey, Calif., June 1983.

[HSI83c] Hsiao, D. K., and Menon, M. J.: "Design and Analysis of a Multi-backend Database System for Performance Improvement, Functionality Expansion and Capacity Growth (Part II)," *Technical Report NPS52-83-007,* Naval Postgraduate School, Monterey, Calif., June 1983.

[KAR81] Karlsson, K.: "Reduced Cover-Trees and Their Application in the SABRE Access Path Model," *Proceedings of the Seventh International Conference on Very Large Data Bases,* Cannes, France, Sept. 1981, pp. 345–353.

[KIT81] Kitsuregawa, M., Suzuki, S., Tanaka, H., Moto-oka, T.: "Relational Algebra Machine Based on Hash and Sort," *IECE Japan Technical Group Meeting,* EC81-35, 1981.

[KIT83a] Kitsuregawa, M., Tanaka, H., and Moto-oka, T.: "Relational Algebra Machine GRACE," *RIMS Symposia on Software Science and Engineering,* 1982, Lecture Note in Computer Science, Springer-Verlag, New York, 1983, pp. 191–212.

[KIT83b] Kitsuregawa, M., Tanaka, H., and Moto-oka, T.: "Application of Hash to Data Base Machine and Its Architecture," *New Generation Computing,* vol. 1, no. 1, 1983, pp. 63–74.

[KIT84] Kitsuregawa, M., Tanaka, H., and Moto-oka, T.: "Architecture and Performance of Relational Algebra Machine GRACE," *Proceedings of the International Conference on Parallel Processing,* IEEE, Bellaire, Mich., 1984, pp. 241–250.

[KIT85] Kitsuregawa, M., Fushimi, M., Tanaka, H., and Moto-oka, T.: "Memory Management Algorithms in Pipeline Merge Sorter," *Proceedings of the Fourth International Workshop on Database Machines,* DeWitt, D. J., and Boral, H. (eds.), Springer-Verlag, New York, 1985, pp. 208–232.

[MIS81] Missikoff, M., and Terranova, M., "An Overview of the Project DBMAC for a Relational Database Machine," *Proceedings of the Sixth Workshop on Computer Architecture for Non-numeric Processing,* Hyeres, France, 1981.

[MIS82] Missikoff, M.: "A Domain-Based Internal Schema for Relational Database Machines," *1982 ACM-SIGMOD Conference,* Orlando, Fla., 1982, pp. 215–224.

[MIS83] Missikoff, M., and Terranova, M.: "The Architecture of a Relational Database Computer Known as DBMAC," in *Advanced Database Machine Architecture*, D. K. Hsiao, (ed.), Prentice-Hall, Englewood Cliffs, N.J., 1983, pp. 87–108.

[NIC80] Nickens, D. O., Genduso, T. B., and Su, S. Y. W.: "The Architecture and Hardware Implementation of a Prototype MICRONET," *Proceedings of the Fifth Conference on Local Computer Networks*, Minneapolis, Mn., Oct. 1980, pp. 56–64.

[SCH83] Schweppe, H., Zeidler, H. C., Hell, W., Leilich, H. O., Stiege, G., and Teich, W.: "RDBM—A Dedicated Multiprocessor System for Database Management," in *Advanced Database Machine Architecture*, D. K. Hsiao (ed.), Prentice-Hall, Englewood Cliffs, N.J., 1983, pp. 36-85.

[SEK82] Sekino, A., Takeuchi, K., Makino, T., Doi, T., Goto, T., and Hakozaki, K.: "Design Considerations for an Information Query Computer," *Proceedings of the International Workshop on Database Machines*, San Diego, Calif., Sept. 1–3, 1982.

[SEQ78] Sequine, C. H., Despain, A. M., and Patterson, D. A.: "Communication in X-Tree, a Modular Multiprocessor System," *Proceedings of the ACM*, Washington D.C., 1978.

[SHA82] Shaw, D. E.: "A Parallel Algorithm for External Sorting, NON-VON Supercomputer," *Technical Report*, Computer Science Dept., Columbia University, New York, August 1982.

[SHU81] Shultz, R. K.: "A Multiprocessor Computer Architecture for Database Support," Ph.D. dissertation, Computer Science Dept., Iowa State University, Ames, Iowa, 1981.

[SHU84] Shultz, R. K., and Zingg, R. J.: "Response Time Analysis of Multiprocessor Computers for Database Support," *ACM Transactions on Database Systems*, 1984, pp. 14–17.

[SU78] Su, S. Y. W., Lupkiewicz, S., Lee, C., Lo, D. H., and Doty, K. L.: "MICRONET: A Microcomputer Network System for Managing Distributed Relational Databases," *Proceedings of the Fourth International Conference on Very Large Data Bases*, Berlin, West Germany, 1978, pp. 288–298.

[SU82] Su, S. Y. W., and Mikkilineni, K. P.: "Parallel Algorithms and Their Implementation in MICRONET," *Proceedings of the Eighth International Conference on Very Large Data Bases*, Mexico City, Mexico, Sept. 1982, pp. 310–321.

[SU83] Su, S. Y. W.: "A Microcomputer Network System for Distributed Relational Databases: Design, Implementation, and Analysis," *Journal of Telecommunication Networks*, vol. 2, no. 3, 1983, pp. 307–334.

[SU84] Su, S. Y. W., and Baru, C. K.: "Dynamically Partitionable Multicomputers with Switchable Memory," *Journal of Parallel and Distributed Computing*, vol. 1, no. 2, Nov. 1984, pp. 152–184.

[SWA77] Swan, R. J., Fuller, S. H., and Siewiorek, D. P.: "Cm*—A Modular Multi-Microprocessor," *Proceedings of the National Computer Conference*, Dallas, Tex., 1977, pp. 637–644.

[TAN80] Tanaka, Y., Noxaka, Y., and Masuyama, A.: "Pipeline Searching and Sorting Modules as Components of a Data Flow Database Computer," *Information Processing 80*, S. H. Lavington (ed.), North-Holland Publishing Co., 1980, pp. 427–432.

[TAN82] Tanaka, Y.: "A Data-Stream Database Machine with Large Capacity," *Proceedings of the International Workshop on Database Machines*, San Diego, Calif., September 1–3, 1982. Also in *Advanced Database Machines*, D. K. Hsiao (ed.), Prentice-Hall, Englewood Cliffs, N.J., 1983, pp. 168–202.

[TEI81] Teich, W.: "The Sort Processor of the RDBM," *Sixth Workshop on Computer Architecture for Non-numerical Processing*, Hyeres, France, June 1981.

[TER84] Teradata Corporation: "DBC/1012 Data Base Computer Concepts and Facilities," Release 1.1, C02-0001-01, Los Angeles, Calif., 1984.

[THA87] Thakaore, A. K., and Su, S. Y. W.: "Matrix Inversion and LU Decomposition on a Multicomputer System with Dynamic Control," *Proceedings of the Second International Conference on Supercomputing*, vol. 1, International Supercomputing Institute, Inc., 1987, pp. 291–300.

[UEM80] Uemura, S., Yuba, T., Kokubu, A., Ooomote, R., and Sugawara, Y.: "The Design and Implementation of a Magnetic-bubble Database Machine," *Information Processing 80*, S. H.

Lavington (ed.), North-Holland Publishing Co., Amsterdam, Netherlands, 1980, pp. 433–438.

[UEM83] Uemura, S.: "Database Machine Activities in Japan," *IEEE Database Engineering,* vol. 6, no. 1, 1983, pp. 63–64.

[VAL82*a*] Valduriez, P., and Gardarin, G.: "Multiprocessor Join Algorithms of Relations," *Second International Conference on Data Bases: Improving Usability and Responsiveness,* Jerusalem, June 1982.

[VAL82*b*] Valduriez, P.: "Semi-join Algorithms for Multiprocessor Systems," *ACM-SIGMOD International Conference on Management of Data,* Orlando, Fla., June 1982, pp. 225–233.

[VAL84] Valduriez, P., and Gardarin, G.: "Join and Semijoin Algorithms for a Multiprocessor Database Machine," *ACM Transactions on Database Systems,* vol. 9, no. 1, March 1984, pp. 133–161.

[VIE82] Viemont, Y., and Gardarin, G.: "A Distributed Concurrency Control Based on Transaction Commit Ordering," *Twelfth International Conference on FTCS,* Los Angeles, Calif., June 1982.

CHAPTER
7

MULTIPROCESSOR DATABASE COMPUTERS: SYSTEMS WITH DISTRIBUTION OF FUNCTIONS

This chapter describes a number of multiprocessor systems in which database management functions are distributed and processed by a number of dedicated component systems. Some of these component systems may be special-purpose processors, and others may be conventional general-purpose computers programmed to do specific database management functions. This category of multiprocessor systems is divided into two subcategories: dedicated database computers and systems with functionally specialized processors. The first subcategory represents one method of functional distribution—a method that uses a single dedicated computer to handle all the database management functions. It contains systems that are commonly called *back-end computers*; a term that is not suitable for our classification since almost all existing database machines are back-end processors to some host or front-end computer. Examples of this subcategory include XDMS, IDM, iDBP, and IQC. The second subcategory represents another method of functional distribution—a method that uses a number of processors to perform different database management functions. Examples of this subcategory include DBC, SABRE, RDBM, DELTA, DDM, CADAM, systolic arrays, and VLSI tree machines. The architectures, data organizations, and processing techniques used in these systems are described below.

320

7.1   DEDICATED DATABASE COMPUTERS

In a conventional computer system that supports a database management system, the central processor is overburdened with not only all the database management functions (e.g., query translation, query optimization, transaction management, integrity and security control, concurrency control, error recovery, etc.), but also with the usual operating system functions (e.g., as job management, task management, resource allocation, I/O and file management, etc.). Also, since the operating system and the DBMS software are so closely coupled, changes made in one may have undesirable effects on the other. Furthermore, since these two software subsystems run on the same computer, software or hardware failures may compromise the security and integrity of the DBMS and its databases. One solution to these problems is to download all or most of the DBMS functions to a dedicated computer (see Figure 7.1). The host computer takes care of only the user interface, application program execution, and operating system functions. It sends all database commands to the dedicated database computer for processing against the databases stored in the secondary storage devices. This architecture has the following advantages:

1. Since the database computer is dedicated to database management functions, its hardware and software can be configured and tailored to suit these specific functions. Thus, greater efficiency can be achieved.

2. The host computer can be relieved of the tedious and time-consuming operations of database manipulation, maintenance, and control.

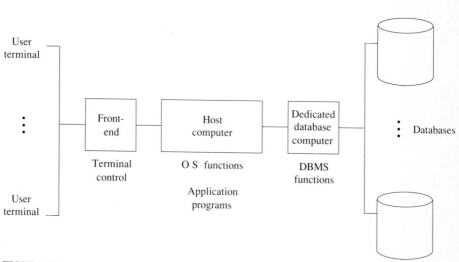

FIGURE 7.1
System configuration with a dedicated database computer.

3. System performance can be increased by running the host and the database computers concurrently, each executing its own functions.

4. A number of host computers can be connected to a single dedicated database computer (see Figure 7.2*a*) to share the same database.

5. A database system can be easily expanded by adding more database computers and their associated databases to a host computer (see Figure 7.2*b*).

6. Since the database and the DBMS software are isolated from the application programs and other system software running on the host computer, they can be

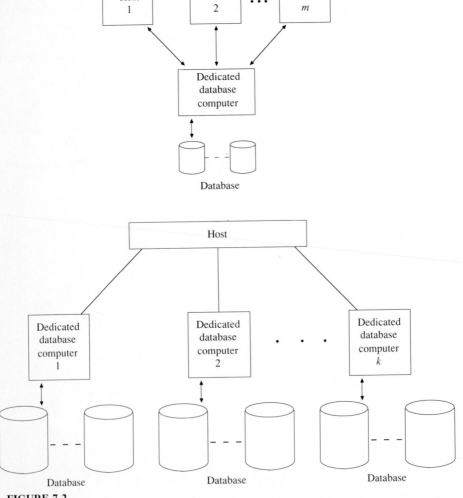

FIGURE 7.2
(a) Multiple host configuration. *(b)* Multiple dedicated database computers.

more easily protected from the security point of view. Greater reliability can also be achieved due to the localization of system errors on both computers, that is, errors will not propagate from one computer to the other.

7. Most importantly, minimal changes to the existing database and host computer software are required to incorporate a dedicated database computer. This is the main reason that the first commercial database machine introduced is a dedicated database computer (i.e., Britton Lee, Inc.'s IDM 500) which has been quite well accepted by the database community.

On the other hand, the dedicated database computer is not without its disadvantages. First, one incurs the cost of an additional computer. Second, the configuration may result in an unbalanced resource utilization, since either the host or the database computer may be overloaded while the other is idling. Finally, the query response time may increase due to the fact that the retrieved data need to be handled by an additional computer before they can be output to the user. With these advantages and disadvantages in mind, the systems in this subcategory will be examined.

7.1.1 XDMS

The Experimental Data Management System (XDMS) was designed and proto-typed at Bell Laboratories during 1970 to 1972 [CAN74]. It was the first known system to use a dedicated database computer to improve the overall performance of a DBMS. To demonstrate how the database management and other system functions are distributed between the host and the dedicated database computer, Figure 7.3 shows the key components of a database management system running on a host computer, the UNIVAC 1108. The DBMS uses the data model recom-mended by the Data Base Task Group (DBTG) of the Conference on Data System Language. As shown in the figure, a schema description using a data definition language (DDL) is compiled by a DDL compiler into a set of schema tables at compilation time. The schema tables are used by a data manipulation language (DML) and a high-level language compiler (COBOL) to translate application pro-grams, which contain embedded DML statements, into object modules. During execution time, an application program (the object code) is executed. The codes for the original DML commands make calls to data management routines to access the data stored on disks. The retrieved results are transferred to the application program area for further processing, and the final results are presented to the user on a terminal from which ad hoc queries are issued.

To relieve the host computer from all the database management tasks, a Digital Scientific META-4 computer is used in XDMS as a dedicated database computer to manage and manipulate the database (see Figure 7.4). An XDMS interface (a software component) is added in the host to transmit translated DML commands to the XDMS back-end for execution and to receive data from it. It is reported by Canaday, et al. [CAN74] that the entire effort of converting the configuration shown in Figure 7.3 to that of Figure 7.4 required 6 man-years and

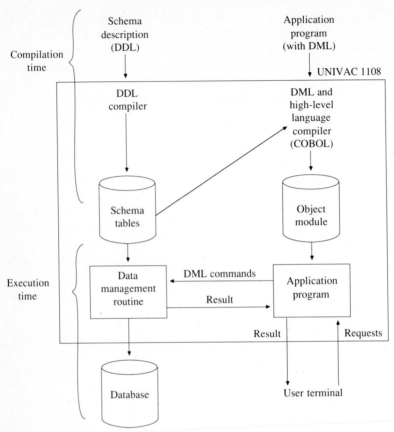

Compilation time

Execution time

FIGURE 7.3
DBTG data management system configuration. (*Source:* [CAN74] ©1974, Association for Computing Machinery, Inc., reprinted by permission)

$60K in equipment. The software in the back-end occupies 15K 16-bit words and 17K of memory for the I/O buffer. The XDMS interface module occupies 4.5K of 36-bit words and 1K of buffer space.

7.1.2 IDM

The Intelligent Database Machine (IDM) can be considered the first commercial database machine that has survived the test of time and market competition against conventional database management hardware and software systems. The product was introduced by Britton Lee, Inc. of Los Gatos, California in 1981 [BRI81*a* and BRI81*b*]. There are two product series, IDM500 and IDM200. The latter, introduced in 1982, is essentially a stripped-down version of the former. The IDM is an integrated hardware/software database computing system that provides complete database management services to multiple intelligent terminals and/or large-scale host computers. It manages large databases stored on disks.

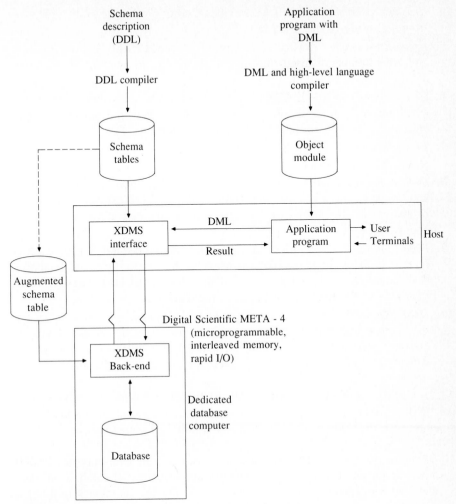

FIGURE 7.4
XDMS configuration. (*Source:* [CAN74] ©1974, Association for Computing Machinery, Inc., reprinted by permission)

The database management functions performed by the IDM are as follows:

1. *Transaction management.* IDM guarantees database consistency by ensuring that database operations, which form a transaction, are either executed to their completion or not executed at all by restoring the database to its preexecution state.
2. *Optional logging of database changes.* IDM optionally logs all commands that change the database to establish an audit trail for auditing purposes.
3. *Indexing of data.* IDM allows selected data fields to be indexed to facilitate fast data access and update.

4. *Crash recovery facilities*. IDM provides facilities to handle system recovery from software and hardware failures.
5. *Large RAM cache*. IDM contains large, high-speed RAM for storing indices and other frequently used information to reduce the number of secondary storage accesses, thus improving system performance.
6. *Concurrency control*. IDM allows multiple users to query the same database simultaneously. It has a concurrency control mechanism to prevent the concurrent processes from interfering with one another.
7. *Protection feature*. IDM has facilities to deny or permit each user the access to and manipulation of a database.
8. *Data definition facilities*. IDM provides data definition facilities to define and create databases before application programs are executed against the databases. It also allows new relations to be defined at run time by the application programs.
9. *Data manipulation facilities*. A high-level, nonprocedural language called Intelligent Data Language (IDL) is provided for use to query the databases. The language can also be embedded in a high-level host language (e.g., FORTRAN) to access and manipulate the databases.
10. *Data independence*. IDM runs a relational database management system that has the following two features: (a) the user does not have to know the physical organization of the database and (b) changes made on the internal structures of the database will not affect the application programs.

7.1.2.1 IDM'S HARDWARE ARCHITECTURE. The hardware architecture of the IDM is shown in Figure 7.5. It consists of the following single-board components, each of which can be plugged into an internal high-speed bus.

1. *Database processor*. The database processor is a general-purpose, Z8000-based processor. It manages all resources and executes all database management software except when a database accelerator (see number 4 in this list) is used to handle some of the time-critical functions.
2. *I/O channel processors*. The IDM allows up to 8 I/O channel processors, which connect front-end devices (intelligent terminals and host computers) to the IDM. The main functions of a channel processor are (a) to receive commands from a front-end device and to return results to the device, (b) to perform all host-dependent hand-shaking, including checking for the correct transmission of data and coordinating data retransmission in case of error, and (c) to convert various host data types to a standard IDM format. There are two types of I/O channel processors: parallel (PIO) and serial (SIO). The PIO processor provides byte-parallel transmissions at up to 250K bytes per second. One of the I/O processor boards controls an IEEE-488 bus (GPIB). The standard back panel on the IDM has room for 4 independent GPIB buses. Thus, 4 host computers can be connected to an IDM via 4 dedicated buses. Several host computers can also be connected to a single GPIB bus. The serial

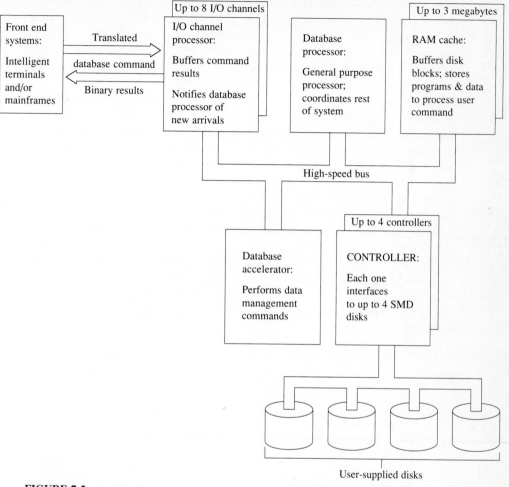

FIGURE 7.5
IDM hardware architecture. (*Source:* [BRI81*a*] reprinted by permission of Britton Lee, Inc.)

I/O channel processor is connected to the back panel of the IDM through 1 50-pin connector. This connector provides up to 8 separate, RS232-compatible, bit-serial lines. Each line is capable of transmitting data at speeds from 110 bits per second to 19,200 bits per second. The IDM back panel has room for up to 8 connectors. This allows 8 SIO channel processors to control up to 64 serial lines.

3. *Disk controller.* The main function of the disk controller is to move data between disks and the IDM's main memory. The controller-disk interface is SMD CDC 9760 compatible. This allows many different disk drives to be connected to the controller. A controller can manage up to 4 disk drives, and

there can be up to 4 controllers in the system, thus allowing a total of up to 16 disk drives. A disk drive can be connected to a disk controller without changing the controller board. All disk drive parameters (e.g., number of cylinders, number of bytes per track, number of heads, etc.) can be supplied via the software. These parameter values are stored on the disk and are accessed by the controller to determine its actual logical device name.

4. *Database accelerator.* This is a special-purpose database processor with a speed of up to 10 MIPS or 100 nsec instruction time and with an instruction set specifically designed to support a relational database. This is an optional component and operates under the control of the database processor. It can initiate disk activity and is able to search data pages as they are being transmitted from the disks into the RAM cache (see number 5 in this list). The software of the IDM is structured in such a way that if the accelerator is used, then time-consuming operations are performed by the accelerator.

5. *RAM cache.* The system can have up to 12 semiconductor memory storage boards, each of which contains 256K bytes of memory. The memory is used to buffer the disk pages and to store the program instructions and data of the user processes. It reduces the amount of I/O activity and accelerates the execution of user processes. The memory subsystem is controlled by a memory timing and control unit that provides single-bit error correction and double-bit error detection.

The IDM 500 series has three system configurations: 500E, 500X, and 500XL. Their components and options are shown below:

IDM 500E
    Configuration
        IDM 500/0
        1M byte RAM
        8-port serial I/O
        160M byte Winchester disk
        300M byte cartridge tape
        40-inch DEC cabinet
    Options
        8 RS-232 I/O channels; or
        1 IEEE-488 I/O channel; or
        1 Ethernet LAN I/O channel
IDM 500X
    Configuration
        IDM 500/1
        1M byte RAM
        8-port serial I/O
        320M byte Winchester disk
        300M byte cartridge tape
        60-inch DEC cabinet

Options
    1 to 5 megabytes additional RAM memory
    Mirrored disk (redundant disks)
    1 160M byte disk drive
    Disk expansion units (14 additional disk drives)
    56 RS-232 I/O channels; and/or
    7 IEEE-488 I/O channels; and/or
    4 Ethernet LAN channels; and/or
    4 Block multiplexer channels
IDM 500XL
  Configuration
    IDM 500/2
    2M bytes RAM
    8-port serial I/O
    8 MIPS accelerator
    60-inch DEC cabinet
    1.02-megabyte Winchester disk
    500M byte cartridge tape
  Options
    1 to 4M bytes additional RAM memory
    Mirrored disk (redundant disks)
    Disk expansion units (13 additional disk drives)
    56 RS-232 I/O channels; and/or
    7 IEEE-488 I/O channels; and/or
    4 Ethernet LAN channels; and/or
    4 Block multiplexer channels

7.1.2.2 IDM SOFTWARE ARCHITECTURE. The database in the IDM system is logically represented as a set of relations. The definition information of these relations, that is, the dictionary information, is also stored in the form of relations. Thus, the dictionary information can be accessed and manipulated just like the rest of the database. Physically, the relations are stored on the disk drives along with the disk drive parameter values. The IDM uses the parameter values to format the drive and to allocate space on the drive. A disk drive is divided into a number of zones, each of which contains a number of cylinders. A zone is divided into a number of pages, each containing 2K bytes. A page is the basic unit of storage allocation as well as the unit of I/O. Pages are allocated to accommodate the dynamic growth of relations.

To access a database, the user's database commands must be translated by the front-end device into an internal query representation recognized by the IDM. Three user-interface methods are provided by the IDM, each having its own requirements.

1. *Subroutine calls.* The user can write a number of subroutines, which contain calls to the IDM, to perform some limited database management functions.

These routines become a part of the operating system's subroutine library. An existing application program can then be modified to contain calls to these routines. During program execution time, the subroutine calls will cause the subroutine parameters to be passed to the IDM by the operating system. The IDM will perform the specified operations and return the results to the application program. To use this interface method, the existing operating system needs to be modified to interface with the IDM, and the existing programs need to include calls to the IDM for the various database functions.

2. *Data manipulation language.* IDM provides a general-purpose query language, called the Intelligent Database Language (IDL), for the user to issue ad hoc queries against a database [BRI81*b*]. The language has a syntax similar to QUEL of the INGRES database management system developed at the University of California at Berkeley. It contains commands for (a) initializing a database, (b) entering a database, (c) loading data into relations, (d) accessing data in a database, (e) creating views or virtual relations, (f) modifying data, (g) denying or granting access right to users, (h) defining and aborting transactions, (i) creating audit trails, and (j) dumping databases for error-recovery purposes. In addition, the IDL allows "new" commands to be defined, preprocessed, and stored in the IDM. The stored commands are named or assigned with numbers. The program running on the front-end device can use the names or numbers to cause the preprocessed commands to be executed. This facility not only makes the execution of queries more efficient, since the queries have been preprocessed, but it also reduces the amount of information that needs to be transferred to the IDM. This is because the names or numbers of the stored commands and parameters are all that are necessary to activate the prestored commands. To use this interface method, a parser needs to be implemented for the query language. In addition, routines to transfer data to and from the IDM and routines to format data received from the IDM would also be necessary.

3. *Embedded query language.* The IDL can also be embedded into a general-purpose host programming language. The IDL statements are specifically marked in an application program. They are processed by a preprocessor, which parses them and sends them to the IDM as stored commands. The preprocessor replaces these statements by host language calls to the run-time subroutines that interface to the IDM. After the replacement, the resulting program contains only the host language statements, which are then compiled by the regular compiler. To use this interface method, the preprocessor and the parser need to be implemented. The operating system needs to be modified to interface with the IDM.

7.1.3 IQC

The Information Query Computer (IQC) is a dedicated database computer designed and prototyped by the Nippon Electric Co., LTD. of Japan [SEK82]. It is a follow-up work of another experimental system, the Generalized Database

Subsystem (GDS) [HAK77]. IQC is designed to serve as a dedicated database computer not only for a number of hosts but also for a network of microcomputers, minicomputers, and main-frame computers of different makes and architectures (see Figure 7.6). The database management system that runs on IQC is a relational-like system (NEC's DBMS called INQ) with an added feature whereby multivalued domains (or repeating groups) are allowed. Thus, a database in INQ is a set of nonnormalized relations. A high-level data manipulation language is available so the user can retrieve and manipulate the database.

The main software components residing in the host and the IQC are shown in Figure 7.7. The IQC software consists of a control program, a message handler, some protocol tasks, and a database management system. The control program supervises and controls all activities of the IQC. The message handler is

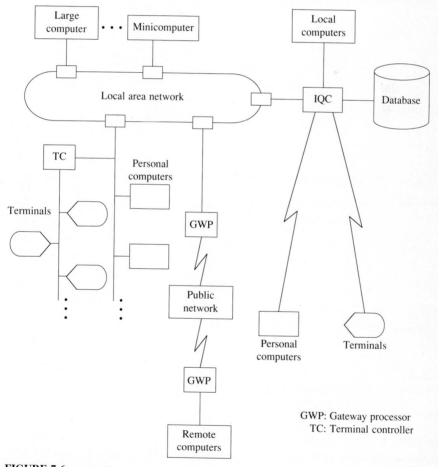

FIGURE 7.6

The IQC system configuration. (*Source:* [SEK82] copyright ©1982. Spinger-Verlag, reprinted by permission.)

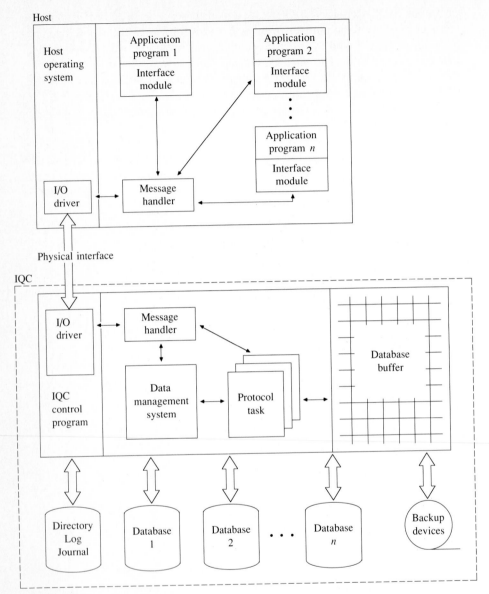

FIGURE 7.7
The main software components of the host and the IQC. (*Source:* [SEK82] copyright ©1982. Springer-Verlag, reprinted by permission.)

responsible for maintaining smooth communication with the host(s) in accordance with some predetermined communication protocols. A command from the host computer is received by the message handler as a message that is passed to a protocol task. The protocol task executes the command with the help of the DBMS and returns the result to the message handler, which in turn forwards it to the host computer. A very large database buffer is assumed to allow large quantities of data to reside in the main memory, thus facilitating fast data accesses.

On the host side, the main software components are a message handler and interface modules for individual application programs. The message handler is responsible for sending and receiving messages to and from the IQC. It also passes and receives these messages to and from the interface modules of application programs and renders IQC access services to the application programs. The interface modules, on the other hand, provide the corresponding application programs with access entries for individual database commands. They receive an IQC access request in the form of a "CALL IQC" statement in an application program, prepare a message in the prescribed data format, and pass it to the message handler.

The logical interface between the IQC and the host occurs at the database query level. High-level queries are passed from the host to the IQC for processing and the results are returned to the host. This level of interface is chosen instead of, for example, the data manipulation language, the logical record I/O, or the physical record I/O level, for the following reasons. First, it offers the most natural interface between independent application programs and the DBMS. Second, an analysis conducted by Sekino et al. [SEK82] shows that the frequency of host-IQC communication is minimized at the database query level. This is important for achieving efficiency in query execution. Third, the software required on the host computer is minimized so that a small computer or an intelligent terminal can be used as a host to the IQC.

The storage access technique of the IQC is the traditional indexing technique using a B-tree organization. Indexes are established for some selected attributes to provide direct access to records or tuples containing certain attribute values. The IQC also manages a large database buffer in the main memory using the least recently used (LRU) algorithm for the replacement of data pages. Thus, data pages that contain frequently used indices tend to remain in the main memory.

7.1.4 iDBP

The Intel Database Processor (iDBP) is a dedicated database computer introduced by the Intel Communications in 1982 [INT82*a*, INT82*b*, INT82*c*, and INT82*d*]. It is designed to serve a number of different functions depending on the application environments in which the system is used. It serves as (1) a database engine that contains a powerful database management system running on a separate processor, (2) an intelligent controller that manages its own dedicated storage, (3) a back-end building block that provides a structured application interface to multiple host computers, and (4) a database server that provides shared information for workstations in a local area network. It is a microcomputer system that performs file and database management services for applications that run on some front-end devices.

7.1.4.1 THE SYSTEM CONFIGURATION OF iDBP. The database management functions performed by the iDBP are realized by several subsystems of integrated

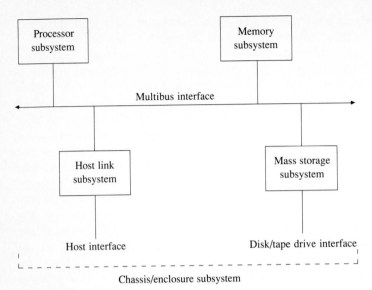

FIGURE 7.8
iDBP subsystems. (*Source:* [INT82a] Reprinted by permission of Intel Corporation)

hardware, firmware, and software. Figure 7.8 shows the various subsystems, connected by a Multibus, that form the iDBP. Descriptions of the functions of the subsystems follow.

1. *Processor subsystem.*   It consists of an SPU II board featuring an 8086 microprocessor with 128K bytes of on-board RAM. It executes all the DBMS and operating system software and manages hardware resources such as host communication links, disk controllers, and system memory.
2. *Memory subsystem.*   It consists of a primary CSU II board and an optional memory expansion board that provide the processor subsystem with up to one megabyte of ECC-protected memory.
3. *Host link subsystem.*   It consists of the Intel Communications front-end processor (FEP) with various personality interface modules (PIMs) that implement communication with the host(s).
4. *Mass storage subsystem.* It consists of Winchester or SMD-compatible disks and optional tape controllers.
5. *Chassis/enclosure subsystem (optional).* It includes the Multibus backplane, card cage, connector panel, front panel, cooling fans, and power supplies.

iDBP comprises a family of compatible products and product levels. There are two basic system configurations: the iDBP 86/440 Database Processor and the iDBP 86/441 Database Processor Starter System. The 86/440 Database Processor includes the following four product levels:

Level 1: Printed circuit boards

Level 2: Level 1 plus backplane and card cage

Level 3: Level 2 plus power supply, cooling fans, front panel with switches, internal cables, and rear connector panel in a 19-inch rack-mountable chassis.

Level 4: Level 2 plus power supply, cooling fans, front panel with switches, internal cables, and rear connector panel in a stand-alone enclosure.

With this configuration, the iDBP is used as a microprocessor-based database machine that functions as a mass storage controller for one or more host computers.

The Starter System is a single-level product. It combines the iDBP database processor with the following hardware facilities:

1. An 84 megabyte Fujitsu disk drive housed in an attached peripheral enclosure
2. An integral $5\frac{1}{4}$-inch floppy disk drive
3. An intelligent CRT terminal

This configuration facilitates applications integration by combining the Database Processor with a simple terminal-user interface.

7.1.4.2 THE DBMS OF iDBP. Central to the iDBP system is its DBMS software, which manages files for the front-end host(s). The DBMS has the following special features:

1. It manages both structured files as well as unstructured files.
2. It supports all three popular data models, namely relational, hierarchical, and network models. For the relational model, it provides a set of relational operators that can dynamically transform stored data into application-oriented relations and can define "views" over stored files. For the hierarchical model, it provides tools to implement hierarchical structures of unlimited width and depth (limited only by the available storage space). For the network model, it provides tools to implement set-types and many-to-many relationships.
3. It allows attributes in records to serve as "record pointers" the values of which point to related records in the same or different files. Using these record pointers, iDBP can connect files and records by creating parent-child-sibling or owner-member relationships.

The educational database of Chapter 2 will be used here as an example to illustrate some of these features. Suppose, in addition to the COURSE relation or file shown in Figure 7.9, there is a text file containing the textual descriptions of all the courses offered. In iDBP, the text file is treated as a long byte stream. A byte count can uniquely identify a text that describes a course. To relate these two existing files, iDBP provides the following command to define a view that connects these two files.

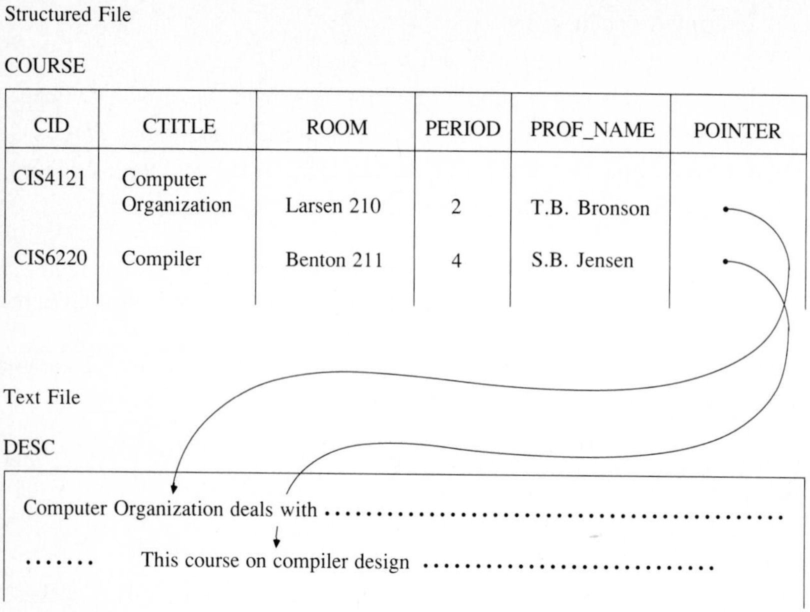

Structured File

COURSE

CID	CTITLE	ROOM	PERIOD	PROF_NAME	POINTER
CIS4121	Computer Organization	Larsen 210	2	T.B. Bronson	•
CIS6220	Compiler	Benton 211	4	S.B. Jensen	•

Text File

DESC

Computer Organization deals with ·· ·····

······· This course on compiler design ···························· ·····

FIGURE 7.9
COURSE and DESC files.

> DEFINE   VIEW   view = COURSE_DESC   CONNECT   file = COURSE
> pointer = DESC_PTR file = DESC

The result of this command is the view of the data file shown in Figure 7.10. The user can regard this file as physically available in the database. Each record is a composite of the original course record plus the pointer and the associated text string. The iDBP will manage the pointers and relate the structured record with the unstructured text string for the user.

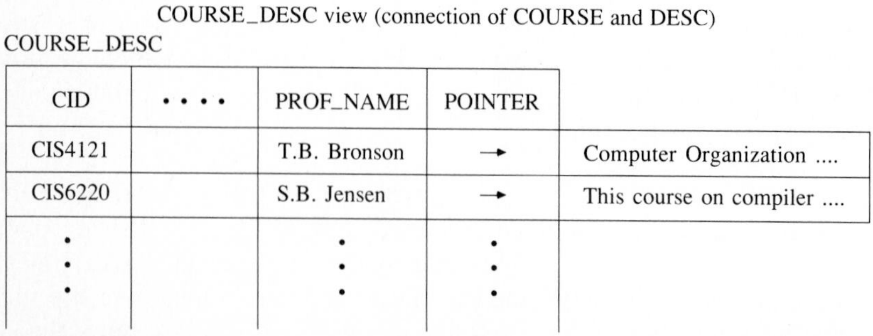

COURSE_DESC view (connection of COURSE and DESC)

COURSE_DESC

CID	· · · ·	PROF_NAME	POINTER	
CIS4121		T.B. Bronson	→	Computer Organization ....
CIS6220		S.B. Jensen	→	This course on compiler ....
·		·	·	
·		·	·	
·		·	·	

FIGURE 7.10
A view that connects a structured file and a text file.

The DBMS performs a wide range of data management functions, [INT82*d*] including:

1. Data definition, selection, retrieval, update, and deletion
2. Access control (data security)
3. Concurrency control
4. Transaction logging, recovery, and restart
5. File and database backup and recovery
6. Performance tuning
7. Parameter-driven macros (catalogued sequences of elementary commands)
8. Text searching and editing
9. Linked-list support
10. Integrated data dictionary control
11. Interfile relationship definition for structured and unstructured files

7.2 SYSTEMS WITH FUNCTIONALLY SPECIALIZED PROCESSORS

The other method of distributing database management functions will now be examined. Instead of using a single dedicated computer to handle all or most of the database management functions, this method distributes some frequent functions such as Selection, Join, Projection, Sort, Index Processing, Security Enforcement, and so forth to a number of specialized processors, each of which carries out one or a few functions. These processors can be special-purpose processors or general-purpose processors programmed to do special functions. The hardware and/or software of these specialized processors are tailored to perform the functions at high speed. Data to be processed by them are transferred from one processor to another. Each processor takes the input data and transforms them to produce the output according to the database function(s) built into the processor. The output data are passed to another processor according to the operation required for a specific query. In order to increase the response time and execution time of a single query or the overall system throughput, the operations of a single query or multiple queries are pipelined to increase the degree of parallelism. Thus, the specialized processors can concurrently perform their functions over different data streams for the same or different user queries.

In this subsection, a number of database machines are used as examples to show (1) which database management functions are assigned to specialized processors and how they are distributed among the processors in different architectural frameworks and (2) what novel data organizations and processing techniques are used to process queries.

7.2.1 Distribution of Functions

In order to build a cost-effective and cost-efficient multiprocessor database machine, it is necessary to select the proper database management functions for specialization by hardware and/or software. These should be the basic functions frequently performed by a database management system. The increased speed of a specialized processor should justify the cost of the processor and the overhead involved in transporting data between processors and in interprocessor communication and synchronization. The set of basic operations that are good candidates for specialization are very much dependent on the underlying data models used by different database computers. For example, in a relational model–based system, the relational algebraic operations such as Join, Selection, and Projection are very frequent operations. Other frequently used operations (e.g., the aggregate functions Sum, Count, Average, etc. and sorting) are very time-consuming. If a hardware sorter is available, the sorting of a relation or relations can be the first step before performing other time-consuming operations (e.g., Join, Elimination of Duplicates, Set-intersection, Set-union, Set-difference, Aggregation, etc.) Some or all of these operations have been assigned to specialized processors in relational systems such as SABRE, RDBM, DELTA, DDM, CADAM, systolic arrays, and VLSI tree machines. Table 7.1 shows a list of basic operations that are assigned to specialized processors in the relational multiprocessor systems to be discussed in this category.

In a system such as The Ohio State University's Data Base Computer (DBC), which uses an attribute-based data model, the basic operations are quite different from the relational systems. They include the transformation of attribute names to internal representations, the processing of indices to locate data in the mass memory, and the intersection of sets of index terms. In addition, DBC uses a specialized processor to implement security rules to enforce data security.

7.2.2   Architectures and Processing Techniques

This subsection describes the architectures of the previously mentioned systems to show how some of the database functions are distributed and implemented.

7.2.2.1   THE ARCHITECTURE AND PROCESSING TECHNIQUES OF DBC.
DBC was the first multiprocessor system in this subcategory. It was designed and analyzed at The Ohio State University beginning in 1975. (Hsiao provides a collection of the major publications [HSI80]). The five design goals of the DBC [BAN79] are:

1. To permit the handling of a very large ($10**10$ bytes) on-line database
2. To use hardware available at the time rather than basing the design on emerging and commercially unavailable technologies
3. To compete favorably with available software-implemented database systems
4. To include in the design hardware a security mechanism
5. To permit the use of high-level commands that are able to support different database organizations.

TABLE 7.1
Distribution of functions to specialized processors

System	Selection	Projection	Join	Sort	Set operation	Divide	Merge	Aggregation	Elimination of duplicates	Insertion and deletion
SABRE	✓	✓	✓	✓				✓		✓
RDBM	✓	✓	✓	✓		✓		✓		✓
DELTA	✓	✓	✓	✓	✓					
DDM	✓	✓	✓	✓	✓		✓			
CADAM	✓	✓	✓		✓			✓	✓	✓
Systolic array	✓		✓		✓	✓		✓	✓	
VLSI	✓	✓	✓	✓	✓	✓			✓	✓
tree machines										

The DBC hardware is designed to support the processing of the attribute-based data model already described in Section 6.3.1.2. The data model used in the MDBS described in that section was adopted from the DBC, which is the predecessor of the MDBS but which has a very different architecture.

The overall architecture of the DBC is shown in Figure 7.11. The DBC consists of two connected loops of processors: a data loop and a structure loop [BAN79]. The data loop contains a mass memory subsystem (MM) and a security

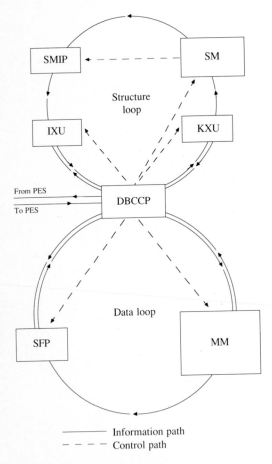

———— Information path
– – – – Control path

DBCCP: Database command control processor
KXU: Keyword transformation unit
SM: Structure memory
SMIP: Structure memory information processor
IXU: Index translation unit
MM: Mass memory
SFP: Security filter processor
PES: Program execution system

FIGURE 7.11
Architecture of DBC. (*Source:* [BAN79] ©1979 IEEE)

filter processor (SFP). The structure loop contains a keyword transformation unit (KXU), a structure memory (SM), a structure memory information processor (SMIP), and an index transformation unit (IXU). These two loops are connected to a database command and control processor (DBCCP), which controls the operations and data transfer in these loops.

These processors and subsystems are designed to support three software processing techniques: data clustering, indexing, and object classification for security enforcement. In DBC, as in MDBS, data records are grouped to form disjointed clusters based on their contents, that is, based on whether they satisfy a set of descriptors (see the description of the data organization of MDBS in Section 6.3.1.2). These clusters of records are placed together on disk cylinders to reduce the number of disk accesses required in query processing. The indexing technique used in this system associates a number of expected retrieval keywords or attribute-value pairs with the cylinders that contain records having these keywords. This technique allows relevant cylinders to be accessed and processed directly in response to search and retrieval queries. The processing of indices is supported in the DBC by the KXU, SM, SMIP, and IXU components to be described later in this section.

The object classification technique used for security enforcement requires an explanation. In DBC, records of a file are classified according to whether they satisfy some security constraints. A security constraint can be expressed by a canonical expression of *security keywords,* that is, attribute-value pairs used in expressing the constraints. For example, if the employee records containing salary values in the range of $20K to $100K need to be protected, a constraint can be stated in the following expression of security keywords,

$$(SAL \geq 20K) \text{ AND } (SAL \leq 100K)$$

A set of records that satisfies a canonical expression of security keywords is called a *security atom.* To simplify the access control operations and the access of data records, the database creator is required to define security constraints in such a way that security atoms contain disjointed sets of records. For example, if there are different security requirements for the following two overlapping salary ranges,

$$(SAL \geq 20K) \text{ AND } (SAL \leq 70K)$$
$$(SAL \geq 50K) \text{ AND } (SAL \leq 100k)$$

then the record sets of the security atoms formed by these two constraints would overlap. In this case, the ranges can be respecified as:

$$(SAL \geq 20K) \text{ AND } (SAL < 50K)$$
$$(SAL \geq 50K) \text{ AND } (SAL \leq 70K)$$
$$(SAL > 70K) \text{ AND } (SAL \leq 100K)$$

so that three nonoverlapping security atoms can be formed.

When a user makes a database request to the system, a prestored security profile of the user is accessed. This profile contains a number of *atomic access privileges* of the user. Each atomic access privilege specifies a security atom and the operation(s) that the user can legitimately perform. For example, user U1 may retrieve and delete atom S1, retrieve atom S2, and update atom S3. Using the access privileges, the DBCCP can determine if there is an expression of security keywords, which forms an atom referenced in the access privileges and satisfies the user's request. If there is such an expression, the operation specified in the user's request is compared with the operations associated with the security atom. If the user's operation is authorized, then the operation on the atom is permitted and subsequently carried out by the mass memory. Otherwise, the query is rejected due to security violations. This method allows the DBCCP to control accesses at the record level. Attribute-level (or field-level) accesses are controlled by the security filter processor (SFP) discussed later in this section.

The DBC is meant to serve as a back-end system to a host computer. Database queries issued at the host are sent to the DBCCP for execution. The DBCCP uses the structure loop (see Figure 7.11) to process the relevant indices of a given query and to determine the corresponding set of cylinders in the mass memory that need to be processed. The data loop is then used to access and process the contents of the selected cylinders in the content-addressed mass memory. The output of the mass memory is further screened by the SFP, which enforces field-level security to filter out data that should not be accessed by the user. The filtered results are sent to the DBCCP, which in turn forwards the results to the host. Given this general procedure, the components and their functions will be described in detail beginning with the control processor, DBCCP.

The main functions of the DBCCP are to receive a database request from the host, control the processing of the request by the processors in the structure and data loops, and return the results to the host. It also manages the cylinder space in the mass memory and the cluster information and enforces record-level security checking. A database request given to the DBCCP is in the form of a query conjunction, such as,

$$(AGE \geq 22) \text{ AND } (SUBJECT = \text{`computer'}) \text{ AND } (STATUS = 5)$$

where AGE, SUBJECT, and STATUS are attribute names and AND is the logical AND condition of the three predicates. The predicates in a query conjunction are passed to the key transformation unit (KXU).

The main function of the KXU is to convert the variable-length keywords to fixed-length keywords in order to standardize their internal representation and to facilitate their matching. A unique identifier is assigned to each attribute in the database and in the user's query. The mappings between attributes and their identifiers are stored in an attribute information table. For each attribute, the table contains the minimum and maximum values, the data type, and the number of ranges into which the attribute values may be divided (usually for numerical attributes). Different hash functions are stored in a hash algorithm library and are used to transform variable-length attribute values into their corresponding fixed-length hash codes. For example, the keyword (AGE, 22) would be transformed into a fixed-length keyword having format (a, r, v) where 'a' stands for the AGE identifier, 'r' for a range number to which the value 22 belongs, and 'v' for the hash code of the value. The (a, r) pair is called the *bucket name* of the keyword. It is used to access the structure memory. A KXU control processor takes variable-length keywords and predicates as input and uses the prestored hash algorithms and attribute information to produce fixed-length keywords or bucket names.

The structure memory (SM) is used to store and access the index information associated with the keywords chosen by the database designer for indexing purposes. Indices are maintained in the SM on these selected keywords and their ranges. The keywords and value ranges used to form clusters of records are the natural candidates for indices, since most query conjunctions are expected to contain one or more of these keywords. Associated with each indexed keyword is a list of index terms, each of which contains, among other items, a pair (f, s) where f is a relative cylinder number and s is a security atom identifier. The cylinder number specifies the relative location of a physical disk cylinder of the mass memory in which at least one and possibly more records containing the keyword can be found. The record(s) belongs to the security atom s. For example, the following keywords and index terms may be stored in the SM.

> (AGE, $r1$) {($f1$, $s1$), ($f2$, $s2$)}
> (AGE, $r2$) {($f3$, $s3$), ($f4$, $s4$), ($f5$, $s5$)}
> (AGE, $r3$) {($f6$, $s6$), ($f7$, $s7$), ($f8$, $s8$)}
> (AGE, $r4$) {($f9$, $s9$), ($f10$, $s10$)}
> (SUBJECT, computer) {($f4$, $s4$), ($f10$, $s10$)}
> (STATUS, $r1$) {($f11$, $s11$)}
> (STATUS, $r2$) {($f4$, $s4$), ($f10$, $s10$)}

In these terms, the $r1$ associated with AGE represents the age range between 10 to 21, $r2$ the age range between 22 and 26, $r3$ the age range between 27 and 40, and $r4$ the age range above 40. The f's represent relative cylinder addresses and the s's represent security atom identification. The $r1$ associated with STATUS represents the status range between 1 and 4, and $r2$ represents the status range greater than 4.

Given these keywords and index terms, the example query conjunction will cause the SM to retrieve the index terms associated with (AGE, $r2$), (AGE, $r3$), (AGE, $r4$), (SUBJECT, computer), and (STATUS, $r2$). The intersection of these five sets of index terms will provide the cylinder addresses for accessing these records that satisfy the query. The Intersection operation is carried out by the SMIP, which will be described later in this section.

To facilitate the high-speed retrieval of index terms, a content-addressable, intelligent SM is used. The organization of the SM is shown in Figure 7.12. It consists of a bucket memory system, a controller-processing element bus, a structure memory controller, and a look-aside buffer. The bucket memory system itself consists of an array of memory-unit and processing-element pairs, similar in concept to the cellular-logic devices described in Chapter 3. Each memory unit is divided into a number of modules or blocks in which the keywords and index terms are stored. In the DBC, a bucket is defined as all keywords and their index terms

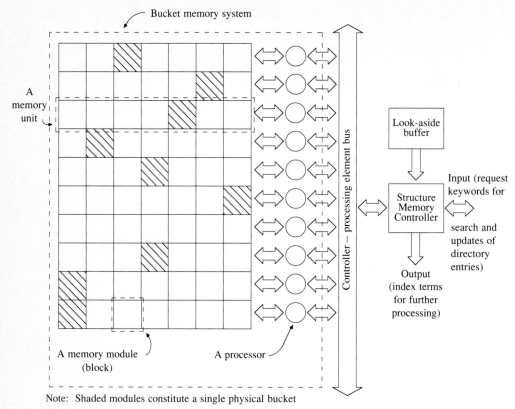

Note: Shaded modules constitute a single physical bucket

FIGURE 7.12
Organization of the structure memory. (*Source:* [BAN79] ©1979 IEEE)

corresponding to a particular attribute, the values of which fall within a given value range. These keywords and index terms are spread as evenly as possible across the memory units to allow the corresponding processing elements to access and search the bucket in parallel. The structure memory controller contains a RAM for storing a bucket table. Each entry of this bucket table contains a bucket name (i.e., attribute identification plus a range number) and a set of memory module numbers indicating the memory blocks that contain the index terms of the bucket.

When keywords in a query conjunction are provided to the structure memory controller, the controller uses the bucket table to locate the proper memory modules to retrieve the index terms. The look-aside buffer is used to store update requests temporarily. The data in the bucket memory system are not updated immediately when the update requests are received. These accumulated update requests are delayed until either the loading of the buffer reaches a certain threshold value or the structure memory encounters a slack period with no new requests awaiting execution. Thus, update requests will have less effect on the performance of the SM. In the case of a retrieval operation, the set of index terms retrieved for a keyword need to be adjusted according to the update requests stored in the look-aside buffer so that the adjusted index terms will reflect the actual contents of the SM.

As explained and illustrated previously, several sets of index terms will normally be retrieved by the SM and passed to the SMIP, the next processor in the structure loop. The main function of the SMIP is to intersect these sets of index terms. The SMIP, as shown in Figure 7.13, also has a cellular-logic architecture. It consists of an SMIP controller and an array of memory-unit and processing-element pairs. Two buses are used, one to connect the controller to the processing-element array and the other to connect the memory elements. The processing elements are microprocessors, and the memory units are RAM modules.

The SMIP controller receives several sets of index terms. For each index term, two hash functions are applied. The first determines the processing element number, and the second determines the memory location of the index term. The

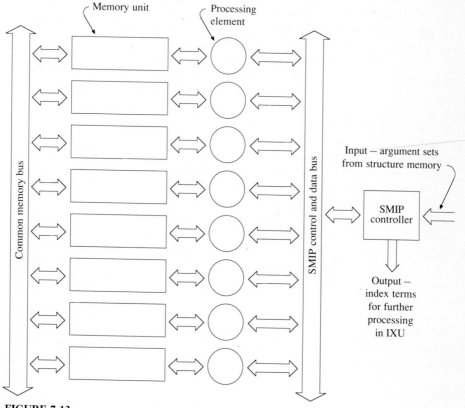

FIGURE 7.13

Organization of the structure memory information processor (SMIP). (*Source:* [BAN79] ©1979 IEEE)

index term is stored along with a counter that keeps track of the number of identical index terms that are hashed to that location. In the case of collision, the index term is stored in the nearest available location in the same memory unit. If a particular memory unit overflows, then space from some other memory unit is used. In this case, the index term is transferred through the common memory bus shown in the figure. It should be noted that by using this scheme all processing elements can receive index terms and operate in parallel.

After the input sets have been hashed, an index term whose counter value equals the number of input sets processed would indicate that it is a member of the set intersection. Using the previous example, the set of index terms formed for the example conjunction would be $\{(f4, s4), (f10, s10)\}$. All the members of the intersection are then output to the next processor, the IXU, which converts the relative cylinder numbers in each index term into physical cylinder numbers. The output set is denoted by $\{(c101, s4), (c127, s10)\}$. This set is then given to the DBCCP, which performs the record-level access checking to determine if the user has the access right on records belonging to the security atoms $s4$ and $s10$. If an access violation is detected, the corresponding index term will be removed from the set. Assuming no violation exists, the physical cylinder numbers $c101$ and $c127$ are passed to the mass memory, which reads and processes the cylinders' contents.

The organization and the operation of the mass memory has been given in Chapter 4. The mass memory (MM) is an elaborate filter that is capable of reading the contents of n disk tracks of a cylinder in parallel to n track information processors (TIPs) shown in Figure 4.19. The TIPs simultaneously examine the records stored in their corresponding tracks to determine which records satisfy the predicates in a query conjunction. The selected records are then passed to the security filter for attribute-level security checking. The physical cylinder numbers provided by the DBCCP are used to search the proper cylinders one at a time.

In order to allow the contents of disk tracks to be searched on the fly as they are transferred to the TIPs, the DBC organizes records and query conjunctions in the formats shown in Figure 7.14. Each record in the mass memory has a cluster number, a security atom identifier, the number of keywords in the record, and a set of keywords (or attribute-value pairs). The keywords are ordered in ascending order by the fixed-length attribute identifiers. The value part consists of a length indicator and the variable-length value. In a similar format, a query conjunction is represented internally by the number of predicates in the conjunctive expression followed by a set of triplets. Each triplet consists of a fixed-length attribute identifier, a relational operator, and a variable-length value with a length indicator. The set of triplets is ordered in ascending order by their attribute identifiers. Since the records and the query conjunction are ordered, the TIPs are able to perform the search using bit-by-bit comparison without repeatedly scanning the record contents.

The security filter processor (SFP) of the DBC performs a number of important functions. It enforces the attribute-level security of the database, performs aggregate functions (e.g., Maximum, Minimum, Average, etc.) on the records

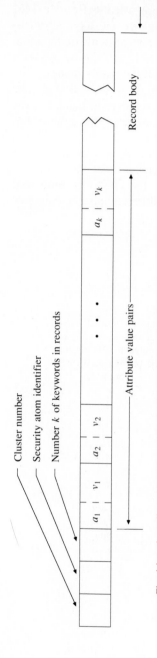

Cluster number

Security atom identifier

Number k of keywords in records

a_1 | v_1 | a_2 | v_2 | $\cdots$ | a_k | v_k

Attribute value pairs

Record body

a_i: Fixed-length attribute identifier of the i th keyword of the record

v_i: Variable-length value with length indicator of the i th keyword

$$a_1 < a_2 < a_3 < \cdots < a_k$$

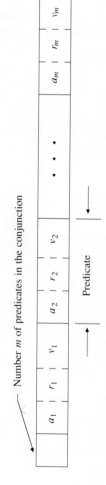

Number m of predicates in the conjunction

a_1 | r_1 | v_1 | a_2 | r_2 | v_2 | $\cdots$ | a_m | r_m | v_m

Predicate

a_i: Fixed-length attribute identifier of the i th predicate of the conjunction

r_i: Relational operator of the i th predicate

v_i: Variable-length value with length indicator of the i th predicate

$$a_1 \leq a_2 \leq a_3 \leq \cdots \leq a_m$$

FIGURE 7.14

(a) The format of a record R in the mass memory. (*Source:* [BAN79] ©1979 IEEE) (b) The format of a query conjunction. (*Source:* [Ban79] ©1979 IEEE)

passed to it by the MM, and carries out the projection function by selecting the record fields that pass the security check and outputting them to the DBCCP. The organization of the SFP is shown in Figure 7.15. The input records from the MM are stored in the RAM. The access authorization unit uses the prestored attribute-level security rules associated with the user to determine what fields on the input records can be seen by the user. The postprocessing unit performs aggregation functions over the input records if they are called for in the user's request. The field extraction unit selects the legitimate fields for output to the DBCCP. The output of the SFP may be used for updating the mass memory. In that case, the output is routed to the MM via the DBCCP. The operations of the submodules contained in the SFP are controlled by the SFP controller.

From the description of the DBC architecture and the processing techniques given here, the reader can see that the database management functions associated with the attribute-based model, the indexing scheme, the cluster scheme, and the security mechanism used in the DBC are distributed in a number of elaborate

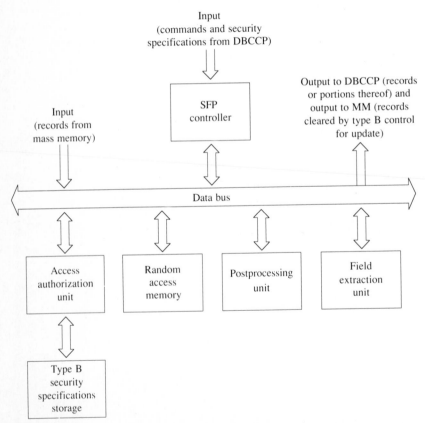

FIGURE 7.15
Organization of the security filter processor (SFP). (*Source:* [BAN79] ©1979 IEEE)

subsystems. Each of the subsystems, in turn, contains a number of processors and memory modules to carry out its subfunctions. This is a good example of a hardware system designed to support a number of software techniques that have been recognized to be effective for managing very large databases. The speed of this system is not only achieved by functional specialization but also by pipelined processing of queries by the subsystems. The hardware architecture of the DBC incorporates a number of database computer design concepts such as database filter, associative memory, and cellular-logic device. This system was designed and quite thoroughly analyzed; however, no implementation effort was undertaken.

7.2.2.2 THE ARCHITECTURE AND PROCESSING TECHNIQUES OF SABRE. Système d'Accès a des Bases Relationneles (SABRE) is a relational multiprocessor database machine designed and prototyped at INRIA, France [GAR81, VAL82a, VAL82b, KAR81, and GAR83]. The main objective of the project is to develop an efficient, extensible, portable, and reliable database manager that can be used as a basic tool to build integrated and distributed database systems.

This system has a number of features for improving the speed of I/O and query response and execution time. To improve I/O speed and reduce I/O overhead, SABRE uses database filters. It also uses new access methods and a multiclustering strategy to improve the speed of secondary storage accesses [KAR81]. Furthermore, it uses a large cache memory to increase the effective speed of the secondary memory. To increase query response and execution times, SABRE allows both interquery and intraquery parallelism. Multiple queries are processed simultaneously by general-purpose processors that are programmed in software to perform specific database management functions.

The functional architecture of SABRE is shown in Figure 7.16 [GAR83]. It contains a number of virtual processors, each of which is assigned a major database management function. The main functions of these processes are as follows:

1. *View and integrity processor (VIP).* The functions of this processor are (a) to verify the user's access right on the view he or she wants to process, (b) to manage the mapping between views and the conceptual database and to translate requests expressed on relations in views to the relations defined in the conceptual model, and (c) to perform integrity control on update requests.

2. *Request evaluation processor (REP).* The processor decomposes queries into relational algebraic operations and performs query optimization.

3. *Relation access processor (RAP).* This processor manages access paths to partitions of tuples (or records) to determine those that need to be scanned or updated.

4. *Join, sort, and aggregate processors (JSP).* These processors perform the relational join, sort, and aggregate functions on partitions of relation(s). Several of these processors can be used to implement parallel algorithms for these operations.

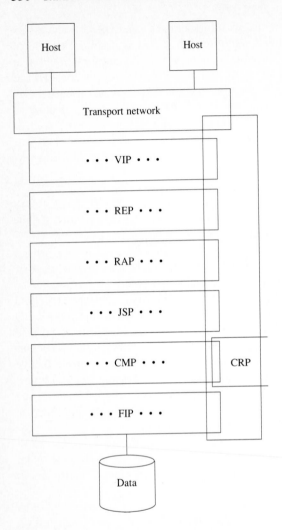

FIGURE 7.16
The functional architecture of SABRE.
(*Source:* [GAR83])

5. *Concurrency control and recovery processor (CRP).* This processor handles concurrency control using an algorithm that is based on a time-stamping method [VIE82]. It also keeps a log for updates and manages a two-step commitment protocol [BAE81].

6. *Cache memory processor (CMP).* This processor manages the cache memory and allocates space in both the cache and secondary memories. It is responsible for moving memory pages between the memory devices.

7. *Filtering processors.* These processors are paired with the disks used in the system. They perform Selection, Insertion, and Deletion operations on relational tuples as they are transferred from disks to the cache memories.

   These virtual processors are mapped to a number of physical processors. The number of physical processors used to implement their functions would depend on a specific implementation. In fact, the first version, SABRE.VO, was implemented on a single general-purpose computer running MULTICS. It is a single-user system used to validate the initial design of SABRE. The second version, SABRE.V1, was extended to support multiuser and multiprocess operations but was still running on a single computer. The third version, SABRE.V2, involves three 68000 computers and a 256K common memory. The hardware system, called SM90, was developed by the French PTT (CNET). The planned distribution of the database functions are shown in Figure 7.17.

As shown in the figure, Processor A implements the user interface for multiple hosts and the view and integrity processor (VIP). Processor B implements the request evaluation processor (REP) and the relation access processor (RAP). Processor C implements the join-and-sort processor (JSP), the cache memory processor (CMP), the concurrency and reliability control processor (CRP), and the filter processor (FIP). These three physical processors are connected to a common bus and have access to 256K bytes of shared memory.

7.2.2.3 RDBM. The Relational Database Machine (RDBM) was designed and developed at the Technical University of Braunschweig, West Germany [AUE81 and SCH83]. The research and development work on this machine is being carried out by the same group that developed the SURE system described in Chapter 4. This system uses (1) a number of special-function processors for performing join, sort, main memory management, and data conversion, (2) a common memory

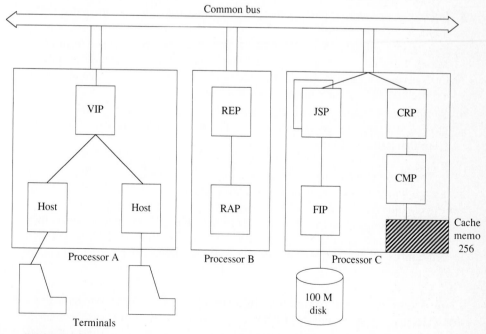

FIGURE 7.17
Functional distribution of SABRE.V2. (*Source:* [GAR83])

for staging data to be processed by the special-function processors and their communication and synchronization, and (3) a secondary memory system, which employs a logical data access interface and contains special-function processors to perform restriction (or selection), update, and secondary storage management.

The overall organization of RDBM is shown in Figure 7.18. It consists of the following main components:

1. *Database supervisor (DABS).* This is a general-purpose minicomputer that provides communication interface to a host computer, translates and optimizes queries to produce codes for execution by other components, and controls their execution.

2. *Content-addressable memory (CAM).* This memory system consists of a secondary memory and its manager as well as a database filter for performing restriction and update operations using a linear array of specialized processors (RUPs).

3. *Main memory (MAM).* This memory is shared by the other components and is managed by a special-purpose hardware system, the main memory manager (MAMM).

4. *Conversion processor (COP).* This processor serves to convert data from external to internal system data format and vice versa, eliminate attributes (i.e., perform projection) and alter their order within a tuple for output generation, and buffer the data transferred between the DABS and the MAM which have different data rates.

5. *Interrecord processor (IRP).* This processor performs operations that involve multiple records of the same or different relations. Its main functions are the joining of relations, the evaluation of aggregate functions (e.g., Minimum, Maximum, Sum, Average, etc.), and the evaluation of set comparison operations necessary for performing the relational division and for evaluating query expressions that contain universal quantifiers.

6. *Sort processor (SOP).* This is a special hardware processor for sorting relations using a four-way merge-sort algorithm. The interrecord operations can benefit from the sorted relations.

These components are interconnected by three buses (shown in Figure 7.18 as one): a data bus, an instruction bus, and a status bus. The hardware and software techniques of the main memory system, the content-addressable memory, and the interrecord processor will be described here in some detail, since they are the special features of the RDBM. Readers who are interested in the detailed description of all the components of this system should refer to the article by Schweppe, et al. [SCH83].

Logical addressing and common main memory. In the RDBM, database functions are distributed among a number of processors. These processors need to cooperate in order to correctly execute queries. These processors also need to communicate with one another to synchronize their operations and to pass data

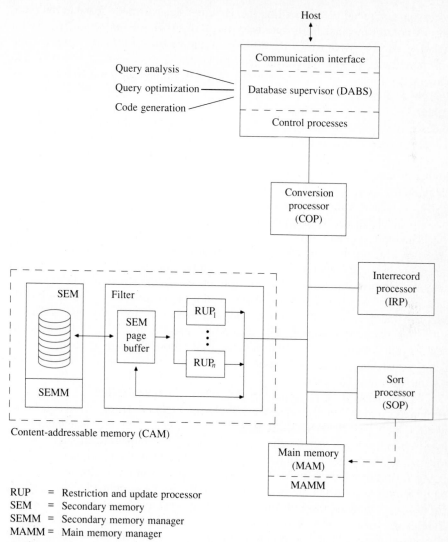

FIGURE 7.18
Overall organization of RDBM. (*Source:* [SCH83])

among them. One common method is to use message passing and data passing directly between processors. This method can be quite time-consuming and may cause bus contention in a common-bus architecture like the RDBM. Instead, the RDBM uses a common main memory for interprocessor communication and synchronization. All components except the DABS have direct access to the common memory for data and processing status.

Using the common memory method, accesses to the memory by these special-purpose processors would still need to be synchronized to prevent different processors from reading and writing the same physical memory space at the same time. A control mechanism is necessary to regulate the memory accesses. There are two general ways in which memory space can be assigned to a processor. One is to preallocate physical space to each processor that stores and accesses data or messages to and from the designated space. Data are accessed by specifying their physical addresses. Physical addressing of data has a number of well-known problems. One is the inflexible use of the memory, since each processor needs the predesignated space to operate. The other is the fragmentation of main memory, that is, pockets of unusable spaces scattered throughout the memory, due to the release of a space by one processor that does not fit the memory need of another processor. A third problem is that memory space is often wasted because a maximal space is reserved for each processor in order to prevent space overflow. Lastly, the space, which can be assigned to a processor, is limited to the physical space available in the main memory.

The other method, the one used in the RDBM, assigns a logical space to a processor which is dynamically mapped to some physical space. The processor, in effect, sees a contiguous logical space that is not bound by the size of the physical memory. At run-time, when data are referenced by their logical addresses, the main memory manager allocates physical blocks (generally nonconsecutive) in the main memory and translates the logical addresses into physical addresses before the data are accessed. The techniques used in the RDBM for dynamic memory allocation and dynamic address translation are similar to the virtual memory management scheme based on segmentation and paging concepts used in some operating systems.

In the RDBM, a relation occupies a logical space called a *segment*. A segment is divided into 8K-byte pages. Tuples of a relation are accessed and stored by GET.NEXT or PUT.NEXT functions, respectively. The physical memory is divided into frames, which are the same size as pages. Frames are allocated at run-time to store the pages of different segments loaded from the secondary memory. Figure 7.19 shows the structure of the main memory system. A command to access main memory arrives via the instruction bus (IB) to the command waiting queue (FIFO). If a command from the queue cannot be executed due to the unavailability of relevant data in the main memory, then it is put back into the queue. Otherwise, the command is executed by the universal processor shown in the figure. If the command is a data transfer command, the logical address referenced by the command needs to be translated into a physical address. This translation is achieved by using information stored in two sets of hardware implemented tables: the segment tables and the frame description tables. The first set contains a segment name table and a segment description table. The segment name table is implemented by a 32 × 32 content-addressable memory. This memory uses a hashing technique to store the segment names or names of relations that have been staged into the main memory. A content search of this table provides an entry into the second table, which is implemented by a 256 × 16 RAM. This second table stores a frame number, which specifies the physical space holding the current page of the segment being searched, and a tuple number, which specifies the relative

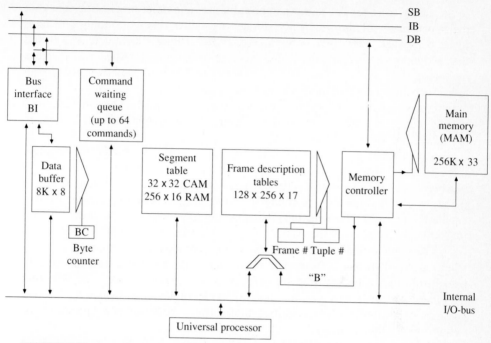

FIGURE 7.19
Structure of the main memory hardware (MAMM). (*Source:* [SCH83])

location of the tuple inside the page. The frame number is used to address the proper table out of the set of frame description tables. The tuple number is used as an offset to address an entry in the frame description table. This table contains, among other data, the starting address of the tuple in that physical frame. Thus, the processor can thus form the physical address of the tuple being searched by concatenating the frame number and the starting address of the tuple.

The contents of these two sets of tables are automatically filled by decoding, on the fly, the delimiters separating attributes and tuples. Whenever a tuple delimiter signaling the start of a tuple is encountered during write operations, the 13 least significant bits of the current main memory address are stored in the frame description table selected by the 7 most significant bits of the address.

Besides the components described here, the main memory system contains a 256K × 33 RAM, a memory controller, and a 8K × 8 data buffer for buffering pages of data being moved in or out of the main memory.

Filtering functions and secondary memory system. Since databases are generally too large to be stored in the main memory, they are stored in secondary storage devices. In the RDBM, pages of relations are moved very frequently between the main memory and the secondary storage. To achieve this, the logical addresses in terms of relation names need to be translated into physical addresses in secondary storage. The address translation task and other tasks associated with the management of the secondary storage are rather time-consuming and need to be performed very frequently to support the paging scheme. It is believed that assigning these functions to the database supervisor (DABS) will create a bottleneck. The DABS is a conventional processor that is already overloaded with tasks such as communication with the host, parsing, user task analysis, query optimization, control of specialized processors, and so forth. Thus, the memory management tasks are downloaded to a content-addressable memory system in the RDBM.

Moving large quantities of data from the secondary storage to the main memory will restrict the performance of the system based on the data access and transfer rates. It is obviously advantageous to reduce the length and width of the accessed relations by performing selection and projection operations using a database filter prior to moving data to main memory. In the RDBM, these filtering functions are handled by the content-addressable memory system.

The content-addressable memory (CAM) consists of a secondary memory manager (SEMM) and a filter. The main functions of CAM are to access data pages from the secondary storage, perform content searches (i.e., the Selection operation) on the pages to filter out irrelevant tuples, and select the needed columns or attributes of the qualified tuples (i.e., the Projection operation) for output to the main memory.

The structure of the SEMM is shown in Figure 7.20. Similar to the structure of the main memory system, a universal processor, which implements the secondary memory management functions, is connected via a bus interface to the RDBM bus system. Secondary memory reference commands received from the DABS or MAMM are queued in a buffer. When the processor is free to process a command, it takes a command from the queue and translates its logical page address into a physical address using the address mapping information stored in the management information buffer. If the mapping information is not in the buffer (it is assumed that all management information cannot fit into the buffer), then it is fetched by the secondary memory (SEM) controller into a management information I/O buffer and then moved to the management information buffer using a least recently used (LRU) replacement strategy for buffer management, that is, the least recently used space in the management information buffer is used to load the data from the I/O buffer.

Depending on the type and source of a command to the SEMM, data from the secondary memory are moved to different data buffers with different priorities. If the command is to search a relation, a series of physical addresses are generated by the universal processor for accessing the pages of the relation. These addresses are stored in a FIFO page address buffer and are used by the secondary memory controller to fetch the pages from the secondary storage to two alternating page buffers of the restriction and update processor (RUP). These two buffers implement a double-buffering technique to allow the data transfer time to overlap with the processing of their contents. A number of RUPs are used to perform a content search on data pages to carry out the filtering and update functions.

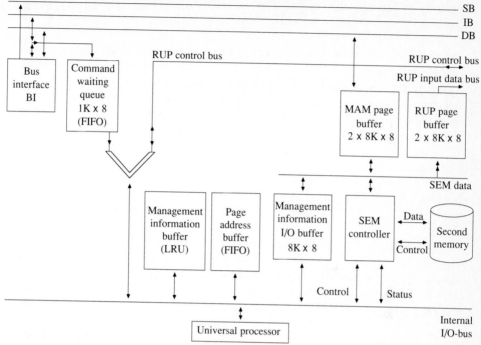

FIGURE 7.20
Structure of the secondary memory manager hardware (SEMM). (*Source:* [SCH83])

Data pages fetched from the secondary storage are distributed to RUPs, each of which receives a subset of the tuples of the relation. Each RUP contains a 4K × 8 input tuple buffer to hold the received tuples for processing by the processor unit. All the RUPs simultaneously execute the same query or queries against their corresponding tuples. Those tuples that satisfy the qualification condition specified in a search query form the selection results. A projection over a subset of the attributes of these selected tuples can also be performed to further reduce the size of the resulting relation. The resulting tuples are moved to an output tuple buffer, from which data are transferred via the data bus to any processor in the system that requires the data.

If the command to the SEMM is from the main memory manager, which generally requests for a particular page, it is given a higher priority than the processing of page addresses just discussed. The main memory manager requests are made very frequently in connection with page replacement in the main memory. Thus, data pages need to be supplied quickly so as not to block other processors in the system from obtaining access to the main memory. For this command, the requested page is moved to the MAM page buffer from the secondary storage.

Commands received from the RUPs via the RUP control bus are given even a higher priority, since they may contain locking requests in the context of update operations. Fast response to these commands are important to allow the contents of the RUP data buffer to be locked for updates.

Interrecord operations and interrecord processor. Many relational operations involve the processing of more than one tuple to obtain the desired result. Some examples are: the evaluation of aggregate functions such as Average, Min, Max, and Sum, set operations, and the relational Join and Divide. These operations are processed in the RDBM by an interrecord processor (IRP). They are carried out in a pipelined fashion by overlapping the operation of the IRP with other processors. For example, an aggregation operation is usually performed on a set of tuples that satisfy some selection conditions. As tuples are evaluated by the RUPs, the qualified tuples are staged in the main memory. The IRP can then calculate the aggregate value while more tuples are being generated by the RUPs. The final aggregate value can thus be obtained soon after the last tuple is selected by the RUPs.

In RDBM, a Join operation can be performed using different algorithms depending on the data characteristics of the involved relations. Usually a join operation is done on two relations that have been reduced in size by a selection and/or a projection operation. The reduced relations can then be sorted to facilitate the final join. In RDBM, the sorting of relations is done by the sort processor (SOP) shown in Figure 7.18. In general, an equi-join operation is represented by the expression $R(Q)(A = B)S(P)$, where Q and P represent selection and/or projection conditions, where A is an attribute of relation R, and where B is an attribute of relation S. The following steps illustrate one possible algorithm for the Join operation:

1. The relation R is fetched by the secondary memory manager and processed by the filter. The reduced relation is stored in the main memory. Here, it is assumed that the main memory is large enough to store the reduced relation.
2. The following two substeps are carried out in parallel: (a) the reduced R is sorted by the sorter processor, and (b) the relation S is processed by the content-addressable memory as in step 1.
3. The reduced S is then sorted by the sort processor.
4. The Join operation is performed on the two sorted relations by concatenating their corresponding tuples if the value of A in one relation is equal to the value of B in the other relation. The results are established in the main memory ready for use by a subsequent operation.

To support the interrecord operations, the interrecord processor uses a universal microprocessor, two 8K × 8 input buffers and a 4K × 8 output buffer (see Figure 7.21). Two input buffers allow double-buffered access to each of the two relations involved in a join operation. To facilitate the random access to the tuples, an internal attribute pointer address table is established for each input buffer when a data page is loaded into the buffer. The result of an interrecord operation is assembled in the output buffer, from which data are transferred to the main memory.

The functions and the hardware structures of the three key components of the RDBM have been described. A prototype system was developed using the same disk as that used in the SURE project described in Chapter 4. The HP2100 minicomputer of the SURE project is used as the disk controller. The special-function processors of the RDBM are built around a standardized 8-bit microprocessor unit. A NORSK DATA NORD-100 minicomputer with a 512K-byte memory is used to control the overall operation of the RDBM. It is also used to simulate and test the various hardware components not yet implemented.

7.2.2.4 DELTA. DELTA is a relational database machine designed and implemented by the Institute for New Generation Computer Technology (ICOT) as a part of the Japanese effort on fifth generation computers [MIY84, SHI84*a*, SHI84*b*, SAK84, KAK84, and IWA84]. It is one of the two key components of a knowledge base machine (KBM). It provides relational database management

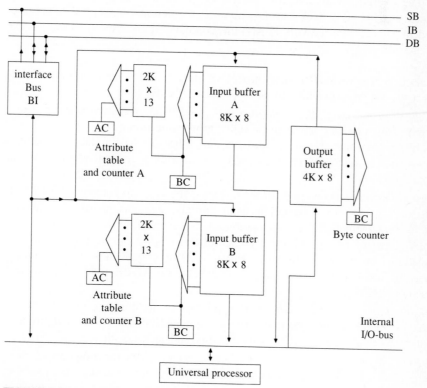

FIGURE 7.21
The structure of the interrecord processor (IRP). (*Source:* [SCH83])

support to the other component—the sequential inference machine (SIM)—which is a hardware system for processing the logic programming language, PROLOG.

Unlike other database machines that are designed to support only business data processing, DELTA's design is strongly influenced by the requirements of logic programming. In logic programming, the extensional knowledge is represented as a set of facts that can be stored as relations in a relational system. Whereas, the intensional knowledge is represented by rules that are used by an inference engine to draw logical inferences. Relations required to support logic programming contain very few attributes. These attributes are often accessed in a nondeterministic manner, that is, there are no fixed/known subsets of attributes through which tuples of relations are accessed. Thus, the traditional key-based database access methods and tuple-oriented data organization are unsuitable, and, instead, DELTA employs an attribute-based internal schema. Other features of DELTA include the use of a relational database engine (RDBE), which contains special-purpose hardware for sorting and merging data at high speeds. The sort-merge hardware forms the basis for all the relational algebraic operations and aggregation functions. DELTA also uses a large-capacity semiconductor memory as disk cache to increase the effective speed of the conventional disks.

The overall architecture of DELTA is shown in Figure 7.22. DELTA is intended to serve as a back-end to a number of inference machines' SIMs connected in a local area network (LAN) environment. It consists of the following components:

1. *Interface processor (IP)*. This processor manages interface functions to connect the database machine to an LAN and a Multibus.

2. *Control processor (CP)*. This processor provides a centralized control of distributed operations performed by separate working processors. It controls not only the data-intensive operations but also other database management functions such as recovery, security control, concurrency control, and transaction management.

3. *Relational database engine (RDBE)*. This is the key component of DELTA. It performs the relational operations using Sort and Merge as the basic operations. It is implemented by a combination of a general-purpose processor and a specialized processor. Multiple copies of this engine can be used to support relational operations as shown in Figure 7.22 by dotted lines. Two channels, one for input and one for output, connect each RDBE to the hierarchical memory (HM).

4. *Maintenance processor (MP)*. This processor monitors the operations and status of other components to determine if any malfunction occurs and provides functions that enhance DELTA's reliability and serviceability.

5. *Hierarchical memory (HM)*. This component provides functions for storing, accessing, clustering, and maintaining relations stored on disks. It consists of a general-purpose processor as a controller, a large-capacity semiconductor memory as a disk cache, and large-capacity moving-head disks. High-speed

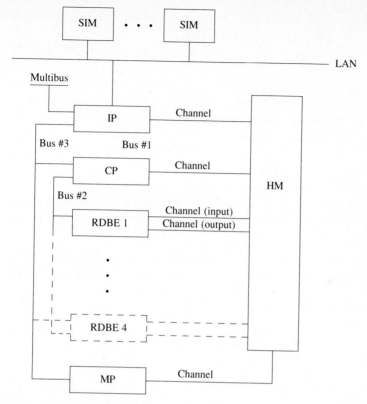

SIM: Sequential inference machine
IP: Interface processor
CP: Control processor
RDBE: Relational database engine
MP: Maintenance processor
HM: Hierarchical memory

FIGURE 7.22
The overall organization of DELTA. (*Source:* [SAK84] reprinted by permission of the authors.)

channels connect the HM to other system components. The RDBE(s) sees the HM as a large buffer with a very short latency and fast transfer speed.

6. *Buses.* Besides the LAN and Multibus, which connect DELTA to the host computers, there are three other system buses: the first connects the IP and CP (bus #1), the second connects the CP to all the RDBEs (bus #2), and the third connects the IP, CP, RDBEs, and MP (bus #3). In the implementation, IEEE-488 standard buses are used.

The RDBE is the main hardware component of DELTA and is described in some detail here. The configuration of RDBE is shown in Figure 7.23. It consists of the following modules:

1. *A general-purpose CPU with a main memory.* A 16-bit CPU is used as the controller.

2. *HM adapters.* Two adapters serve as interfaces between the RDBE and the HM.

3. *IN module.* This module transforms the input data into an internal format that is suitable for the sorters and the merger. The data transformation operations handled by this module include reordering data fields, converting data types, and generating null value signals to the sorter.

4. *Sorter.* This is a special-purpose machine that implements a two-way merge-sort algorithm to produce sorted relation tuples. The sorter consists of twelve sorting cells and a sorting checker whose functions will be explained later.

5. *Merger.* This is a special-purpose machine that performs external sorting and relational database operations using algorithms that are based on a two-way merge operation.

The DT, PT, NL, and DP lines shown in the figure stand for data lines, parity lines, null lines, and a duplicate line, respectively. The null line is used

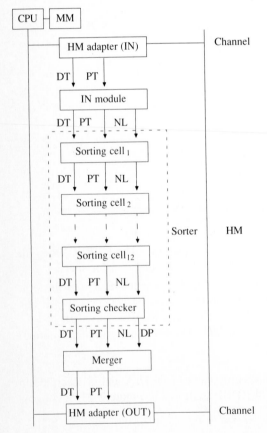

FIGURE 7.23
The organization of RDBE. (*Source:* [KAK84] reprinted by permission of the authors.)

to signal to a sorting cell that a tuple with a null value key is on the data lines. The duplicate line is used to signal to the merger that there is a tuple having the same key value as the subsequent one on the data lines.

The sorter itself consists of a linear array of sorting cells (12 in the current implementation) and a sorting checker as shown in the figure. These cells operate in parallel in a pipelined fashion. There are two FIFO memories, a comparator, a control circuit, and a selector in each cell. The FIFOs are used to store two sorted sequences of tuples (transformed by the IN module) that are to be merged into a longer sequence. In the ascending (or descending) sort, the sorter compares the top elements of these FIFOs and the selector selects the smaller (or larger) element for output to the next cell. The operation of a cell on every two bytes of data (restricted by a 16-line data bus) consists of three cycles: one memory read from one short sequence, one memory read from the other short sequence, and one for the comparator to compare the two words and the selector to output the smaller (or larger) word. In the last cycle, the word sent from the previous sorting cell is stored in the memory. It is reported that each cycle takes 220 nsec, and the two-byte merge operation takes 660 nsec [SAK84]. The sorter performs the internal sort; all tuples to be sorted are stored in the memories. The maximum number of tuples that can be processed by the sorter is restricted to $\min(2 ** N, (M/L))$, where N is the number of sorting cells, M is the memory size of the last sorting cell (64K bytes), and L is the tuple length.

During the sorting process, the sorting checker compares the key field of each tuple with that of the next tuple. It verifies the result to ensure the reliability of the sorter. It also generates a duplicate signal to the merger when the values are the same. The signal is used by the merger in carrying out different relational operations.

The merger is the key component of the RDBE, which performs relational operations. It operates similarly to the merge sorter, since all operations carried out by it are based on the two-way merge-sort. The organization of the merger is shown in Figure 7.24. It consists of two sections: an operation section and an output section. The main components of the operation section are (1) two 64K-byte FIFO memories (named U-memory and L-memory) for storing sorted data streams provided by the sorter, (2) a 1K word × 10-bit ROM table that contains control information for performing various operations, (3) a comparator that compares the keys of the two tuples read from the two FIFOs, and (4) a command register that stores the command to be performed by the merger (e.g., the Join, Restriction, Sort, or Comparison command). The output control section consists of (1) two 16K-byte tuple memories for storing the two tuples operated on by the operation section, (2) two field-reordering circuits for reordering the fields of the corresponding tuples, (3) two data-type-transformation circuits for converting data types, (4) two field-selection circuits for selecting fields of these tuples, (5) a new tuple identifier generator for adding a tuple identification to an output tuple, (6) a selector that transfers the tuple to the HM adapter, and (7) an output sequence controller that controls the operations of this section.

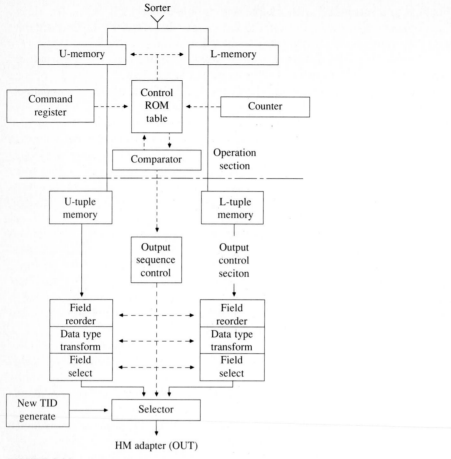

FIGURE 7.24
The organization of merger. (*Source:* [IWA84] reprinted by permission of the authors.)

The remainder of Section 7.2.2.4 will examine how this merger implements some basic operations. The algorithms for these operations are taken from a paper by Shibayama et al. [SHI84b].

1. *Simple selection.* This is a selection operation with a single qualification condition (e.g., student's age equal to, greater than, less than, or other relational operator) as a constant. This operation is carried out by placing the constant value on the top of the first FIFO and passing the stream of tuples to be selected through the second FIFO. The merger operation is performed on the data emerging from these two FIFOs. The selector outputs only those tuples that satisfy the selection condition.

2. *Range selection.* This selects tuples whose attribute values fall in a given

value range (e.g., $22 \leq AGE \leq 40$). This operation is carried out by placing the range values $V1$ and $V2$ in sorted order in the first FIFO and passing the attribute values to be selected (the target values that have been sorted by the sorter) through the second FIFO. The merger discards the target values until the top element exceeds $V1$, advances the first FIFO so that $V2$ now appears on the top, and outputs the target values until the top element of the second FIFO exceeds $V2$.

3. *Equi-join.* The Equi-join operation is performed using the following procedure. The first FIFO is filled with the values of the join attribute of one relation, and the second FIFO is filled with that of the second relation. The top two elements are compared. Assuming that the relations have been sorted in descending order, if the first FIFO contains the larger value, it is advanced to the second element. If the second FIFO contains the larger value, the second FIFO is advanced. If the two top elements are equal, both values are output, or in the case of a natural join, only one of them is output.

7.2.2.5 DDM. The Data-stream Database Machine, which we shall abbreviate as DDM, is designed and partially prototyped at the Hokkaido University in Sapporo, Japan, by Professor Y. Tanaka and his associates [TAN82]. It is an extension of an earlier work on a data flow database computer reported in [TAN80]. It is a relational database machine with the following distinct features:

1. It utilizes a highly parallel and functionally distributed architecture realized by the extensive use of VLSI technologies.
2. It employs a hardware encoding and decoding subsystem to transform data between the external representation, which has variable-length attributes and values, and the internal representation, which uses fixed-length attributes and values. This subsystem contains, among other components, a number of file processing modules for parallel searching of file segments distributed across many disk units.
3. A data-stream processing technique is used to overlap the processing of file segments by specialized function processors and the transfer of the file segments to these processors. The relation tuples contained in a file segment are sorted by a hardware sorter when they are passed among a number of specialized processors that perform various relational operations.

This subsection describes the DDM's abstract architecture, the encoding/decoding scheme and its hardware support, and the data-stream processing technique and associated hardware modules.

Abstract architecture. The abstract architecture of the DDM is shown in Figure 7.25. It consists of an encoder/decoder subsystem and a kernel database machine, which in turn consists of three subsystems: a tuple selection (TS) subsystem for selecting tuples that satisfy some selection conditions, a tuple construction (TC)

Kernel database machine

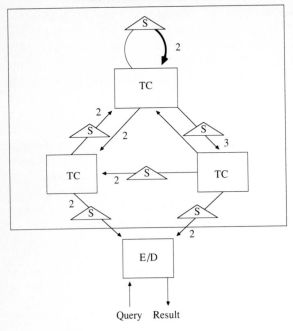

S: Sorter
TS: Tuple selection
TC: Tuple construction
AO: Aggregate operation
E/D: Encoder/decoder

FIGURE 7.25
An abstract architecture of DDM. (*Source:* [TAN82])

subsystem for converting a tuple identifier to a tuple with specified attributes and their values, and an aggregate operation (AO) subsystem for grouping tuples with the same value and performing aggregate functions over the groups formed. The subsystems of the kernel are indirectly connected to each other (or to itself in the case of TC) through a number of logical hardware sorters, which are realized by a number of physical sorters. Each sorter takes an unsorted file segment as input from a source subsystem and sorts the tuples in the segment over some specified attribute or tuple identifier before passing the sorted tuple stream to a target subsystem. Sorted segments of files are passed along (see Figure 7.25) during the execution of various relational database operations. The numbers labeling the sorters indicate the width of words handled by the sorter. A number 3 on the sorter between TC and AO means that the width of the tuple stream passed between them is limited to 3 times the width of an encoded word. A query issued to the DDM is first encoded by the encoder/decoder subsystem using the same encoding method that is applied to the data. The encoded query is processed by the kernel, and the results are decoded to the external data representation before passing them to the user on a terminal or to a host computer.

Encoding/decoding technique and encoder/decoder subsystem. In order to simplify the design and implementation of hardware systems that process data files and to conserve main memory space and secondary storage, a common practice employed by many database computers (e.g., CASSM and DBC) is the encoding of external data (usually variable in length) into some standardized internal format that has fixed-length data representation. The DDM also employs such a scheme. An obvious way of achieving this conversion is to set up a directory to contain the external representations of file names, attributes, and values and their corresponding internal representations. Thus, encoding and decoding operations can be carried out by directory look-ups. However, a directory look-up can be rather time-consuming if the number of directory entries is large. Also, the directory needs to be updated often to accommodate the new variable-length names or values entered into the system. Therefore, it is necessary to have a scheme for organizing the directory to allow fast encoding and decoding of data and to provide a flexible way of adding new data into it. The DDM adopts the extendible hashing technique proposed by Fagin, et al. [FAG79] (with some extensions) to encode and decode data.

In DDM, only the attributes and values of some selected data types (referred to as code types) are encoded. These data types are identification numbers (e.g., social security numbers), short character strings (e.g., names of students), and long character strings (e.g., textual descriptions of course contents). All attributes and values of these data types are replaced in a file by their corresponding encoded values and are stored in the secondary storage devices (disks). The coding technique used is as follows. For each attribute of a code type, two hash functions are used to transform a value of that attribute into a string of binary digits (see Figure 7.26). The first hash function, h_1, is an order-preserving hash function (i.e., $h_1(a) > h_1(b)$ if $a > b$). It transforms a value v into a binary number of length l_1. The second hash function, h_2, hashes the same value v into another bit string of length l_2. The concatenation of these two bit strings is the hash code of v with length, $l = l_1 + l_2$. This concatenated code and the extension code (to be explained next) shown in the figure form the encoded value of v. All attribute values that are hashed to the same hash code by h_1 form a group that has a binary tree associated with it. The binary tree is constructed by using the hash codes generated by h_2 for the values in that group. The leaves of the binary tree specify entries to a segment table that stores the disk addresses of the data segments. Each segment contains the original attribute values and some associated information of those values with the same $h_2(v)$. For example, assume that the values of course identifiers (CID) are to be encoded. The first hash function, h_1, can be specified simply as a range table that partitions the values of CID into a number of ranges (see Figure 7.27). In the example, the CIDs whose first letter falls into the range A to D form a group, E to K form another, and so on. The first range is represented

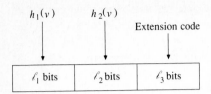

FIGURE 7.26
The structure of hash codes.

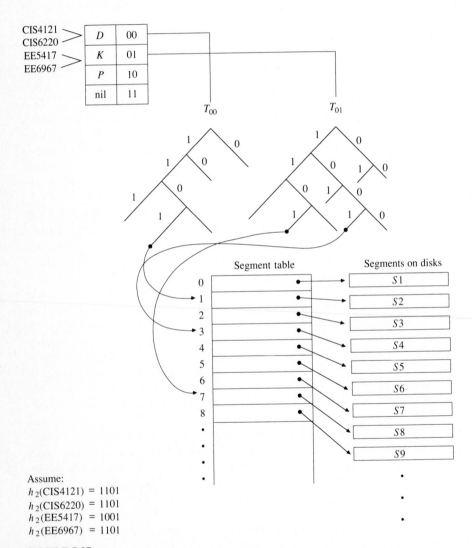

Assume:
$h_2(\text{CIS4121}) = 1101$
$h_2(\text{CIS6220}) = 1101$
$h_2(\text{EE5417}) = 1001$
$h_2(\text{EE6967}) = 1101$

FIGURE 7.27
A directory of segments.

by the binary value 00 which addresses a binary tree, and so on for the other ranges. The hash codes of these CIDs produced by h_2 are used to determine the proper leaves of the tree where the pointers to the segment table are stored. In the example, the course identifiers CIS4121 and CIS6220 are stored in segment $S2$, and EE5417 and EE6967 are stored in segments $S4$ and $S8$ respectively.

As the database expands and the number of distinct values of an attribute increases, it is possible for a segment to overflow. In this case, the segment is split into two by adding another level to its corresponding leaf node, and the values and their associated information in the original segment are distributed to these two segments according to their hash values. The extension code is used to uniquely identify the synonyms that have a common hash value. It can grow to l_3 bits, as illustrated in Figure 7.26. The values in a segment are not necessarily arranged in sorted order. Each segment consists of an entry portion and a record portion. The entry portion stores the concatenated hash codes (length l) and a pointer to the record portion. The hash codes stored in the segment table are directly addressable by the last l_2 bits of the concatenated hash codes. The pointer points to a list of synonymous values, their extension codes, and so forth stored in the record portion.

To verify if a given value is in the encoding directory, it is first hashed by the h_1 and h_2 functions associated with its attribute. A proper binary tree is located based on the h_1 hash code and the tree is searched, based on the h_2 hash code, to determine the proper segment address stored in the segment table. The segment is then fetched from the disk. The concatenated hash code is searched in the entry portion of the segment, and the pointer is taken to locate the list of synonyms stored in the record portion. The list is sequentially searched to check for the given value.

Using this encoding and decoding scheme, every attribute in a database whose data type is one of the three code types (i.e., identification number, short character string, and long character string) is replaced by its encoded value. Query processing is performed on these encoded values, and the results of the query are decoded to their original values by the encoder/decoder subsystem.

To support these encoding and decoding functions, DDM uses two basic hardware techniques: the distribution of encoding/decoding functions to a number of specialized function processors and the use of a number of file processors to do parallel search and processing of the encoding directory. These processors are connected to form the encoder/decoder subsystem shown in Figure 7.28. The subsystem consists of a directory processor and a number of file processors interconnected by a common bus. The directory processor is composed of a controller and a number of specialized function processors. Inputs to the controller are a transaction identification, a command code specifying a search or an insertion, and an attribute code (A) and a value (v) that is to be encoded or an attribute code and an encoded value (e.g., which is represented by a hash code and extension) that is to be decoded. The attribute code is converted into a subtype code by the subtype table searcher. The subtype code is used to locate the range table, which partitions the values of the attribute into groups. A range table searcher is used

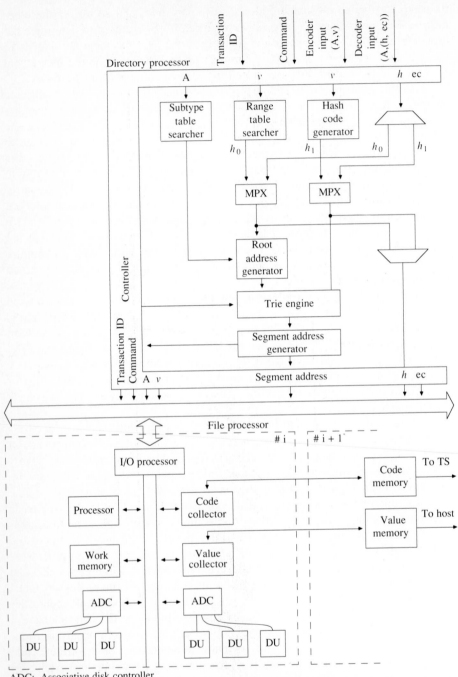

ADC: Associative disk controller
DU: Disk unit

FIGURE 7.28
The architecture of the encoder/decoder subsystem. (*Source:* [TAN82])

to search the range table for the hash value $h_1(v)$. A hash code generator is used to compute the $h_2(v)$ value, the second portion of the hash code. A root address generator uses the subtype code and $h_1(v)$ to determine the root address of the binary trie that encodes the values in a group. The root address and the $h_2(v)$ value are sent to the trie engine which uses the $h_2(v)$ value to traverse the trie to identify the pointer to the segment table described previously. A segment address generator uses the pointer to access the segment address on a disk from the table. The address is then passed to a proper file processor for fetching the segment.

A file processor is in itself an elaborate subsystem. It consists of the following main components:

1. An I/O processor serves as an interface to the common bus.
2. A processor unit, which accesses the segment into the work memory, searches the entry portion using the concatenated hash value to find the pointer to the list of synonyms. In the case of encoding a value, the processor searches the list for the original value v. The extension code associated with v is accessed and stored together with the transaction identification in a code memory. The code and the identification are read by a code collector. In the case of decoding an encoded value, the list of synonyms are searched and the stored extension codes are matched against the extension part of the encoded value. Once a match is found, the corresponding original value v is accessed into the value memory together with the transaction identification. The value and the transaction identification are read by the memory collector.
3. A disk subsystem that consists of an associative disk controller and a number of disk units is another main component. It is proposed that double actuator disk units be used to reduce the seek time and latency time. A cache memory is used for each read/write head, as illustrated in Figure 7.29. The direct

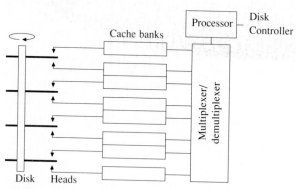

FIGURE 7.29
A disk unit with a cache bank for each head. (*Source:* [TAN82])

connection of each head to a disk cache allows the contents of a cylinder to be read in parallel. These memory units are connected to a dedicated processor through a multiplexer/demultiplexer. The processor manages and accesses the disk caches and communicates with the disk controller. It is suggested that some associative search functions be built into the disk controller to improve its processing capability.

Data-stream processing and the kernel database machine. In a functionally distributed system such as the DDM, large quantities of data often need to be transferred from one function processor to another. If data are transferred sequentially and the transfer time cannot overlap with the processing time, then the performance of the system will be rather poor. The so-called data-stream processing allows for the overlapping of processing with sequential data transfer. The components of the DDM are designed to achieve such an overlap. The algorithms for relational database operations are also designed to take advantage of this type of processing.

To illustrate how the relational selection and join are performed in this system, assume that $R1(A1, A2, A3)$ and $R2(B1, B2, B3)$ are two relations. TID1 and TID2 are two attributes that are added to these two relations respectively. The values of these attributes uniquely identify their tuples. Some attributes of relations in a database are designated as index attributes for which indices are built for direct access of tuples containing a specific value. To perform a relational operation, a continuous stream of tuples is passed through the key components of the kernel. Each component operates on the stream, transforms as required, and passes the transformed stream of tuples onto the next component. For example, the selection of $R1$ tuples satisfying the condition $A1 = $ 'a' and the projection of these tuple over $A2$ and $A3$ would take the following steps:

1. The encoder/decoder subsystem encodes the value 'a' and outputs the encoded value to TS (see Figure 7.25).
2. TS searches the tuples of $R1$ for those tuples whose encoded $A1$ value equals 'a'. TC projects the resulting tuples over TID1, the added attribute, and outputs the resulting relation $S1$ to TC through a sorter, which sorts $S1$ on TID1.
3. TC joins the sorted $S1$ with the original relation $R1$ and projects the result over $A2$ and $A3$. The resulting relation, $S2$, is sorted on $A2$ and $A3$ and sent to AO.
4. AO removes the duplicates from the sorted $S2$ and outputs the result to the encoder/decoder. The decoded data are then transferred to the source of the query.

In the second example, an equi-join is performed between selected tuples of $R1$, where $A1 = $ 'a', and all tuples of $R2$, over the join attributes $A2$ and $B1$. The result is projected over $A2$, $A3$, and $B3$. The following steps illustrate the execution of this query.

1. TS selects those tuples of $R1$ whose $A1$ values equal 'a' and projects over TID1. The resulting relation $S1$ is sorted and passed to TC.

2. TC joins the sorted $S1$ with the original relation $R1$ and projects over $A2$ and TID1. The resulting relation $S2$ is sorted by a sorter and sent back to TS.

3. TS joins the sorted $S2$ with $R2$ over ($A2 = B1$) and projects the result over TID1 and TID2. The result of projection is named $S3$. It contains a set of pairs of TID1 and TID2 and is sorted enroute to TC.

4. TC projects $R1$ over TID1, $A2$ and $A3$ and joins the resulting relation with the sorted $S3$. The result is projected over TID2, $A2$, and $A3$. The resulting relation is named $S4$. Now $S4$ is split into two relations $S5[@,A2,A3]$ and $S6[@, \text{TID2}]$ where @ is a special attribute to keep track of the tuple counts of the tuples of $S4$. The reason for this split is that the word width for the sorter between each pair of the three subsystems TS, TC, and AO is restricted to twice or three times the width of an encoded word (see Figure 7.25). Since we need to join $S4$ and $R2$ over their TID2 to get $B3$ for the output, and since the word width of the sorter connecting TC to itself is twice the width of an encoded word, the split allows $S6$ (which has only two attributes) to be sorted by the sorter. The sorted $S6$ is given to TC at step 5, and $S5$ is passed to AO in step 6.

5. TC projects $R2$ over TID2 and $B3$ and joins the result with the sorted $S6$ over TID2. A projection over $[@, B3]$ is taken to produce the resulting relation $S7$, which is again sorted enroute to AO.

6. AO joins $S5$ with the sorted $S7$ over the attribute @ and projects the resulting relation over $A2$, $A3$, and $B3$ to get the output attributes needed for output. It then removes duplicates from the result of projection and outputs the remaining tuples to the encoder/decoder.

This process appears to be a complicated way of performing a simple query. However, the main reason for these steps is to replace the time-consuming "strict" Join operation by a number of so-called linear joins. In these steps, each Join is performed between a relation and a sorted relation. Thus, they can be performed in one scan of the two relations. This simplifies the specialized hardware and allows data-stream processing to be carried out on the data passed between them.

The subsystems of the kernel database machine are designed around two main hardware components: a search engine and a sort engine. Their designs are given in detail by Tanaka [TAN82]. Their key components will be described here. The search engine is a data-stream processing hardware that searches a set of sorted keywords for a given input key. The set of sorted keywords is organized in a left-sided binary trie, as illustrated by Figure 7.30. The loading of the keywords 3, 4, 7, ..., etc. into the trie follows the order 0, 1, 2, ..., marked by labeled circles in the figure. To search for an input key, say 28, the trie is traversed by taking the right or left branches, according to the result of the comparison between the input key and the stored key at each node, until a leaf node is reached. A null value at a node is assume to be a very large value. The concatenation of the binary digits forms the address of a table where the tuple containing the key

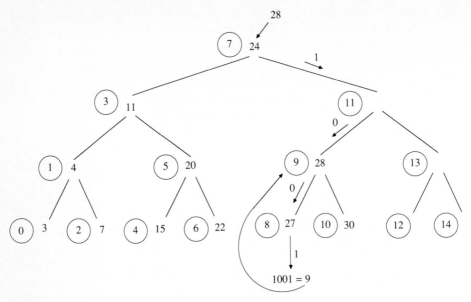

FIGURE 7.30
Trie traversing in a search engine. (*Source:* [TAN82])

can be found. The engine is used to support the selection, linear join, insertion, and deletion operations handled by the TS subsystem and the tuple construction, duplicate removal, group-by operation, and set operation of the TC subsystem.

The sort engine uses the heap-sort algorithm to sort a stream of keys. A *heap* is a binary trie with the keys stored on each path from the root to a leaf in sorted order. The sort engine constructs such a binary trie during the input keys. Keys are added to a heap starting from the root in left-to-right order. A heap of L levels will hold $2**L - 1$ keys. During the output phase, the root is first output. A hole is created at the root. The hardware circuit compares its left and right sons to determine which key should be moved up to fill the hole. In so doing, a new hole is created at the next level. The same comparison is carried out at the next level. The process of outputting keys from the root and moving keys up to the root continues until all the keys in the heap have been sent out.

The hardware implementations of these two engines are similar. They consist of a linear array of special circuits, each of which has a local memory and manages the keys of one level of a binary trie stored in it. Prototypes of these two engines have been constructed using discrete logic circuits. Each has 12 levels and a 16-bit word width. It is reported by Tanaka [TAN82] that the prototype search engine can input a search table with 4,095 keywords in 4 ms, and can search input keys at the rate of $10**6$ keys per second. The prototype sort engine can sort 4,095 keys in 16 ms. It is expected by the designer that the VLSI implementation of these engines will be 10 times faster than their prototypes.

7.2.2.6 CADAM. The Content-Addressable Database Access Machine (CADAM) is another Japanese database machine effort undertaken by the OKI Electric Industry Company in Tokyo [HIK81]. It is a relational database machine that is to be used as a back-end processor to a host computer. The system has the following features:

1. It uses a cache memory to buffer the data read from a moving-head disk for content search by a number of processing elements.
2. Tuples of a relation are clustered based on the value ranges of some selected attributes and are physically placed together on disks for fast I/O.
3. The functions of selection and projection are distributed to an array of processing elements, whereas the functions of join, set operations, and aggregation operations are handled by a separate processor. These processors can operate on data concurrently, thus achieving overlapping of these functions.
4. Transactions are queued, and their executions are reordered on the basis of disk access efficiency. By this method, a transaction that requests a physical data access unit (PAU) closest to the present disk head position is executed first.

The clustering technique will be detailed next as will be the hardware architecture of CADAM for supporting these techniques. The attributes of a relation in this system are partitioned into two categories: clustering and nonclustering attributes. The possible values of a clustering attribute are divided into a number of predefined ranges. A relation is partitioned into a number of segments, each of which contains records whose values of a clustering attribute fall in a given range. If there is more than one clustering attribute defined for a relation, each segment will contain all the records that satisfy a combination of these attribute ranges. Each segment may contain a different number of records (or tuples) of a relation. A segment is stored on the disk in one or more fixed-length PAUs. Thus, records with similar contents are physically clustered together. Furthermore, CADAM clusters those PAUs belonging to the segments defined by adjacent attribute ranges.

To retrieve data from the database, the clustering attribute(s) and value(s) provided in the query are used to determine the segment that may contain tuples satisfying the search conditions. This process involves some table look-up(s) to search the predefined attribute ranges and to access the corresponding segment number. A mapping table is used to convert from a segment number to a PAU number or numbers. Independently retrieved PAU numbers for each search condition specified in the query are logically ANDed or ORed based on the Boolean conditions of the query to determine the final set of PAUs. These PAUs are then accessed from disks, and their contents are searched by an array of processing elements in an associative manner for those tuples satisfying the search.

The hardware organization of CADAM is shown in Figure 7.31. CADAM consists of three processors: the interface processor (INP), the directory processor

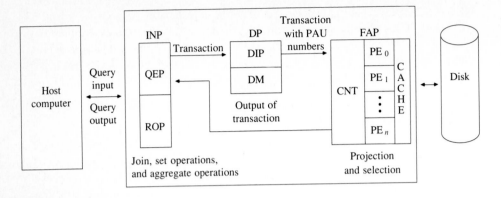

INP: Interface processor
DP: Directory processor
FAP: File access processor
QEP: Query processing submodule
ROP: Relational operations submodule
DIP: Directory processing submodule
DM: Directory memory submodule
CNT: Controller submodule
PE: Processing element submodule
CACHE: Cache memory submodule

FIGURE 7.31
Basic operation of CADAM. (*Source:* [HIK81] copyright ©1981. AFIPS, reprinted by permission of AFIPS Press.)

(DP), and the file access processor (FAP). The IP consists of the query processing submodule (QEP) and the relational operation submodule (ROP). The QP submodule receives a query from the host computer. It analyzes the query and decomposes it into a structure of basic database operations. Those operations, which involve the projection and/or selection on a single relation (called "transactions" in this system) are sent to the DP and FAP for processing. The selected and/or projected relation is further processed by the ROP submodule, which is responsible for carrying out operations such as join, set operations, and aggregate operations. The retrieval results of the query are sent to the host by the QEP.

The DP also consists of two submodules: a directory processing (DIP) submodule and a directory memory (DM) submodule. The DIP submodule uses a mapping table stored in the DM submodule to convert attribute value(s), provided in a transaction as the search condition, into PAU address(es). The address(es) is used by the FAP to fetch the physical unit(s), which contain tuples that may satisfy the search condition.

The FAP consists of a controller, an array of processing elements and a cache memory. The controller queues the transaction numbers and the PAU addresses received from the DP and selects one of the PAU addresses in the queue, which addresses a PAU that can be accessed in the shortest time, based on the current position of the read/write heads of the disk. This system reorders the sequence of transaction execution in order to gain speed in secondary storage accesses. The fetched PAU is stored in the cache memory, and a number of processing elements are dynamically assigned to carry out the selection and/or projection operations on the data. The results are sent to the QEP by the controller.

7.2.2.7 VLSI PROCESSORS.

Recent advances in large-scale integration (LSI) and very large-scale integration (VLSI) technologies has drastically changed the way computers are built and even the way computational problems are solved. These technologies allow thousands of devices to be fabricated on a single chip. Thus, a large amount of logic can be implemented very inexpensively using these technologies. These technologies have opened the door for building special-purpose processors cost efficiently and effectively. One of the design requirements for using VLSI technology is that the design of a device should be very regular, that is, the device should consist of a large number of identical or very similar cells (e.g., processing elements) interconnected in a regular structure. Each cell is very simple and, by itself, can perform a very limited calculation. For example, Figure 7.32 represents a general cell containing some logic and memory and a number of input and output lines. Data taken from the input lines and those stored in the memory are processed by the logic, and the results are sent out via the output lines. For example, the same input data may be sent out without any modification.

Although the computational capability of a single cell is usually very restricted, a number of such cells can be connected together in a regular structure to perform a complex computational task. Data produced by one cell can be passed to another cell in a pipelined fashion. Algorithms for solving complex problems can be formulated to take advantage of the structural characteristics and processing techniques applicable to these cells. In this subsection, we shall examine two cell interconnection structures (array and tree) that have been proposed for implementing database processors using the VLSI technology.

Systolic arrays. The systolic array approach was proposed by Kung of Carnegie-Mellon University as a cost-efficient way of solving a wide variety of computational problems, such as matrix computations [KUN79b], pattern matching

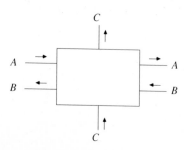

FIGURE 7.32
A processing cell.

[FOS80], signal and image processing [KUN80*b*, KUN81*a*, and KUN81*b*], transitive closure and dynamic programming [KUN79*a*], and database management [KUN80*a*].

In this approach, cells are connected in a linear (Figure 7.33*a*), orthogonal (Figure 7.33*b*), or other more complex structures. All the cells receive data, perform computations, and output data synchronously in each cycle, analogous to the cells in a heart—thus, the name, *systolic array*. More than one data stream can be moving at constant velocity inside an array. These data streams may interact with one another depending on the algorithm that the array is designed to perform. Systolic algorithms for relational database operations have been presented by Kung and Lehman [KUN80*a*]. In the notation used, relations are denoted by A, B, C, and so forth; the tuples of a relation, say relation A, are denoted by a_1, a_2, and so on; and values in a tuple a_i, are denoted by $a_{i,1}$, $a_{i,2}$, ... $a_{i,m}$, where where m is the number of elements in a tuple. A matrix T represents the results of logical operations. The entry $T_{i,j}$ denotes the result of comparing the ith element of a tuple in one relation with the jth element of a tuple of another relation. The notation $T_{i,j}(k)$ denotes the value of $T_{i,j}$ at time k.

Comparison of tuples of two relations. Let two relations be defined over the same set of domains or two sets of comparable domains, and compare two tuples of these two relations for equality. The tuples are fed to the linear array of cells from opposite ends (see Figure 7.34). The first elements of the tuple from each relation meet in the left-most cell. They are compared, and the result is ANDed with the TRUE input to produce the TRUE/FALSE output of the left-most cell. In the next cycle (time step), the output goes to the second left-most cell, where the second elements of each tuple meet. Each subsequent element of the tuple is fed and compared with the corresponding element of the tuple in the other relation at each

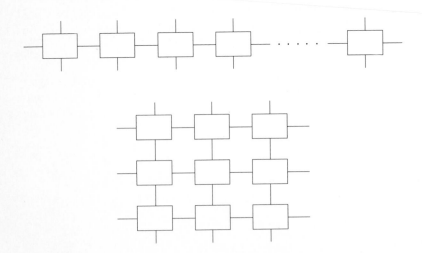

FIGURE 7.33
(*a*) A linear structure of cells. (*b*) An orthogonal structure of cells.

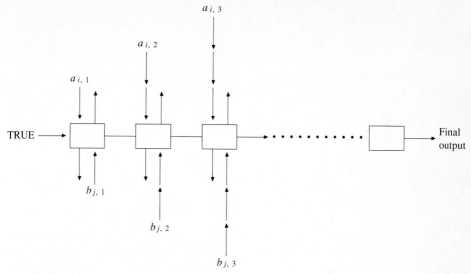

$a_{i,3}$

$a_{i,2}$

$a_{i,1}$

TRUE

$b_{j,1}$

$b_{j,2}$

$b_{j,3}$

FIGURE 7.34
Tuple comparison in a linear structure of cells.

succeeding time step. The final output is TRUE only if the two tuples compared
are identical.

Using the same technique in an orthogonal structure of cells, the tuples of two
relations can be compared simultaneously (see Figure 7.35). In this structure, the
tuples of relation A and B are fed to the two-dimensional array from top and bottom,
respectively. Here also the elements of tuple a_i will be fed at such times that
elements $a_{i,k}$ is one step ahead of $a_{i,k+1}$. Each tuple is two steps behind the tuple
that precedes it. The same operation is performed as illustrated in the linear case,
and the final results are produced by the cells in the right column. If the results
are accumulated in a matrix T, then the following equations hold:

$$T_{i,j} = \text{TRUE if } T_{i,j}(\text{initial}) = \text{TRUE and } a_{i,k} = b_{i,k} \text{for}$$
$$\text{all } k \text{in the range } 1 \leq k \leq m$$
$$= \text{FALSE otherwise}$$

Set intersection. Using the orthogonal structure described previously, the intersection of two relations defined over comparable domains can be performed
using the structure given in Figure 7.36. An accumulation array is added to the
right for storing the output from the comparison array. Based on the configuration shown in the figure, $a_{1,1}$ will meet $b_{1,1}$ at the third time step at cell
$C31$. The result of comparing tuples a_1 and b_1 will reach cell $M3$ at the sixth
time step. The inputs of each M cell are logically ORed (note that the initial
input to $M1$ is FALSE). From there, the result travels downward. At the ninth
time step, the output of $M5$ indicates whether a_1 and b_1 are equal or not and
should or should not be included in the resulting set intersection. A TRUE output indicates that the identical tuples should be included in the resulting relation.

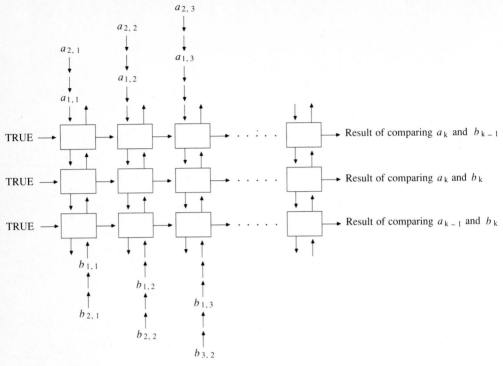

FIGURE 7.35
Tuple comparison in an orthogonal structure of cells.

Elimination of duplicates. This operation can be performed by feeding the same relation into both ends of an orthogonal structure and recording the output of the cells in the right-hand column in a matrix T. $T_{i,j}$ is TRUE if $T_{i,j}$(initial) is TRUE and $a_{i,k} = a_{j,k}$ for $1 \leq k \leq m$. $T_{i,j}$ is FALSE otherwise. In this matrix, the elements in the diagonal are all TRUE, and $T_{i,j}$ and $T_{j,i}$ are TRUE if $a_i = a_j$ for $i \neq j$. Thus, the matrix is symmetric. To eliminate the duplicate tuples of relation A, all tuples a_i corresponding to TRUE values in the lower (or upper) triangle of the matrix T must be removed. There are two ways to do this. One is to OR all the elements of each row of T in the lower triangle matrix (excluding the diagonal). The other is to set the diagonal and upper triangle elements to FALSE and then take the OR across the whole row. The diagonal and the upper triangle can be set to FALSE by setting the initial input of the corresponding rows of the comparison array to FALSE. To produce relation A' from A by eliminating the duplicates in A, the user eliminates tuples of A whose corresponding T_i is TRUE after ORing its elements by one of these methods.

Union. The union of relations A and B is formed by appending the tuples of B to those of A to produce the relation C. Relation C is then fed into both ends of the comparison array to remove the duplicates in it.

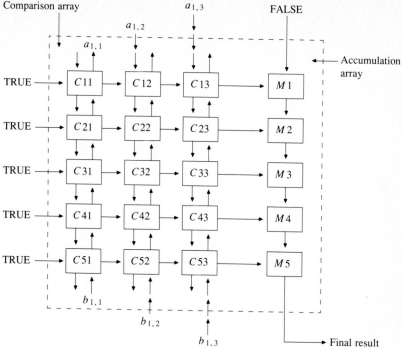

FIGURE 7.36
Cell configuration for set intersection.

Projection. The Projection operation is done by projecting over the selected attributes and feeding the projected result into both ends of the comparison array to eliminate duplicates.

Subtraction. $C = A - B$ is a relation whose tuples are those found in A but not in B. This operation can be carried out by using the output of the Intersection operation described previously. Recall that in the case of intersection, T_i is TRUE whenever a tuple a_i is present in both A and B. It is FALSE for any a_i present in A but not in B. The Subtraction operation can be carried out by simply inverting the output line of the accumulation array.

Join. Let relation C be the result of joining relations A and B over a common attribute X. A linear array of cells is used for this operation (see Figure 7.37). The attribute values of $A.X$ and $B.X$ denoted in the figure by a_{53}, b_{11}, and so forth are fed into the linear array from the two ends, respectively. These values are compared as they pass each other in the cells. The comparison results are given out as a matrix T where $T_{i,j}$ is TRUE if $A_i.X = B_j.X$ and FALSE otherwise. For every $T_{i,j} = $ TRUE, the corresponding A_i and B_j are retrieved and concatenated to form a tuple of C. One can extend this technique to perform

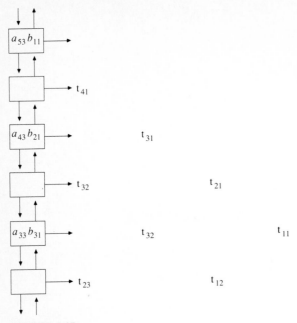

FIGURE 7.37
Cell configuration for a join operation.

the Join operation over composite domains by simply using multiple columns of cells.

A VLSI tree machine. Bentley and Kung designed a tree machine for searching data and performing storage operations in a single file [BEN79]. This machine was later extended for other database applications by Song [SON80 and SON81]. Its implementation using the VLSI technology has been studied. The overall system configuration of this machine is shown in Figure 7.38. The main component of this system is the tree machine. It is controlled by a tree controller and is used as a back-end processor to a host computer. The typical sequence of operations of this machine is as follows. Data retrieval and manipulation commands are submitted to the host computer, which transfers the commands to the tree controller. The controller uses some preestablished directories to determine the locations in the mass storage where the needed data reside. Data clustering in the mass storage is assumed. The tree controller then commands the the I/O controller to fetch the needed data and to load them into the tree machine. Once loaded, it issues commands to the tree machine to carry out the intended operations. The resulting data from the tree machine are returned to the host computer.

The structure of the tree machine. The tree machine itself has the structure of a mirrored tree (see Figure 7.39). It consists of three types of processing nodes: circles, squares, and triangles. The circles are organized in a binary tree structure with the root serving as the input processor for receiving data and/or commands from the tree controller. The function of these circles is to broadcast data and/or commands to their sons until they reach the square nodes. The square nodes have

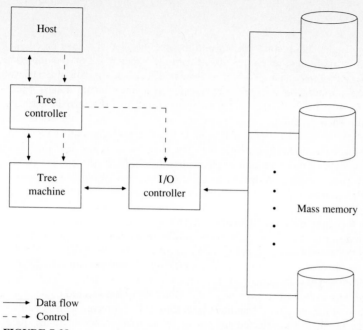

FIGURE 7.38

The overall system configuration of the tree machine. (*Source:* [SON80] ©1980 IEEE)

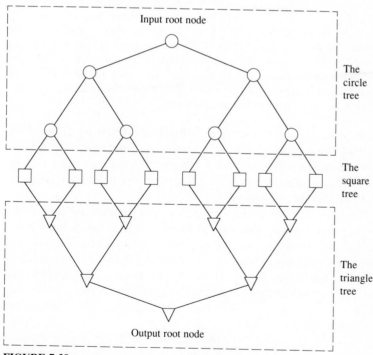

FIGURE 7.39

The structure of the tree machine. (*Source:* [SON80] ©1980 IEEE)

memory to store the data records loaded into the tree machine and have processing logic to carry out a limited repertoire of instructions. The actual data manipulation operations are performed in parallel in the square nodes and, in the case of a retrieval operation, the retrieved data records are transferred to the triangle nodes, which form the reflection of the circles. The triangles are again organized in a binary tree structure. Their function is to combine the results produced by the squares to obtain the final results. The root of the triangle tree serves as the output processor for transferring data to the tree controller. The three node types described here are special processors designed and implemented in VLSI for performing specific retrieval and data manipulation operations. The machine operates in a synchronized fashion. Different node types perform different functions in synchronized time steps.

Algorithms for some database operations. This subsection examines how Selection, Join, and storage operations (Insertion and Deletion) can be carried out in this machine. In the case of a selection operation, records to be selected are preloaded into the memory of the square nodes. A complex query may contain a number of search conditions. They are broadcast down the circle tree one following the other to the square nodes. The squares do the comparison against their stored data records and keep track of the conditions that have been satisfied. If a record satisfies all the conditions given, then it is selected for output to the triangle nodes. If the query asks only for a count of the records that satisfy the search conditions, each square would simply keep a count and output it instead of the records themselves. In either case, the triangle nodes would combine the results by either taking the union of the output records or summing the counts to produce the final result. If more than one square node has records that satisfy the search conditions, they are sent to the triangle nodes in turn at different time steps. In the Selection operation, all the N square nodes of the tree machine (N is a power of two) can receive a search condition initiated by the input root node in $O(\log N)$ time, and it takes the same time for an output of a square node to reach the output root of the triangle tree. If the multiple search conditions are pipelined, the time for the Selection operation would be linear in the number of search conditions.

In addition to the Selection operation, it has been shown by Bentley and Kung [BEN79] that many other search operations (e.g., finding a member of a set, counting the number of occurences of an element in a multiset—that is, a set with duplicated elements, finding the nearest neighbor of a given element, etc). can be easily and efficiently implemented.

The Join operation is a more complicated one. A procedure for performing the operation is proposed by Song [SON80] as follows. It is assumed that the join is to be performed over two relations whose tuples, tuples identifications, and relation identifications (which constitute the A-tuples and B-tuples) are arbitrarily scattered in N square nodes (see Figure 7.40). It is further assumed that the tree controller has an associative memory of the kind presented in Chapter 5 for storing and searching $\log N$ entries of tuples and their identifications. These entries are to be used for forming the join results.

First, a command is broadcast down the circle tree to all the squares instructing those that hold A-tuples to send out their tuples and tuple identifications (referred to as A-information) to their triangle nodes. After $\log N$ time steps, the first

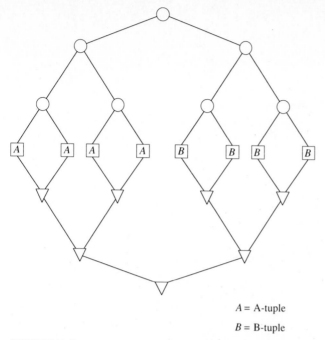

A = A-tuple

B = B-tuple

FIGURE 7.40
Two relations residing in the tree machine. (*Source:* [SON80] ©1980 IEEE)

A-information will reach the output triangle node and the rest of the A-information will emerge from the root node in a pipelined fashion. The A-information is then stored in the associative memory of the controller. The A-tuples and the attribute values, over which the Join is to be performed, are redirected to the circle tree to be broadcast down to the squares. These data are denoted as a-information in Figure 7.41, which illustrates the rebroadcasting process. This time, all squares that contain the original A-information will simply ignore the a-information until the Join is completed. Whereas, all squares that hold the B-information are instructed to compare the a-attribute value against each b-attribute value of its B-tuples. If the Join condition is satisfied, each B square will send out its B-tuples in turn, together with the received A-tuple identification (or B-information), to their corresponding triangle nodes. This B-information would descend the triangle nodes in a pipelined fashion. In log N steps, the first B-information will emerge from the output root, which transfers the result to the controller. The associated A-tuple identification of each piece of B-information is used to search the associative memory for fetching the stored A-tuple. Concatenation of the A-tuple with the B-tuple will form the desired join tuple for output to the host computer.

In the triangle tree, the outputting of the A-information in the first pass may conflict with the outputting of the B-information during the second pass, since the output process is done in a pipelined fashion (see Figure 7.42). During the output process, a higher priority is given to the outputting of the B-information. This is because each a-information may generate many B-information outputs,

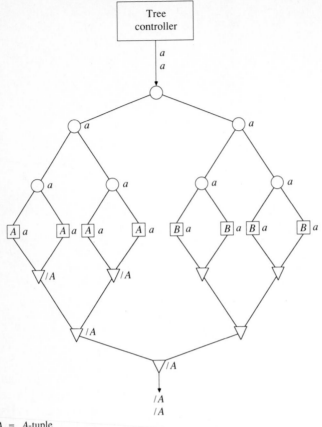

A = A-tuple

B = B-tuple

/A = A-information

a = a-information

FIGURE 7.41
The rebroadcasting of a-information. (*Source:* [SON80] ©1980 IEEE)

therefore, it is important to empty the *B*-information to allow the controller to perform the final concatenation of *A*-tuples and *B*-tuples.

Two different versions of insertion and deletion algorithms have been proposed by Bentley and Kung [BEN79] and Song [SON80], respectively. Song's method will be described here. For both insertion and deletion, it is assumed that the tree controller keeps a pool of "free squares"—that is, squares that currently do not contain data records—and a pointer FIRSTFREE, which specifies the first free square for insertion of a new data record. Each square node is assumed to contain two fields: a Node.Freeposition and a Node.Content. If a square is free, its Node.Freeposition will contain an integer from 0 to $N - 1$ to specify the square number of the next free square. To insert a new record X, the controller will generate an insert instruction that contains the free position for insertion and the content to be inserted. The instruction is broadcast to all the squares. The one addressed by the Freeposition value will store the broadcast content and set its Freeposition value to null. The controller will reset the FIRSTFREE pointer to point to the next free square in the free square pool.

To delete a record from a square, the content of the record is broadcast to all the squares together with the location of the current free square specified

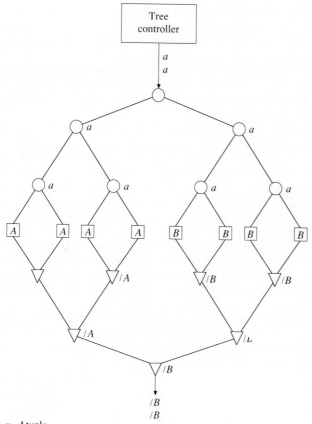

A = A-tuple

B = B-tuple

$/A$ = A-information

$/B$ = B-information

a = a-information

FIGURE 7.42

Pipelining the input and output of A and B tuples. (*Source:* [SON80] ©1980 IEEE)

by the FIRSTFREE counter. The square whose Node.Content matches the given record is the one to be deleted. It sets the Node.Content field to null and the Node. Freeposition field to the location of the free square provided in the deletion instruction. The FIRSTFREE content is reset by the controller to the square just deleted (freed) to maintain the pool of free squares.

Implementation considerations. This tree machine is designed for implementation using VLSI technology. One of the key considerations is the pin limitation problem. A VLSI chip can contain a considerable number of processing elements. However, each chip has a very limited number of pins for connecting to other chips or external devices. To overcome the pin-out problem, the designers of the machine propose to use the bit-serial, shift register technology of VLSI to implement the tree processors [BEN79]. Data and/or commands going in or coming out of a chip are transmitted in bit-serial fashion to reduce the pin requirement. Memory words needed in the various types of processing nodes are implemented using shift registers. Another consideration is the mapping of the mirrored tree on a chip. It is proposed that the user first unmirror the tree and then lay out a binary tree on a chip using the space-economical layout technique introduced by Bentley and Kung [BEN79] as illustrated in Figure 7.43.

Since a chip can fit only a small number of processors (the circles, squares, and triangles), a number of chips will be needed to implement a tree machine. The packaging of chips is therefore an important consideration. It is proposed by Bentley and Kung [BEN79] that two kinds of chips be constructed to implement the tree machine: the leaf chips and the internal chips. The leaf chips contain, as estimated, 16 squares, 15 circles, and 15 triangle nodes (see Figure 7.44). Each leaf chip has only 2 wires for input and output purposes. Thus, only 2 communication pins will be needed for data transmission. This leaves room for increasing the number of processing elements on a leaf chip as VLSI technology advances without being bounded by pin limitations. The internal chips can be constructed with 7 circles and 7 triangles on them. In this configuration, there will be a pair of input-output wires at the top of the chip and 8 pairs at the bottom (see Figure 7.45). The internal chips will be pin-bound even in today's fabrication technology.

Besides the hardware implementation considerations discussed here, many timing considerations for controlling the pipelining operations of the tree machine have been studied and discussed by Song [SON80 and SON81]. Interested readers should refer to these works for more information.

7.3   ANALYSIS

This section provides the analyses of the four representative database operations in the abstract models for systems that use a dedicated database computer and systems that use functionally specialized processors. Important performance parameters of some selected algorithms for these operations will be identified, and cost formulas in terms of execution or response time will be derived. The general assumptions made for the analysis in Chapter 2 are used in this chapter.

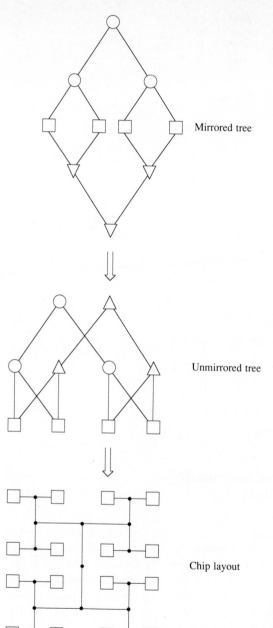

Mirrored tree

Unmirrored tree

Chip layout

FIGURE 7.43
Chip layout for a tree machine. (*Source:* [BEN79] ©1979 IEEE)

Input   Output
pin   pin

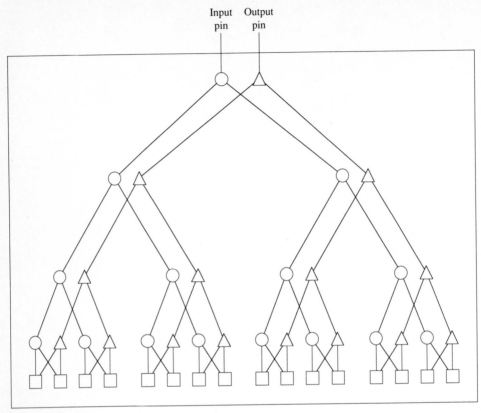

FIGURE 7.44
A leaf chip. (*Source:* [BEN79]   ©1979 IEEE)

7.3.1   An Abstract Model for Functionally Distributed Systems with a Dedicated Database Computer

The abstract model for this category of database machines is shown in Figure 7.46. It consists of a terminal, a host computer, a high-speed dedicated database computer, and a disk. A user's query is submitted through the terminal to the host computer. It is compiled and transformed into an internal structure suitable for the dedicated database computer. The internal structure of the query is then passed to the dedicated database computer for execution. It is assumed that the dedicated computer has an accelerator that can process data much faster than a conventional processor. The speed of the accelerator is modeled by an acceleration factor denoted by acc_fac, which is a real value between 0 and 1. The value is multiplied with the processing time of a conventional computer to account for the effect of acceleration. Acc_fac = 1 means no acceleration, and acc_fac = 0 means infinite acceleration. During the execution of each primitive operation of the query, the referenced relation(s) or data file(s) stored on the disk is accessed and

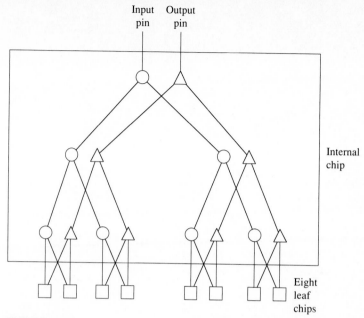

Input pin   Output pin

Internal chip

Eight leaf chips

FIGURE 7.45
An internal chip. (*Source:* [BEN79] ©1979 IEEE)

processed. The resulting relation of the operation is either transferred to the host computer for output to the user's terminal or written back (in the case of update) to the disk. A communication interface is necessary between the host computer and the dedicated database computer since the dedicated database computer is an independent computer system and typically has an interface to connect to an arbitrary host computer. It is assumed that queries and data passed between these two systems need to be transformed to suit the structural or format requirements of these two systems.

7.3.2 Analyses of Algorithms

As before, the cost formulas will be derived for the four representative database operations: Select, Join, Statistical Aggregation, and Update. Table 7.2 gives a list of basic parameters used in the analyses.

7.3.2.1 SELECT. The selection command is received by the host computer, which compiles it and transforms the compiled output to some internal structure suitable for the dedicated computer. The query structure is then transferred to the dedicated computer for execution. The instruction flow time is

$$t[\text{inst\_flow}] = t[\text{comp}] + t[\text{trans}] + t[\text{tp\_xfer}]$$

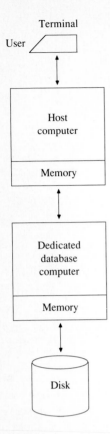

FIGURE 7.46
An abstract model for systems with a dedicated database computer.

Since the dedicated database computer is just another conventional computer with an accelerator for improving its processing speed, the analysis of the select algorithm and those for the other subsequent algorithms are similar to the ones presented in Chapter 2 except that the acceleration factor, acc_fac, is included in the cost formulas. The time required to read q pages of the referenced relation R by the dedicated computer is

$$t[\text{read\_q\_pg},R] = q * t[\text{I/O}]$$

The time necessary to process q pages of R is

$$t[\text{proc\_q\_pg},R] = q * t * t[\text{proc\_tuple},R] + q * t * sel\_fac * t[\text{mov}]$$

where $t[\text{proc\_tuple}, R] = x * \text{acc\_fac} * (2 * t[s] + t[\text{cpu}])$.

The time required to output all the selected pages to the disk has been derived in the conventional system model as $t[\text{I/O}, L]$.

The total data processing time for m pages of R is therefore

$$t[\text{process}] = 2 * t[\text{access}] + (m/q) * \{t[\text{read\_q\_pg},R] \\ + t[\text{proc\_q\_pg},R]\} + t[\text{I/O}, L]\}$$

TABLE 7.2
Performance parameters

Parameter	Definition
R	Name of a referenced relation
m	Number of pages in relation R
S	Name of the inner relation in a join operation
s	Number of pages in relation S
L	The resulting relation of an operation
acc_fac	An acceleration factor of a dedicated database computer
c_fac	Collision factor; a value greater than 1 to account for the extra processing needed due to collisions in hashing
d	Number of S pages necessary to produce one page of L when they are joined with one tuple of R
jn_fac	Join selectivity factor; i.e., the ratio of the number of tuples of L to the number of tuples of the cross-product between R and S
$n1$	Number of entries in an attribute information table
$n2$	Number of cylinders to be searched for producing one page of output
nc	Number of cylinder addresses retrieved by the structure memory
psize	Page size in bytes
p	Number of processing elements
q	Number of tracks in a disk cylinder
r	Average time interval for producing one page of output
sel_fac	Selectivity factor for the selection operation; i.e., the ratio of the number of selected tuples of a referenced relation to the number of tuples of that relation
t	Number of tuples per page of R or S
u	Total number of pages of L produced by joining relations R and S
w	Number of distinct categories in statistical aggregation
x	Number of attributes involved in selection conditions or number of category attributes
$x1$	Number of indexed predicates
$t[access]$	Disk seek time plus latency
$t[comp]$	Compilation time for a simple query

TABLE 7.2
Performance parameters (*Continued*)

Parameter	Definition
t[cpu]	Time for comparing two values in registers or an arithmetic operation
t[hash]	Time for performing a hash function over an attribute or value
t[I/O]	Track (page) read/write time
t[mov]	Time for moving a tuple of R or S
t[msg]	Time for transferring a sort message between two processors
t[s]	Time to load a value from the memory to a register
t[tp_out]	Time for transferring one tuple to a terminal
t[trans]	Time for transforming a compiled query or a data page
t[xfer]	Time for transferring a page between two processors

where $2 * t$[access] accounts for the seek time and latency time for the reading of the first page of R and for the writing of the first page of L.

This process will produce ceil(sel_fac $* m$) output pages of the resulting relation L. The collection of the pages of L consists of (1) the reading of the pages of L from the disk, (2) the transformation and transfer of these pages of L to the host, and (3) the output of all the tuples of L to the user's terminal. The total data collection time is

$$
\begin{aligned}
t[\text{data\_collect}] = {} & [\text{access}] + \text{ceil}(\text{sel\_fac} * m) \\
& * \{t[\text{I/O}] + t[\text{xfer}] + t[\text{trans}]\} \\
& + m * t * sel\_fac * t[\text{tp\_out}]
\end{aligned}
$$

Without considering the possible overlap in the above time components, the total execution time for this algorithm is

$$t[\text{Select}] = t[\text{inst\_flow}] + t[\text{process}] + t[\text{data\_collect}]$$

7.3.2.2 JOIN. This section considers the same join algorithms used in the conventional system model presented in Chapter 2, namely the nested-loop–join algorithm and the sort-merge–join algorithm.

Nested-loop–join algorithm. Similar to the select algorithm described above, the instruction flow time is

$$t[\text{inst\_flow}] = t[\text{comp}] + t[\text{trans}] + t[\text{tp\_xfer}]$$

The times for reading a page of R and q pages of S are the same as those derived for the conventional system model. They are $t[\text{read\_pg}, R]$ and $t[\text{read\_q\_pg}, S]$, respectively.

The time required for joining these pages is

$$t[\text{jn\_Rpg\_Sq}] = t * q * t * acc\_fac * \{2 * t[\text{s}] + t[\text{cpu}] + jn\_fac * 2 * t[\text{mov}]\}$$

which is similar to the expression given in Section 2.3.2.

Including the reading of one R page, the reading of the pages of S, and the processing of this page against all s pages of S, the total time for processing one page of R is

$$t[\text{proc\_pg}, R] = t[\text{read\_pg}, R] + (s/q) \\ * \{t[\text{read\_q\_pg}, S] \\ + t[\text{jn\_Rpg\_Sq}]\}$$

The time necessary for writing the output pages of the resulting relation L is

$$t[\text{write\_j1}, L] = u * t[\text{I/O}]$$

where $u = \text{ceil}((jn\_fac * s * t * m * t)/(t/2))$ is the number of output pages for joining R and S.

Including the writing of L, the total processing time to join m pages of R with all the pages of S is

$$t[\text{process}] = (2 + m) * t[\text{access}] + m * t[\text{proc\_pg}, R] + t[\text{I/O}, L]$$

where $(2 + m) * t[\text{access}]$ accounts for the seek and latency times for the reading of the pages of relation R, the reading of the pages of relation S (m times), and for the writing of the pages of L.

The data collection time consists of (1) the reading of the pages of L from the disk to the main memory and (2) the transformation and transfer of these pages to the host for output to the user's terminal.

$$t[\text{data\_collect}] = t[\text{access}] + u * t[\text{I/O}] + \\ t[\text{trans}] + t[\text{xfer}] + jn\_fac * \\ m * t * s * t * 2 * t[\text{tp\_out}]$$

The total execution time for this algorithm is

$$t[\text{Join\_nested\_loop}] = t[\text{inst\_flow}] + t[\text{process}] + t[\text{data\_collect}]$$

Sort-merge join algorithm. The instruction flow time is

$$t[\text{inst\_flow}] = t[\text{comp}] + t[\text{trans}] + t[\text{tp\_xfer}]$$

As in the conventional system model, the time to load the outer relation pages is

$$t[\text{read}, R] = t[\text{access}] + m * t[\text{I/O}]$$

Taking the acceleration factor into consideration, the time to perform $m/2$ two-page merge operations is

$$(m/2) * 2 * t * \text{acc\_fac} * \{2 * t[\text{s}] + t[\text{cpu}]\}$$
$$= m * t * \text{acc\_fac} * \{2 * t[\text{s}] + t[\text{cpu}]\}$$

Including the reading and writing of the relation R, the time to implement one merge-sort subphase of a four-way external merge sort algorithm is

$$t[\text{merge\_sort\_pg}, R] = 2 * \{t[\text{access}] + m * t[\text{I/O}]\} +$$
$$m * t * \text{acc\_fac} * \{2 * t[\text{s}] + t[\text{cpu}] + t[\text{mov}]\}$$

Since there are $\log_4(m)$ subphases, the time for sorting R is

$$\log_4(m) * t[\text{merge\_sort\_pg}, R]$$

Similarly, the time for sorting S is

$$\log_4(s) * t[\text{merge\_sort\_pg}, S]$$

where

$$t[\text{merge\_sort\_pg}, S] = 2 * \{t[\text{access}] + s * t[\text{I/O}]\} +$$
$$s * t * \text{acc\_fac} * \{2 * t[\text{s}] + t[\text{cpu}] + t[\text{mov}]\}$$

After this sorting phase is completed, the next phase of the operation is to merge the sorted R and S. The time for performing approximately $(m + s)/2$ two-page merge operations is

$$\{(m + s)/2\} * 2 * t * \text{acc\_fac} * \{2 * t[\text{s}] + t[\text{cpu}] + t[\text{mov}]\}$$
$$= (m + s) * t * \text{acc\_fac} * \{2 * t[\text{s}] + t[\text{cpu}] + t[\text{mov}]\}$$

Including the reading of the R and S relations and the forming of the output tuples of L, the total time to perform the actual join-by-merge operation is

$$t[\text{merge}] = (m + s) * t * \text{acc\_fac} * \{2 * t[\text{s}] + t[\text{cpu}] + t[\text{mov}]\}$$
$$+ 2 * t[\text{access}] + (m + s) * t[\text{I/O}]$$
$$+ u * t/2 * 2 * \text{acc\_fac} * t[\text{mov}]$$

where $u = \text{ceil}(m * t * s * t * \text{jn\_fac}/(t/2))$ is the total number of the output pages of L.

Since all the output pages need to be written to the disk, the time required is

$$t[\text{I/O}, L] + u * t[\text{I/O}]$$

Adding all the time components, the total time for data processing is

$$t[\text{process}] = \log_4(m) * t[\text{merge\_sort\_pg}, R]$$
$$+ \log_4(s) * t[\text{merge\_sort\_pg}, S]$$
$$+ t[\text{merge}] + t[\text{access}] + t[\text{I/O}, L]$$

The cost formula for data collection time for this algorithm is the same as the one derived for the nested-loop–join algorithm described in this section.

The total execution time for this algorithm is

$$t[\text{Join\_sort\_merge}] = t[\text{inst\_flow}] + t[\text{process}] + t[\text{data\_collect}]$$

7.3.2.3 STATISTICAL AGGREGATION.

This section considers the same algorithms used for this operation in the conventional system model presented in Chapter 2.

Sort-merge aggregation algorithm. The instruction flow is the same as for the previous operations

$$t[\text{inst}] = t[\text{comp}] + t[\text{trans}] + t[\text{tp\_xfer}]$$

The time to sort relation R has been shown to be

$$\log_4(m) * t[\text{merge\_sort\_pg}, R]$$

in the sort-merge–join algorithm given previously.

The time needed to calculate the summary attribute values for the w categories is

$$m * t * \text{acc\_fac} * \{t[\text{s}] * t[\text{cpu}]\} + w * t[\text{mov}] * \text{acc\_fac}$$

The data processing time is therefore

$$t[\text{process}] = \log\_4(m) * t[\text{merge\_sort\_pg}, R]$$
$$+ m * t * \text{acc\_fac} * \{t[\text{s}] + t[\text{cpu}]\} + w * t[\text{mov}] * \text{acc\_fac}$$

The data collection time for the resulting relation, which has $\text{ceil}(w/t)$ pages is

$$t[\text{data\_collect}] = \text{ceil}(w/t) * \{t[\text{trans}] + t[\text{xfer}]\} + w * t[\text{tp\_out}]$$

Hash aggregation algorithm. The instruction flow is the same as before

$$t[\text{inst\_flow}] = t[\text{comp}] + t[\text{trans}] + t[\text{tp\_xfer}]$$

The processing time is very similar to the one derived for the conventional system model in Chapter 2. The time for reading relation R is $t[\text{read}, R]$. The time for hashing x category attribute values in $m * t$ tuples of R is

$$m * t * \text{acc\_fac} * x * t[\text{hash}]$$

The time for collision checking of $m * t$ tuples of R is

$$m * t * \text{c\_fac} * \text{acc\_fac} * \{2 * t[\text{s}] + t[\text{cpu}]\}$$

The computation time for calculating the aggregate values is

$$m * t * \text{acc\_fac} * \{t[\text{s}] + t[\text{cpu}]\}$$

The time to establish w tuples of the resulting relation in the output buffer is

$$w * t[\text{mov}] * \text{acc\_fac}$$

The total processing time for this algorithm is therefore

$$
\begin{aligned}
t[\text{process}] &= t[\text{read}, R] + m * t * \text{acc\_fac} * \{x * t[\text{hash}] \\
&\quad + \text{c\_fac} * \{2 * t[s] + t[\text{cpu}]\} + \{t[s] \\
&\quad + t[\text{cpu}]\}\} \\
&\quad + w * t[\text{mov}] * \text{acc\_fac}
\end{aligned}
$$

As in the sort-merge case, the data collection time for this algorithm is

$$t[\text{data\_collect}] = \text{ceil}(w/t) * \{t[\text{trans}] + t[\text{xfer}]\} + w * t[\text{tp\_out}] * \text{acc\_fac}$$

The total execution for this algorithm is

$$t[\text{Aggregate}] = t[\text{inst\_flow}] + t[\text{process}] + t[\text{data\_collect}]$$

7.3.2.4 UPDATE. The instruction flow time is the same as the ones for the other operations described above, and again, the analysis of data processing for this operation is very similar to the one for the conventional system model. The reading of q pages of R is

$$t[\text{read\_q\_pg}, R] = q * t[\text{I/O}]$$

For these q pages, assuming there are x attributes involved in the search conditions, the time to select tuples for updating is

$$q * t * x * \text{acc\_fac} * \{2 * t[s] + t[\text{cpu}]\}$$

There are $q * t * \text{sel\_fac}$ tuples to be updated. The time needed is

$$q * t * \text{sel\_fac} * \text{acc\_fac} * \{2 * t[s] + t[\text{cpu}]\}$$

Assuming all q pages of R have been modified, the time to write them back to the disk is

$$q * t[\text{I/O}]$$

The total time for processing (m/q) cylinders of R is

$$
\begin{aligned}
t[\text{process}] &= 2 * t[\text{access}] + (m/q) * q * \{t[\text{I/O}] + t * x \\
&\quad * \text{acc\_fac} * (2 * t[s] + t[\text{cpu}]) + \text{sel\_fac} * t \\
&\quad * \text{acc\_fac} * (2 * t[s] + t[\text{cpu}]) + t[\text{I/O}]\} \\
&= 2 * t[\text{access}] + m * \{2 * t[\text{I/O}] + t \\
&\quad * \text{acc\_fac} * (2 * t[s] + t[\text{cpu}]) * (x + \text{sel\_fac})\}
\end{aligned}
$$

The total execution time for this algorithm is

$$t[\text{Update}] = t[\text{inst\_flow}] + t[\text{process}]$$

7.3.3 An Abstract Model for Systems with Functionally Specialized Processors

This model is a simplified model of the DBC system. Since hardware for security enforcement has not been considered in the other categories of database computers, the security filter component will be taken out of the data loop of the DBC system and the data and data structure for security processing will be taken out of the components of the structure loop. The resulting abstract model is shown in Figure 7.47. While it is assumed here that the general sequence of query processing and data flow as well as the architectures and functions of the components in this model are the same as those of the DBC system, the following analyses are made based on assumptions that are consistent with those made in the analyses for the other abstract models but not necessarily the same as the analyses made by the DBC researchers. For this reason, it is important that the reader should not interpret the cost formulas for this model to represent the DBC's actual performance. The DBC system is used as the basis for our abstract

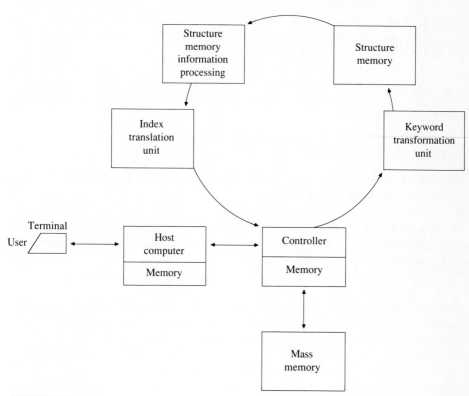

FIGURE 7.47
An abstract model for systems with functionally specialized processors.

model since it uses specialized hardware to support parallel data searches and uses the processing of auxiliary data structures for indexing, table look-up, and data clustering. For a better understanding of the analyses presented in this section, the reader is urged to review the material on the DBC system described in Section 7.2.2.1.

As in the previous analyses in this book, it is assumed that data are transferred between component systems in units of pages, each of which corresponds to a disk track. The processing of pages is performed in a pipelined fashion, that is, each component system receives one or more than one input page to produce an output page that is immediately transferred to the next component system. The operations of these component systems overlap one another most of the time. In a pipelined system, computing the execution time is rather difficult because different component systems operate at different speeds and the delay in one system will effect the "smoothness" of data flow. The following analyses of algorithms consider only the response time of each algorithm, which is the time elapsed from the start of execution of an operation to the time the first page of output is produced by the last component system in the chain of processors that carry out the processing tasks. To determine the system response time, the time to produce the first block of output in each component system needs to be calculated.

The following analyses do not consider the time for establishing the result of an operation as a relation in the database. This is because the creation of a relation in the database will involve the building of indices and clustering of its records to facilitate the future processing of the relation. The time required to do this represents a considerable overhead in systems that use indexing and clustering techniques.

7.3.4 Analyses of Algorithms

The same representative data operations are used in this section as have been used throughout this book in our analyses.

7.3.4.1 SELECT. In this model, the query is first received by the host computer, which performs the compilation and transfers the compiled query to the controller. The instruction flow time is

$$t[\text{inst\_flow}] = t[\text{comp}] + t[\text{tp\_xfer}]$$

Let the selection query contain $x1$ predicates whose attributes are indexed. Each predicate has the form, attribute-relation-value, and is used as a part of the search condition expressed by a query conjunction in the Select operation. These predicates are sent, one at a time, to the keyword transformation unit (KXU), which transforms the variable-length predicate to fixed-length codes. The transformation task involves two steps. First, a table look-up is performed to retrieve a hash function for each predicate. If $n1$ is the number of entries in the attribute information table, an average of $n1/2$ comparisons would be necessary to search for an attribute. Second, the hash function is applied to compute the fixed-length code for the predicate. A part of this code forms the bucket name. This name is used by the structure memory to access the index terms associated with the predicate. As these fixed-length codes are produced, KXU pipes the codes to the structure memory (SM). The time to send a code to SM is assumed to be $t[msg]$. The time for completing the processing of the first predicate in the KXU is

$$t[\text{KXU, first}] = n1/2 * (2 * t[s] + t[cpu]) + t[hash] + t[msg]$$

The SM contains a set of p processing elements, each of which has a memory unit containing a set of memory modules. It is assumed that these memory modules are fast memory devices (e.g., CCDs) and the data stored in them can be searched on the fly by the processing elements. Assume that the memory modules contain only the relative cylinder addresses. The security atoms of the DBC are not considered. The records, which may satisfy the coded predicates received from the KXU, are stored in these cylinders. Since index terms associated with predicates are stored across the memory units of the SM, it is assumed that not more than one memory module in a memory unit contains cylinder addresses associated with a referenced predicate code. However, several modules across different units may contain cylinder addresses associated with a predicate code. In order to access the index terms associated with a predicate, a table look-up is performed by the controller of the SM, using the predicate code to determine which memory modules need to be searched. The table look-up time is approximated by $t[cpu]$ plus the time for accessing a maximum of p memory module identification numbers—that is, $p * t[s]$. The time for examining a memory module's contents on the fly by a processing element is equivalent to $t[xfer]$. Thus, the time for processing the first predicate code by the SM is

$$t[\text{SM}] = t[cpu] + p * t[s] + t[xfer]$$

The cylinder addresses found by all the processing elements are then transferred to the next component system in the structure loop, that is, the structure memory information processor (SMIP). The time for transferring these addresses would depend on the number of addresses found. The referenced relation R occupies $ceil(m/q)$ cylinders, and $sel\_fac * ceil(m/q)$ of them would contain the relevant data. Since there may be other cylinder addresses included in this process due to collisions when attributes are first hashed, a collision factor, c_fac (> 1), needs to be considered. The number of cylinder addresses retrieved by the SM is

$$nc = sel\_fac * ceil(m/q) * c\_fac$$

If a logical cylinder address has four bytes and the size in bytes of a page is denoted by $psize$, then the number of page transfers involved would be $(nc * 4/ psize)$. Since the SM operates in a pipelined fashion, only one $t[xfer]$ needs to be considered in the transfer time for transferring the index terms of the first predicate code.

The SMIP receives x sets of logical cylinder addresses, each of which corresponds to one predicate processed by the KXU and the SM. It performs a set intersection operation on these sets to obtain the addresses of the set of cylinders in the mass memory whose contents are to be examined. Using the scheme proposed in the DBC system, the Intersection operation involves two hashing operations for each cylinder address. Thus, including the input time, the time for performing the intersection is

$$t[\text{intersect}] \ = \ \text{ceil}((nc * 4)/p\text{size}) * t[\text{xfer}] \ + \ nc * 2 * t[\text{hash}]$$

The result of the Intersection is a set of cylinder addresses, which needs to be transferred to the next component system, the index translation unit (IXU). This set should contain less than nc cylinder addresses since some addresses may not be in the intersection of the input sets. But the number of cylinder addresses should be greater than or equal to $\text{ceil}(m/q) * \text{sel\_fac}$, since the possibility of collisions in the initial hashing of attributes may introduce cylinder addresses that should not have been included. A smaller c_fac value, which we denote as c_fac$'$, will be used here in the expression for nc. The time required to transfer all the cylinder addresses to the IXU is

$$\text{ceil}(\text{ceil}(m/q) * \text{sel\_fac} * \text{c\_fac}' * 4/p\text{size}) * t[\text{xfer}]$$

Again, if the effect of pipelining is considered, the first $t[\text{xfer}]$ is what is important for determining the response time of the algorithm. The time needed for the SMIP to produce and transfer the first page of output is

$$t[\text{SMIP}] \ = \ t[\text{intersect}] \ + \ t[\text{xfer}]$$

The IXU contains a cylinder address table for converting the logical cylinder addresses to physical cylinder addresses by which the mass memory accesses the data stored on the secondary storage. Since the IXU is a special-purpose processor designed specifically for the conversion task, it is assumed that $t[\text{cpu}] \ + \ t[\text{s}]]$ is adequate to perform the table look-up for each logical address. Considering the effect of pipelining, the time required to produce the first page of physical addresses is

$$t[\text{convert\_pg}] \ = \ \text{ceil}(p\text{size}/4) * \{t[\text{cpu}] \ + \ t[\text{s}]\}$$

The time to transfer the first page to the controller is $t[\text{xfer}]$. The processing time for the first page of output from IXU to the controller is

$$t[\text{IXU}] \ = \ t[\text{convert\_pg}] \ + \ t[\text{xfer}]$$

The total time required for the first page of data to be received by the controller, which is also the response time of the structure loop, is

$$t[\text{response\_str\_loop}] \ = \ t[\text{KXU}] \ + \ t[\text{SM}] \ + \ t[\text{SMIP}] \ + \ t[\text{IXU}]$$

The physical cylinder addresses received by the controller are then used by it to direct the mass memory to perform the actual Selection operation on the cylinders. The mass memory has q track information processors (TIPs), which can simultaneously search q tracks of a cylinder on the fly. The time required to process q tracks is the same as for reading one track, that is, $t[\text{access}] \ + \ t[\text{I/O}]$. Since we assumed earlier that $\text{ceil}(m/q) * \text{sel\_fac} * \text{c\_fac}'$ cylinders contain tuples that would satisfy the selection conditions, the total processing time of the MM would be

$$\text{ceil}(m/q) * \text{sel\_fac} * \text{c\_fac}' * \{t[\text{access}] + t[\text{I/O}]\}$$

Here, it is assumed that tuples of a relation are clustered in a cylinder but a relation need not occupy consecutive cylinders; thus, one $t[\text{access}]$ is involved along with each $t[\text{I/O}]$. Also, q tracks of data can be transferred to the TIPs in parallel, that is, in one $t[\text{I/O}]$. The MM should produce $\text{ceil}(m * \text{sel\_fac})$ pages of output of the resulting relation L. These pages are produced over time as the MM receives the physical cylinder addresses in an input data pipeline. In turn, the MM outputs these pages to the controller as they are produced. If, on an average, $n2$ cylinders ($n2 \geq 1$) need to be searched to produce one page of output, the time required to produce the first page of data for the controller by the MM is

$$t[\text{MM}] = n2 * \{t[\text{access}] + t[\text{I/O}]\} + t[\text{xfer}]$$

This first page is then transferred by the controller to the host computer, which in turn sends the tuples to the user's terminal. The time required for these two steps is

$$t[\text{collect\_pg}] = t[\text{xfer}] + t * t[\text{tp\_out}]$$

Adding these time components, the response time for the algorithm can be represented by

$$t[\text{Select\_response}] = t[\text{inst\_flow}] + t[\text{response\_str\_loop}]$$
$$+ t[\text{MM}] + t[\text{collect\_pg}]$$

7.3.4.2 JOIN. Since the feature of this model is the hardware-assisted processing of indices to minimize the disk search time, this feature is used to perform the relational join. The basic algorithm to be described is the nested-loop algorithm. The outer relation R is first read into the controller's main memory from the MM. Here, we assume that the controller is capable of reading a relation without going through the structure loop. This is different from the way the DBC is designed. For each tuple of R, the join attribute and its value in that tuple are used as the predicate for accessing the tuples of the inner relation S that satisfy the join condition. The retrieval of S tuples is through both the structure loop and the data loop, as described previously in the Selection operation. These S tuples are transferred, page by page, from the MM to the controller. The tuples in these pages are joined with the R tuple currently being processed to produce the resulting relation L. As soon as a page of L is produced, it is transferred to the host computer for output to the user's terminal. The algorithm terminates after the last R tuple has been processed.

The instruction flow for this operation is

$$t[\text{inst\_flow}] = t[\text{comp}] + t[\text{tp\_xfer}]$$

The time required to read a cylinder containing q pages of R is,

$$t[\text{read\_q\_pg}, R] \;=\; t[\text{access}] \;+\; t[\text{I/O}]$$

The join attribute value in each tuple of R is extracted to form a predicate with the join attribute. The time for forming a predicate is estimated to be

$$t[\text{form\_predicate}] \;=\; 2 * \{t[s] \;+\; t[\text{cpu}]\}$$

The predicate is used to retrieve the S tuples that satisfy the join condition. The first page of S tuples will take the following time to produce, as derived in the selection algorithm.

$$t[\text{receive\_st\_pg}, S] \;=\; t[\text{response\_str\_loop}] \;+\; t[\text{MM}]$$

After the first page, the pages of S will flow through the pipeline at a varying rate depending on the characteristics of the S tuples, the speed of the component systems, and other factors. Assume that d pages of S are necessary to produce one page of L when joining with the tuple of R. If the average time interval for receiving a page from the pipeline between the MM and the controller is r, then the time required to receive d pages of S by the controller would be

$$t[\text{receive\_d\_pg}, S] \;=\; t[\text{receive\_st\_pg}, S] \;+\; (d - 1) * (r \;+\; t[\text{xfer}])$$

Tuples in these d pages are joined with the tuples of R in the controller to produce one page of L. The Join operation will take the following time

$$t[\text{jn\_Rt\_Spg}] \;=\; d * t * 2 * t[\text{mov}]$$

where $2 * t[\text{mov}]$ has been used in the previous analysis to represent the time to move one tuple of R and one tuple of S to form a tuple of L. The page of L is then transferred to the host computer for output to the user's terminal. Since each tuple of L is roughly twice as large as a tuple of R or S, there are only t / 2 tuples in a page, and each tuple will take $2 * t[\text{tp\_out}]$ to output. The data collection time for the first output page is

$$t[\text{data\_collect\_pg}] \;=\; t[\text{xfer}] \;+\; t * t[\text{tp\_out}]$$

Therefore, the response time of the Join operation is

$$\begin{aligned}
t[\text{Join\_response}] \;=\; & t[\text{inst\_flow}] \;+\; t[\text{read\_q\_pg}, R] \\
& + \; t[\text{form\_predicate}] \;+\; t[\text{receive\_d\_pg}, S] \\
& + \; t[\text{jn\_Rt\_Spg}] \;+\; t[\text{data\_collect\_pg}]
\end{aligned}$$

7.3.4.3 STATISTICAL AGGREGATION. In this model, it has been assumed that records are clustered based on their contents, just like the scheme used in the DBC system. In order to highlight the clustering feature, it is assumed that records, which belong to the same category in a statistical aggregation operation, have been clustered and stored together in cylinders. There are w categories of records that need to be retrieved, and the values of the summary attribute (assuming one is involved) in each category are to be aggregated to produce one output tuple. This algorithm involves (1) the retrieval of R records to determine the category attribute values, (2) the use of category attribute values of each category to retrieve the records of R that belong to the category, and (3) the aggregation of the summary attribute values of these records to produce an output tuple. These steps continue until the output relation L is produced. As pages of L are produced, they are transferred to the host computer for output to the user.

The instruction flow time remains the same:

$$t[\text{inst\_flow}] = t[\text{comp}] + t[\text{tp\_xfer}]$$

The initial retrieval of a cylinder-full of tuples of R has been defined as

$$t[\text{read\_q\_pg}, R] = t[\text{access}] + t[\text{I/O}]$$

The category attribute values of each tuple are examined by a table search to determine if the current values form a new category. If they do, these values are used to form a query conjunction that is to be processed by the structure loop and then by the MM to retrieve all the records belonging to the category. The category table contains w entries, and on an average $w/2$ comparisons are necessary to determine the correct category. The time necessary for forming the query conjunction depends on the number of category attributes involved. Assume there are x category attributes. The time for this step would be

$$t[\text{form\_query\_conj}] = w/2 * \{2 * t[s] + t[\text{cpu}]\} + x * \{2 * t[s] + t[\text{cpu}]\}$$

Now the query conjunction is used as the search conditions for a selection operation. Based on the analysis of the Selection operation, it takes the following time to receive the first page of R records by the controller from the MM.

$$t[\text{receive\_st\_pg}, R] = t[\text{response\_str\_loop}] + t[\text{MM}]$$

Assuming tuples of R are evenly distributed over w categories, each category will have $\text{ceil}(m/w)$ pages. These pages will take the following amount of time for the controller to receive:

$$t[\text{receive\_all\_pg}, R] = t[\text{receive\_st\_pg}, R] + \{\text{ceil}(m/w) - 1\} * \{r + t[\text{xfer}]\}$$

where r is the average interval for the controller to receive a page from the output pipeline of the MM.

The tuples in the received pages of R are to be aggregated. The time necessary for this operation is

$$t[\text{aggr}] = m/w * t * \{t[s] + t[\text{cpu}]\}$$

The result is a tuple for the output relation L. It is moved to the output buffer. The total time for producing a tuple of L is

$$t[\text{produce\_tuple}, L] = t[\text{form\_query\_conj}] + t[\text{receive\_all\_pg}, R] + t[\text{aggr}]$$

The processing steps represented by the three terms in this expression are repeated for each distinct category found in the relation R. Assuming the first q pages of R read earlier contain category values that belong to t distinct categories, the time needed to produce t tuples of L would be

$$t[\text{produce\_pg}, L] = t * t[\text{produce\_tuple}, L]$$

This page of L is then collected for output to the user. The collection time is

$$t[\text{data\_collect\_pg}] = t[\text{xfer}] + t * t[\text{tp\_out}]$$

Therefore, the response time for this algorithm is

$$t[\text{Aggr\_response}] = t[\text{inst\_flow}] + t[\text{read\_q\_pg}, R]$$
$$+ t[\text{produce\_pg}, L] + t[\text{data\_collect\_pg}]$$

7.3.4.4 UPDATE. The Update operation is similar to the Selection operation except that the updated tuples of the relation R need to be written back to the database in the MM's secondary storage. Also, the Update operation may require that the indices and tables for managing the clusters and cylinder addresses be modified accordingly. The time required for updating the auxiliary information of a relation would depend on the internal data structures used for the indices, tables, and directories. The analysis for updating the auxiliary data structures in this model would be the same as that of a conventional database system since indexing and clustering are software techniques commonly used in conventional systems. For this reason, it will not be covered in this book.

7.4 SUMMARY AND DISCUSSION

This chapter as well as Chapter 6 have presented two major categories of multi-processor systems: systems with replication of functions and systems with distribution of functions. The first category of systems distribute a database across processors, which are programmed to do a number of database management functions (i.e., the functions are replicated among the processors). Instructions or database commands are transferred to these processors for execution against the distributed data in some parallel fashion. This type of system generally requires the capability of broadcasting commands and data to the processors. Although many database operations involve only the broadcasting of commands (a small amount of transfer time), several operations still require the movement and exchange of large quantities of base or temporary data among processors. Furthermore, since operations are performed on distributed data by multiple processors simultaneously, processes often need to be synchronized to ensure their orderly executions. Therefore, the main challenge of this type of system is to be able to transfer and/or exchange the distributed data or computed results and to synchronize and communicate among cooperating processors at a high speed.

The second category of systems use a number of general-purpose or special-purpose processors to perform various database functions. Data are stored in some secondary storage devices and are routed through these processors. If data cannot be moved at a high speed, and the functionally specialized processors can only be invoked sequentially, the performance of this type of system will not be very good even if individual operations can be executed at high speed. Therefore, the main requirement of this type of system is to have high bandwidth in communication links and in secondary storage accesses. It is important to overlap the processing time with data transfer time in various database operations. The pipelining approach of data processing is very desirable and is commonly used by this type of system.

Besides performance considerations, these two categories of systems have advantages and disadvantages with respect to expandability and reliability. The first category can be easily expanded by adding new processors, main memory, and secondary storage devices to increase computational power, whereas, the second category can be expanded by adding new functional processors to increase their functionalities. A failed processor in the first category may render a portion of the distributed database inaccessible, whereas, in the second category, a function or functions implemented by that processor would become unavailable. In both categories, some type of system redundancy would be necessary to achieve high reliability.

Despite the fact that the architectures and basic data processing approaches of these two categories of systems are rather different, there are a number of hardware, processing, and data organization techniques that are common to systems in both categories.

1. *Hardware techniques.* The idea of pairing processors with secondary storage devices as a way of increasing the bandwidth of these devices through parallel I/O is used in MICRONET, EDC, MDBS, GAMMA, Cube-connected Multicomputer, and DBC/1012. The idea of using disk cache to accelerate the effective bandwidth of disk storage devices is used in DIRECT, CADAM, IDM, DDM, GRACE, SABRE, and DELTA. Besides disks, magnetic bubble memories are also used as secondary storage devices, as seen in GRACE and EDC. The use of a global shared memory as a way to facilitate the passing of data, status, and messages among a number of cooperating processors is seen in DBMAC, SABRE.V2, AND RDBM. The use of switchable memory modules to achieve the same purposes is used in SM3. Other special hardware for enhancing the speed of data processing include (a) hardware sorters used in DDM, DBC/1012, GRACE, and RDBM and (b) control lines for fast interprocessor synchronization and communication used in MICRONET and SM3. A number of other database machine approaches presented in the preceding chapters have been adopted in these systems. For example, the cellular-logic approach of Chapter 3 (i.e., the associative secondary storage concept) is used in EDC and DBC. The database-filtering approach of Chapter 4 is used in GRACE, CADAM, DBC, SABRE, and RDBM. The content-addressing approach of Chapter 5 is used in DBC, CADAM, HYPERTREE, and DDM.

2. *Processing techniques.* A number of processing techniques are shared by several systems presented in this chapter. For example, the idea of encoding and decoding the data as a way of standardizing the internal data representation and of conserving the storage is used in DBC, DDM, RDBM, and DELTA. The pipelining technique is widely used to achieve fast response time and elapse time. GRACE, DDM, DBC, DBMAC, DELTA, and RDBM all use

some form of the pipelining concept to gain processing speed. Unary operations such as Selection and Projection with Duplicate Removal are either processed by some hardware filters or by software techniques. The binary relational operation Join uses one of the following three popular algorithms: the nested-loop–join used in MICRONET and DIRECT, the hash join used in HYPERTREE, GAMMA, DBC/1012, and GRACE, or the sort-merge–join used in DBC/1012, GAMMA, REPT, DDM, and RDBM. It should be stressed here that if the processors used in a multiprocessor system are general-purpose processors, then they can be programmed to perform different algorithms developed for various database operations.

3. *Data organization.* Massive parallelism and specialized hardware are not necessarily cost effective for replacing the traditional software techniques used for reducing the search space of a large database. A number of systems presented in the above two chapters use a number of familiar software techniques for structuring data and for placing data in secondary storage to enhance data retrieval and manipulation. For example, the indexing techniques used in DBC, MDBS, DBC/1012, IDM, and IQC, the inverted structures used in MICRONET, DBMAC, and DELTA, and the clustering techniques used in DBC, MDBS, SABRE, and CADAM are good examples of combining both hardware and software techniques for achieving high performance.

7.5 BIBLIOGRAPHY

[AHU82] Ahuja, S. R., and Asthana, A.: "A Multi-Microprocessor Architecture with Hardware Support for Communication and Scheduling," *Proceedings of Architectural Support for Programming Language and Operating Systems,* Palo Alto, Calif., March 1982, pp. 205–209.

[AUE81] Auer, H., Hell, W., Leilish, H. O., Schweppe, H., Stiege, G., Seehusen, S., Lie, J. S., Zeidler, H. C., Teich, W.: "RDBM—A Relational Database Machine," *Information Systems,* vol. 6, no. 2, 1981, pp. 91–100.

[BAB79] Babb, E.: "Implementing a Relational Database by Means of Specialized Hardware," *ACM Transactions on Database Systems,* vol. 4, no. 1, 1979, pp. 1–29.

[BAE81] Baer, J. L., Gardarin, G., Girault, C., and Roucairol, G.: "The Two-Step Commitment Protocol: Modeling Specification and Proof Methodology," *Fifth International Conference on Software Engineering,* San Diego, Calif., March 1981, pp. 363–373.

[BAN78] Banerjee, J., Baum, R. I., and Hsiao, D. K.: "Concepts and Capabilities of a Database Computer," *ACM Transactions of Database Systems,* vol. 3, Dec. 1978, pp. 347–384.

[BAN78a] Banerjee, J., Hsiao, D. K., and Ng, F. K.: "Data Network—A Computer Network of General-purpose Front-end Computers and Special-purpose Back-end Database Machines," *Proceedings of the International Symposium on Computer Network Protocols,* A. Danthine, (ed.), Liege, Belgium, Feb. 1978, pp. D6-1–D6-12.

[BAN78b] Banerjee, J., and Hsiao, D. K.: "Performance Evaluation of a Database Computer in Supporting Relational Databases," *Proceedings of the Fourth International Conference on Very Large Data Bases,* Berlin, Germany, Sept. 13–15, 1978.

[BAN78c] Banerjee, J., and Hsiao, D. K., "A Methodology for Supporting Existing CODASYL Databases with New Database Machines," *Proceedings of the ACM '78 Conference,* Dec. 1978, pp. 925–936.

[BAN79] Banerjee, J., Hsiao, D. K., and Kannan, K.: "DBC—A Database Computer for Very Large Databases," *IEEE Transactions on Computers,* vol. C-28, no. 6, June 1979, pp. 414–429.

[BAN80] Banerjee, J., Hsiao, D. K., and Ng, F. K.: "Database Transformation, Query Translation and Performance Analysis of a New Database Computer in Supporting Hierarchical Database Management," *IEEE Transactions on Software Engineering,* SE-6, no. 1, Jan. 1980, pp. 91–108.

[BEN79] Bentley, J. L., and Kung, H. T.: "A Tree Machine for Searching Problems," *Proceedings of the 1979 International Conference on Parallel Processing,* IEEE, Aug. 1979, pp. 257–266.

[BRI81*a*] Britton Lee, Inc., "IDM 500: Intelligent Database Machine Product Description," Britton Lee, Inc., 1981.

[BRI81*b*] Britton Lee, Inc., "IDL Tutorial," Britton Lee, Inc. 1981.

[CAN74] Canaday, R. H., et al.: "A Back-end Computer for Data Base Management," *Communications of the Association on Computing Machinery,* vol. 17, Oct. 1974, pp. 575–582.

[FAG79] Fagin, R., Nievergelt, J., Pippenger, N., and Strong, H. R.: "Extendible Hashing—A Fast Access Method for Dynamic Files," *ACM Transactions on Database Systems,* vol. 4, no. 3, 1979, pp. 315–344.

[FOS80] Foster, M. J., and Kung, H. T.: "The Design of Special-purpose VLSI Chips, *COMPUTER,* 13:(1), Jan. 1980, pp. 26–40.

[GAR81] Gardarin, G.: "An Introduction to SABRE: A Multi-Microprocessor Database Machine," *Proceedings of the Sixth Workshop on Computer Architecture for Non-Numeric Processing,* Hyeres, France, June 1981.

[GAR83] Gardarin, G., Bernadat, P., Temmerman, N., Valduriez, P., and Viemont, Y.: "SABRE: A Relational Database System for a Multimicroprocessor Machine," in *Advanced Database Machine Architecture,* D. K. Hsiao (ed.), Prentice-Hall, Englewood Cliffs, N.J., 1983, pp. 19–35.

[HAK77] Hakozaki, K., et. al.: "A Conceptual Design of a Generalized Database Subsystem," *Proceedings of the Third International Conference on Very Large Databases,* 1977, pp. 246–253.

[HEL81] Hell, W.: "RDBM—A Relational Database Machine Architecture and Hardware Design," *Proceedings of the Sixth Workshop on Computer Architecture for Non-numerical Processing,* Hyeres, France, June 1981.

[HIK81] Hikita, S., Yamazaki, H., Hasegawa, K., Mitsushita, Y.: "Optimization of the File Access Method in Content-Addressable Database Machine (CADAM), *NCC Proceedings AFIPS,* Chicago, Ill., 1981, pp. 507–513.

[HSI78] Hsiao, D. K., and Kannan, K.: "Simulation Studies of the Database Computer (DBC)," *Technical Report OSU-CISRC-TR-78-1,* The Ohio State University, Feb. 1978.

[HSI80] Hsiao, D. K. (ed.): "Collected Readings on a Database Computer (DBC), The Ohio State University, Columbus, Ohio, April 1980.

[INT82*a*] Intel Corporation, "iDBP Host Lind Reference Manual," Order number: 222102-001, Intel Corporation, 1982.

[INT82*b*] Intel Corporation, "iDBP Operations Manual," Order number: 222101, Intel Corporation, 1982.

[INT82*c*] Intel Corporation, "Guide to iDBP," Order number: 222104, Intel Corporation, 1982.

[INT82*d*] Intel Corporation, "iDBP DBMS Reference Manual," Order number, 222100, Intel Corporation, 1982.

[IWA84] Iwata, K., Kamiya, S., Sakai, H., Matsuda, S., Shibayama, S., and Murakami, K.: "Design and Implementation of a Two-Way Merge-Sorter and Its Application to Relational Database Processing," *Technical Report: TR-006,* Institute for New Generation Computer Technology, Tokyo, Japan, May 1984.

[KAK84] Kakuta, T., Miyazaki, N., Shibayama, S., Yokota, H., and Murakami, K.: "The Design and Implementation of Relational Database Machine Delta," *Technical Report: TR-089,* Institute for New Generation Computer Technology, Tokyo, Japan, Nov. 1984.

[KAR81] Karlsson, K., "Reduced Cover-Trees and Their Application in the SABRE Access Path Model," *Proceedings of the Seventh International Conference on Very Large Data Bases,* Cannes, France, Sept. 1981, pp. 345–353.

[KUN79a] Kung, H. T., Guibas, L. J., and Thompson, C. D.: "Direct VLSI Implementation of Combinatorial Algorithms," *Proceedings of the Conference on Very Large Scale Integration: Architecture, Design, Fabrication,* California Institute of Technology, Jan. 1979, pp. 509–525.

[KUN79b] Kung, H. T., and Leiserson, C. F.: "Systolic Arrays (for VLSI)," in Duff, I. S. and Stewart, G. W. (ed.), *Sparse Matrix Processings 1978,* SIAM, 1979, pp. 256–282. A slightly different version appears in *Introduction to VLSI Systems* by C. A. Mead and L. A. Conway, Addison-Wesley, Reading, Mass., 1980.

[KUN80a] Kung, H. T., and Lehman, P. L.: "Systolic (VLSI) Arrays for Relational Database Operations," *Proceedings of the ACM SIGMOD 1980 International Conference on Management of Data.* ACM, Santa Monica, Calif., May 1980, pp. 105–116.

[KUN80b] Kung, H. T.: "Special-Purpose Devices for Signal and Image Processing: An Opportunity in VLSI," *Proceedings of the SPIE,* vol. 241, Real-Time Signal Processing III, The Society of Photo-optical Instrumentation Engineers, July 1980, pp. 76–84.

[KUN81a] Kung, H. T., and Song, S. W.: "A Systolic 2-D Convolution Chip," *Technical Report CMU-CS-81-110,* Carnegie-Mellon University, Computer Science Department, March 1981.

[KUN81b] Kung, H. T., and Picard, R. L.: "Hardware Pipelines for Multi-dimensional Convolution and Resampling," *Workshop on Computer Architecture for Pattern Analysis and Image Database Management,* Hot Spring, Va., Nov. 1981.

[LOW74] Lowenthal, E. I.: "Computing Subsystems for the Data Management Function," *Proceedings of the Third Texas Conference on Computing Systems,* IEEE, 1974.

[MAR76] Maryanski, F., et. al.: "Evaluation of Conversion to a Backend Data Base Management System," *Proceedings of the Annual Conference of the ACM,* Houston, Tex., Oct. 1976, pp. 293–297.

[MIY84] Miyazaki, N., Kakuta, T., Shibayama, S., Yokota, H., and Murakami, K.: "An Overview of Relational Database Machine Delta," *Proceedings of the Advanced Database Symposium,* Information Processing Society of Japan, Tokyo, Dec. 1984, pp. 11–20.

[SAK84] Sakai, H., Iwata, K., Kamiya, S., Abe, M., Tanaka, A., Shibayama, S., and Murakami, K.: "Design and Implementation of the Relational Database Engine," *Technical Report: TR-063,* Institute for New Generation Computer Technology, Tokyo, Japan, April 1984.

[SCH83] Schweppe, H., Zeidler, H. C., Hell, W., Leilich, H. O., Stiege, G., and Teich, W.: "RDBM—A Dedicated Multiprocessor System for Database Management," in *Advanced Database Machine Architecture,* D. K. Hsiao (ed.), Prentice-Hall, Englewood Cliffs, N.J., 1983, pp. 36–86.

[SEK82] Sekino, A., Takeuchi, K., Makino, T., Doi, T., Goto, T., Hakozaki, K.: "Design Considerations for an Information Query Computer," *Proceedings of the International Workshop on Database Machines,* San Diego, Calif., September 1–3, 1982.

[SHI84a] Shibayama, S., Kakuta, T., Miyazaki, N., Yokota, H., and Murakami, K.: "A Relational Database Machine with Large Semi-Conductor Disk and Hardware Relational Algebra Processor," *New Generation Computing,* vol. 2, no. 2, Ohmsha, Ltd. and Springer-Verlag, March 1984, pp. 131–155.

[SHI84b] Shibayama, S., Kakuta, T., Miyazaki, N., Yokota, H., and Murakami, K.: "Query Processing Flow on RDBM Delta's Functionally-Distributed Architecture," *Technical Report: TR-064,* Institute for New Generation Computer Technology, Tokyo, Japan, April 1984.

[SHU81] Shultz, R. K.: "A Multiprocessor Computer Architecture for Database Support," Ph.D. dissertation, Department of Computer Science, Iowa State University, Ames, Iowa, 1981.

[SHU84] Shultz, R. K., and Zingg, R. J.: "Response Time Analysis of Multiprocessor Computers for Database Support," *ACM Transactions on Database Systems,* 1984, pp. 14–17.

[SON80] Song, S. W.: "A Highly Concurrent Tree Machine for Database Applications," *Proceedings of the 1980 International Conference on Parallel Processing,* IEEE, Aug. 1980, pp. 259–268.

[SON81] Song, S. W.: "On a High Performance VLSI Solution to Database Problems," Ph.D. dissertation, Computer Science Department, Carnegie-Mellon University, Aug. 1981.

[SWA77] Swan, R. J., Fuller, S. H., and Siewiorek, D. P.: "Cm * —A Modular Multi

Microprocessor," *Proceedings of the National Computer Conference,* Dallas, Tex., June 1977, pp. 637–644.

[TAN80] Tanaka, Y., Noxaka, Y., and Masuyama, A.: "Pipeline Searching and Sorting Modules as Components of a Data Flow Database Computer," *Information Processing 80,* North-Holland Publishing Co., Amsterdam, Netherlands, 1980, pp. 427–432.

[TAN82] Tanaka, Y.: "A Data-Stream Database Machine with Large Capacity," *Proceedings of the International Workshop on Database Machines,* San Diego, September 1–3, 1982. Also in *Advanced Database Machines,* D. K. Hsiao (ed.), Prentice-Hall, Englewood Cliffs, N.J., 1983, pp. 168–202.

[TEI81] Teich, W.: "The Sort Processor of the RDBM," *Proceedings of the Sixth Workshop on Computer Architecture for Non-numerical Processing,* Hyeres, France, June 1981.

[TER84] Terradata Corporation, "DBC/1012 Data Base Computer Concepts and Facilities," Release 1.1, CO2-0001-01, Los Angeles, Calif., 1984.

[UEM80] Uemura, S., Yuba, T., Kokubu, A., Ooomote, R., and Sugawara, Y.: "The Design and Implementation of a Magnetic-bubble Database Machine," *Information Processing 80,* S. H. Lavington (ed.), North-Holland Publishing Company, 1980, pp. 433–438.

[UEM83] Uemura, S.: "Database Machine Activities in Japan," *IEEE Database Engineering,* vol. 6, no. 1, 1983, pp. 63–64.

[VAL82a] Alduriez, P., and Gardarin, G.: "Multiprocessor Join Algorithms of Relations," *Second International Conference on Data Bases: Improving Usability and Responsiveness,* Jerusalem, June 1982.

[VAL82b] Valduriez, P.: "Semi-join Algorithms for Multiprocessor Systems," *ACM-SIGMOD International Conference on Management of Data,* Orlando, Fla., June 1982, pp. 225–233.

[VIE82] Viemont, Y., and Gardarin, G.: "A Distributed Concurrency Control Based on Transaction Commit Ordering," *Twelfth International Conference on FTCS,* Los Angeles, Calif., June 1982.

CHAPTER
8

TEXT
PROCESSORS

Most of the recorded data used by individuals and organizations are in textual form. Books, journals, newspapers, magazines, letters, memos, and so forth contain vast amounts of information that are used daily. A text string is indeed the most high-level, natural data structure that most information users are familiar with, since everyone is taught to read and write texts at a very early age. The encoded data in fixed-format fields, commonly found in file and database management systems, are used only for the ease of representation in computers and for their efficient processing. They are not in the best form for ordinary users.

Many application areas require that data be represented in the form of a *text*, which is a string of characters with widely varying lengths. In office automation applications, for example, electronic mail, letters, and documents are stored and transported in textual format among offices. In the area of document retrieval, index records, abstracts, and book and periodical titles (again in the textual form) are processed and searched. In the area of database management, many applications also require that data be stored as text. For example, engineering design databases store long textual descriptions of objects. The speed of processing large quantities of textual materials and extracting the relevant information from them is of paramount importance to our information-oriented society.

Processing text using the existing Von Neumann computers is a clear case of mismatch between the computer's processing capability and application needs. This is due to the fact that the basic operations used in text processing are very different from the primitive operations supported by today's computers.

Sophisticated and expensive software systems must be developed to process text. There are several well-known text information retrieval systems available commercially. The National Library of Medicine's MEDLINE, the System Development Corporation's ORBIT, the Mead Data Central's LEXIS and NEXIS, and the Lockheed Information Systems' DIALOG are a few examples. It is quite time-consuming and costly to process large volumes of text in these systems. For example, it is pointed out by Hollaar [HOL79] that a legal text retrieval system would be required to store about 30 billion characters. Even if it is searched by a conventional high-speed processor at a rate of about 200K characters per second, more than 40 hours of search time would still be necessary. Another example given by Hollaar, et al. [HOL83] shows that a system for the U.S. Patent and Trademark Office stores about 65 billion characters. It is estimated that 1,500 search requests will be issued against the database per hour. If a high-speed computer can search 1 million characters per second, it will still take over 18 hours to search the database. For this reason, in most of the conventional text processing systems, full text searching is performed only on selected documents. Documents are represented by keywords, index terms, subject headings, or special classification codes that are processed first by computers to select a subset of documents that satisfy the search condition. The science of assigning index terms, subject headings, and so forth in library terms is called *cataloguing*. It is an extremely tedious and time-consuming task and is highly error prone. Also, some of the information in the original text may be lost in the process. It is obviously an advantage if full text can be searched at high speed by the hardware directly. It will also be advantageous if hardware can be used to support the traditional software techniques in text processing such as inverted files, indexing, and superimposed coding.

This chapter describes (1) the characteristics of text databases and how they differ from business-oriented databases supported by the database computers described in the preceding chapters, (2) the basic structure of a text retrieval system, and (3) text processing techniques such as full text scanning, inverted file and index processing, and superimposed coding. Several term comparator designs and hardware systems for supporting these processing techniques will also be described.

8.1 CHARACTERISTICS OF TEXT DATABASES

Text databases are quite different from the business-oriented databases of the commercial database management systems. They are different in structure, primitive operations, and operational requirements.

8.1.1 Structure

Texts are relatively unstructured when compared with business-oriented data records with fixed-length, formatted fields. Although there are punctuation marks, blanks, special symbols to mark the beginning and end of words, clauses, sentences, and paragraphs in a text string, their positions in the text string cannot always be predetermined. It is necessary to scan the text string by explicitly examining each character in it, in order to identify its elements. In a text processing system that does not support full text scan, a text such as a document is represented by a list of keywords or index terms. For example, this book can be represented in contents by such terms as "database computers," "cellular-logic devices," "database filters," "associative memory," "multiprocessor systems," and so forth. Although each of these terms is formatted and can be stored in a fixed-length field, just like an attribute in a business-oriented data record, the keyword list has a variable length as opposed to a fixed number of attribute values. Another common representation of a document is a vector that is defined in N-dimensional space, where N is the number of keywords or index terms that characterize a document collection. N is generally rather large (10,000 or more) and this value can change when new documents that require new keywords or index terms to characterize them are added to the collection. In the vector representation, a large number of elements in a vector are zeros, indicating that the corresponding keywords or terms are not applicable to the document. The storage and processing of this vector representation can be expected to be quite different from that of fixed-formatted records.

8.1.2 Primitive Operations

The primitive operations required in text processing are again quite different from those of the formatted record processing. Text retrieval often involves searching for a number of terms of varying lengths with different "don't-care" conditions and, finally, Boolean operations are applied to the results of term comparisons. The specification of search context (e.g., within a sentence/paragraph) is either explicit or implicit. More complications also arise due to inconsistent spellings, words with many different meanings, acronyms, synonyms, and other anomalies.

In order to support text processing, a powerful query language is needed to allow the user to specify at a high level what he or she is looking for in a text. From the application point of view, the operations expressible in the language are the primitive operations, which should be executed by a text processing system with high efficiency. A list of typical text processing operations has been compiled by Hollaar [HOL79] and is shown in Table 8.1.

The list of operations shown in the figure are self-explanatory. However, the fixed-length "don't care" (FLDC) and variable-length "don't care" (VLDC) conditions of the last two operations create considerable problems in character matching. If the head-per-track approach proposed by Slotnik [SLO70], is used, which is also the basic concept of the cellular-logic devices described in Chapter 3, where character strings are stored in a bit-serial word-serial fashion, then the search is performed in parallel by a linear array of bit-serial comparators. But a search for the term "ISSIP" in the character string "MISSISSIPPI" will result in a failure even though the substring is in it. This is because a serial comparator finds a match of the character "I" at the second position of "MISSISSIPPI" and

TABLE 8.1
Typical text retrieval operations (*Source:* [HOL79]
©**1979 IEEE)**

Operation	Definition
A	Finds any document that contains the word A.
@A	Directly substitutes the previously defined value of A in the expression [macro].
A OR B	Finds any document that contains either the word A or the word B.
A AND B	Finds any document that contains both the word A and the word B anywhere in the document.
A AND NOT B	Finds any document that contains the word A but not the word B.
A AND B IN SENT	Finds any document that contains both word A and word B in the same sentence [specified context].
A B	Finds any document that contains the word A immediately followed by the word B [finds a contiguous word phrase].
A ... B	Finds any document that contains the word A followed (either immediately or after an arbitrary number of words) by the word B.
A .n. B	Finds any document that contains the word A followed by the word B within n words [directed proximity].
$<$A,B$>n$	Finds any document that contains the words A and B within n words of each other [undirected proximity].
(A,B,C,D)%n	Finds any document that contains at least n of the different words A, B, C, or D. Note that if n = 1, this operation is an OR, while if n equals the number of different words specified, it is an AND [threshold OR].
A!!B	Matches the character string A, followed by two arbitrary characters, followed by the string B [fixed-length don't care].
A?B	Matches the character string A, followed by an arbitrary number of characters (possible none), followed by the string B. Note that ?A matches A with any prefix, while A? matches A with any suffix [variable-length don't care].

proceeds from there in serial fashion. At the sixth position of the string, a serial comparator would find that "ISSIP" does not match with "ISSIS" and would start to look for the pattern "ISSIP" in the remaining character string. The pattern obviously cannot be found in a serial search since the two leading characters "IS" the fifth and sixth positions have already passed the comparator. For the reason illustrated by the example, many text processor designs pay great attention to the handling of don't care conditions as we shall see in Section 8.3. The challenge in text processor design is to make the hardware perform operations as close to the operations listed in Table 8.1 as possible.

8.1.3 Operational Requirements

Unlike business-oriented databases, updates (in terms of modifications to and deletions from text databases) are seldom performed in text databases. Once textual data have been verified and entered into a database, they usually stay unchanged for a long period of time. Insertion operations, on the other hand, occur very often. They can usually be batched in a document retrieval system. However, in an office automation environment, insertions need to be carried out in real-time, as they are issued by the users. In addition to these differences in storage operations, the retrieval pattern in text databases is also somewhat different from other types of databases. The frequency of accessing a text decreases with the time it has been entered into the database.

Since a full text database is generally very large and the search time is long, these operational characteristics can be used to affect more efficient processing of text. For example, auxiliary storage structure can be introduced to accelerate search and retrieval operations without having to be concerned with the overhead of updating the auxiliary structure, because data modifications and deletions are infrequent. Also, data that are more recently entered into a database can be stored in faster memory devices in a storage hierarchy since they will be more frequently accessed. Thus, the designers of text processors can take advantage of these operational requirements in their designs.

8.2 BASIC STRUCTURE OF A TEXT RETRIEVAL SYSTEM

The main components of a typical text retrieval system is shown in Figure 8.1. It consists of (1) a control module, (2) a query translator, (3) an index file processing module, and (4) a full text search module. The control module's functions are similar to the transaction manager in a database management system. It receives search queries from the users, translates the queries using the query translator, allocates resources and sequences the execution of translated queries, receives retrieved text from the full text search module, and forwards the results to the user. The function of the index file processing module is to use the keywords or terms in the query identified by the query translator to search index files usually stored in the secondary storage. The purpose of this search is to identify a subset of texts (documents) that may satisfy the query. Here, "index file processing" is

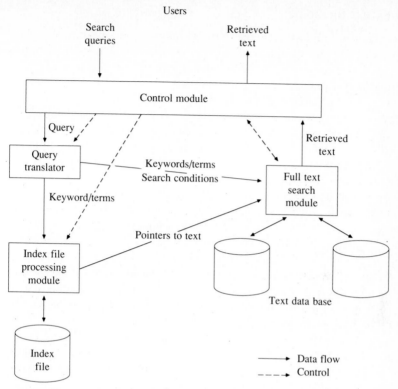

FIGURE 8.1
The basic structure of a text retrieval system.

used in a very general way. It may involve the processing of indices, inverted files, or superimposed files, depending on the particular software access method used in a text retrieval system to reduce the search space of a text database. The query keywords/terms identified by the query translator and the references (pointers or text identifiers) to the subset of texts produced by the index file processing module are used by the full text search module to scan the texts. Those texts that satisfy the search conditions specified in the query are retrieved and output to the user.

The main modules of a text retrieval system can be implemented by using a number of general-purpose and/or special-purpose processors. Hardware enhancements to a text retrieval system can improve its speed and reduce the cost of searching a large text database.

8.3 TEXT PROCESSING TECHNIQUES

Three commonly used text processing techniques are described in this section together with hardware systems that support them. They are full text scanning, inverted file and index processing, and superimposed coding.

8.3.1 Full Text Scanning

In a text processing system, the text database is generally stored in some secondary storage due to its size. In full text scanning, an entire document in the database is read into the main memory from the secondary storage and is matched against a search string (word, phrase, or other textual unit) to determine if it appears in the document. Every character of the document is scanned and compared. This method of processing a text has several advantages. First, it is conceptually very simple. Second, it does not require the use of any auxiliary data (e.g., indices) for providing direct access to portions of the text. Thus, it requires minimal storage space and eliminates the usual problem of updating the auxiliary data as a result of data insertion and deletion or occasional update. However, two serious disadvantages of full text scanning are its slow response time (the time elapsed from the time a search request is issued to the time output is first received) and its long execution time (the time elapsed from the issuing of the search request to the time the full text is scanned). A full text scan requires $O(m \times n)$ comparisons, where m is the length of the search string and n is the length of the text in characters. Many software algorithms have been introduced to reduce the number of comparisons required. For example, Knuth et al. [KNU77] have proposed an algorithm that can search a full document in $O(m + n)$ comparisons. Boyer and Moore [BOY77] have proposed another algorithm that usually requires less than $O(m + n)$ comparisons. However, both schemes require the preprocessing of the search string. If the text database is very large, the processing time required for a full text scan will not be acceptable in many applications. Special-purpose hardware would be required to accelerate the search.

8.3.2 Hardware for Supporting Full Text Scanning

The basic structure of a back-end full text search system described by Hollaar [HOL79] is shown in Figure 8.2. It consists of five main components: search controller, disk controller, term comparator, query resolver, and search database. The search controller's main functions are (1) to receive search requests from a host computer system, (2) to coordinate the overall operation of text search, and (3) to forward search conditions and programming information to the term comparator and the query resolver and to forward commands to the disk controller. The disk controller takes care of the I/O operations of the disk(s) where the text database is stored. In the case of text retrieval, the disk controller reads data from the search database into the term comparator. The term comparator examines the input data and determines whether it matches with any of the words or phrases specified in the search query. The results of matching these words and phrases are represented by logical values of 1's and 0's, which are passed to the query resolver. The resolver takes the results of individual term matches and evaluates them to determine if they satisfy the Boolean conditions provided in the original search query. The textual data that satisfy the search conditions are then transferred to the host computer.

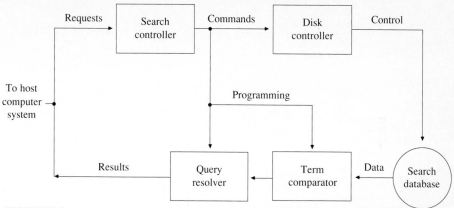

FIGURE 8.2

Basic structure of a back-end full text search system. (*Source:* [HOL83] copyright ©1983. Prentice-Hall, Inc., reprinted by permission.)

A number of back-end full text search systems can be paired with many individual disks or clusters of disks in order to search a large text database in parallel. This architectural structure would be the same as the multiprocessor systems with static processor-memory interconnection (see Chapter 6). It not only allows multiple text search systems to process different portions of the text database simultaneously, but also provides a text retrieval system with a parallel I/O capability.

The key component of the full text search system is the term comparator. It is the central processing unit of the system. Its text processing capabilities and efficiency determine, to a great extent, the functionality and speed of the text retrieval system. For supporting full text scanning, if the comparator can perform at a speed equal to or better than the speed at which text can be read into the main memory from the secondary storage, the text scanning time can overlap with the text input time, thus becoming transparent. Therefore, the design and implementation of the comparator is critical. There are three hardware techniques used in the design of term comparators. They are (1) parallel comparators, (2) cellular comparators, and (3) finite state automata (FSA).

8.3.2.1 PARALLEL COMPARATORS. In this design, a number of comparators are preloaded with different search operands (keywords or strings with or without don't care conditions). The text string to be searched is transferred (broadcast) to these comparators, which simultaneously match their respective operands with the input string. The results of individual term comparisons are sent to a query resolver for evaluation. This design was first proposed by Stellhorn [STE74] and modified by Hollaar [HOL79]. It is shown in Figure 8.3. The delimiter detector looks for the presence of control characters marking the start and end of the desired search context. When the start marker (e.g., beginning of a sentence or word) is encountered, the match of the search operands against the text string starts. The data window buffer is a modified form of a shift register with parallel output. It holds a substring of characters shifted in from the serial input source.

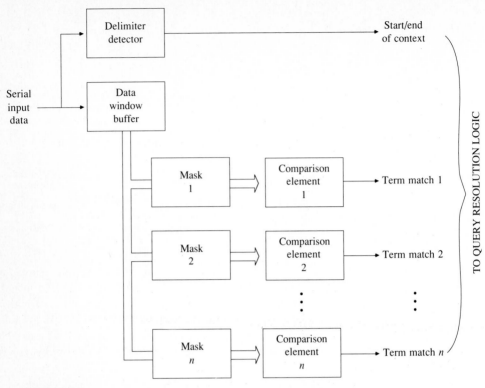

FIGURE 8.3
A multiterm parallel comparator. (*Source:* [HOL79] ©1979 IEEE)

The substring is compared in parallel with the search terms preloaded in the comparison elements. The masks corresponding to these comparison elements are for selecting the proper characters from the substring for comparison. Input data are continuously shifted into the buffer, and, for each character shifted into the buffer, the new substring is compared in parallel with the contents of the comparison elements. When a match occurs, the output of the respective comparison element will be true. The output of all the comparison elements are passed on to the query resolver, where Boolean and proximity conditions will be tested after the end of context signal is received from the delimiter detector. This type of comparator has the MISD architecture. The same approach is used in the database filters CAFS and SURE described in Chapter 4.

   The multiterm parallel comparator can handle fixed-length don't cares (FLD-Cs) and initial and terminal variable-length don't cares (VLDCs). FLDCs are handled by masking out the characters from the input string that corresponds to the don't care characters. For an initial VLDC, the match will start when the desired substring has been shifted into the buffer. All the leading characters will thus be ignored. For a terminal VLDC, the match will be indicated before the unspecified characters (i.e., the trailing characters) are encountered. This comparator also eliminated the problem associated with the serial comparator mentioned previously. The matching of "ISSIP" in the string "MISSISSIPPI" will be successful since the whole term "ISSIP" is matched against the string for every character shifted into the buffer. However, one problem with this design is that the length of a term to be matched is limited to the size of the buffer and that of the comparison elements. Some search terms can be very long (some chemical names may contain as many as 1,900 characters). In that case, the buffer and the comparison elements need to be expanded to a size that prevents it from being cost effective. Furthermore, the system does not handle embedded VLDCs.

The idea of parallel comparison of a character string against multiple terms can be implemented in associative memory of the type described in Chapter 5. Here, the associative memory acts as the comparison device. A word from the input data stream is used as an argument for an associative search of a memory loaded with search terms and flags. If no match occurs, then the word was not a part of the query and processing continues. When a match occurs, flags are sent to a query resolver to indicate that the terms matched. The Associative File Processor designed and manufactured by Operating Systems, Inc. is a text processor based on this concept [BIR77 and OPE77]. It can simultaneously process multiple queries, each of which can have a number of terms. Their corresponding flags are used to indicate to the query resolver which queries have resulted in a match. It is reported that this processor can search for a maximum term length of 8,192 characters (equivalent to approximately 1,200 English words). For an average query with 25 terms, it can simultaneously process queries from 50 different users in a batch.

One problem with the use of associative memory for term comparison is that, if the number of terms involved is large, the cost of the associative memory can become prohibitive. A cost-effective hardware hashing scheme was proposed by Burkowski [BUR82]. This scheme examines the characters of the document and query terms to identify the smallest number of characters that can best discriminate the terms. This scheme allows an expensive associative memory to be replaced by a RAM.

The configuration of the system is shown in Figure 8.4. The system consists of (1) a RAM for storing the document terms, (2) a shift register, which takes a serial text stream as input and provides parallel output of the characters shifted into the register, (3) a mapping module, which accepts a subset of the parallel-out lines of the shift register and computes a mapping function for producing an address for accessing the RAM, (4) a parallel comparator, which compares the term accessed from the RAM with the contents of the shift register to certify if they indeed match, and (5) a hit line, which is used to indicate the match result.

The key feature of the system is the mapping module. We shall therefore focus on it. The mapping technique used by the module is based on the theory of the bipartite graph. A *bipartite graph* consists of two sets of vertices and one set of edges. These two vertex sets are named *boys* and *girls*. An edge links a boy and a girl if there is a certain relationship between them. As an example, consider the following terms: "MARS," "MARTIAN," "STAR," and "ARTIST." All of the two-character substrings of these four terms form the set { RS, MA,

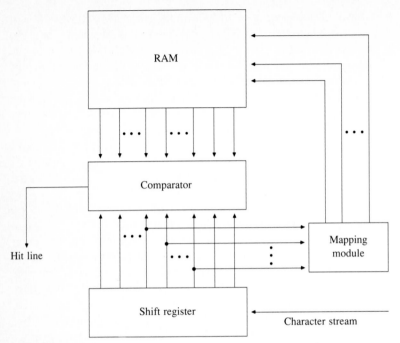

FIGURE 8.4
A term comparator with a RAM storage. (*Source:* [BUR82] ©1982 IEEE)

AR, RT, TI, IA, AN, TA, IS, ST}. Let the *boy set* be the set of four terms and the *girl set* be the set of substrings. If a member of the girl set is a substring of a member of the boy set, an edge will connect the boy and the girl. Figure 8.5 shows the bipartite graph for these terms and substrings. If no two edges share a vertex (either a boy or a girl), then a subset of edges in the graph is called a *matching*. For example, the edge sets { 2, 7}, { 3, 4, 13, 15}, and { 1, 5, 14, 15} are example of matchings. Within a matching, if every boy is connected with a certain girl, then the matching is called *saturating*. A saturated matching may not be achieved within a bipartite graph. (A similar situation exists when some boys in a party do not match the girls whom they like, even if the number of girls is larger than the number of boys). There is a fast algorithm [HOP73] for finding a maximal matching—that is, a matching that comes close to a saturating

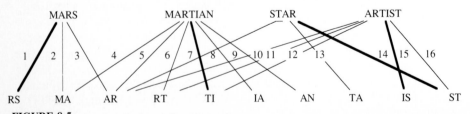

FIGURE 8.5
A bipartite graph for two-character substrings of four terms. (*Source:* [BUR82] ©1982 IEEE)

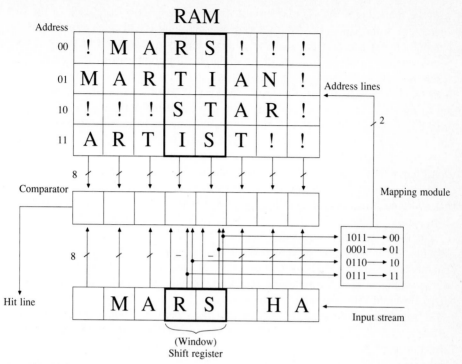

FIGURE 8.6
Storage formats of terms and mapping information. (*Source:* [BUR82] ©1982 IEEE)

in the sense that there is no other matching with more edges. An example of a saturating is shown by the heavy lines in the figure. In this case, it is also a maximal matching.

The proposed hardware system uses the substring of the shift register as a key to address a specific term stored in the RAM. The substring-to-address mapping is done using the matching function of the bipartite graph. In our example, a two-character window is defined at the center of the shift register. The four terms are loaded into the RAM storage with their characters located in such a way that their girls in the saturated matching are lined up with the window of the shift register. The format is illustrated in Figure 8.6. Here, it is assumed that the RAM storage is a 4 × 8 matrix and the shift register is a 1 × 8 array. Character "!" represents the don't care character. The mapping module contains a RAM that stores the information about the saturated matching of the bipartite graph: substring "RS" corresponds to term "MARS" with address '00'b; substring "TI" corresponds to term "MARTIAN" with address '01'b; substring "AR" corresponds to term "STAR" with address '10'b; and substring "IS" corresponds to term "ARTIST" with address '11'b. The parallel-out lines of the two-character window are plugged in the RAM of the mapping module. A subset of these lines is used by the mapping module to perform a contents-to-address mapping (or hashing) to address the mapping RAM. In this example, only the last two significant bits are connected with the mapping RAM. They form a four-bit address (two from each of the two characters in the shift register) to access the mapping RAM. The contents of the mapping RAM location are used to address the term stored in the other RAM, which releases a term to the parallel comparator for comparison. In the example, when the input text is shifted in the shift register with the format shown in Figure 8.6, the RAM will release the term "!MARS!!!" to the comparator. Since any substring RS in the input text stream will also cause the mapping module to hash it to the first term of the RAM, the comparator needs to match the term against the contents of the shift register to certify a match.

In this system, the FLDC problem can be handled simply by putting the don't care characters into the specific character locations in the RAM. However, there does not seem to be an easy solution for handling embedded VLDCs. The hardware hashing scheme also faces a problem similar to the problem associated with parallel comparators. It is difficult to determine the optimal length and width of the RAM storage. The usual hashing collision problem also occurs in this scheme. Perfect hashing of substrings to the mapping RAM addresses cannot be guaranteed. Burkowski [BUR82] used several methods to improve the efficiency of the proposed system, including recoding the data, increasing the window size, and using multiple scanning modules.

Another text processing system that uses parallel comparators is General Electric's GESCAN system [GE85a, GE85b, and GE87]. Its main component is a text array processor (TAP), which is a special-purpose processor for performing high-speed sequential searches of texts. This processor is designed to operate with the VAX-11 family of computers. The general operation of GESCAN is as follows. A text database is stored on the disks of a VAX computer. A user's query is entered from a terminal and is processed by software running on the VAX. A formatted query table is generated and downloaded to the TAP. The VAX computer also reads up to 128K-bytes of textual material from a disk (which forms a text block) and downloads 32K-bytes of data at a time to the TAP. Each load of 32K-bytes of data is searched against the formatted query table to match the terms in it. If any document in each load satisfies the search conditions represented by these query terms and their logical relationships, its identification number is written to an output buffer. Another load of 32K-bytes will then be searched by the TAP. This process continues until the entire 128K-byte block is processed. At this time, the document identification numbers in the output buffer are sent to the VAX computer, which then sends another 128K-bytes of textual data to the TAP. This process continues until the entire text database is processed. The VAX computer (the host) will then use the document identification numbers to retrieve the documents from its disks.

The TAP consists of an array of parallel processors. The block diagram of its architecture is shown in Figure 8.7. The operation of the TAP is controlled by an interface control unit, which receives control information from the host and provides status data to the host. Each term match processor (TMP) has a 1K-byte memory. The TMPs are loaded with query terms, which are compared against the input text stream in parallel. Exact matching of terms or matching with don't

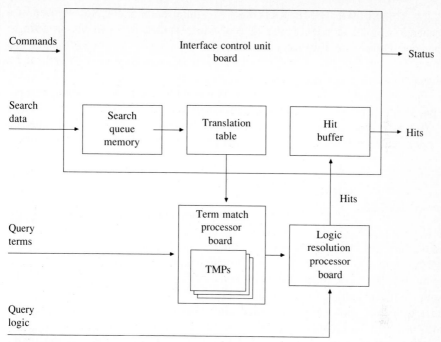

FIGURE 8.7
Architecture of GESCAN Text Array Processor (*Source:* [GE87] ©1987, General Electric)

cares will cause the TMPs to send match signals to the logic resolution processor (LRP). The LRP is a microprogrammable sequencer that can be programmed to perform threshold counts, proximity counts, and evaluate Boolean expressions specified in the user's query. It reports document identification information to the host computer if documents that satisfy the search have been found.

Textual data to be searched by the TMPs is first downloaded from the host computer's memory into a 64-byte search queue memory. The memory serves as a data buffer to allow the search data to be prefetched from the host. The search data are routed through a 256-word translation table. This table is used to identify control characters in the input text stream (i.e., characters for marking the beginning or end of fields and documents) and to convert all noncontrol characters to upper case as a way of standardizing the internal representation of the text.

The TMPs perform term matching with no concern for the relationships among terms. It is the LRP's job to determine if logical relationships of query terms are satisfied. The LRP is a programmable state machine that can perform a variety of query logic functions. Each time a match is reported to it by a TMP, a microprogram for that term is executed. This program may increment a threshold counter, set a match flag, check for a proximity condition, or perform other operations. The Boolean conditions of a query are also represented by a microprogram, which is executed at the end of each document that has been scanned by the system.

8.3.2.2 CELLULAR COMPARATORS.

A cellular comparator is composed of a number of simple, identical cells, each of which is capable of matching a single character. Figure 8.8 illustrates the structure of a basic cell and its input and output. The cell contains a state flip-flop (F), which can have value 0 or 1, and a register for storing a single character. A single match character (C) is preloaded into the holding register. It is compared with one character, X, found in the input character stream. If the character matches with the input character and the state flip-flop is 1, then the match output (M) is 1. Otherwise the output is 0. The cell operates synchronously. The output function M at time t is defined as follows:

$$M = 1 \text{ if } F = 1 \text{ and } C = X \text{ at time } t - 1$$

$$M = 0 \text{ otherwise}$$

The state of F can be initialized by the setup/control signal to 0 or 1 and subsequently controlled by the input E by taking its value. Although a single cell can do very little in terms of text matching, cascading of a large number of cells together would allow more interesting searches to be performed. For example, Figure 8.9 shows a linear array of cells designed to match a multicharacter string. In this example, the five cells are preloaded with the search term "ISSIP," and the anchor (the left-most enable signal) is set to 1. The character string "MISSISSIPPI" is broadcast to these cell one character at a time. At time $t = 1$, the character M is broadcast. Since no cell contains the character, the output signals of these cells, which are labeled 1, 2, 3, 4, and the output are all 0's. This is shown in the figure under the character M. At time $t = 2$, the second character, I, is broadcast to all the cells. This time, the output of cell 1 is 1 and all others are 0's. Note here that although cell 4 contains the character I, its enable input from cell 3 is 0. It therefore does not produce 1 as output. The process continues until time $t = 9$, when the match output equals 1, which indicates that

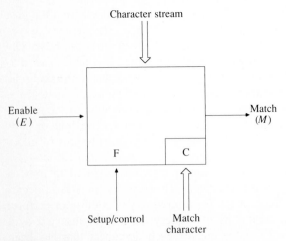

FIGURE 8.8
A comparison cell. (*Source:* [HOL79] ©1979 IEEE)

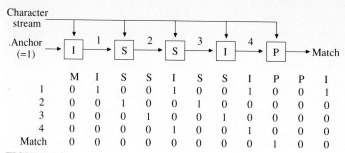

	M	I	S	S	I	S	S	I	P	P	I
1	0	1	0	0	1	0	0	1	0	0	1
2	0	0	1	0	0	1	0	0	0	0	0
3	0	0	0	1	0	0	1	0	0	0	0
4	0	0	0	0	1	0	0	1	0	0	0
Match	0	0	0	0	0	0	0	0	1	0	0

FIGURE 8.9
Cascaded cells for term matching. (*Source:* [HOL79] ©1979 IEEE)

the search term matches the input character string. This processing strategy is said to be operating in an *unanchored* mode, a term borrowed from the SNOBOL programming language [GRI68], since the anchor was set to 1 at all times to allow the search term to occur anywhere in the input character stream. For the search term to occur only at a specific point in the input (i.e., search in an anchored mode), the enable input to the first cell will be pulsed TRUE when the desired point is encountered in the input. For example, to determine whether the search term "ISSIP" matches the input string starting at location 5, the enable input of the first cell will be set to 1 at $t = 5$.

In order to compare an input stream against a number of terms at the same time, a cascaded, two-dimensional array of cells can be used in parallel, and the

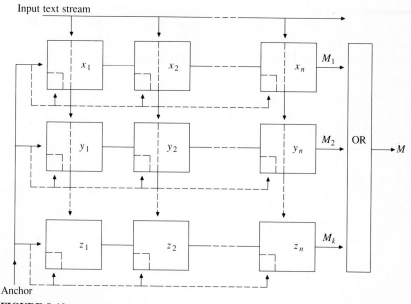

FIGURE 8.10
A cascaded array for matching multiple terms. (*Source:* [MUK78] ©1978 IEEE)

outputs of the array can be logically ORed and passed to a query resolver (see Figure 8.10). As shown in the figure, k terms are compared in parallel against the input text. $M_1, M_2,...M_k$ are the output match bits of these terms. They are ORed to produce the final match signal, M. The dotted lines connecting the cells are for setting anchors to allow searching text in an anchored mode and allow subpatterns of these terms to be matched against the input text. For example, if the ith cell anchor flip-flop of the term $x_1, x_2,...x_n$ is set to 1 at time t, then the existence of the subpattern $x_i, x_{i+1},...x_n$ in the text can be detected. The reader should recognize that the structure and the principle involved here are similar to the associative memories described in Chapter 5. In addition to cascading a number of cells to match multiple search terms, it is possible to connect the basic cells to form more complex match patterns. Figure 8.11 illustrates a structure of cells for checking if the input stream contains the words BOY, TOY, or CART. Each of these words is preceded and followed by a blank, which is shown in the figure by a square symbol.

Cellular comparators allow the implementation of don't cares quite easily. For an FLDC, the cell delays the propagation of the enable signal for as many input characters as there are FLDC characters, thus allowing the characters corresponding to the don't care characters to pass without affecting the output signals of the cells. For initial or terminal VLDC, no special action needs to be taken. Embedded VLDCs can be handled by introducing a cell whose output is TRUE when its enable input is TRUE, and remains TRUE throughout the remaining matching operations.

The uniformly structured cellular hardware is particularly suitable for LSI/VLSI implementation. Mukhopadhyay [MUK78] has demonstrated that cells can be connected to perform the functions used in SNOBOL, such as Span, Break, Len, Tab Pos, Arb, and Arbno operations. Database operations such as Delete, Insert, and Retrieval can also be implemented using this technique. The circuits for these operations have been designed and presented by Mukhopadhyah

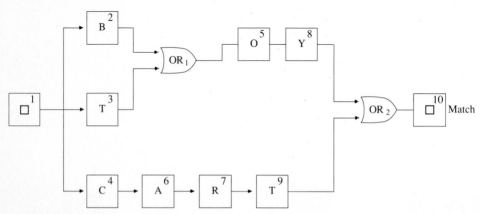

FIGURE 8.11
Gated cascaded cells for complex patterns.

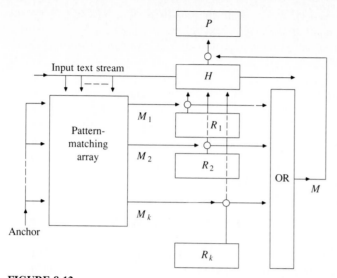

FIGURE 8.12

A circuit for pattern matching with conditional and immediate value replacement. (*Source:* [MUK78] ©1978 IEEE)

[MUK78]. As an example, the circuit for pattern matching with conditional and immediate value replacement will be shown here.

The pattern-matching problem of interest is as follows. A text stream is to be searched. If it contains any one of a set of k terms ($x_1,x_2,...x_n$, $y_1,y_2,...y_n$, $z_1,z_2,...z_n$), a corresponding immediate value will be used to replace the term found in the text stream. Figure 8.12 shows the circuit for this operation. The terms are stored in the pattern-matching array. Their corresponding immediate values are stored in the registers R_1, R_2,...R_k. Register H is a shift register that holds x number of input characters—the same size as the R registers. The input text stream is shifted into the H register, one character at a time, as it is transferred to the pattern-matching array. If a substring of the input matches with any one of the match terms, say term i, the match output M_i of that term will be 1. The final match signal M will also be 1, which activates the gates shown in the figure as a circle between registers H and P. At this time, H register holds the substring of the input text. Its contents will be transferred to the P register, and the contents of register R_i (the immediate value for replacement) will be transferred into H. Thus, the term found in the text stream is replaced.

Before leaving this section, it should be reemphasized that the cellular approach for comparator design and implementation is most suitable for the VLSI implementation. Text processing operations can be directly implemented on VLSI chips and can perform efficiently. However, since the cell structures are built for specific operations, they cannot be changed easily.

8.3.2.3 FINITE STATE AUTOMATA. The third approach for the implementation of term comparators is by using finite state automata. The reader should recall that the same approach was used in the database filter VERSO described in Chapter 4. Two types of finite state automata and their hardware support will be examined in this section: finite state automaton (FSA) and partitioned finite state automaton (PFSA).

Finite state automaton. An FSA can be formally defined as a five-tuple (A, S, M, B, F), where

> A : A set of input alphabets
> S : A set of elements called states
> M : A mapping from $A \times S$ into S
> B : A member of S, called the initial state
> F : A non-empty subset of S, called the final states

In text processing using an FSA, the input text stream is formed by the alphabets in A. The operation of the FSA starts at the initial state B. As each character of the input stream is examined, the mapping M is used to determine the next state of the FSA based on the input character and the current state of the machine. The process continues until a final state is reached or a delimiter, which indicates a search context, is detected. If a delimiter is detected before a final state is reached, the match fails. Otherwise, the input text stream matches a specified pattern defined by the FSA.

A state transition diagram is a common way to show the mapping function M of an FSA. Figure 8.13 shows the state transition diagram of an FSA for recognizing the character string "COMPUTE." In the figure, the numbered circles represent the states of the FSA. The transitions from one state to another are indicated by arrows, which are labeled by the input characters that cause the transitions. The process of matching starts from state 0, the initial state. An input character "C" will cause the automaton to enter state 1, while any other character, denoted by the symbol #, will cause it to remain in state 0. The transitions from state to state are thus driven by the characters of the input stream until the final state, 7, is reached. In this case, the automaton can determine that the character string COMPUTE exists in the text stream.

This FSA not only matches the word COMPUTE but also matches any string containing the characters COMPUTE, such as the word COMPUTER. To design

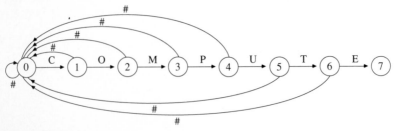

FIGURE 8.13
The transition diagram for the string "COMPUTE."

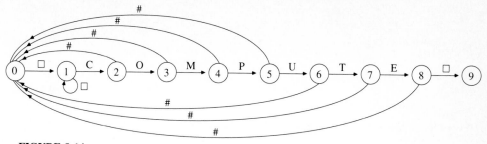

FIGURE 8.14
The state transition diagram for the word "COMPUTE."

an FSA to recognize only the word COMPUTE, blanks need to be added as a part of the transition diagram (see Figure 8.14). The arrows labeled by blanks (□) are used as the delimiters to isolate the individual word "COMPUTE."

For detecting a substring embedded in another substring, as is the case in the previous example of "ISSIP" within the word "MISSISSIPPI," a proper transition diagram for the FSA is shown in Figure 8.15. Note that there is a transition from state 4 back to state 2 to reinitiate the matching process when an input character "S" occurs. This is because the character "I" repeats twice in the first and fourth positions of the substring "ISSIP." The transition from state 4 to state 2 due to character "S" is equal to the transition from state 1 to state 2. In states 1, 2, and 4, an input character "I" will cause the FSA to return to state 1 to restart the process.

In order to handle the FLDCs, the FSA approach adds a state to the FSA for each don't care character. The transition from this added state to the next state is caused by any character except the blank delimiter. For example, Figure 8.16 contains the state diagram for recognizing all words with the pattern "!!!ING," which has three initial don't care characters. Words such as "COMING," "ROWING," "SAYING," and so forth will all match the pattern. The VLDCs can be implemented without additional state. For example, in the case of initial VLDCs, such as the pattern "?ING," the transition diagram for the FSA is given in Figure 8.17. All the arrows labeled #, except that of state 0, return to state 1; all those labeled "I" return to state 2. If the last state of Figure 8.14 is removed, the

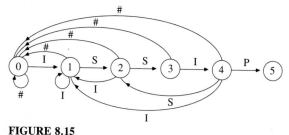

FIGURE 8.15
The state transition diagram for the substring "ISSIP." (*Source:* [HOL79] ©1979 IEEE)

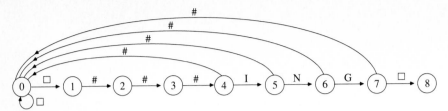

FIGURE 8.16
The state transition diagram for matching "!!!ING" (initial FLDC).

resulting transition diagram becomes one for detecting the terminal VLDC of the word "COMPUTE?" as shown in Figure 8.18.

Building a comparator for handling embedded VLDCs is quite complicated using either the parallel or cellular approach. However, it is quite simple in an FSA. An embeded don't care character divides a string into two substrings: prefix and suffix substrings. A transition from the prefix substring to the suffix substring occurs only if the first character of the suffix substring is encountered in the input text stream. Otherwise, the FSA will remain in the last state of the prefix substring. For example, Figure 8.19 shows the state transition diagram for detecting words with the pattern "RE?ING," such as "REWARDING," "READ-ING," and so forth. The arrow labeled #in state 3 keeps the FSA in the same state until the starting character "I" of the suffix is encountered.

Two general methods can be used to implement FSAs: software and hardware methods. By software means, a conventional computer can be programmed to emulate an FSA. According to the software emulation work done by Aho and Coranck [AHO75], the speed of a bibliographic search can improve five to ten times. This performance still suffers from the same cost-efficiency problem of other approaches used in conventional computers. The alternative solution is to use special-purpose hardware to implement a variety of FSAs. A simple implementation using a block memory will now be described.

The state transition mapping of an FSA can be stored as a transition table in a memory (see Figure 8.20). A block of memory is used to store the data associated with each state. The length of each block is equal to the number of the input alphabet, A. Each element of the block memory contains the next state number. Figure 8.20 shows the transition table for matching the word "COMPUTE." A register is used to keep the current state number. When an input character is examined, it is used as an index to the block memory element, which corresponds to the current state. The next state number retrieved from the specific location in

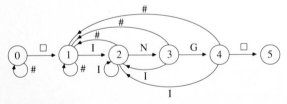

FIGURE 8.17
The state transition diagram for matching "?ING" (initial VLDC).

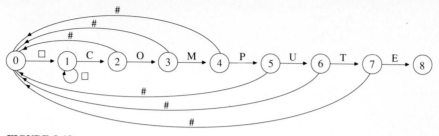

FIGURE 8.18
The state transition diagram for matching "COMPUTE?" (terminal VLDC).

the block memory is placed in the state register. There it is compared with the final states to determine if a final state has been reached.

One obvious problem with this approach is that it requires a large memory. A transition table often contains many *default* states, which point to the beginning state to reinitiate the matching. Also, the table is often quite sparse. Some method should be applied to reduce the size of the sparse transition table. One way of reducing the memory size is to condense each block of memory by including only those entries that correspond to those input alphabets that cause transitions to states other than the default transition. A special entry is also kept to specify the default transition. Assuming 8-bit ASCII code is used to store each character, the memory of this condensed state table can be reduced by a factor of about 100. However, it will substantially increase the processing time per character since it is necessary to search for the proper transition.

Bird et al. [BIR77] suggested a solution to these memory and speed problems through the use of associative/parallel processors. In their method, state transitions are distinguished into two types: sequential and index. Sequential states are used to match single characters. They contain characters that cause the FSA to sequentially advance from the beginning state to the final state. These characters are stored sequentially in the memory. The state register is used to indicate the current state in the sequence. When an input character matches the character indicated by the state register, it causes the state register to be incremented by 1 automatically. In this method, nine bits are required to represent a sequential state—eight for the character and one to distinguish it from an index state.

Index states are those that provide for multiple branches to different states. They contain two fields along with a bit for indicating an index state. The first field

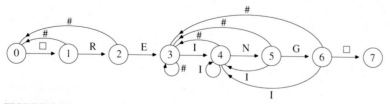

FIGURE 8.19
The state transition diagram for matching "RE?ING" (embedded VLDC).

Input alphabet	States								
	0	1	2	3	4	5	6	7	8
□	1	1	0	0	0	0	0	0	9
A	0	0	0	0	0	0	0	0	0
B	0	0	0	0	0	0	0	0	0
C	0	2	0	0	0	0	0	0	0
D	0	0	0	0	0	0	0	0	0
E	0	0	0	0	0	0	0	8	0
⋮	•••	•••	•••	•••	•••	•••	•••	•••	••
M	0	0	0	4	0	0	0	0	0
N	0	0	0	0	0	0	0	0	0
O	0	0	3	0	0	0	0	0	0
P	0	0	0	0	5	0	0	0	0
⋮	•••	•••	•••	•••	•••	•••	•••	•••	••
T	0	0	0	0	0	0	7	0	0
U	0	0	0	0	0	6	0	0	0
⋮	•••	•••	•••	•••	•••	•••	•••	•••	••

FIGURE 8.20
The transition table for matching the word "COMPUTE."

is called a bit-vector. It has 256 bits, with one bit for each possible input alphabet (assuming 8-bit characters are used). If the bit in the vector corresponding to the input character is 0, the default transition is made, which generally reinitiates the FSA for matching the next word. Otherwise, the number of 1's preceding the bit corresponding to the input character are counted. A parallel adder network can be used for the counting. The count is used as an index to fetch the transition state number contained in the second field of the index state. The state register is replaced by the new state number and compared with the final states. Figure 8.21 shows the sequential and index states for matching the substring "ISSIP." Here, the sequential states contain the ordinal characters "ISSIP" corresponding to the states from 0 to 4, respectively. There are five 256-bit vectors and five second fields representing five index states. To understand the bit settings of the index states in Figure 8.21, the reader should refer back to Figure 8.15 where the transition diagram for "ISSIP" is shown. When the state register is equal to 0 (i.e., the FSA is in the sequential state 0), an input character "I" will cause the state register to be incremented by 1 automatically, thus entering into the next sequential state 1. Any other input character will cause the bit vector to be examined. Since all bits of the left-most bit vector are 0's, the default state (state 0, in this case) is taken. If the FSA is in the sequential state 1, an input character "I" will cause the Ith entry of the corresponding vector to be examined. In this case, the entry contains 1, which will cause all the preceding 1's to be counted. However, there is no 1 preceding the Ith entry. Thus, the count equals 0. The

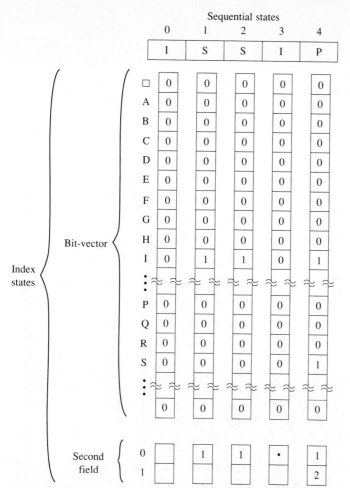

FIGURE 8.21
Sequential and index states for detecting the substring "ISSIP."

0th entry of the second field is fetched. It contains the value 1, which is the state to be entered next. When the FSA is in state 4, an input character "I" will cause state 1 (due to value 1 in the 0th entry of the second field) to be entered, whereas, an input character "S" will cause state 2 (due to value 2 in the first entry of the second field) to be entered.

The storage requirement for a 256-bit vector can be reduced without much loss of information if 6-bit characters rather than 8-bit characters are used. In this case, only 56 bits are needed to represent each bit-vector.

Partitioned finite state automaton. Another method of term comparator design, called partitioned finite state automaton (PFSA), is based on the concept of nondeterministic finite state automaton (NFSA). An NFSA will be defined and its difficulty in implementation will be discussed before detailing the PFSA.

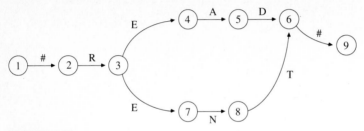

FIGURE 8.22
An example nondeterministic FSA.

An NFSA is a finite state machine that can be in more than one state at a given time. Different from an FSA, in which only one state is active and an input character can cause a transition from the current state to only one state (i.e., deterministic), an NFSA may have a transition to multiple states (nondeterministic) in response to an input character. An NFSA is a convenient way for defining a pattern of terms that share some characters. For example, the words "READ" and "RENT" share the first two characters. They can be defined by the state transition diagram shown in Figure 8.22. In the case of text matching, after the second character "E" has been matched with the input text string, two alternatives "A" and "N" are acceptable as the next character from the input string. The transition from state 3 to multiple states, 4 and 7, is called *forking*. After the fork occurs, these multiple states are active in the sense that their corresponding characters are to be matched with the next character in the input string. At most, only one of them will remain active after the matching since the next input character cannot match different characters at the same time. The rest of the state(s) will terminate. Since a regular FSA is a special case of an NFSA, an NFSA can always perform the operations of an equivalent FSA.

One way to implement an NFSA is to transform it dynamically into a number of regular FSAs every time a forking is encountered. These FSAs include an idle FSA, which will be started every time a possible beginning of a term is recognized [HOP79]. This method requires that the transition table be replicated as many times as the number of FSAs generated. A dynamic scheduling of these FSAs is also needed, which represents a considerable amount of overhead in implementation.

An implementation scheme based on the NFSA concept but without the mentioned drawbacks has been proposed and implemented in hardware by Haskin and Hollaar, et al. [HAS80a, HAS80b, HAS83, and HOL83]. It is called a partitioned finite state automaton (PFSA). It partitions an NFSA into a number of FSAs based on two criteria, which are to be discussed later. Instead of replicating the transition state table for handling the forking situation in an NFSA, this scheme partitions FSAs in such a way that only a small part of the original transition table is needed by each destination state involved in a fork.

An example of PFSA is shown in Figure 8.23. This PFSA is for matching the four terms shown in the figure: #READ#, #RENT, MEN#, and #MOMENT#. The character # is used to denote a delimiter of a term such as blank, comma, or other punctuation marks. In the figure, all states are represented by numbered

Partition 1

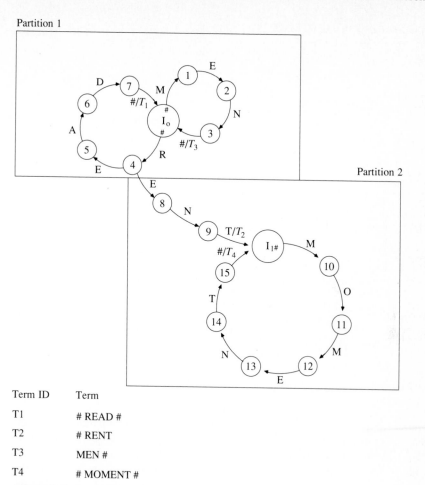

Partition 2

Term ID	Term
T1	# READ #
T2	# RENT
T3	MEN #
T4	# MOMENT #

FIGURE 8.23
A partitioned PFSA for matching four terms.

circles. Two idle states, I_0 and I_1, serve as the initial states for the two partitions, respectively. The token inside an idle state and next to a start-up transition arc indicates the type of the previous character that is necessary for a start-up. The token on a transition arc and outside of a state circle indicates the start-up character for matching the sequence of characters that follows. A term identification ($T1$, $T2$, $T3$, or $T4$) following a slash ($/$) sign on an arc indicates that the term has a match or a hit in that transition. In partition 1, the asterisk symbol (*) indicates that any character can precede the character "M." This is for matching the term "MEN#."

A PFSA is formed by a number of partitions, each of which is an FSA having the property that no two states in it can be simultaneously active. This means that in the course of character matching following a sequence of states in a partition no other transition should force the FSA into another state due to forking or a start-up transition. Two criteria are therefore used to form partitions to represent an NFSA.

TRANSITION TABLE FOR PARTITION 1:

Addr	Hit	Loop	Type	Token	Next	Next left	Next right	State ID
0	0	1	–	–	0	–	–	I_0
1	0	0	0	E	2	–	–	1
2	0	0	0	N	3	–	–	2
3	1	0	1	#	4	–	–	3
4	0	0	0	E	5	–	1	4
5	0	0	0	A	6	–	–	5
6	0	0	0	D	7	–	–	6
7	1	0	1	#	0	–	–	7

Start-up table special entries:

Character	Previous type	Start address
M	#	1
R	#	4

FIGURE 8.24
Transition table and start-up table for partition 1.

First, the destination states involved in a fork must belong to separate partitions. For example, states 5 and 8 are in separate partitions. Second, sequences of states should be assigned to partitions in such a way that when a sequence is followed during character matching, a start-up transition cannot incorrectly interrupt the sequence. For example, if the "MEN#" sequence, that is, states 1, 2, and 3, are grouped in partition 2 together with the sequence "#MOMENT#," both states 12 and 1 will be entered when the input character string contains "#MOM"....This is because the substring "OM" will cause a start-up transition to state 1 (recall that "*" represents any character that precedes "M") as well as causing a transition from state 11 to state 12. Thus, based on the second criterion, the sequence "MEN#" should be in a different partition from that of "#MOMENT#."

The transition tables for partitions 1 and 2 and their corresponding start-up entries are shown in Figures 8.24 and 8.25. The Addr column specifies table index numbers, and the Hit column indicates the transitions that result in the matching of terms. A "1" in the Loop column indicates an idle state. The Type field specifies the token types. The en dash (–) indicates a null value. The Token field stores the tokens to be matched with the input string in different states. The Next field contains the pointer to the next entry of the transition table whose token needs to be matched. Next Left and Next Right are pointers to entries in other transition tables that contain states of a fork. The last column, State ID, stores the identifications of the states.

TRANSITION TABLE FOR PARTITION 2:

Addr	Hit	Loop	Type	Token	Next	Next left	Next right	State ID
0	0	1	–	–	0	–	–	I_1
1	0	0	0	N	2	–	–	8
2	1	0	0	T	0	–	–	9
3	0	0	0	O	4	–	–	10
4	0	0	0	M	5	–	–	11
5	0	0	0	E	6	–	–	12
6	0	0	0	N	7	–	–	13
7	0	0	0	T	8	–	–	14
8	1	0	0	#	0	–	–	15

Start-up table special entries:

Character	Previous type	Start address
M	#	4

FIGURE 8.25
Transition table and start-up table for partition 2.

A hardware implementation of PFSAs has been described by Haskin and Hollaar [HAS83 and HOL83]. It consists of two major components: a match controller and a ring structure of character matchers (CMs) as illustrated in Figure 8.26. The controller serves as the interface between the PFSA and other system components, such as the query resolver and memory systems. An input text string is taken from the secondary storage or the main memory and processed by the controller to determine the start of the character string to be matched. The string

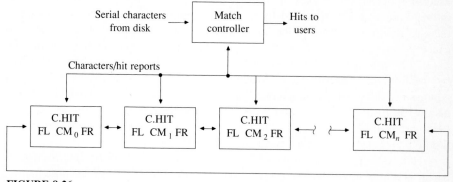

FIGURE 8.26
Block diagram of the PFSA implementation. (*Source:* [HOL83] copyright ©1983. Prentice-Hall, Inc., reprinted by permission.)

is broadcast character by character to all the character matchers, each of which has been assigned with a partition of the PFSA. The character matchers operate in parallel and send hit reports, state addresses, and their identification numbers to the controller. The controller correlates the data and forwards them to other components of the text retrieval system (e.g., the query resolver).

The *character matchers* (CMs) are connected to the controller by a common bus. Each CM is also connected to its two neighbors in the form of a ring. Since a partition of a PFSA is assigned to a CM, activation of multiple CMs will take place when a fork to multiple states is processed. The addresses of these desired states need to be transferred to the proper CMs. In the proposed system, these addresses are represented as fork vectors and are sent to adjacent neighbors through the ring connection. In the ring structure, there are only two immediate neighbors associated with each CM. If there are more than two destination states in a fork, a transformation of the fork structure into a tree structure with a maximum of three branches for each state can be easily performed so that one state will be stored in a CM and the other two will be located in its two adjacent CMs. Thus, the three pointers labeled Next, Next left, and Next right are sufficient for implementing forks.

The structure of a CM is shown in Figure 8.27. It is a direct implementation of the transition tables and start-up tables illustrated in Figures 8.24 and 8.25. Each CM consists of two memories for storing (1) the transition table and the fork table and (2) the start-up table. The transition and fork table memory (TT) is addressed by an address register AREG. The start-up table memory (ST) is addressed by the character of the input text string. The addressed entry provides the type code of the previous character before the actual start-up of a term and the starting address in the transition table. A type comparator is used to compare the type code stored in ST with the type code of the current input character to determine if a start-up condition exists. If it does, the starting address is placed on the address bus to access the transition table.

The processing logic of the CM is centered on the character comparator (CHAR COMP). In this comparator, the input character is compared with the token accessed from the transition table. H, L, T, and C are four control bits used to affect different types of comparison. A successful comparison may cause the next state in TT (specified by the Next pointer) to be entered. In this case, the Next address is gated to the address bus. A successful comparison may also cause the transfer of a fork vector to the CM's left or right neighbors using the FL or FR line drivers shown in the figure. The forking operation is controlled by the fields of the fork table. When a fork vector is received by a CM, the address provided is used to activate the addressed state in TT. A control signal is also given to the type comparator and the character comparator to prevent them from gating other addresses to the address bus, thus giving the fork processing the higher priority over other types of transitions.

The CM has been fabricated as an integrated circuit using the N-channel Metal Oxide Semiconductor (NMOS) fabrication process. Its VLSI implementation has been detailed by Hollaar et al. [HOL83].

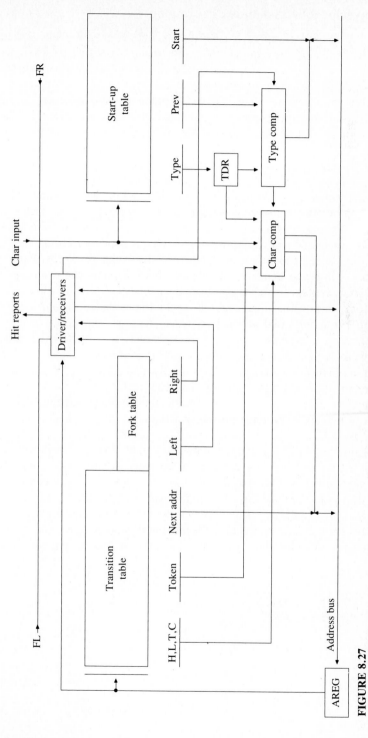

FIGURE 8.27
The organization of a character matcher. (*Source*: [HOL83] copyright © 1983. Prentice-Hall, Inc., reprinted by permission.)

8.3.3   Inverted File and Index Processing

Except in a few applications, such as legal or patent systems, in which exhaustive searches of databases are required to ensure that no existing cases or patents are missed, most applications of text databases do not require that full texts in an entire database be searched. In these cases, a full text scanning would not be cost effective. However, it would be desirable if there is a way to quickly reduce the search to a small subset of documents potentially relevant to a search. Full text scanning can then be carried out over this small subset to select the final documents. The inverted file method and a variety of indexing methods are frequently used for this purpose. Textual material, such as documents, can be represented by a set of keywords or index terms that can be assigned by someone or automatically extracted by computers out of the documents. If these keywords are inverted by storing pointers to the locations of the documents or some references to these documents together with these keywords, the keywords derived from a search query can be used to search this data to determine the subset. Thus, retrieval speed can be greatly improved. If all the keywords representing the documents in a text database are used in this inversion, the resulting file of keywords and pointers to the text is called an *inverted file*. If some selective keywords are used in the inversion, the result file is called an *index file*. The index file is commonly used in database management systems as an access method for searching a database. Figure 8.28 illustrates an inverted file structure. Each keyword is placed in a directory, which is implemented as an index file, along with a pointer to an associated posting list and a counter for keeping track of the number of entries in the posting list. The *posting list* for a keyword contains a list of unique identifiers for all the documents or document subdivisions identified by the keyword. Each posting list is stored in a file called the *posting file*.

Inversion and indexing of a text database can be done to a very low or very high level. At a low level, say word level, an entry in an inverted file or index file associated with a keyword/term will contain pointers to the locations where the word occurs in the database. At a high level, say document level, the entry will have pointers to all the documents that the keyword characterizes. Different levels of inversion determine not only the amount of storage space needed to store the inverted file or index file, but also the amount of text scanning required. A

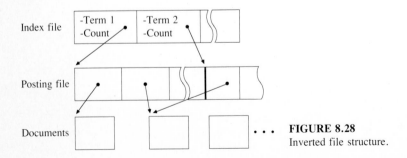

FIGURE 8.28
Inverted file structure.

lower level inversion requires more storage space but less text scanning than a higher level inversion. The selection of inversion level is one of the important performance considerations in a text database system design.

These inverted file and indexing techniques allow the users to combine a list of keyword or index terms and to specify Boolean relationships among them in an expression with AND, OR, and NOT operators. The expression must be satisfied before a document is retrieved. In retrieval, the text processing system will first consult the index file to obtain the posting list addresses and access the posting lists to select those document identifiers that satisfy the search logic specified by the Boolean expression of the index terms. The process of comparing posting lists is known as *term coordination*. It involves merging posting lists and set operations on these lists. This can take a substantial amount of CPU time if there is a large number of index terms or if some of the associated posting lists are very large. For example, individual index terms can reference from 1 to 500,000 documents in the MEDLARS databases [NAT72]. Obviously, a text processing system can benefit from a hardware implementation of the term coordination process.

8.3.4   Hardware for Supporting Inverted File and Index Processing

The system called EUREKA is a good example of a system with hardware support for term coordination. It is an experimental system developed at the University of Illinois for textual information retrieval [HOL76, STE74, and STE77]. It uses the inverted file structure with special hardware for term coordination. The general configuration of EUREKA is shown in Figure 8.29.

The user issues a search request through a front-end processor which translates the request and passes it to a resource scheduling processor. The resource scheduling processor determines the proper hardware subsystems necessary to service the request and sequences their operations. It also reorders the user-specified request in order to reduce the disk latency time and the length of intermediate results during posting list merge. The reordered request is in the form of an ordered set of index terms or keywords, which are given to the index file controller. The controller finds the specified terms of the request in the index file stored on a disk and forwards the proper lists of pointers (to the postings file) to the postings file disk controller. The postings file disk controller operates under the control of the resource scheduling processor to access the document postings lists and transfer them to the list merging processor through a mediate memory (a buffer memory). The list merging processor takes two lists at a time and performs an intersection, or a union, or removal of elements of one list from the other depending on the operation required for that search request. The list-merging operation is repeated over the document postings lists to obtain the final merged list of document identifiers. The merged list is used by the full text scanner to access and scan the full texts stored on disks to determine those documents that satisfy the search conditions. The retrieved documents are transferred to the front-end processor which forwards them to the user.

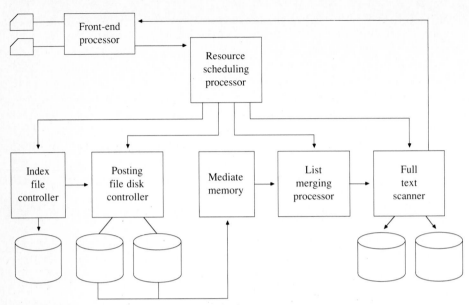

FIGURE 8.29
The general configuration of EUREKA. (*Source:* [STE77] ©1977 IEEE)

The list merging processor is central to the term coordination task. In its simplest form, the list merging processor consists of a comparator, a selector, a logic to access a data memory, and a special sequencer to control these components. Data are fetched from the disk memory and placed in one of the two holding registers, which correspond to the two posting lists. The function of the list merging processor is to combine two ordered lists into a single ordered list. To achieve that, the values in the two lists are compared and the lower of the two is transferred to an output register. For a union operation (i.e., logical OR), the contents of the output register are transferred to a data memory. If the intended operation is a set intersection (i.e., logical AND), the transfer occurs if the two input values are equal. In either case, the register that holds the lower value is loaded with the next entry from the data memory.

The organization of the list merging processor is shown in Figure 8.30. It consists of a Batcher-type even-odd merge network [BAT68], a term coordination network capable of removing unwanted results produced by the merge network, and a data memory for storing the posting lists read from the disk and for storing the final result of a merge. The processing is done in a bit-serial, pipelined fashion. Since the posting lists to be merged generally contain more data than what the registers in the merge network can hold, the lists must be broken into a number of sublists of n elements each. Here, it is assumed that $2n$ elements from two input lists can be held and processed by the merge network. These sublists must be processed by the list merging processor in separate hardware cycles. In each cycle, n of the smallest elements are the final results and are output to a term coordination network, labeled F in the figure. The other n larger elements need

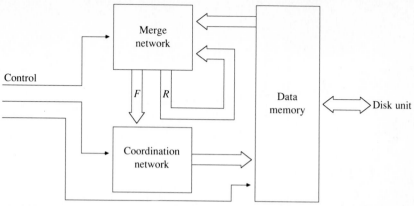

FIGURE 8.30
The organization of the list merging processor. (*Source:* [STE77] ©1977 IEEE)

to be further processed and compared with the subsequent sublists. Therefore, they are returned to the merge network, labeled R in the figure.

To illustrate the operation of the list merging processor, consider the merging of the following two ordered lists:

L1 (3,5,8,10,12,27)
L2 (2,3,5,6,10,13,27,33)

Assume that the search request is (L1 OR L2), and n is equal to 3. These two lists are divided into the following five sublists for the value of n chosen.

L11 (3,5,8), L12 (10,12,27)
L21(2,3,5), L22 (6,10,13), L23(27,33)

The merging process in six cycles is shown in Table 8.2. In each cycle, there are three parallel activities taking place: (1) the reading of data from the disk, (2) the merging and coordination, and (3) the writing of the coordinated results to the disk. In cycle 3, the comparison of L22(6,10,13) with R2(5,5,8) produces two output sections F2(5,5,6) and R3(8,10,13). The value 5 is the smallest value in these sublists. It is combined with the intermediate results of the previous cycle (2,3) to form the coordination result (2,3,5). The next smallest element in F2 is the value 6, which is stored as the intermediate result. R3(8,10,13) is sent back to the merge network for comparison during the next cycle.

In general, if L1 and L2 contain i and j sublists, respectively, the total number of cycles would be $i + j + 2$, which includes the cycle for writing the last result back to the disk. It was estimated that this processor can increase the speed by a factor of 10 or 20.

If a substantial increase beyond this is necessary, a number of list merging processors can be used to perform list merging in parallel [HOL78a and HOL83]. For example, $N - 1$ number of identical merging processors can be structured in a binary tree of merging network to merge N lists in $\log_2 N$ stages as illustrated in Figure 8.31. Each merge processor is a bit-serial, custom-built processor. With the

TABLE 8.2
Cycles in the term coordination process. (*Source:* [STE77] ©1977 IEEE)

Cycle	Feed back	Read in	Merge		Coordination result	Intermediate
1	—	L11(3, 5, 8)	—	R1(3, 5, 8)	—	—
2	R1(3, 5, 8)	L21(2, 3, 5)	F1(2, 3, 3)	R2(5, 5, 8)	—	(2, 3)
3	R2(5, 5, 8)	L22(6, 10, 13)	F2(5, 5, 6)	R3(8, 10, 13)	(2, 3, 5)	(6)
4	R3(8, 10, 13)	L12(10, 12, 27)	F3(8, 10, 10)	R4(12, 13, 27)	(6, 8, 10)	—
5	R4(12, 13, 27)	L23(25, 27, 33)	F4(12, 13, 25)	R5(27, 27, 33)	(12, 23, 25)	—
6	R5(27, 27, 33)	—	F5(27, 27, 33)	—	(27, 33)	—

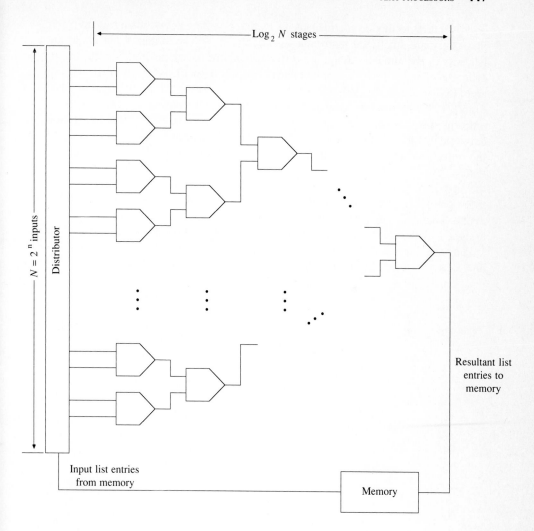

FIGURE 8.31
A list merging network. (*Source:* [HOL83] copyright ©1983. Prentice-Hall, Inc., reprinted by permission.)

available integrated circuit technology, it has been estimated that a 127-processor list merging network should be able to process a 100-term query in just over a second.

The merging network in Figure 8.31 can merge as many lists in one pass as there are leaf-processors in the binary tree. If the number of lists to be merged exceeds the number of leaf-nodes, these lists will have to be merged in multiple passes through the network. This will not give very good performance since intermediate results must be accumulated and possibly written to and read from the secondary storage. Increasing the number of nodes in the network is not a good solution to this problem since, in many cases, the keywords/terms involved in a query are small and many merge processors will be idling. What is needed is a way of dynamically assigning different sizes of merge networks to queries of different complexities. A two-level list merging network is proposed by Huang and Hollaar et al. [HUA80 and HOL83] as a solution to the problem addressed. Figure 8.32 shows the structure of the network. It consists of two levels of uniform-sized merge trees. These two levels are interconnected by a connection network that allows the output of a tree at one level to be connected directly to the output buffers or to the input of a tree at another level. For simple queries with a few keywords/terms (thus, involving a few lists), the merging is done at the first level and the results are transferred directly to the output buffers. For a more complex query, some merge trees at the second level are assigned to the query. They take input from those merge trees at the first level, which have been assigned to the query, as well as from the input buffers. A direct access mass storage system is used to read lists from the secondary storage to the input buffers and to write results from the output buffers to the secondary storage.

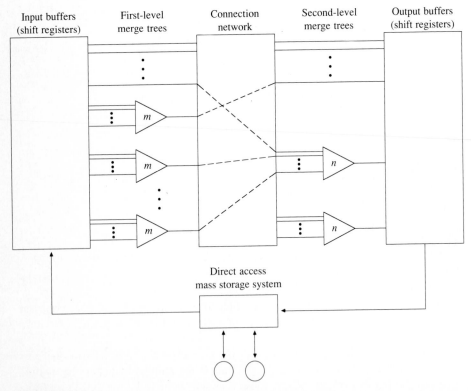

FIGURE 8.32
A two-level list merging network. (*Source:* [HOL83] copyright ©1983. Prentice-Hall, Inc., reprinted by permission.)

8.3.5 Superimposed Coding

The technique of superimposed coding and its variations have been used in many text processing studies [GUS71, ROT74, RIV76, AHO79, LLO80, TSI83, LAR83, CHR84, and LEE86]. A document can be represented by a number of assigned keywords or index terms or by the "content words" (i.e., words other than prepositions, articles, etc.) appearing in the document. In a multiattribute hashing scheme, each keyword can be hashed to a fixed-length bit pattern by a hash function. The resulting patterns for these keywords can be superimposed by forming the logical OR operation over them to obtain a single bit pattern with the same length. The resulting bit pattern is called the *superimposed code word* or the *signature* of the document. Figure 8.33 shows an example of a superimposed code.

The signatures $S_i(1 \leq i \leq n)$ of a collection of n documents, which form the text database, are stored in a signature file, the function of which is similar to an index file commonly used in database management applications—that is, to filter out irrelevant documents in a document search. A search query provides a number of search keywords. These keywords are hashed in the same fashion as those for the documents using the same hash function. The signature of the query, S_q, is obtained and is compared against the signatures of the documents. A document signature S_i qualifies for a search, if and only if for all the bit positions in S_q that are set to 1, the corresponding bit positions of S_i are also set to 1. The condition is known as the *inclusion condition*. More formally, the set of qualified document signatures can be defined as follows:

$$\{S_i | S_i \wedge S_q = S_q \text{ where } 1 \leq i \leq n\}$$

A disqualified signature indicates that the associated document is guaranteed not to contain the keyword(s) specified in the query. However, a qualified signature only means that the corresponding document block is very likely to satisfy the query. That is, there is still a chance that the text block may not contain the keyword(s) being searched for (i.e., a false drop). Therefore, the documents must be further searched to eliminate false drops. Such a false drop can be largely avoided by using a suitable signature-generating algorithm, which will ensure that 50 percent of the bits in a signature are 1's [ROB79].

This superimposed coding technique can be applied to logical blocks of documents rather than to entire documents [CHR84]. The text database is divided

Keywords	Hashed code
Database	001 101 001 010
Machine	100 101 011 000
Application	001 000 010 110
Signature	101 101 011 110

FIGURE 8.33
An example of superimposed coding.

into a number of fixed-length blocks, B_n. Each text block, B_i, is associated with a signature S_i (the length of the signature is fixed, say m). The signature is obtained from its associated text block by means of hashing each content word in the block to a bit string of fixed length, say m. The logical OR of all the bit strings representing all the words in the block form the superimposed code word or signature S_i. This scheme is an extension of hash coding and inverted list techniques.

8.3.6   Hardware for Supporting Superimposed File Processing

The simplest approach to search a signature file is to store the signature file sequentially on disks and scan it bit serially. It would take $(n \times m)$ time units to search n signatures of m bits each. This time is significant, if n is a large number. To accelerate the search of a signature file, Ahuja and Roberts [AHU80] proposed a word-serial and bit-parallel (WSBP) approach in which the whole signature file is stored in fast memories, such as magnetic bubble memories or RAM modules. These memories have a very high bandwidth, not only for their high memory access rate, but also for their capability to access a large bit-vector in a single access. Hence, a substantial increase in search speed is achieved, compared to bit-serial or byte-serial access of disks.

The system configuration is shown in Figure 8.34. It has the same architecture as the cellular-logic devices described in Chapter 3 except that the data layout in this system is in word-serial and bit-parallel fashion (WSBP). It consists of a linear array of signature processor modules and a controller interconnected by a multibus. Each signature processor module consists of a signature store and a query mask. Signatures are read from the signature file in a sequential manner and masked by S_q. Only the masked bits are ANDed together to produce a hit signal, indicating that a match has occurred. Because of the parallel nature of the system, the time taken to search all the modules is the same as the time taken to search one module.

The system was implemented and tested on experimental databases ranging in size from 48,000 records to 100,000 records. It was reported by Ahuja and Roberts [AHU80] that this special hardware yielded a 100-fold speed improvement over a corresponding software implementation.

A further modification to this arrangement was suggested by Lee [LEE86]. Since it is necessary to examine only the bit positions which are 1's in S_q, a transposed file organization would reduce the amount of data to be read from the signature file. The module for such a system is shown in Figure 8.35. The signature store is partitioned into a number of signature blocks. Each block, B_i, has a capacity of n_b signatures of the same length m_i. Initially, the first block occupies addresses from 1 to m_1, the second block from $m1 + 1$ to $m1 + m2$, and so on (for convenience, memory locations start from 1). Signatures within a block are searched in parallel, while signature blocks are processed sequentially. Thus, the data organization of this system is word-parallel and bit-serial (WPBS). S_q is sent to the controller, which then addresses the signature store according

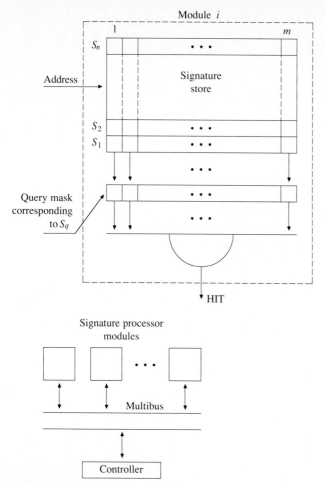

FIGURE 8.34
A signature processor based on WSBP organization. (*Source:* [AHU80] ©1980 IEEE)

to the bits set in S_q. If the ith bit of S_q is set, the ith word of a signature block that contains the ith bit from every signature in the block is read. It forms an output word. The output words formed by processing all the 1's in S_q are logically ANDed together by the comparator, C. At the end of the operation, the ith bit of C will be set to 1 if and only if S_i includes S_q (i.e., if and only if S_i qualifies). The bit-vector from C is used to retrieve the qualified text pointers from the pointer store. After a signature block is searched, the next block can be processed in the same manner except that the addresses are offset by the signature length, m_1. In other words, if the ith bit of S_q is set, the signature store will be addressed by the controller at locations $i, m1 + i, m1 + m2 + i$, and so on, until all the signature blocks have been processed. By using a little extra hardware (i.e., the MRR and pointer store in Figure 8.35), the speed of text retrieval can be significantly improved.

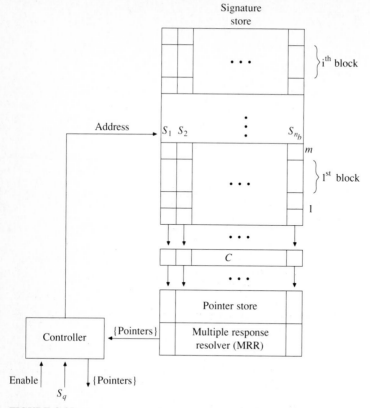

FIGURE 8.35
A WPBS signature processor. (*Source:* [LEE86] ©1986 IEEE)

While the hardware-assisted superimposed coding is fast and can do parallel searches, it has a storage overhead of 10 to 20 percent of the size of the text database. Also, the efficiency of the method largely depends on the efficiency of the coding algorithm; more false drops mean that a lot of time will be wasted examining wrong documents. Also the signature file grows linearly with the text database. Hence, it is important that the system allows the easy addition of processors onto the multibus.

8.4 SUMMARY AND DISCUSSION

In this chapter, the following three main topics have been covered:
1. The characteristics of text databases have been presented in terms of their structure, primitive operations, and operational requirements. It has been established that text databases are quite different from conventional, formatted databases used in business-oriented applications. To achieve efficient processing and manipulation of this type of databases, it is necessary to use special purpose processors and hardware systems that are tailored for text processing.

2. The basic structure of a text retrieval system has been presented. Its main components and their functions were described. It was pointed out that text processing involves two general processes: index file processing and full text scanning. The first process aims to reduce the search space by using software techniques such as indexing, inverted file processing, hashing, and superimposed coding. The second process does full text scanning over some selected texts (or documents) to determine the ones that satisfy a search query.

3. The techniques commonly used in text processing were examined, and the hardware support extended by these techniques was described. The software and hardware techniques were presented in three categories: full text scanning, inverted and index processing, and superimposed coding.

    a. For supporting full text scanning, the use of special hardware comparators is the key to achieve the needed efficiency. Three comparator designs were presented: parallel comparators, cellular comparators, and finite state automata. Their methods for handling different types of don't cares were emphasized. The hardware systems using these different types of comparators were also described. The work of Burkowski [BUR82] and the products of Operating Systems, Inc. (Associative File Processor) and General Electric (GESCAN) are examples of systems using parallel comparators. The work of Mukhopadhyay [MUK78 and MUK80] was used as an example of systems using cellular comparators. The hardware implementation of regular finite state automaton was illustrated by the work of Bird, Tu, and Worthy, [BIR77], and the hardware implementation of the partitioned finite state automaton was illustrated by the work of Haskin and Hollaar [HAS80a, HAS80b, HAS83, HOL76, HOL78a, HOL78b, HOL79, and HOL83].

    b. The second category of text processing techniques is the inverted file and index processing. For this type of processing, the speed at which terms and their associated pointers in a posting file or index file are coordinated is very important to achieve system efficiency. For this reason, the task of term coordination is an obvious target for hardware implementation. It involves the merging of lists of pointers to determine the set of documents that may satisfy the search conditions specified in a query. The list merging processor used in EUREKA, the parallel list merging architecture proposed by Hollaar, and the two-level list merging architecture proposed by Hua and Hollaar are examples of hardware systems for list merging.

    c. The third category of text processing technique is the superimposed coding. There are variations of superimposed coding techniques. However, they all involve the processing of signature files. It is important to keep the storage requirement of a signature file and its processing time low. To achieve this, hardware systems for supporting superimposed coding have been proposed. The word-serial and bit-parallel approach for signature file processing proposed by Ahuja and

Roberts [AHU80] and its refinement proposed by Lee were described in this chapter as examples.

From this chapter, it should be clear to the reader that the solution to efficient text processing is not just using hardware alone but using a combination of software and hardware techniques. It is too time-consuming to do a full text scan of a very large text database even if high-speed hardware is used for the task. It is necessary to first reduce the search space to a manageable size using traditional software techniques such as indexing, fully inverted file technique, hashing, and superimposed coding, and then to apply the full text search techniques. Special text processors can be used to improve the speed of a text retrieval system in two ways: (1) by providing hardware support to process index, inverted, or signature files to select a subset of documents for further processing and (2) by providing high-speed text scanning capability to verify the selected documents.

Several issues about text processing in general and text processors in particular are possible topics for further research on the subject.

1. *Access methods for text.* A survey on access methods used in text processing is given by Faloutsos [FAL85]. There are many ways textual data can be organized and accessed in main memory and secondary storage. Quantitative evaluation of these access methods needs to be conducted to determine under what conditions (i.e., data characteristics and processing requirements) one method is better than another. It is generally believed that superimposed coding methods are better than inverted files, indexing, or hash-based methods. However, this conclusion has not been established quantitatively. Special-purpose hardware can be built to support any of the access methods used. It is also possible to build hardware to support a number of access methods if it can be quantitatively established that they are the better ones under most conditions.

2. *Text compression.* In order to reduce the storage requirement of a large text database, it is necessary to compress the data in some way before storing them on secondary storage. Recent surveys on text compression techniques were conducted by Severance and Welch [SEV83 and WEL84]. Text compression is a transformation of textual data. This function seems to be a natural candidate for hardware implementation. A database filter of the type described in Chapter 4, which is located between secondary storage devices and the main memory, should be able to perform the transformation on the fly as compressed data are read from the secondary storage or as the uncompressed data are written into the secondary storage. Another problem needing investigation is whether full text scanning can be done directly on compressed data without transforming texts back to their original forms.

3. *Data placement strategies.* The way in which textual data, or any other type of data, are placed in the secondary storage has a great impact on access efficiency. For example, if documents that are related and are likely to be requested together are stored together in the adjacent tracks or cylinders on a disk, secondary storage access time for these documents can be significantly

reduced. Recall that clustering techniques have been used in database computers like DBC and MDBS described in chapters 6 and 7. It is also heavily used information retrieval [SAL83]. Another method for achieving processing efficiency is to pair secondary storage devices with full text scanning devices so that parallel I/O and processing of documents are possible. This approach would be the same as the one used in cellular-logic devices (see Chapter 3) and in multiprocessor systems with static processor-memory interconnection (see Chapter 6). Other data placement strategies suitable for textual data need to be investigated.

4. *Integration of hardware techniques for formatted data and textual data.* It has been clear to the database system community that an extension of the existing database management systems to handle text is necessary to support many database applications. Haskin and Lorie's extension of the System R to handle "long" fields [HAS82], Tsichritzis et al.'s use of superimposed coding for both formatted and textual data [TSI83], and Stonebraker's extension of INGRES to provide text processing facility are some good examples of the efforts in this direction [STO83]. The question that can be raised with respect to the database computers is whether the hardware techniques used in processing formatted and textual databases can be integrated so that a single system can be built to process both types of data efficiently. It is clear that the access methods used in text processing, such as inverted file and index processing, are typical methods used in formatted data processing. The superimposed coding, hashing techniques, and data clustering strategies used in text processing have also been used for processing formatted data. Hardware for supporting these access methods will benefit both types of databases. If the hardware for supporting full text scanning is integrated with other components designed for processing formatted data, much more textual data (e.g., textual description of objects in a database, explanations to be given to the user to provide information about searches and instructions for query formation, etc.) can be incorporated into a database. This would be very useful for building a high-level, user-friendly database system. The objective of integration should be to eliminate redundant hardware and to facilitate better communication among hardware components so that the cost of building an integrated system can be reduced and the efficiency of the system can be increased.

5. *Distributed text database systems.* Just like business-oriented, formatted databases, text databases may have been created and used by different organizations or different branches of an organization. These databases often need to be shared among organizations or branches. They may either be geographically distributed or centralized and may be implemented on either the same type of computers (homogeneous systems) or different types of computers (heterogeneous systems). The same problems that exist in distributed formatted databases will also exist in distributed text databases. However, in text databases, the quantity of data to be transferred among distributed component systems can be expected to be much larger. Data communication time is a predominant factor in a distributed text processing system. It will be interesting to study how this affects the various access methods, data placement strategies, text

processing algorithms, full text scanning techniques, and alternative hardware designs and implementations. Research into these problems would be beneficial and fruitful.

8.5 BIBLIOGRAPHY

[AHO75] Aho, A. V., and Coranck, M. J.: "Efficient String Matching: An Aid to Bibliographic Search," *Comm. of ACM,* vol. 18, no. 6, June 1975, pp. 333–340.

[AHO79] Aho, A. V., and Ullman, J. D.: "Optimal Partial Match Retrieval when Fields are Independently Specified," *ACM Transactions on Database Systems,* vol. 4, no. 2, June 1979, pp. 168–179.

[AHU80] Ahuja, S. R., and Roberts, C. S.: "An Associative/Parallel Processor for Partial Match Retrieval Using Superimposed Codes," *Proceedings of the Annual Symposium on Computer Architecture,* 1980, pp. 218–227.

[BAT68] Batcher, K. E.: "Sorting Networks and Their Applications," *Spring Joint Computer Conference,* 1968, pp. 307–314.

[BIR77] Bird, R. M., Tu, J. C., and Worthy, R. M.: "Associative/Parallel Processors for Searching Very Large Textual Data Bases," *Proceedings of the Third Non-numeric Processing Workshop,* Syracuse, New York, May 1977, pp. 8–16.

[BOY77] Boyer, R. S., and Moore, J. S.: "A Fast String Searching Algorithm," *Comm. of ACM,* vol. 20, no. 10, Oct. 1977, pp. 762–772.

[BUR82] Burkowski, F. J.: "A Hardware Hashing Scheme in the Design of a Multiterm String Comparator," *IEEE Transactions on Computers,* C-31, no. 9, Sept. 1982, pp. 825–834.

[CHR84] Christodoulakis, S., and Faloutsos, C.: "Design Considerations for a Message File Server," *IEEE Transactions on Software Engineering,* SE-10, no. 2, March 1984, pp. 201–210.

[COP78] Copeland, G. P.: "String Storage and Searching for Data Base Applications: Implementation on the INDY Backend Kernel," *Proceedings of the Fourth Non-numeric Processing Workshop,* Syracuse, N.Y., Aug. 1978, pp. 8–17.

[FAL85a] Faloutsos, C.: "Design of a Signature File Method that Accounts for Nonuniform Occurrence and Query Frequencies," *Proceedings of the Eleventh Conference on Very Large Data Bases,* Stockholm, Sweden, Aug. 1985, pp. 165–170.

[FAL85b] Faloutsos, C.: "Signature Files: Design and Performance Comparison of Some Signature Extraction Methods," *Proceedings of the ACM SIGMOD Conference,* Austin, Texas, May 1985, pp. 63–82.

[FAL85c] Faloutsos, C.: "Access Methods for Text," *Computing Surveys,* vol. 17, no. 1, March 1985, pp. 49–74.

[GE85a] General Electric: *Text Array Processor Reference Manual,* Aug. 1985.

[GE85b] General Electric: *GESCAN Reference Guide, Version 3.3,* Aug. 1985.

[GE87] General Electric Company. GESCAN Technical Summary, Part No. 326A4147X1, June 1987.

[GRI68] Griswold, R. E., Poage, J. F., and Polonsky, I. P., *The SNOBOL4 Programming Language,* Prentice-Hall, Englewood Cliffs, N.J., 1968.

[GUS71] Gustafson, R. A.: "Elements of the Randomized Combinatorial File Structure," *Proceedings of the ACM SIGIR Symposium on Information Storage and Retrieval,* University of Maryland, April 1971, pp. 163–174.

[HAS80a] Haskin, R. L.: "Hardware for Searching Very Large Text Databases," *Workshop on Computer Architecture for Non-numeric Processing,* March 1980, pp. 49–56.

[HAS80b] Haskin, R. L.: "Hardware for Searching Very Large Text Data Bases," Ph.D. dissertation, Computer Science Dept., University of Illinois, Urbana-Champaign, *Technical Report UIUCDCS-R-80-1027,* Aug. 1980.

[HAS82] Haskin, R. L., and Lorie, R. A.: "On Extending the Functions of a Relational Database System," *Proceedings of the ACM SIGMOD Conference,* Orlando, Florida, 1982, pp. 207–212.

[HAS83] Haskin, R. L., and Hollaar, L. A.: "Operational Characteristics of a Hardware-based Pattern Matcher," *ACM Transactions on Database Systems,* vol. 8, no. 1, March 1983, pp. 15–40.

[HOL76] Hollaar, L. A., et al.: "The Design of System Architectures for Textual Information Retrieval," *Proceedings of the ACM National Conference,* 1977, pp. 697–702.

[HOL78a] Hollaar, L. A.: "Specialized Merge Processor Networks for Combining Sorted Lists," *ACM Transactions on Database Systems,* vol. 3, no. 3, Sept. 1978, pp. 272–284.

[HOL78b] Hollaar, L. A., and Roberts, D. C.: "Current Research into Specialized Processors for Text Information Retrieval," *Proceedings of the Fourth International Conference on Very Large Data Bases,* West Berlin, Germany, Sept. 1978, pp. 270–279.

[HOL79] Hollaar, L. A.: "Text Retrieval Computers," *IEEE Computer,* vol. 12, no. 3, March 1979, pp. 40–50.

[HOL83] Hollaar, L. A., Smith, K. F., Chow, W. H., Emrath, P. A., and Haskin, R. L.: "Architecture and Operation of a Large, Full-text Information-retrieval System," in *Advanced Database Machine Architecture,* D. K. Hsiao (ed.), Prentice-Hall, Englewood Cliffs, N.J., pp. 256–299.

[HOP73] Hopcroft, J. E., and Karp, R. M.: "An n 5/2 Algorithm for Maximum Matchings in Bipartite Graphs," *SIAM J. Comp.,* vol. 2, no. 4, Dec. 1973, pp. 225–231.

[HOP79] Hopcroft, J. E., and Ullman, J. D.: *Introduction to Automata Theory, Languages and Computation,* Addison-Wesley, Reading, Mass., 1979.

[HUA80] Huang, H. M.: "On the Design and Scheduling of an Index Processing System for Very Large Databases," Ph.D. dissertation, University of Illinois, Urbana-Champaign, Aug. 1980.

[KNU77] Knuth, D. E., Morris, J. H., and Pratt, V. R.: "Fast Pattern Matching in Strings," *SIAM J. Comp.,* vol. 6, no. 2, June 1977, pp. 323–350.

[KUC77] Kuck, D. J., Lawrie, F. H., and Samch, A. H. (eds.): "High Speed Computer and Algorithm Organization," *Proceedings of the Symposium on High-Speed and Algorithms Organization,* University of Illinois, April 1977, pp. 13–15.

[LAR83] Larson, P. A.: "A Method for Speeding up Text Retrieval," *Proceedings of the ACM SIGMOD Conference,* San Jose, Calif., 1983.

[LEE86] Lee, D. L.: "A Word Parallel, Bit-Serial Signature Processor for Superimposed Coding," *Proceedings of the International Conference on Data Engineering,* Los Angeles, Feb. 1986, pp. 352–359.

[LLO80] Lloyd, J. W.: "Optimal Partial-match Retrieval," *BIT 20,* pp. 406–413.

[MUK78] Mukhopadhyay, A.: "Hardware Algorithms for Nonnumeric Computation," *Proceedings of the Fifth Symposium on Computer Architecture,* Palo Alto, Calif., April 1978, pp. 8–16. (Also *IEEE Transactions on Computers,* vol. C28, no. 6, June 1979, pp. 384–394.)

[MUK80] Mukhopadhyay, A.: "Hardware Algorithms for String Processing," *Proceedings of the IEEE International Conference on Circuits and Computers,* New York, Oct. 1–3, 1980.

[NAT72] National Library Medicine Master MESH, Nov. 1972.

[OPE77] Operating Systems, Inc.: High-speed Text Search Design Contract, *Interim Report,* Report 77-002, 1977.

[RIV76] Rivest, R. L.: "Partial Match Retrieval Algorithms," *SIAM J. Comp.,* vol. 5, no. 1, March 1976, pp. 19–50.

[ROB77] Roberts, D. C. (ed.): "A Computer System for Text Retrieval: Design Concept Development," Office of Research and Development, Central Intelligence Agency, Washington, D.C., Report RD-77-10011, 1977.

[ROB78] Roberts, D. C.: "A Specialized Computer Architecture for Text Retrieval," *Proceedings of the Fourth Non-Numeric Workshop,* Syracuse, N. Y., Aug. 1978, pp. 51–59.

[ROB79] Roberts, C. S.: "Partial-match Retieval via the Method of Superimposed Codes," *Proceedings of the IEEE,* vol. 67, no. 12, Dec. 1979, pp. 1624–1642.

[ROT74] Rothnie, J. B., and Lozano, T.: "Attribute-based File Organization in a Paged Memory Environment," *Comm. of the ACM,* vol. 17, no. 2, Feb. 1974, pp. 63–69.

[SAL83] Salton, G., and McGill, M. J.: *Introduction to Modern Information Retrieval,* McGraw-Hill, New York, 1983.

[SEV83] Severance, D. G.: "A Practitioner's Guide to Database Compression," *Inf. System,* vol. 8, no. 1, pp. 51–62.

[SLO70] Slotnick, D. L.: "Logic per Track Devices," in *Advances in Computers,* vol. 10, F. Alt (ed.), Academic Press, New York, 1970, 00. 291–296.

[STE74] Stellhorn, W. H.: "A Processor for Direct Scanning of Text," presented at the first Non-numeric Workshop, Dallas, Oct. 1974.

[STE77] Stellhorn, W. H.: "An Inverted File Processor for Information Retrieval," *IEEE Transactions on Computers,* vol. C26, no. 12, Dec. 1977, pp. 1258–1276.

[STO83] Stonebraker, M., Stettner, H., Lynn, N., Kalash, J., and Guttman, A.: "Document Processing in a Relational Database System," *ACM Transactions on Office Information Systems,* vol. 1, no. 2, April 1983, pp. 143–158.

[TSI83] Tsichritzis, D., and Christodoulakis, S.: "Message Files," *ACM Transactions Office Information Systems,* vol. 1, no. 1, Jan. 1983, pp. 88–98.

[WEL84] Welch, T. A.: "A Technique for High-performance Data Compression," *IEEE Computer Magazine,* vol. 17, no. 6, June 1984, pp. 8–19.

[WIN79] Wing, J. M.: "Partial-match Retrieval Using TRIES, Hashing and Superimposed Codes," Master's thesis, MIT, Boston, June 1979.

CHAPTER
9

RETROSPECT
AND PROSPECT
OF DATABASE
COMPUTERS

In the preceding chapters, the principles, architectures, and techniques used in five categories of database computers have been described. The key features of many laboratory and commercial systems also have been described. However, many other worthwhile research efforts and systems are not included in this book due to time and space limitations. The field of database computers has grown considerably since its birth in the early 1970s. The number of researchers in industrial research laboratories and universities who are actively pursuing research in this field has steadily increased. The number of technical conferences at which papers on this subject have regularly appeared has also increased. Presently, the author knows of two annual workshops that are dedicated to this subject and that have served as forums for researchers and developers to exchange ideas and present results of their investigations. They are (1) the Syracuse University Minnowbrook Workshop on Data Base Machines organized by Professor Bruce Berra of the Syracuse University and (2) the International Workshop on Database Machines organized by the international research community and held in different locations outside the United States. A working group on database machines established by the Naval Data Automation Command in 1981 has also been active in promoting the database machine technology. This group is formed by military personnel, researchers from universities, industry people, and vendors of database computers. It has over 660 members in over 285 organizations. In addition to these activities, several established technical conferences, such as the International Conference on Very Large Data Bases organized by the VLDB Foundation,

ACM's International Conference on Management of Data (SIGMOD), IEEE's International Conference on Parallel Processing, IEEE's International Symposium on Computer Architecture, and AFIPS's National Computer Conference (NCC), regularly contain papers and panels on this subject. Among the technical journals, ACM's *Transactions on Database Systems*, IEEE's *Transactions on Software Engineering*, IEEE's *Transactions on Computers*, and the *Journal on Parallel and Distributed Computing* (published by Academic Press, Inc.) publish most of the articles in this field.

Despite past and present activities in the field of database computers, the following questions have often been raised by researchers as well as users of database computers:

1. What has been accomplished in the almost 20 years of research and development on database computers?
2. Why are there not more commercial database computers available and more organizations using the available database computers?
3. What is the prospect of database computers, and what are the likely future research directions?

In this chapter, these questions will be addressed. The material presented in this chapter represents the author's own view of the past accomplishments and future prospect and directions of this field of study. Readers are cautioned not to take this as the general consensus of the many distinguished researchers in this field.

9.1 PAST ACCOMPLISHMENTS

It is easier to look back and identify the accomplishments of a field of study than it is to predict the future; however, it is impossible to provide a complete list of accomplishments made by many workers in this field. In the following subsections, several key accomplishments are summarized.

9.1.1 The Identification of Problems and Limitations of Conventional Computers for Database Applications

The past efforts in research and development on database computers have definitely identified the problems and limitations of using the conventional computers for managing large databases. Recall that in Figure 1.7 the limitations of the existing secondary storage devices, main memories, processors, and two bottlenecks (i.e., I/O and Von Neumann bottlenecks) created by these limitations were shown. Due to the fact that a secondary storage device is not able to do meaningful search operations on the data stored in it, large quantities of data need to be moved from the secondary storage device to the main memory of a computer (i.e., the staging problem discussed in Chapter 1). The bandwidth of data transfer between them is restricted by the low speed of the storage device's mechanical motion and the speed of the communication channel. The space limitation of the main memory further requires that large quantities of data be moved to the secondary storage to make room for the multitude of application programs in execution and for the data these programs use. This I/O bottleneck is a very serious problem in large database applications.

Another equally serious problem is the limitations of the Von Neumann processors used in conventional computers. These processors are designed to perform a set of basic operations, which are primitive operations for numeric processing. They do not match with the primitive operations frequently used in nonnumeric processing. As a result, layers of software are built in the conventional system to bridge the gap between the hardware and the database applications. This is the main cause of inefficiency and the main reason for the high software development cost of a database application. If a computer can be built to perform high-level operations needed by database applications, the software development effort can be greatly simplified. This point has been overlooked even by database computer professionals since the justification given by the researchers and developers of database computers in the past has been the speed advantage of database computers over conventional systems. The simplification of software development and programming ease of these computers, although more difficult to quantify, has not been considered. The SISD architecture of conventional single-processor systems inherently restricts their capability in serving large number of concurrent users and programs. This Von Neumann bottleneck causes the inability of conventional systems to efficiently service a large number of users who concurrently access and manipulate large databases.

9.1.2 The Introduction of Computer Architectures, Special-purpose Processors, and Techniques for Solving Nonnumeric Processing Problems

The past efforts on database computers have produced a large number of architectural designs of database computers, special-purpose processors, and software and hardware techniques for the control and operation of these machines. The SISD architecture of conventional computers has been replaced by SIMD and MIMD architectures in most database computers. The intelligent secondary storage devices and the database filters described in Chapters 3 and 4 were designed mainly to solve the data-staging problem and to relieve the I/O bottleneck discussed earlier. The main design principles and hardware and software techniques introduced in these systems include: (1) the pairing of processing elements and memory elements, (2) content-addressing and context-addressing techniques applied over blocks of data, (3) mark bits and bit manipulation to resolve complex search conditions, (4) hardware garbage collection on rotating memory devices, (5) the modification of the major-minor loop architecture for relational database processing, (6) the content-to-address mapping technique and its application to relational operations, (7) associative programming techniques and their application to integrity and security control, and (8) techniques for on-the-fly processing of data transferred between disk and main memory.

The associative memory systems discussed in Chapter 5 alleviate the limitations of the conventional main memory by using content addressing and parallel searching of memory contents at the bit or word level. Techniques for implementing complex data structures in these memory devices have been introduced. The use of multiple associative memory modules for supporting index processing and directory lookups have been demonstrated in these systems.

The multicomputer systems presented in Chapters 6 and 7 use parallel-processing techniques to resolve the Von Neumann bottleneck problem addressed. A variety of data placement strategies have been studied and their effects on system performance have been evaluated. Parallel algorithms for supporting relation operations such as Join, Select, and Aggregate have been introduced, and their performances have been thoroughly analyzed and compared in the works reported in these chapters. A variety of interconnection schemes have been used in the proposed systems for connecting memory modules, processors, and secondary storage devices. They include common bus, ring, tree, hypertree, and hypercube interconnections.

Many special-purpose processors have been introduced to perform sorting, merging, and relational operations efficiently. Text processors described in Chapter 8 are also special-purpose processors. The integration of special-purpose processors with general-purpose processors to form database computers has been demonstrated. Query processing techniques such as data flow, pipelining, and query decomposition into parallel tasks, have been used and evaluated in multicomputer systems.

9.1.3 Prototyping and Commercialization of Database Computers

Another main achievement of the field of database computers is the prototype development and commercialization of several systems. Although many systems described in this book and many others not included in it are "paper designs," several systems have been prototyped and tested in industry laboratories and universities. These prototypes, although far from meeting the requirements of commercial products, have served to demonstrate many new concepts and techniques introduced by different researchers.

A few database computers have also become commercially available. Among them, Britton Lee's IDM and Teradata's DBC/1012 have been quite successful. As the vendors of these computers continue to develop improved software for supporting various applications, these systems can be expected to be even more successful commercially in the future. Although one can be optimistic about the commercial future of the present generation of database computers, one should not lose sight of the fact that these systems will continue to face strong competition from conventional computers, which continue to improve in performance due to technology advances. It is also important to point out that the users of and organizations with large databases and application systems will continue to resist adopting database computers due to their incompatibility with the existing systems. Most changes to the existing database systems are evolutional rather than revolutional. The commercial future of the existing database computers and the future systems depend on how compatible they are with the existing hardware and software facilities or, if they are not compatible, how easy it would be to convert the existing applications to the new systems. These issues on the performance and compatibility of database computers will be further elaborated in the next section.

9.1.4 Fostering the Cooperation and Collaboration of Computer Scientists and Engineers

Most of the complex problems we face in this modern society require the integration of many technologies and the collaboration of many capable people in different disciplines in order to find the solutions. The field of database computers has drawn a great number of computer scientists and engineers together to investigate software and hardware solutions to database management problems. The solutions to these problems require the integration of technologies introduced by such disciplines as computer architecture, database management, software engineering, programming languages, very large scale integration, artificial intelligence, and computer theory. The existing laboratory and commercial database computers are the results of cooperation and collaboration of many fine computer scientists and engineers. This, in itself, represents a significant contribution by the field of database computers to the advancement of new technologies.

9.2 THE FACTORS THAT LIMIT THE GROWTH OF DATABASE COMPUTERS

The problem of efficient and effective management of large databases is common to all large organizations worldwide. There is definitely a need for more efficient computers for data management and for a more effective way of managing data to support decisionmaking. If database computers can provide better service to the database users as suggested by researchers and developers of database computers, then why are there not more database computers available and more organizations using them? The following subsections attempt to answer this question.

9.2.1 Performance Improvements in Conventional Systems

The advent of a new technology generally effects computing systems in one of the following ways: (1) it serves to improve the performance of already existing systems by making them faster, more efficient, more reliable, and less expensive; or (2) it stimulates totally new approaches and directions in system and architectural designs and implementations and make possible the development of new application areas. Several technologies have made a great impact on the development of database computers in the past and will continue to determine and shape the future. They are: CPU technologies, memory and storage technologies, and interconnection technologies. While these technologies enable the development of database computers and give them the advantage over existing conventional systems, they also have improved the new conventional systems tremendously and made the advantages of database computers less significant. The technologies change and improve so rapidly that it is difficult for any database computer to maintain a significant edge over new conventional systems. If the performance of database computers is not significantly superior to the existing systems, then there would be no reason for an organization to adopt a totally new system that might disrupt the existing applications. An easier alternative and perhaps a less expensive way to improve a present system is to simply upgrade it to the next model provided by the same computer vendor. It is commonly believed among researchers in the field of database computers that unless a database computer can demonstrate at least one order of improvement in speed over conventional systems, it would not be acceptable to the potential users.

The key issues that need to be addressed are (1) at what rate the improvement of conventional systems can continue and (2) what strategies the researchers and developers of database computers should follow to invent computers that are far superior to the conventional systems. Let us consider the CPU, memory, and interconnection technologies in turn.

9.2.1.1 CPU TECHNOLOGIES. The CPU is still the most complex part of a computer. Integrated circuit (IC) technology has had a great impact on CPU design and complexity. Many CPUs today are no longer based on the SISD architecture. They contain parallel-processing modules that can perform complex functions concurrently. At the same time, the constraints of large scale integration (LSI) and very large scale integration (VLSI) are most visible in these designs. For example, the functions of a CPU cannot be arbitrarily increased since the pin-out is highly restricted for each chip. A regular design is much easier and much more reliable to implement than an irregular design. Besides the limitation on functionality, the speed improvement that can be made on CPUs has a physical limit due to the heat dissipation problem in chips. Although the improvement in speed and functionality of CPUs is expected to continue, the rate of improvement is not going to be as fast or as dramatic as it was in the past decade. If the rate of improvement of CPUs remains low in supporting the conventional primitive operations (a mismatch with the nonnumeric processing primitives) and if the demand continues for higher functionality and speed from the database users, the CPU limitations in supporting database applications will remain.

It is this author's opinion that the database computer researchers should not simply adopt the available CPUs in their design of database computers, even though it is convenient for them to build a functioning system quickly to simulate their research ideas. These two approaches should be followed.

1. Develop special-function chips for dedicated applications to enhance system performance. For example, function chips can perform primitive database operations (e.g., Sort, Join, Set operations, Duplicate Elimination, etc.) more

efficiently and can perform other database management functions as well (e.g., query translation, index processing, query optimization, transaction management, concurrency control, error recovery, integrity control, and security control). In the existing works, the use of special-purpose devices for performing the primitive database operations and algorithms for executing these operations in conventional computers has been studied extensively. Except in a few isolated cases (e.g., the index processing in DBC and RELACS, security control in DBC and CASSM, and integrity control in CASSM), the latter category of database management functions has not been studied in the context of database computers. In most of the multicomputer systems, it is generally assumed that a host computer is used to handle this second category of functions. If database computers are designed solely for supporting primitive operations, then, as very convincingly argued by Boral and DeWitt [BOR83], there is no need to use special function chips or microcode-driven systems. Conventional off-the-shelf processors will suffice since they can process data as fast as data can be transferred into the main memory from the secondary storage. I/O bandwidth is the limiting factor in system performance. However, if other high-level database functions are considered, a conventional database management system has been found to be CPU-bound; the use of special-purpose devices for supporting these functions would be desirable and, most likely, necessary. The processing of high-level database functions by database computers was ignored in Boral and DeWitt's observation.

2. Use new technologies to implement novel architectures. For example, develop architectures that support the processing of multimedia databases (e.g., texts, images, voice data, and regular formatted data), graphics-oriented processing, direct processing of high-level languages, and object-oriented computing (to be discussed further in section 9.3.1.2). Database management is no longer limited to business-oriented processing of formatted data. Many new database applications (e.g., image processing, computer-aided design and manufacturing, office automation, etc.) require the processing of image, voice, graphic, and textual data. In order to achieve at least one order of speed advantage over conventional computer systems in processing these diverse data, researchers in database computers cannot simply adopt what is available. They need to create new devices and invent new architectures based on new technologies.

9.2.1.2 MEMORY AND STORAGE TECHNOLOGIES. There is no doubt that the advent of memory and storage technologies has had a significant impact on both conventional systems and database computers. In the past, direct access storage has been dominated by two distinct technologies: (1) ferrite core and MOS LSI memories and (2) rotating magnetic disks. The former is more costly but has microsecond access time; the latter is cheaper but has millisecond access time. There has been a gap between these two extremes of memory technology. However, a number of new technologies have emerged in recent years. CCD, magnetic bubble memory, electronic beam addressable memory, VLSI memory, and optical disks are devices that fill the storage gap. The densities of these new devices and disks have steadily increased over the years. The most dramatic density increase is in VLSI memory chips. It was pointed out in the preceding section that the pin-out problem is a major bottleneck in the VLSI implementation of CPU chips. However, in the case of memory chips, a 100 percent increase in the number of bits per chip requires only a single additional pin; an eight-fold increase requires only three pins. It is clear that VLSI technology has immediate benefits for memory chips. On the other hand, the density improvement in magnetic disks is not by orders of magnitude as is true for VLSI memory chips. In fact, disk manufacturers are currently pushing the limits of technology in order to increase disk densities. An advance in this direction is the introduction of optical disks. The earlier optical disk produced by RCA can already record 5×10^{10} bits on one side of an optical disk at rates greater than 100 Mbits per second [KEN82]. The disk's area density of 10^9 bits per square inch is an order of magnitude greater than the generally accepted limit of 10^8 bits per square inch in magnetic disks. The density of optical disks has since increased considerably.

Given a wide range of memory and storage devices with different speeds, capacities, and costs, a cost-effective approach is to establish a memory hierarchy in a database computer to take advantage of these differences. The concept of memory hierarchy has been used in several database computers such as DIRECT.

Although the density of secondary storage devices has improved considerably in the past, the bandwidth (measured by megabyte per second data transfer rate) of these devices has not increased at the same rate. In fact, as pointed out by Boral and DeWitt [BOR83], if the same amount of data is packed in a high-density, high-speed disk drive as opposed to a number of low-density, low-speed drives, the total available bandwidth for accessing the data from the high-density disks actually decreases. This is because the data in a high-density drive can only be read sequentially; whereas, in multiple low-density drives, data can be transferred out in parallel. Thus, database computers that have a large number of processors sharing a number of disks will have the bandwidth problem. A solution to this problem is to build disks that have the parallel read-out capability such as the Winchester drives built by CDC. However, they are very expensive to build. Their reliability is also a problem when the number of parallel read heads increases due to head alignment and synchronization difficulties.

Also, the increase of the bandwidth of a disk drive may not solve the problem of accessing a large quantity of data stored in it unless the speed of the I/O processor(s) associated with the disk can match the disk transfer rate. A solution to this problem seems to be the adoption of the idea of pairing a memory element (in this case, a disk) with a processing element (a general-purpose processor) introduced in cellular-logic devices. Parallel I/O and processing capabilities of a large number of processor-disk pairs can increase the total bandwidth for accessing large databases even if the individual processor's speed and the individual disk's bandwidth is not very high. This approach has been used in MICRONET, MDBS, DBC/1012, GAMMA, and the Cube-Connected Multicomputer System.

The advent of VLSI memory technology has driven the price of memory chips down, and the price is expected to continue to decrease. The density of these chips, on the other hand, has increased tremendously. Soon a gigabyte of memory per processor will be common. If a large amount of main memory is made available in a computer system used for database management, large quantities of data, indexing information, and directories, dictionaries, which are very frequently used by a DBMS, can be kept in the main memory [GAR84]. This will greatly reduce the amount of I/O operations needed to page these data in and out of the main memory from the secondary storage devices, as is the case in a conventional DBMS. Furthermore, new implementation techniques and special index structures can be introduced to process the memory-resident data [DEW84, LEH86a, and LEH86b]. The availability of huge main memory may change the way large databases are physically organized and processed. High-density, low-cost memory chips can also be used as disk caches for prefetching the data from disks, thus providing a higher effective bandwidth to disks.

9.2.1.3 INTERCONNECTION TECHNOLOGIES. The motivations for interconnecting processors can be classified into two broad categories: (1) system enhancement and (2) distributed processing. For system enhancement, various components of a computer system are interconnected via communication links in order to speed up communications among them and to increase the overall throughput of the system by balancing the utilization of system resources. For distributed processing, independent computer systems, which are located in different geographical areas (restricted or long distance), are interconnected for the purpose of resource sharing and parallel processing of distributed data. Major developments in the interconnection of computers have been those of packet switching and circuit switching. Packet switching allows messages between computers to travel in fixed-sized packets from source to destination through some available path; this is used extensively in computer networks that span long distances. Circuit switching utilizes actual electronic switches to establish connections among processors and is often used in "tightly-coupled" architectures. The advent of interconnection technologies has had considerable impact on the development of database computers. Most of the multicomputer systems described in Chapters 6 and 7 take advantage of the commercially available off-the-shelf processors and interconnection technologies.

For solving large database problems, the interconnection of processors is not the only concern. It is still a real challenge for designers of database computers to provide the interconnection of processors, man memory modules, and secondary storage devices in a flexible and reliable way so that large quantities of data can be moved and processed efficiently. Dynamic reconfiguration of interconnections among processors, main memories, and storage devices in order to achieve maximum resource utilization and to support MIMD processing of multiple database queries would be necessary.

The three categories of technologies (CPU, memory, and interconnection technologies) discussed here have had great impact on the development of both conventional systems and database computers. However, it is this author's belief that interconnection technologies have a more profound effect on the efficiency of database computers than the other two categories since parallel processing is the solution to large database problems and interconnection technologies are the backbone of parallel processing. The recent development of fiberoptic communication lines and optical interconnection networks offers great potential to the development of a new generation of database computers. The prospect of this new development and its possible impact on research and development of database computers will be discussed in section 9.3.2.2.

9.2.2 Compatibility Problems

The potential users of database computers are those organizations that have large databases and many application systems and programs which have already been developed and are in operation. The computing systems of these organizations have reached their performance limits and are no longer capable of supporting the growing computational demands efficiently. These organizations are tired of upgrading their systems to the next model offered by their computer vendors every five to ten years and have turned to database computer manufacturers for solutions to their database management problems. Their main concern is to set up quickly a new working system that can satisfy their present and forseeable future needs and to immediately set up their existing software systems, application programs, and databases to support the organization's daily functions.

Unfortunately, many proposed solutions to problems of managing large databases require computers that have rather different architectures, software systems, data organizations, and algorithms from those of conventional computers. In order to establish the existing applications on these new database computers, new software systems may be required, databases may have to be reloaded or converted to fit the new organization and structure, and application programs may need to be either rewritten or modified. System conversion is an extremely expensive and time-consuming task. Few organizations will have the time and resources to perform a major system conversion. This may explain why so many novel architectures and ideas that have appeared in the database computer literature have not turned into commercial products. Commercial systems such as iDBP, IDM, and DBC/1012 require minimal changes to the existing applications.

As mentioned earlier, most organizations accept evolutional changes rather than revolutional changes to their computing systems, unless the performance and other advantages of a new database computer such as availability of maintenance, vendor service, education, a user group, and software are so much better than the possible upgrades that the cost of a total system conversion could be justified. Of course, if the vendor of a new database computer can provide effective tools to assist its customers to carry out the necessary conversion and provide programs to educate its personnel to operate, maintain, and use the new system, it will also help the sale of the product. The ease of conversion and hardware-assisted conversion facilities should be included in the design and development considerations of the new generation of database computers. The problem of compatability is definitely one of the main reasons why there are not more commercial database computers on the market and more organizations using the available products.

9.2.3   Limitations of the Underlying Data Model

With a few exceptions, most database computers proposed to this date are based on the relational data model. The systems are designed to operate on the primitive relational operations (Join, Project, and Select), set operations (Union, Intersect, and Difference), storage operations (Delete, Insert, and Update), and aggregation operations (Sum, Max, Min, etc.). Much effort has been put into the development and evaluation of algorithms and hardware to perform these operations. Even if we are successful in achieving the efficient support of relational database processing, we will still have two significant problems: performance and functionality. As regards performance, the relational data model forces all data to be normalized into flat tables containing atomic values. It then uses the Join operation to correlate data in different tables. Consequently, a query with moderate complexity may involve a number of Join operations, which are very time-consuming to perform. No matter how fast one can make a database computer or a special function unit perform the Join operation, if a system has to execute the operation very often, it still will not be able to execute queries efficiently. Therefore, it is important that the underlying data model of a database computer should allow data to be logically and physically structured together in a nonnormalized structure if the semantic relationship of the data does not call for a normalization. Functionally, the relational data model has been found by many researchers in database management to be inadequate in modeling scientific, engineering, and statistical databases. For example, constructs and techniques for modeling and processing unformatted data, ranges of values, statistical summaries, versioning, long transactions, complex data types, multimedia data, computation formulas being values of attributes, and so forth, are necessary to represent the true high-level application views of databases. The implementation of the concepts of generalization hierarchy and inheritance of attributes and operations, which have long been recognized as important to database management, will also increase the functionality of a database computer and its DBMS dramatically. The use of so-called semantic models as the underlying data models for database computers is a promising approach to achieve both efficiency and functionality. It will be discussed in Section 9.3.1.1.

9.2.4   Limited Performance and Functional Improvement Demonstrated by Laboratory Systems

The improvements in performance and functionality demonstrated by the existing research database computers have been quite limited. There are several reasons for this. First, so far, all the research efforts have concentrated on finding hardware and software means to accelerate retrieval and storage operations. Very few projects take a critical look into hardware or architectural support for many of the other important database management functions such as security and integrity control, concurrency control, transaction management, query optimization, view mapping and update, recovery, report generation, and auditing. These DBMS functions take a large portion of the processing time of a DBMS, and their complexity increases as the number of concurrent users or programs increases. They too need hardware or architectural support as do data retrieval and manipulation operations.

Second, the prototype systems developed in many research projects are for the purpose of demonstrating the ideas and techniques proposed by the researchers. They are rarely developed as production systems nor do the researchers intend to turn them into commercial products. Instead, they provide a testing ground for the analysis, simulation, and evaluation of new architectures and techniques. The efficiency of the physical system is not always the main concern of the investigators. Almost all prototype systems, with the exception of a few systems built in Japan, do not use the most up-to-date technologies in their implementations. Thus judging the performance and functionality of a database computer by its prototype is a common mistake made by critics of database computers.

Third, most research projects in database computers were initiated by universities, and their prototype systems were developed in university laboratory environments. Very few universities in the world are adequately equipped to do large-scale system development tasks. The lack of engineer and system programmer support, inadequate fabrication and testing facilities, the short-term commitments from student assistants, and the absence of long-term research support are examples of deep-rooted problems that hinder the development of large database computers and their supporting software systems in universities. University researchers would be more successful in developing a functional system if computer manufacturers would collaborate on development work.

9.3 FUTURE PROSPECT AND RESEARCH DIRECTIONS

It is difficult to accurately predict the distant future of the database computer field when there is such rapid development and changeover of the many technologies on which the database computer technology is based. Nevertheless, if one examines the general course of computer technology in the past along with the present technological development, it is possible to predict the general trend and research directions of the near future with some degree of confidence.

The future prospect of research and development in the database computer field is very good for two reasons. First, the need for a more efficient and effective method of database management will continue to increase; thus there is always a place for research and development in this area. Commercial products should continue to gain popularity due to this need. Second, recent development of several software and hardware technologies presents new challenges and opportunities to database computer designers and can potentially increase the functionality and efficiency of future database computers.

It has often been said that our need for computational power and memory space can never be satisfied. As soon as more computational power and more memory space are made available, new applications will be found for which more power and space will be needed. Our society's appetite for data is the same. If an organization is making decisions based on 10 billion bytes of data today, it will soon be demanding more data to be collected and made available so that more complete information can be obtained to aid in decision making. Also, we always seem to be able to find new applications for which the present systems are not adequate. The computing system for supporting the Strategic Defense Initiative (SDI) program is an example. Newer and more complex computing systems always involve database management problems, even if the systems are designed mainly for applications other than nonnumeric applications. For example, the existing supercomputers such as CYBER 205, CRAY-X-MP, Fujitsu VP-200, and Hitachi S810/20 are mainly used to solve large-scale numeric problems found in fluid mechanics, geophysics, particle physics, and other fields. In these problems, very large data files are processed (e.g., manipulation of 100,000 by 100,000 matrices). Data movement between secondary storage devices and main memory and movement within main memory are database management problems that need to be solved in order to efficiently solve numeric problems. The effective and efficient management of large databases will always be a necessity to computer users solving complex problems and will continue to be a challenge to the computer scientists and engineers. The challenge will be to develop database computers that meet application requirements in both functionality and efficiency and at reasonable cost. There is no doubt that research and development on database computers in universities and major industry laboratories will continue to work to meet the challenge.

As far as the commercial future of database computers is concerned, the author believes that there will be a slow but steady growth for the reasons presented in Section 9.2. Database computers that can be easily integrated into the existing systems will be most welcomed by users. These include dedicated database computers, special-purpose VLSI chips that perform specific DBMS functions, database filters, and multicomputer systems that use off-the-shelf processors and peripheral devices. Database computers will never gain real popularity unless the new generation of products can be built far better in both functionality and speed than the existing DBMS running on conventional systems. In order to achieve both high functionality and speed, the next generation of database computers needs to take full advantage of a number of software and hardware technologies that have become or are becoming available. Three areas of software technologies offer great opportunities to researchers and designers of future systems. They are (1) semantic modeling, (2) object-oriented paradigm, and (3) knowledge base management. The hardware technologies that offer the needed speed are (1) optical disk and (2) optical communication, interconnection, and computing. These technologies and their implications to database computer research and development are discussed in the following subsections.

9.3.1 Software Technologies

This section describes three current research directions that hold promise to the development of more intelligent and powerful database management systems. Research in these directions has introduced a number of models and techniques that can be implemented in a database system to give more functionality to the system. However, their implementation on a conventional system will add more overhead and further slow down the performance of a DBMS. Implementation of these models and techniques on database computers may achieve the needed functionality and efficiency at the same time.

9.3.1.1 SEMANTIC MODELS. Motivated by the need for more powerful data models for defining and processing business-oriented data as well as scientific, engineering, and statistical data, a number of so-called semantic models have been proposed. These are data models that contain some general semantic constructs for defining the structural relationships, constraints as well as the behavioral aspects (or operational characteristics) of data. Some examples are reported in [CHE76, SMI77, SHI79, MYL80, HAM81, SU83, ABI84, and SU86]. These models allow database designers and users to more explicitly define the semantic properties of their data. They provide a higher level of data representation than, say, normalized relations in the relational model. A DBMS, which uses this type of model, will be able to make use of the semantics of data captured in the schema of the database to behave more "intelligently," such as automatically resolving ambiguities in users' queries, providing explanations to the user, and enforcing the constraints automatically to keep the database in a consistent state.

Although a semantic model can add many functionalities to a DBMS, its implementation using the traditional software means will greatly complicate the DBMS software. This may explain why developers of commercial DBMSs are slow in adopting some of the ideas and techniques introduced in the existing semantic models. The present generation of database computers provides hardware or architectural support to the data models used in the existing DBMSs. Even if other functionalities of these models have been implemented in database computers, the functionalities of the resulting systems will be the same as the commercial DBMSs. One fruitful direction of research for database computer researchers would be to design and develop database computers to directly support the processing of data in various semantic constructs. For example, the processing of complex objects represented by nonnormalized structures and the handling of attribute inheritance in a generalization hierarchy can be carried out or assisted by hardware. This will increase not only the functionality of a database computer but also the overall efficiency of the system, since the gap between the application's view of data and data relationships and their hardware representations can be greatly narrowed. Many levels of software mapping of data and instructions can be eliminated. Furthermore, if the hardware is able to perform operations on high-level data abstractions, it should also greatly simplify the application development, since high-level commands will become available to system developers and application programmers.

9.3.1.2 OBJECT-ORIENTED PARADIGM. The object-oriented paradigm, which was introduced in programming languages such as SIMULA 76 [BIR73] and SMALLTALK [GOL83] and used in software systems such as KEE [KEE84], LOOPS [BOB83], and FLAVOR [MOO86] can be extended to provide the basis for the development of more powerful database management systems. A good example is GEMSTONE [GEM86a and GEM86b] by Servio Logic Development Corporation of Oregon. Several key concepts of the object-oriented paradigm are important and useful for a wide variety of database applications. They are outlined below.

High-level data abstraction. Complex objects found in engineering design and manufacturing tasks can be explicitly defined in terms of other objects. For example, a design object such as an automobile can be defined in terms of objects such as the chassis, body assembly, engine assembly, wheel and brake assembly, and so forth. The object, such as the body assembly, can in turn be defined by such objects as top, doors, interior, fenders, and so forth. The user of an object-oriented system is able to address all the components as independent objects by names as well as the complex object defined by the top level of abstraction. Engineers can directly define and manipulate objects they deal with in their applications instead of dealing with the implementation representation of objects such as relations in a relational DBMS.

Uniform representation and communication. All things of interest in a complex application system such as physical devices (tools, machines, computers, manufacturing parts, etc.) and software entities (control programs, procedures, functions and low-level system entities such as buffers, stacks, and queues) can be uniformly treated and represented as objects. Each object has its own private memory and a public interface. Communication among objects is by message passing. This uniform representation and communication methodology is the key to increasing the functionalities and modularity of a DBMS and its incremental implementation.

Separation of object specification and definition. In an object-oriented system, the specification of an object class in terms of an object class name, superclass and subclass relationships, instance variables, operations and parameters, and so on are separated from the class definition, which contains the actual procedures and functions (i.e., the methods) for executing the specified operations. This separation allows not only the ease of changing the implementation strategies (i.e., the procedures and functions) without affecting the user's view of the object classes, but it also provides the next very important property of the object-oriented paradigm.

Information hiding. In order to make use of an object, the user (human user or program) only needs to know the specification part of the object class and not the inner workings of the procedures and functions of that class. The user does not need to know in which programming languages the procedures and functions are written and in what hardware systems the programs are run. This information-hiding property not only simplifies user programming tasks, but also allows accessing and sharing of the procedures and functions implemented by different people and organizations.

Inheritance. In the object-oriented paradigm, the objects of a subclass can automatically inherit the attributes (or instance variables) and operations of its superclasses. This is similar to the concepts of generalization and generalization hierarchy introduced by Smith and Smith in the database field [SMI77]. This concept can be extended so that constraints and knowledge rules associated with objects and object classes can also be inherited. If a new object class can be inserted into a proper place in an object class hierarchy, the structure properties, operational characteristics, and knowledge rules associated with its superclasses can automatically be inherited without tedious respecification and definition. Furthermore, the implemented procedures and functions for performing the operations and for enforcing the constraints and rules of these superclasses can also be used. This leads to the next very important property of object-oriented systems.

Reusable codes. Programs written for an object-oriented system are broken down into independent modules with well-defined interfaces. These modules are treated as objects and can be activated by passing the proper messages to them. They can be reused and incorporated into other programs since their functionalities and interfaces are well-defined. Thus, in a sense, programming in an object-oriented system involves composing a new program using the existing coded modules and adding new codes. Also, programs coded for an object class can be inherited by its subclasses. Thus, recoding of these programs for the subclasses is not necessary.

Polymorphism. An operator, function, or procedure (in the form of a message) in an object-oriented system can be implemented in different codes and can operate differently depending on the type of object to which the message is sent. For example, an operation named PRINT can be implemented by two different procedures to print a character string or an integer, depending on whether the object to be printed is a character string or an integer. Instead of naming the procedures differently, they are given the same name (operator overloading). The proper procedure of the PRINT operation is dynamically bound to an object at run-time once the type of the object is known. This feature gives the user great flexibility in naming operations associated with object classes and relieves the user from the burden of remembering different operations for different objects.

Integration of data and metadata. In the object-oriented paradigm, the specification and definition (i.e., the metadata) of an object class is itself an object that can be accessed and manipulated. No clear line needs to be drawn between data and metadata. This property suits many database application areas in which data and metadata are made accessible to the users in order to facilitate the full use of these data resources.

IMPLEMENTATION OF OBJECT-ORIENTED LANGUAGES. The preceding properties are all very ideal for adoption in a DBMS. However, the efficient implementation of these properties is the main difficulty. The key issues that affect the efficient implementation of object-oriented languages such as SMALLTALK and database systems based on this type of language are discussed below.

Use of byte code interpreter. The programming language SMALLTALK-80 has been defined for a virtual machine with a set of instructions called *byte codes*. Methods of object classes written in SMALLTALK are first compiled into byte codes, which are interpreted by an interpreter during run-time. The advantage of the interpretation approach is that it makes the language portable, since interpreters for different computers can be easily implemented. However, the performance is poor due to the overhead involved in interpreting the instruction set at run-time. A software solution to this problem is to translate the language into the instruction set of a computer as is done by the system being developed at the University of Toronto called SWAMP [LEW86]. A second solution introduced by XEROX's DORADO is to use a microcode kernel implementation of the interpreter [PIE83 and DEU84]. A third solution, used in the system SOAR developed at the University of California, Berkeley [UNG84 and SAM86], is to directly compile the language into the native machine code of a computer.

Method lookup. During the execution of a program in an object-oriented system, every procedure call is made to an abstract procedure corresponding to the name of a message, which must be combined with some run-time information to resolve the message with the actual piece of code (i.e., the method). There is no statically determinable information on data types to allow the procedure to be properly performed. This offers the property of polymorphism discussed earlier. However, the dynamic association mechanism is quite costly in comparison with the overhead associated with the procedure calls in conventional programming languages. A number of solutions to this problem have been introduced: SOAR uses an in-line cache for fast method lookup, SWAMP uses a hardware cache, and the Caltech Object Machine (COM) uses some instruction translation look-aside buffers to cache the associations to the methods during instruction decoding [DAL85].

Pure object orientation. Most implementations of object-oriented languages treat everything uniformly as objects, and the communication between objects is achieved by message passing. For example, an arithmetic operation such as 2 + 2 is processed by passing a message that contains an object 2 and an addition operator to another object 2. Although this technique has the advantage of uniformity in program execution, message handling for frequent, low-level operations contributes to a significant amount of overhead in object-oriented systems. Obviously, a reduction in the number of calls and message processing operations would be desirable. SOAR maintains a registry of frequently used objects, which can be used by run-time supporting routines. SWAMP incorporates a field in the object address of a small object such as an integer to indicate that the object itself is the data.

Context allocation and deallocation. Activation records associated with procedure or function calls in conventional programming systems are called *contexts* in object-oriented systems. Each time a message is sent to an object, a context must be established in a heap structure and several fields of data are initialized. Since there is a large number of objects and, thus, contexts established and removed from the system, the allocations and deallocations of contexts during run-time slow down the system considerably. Measurements on a SMALLTALK implementation show that 85 percent of all object allocations and deallocations involve contexts, and over 90 percent of all memory references are to contexts. For this reason, techniques are needed to reduce the number of context references and the access time. The strategy used in SOAR is to keep context residence on the machine stack and moved to the heap space only when necessary. A similar approach is taken in COM, which uses context caching in conjunction with a free list that operates like a stack. SWAMP uses a microcode context cache and some hardware registers to keep track of the condition of a context.

Garbage collection. The current implementation of SMALLTALK-80 addresses objects indirectly through an object table and uses reference counting as the method of garbage collection. This method is rather slow because every reference to a field of an object takes two memory references and involves the overhead of reference counting. In SOAR and SWAMP, object references directly point to memory locations. This scheme involves an alternate garbage collection method called *generation scavenging*.

From this above discussion, it should be clear that there are a number of efficiency problems involved in the implementation of object-oriented languages. These problems will also be in any implementation of an object-oriented DBMS on a conventional computer. Although research has been conducted to seek effective means of processing objects as demonstrated in the SOAR, COM, and DORADO systems, it has been restricted to small granules of objects and operating system support issues. One fruitful direction of research in the database computer area is to investigate hardware techniques and architectures to support the processing of large granules of objects and database management support of an object-oriented computing system. Meaningful research efforts include: (1) special-purpose hardware or microcode techniques for supporting the manipulation of complex data structures that model complex objects; (2) the inheritance of attributes, operations, and knowledge rules associated with object classes in object class lattice; (3) the handling of historical data associated with objects; (4) the processing of messages; and (5) context allocation and deallocation.

9.3.1.3 KNOWLEDGE BASE MANAGEMENT.

Knowledge base management is a relatively new field of study that has resulted from the marriage of two technologies—database management technology and artificial intelligence technology. A knowledge base management system (KBMS) is an intelligent system that provides the traditional database management functions such as database retrieval and manipulation, integrity and security control, concurrency control, recovery, report generation, and so forth. It also provides deductive (some with inductive) capabilities and is able to perform different types of reasoning. A KBMS can better meet the functional requirements of many database applications than a DBMS can, since the incorporation of knowledge rules (which may represent semantic constraints, general inference rules, and domain specific expert rules) are generally needed in real-world applications. Presently, there are four general approaches that have been taken in the development of KBMSs. They are: (1) the extension of an existing DBMS to incorporate knowledge rules (e.g., the POSTGRES system being developed at the University of California, Berkeley [STO86]), (2) the bridging of an existing DBMS with an AI system (e.g., the effort undertaken at the New York University [JAR84], (3) the extension of an existing AI system to provide database management functions (e.g., [WAR84]), and (4) the integration of functions and components of a database management system with those of an AI system (e.g., [WIE83, SHE84, and RAS87]).

The key features of a knowledge base management system are its knowledge representation scheme and reasoning mechanism. There are a number of popular knowledge representation schemes and corresponding reasoning mechanisms used in the existing systems [BAR81]: (1) logical representational scheme, (2) production scheme, (3) semantic network scheme, (4) frame-based scheme, and (5) procedural scheme.

The logical representational scheme represents knowledge by a collection of independent facts and a set of rules expressed in the form of logical formulae, which consist of predicates, logical connectives, quantifiers, and functions. Reasoning is achieved by applying a set of well-defined inference rules.

The production scheme represents knowledge in the form of a set of independent production rules, each of which contains a condition and an action, and an inference engine, which controls the execution of production rules. The reasoning mechanism generally involves the matching of some data conditions against either the right-hand or left-hand side of the production rules, depending on whether the forward-chaining or backward-chaining control strategy is used. If a match is found, the right-hand side condition or the left hand side action is undertaken. This matching process may result in more than one rule matched with the data conditions. In this case, a conflict resolution phase is taken in the control mechanism to determine the rule that should be applied first.

The semantic network representation scheme represents knowledge in the form of a network of interrelated objects or concepts. Each link in the network represents an association between a pair of objects or concepts. Data are processed by traversing the network. The reasoning mechanism used in this representation constructs a fragment of the network representing a query and then matches the fragment against the network for an exact match. The pattern matcher can make inferences by creating network structures that are explicitly in the network.

The frame-based scheme represents knowledge by frames, which are structures for representing stereotypical situations. Each frame contains a number of slots, which contain knowledge within the context of a frame, and procedural attachments, which describe how the knowledge can be used. Two popular reasoning mechanisms are used in this scheme: data-driven and expectation-driven. In the data-driven mechanism, procedural attachments associated with slots are triggered when the slots have prespecified values. In the expectation-driven mechanism, an expectation is verified in a selected context and the procedural attachment to a slot can be activated to fill in the slot on confirmation of the expectation.

The procedural scheme represents knowledge in the form of a collection of active agents or procedures. Reasoning is done by activating these procedures in a controlled manner. Specialized inference procedures, which implement heuristic rules, give this representation scheme a sense of direction in problem-solving activities, thus avoiding wasteful searches.

The efficient implementation of a knowledge base system that uses any of these knowledge representation schemes and the corresponding reasoning mechanisms is a very difficult task. This is particularly true on a conventional system for the following reasons. First, many AI algorithms are nondeterministic in nature. It is not possible to first plan the actions that need to be taken in problem-solving activities. Consequently, a large number of search paths often need to be exhaustively explored. Second, due to the first reason, an AI system needs to dynamically create new data structures and incorporate new functions during the solution process. This can greatly slow down the system. When AI problems are combined with the large database problems in a KBMS, the problems are multiplied; they become unmanageable in conventional systems. This explains why most of the AI systems in use are small systems with a small fact base and a small rule base.

One of the features of AI computation is that AI systems have high potential for parallel and distributed computations [WAH87]. In many AI algorithms, a number of independent tasks must carried out under a given condition. They can be processed concurrently. This exploits the so-called AND-parallelism. AI algorithms often involve exploring multiple search paths, one of which may lead to the solution to a problem. In this case, these search tasks can also be processed concurrently; this is called OR-parallelism. The parallel processing feature suits the objectives of database computers very well since parallel processing is the key feature of these systems. Furthermore, AI computation mainly involves symbolic processing—that is, symbol comparison, set operations, sorting, pattern matching, and retrieval, and so on, which are nonnumeric operations that a database computer can do well. Therefore, one important research direction is to extend the database computer technology into "knowledge base computer technology." In fact, a good number of research projects are being carried out in different countries in this direction [BER83, FAH83, BIC84, TAM84, UCH84, MOL85, MUR85, SHA85, GUP86, STO86, ITO86, TAN86, FAH87, KAN87, WAH87, and HWA87].

9.3.2   Hardware Technologies

The three software technologies discussed in the last section can give the next generation of database/knowledge base computers the needed functionality. In order to achieve efficiency in the implementation of these technologies, it is necessary to apply new hardware technologies in the design and development of future systems. In this section, two hardware technologies and their potential impact on future database/knowledge base computers are discussed.

9.3.2.1   OPTICAL DISK TECHNOLOGY. Many database or knowledge base applications require very large quantities of data (10^{14} bytes or more) to be stored and processed. These data need to be stored in low-cost secondary storage devices. If the present high-density magnetic disks such as IBM's 3380 disks (630 megabyte per drive) are used to store these data, it will take approximately 158,730 disk drives. The cost of so many disk drives would be prohibitive for any application. Other alternatives for meeting the large storage requirement obviously need to be sought. Among the various types of mass storage technologies, the newly emerging optical disk storage technology has a very high potential for very large database/knowledge base applications.

Optical storage media began to draw much attention among researchers and practitioners about the mid-1970s. An optical disk system uses a modulated argon laser beam to record data on an optical disk. A second nonmodulated beam from the same laser is used to reflect off the disk, and the reflected light is detected and demodulated in order to read back the data. Optical disk systems have several advantages over conventional magnetic mass storage media in that they offer huge on-line capacity, fast data access rate, high density, low cost per megabyte of storage, high data transfer rate, and they are small in size [LOU82, ROT83, and HER80]. The existing optical disks can store as many as 600 million bits per square inch. A single disk can store between 800 megabytes and 4 gigabytes of digitally encoded data. This is roughly 1 to 2 million typical typewritten pages of character data or the contents of over 2000 double-sided, double-density floppy disks [SAF85]. If data compression techniques are used, then a six-fold to tenfold improvement can be yielded in storage capacity. The error rate for this type of storage device is low. An error rate of 1 bit per 10 trillion is achieved by using the direct-read-after-write (DRAW) error-correction technique. Continuous improvements in density, capacity, stability, resolution, error rate, and access rate are expected [POP84, OLE85, AMM85, and MEA87].

Presently, there are several products available. They include RCA's Jukebox, LaserData's DataDisc, CLASIX DataPlate produced by Reference Technology Incorporated, and Drexon-coated optical cards produced by Drexler Technology Corporation. Many companies are also involved in research on optical storage media. They include Storage Technology Corporation, Shugart Associates, Optical Storage International, 3M Company, Panasonic Industrial Company, Toshiba Telecom, Integrated Automation Company, Matsushita, Hitachi, Philips, and FileNet. Market surveys show that the future for optical disks is very bright. E. S. Rothschild predicts an installed base of 8.3 million optical disk drives by 1990 [ROT84]. An even more optimistic prediction given by Freeman Associates in 1984 projects that a $9 million optical media market in 1984 will grow to $7 billion by 1990 [MEA87].

What do the features and market potential of optical disks mean to the future of database/knowledge computer development? The answer is that very large, fast, and reliable secondary storage devices will soon be available at an affordable price for very large database/knowledge base applications. Before the reader gets overly optimistic about this technology, it is important to point out that two problems still must be addressed before optical disks can be effectively used for database/knowledge base applications. First, the current optical disks are not read-write devices as are the magnetic disks in use today. They are either read-only (e.g., CD-ROMs) or write-once-read-many (WORM) devices. This property limits its application in the database field since database applications require recorded data to be updated very often. This limitation has been partially eliminated recently by companies such as Matsushita, Corning Glass Works, Sony, and Nippon Telephone and Telegraph, which have successfully developed erasable optical disks. Although the erasable optical disk technology is not yet mature, research on recording materials holds great promise for a breakthrough. Second, the proper integration of this type of storage device into an application environment while maintaining high performance capabilities is still a research issue. Some research effort has been devoted to this issue [HAH83, MOR84, KAN84, YAO85, HEV85, and AMM85]. Fast data access and a high-speed data transmission path (i.e., the bandwidth) have been the main concerns of these studies. This author believes that a combination of the following two approaches can be taken to increase the bandwidth of optical disks: (1) the pairing of an optical disk with a fast processor that matches with the transfer rate of the disk to provide a large system with parallel I/O capabilities (a principle used in cellular-logic devices) and (2) the use of a large cache memory for each disk to increase its bandwidth.

9.3.2.2 OPTICAL COMMUNICATION, INTERCONNECTION, AND COMPUTING TECHNOLOGIES. In order to achieve high efficiency in processing very large databases, parallel and distributed computing is the solution. In parallel and distributed computing—a principle that is used in almost all categories of database computers presented in this book (particularly in the multiprocessor database computers)—data are distributed among the local memory modules of a number of processors. Distributed data are processed by their corresponding processors. If all nonnumeric processing operations can be done independently by these processors over their corresponding data, then there is really no problem in handling large databases since the processing time is reduced to the processing time of a single processor (not counting the data collection, of course). Unfortunately, this is not the case. Many operations require frequent interprocessor communications and synchronizations as well as transfers of data among these processors. Three key factors that determine the speed of performing these operations are: (1) the speed at which communication, synchronization, and transfer of data can be carried out, (2) the reconfigurability of the interconnections among processors, main memory modules, and secondary storage devices so that distributed data can be directly accessed by processors simply by changing the interconnections instead of shipping large quantities of data from one processor to another and (3) the speed of the processors.

Recent developments in optic technology offer potential solutions to meet the need for higher speed in processing and communication and more flexible interconnections. In addition to the optical storage technology discussed in the preceding section, three other areas of optic technology are relevant to the future of database computers. They are: (1) optical communication, (2) optical interconnection, and (3) optical computing. Recent research and development efforts in these three areas of optical technology are reported in two special issues of *Proceedings of the IEEE* published in January 1977 and July 1984, and a special issue on optical computing in the April 1986 issue of *Optics News*.

Fiber optic communication has become a mature technology. Optic fibers have already been used for several years as transmission media in many local area networks. The main advantage of this type of transmission media is its high bandwidth (gigabits per second). Using this media, control commands, messages, status, and data of many processors in a network can be multiplexed and transmitted at very high speed, possibly faster than the computation times required for these processors to do their local tasks. In this case, the interprocessor communication and data transfer time will no longer be the bottleneck of a multicomputer system. Also, if data can be transferred from processor to processor at a gigabits-per-second rate, remote data can be transferred to a processor so fast that they become practically local data to the processor. The speed offered by fiber optic communication should change the way we think about very large database or knowledge base problems and alter the techniques we use to solve them.

Optical interconnection technology is an upcoming technology that will have great impact on the designs of computer chips, boards, and systems. Optical interconnections can be used to link chips on a board, boards within a system unit of a multiboard computer, and processors to processors, or processors to memories in a parallel processing computer. Optics have three main advantages over electronics as a means of computation and communication [CAU86 and GIB86]:

1. *No interaction.* Light pulses do not interact with each other the way electrons do. That is, light beams can cross each other without mutual effect, thus the

problem of "crosstalk" found in electronic devices is not a problem in optic devices. A very large number of communication links can be established in a very small physical space.

2. *Massive parallelism.* A million beams can provide parallel communication or computation between two 1000 X 1000 optical decision plans, which are made of light-sensitive material that serve as optical transistors and logic gates. Light beams carrying information from another plane can cross the same space used by the beams of the first two planes without interaction. This property offers an extremely high degree of parallelism in optical computing and communication.

3. *High speed.* Computation and communication are carried out at the speed of light. The speed of an optical computer is projected to exceed one million billion (10^{15}) bit operations per second, which is 1000 to 10,000 times faster than the speed of modern supercomputers such as Cray.

Recent progress in optical interconnection indicates that it is possible to build very large optical crossbar networks, which provide nonblocking and fully reconfigurable interconnections [CLY85 and SAW87]. If such crossbar networks can be built cost effectively, they can be used to interconnect processors, memory modules, and secondary storage devices of a multicomputer database computer to allow static interconnection as well as dynamic reconfiguration of these processors and devices. In addition to this application, optical interconnection technology may be used to represent and process objects of a large database. One can envision that a database containing a set of interrelated objects and relationships among objects is represented by direct or indirect optical interconnections. For example, "John takes a course entitled Mathematics 101" is represented as a direct connection between "John" and "Mathematics 101." An optical device can implement fixed interconnections between millions of object pairs via holograms. The processing of concurrent queries can be treated as verifications of some specified interconnections and can be carried out by passing commands and data through these interconnections in a parallel fashion.

Another aspect of optics technology is optical computing. It involves the use of optical bistable devices to mimic digital gates and multivalued logic circuits. Two laser pulses can serve as the inputs of a logic gate. Transmission of another pulse represents the output of the gate. It has been demonstrated that various logic gates such as AND, OR, and NOR gates can be implemented by optical means [GIB86]. This offers the potential for constructing an all-optics computer that computes at light speed. However, it is the common opinion of the researchers in optical computing that such a computer is only a possibility. The realization of such a computer is in the far distant future.

Based on the present technological development, optical interconnection technology holds greater promise to become an available technology for the computer industry than all-optics computing technology. The investigation on the use of optical disk technology, fiber optics communication technology, and optic interconnection technology in the future design and development of database/ knowledge base computers is timely and is the most promising approach to the realization of a database/knowledge base computer with high functionality and efficiency.

*   *   *

In view of the current development and progress of the software and hardware technologies discussed in this section and their potential impact on the database computer field, this author would like to end this book on an optimistic note. Database computers are here to stay. The database computer field will continue to develop, flourish, and expand. Organizations that prepare themselves to adopt this new technology will definitely reap the true benefits from its development.

9.4 BIBLIOGRAPHY

[ABI84] Abiteboul, S. and Hull, R.: "IFO: A Formal Semantic Database Model," *Proceedings of the ACM's SIGACT-SIGMOD Symposium on Principles of Database Systems,* Waterloo, Canada, 1984, pp. 119–132.

[AMM85] Ammon, G. J., Calabria, J. A., and Thomas, D. T.: "A High-Speed, Large-Capacity, 'Jukebox' Optical Disk System," *IEEE COMPUTER*, vol.18, no. 7, July 1985, pp. 36–45.

[AND87] Anderson, J. M., Coates, W. S., Davis, A. L., Hon, R. W., Robinson, I. N., Robison, S. V., and Stevens, K. S.: "The Architecture of FAIM-1," *IEEE COMPUTER*, vol. 20, no. 1, Jan. 1987, pp. 55–65.

[BAR81] Barr, A. and Feigenbaum, E. A. (eds.): *The Handbook of Artificial Intelligence*, vol. 1, William Kaufmann, Inc., Los Altos, California, 1981.

[BAR82] Bartolini, R. A.: "Optical Recording: High Density Information Storage and Retrieval," *Proceedings of the IEEE*, vol. 70, 1982, pp. 589–597.

[BEL83] Bell, A. E.: "Optical Data Storage Technology Status and Prospects," *Computer Design*, vol. 22, no. 1, Jan. 1983, pp. 133–138.

[BER83] Berger-Sabbatel, G., Ianeselli, J. C., and Nguyen, G. T.: "A PROLOG Data Base Machine," *Data Base Machines*, Springer-Verlag, New York, Sept. 1983.

[BIC84] Bic, L.: "Execution of Logic Programs on a Dataflow Architecture," *Proceedings of the Eleventh International Symposium on Computer Architecture*, IEEE/ACM, Ann Arbor, Mich., June 1984, pp. 290–296.

[BIR73] Birtwistle, G. M., Dahl, O. J., Myhaug, B., and Nygoard, K.: *Simula Begins*, Auerback, Philadephia, 1973.

[BOB77] Bobrow, D. G., and Winograd, T.: "An Overview of KRL, a Knowledge Representation Language," *Journal of Cognitive Science*, vol. 1, no. 1, 1977, pp. 3–46.

[BOB83] Bobrow, D. G., and Stelfik, M.: *The LOOPS Manual*, Xerox Corporation, 1983.

[BOR83] Boral H., and DeWitt, D. J.: "Database Machines: An Idea Whose Time Has Passed? A Critique of the Future of Database Machines," *Computer Sciences Technical Report #504*, University of Wisconsin, Madison, Wis., July 1983.

[CAU86] Caulfield, H. J.: "Optical Computing Some Hard Questions," *Optics News*, vol. 12, no. 4, April 1986, pp. 9–11.

[CHE76] Chen, P. P. S.: "The Entity-Relationship Model—Toward a Unified View of Data," *ACM Transactions on Database Systems*, vol. 6, no. 1, March 1976, pp. 9–36.

[CLY85] Clymer, B., and Collins, S. A.: "Optical Computer Switching Networks," *Optical Engineering*, vol. 24, Jan. 1985, pp. 74–81.

[COP84] Copeland, G. and Maier, D.: "Making SMALLTALK a Database System," *Proceedings of the 1984 ACM-SIGMOD Conference*, Boston, Mass., 1984, pp. 316–325.

[DAL85] Dally, W. J. and Kajiya, J. T.: "An Object Oriented Architecture," *Proceedings of the*

Twelfth Annual International Symposium on Computer Architecture, Boston, Mass., June 1985, pp. 76–83.

[DEU84] Deutsch, P.: "The DORADO SMALLTALK-80 Implementation: Hardware Architecture's Impact on Software Architecture," in *SMALLTALK-80, Bits of History, Words of Advice*, Glen Krasner (ed.), Addison-Wesley, Reading, Mass., 1984, pp. 113–126.

[DEW84] DeWitt, D. J., Katz, R., Olken, F., Shapiro, L., Stonebraker, M., and Wood, D.: "Implementation Techniques for Main Memory Database Systems," *Proceedings of the 1984 ACM-SIGMOD Conference*, Boston, Mass., June 1984, pp. 1–8.

[FAH83] Fahlman, S. E., and Hinton, G. E.: "Massively Parallel Architectures for AI: NETL, THISTLE and BOLTZMANN Machines," *Proceedings of the National Conference on Artificial Intelligence*, American Association for Artificial Intelligence, 1983, pp. 109–113.

[FAH87] Fahlman, S. E., and Hinton, G. E.: "Connectionist Architectures for Artificial Intelligence," *IEEE COMPUTER*, vol. 20, no. 1, Jan. 1987, pp. 100–108.

[GAR84] Garcia-Molina, H., Lipton, R. J., and Valdez, J.: "A Massive Memory Machine," *IEEE Transactions on Computers*, vol. C-33, no. 5, May 1984, pp. 391–399.

[GEM86a] *Gemstone C Interface Manual*, Servio Logic Development Corporation, Beaverton, Ore., 1986.

[GEM86b] *OPAL Programming Environment Manual*, Servio Logic Development Corporation, Beaverton, Ore., 1986.

[GIB86] Gibbs, H. M.: "Approaching the All-Optical Computer," *Optics News*, vol. 12, no. 4, April 1986, pp. 21–23.

[GOL82] Goldstein, C. M.: "Optical Disk Technology and Information," *Science*, vol. 215, 1982, pp. 862–868.

[GOL83] Golberg, A. and Robson, D.: *SMALLTALK-80: The Language and Its Implementation*, Addison-Wesley, Reading, Mass., 1983.

[GUP86] Gupta, A., Forgy, C., Newell, A., and Wedig, R.: "Parallel Algorithms and Architectures for Rule-based Systems," *Proceedings of the Thirteenth Annual International Symposium on Computer Architecture*, IEEE/ACM, Tokyo, Japan, June 1986, pp. 28–37.

[HAH83] Hahn, E. Z.: "The Library of Congress Optical Disk Pilot Program: A Report on the Print Project Activities (Digitized Electronic MARC [Machine-Readable Cataloging] and Non-MARC Display [DEMAND] System)," *Library of Congress Information Bulletin*, 1983, pp. 374–376.

[HAM81] Hammer, M. and McLeod, D.: "Database Description with SDM: A Semantic DataModel," *ACM TRansactions on Database Systems*, vol. 6, no. 3, 1981, pp. 351–386.

[HER80] Herzog, D. G.: "Optical Disk Approaches as Mass Storage," *IEEE Symposium on Mass Storage Systems*, New York, 1980, pp. 38–41.

[HEV85] Hevner, A. R.: "Evaluation of Optical Disk Systems for Very Large Database Applications," *Working Paper Series MS/S 85-004*, Database Systems Research Center, University of Maryland, College Park, Md., Feb. 1985.

[HIL85] Hillis, W. D.: *The Connection Machine*, MIT Press, Cambridge, Mass., 1985.

[HWA87] Hwang, K., Ghosh, J., and Chowkwanyun, R.: "Computer Architectures for Artificial Intelligence Processing," *IEEE COMPUTER*, vol. 20, no. 1, Jan. 1987, pp. 19–27.

[ITO86] Itoh, H.: "Research and Development on Knowledge Base Systems at ICOT," *Proceedings of the Twelfth International Conference on Very Large Data Bases*, Tokyo, Japan, Aug. 1986, pp. 437–445.

[JAR84] Jarke, M., and Vassiliou, Y.: "An Otimizing Prolog Front-end to a Relational Query System," *Proceedings of the 1984 ACM-SIGMOD Conference*, Boston, Mass., June 1984, pp. 296–305.

[KAN84] Kanazawa, Y., Ito, M., and Abe, S.: "Development of Large Capacity Optical Disk," *SPIE*, vol. 490, Applications of Optical Digital Data Disk Storage Systems, 1984, pp. 12–19.

[KAN87] Kanaegami, A., Yokota, K., and Kawamura, M.: "Kappa-Knowledge Base Management System on PSI," *Technical Report TR-87*, Institute for New Generation Computer Technology, Tokyo, Japan, 1987.

[KEE84] *KEE Reference Manual*, Intelligenetics, Palo Alto, Calif., 1984.

[KEN82] Kenville, R. F.: "Optical Disk Data Storage," *IEEE COMPUTER*, vol. 15, no. 7, July 1982, pp. 21–25.

[LEH86a] Lehman, T. J., and Carey, M. J.: "Query Processing in Main Memory Database Management Systems," *Proceedings of the 1986 ACM-SIGMOD Conference*, Washington, D.C., May 1986, pp. 239–250.

[LEH86b] Lehman, T. J., and Carey, M. J.: "A Study of Index Structures for Main Memory Database Management Systems," *Proceedings of the Twelfth International Conference on Very Large Data Bases*, Tokyo, Japan, Aug. 1986, pp. 294–303.

[LEW86] Lewis, D. M., Galloway, D. R., Francis, R. J., and Thomson, B. W., "SWAMP: A Fast Processor for SMALLTALK-80," *Proceedings of the ACM's Conference on Object-Oriented Programming Systems, Languages and Applications*, Portland, Ore., Sept. 1986, pp. 131–139.

[LOU82] Lou, D.: "Characterization of Optical Disks," *Applied Optics*, vol. 21, no. 9, 1982, pp. 1602–1609.

[MAR86] Margaret, H. E.: "Main Memory Database Recovery," *Proceedings of the Fall Joint Computer Conference*, Dallas, Tex., Oct. 1986, pp. 1226–1232.

[MEA87] Meade, J.: "The Future of Optical Disks in Archival Storage," *Hardcopy Magazine*, Feb. 1987, pp. 63–72.

[MOL85] Moldovan, D. I., and Tung, Y. W.: "SNAP: A VLSI Architecture for Artificial Intelligence Processing," *Journal on Parallel and Distributed Computing*, vol. 2, no. 2, May 1985, pp. 109–131.

[MOO86] Moon, D. A.: "Object-Oriented Programming with Flavors," *Proceedings of the ACM's Conference on Object-oriented Programming Systems, Languages and Applications*, Portland, Ore., Sept. 1986, pp. 1–8.

[MOR84] Mori, M., and Yamamoto, K.: "High Performance Optical Disk Memory System," *SPIE*, vol. 490, Applications of Optical Digital Data Disk Systems, 1984, pp. 2–5.

[MOR86] Morita, Y., Yokota, H., Nishida, K., and Itoh, H.: "Retrieval-by-Unification Operation on a Relational Knowledge Base," *Proceedings of the 12th International Conference on Very Large Databases*, Tokyo, Japan, Aug. 1986, pp. 52–59.

[MUR85] Murakami, K., Kakuta, T., Onai, R., and Ito, N.: "Research on Parallel Architecture for Fifth-Generation Computer Systems," *IEEE COMPUTER*, vol. 18, no. 6, June 1985, pp. 76–92.

[MYL80] Mylopoulos, J., Bernstein, P., and Wong, H.: "A Language Facility for Designing Database-Intensive Applications," *ACM Transactions on Database Systems*, vol. 5, no. 2, June 1980, pp. 185–287.

[NOJ86] Nojiri, T., Kawasaki, S., and Sakoda, K.: "Micro-programmable Processor for Object-oriented Architecture," *Proceedings of the Thirteenth Annual International Symposium on Computer Architecture*, Tokyo, Japan, June 1986, pp. 74–81.

[OLE85] O'Lear, B. T., and Kitts, D. L.: "Optical Device Interfacing for a Mass Storage System," *IEEE COMPUTER*, vol. 18, no. 7, July 1985, pp. 24–32.

[PIE83] Pier, K. A.: "A Retrospective on the Dorado, A High Performance Personal Computer," *Proceedings of the Tenth Annual International Symposium on Computer Architecture*, June 1983, pp. 252–269.

[POP84] Popoff, P., and Ledieu, J.: "Towards New Information Systems: Gigadisc," *SPIE*, vol. 490, Application of Optical Digital Data Disk Storage Systems, 1984, pp. 20–26.

[RAS87] Raschid, L.: "The Design and Implementation Techniques for an Integrated Knowledge Base Management System," Ph.D. diss., Department of Electrical Engineering, University of Florida, August 1987.

[ROT83] Rothchild, E. S.: "Optical Memory Media: How Optical Disks Work, Who Makes Them, and How Much Data They Can Hold," *Byte*, vol. 8, no. 3, March 1983, pp. 86–106.

[SAF85] Saffady, W.: *Optical Disks 1985—A State of the Art Review*, Meckler Publishing Co., Westport, Conn., 1985.

[SAM86] Samples, A. D., Ungar, D., and Hilfinger, P.: "SOAR: SMALLTALK without Byte-codes," *Proceedings of the ACM's Conference on Object-oriented Programming Systems, Languages and Applications*, Portland, Ore., Sept. 1986, pp. 92–103.

[SAW87] Sawchuk, A. A., Jenkins, B. K., Raghavandra, C. S., and Varma, A.: "Optical Crossbar Networks," *IEEE COMPUTER*, vol. 20, no. 6, June 1987, pp. 50–60.

[SHA85] Shaw, D. E.: "NON-VON's Applicability to Three AI Task Areas," *Proceedings of the Ninth International Joint Conference on Artificial Intelligence*, Los Angeles, Calif., Aug. 1985, pp. 61–70.

[SHE84] Shepherd, A., and Kerschberg, L.: "PRISM: A Knowledge Based System for Semantic Integrity Specification and Enforcement in Database Systems," *Proceedings of the ACM-SIGMOD Conference*, Boston, Mass., June 1984, pp. 307–315.

[SHI79] Shipman, D.: "The Functional Data Model and the Data Language DAPLEX," supplement to the *Proceedings of the 1979 ACM-SIGMOD Conference*, Boston, Mass., May 1979, p. 53.

[SMI77] Smith, J. M., and Smith, D. C. P.: "Database Abstractions: Aggregation and Generalization," *ACM Transactions on Database Systems*, vol. 2, no. 2, June 1977, pp. 105–133.

[STO86a] Stonebraker, M. and Rowe, L. A.: "The Design of Postgres," *Proceedings of the 1986 ACM-SIGMOD Conference*, Washington, D. C., May 1986, pp. 340–355.

[STO86b] Stolfo, S. J., and Miranker, D. P.: "The DADO Production System Machine," *Journal on Parallel and Distributed Computing*, vol. 3, no. 2, June 1986, pp. 269–296.

[STO87] Stolfo, S. J.: "Initial Performance of the DADO2 Prototype," *IEEE COMPUTER*, vol. 20, no. 1, Jan. 1987, pp. 75–83.

[SU83] Su, S. Y. W.: "A Semantic Association Model for Corporate and Scientific-Statistical Databases," *Information Science*, vol. 29, 1983, pp. 151–199.

[SU86] Su, S. Y. W.: "Modeling Integrated Manufacturing Data with SAM*," *IEEE COMPUTER*, vol. 19, no. 1, Jan. 1986, pp. 34–49.

[SUZ84] Suzuki, N., Kubota, K., and Aoki, T.: "Sword-32: A Bytecode Emulating Microprocessor for Object-Oriented Languages," *Proceedings of the International Conference on Fifth Generation Computer Systems*, Tokyo, Japan, Nov. 1984, pp. 389–397.

[TAM84] Tamura, N., and Kaneda, K.: "Implementing Parallel Prolog on a Multi-processor Machine," *International Symposium on Logic Programming*, Atlantic City, N.J., May 1984, pp. 42–48.

[TAN86] Tanaka, H.: "A Parallel Inference Machine," *IEEE COMPUTER*, vol. 19, no. 5, May 1986, pp. 48–54.

[UCH84] Uchida, S., and Yokoi, T.: "Sequential Inference Machine: SIM Progress Report," *Technical Report TR-86*, Institute for New Generation Computer Technology, 1984.

[UNG84] Ungar, D., Blau, R., Foley, P., Samples, A. D., and Patterson, D.: "Architecture of SOAR: SMALLTALK on a RISC," *Proceedings of the Eleventh International Symposium on Computer Architecture*, IEEE/ACM, June 1984, pp. 188–197.

[WAH87] Wah, B. W.: "New Computers for Artificial Intelligence Processing," *IEEE COMPUTER*, vol. 20, no. 1, Jan. 1987, pp. 10–15.

[WAL87] Waltz, D. L.: "Applications of the Connection Machine," *IEEE COMPUTER*, vol 20, no. 1, Jan. 1987, pp. 85–97.

[WAR84] Warren, D. S., and Sciore, E.: "Towards an Integrated Database-Prolog System," in *Expert Database Systems*, L. Kerschberg, (ed.), Benjamin Cummings Publishing Co., Menlo Park, Calif., 1986, pp. 293–305.

[WIE83] Wiederhold, G., Milton, J., and Sagalowicz, D.: "Applications of Artificial Intelligence in the Knowledge-based Management Systems Project," *Database Engineering*, vol. 6, no.4, Dec. 1983, pp. 75–84.

[YAO85] Yao, S. B., Hevner, A. R., Silva, E., and Nadkarni, S.: "Design Issues on Optical Disk Systems," *Working Paper Series MS/S 85-014*, Database System Research Center, University of Maryland, College Park, Md., June 1985.

[YOK86] Yokota, H. and Itoh, H.: "A Model and Architecture for a Relational Knowledge Base," *Proceedings of the Thirteenth International Symposium on Computer Architecture*, Tokyo, Japan, June 1986, pp. 2–9.

LIST OF
ABBREVIATIONS

AMP—Access Module Processor

APCS—Associative Processor Computer System

APPLE—Associative Processor Programming LanguagE

ASLM—Associative Search Language Machine

ASP—Association-Storing Processor

CADAM—Content-Addressable Database Access Machine

CAFS—Content Addressable File Store

CASSM—Context Addressed Segmented Sequential Memory

CCD—Charge-coupled Device

CL—Cellular-Logic

COM—Caltech Object Machine

CPU—Central Processing Unit

DBC—Database Computer

DBC/1012—Teradata Corporation's Database Computer

DBM—Data Base Machine

DBMAC—A database machine project sponsored by the Italian Applied Program for Informatics

DBMS—Database Management System

DBTG—Data Base Task Group

DDL—Data Definition Language

DDM—Data-stream database machine

DELTA—A relational database machine implemented by the Institute for New Generation Computer Technology

DIRECT—A relational database computer prototyped at the University of Wisconsin

DML—Data Manipulation Language

DRAW—Direct-Read-After-Write; an error-correction technique

EDC—Electronic-disk Oriented Database Complex

EUREKA—A text retrieval system developed at the University of Illinois

FLDC—Fixed-Length Don't Care

FSA—Finite State Automaton

GAMMA—A relational database computer designed and implemented at the University of Wisconsin

GESCAN—A Text Array Processor manufactured by General Electric
GRACE—A relational database computer system developed at the University of Tokyo
iDBP—Intel Database Processor
IDL—Intelligent Database Language
IDM—Intelligent Database Machine
IFP—Interface Processor
INGRES—A commercial relational database management system
IQC—Information Query Computer
KBMS—Knowledge Base Management System
KXU—Key Transformation Unit
LSI—Large Scale Integration
MDBS—Multi-backend Database System
MICRONET—A relational microcomputer network designed and prototyped at the University of Florida
MIMD—Multiple Instruction Stream and Multiple Data Stream
MISD—Multiple Instruction Stream and Single Data Stream
MM—Mass Memory
NFSA—Nondeterministic Finite State Automaton
NON_VON—A massively parallel supercomputer being developed at Columbia University
PAM—Primary Associative Memory
PFSA—Partitioned Finite State Automaton
QP—Query Processor
RAP—Relational Associative Processor
RARES—Rotating Associative Relational Store
RDBM—Relational Database Machine
RELACS—Relational Associative Computer System
REPT—A relational database computer designed at Iowa State University
SABRE—Système d'Accès a des Bases Relationneles
SAM—Secondary Associative Memory
SAM*—Semantic Association Model
SFP—Security Filter Processor
SM—Structure Memory
SIMD—Single Instruction Stream and Multiple Data Stream
SISD—Single Instruction Stream and Single Data Stream
SM3—A multicomputer system with Switchable Main Memory Modules
SNAP—A VLSI architecture for artificial intelligent processing
STARAN—An associative memory system designed and developed by the Goodyear Aerospace Corporation under the support of the United States Air Force
SURE—A database filter designed and prototyped at the Technical University of Braunschweig
TAP—Text Array Processor
TEQUEL—TEradata QUEry Language
TMP—Term Match Processor
VERSO—A database filter designed and prototyped by INRIA in France
VLDC—Variable-length Don't Care
VLSI—Very Large Scale Integration
WORM—Write-Once-Read-Many; a characterization of disk devices
XDMS—Experimental Data Management System

INDEX